A Bibliography of New York State Communities

— THIRD EDITION —

Compiled by
Harold Nestler

HERITAGE BOOKS
2008

HERITAGE BOOKS
AN IMPRINT OF HERITAGE BOOKS, INC.

Books, CDs, and more—Worldwide

For our listing of thousands of titles see our website at
www.HeritageBooks.com

Published 2008 by
HERITAGE BOOKS, INC.
Publishing Division
100 Railroad Ave. #104
Westminster, Maryland 21157

Copyright © 1990 Harold Nestler

Other books by the author:
A Bibliography of New York State Communities

All rights reserved. No part of this book may be reproduced or transmitted in any form or by any means, electronic or mechanical, including photocopying, recording or by any information storage and retrieval system without written permission from the author, except for the inclusion of brief quotations in a review.

International Standard Book Numbers
Paperbound: 978-1-55613-330-5
Clothbound: 978-0-7884-7522-1

DEDICATION

Dedicated to Bill Kaplan

If he had not acquired so many fine New York books and sold them to me, this volume would not have been written. He can find books in shops where no one else would think to look.

More than once we would be in the same shop at the same time. I would be scanning the shelves and picking out a few odd pieces. Bill would be poking around in some obscure corner, even looking at the books piled up behind the waste basket. He would come up with two or three rarities or unusual items, and sell them to me a week later with a twinkle in his eye as he told me where he found them.

We have spent many delightful hours talking about books and bookmen. He knew many of the old-time New York City dealers, and is a fount of knowledge about them and their times.

TABLE OF CONTENTS

Foreword	vii
Abbreviations	ix
Albany County	1
Allegany County	3
Bronx County	5
Broome County	5
Canals County	6
Catskill Mountains and Delaware Valley	8
Cattaraugus County	12
Cayuga County	14
Central New York	15
Chautauqua County	27
Chemung County	29
Chenango County	29
Clinton County	31
Colonial New York	32
Columbia County	35
Cortland County	38
Delaware County	38
Dutchess County	40
Erie County	44
Essex County	47
Franklin County	49
Fulton County	50
Genesee County	50
Greene County	51
Hamilton County	52
Herkimer County	53
Hudson Valley	54
Indians	84
Jefferson County	96
Kings County	99
Lewis County	101
Livingston County	101
Long Island	103
Madison County	105
Maps	106
Martin Van Buren	111
Monroe County	114
Montgomery County	118

Munsell's Historical Series	119
Nassau County	120
New York County	123
Niagara County	144
Northern New York	146
Oneida County	162
Onondaga County	165
Ontario County	168
Orange County	170
Orleans County	173
Oswego County	173
Otsego County	174
Putnam County	178
Queens County	179
Reference Books	179
Rensselaer County	189
Revolutionary War	190
Richmond County	209
Rockland County	210
St. Lawrence County	212
Saratoga County	213
Schenectady County	215
Schoharie County	216
Schuyler County	218
Seneca County	218
Shakers	220
State Wide	222
Steuben County	232
Suffolk County	233
Sullivan County	239
Tioga County	240
Tompkins County	240
Tryon County	242
Ulster County	242
Van Buren, Martin	111
Warren County	245
Washington County	245
Wayne County	247
Westchester County	250
Western New York	255
Wyoming County	262
Yates County	263
Index	265

FOREWORD

"Nestler! Pay attention! Why in the world did you do that instead of the lesson I assigned to the class?" I can still hear my history and geography teachers in New York state back in the 1930's. I never was a good student, and even though history and geography were my favorite subjects I did not get really good grades in them. For instance, the class would be given a paper to write on the Inauguration of Washington as President, which took place in New York City. I would start out on the assignment but would get side-tracked by more interesting things, such as: what route did he take to get there, where did he stay each night, how many miles did he travel a day, what was the name of his horse? The teachers did not appreciate my assiduous researches along those lines. My proclivity for the obscure and entertaining facts that liven up dry history was to stand me in good stead in years to come.

Over the years I have received a great many catalogs from booksellers specializing in Americana. A number of them are as dry as vacuum-cleaner dust, giving only the author, title, number of pages, and price. I like to be entertained at least a little bit when I read a catalog.

Throughout the years I have issued at least thirty catalogs on New York State Americana, listing approximately 15,000 titles including duplicates. I try to make comments on at least half of the items listed to make it more interesting for my readers. A number of them have told me they really enjoy my annotations, and I happily take their word for it.

This book contains approximately 2500 titles. About one-third of them are an arbitrary selection of titles from my catalogs, most of them with comments. I have embellished many of the comments, and added some anecdotes and memories of other booksellers. (There are probably a dozen or so books that I have never had but which I had notes on in my files.) I have tried to put them in categories, but that is somewhat arbitrary, too, as some of them could be placed under two or more headings.

The other two-thirds are a bibliography of New York State towns and counties. Many of these books I have never had, but gathered the titles by extensive research in libraries throughout the state. Here is the reason I compiled the bibliography:

There has long been a need for a bibliography of New York State town and county histories, particularly for the use of librarians, book dealers, historians, genealogists, and collectors. The increase in recent years of interest in the history of the state, and the resultant demands upon libraries and book stores, makes it doubly important that such a work be published.

This volume is an attempt in that direction, listing approximately 85% of the important books and pamphlets published from 1900 through 1987, and a large portion of those issued in the previous hundred years. Limitations, of course, had to be imposed because of lack of time and space. All community, town, and county histories located have been listed, but histories of churches, businesses, organizations, military units, and gazetteers and directories have for the most part been eliminated. The inclusion of the thousands of such publications would make the bibliography too cumbersome. Not included also are the many articles which have appeared in newspapers, magazines, and historical society publications; and manuscript histories on deposit in public libraries or in the archives of historical societies. General histories of New York State have not been included in the bibliography. However, because of its importance in any phase of New York history, the monumental ten volume *History of the State of New York*, edited by Alexander C. Flick (Columbia Univ. Press 1933-1937, reissued 10 volumes in 5, Ira J. Friedman, Inc. 1962) deserves special mention.

Emphasis has been placed mainly upon the smaller towns and communities. The larger cities, such as New York, Brooklyn, Albany, Saratoga, Utica, Syracuse, Rochester, Buffalo, Niagara, and Schenectady should be the subject of exhaustive bibliographies compiled by someone with the patience and time for prolonged research.

A number of entries will be found listing "advertisements." These were usually issued by centennial committees, and contain paid ads of local merchants to help pay for the cost of printing. The historical articles are usually brief, but often a longer well-researched essay is found. An important feature of a number of these publications are the photographs of the community "before" and "after" a certain date of event. These particular photos can often be found nowhere else, and are a valuable record of the history of the community. These pamphlets, as most of them are less than fifty pages in length, were usually given away or sold cheaply during a centennial celebration. Many of them disappeared forever shortly after the festivities. Consequently many are scarce, and they are getting scarcer as the local townspeople do their Spring and Fall house cleaning.

A great many historical publications were issued during 1876, the centennial year of American Independence. No doubt a major reason for this was a Public Resolution passed by Congress and approved by the President, March 13, 1876. "Joint Resolution on the celebration of the Centennial in the several counties and towns. Be it resolved by the Senate and House of Representatives of the United States of America in Congress assembled, That it be, and is hereby recommended by the Senate and House of Representatives to the people of the several States that they assemble in their several counties or towns on the approaching centennial anniversary of our national independence, and that they cause to have delivered on such day an historical sketch of said county or town from its formation, and that a copy of said sketch may be filed, in print or manuscript, in the clerk's office of said county, and an additional copy, in print or manuscript, be filed in the office of the librarian of congress, to the intent that a complete record may thus be obtained of the progress of our institutions during the first centennial of their existence."

In the late 1800's and early 1900's a number of biographical volumes, or "mug books" as they are known in the book trade, were published. Until a few years ago they were considered vanity books and unimportant, but they do contain a lot of information unavailable elsewhere and are now being sought after and used by historians and genealogists. They are called vanity books because they contain the biographies and photos of those citizens who supplied the pictures and details of their life. These same people, of course, subscribed to the work, thus assuring the publisher a sure sale and profit before the book was printed. In 1882 a man paid W. W. Munsell & Co. $150.00 to have his portrait and biography published in one of their publications. In return, he was to receive one copy of the work, and twenty extra prints of his portrait. These biographical volumes usually covered one county or city. Occasionally two counties were included in one volume with both county names appearing in the cover title; but sometimes only the name of one of the counties is given in the cover title.

The main libraries visited by the compiler were: Long Island Historical Society, Brooklyn; New York City Public Library; New York State Library, Albany; Cornell University Library, Ithaca; New York State Historical Association, Cooperstown; Jefferson County Historical Society, Watertown; Rochester Public Library; Buffalo Public Library; State University Library at Cortland; University of Rochester Library; Westchester County Historical Society. The Compiler is deeply in debt to the librarians of those institutions for their aid, suggestions, and encouragement. In addition, many smaller libraries were visited and their resources utilized.

I wish to express my thanks to the hundreds of librarians and local historians who answered my countless queries and questionnaires. A special note of appreciation must be made to Dr. Louis C. Jones of the New York State Historical Association who graciously allowed me to use the bibliographical notes begun by Mrs. C. Elts Van Norman, Geneseo State University College, which are on deposit at the Association's Library in Cooperstown.

This bibliography is arranged alphabetically by counties. Under each county, the county histories are listed first, then the community and town histories in alphabetical order.

Abbreviations used in the *Bibliography*:
AAS	American Antiquarian Society, Worcester, MA
ABS	American Bible Society
advts.	advertisements
anon.	anonymous
BAE	Bureau of American Ethnology
bib.	bibliography
biog.	biographical/biography/biographies
CA	California
ca	about
co.	county/counties
comp.	compiler
CT	Connecticut
DAB	*Dictionary of American Biography*
ed.	editor(s)/edition(s)

hist.	history/historical
illus.	illustration(s)/illustrated
lmtd.	limited
MA	Massachusetts
ME	Maine
MI	Michigan
mimeo.	mimeographed
mss.	manuscript
NC	North Carolina
n.d.	no date
NH	New Hampshire
NJ	New Jersey
NY	New York
NYC	New York City
OH	Ohio
PA	Pennsylvania
P.L.	public library
port.	portrait
ports.	portraits
pp.	pages
prntd.	printed
pub.	publish(ed)/publisher(s)
pvtly.	privately
reprnt.	reprint
reprntd.	reprinted
repub.	republished
RI	Rhode Island
soc.	society
TN	Tennessee
U. S.	United States
vol.	volumes
VT	Vermont
wrps.	wrappers

Many of the city names have been abbreviated.

Library Abbreviations:

ARPL	Arcade Public Library
BHS	Buffalo & Erie County Historical Society
BIPL	Binghamton Public Library
BMLR	Brighton Memorial Library, Rochester
BPL	Buffalo Public Library
BRPL	Brockport Public Library
CPLR	Chili Public Library, Rochester
CU	Cornell University Library, Ithaca
DHS	DeWitt Historical Society, Ithaca
ERPL	East Rochester Public Library
FPL	Fairport Public Library
HHK	House of History, Kinderhook
HIPL	Hilton Public Library
HPL	Honeoye Public Library
IPLR	Irondequoit Public Library, Rochester

JCHS	Jefferson County Historical Society, Watertown
LIHS	Long Island Historical Society, Brooklyn
LPL	Lyons Public Library
NEPL	Newark Public Library
NFPL	Niagara Falls Public Library
NKPL	Nyack Public Library
NUPL	Nunda Public Library
NYHS	New York Historical Society, New York City
NYPL	New York City Public Library
NYSHA	New York State Historical Association, Cooperstown
OCHS	Ontario County Historical Society, Canandaigua
PCHS	Putnam County Historical Society, Cold Spring
POPL	Poughkeepsie Public Library
PPL	Pittsford Public Library
RPL	Rochester Public Library
RUPL	Rush Public Library
SLA	State Library, Albany
SPL	Syracuse Public Library
SUC	State University Library, Cortland
TPL	Troy Public Library
UR	University of Rochester Library
VPL	Vernon Public Library
WCHS	Westchester County Historical Society
WEPL	Webster Public Library
WOPL	Wolcott Public Library
WPL	Watertown Public Library

Harold Nestler

ALBANY COUNTY

ALBANY COUNTY

Anon. *Farmers' & Country Merchants' Almanac & Ready Reference Book.* Hist. sketches for co. of: Albany, Rensselaer, Washington, Warren, Schenectady, Saratoga, Rutland & Bennington. Albany. (1870). advts. 207 pp.

Anon. *History of Albany Co., 1683-1867* Syracuse. 1867. advts. wrps. 50 pp. (pub. by Hall & Patterson advt. agents.)

Bennett, A. P. *The People's Choice. A History of Albany County in Art and Architecture.* Albany. July 1980. illus. maps. bib. wrps. 135 pp.. Lmtd. to 1000 copies. 2nd printing, November 1980, lmtd. to 750 copies.

Howell & Tenney. *History of the Co. of Albany 1609-1886.* NY 1886. 995 pp. (Includes: hist. of co. of Schenectady 1662-1886.)

Kimball, F. *The Capital Region of NY State.* Albany, Rensselaer, Greene, Montgomery, Herkimer, Columbia, Schenectady, Schoharie, Fulton, Otsego Cos. NY. 1942. illus. 3 vol.

Parker, A. *Landmarks of Albany County.* Syracuse. 1894. 3 vol. in 1.

--- *Landmarks of Albany Co.* Syracuse 1897. 2 vol.

Preston, J. *A Statistical Report of the County of Albany, for ... 1820.* Albany. 1823 wrps. 30 pp. (A description of the co., including: type of farming, number of factories, mills, breweries, timber, suggestions for better agriculture, other data.)

ALBANY, Albany Co. (American Guide Series) *Albany.* n.d. (1930's.) map. illus. wrps. 28 pp..

Banks, A. *Albany Bicentennial. Historical Memoirs.* 1686-1886. Albany. 1888. 461 pp..

Barnes, T. *Settlement & Early History of Albany.* (1609-1686) Albany. 1851. 25 pp. lmtd. 300 copies.

Barnes, T. *Settlement & Early History of Albany.* 2nd. ed. Albany. 1864. illus. wrps. lmtd. 300 copies. 100 pp..

(Davis?) *Olden Times of Albany and Schenectady. First Known Discoveries of America.* Schenectady. 1845. wrps. 16 pp.

Fernow, B. *Albany & Its Place in the History of the U. S.* Albany. 1886. 98 pp.

Fitzgerald, C. *History of the City of Albany.* Masters Thesis 1929. State Teachers' College. Albany.

Hill, D. (Gov.) 1686-1886. *Oration Delivered at the Bicentennial Celebration at Albany July 22, 1886.* n.d. 46 pp.

Hislop, C. *Albany: Dutch, English, & American.* Albany 1936. illus. map. 413 pp.

Jackel, A. (ed.) *Source Materials for Black History.* Albany, NY, comp. by Harmanus Bleecker Lib. & NY State Lib. with bib. by F. Cady. 1972. (Extensive collection of photocopies of prntd. source material.) Lmtd. 15 copies placed in Albany schools.

Kenney, A. *Albany - Crossroads of Liberty.* 1976 wrps. 82 pp.

(Kimball, F.) *Albany, A Cradle of America.* Albany. 1936. illus. 62 pp.

Miller, G. A. *Retrospect of Two Centuries.* Albany. 1886. 16 pp.

Munsell, J. *Annals of Albany.* Albany 1850-59. 10 vol. (Vol. 3: 500 copies. Vol. 4: 500 copies. Vol. 5: 500 copies.

Vol. 6: 500 copies. Vol. 8: 350 copies.) Vol. 10: 350 copies.)
Munsell, J. Annals of Albany. 2nd. ed. Alby. 1869-71. 4 vol.
Munsell, J. Collections on the History of Albany. Albany 1865-71. maps. illus. 4 vol. (Vol. 1: 200 copies. Vol. 3: 240 copies.) Vol. 1 2nd ed. pub. in 1869.
Munsell, J. Collections on the History of Albany. Another ed. microfilmed by Bell & Howell, Cleveland, Ohio. 1964.
--- Men & Things in Albany Two Centuries Ago. Albany 1876. wrps. illus. 48 pp. (reprntd. in Transactions of Albany Institute 1879.)
Priest, J. A Copy of the Grants to the Van Rensselaer & Livingstone Families, Together With a History of the Settlement of Albany. Gathered from Authentic Sources, & Pub. for the Information of the Renters. Albany. Munsell. 1844. 32 pp.
Proctor, L. Albany as an Historical City, 1893. 15 pp.
Reynolds, C. Chronicles. A History of the City Arranged Chronologically From the Earliest Settlement to the Present Time. Albany. 1906. illus. map. 817 pp.
Springer, A. (comp.) Albany Bicentennial. A Chronicle of Local Events 1686-1886. Albany. 1886. 48 pp.
Tenney, J. New England in Albany. Boston 1883. 126 pp.. (Much data on New Englanders who were influential in Albany, with 60 pp. of brief biog.)
Weise, A. The History of the City of Albany. Albany. 1884. illus. map. 520 pp.
(Worth, G.) Random Recollections of Albany 1800 to 1808 by Ignatius Jones. 1849. wrps. 57 pp.
(Worth, G.) Random Recollections of Albany 1800 to 1808, by Ignatius Jones. 2nd. ed. Albany 1850. 90 pp.
(Worth, G.) Random Recollections of Albany 1800 to 1808, by Ignatius Jones. 3rd. ed. Albany 1866. With notes by Joel Munsell, the pub. illus. 139 pp.. lmtd. 450 copies. 3rd ed. reprntd. 1867. 144 pp. lmtd. 350 copies.

ALTAMONT, Albany Co.
Gregg, A. Below the Heldebergh: the Story of Altamont. 1965. illus. 26 pp.

BERNE, Albany Co.
Stapleton, E. Our Heritage. 1750-1900. 1977. illus. map. bib. wrps. 144 pp.

COEYMANS, Albany Co.
Giddings, E. Coeymans & the Past. Coeymans. 1973. illus. 135 pp.
Munsell, J. The Hudson River, Overslagh & Coeymans Bowery. Albany 1875. illus. 8 pp.

COHOES, Albany Co.
Bean, W. Cohoes, its Past & Present History, and Future Prospects. Cohoes. 1873. illus. wrps. 92 pp.
(Masten, A.) The History of Cohoes, From Earliest Settlement to Present. Albany 1877. 327 pp. (Copy at SLA interleaved with blank pages.) Reprntd. 1969. wrps.

GREEN ISLAND, Albany Co.
Hutchinson, S. A. History of the Village of Green Island. Troy 1934. wrps. 30 pp.

GUILDERLAND, Albany Co.
Brinkman, W. Historical Data of ... Guilderland. 1945. mimeo. 37 pp.

Gregg, A. *Outline History of Town of Guilderland.* 1951. 8 pp.

HELLEBERGH, Albany Co.
Gregg, A. *Old Hellebergh: Historical Sketches of the West Manor of Rensselaerwyck.* Altamont. 1936. illus. maps. wrps. 188 pp. reprntd. 1975. reprntd. 1978.

NISKAYUNA, Albany Co.
Becker, H. *Canastigione. The Early History of the Formation of That Part of Canastigione on the North Side of the Mohawk River at Niskayuna Including Village of Vischers Ferry & the Lower End of the Town of Clifton Park.* Rexford 1953. maps. 360 pp.

RENSSLAERVILLE, Albany Co.
Anon. *People Made It Happen Here. History of the Town. 1788-1950.* Rensselaerville Hist. Soc. 1977. illus. index. bib. 294 pp. reprntd. 1979. 305 pp.
Keller, W. *Rensselaerville, an Old Village of the Helderbergs.* wrps. 1924.
Torrance, M. *The Story of Old Rensslaerville.* 1939. pvtly. prntd. illus. maps. 72 pp.
Washbon, H. *Rensslaerville Reminiscences & Rhymes.* Rreprntd. from Village newspapers. Albany 1890. map. 93 pp. (First pub. in Rensslaerville Press in 1873)

VISCHER FERRY, Albany Co.
Becker, H. *Early Views of the Vischer Ferry Area.* Rexford. 1971. (1 copy only.)

WATERVLIET, Albany Co.
Myers, J. *History of City of Watervliet 1630-1910.* Troy (1910) illus. wrps. 124 pp.

WESTERLO, Albany Co.
Blaisdell, T. H. *Town of Westerlo, Then and Now.* 1976. wrps. 32 pp.

ALLEGANY COUNTY

ALLEGANY COUNTY
Beers, F. (ed.) *History of Allegany Co. 1806-1879.* NY. 1879. illus. map. 392 pp. 3 tinted plates. Reprntd. 1978 with name index.
Doty, L. (ed.) *The Genesee Country.* Allegany, Cattaraugus, Chautauqua, Chemung, Erie, Livingston, Monroe, Niagara, Ontario, Orleans, Schuyler, Steuben, Wayne, Wyoming, Yates Cos. Chicago 1925. illus. maps. 4 vol.
Flanagan, M. *History & Folklore of Allegany Co.* (Albany.) 1939. map. 120 pp. typed mss. at NYSHA.
Minard, J. *Allegany Co. & Its People.* Alfred. 1896. illus. maps. 2 vol.
--- *Recoll. of the Log School House Period, Sketches of Life & Customs in Pioneer Days.* Cuba. 1905. illus. 140 pp.

ALFRED, Allegany Co.
Clawson, C. *Hist of ... Alfred.* Alfred. 1926. illus. maps. 85 pp.

ALMA, Allegany Co.
Shear, H. *The Alma Story 1795-1850.* pub. by the author. Wellsville 1959. wrps. map. 85 pp.
Shear, H. *The Alma Story 1850-1900.* Part 2. pub. by author. 1960. wrps. map. 84 pp.

ALMOND, Allegany Co.
Reynolds, J. *The Almond Story. The Early Years.* Hornell 1962. wrps. 120 pp.

ANDOVER, Allegany Co.
Mulconery, B. (local historian.) (Beginning in 1951, and continuing for some years, a mimeo. 15- to 20-page local hist. was compiled each year, and given away to 400 or 500 interested people, usually in March.)

ANGELICA, Allegany Co.
Newman, L. *Angelica Sesquicentennial 1805-1955.* wrps. 58 pp. (Includes: Alfred, Allen, Belfast, Belmont, Belvidere, Birdsall, Cuba, Fillmore, Friendship, Rushford, Scio, West Almond, Wellsville.)
Stillwell, L. *Angelica Collectanea.* Angelica. 1955. illus. map. 208 pp.

BOLIVAR, Allegany Co.
Herrick, J. *Bolivar, Pioneer Oil Town.* Los Angeles, Cal. 1952. map. 150 pp. (Map is on dust jacket, not in book.)

CENTERVILLE, Allegany Co.
(Fiegl, E. comp.) *Centerville Sesquicentennial 1808-1958.* mimeo. illus. 22 pp.

CERES, Allegany Co.
Mann & King. *History of Ceres & Its Near Vicinity From Its Earliest Settlement in 1798 to the Present.* Olean. 1896. 150 pp. (Settled in 1798 near the NY-PA border. During a boundary resurvey in 1877, it was found to be in PA.)

CUBA, Allegany Co.
Anon. *Cuba, Incorporated as a Village for a Century 1850-1950.* Cuba. 1950. illus.
Minard, J. *Civic History & Illustrated Progress of Cuba 1822-1910.* Cuba. 1911. illus. 340 pp.

FRIENDSHIP, Allegany Co.
McCarthy, B. (and others.) *History of Friendship.* Bolivar. 1965. illus. map. advts. wrps. 72 pp. (Includes Nile & Belvidere.)
Olean Times Herald, 1965, had series of articles on Friendship hist.

GRANGER, Allegany Co.
Barney, D. Early Settlement of Granger. Newspaper articles in *Northern Allegany Observer.* March-April 1962.

HUME, Allegany Co.
Minard, J. *Pioneer Sketches. A History of Early Times.* Fillmore 1888. 79 pp. (Revised & enlarged ed. of article in *Angelica Reporter* ca 1868.)

RUSHFORD, Allegany Co.
Anon. *The Rushford Centennial. With Other Data & Reminiscences.* NY. (1908.) illus. map. 546 pp.
Gilbert, J. (ed) *Rushford & Rushford People.* Rushford. 1910. illus. map. 572 pp.

WELLSVILLE, Allegany Co.
Anon. *Centennial Book. Wellsville 1857-1957.* 1957. illus. advts. 80 pp.
Howe, M. *A History of the Town of Wellsville.* Wellsville. 1963. pub. by author. wrps. index. 224 pp.
Shear, H. *The Wellsville Story. Pioneer Days 1807-1850.* No. 1 of a series. (1957.) pub. by author. wrps. map. 75 pp.

WILLING, Allegany Co.
Shear, H. *The Willing Story 1795-1850.* Welsv. 1960. pub. by author. map. wrps. 113 pp.

WIRT, Allegany Co.
Thompson, E. (town historian.)

A History of the Town of Wirt and Village of Richburg. 1963. illus. 46 pp.

BRONX COUNTY

BRONX COUNTY
Anon. *Borough of the Bronx.* Pub. by North Side Board of Trade. 1897. illus. map. 248 pp.
Anon. *Bronx & Its People 1609-1927.* 1927. illus. 4 vol.
Cook & Kaplan. *The Borough of the Bronx 1639-1913.* 1913. pub. by authors. illus. 198 pp.
Jenkins, S. *The Story of the Bronx 1639 to Present.* NY. 1912. illus. maps 451 pp.
McNamara, J. *History in Asphalt. Origins of Bronx St. & Place Names.* 1978. illus. map. 522 p
Ultan, L. *The Beautiful Bronx. (1920-1950).* 1979. illus. index. 192 pp.

HIGH BRIDGE, Bronx Co.
Allyn, D. A. *Short Hist. Sketch of the High Bridge Neighborhood.* 1958. mimeo. 20 pp.

BROOME COUNTY

BROOME COUNTY
Anon. *Biographical Review. Sketches of the Leading Citizens of Broome County.* Boston. 1894. illus. 836 pp.
Anon. *History of Broome Co. 1806-1867.* Syrce. 1867. 34 pp.
Burr, G. *Historical Address Relating to the County of Broome.* Binghamton. 1876. 55 pp.
Hinman, M. *Creation of Broome County, NY. 175th Anniversary of the Co. 1806-1981.* Pub. by author. Windsor, NY. 1981. wrps. maps. bib. 33 pp.
Smith, H. (Ed.) *History of Broome Co.* Syracuse. 1885. illus. 2 vol. Also issued in 1 vol. Reprntd. ca 1978 with index.

BINGHAMTON, Broome Co.
Anon. *Binghamton Centennial Celebration 1834-1934.* ca 1934. illus. wrps. unpaged.
Anon, *Binghamton Past & Present. Descriptive. Historical.* Evening Herald Co. 1894. illus. advts. 120 pp.
Lawyer, W. (Ed) *Binghamton, Its Settlement, Growth, Development. 1800-1900.* 1900. illus. maps. 1035 pp. Lmtd. 550 copies.
Seward, W. (ed) *History of Binghamton & Broome Co.* NY. 1924. illus. maps. 3 vols.
Wilkinson, J. *The Annals of Binghamton, and of the Country Connected With It, From the Earliest Settlement.* 1840. lmtd. printing. 256 pp. (10-page typed index, comp. by E. Thomas, Oswego, in SLA.)
--- *The Annals of Binghamton. Reprinted With Notes, & Appendix, From the Original Edition Published in 1840.* Binghamton Times Assn. 1872. map. 312 pp. (This ed. was actually prntd. in 1873, and a few references to events in 1873 are in the book.)
Reprntd. 1967. *Appraisal 1840-1967, by Tom Cawley.* illus. by John Hart.
Reprntd. 1970 with separate index, comp. by M. Fuller.

CASTLE CREEK, Broome Co.
Lilly, J. *Annals of Castle Creek & Vicinity.* Whitney Point 1903. wrps. 32 pp.

CHENANGO, Broome Co.
Mss. on hist. in prvt. collection.

COLESVILLE, Broome Co.
Jacob, R. *Famines, Fires, & Festivals. A History of Colesville, 1785-1978.* 1978. illus. map. bib. 192 pp.

LISLE, Broome Co.
Lewis, F. *Lafayette & Lisle*, Seattle, Wash. (ca 1924) illus. 12 pp.
"Natt Odd." *A Geographical & Historical View of the State of Lisle*. 1842. pamphlet. (This humorous work has been attributed to several people: Mr. Cook, R. J. Ketchum, Nehemiah Randall.)
Walker, O. (town historian.) *Lisle. State, Town, Village.* Whitney Point 1962. illus. wrps. 127 pp.

NIMMONSBURG, Broome Co.
Page, F. *Early History of Nimmonsburg*. 1950. mimeo. 10 pp.

SANFORD, Broome Co.
Colwell, E. *The Hills of Home. Hunters' Tales, Early Settlers.* Bainbridge. 1944. 53 pp. typed mss. at SLA.

WHITNEY POINT, Broome Co.
Seymour, G. *Whitney's Point, Old & New. 1791-1898.* Whitney Point Reporter. Souvenir ed. April 23, 1898. illus. 47 pp.

CANALS

--- *An Act to Provide for the Improvement of the Internal Navigation of the State. Passed April 8th. 1811.* Broadside, 8 x 9 inches. (This Act appointed commissioners to consider a canal between the Great Lakes and the Hudson River, acquire lands and loans, employ personnel, and report to the legislature. This was the major step in implementing the building of the Erie Canal.)
Campbell, W. W. *Life and Writings of DeWitt Clinton*. NY. 1849. port. 381 pp. (The most important section of this work is the 177 pp which include the first printing of Clinton's private journal of his trip, with the other Canal Commissioners, in 1810, up the Mohawk and throughout western NY to learn the feasibility of constructing a canal from Albany to Lake Erie.)
(Carey, Mathew) *Internal Improvement. New Series No. II* Phil. Carey. Jan. 31, 1826. 4 pp. signed in type "Fulton." (The author, probably Carey, discusses the remarkable amount of tolls collected on the Erie Canal. It includes a letter from Carey to Gov. DeWitt Clinton in Dec. 1825 asking questions about the canal, and Clinton's two answering letters, dated Jan. 12 and 13, 1826. Clinton details a new proposal on the number of horses and men for each canal boat and a new system of work and rest. "This plan will also have a beneficial effect in protecting the morals of the young men employed as drivers, who will always be under the eye of the masters of the boats, instead of remaining at stands for a considerable time, and indulging in dissipation." About this time Carey issued a number of pamphlets on canals and railroads.)
(Clinton, DeWitt) *Letters on the Natural History and Internal Resources of the State of New York, by Hibernicus.* NY. 1822. prntd. boards. 224 pp. (Clinton had explored the proposed route of the Erie Canal, and wrote these letters about the travel and resources of the region to generate support for its construction.)
Colden, Cadwallader D. *Memoir Prepared at the Request of a*

Committee of the Common Council of the City of New York, and Presented to the Mayor of the City at the Celebration of the Completion of the New York Canals. NY. 1825. maps. plates. 408 pp. (A scarce item and difficult to find in complete condition. Many of the known copies have had some of the fine plates and maps removed. Rink's *Technical Americana* notes three printings in 1825, each with different pagination: 408, 388, and 130. The 408page ed. was reprntd. by University Microfilms, Ann Arbor, MI, in 1967. The seal of the city of NY was impressed on the front cover of some presentation copies of the 1825 ed.)

(Eaton, Amos.) *To Gentlemen Residing in the Vicinity of the Erie Canal.* Troy (NY). Dec. 13, 1822. 10 pp. pamphlet. (In this pamphlet Eaton explains the plan of Stephen Van Rensselaer who proposes to take a geological and agricultural survey of lands adjoining the Erie Canal. He requests data from those living near the canal, and gives directions on collecting and preserving specimens needed. Rink's *Technical Americana* locates only two copies and neither of them are in NY State.)

--- *Erie Canal. New York State Council on the Arts.* 1968. (This is a set of 50 loose pictures, each 11 x 14 inches, pub. for the sesquicentennial of the canal. These illus. depict scenes along the way, canal boat life, early broadsides, and a map. These are great for teaching displays. The Council on the Arts issued at least six other portfolios of loose prints: Farm Life Today, Open Space in the Inner City, Main Street, Neighbors on the Block, Growing Up Black, and the Lower East Side. As these pictures are taken out and displayed, inevitably some will be scattered and lost. In years to come complete portfolios will be more difficult to find. Here is a tip for purchasers of portfolios of prints: do not pay for the item until you have counted the plates and made sure the set is complete.)

--- *(Erie Canal Medal).* A medal, made of white metal, was selectively distributed at the opening of the Erie Canal. It was approximately 1 1/2 inches in diameter. The inscription on the front is, "Erie Canal Comm. 4 July 1817 Comp. 26 Oct. 1825. C. C. Wright, Sc. 1826. Presented by the City of N. York." Obverse inscription is, "Union of Erie With the Atlantic. R. del. W. Sc." (Only a few medals were made. Hibler and Kappen's book containing information on medals calls it "extremely rare." On uncommon occasions it is found in a small round wooden box with the label, "This box was made out of a piece of wood, brought from Erie in the first Canal Boat. *The Seneca Chief.*")

--- (Erie Canal) Printed invitation ticket to attend the Celebration of the completion of the Erie Canal, at NYC, Nov. 4, 1825, and to proceed from there in a Steam Boat to Sandy Hook. It was 5 1/2 x 3 1.4 inches, and was issued by the Corporation of the City of New York. The fine cartouche was drawn and engraved by A. B. Durand.

Platt, J. *The Canals of New York State. A Hindrance to Its*

Commercial Prosperity. 1899. wrps. 15 pp. (A statistical paper showing that it costs more to ship cargo by canal than by railroad. In 1902 Platt wrote another pamphlet in opposition to the Barge Canal. He had a reason for being oppugnant to canals: he was one of the chief promoters of the railroad bridge across the Hudson at Poughkeepsie. The bridge was begun in 1873 and the first train crossed it on December 29, 1888.)

--- *Public Proceedings on the Removal of Hon. DeWitt Clinton, From the Office of Canal Commissioner.* NY. 1824. wrps. 40 pp. (Clinton's political leadership was opposed by the Albany Regency, directed by Sen. Martin Van Buren. They succeeded in removing him as Canal Commissioner. The public was indignant at this, and voted him in as Governor of the state in the same year. This event is discussed in Bobbe's biog. of Clinton.)

--- *To the Honorable the Legislature of the State of New York, the Subscribers, Inhabitants of Black Rock and Other Parts of the County of Niagara on and near Niagara River, Beg Leave Respectfully to Represent ... Black Rock, January 1821.* Folio broadside. (Subscribers give numerous reasons why the Erie Canal should terminate at Black Rock instead of at Buffalo; and gives some proposals for constructing a harbor at Black Rock. There was bitter rivalry for the canal terminus between Black Rock and Buffalo, and Buffalo finally won. Not in *Am. Imprints,* Sabin, or Whitford.)

Vindex (pseud.) *A Review and Refutation of the Statements Made in the Late Report of the Canal Commissioners, to the Legislature of This State.* Albany. 1828. 30 pp. (An expose of the errors made in building the Erie Canal, and a discussion of the quarrel of whether Buffalo or Black Rock should be the western terminus. *American Imprints* locates only one copy of this pamphlet, and that one is incomplete, having only eight pages.)

Williams, W. *The Stage, Canal, and Steamboat Register, for 1831.* Utica. [1830?] 16 pp.. pamphlet. (Mileage charts, Erie Canal tolls, other information of interest to travellers. It has a large folding map of NY State, with inset map of the Hudson River and a profile of the Erie Canal. This is not listed in J. Williams' *An Oneida County Printer. William Williams ... With a Bibliography of the Press at Utica ....* 1906. Reprntd. in 1974.)

CATSKILL MOUNTAINS AND DELAWARE VALLEY

--- (Ashokan Reservoir) *Board of Water Supply Songs. Celebration of the Beginning of Storage of Catskill Water. October 11, 1913.* wrps. (This is a booklet of 27 music-less songs about the new reservoir: Wait Till the Dam is Finished. Shall We Gather at Ashkan? At The Head of the Big Pipe Line. Flow, Flow, Flow. When Its Conduit Closing Time on Contract 3.; plus many more.)

Booth, M. A. *The Delaware and Hudson Canal, With Special Emphasis on Deerpark, New York.* 1965. wrps. maps. bib. 120 mimeo. pp. (This is ac-

tually "a preliminary research report on the proposed reconstruction of a short section of the Delaware and Hudson Canal near Port Jervis, NY." This was primarily written for those who would be working on the project. Probably few copies were made.)
Calder, A. *Miriam's Heritage. A Story of the Delaware River.* NY. 1878. 175 pp. (Delaware Valley fiction of the Beaverkill area, with a background of the NY and Erie Railroad construction, and timber rafting on the river.)
--- Canajoharie and Catskill Rail Road Company. (This company was chartered in April 1830 to run a railroad through the valley of the northern Catskills to connect the city of Catskill on the Hudson River to Canajoharie on the Mohawk River. Only about 26 miles were ever completed. It ran into financial problems, and failed to pay interest on the loans it had received from the state of NY. Roscoe's *History of Schoharie Co.* says, "The business men of Albany city saw the project would be detrimental to their interest, purchased the stock and let the enterprise fail." The road's career was actually ended when a bridge at High Rock collapsed in March 1840, throwing the train into a creek. Several years ago some blank stock certificates of this ill-fated railroad came on the market.)
Cantine and Rainer (eds.) *Prison Etiquette. The Convicts' Compendium of Useful Information.* Bearsville, NY. Retort Press. 1950. wrps. illus. with drawings. 138 pp. (This was written by 15 extreme pacifists who went to prison during World War II. It is "a manual of living-technique for prisoners in general." The main topics covered are: Resistance in Prison, the Prison Community, and Arts and Letters. Bearsville is in the edge of the Catskills near Woodstock.)
Francis, A. M. *Catskill Rivers. Birthplace of American Fly Fishing.* Beaverkill Press. NY. pvtly. prntd. 1983. illus. maps. bib. chronology. index. 258 pp. (An in-depth study of fishing on Catskill Mountain streams from the earliest days. There was a regular trade ed. as well as a Deluxe Ed. lmtd. to 300 copies with full leather binding with gold lettering, marbled end papers, in a slip case.)
--- *The Catskill Water System News, June 20, 1911 through Dec. 20, 1913.* Total of 61 numbers. bound volume. (This was a 4-page newspaper pub. for employees working on the Catskill Aqueduct that would bring water to NYC. It provides a wonderful source of information: history of the area, diagrams, poetry, technical data, personal news, hiking trips, bids, contracts, tunnels.)
Gardner, E. E. *Folklore from the Schoharie Hills.* 1937. index. folding map. illus. bib. 351 pp. (Author collected folklore in the back country of Schoharie Co. in the early 1900s. She had come from "the great world where there lived folks with awful larnin'", and at first was charged with being a "guvment spy." The finest work of its type on a NY co.)
--- *Guide to Rambles From the Catskill Mountain House, By a Visitor.* Catskill. 1862. 8 pp. pamphlet. (A description of

walks for vacationers in the vicinity of this famous hotel which overlooked the Hudson Valley from the eastern rampart of the Catskill Mountains. That grand edifice has been demolished.)

Hunt, W. *The American Biographical Sketch Book.* NY. 1849. Illus. 408 pp. (Hunt compiled the biog. of 126 notable Americans, devoting 40 pages to Zadock Pratt the noted tanner of Prattsville, NY. The front cover has an illus. of Pratt, and of Prattsville as it was in 1824 and in 1849, in gold design. Bindings with illus. of specific towns are exceedingly rare.)

Hutton, Capt. T. *H-A-L-TT!-WHA-ZAA? Being a History of the First Provisional Regiment, and the Answer of a State Militant to the Threat of Berlin.* 1919. illus. map. 506 pp. (A very detailed history of the regiment that guarded the NYC water supply and the Catskill Aqueduct during World War I. In the past 35 years I have only seen one copy of this elusive book.)

Irving, Washington. *Rip Van Winkle.* ca 1920s? wrps. illus. with small drawings. 52 pp.. (Catskill Mountain classic prntd. in Gregg Shorthand.)

Jagendorf, M. *The Marvellous Adventures of Johnny Darling.* 1949. illus. bib. 239 pp. (Tall tales by and about Johnny Caesar Cicero Darling, the Paul Bunyan of Sullivan Co. This unusual bib. consists of names of folk who told these entertaining tales to author.)

Knoepfel, W. H. *An Account of Knoepfel's Schoharie Cave, Schoharie Co., New York. With the History of its Discovery, Subterranean Lake, Minerals, and Natural Curiosities. Illustrated With Engravings.* NY. 1853. 16 pp. (This cave is now known as Ball's Cave. Knoepfel obtained the property from Peter Ball, the original owner, named it Knoepfel's Cave, and pub. this pamphlet with the intention of opening the site to the public. I hope no one came to see the place on the strength of his publication because he never got around to making it accessible. Clay Perry's *Underground Empire, Wonders and Tales of New York Caves*, pub. in 1948, describes this cavern.)

Lichtenthaeler, F. *Storm Blown Seed of Schoharie.* maps. 102 pp. 1944. (This is an hist. gem of a study of the emigration of the Palatines from Schoharie Co., NY, to Pennsylvania, in Vol. 9 of the proceedings of the PA German Folklore Society.)

Newman, J. B. *Wa-Wa-Wanda. A Legend of Old Orange.* NY. Rudd and Carleton. 1860. map of the Minisink Battle Ground on the Deleware River. 180 pp.. (Poetry about the Waywayanda area of Orange Co., NY, with numerous hist. footnotes.)

O'Connor, J. *Works of James O'Connor the Deaf Poet, With a Biographical Sketch of the Author.* NY. 1886 ed. Port. 316 and 76 pp. (O'Connor was a farmer of Andes, NY, born in 1835, who had a poetic pen. He composed many of the poems while working in the field. His book was so well received that he personally sold 500 copies in 35 days.)

--- *Overlook Mountain House.* Woodstock, Ulster County, NY. C. K. Haskell, Prop. An

8-page, illus. advertising pamphlet. ca late 1800s. (Includes terms, and travel routes to this famous hotel.)

(Pratt, Z.) *Biography of Zadoc Pratt, of Prattsville (NY).* ca 1852. port. index. illus. 506 pp. (Pratt was a prominent Tanner in the Catskill Mountains, and was a Congressman. He built a 130-foot long bridge in 3 foot of snow in 11 days without use of ardent spirits.)

(Pratt, Z.) *Chronological Biography of Hon. Zadock Pratt, of Prattsville, New York.* 1862. wrps. 45 pp. (Pratt outlived four wives, and possibily was an eccentric: he once walked forty miles in a day without food or water as a matter of curiosity; and at one time he subscribed to eight daily and thirty weekly newspapers.)

Rusk, S. *An Illus. Guide to the Catskill Mountains, With Maps and Plans. A Book of Facts.* Catskill. 4th. ed. 1881. wrps. index. illus. 142 pp. (One of the scarcest of the Catskill Mountain guide books.)

Schaldach, W. J. *The Wind on Your Cheek, or More Chips From the Log of an Artist Sportsman.* 1972. Rockville Centre, NY. Freshet Press. illus. with drawings. Several colored plates. 159 pp. (Has a chapter on fishing in the famous Beaverkill in the southern Catskills, an illus. of Barnhart's Pool in Beaverkill, and an illus. of a covered bridge. If you drive on route 17 west of Roscoe, NY, during the fishing season, you will see a number of men with rods in the waters of the Beaverkill and other fine fishing streams; and at one point a quick glimpse to the north might spot a covered bridge.)

Searing, A. E. P. *The Land of Rip Van Winkle. A Tour Through the Romantic Parts of the Catskills. Its Legends and Traditions. With Illus.* by Joseph Lauber, Charles Volkmar, and Others. Engraved by E. Heinemann. NY. G. Putnam & Sons. 1884. 147 pp. (A classic of Catskill Mountain literature, with fine illus. of scenery, and a folding frontispiece. Bound in green cloth with gold lettering on the front cover. The authoress was the wife of the secretary of the Overlook Mountain House Company. Reprntd. ca 1891. Alf Evers, in his delightful book *The Catskills* devotes over a full page to this work.)

Tremain, L. *Oration, by ... Delivered at Oakhill, Greene Co., NY, July 4, 1851.* Catskill. 1851. 29 pp.. pamphlet. (Tremain, a U. S. Congressman from Durham, in Greene Co., gave this impressive Fourth of July oration. When he told a story of a brave deed in the Mexican War, he ended with, "That man was an Irishman!" A prntd. note in brackets says, "Loud burst of tremendous ... applause arose at this announcement." To this day there are lots of Irish in Greene Co.)

White, F. *The Spicklefisherman and Others.* NY. Derrydale Press. illus. by A. B. Frost, G. Stevenson, and O. Kemp. 1928. 112 pp. Lmtd. 775 copies. ("Four of the best fishing stories ever written." Fishing on the Beaverkill, one of the top trout streams in the northeast, which flows in the southern Catskills towards the Delaware Valley. The Derrydale Press issued many fine sporting books and prints between the years 1927 and 1942, and a few of them refer to NY state. They even went further afield and in the 1930s prntd. three vol. of the hist. records of the Town of Brookhaven (L.I.) for the town, in an ed. of 200 sets. In 1981 the Angler's and Shooter's Press of Goshen, CT, pub. a comprehensive bibliography of Derrydale Press, which every sporting book collector should have on his reference shelf. [It even has a chapter titled "The Pain and Pleasure of Derrydale Collecting."] Montague Hankin of Summit, NJ, who made his fortune in other enterprises, also bought and sold books, pamphlets, maps, and mss. Over the years I had many a fine lunch at his home, and bought a number of NY state items, including a manuscript from 1743 about the Esopus Indians interfering with the surveying of the Hardenberg Patent in the Catskills. [Once I took "Monty" down to look at a library in a mansion at the NJ shore. He bought some fine items, but I did not find too much. I did buy a tiger skin rug, head and all. On the way back to his home I put it on the back seat of the car with the head looking out of the window. That brought a number of incredulous stares from passing motorists.] To get back to the Derrydales: "Monty" was a specialist in them. He had them stacked all over the place, including piles of duplicates squirreled away in odd corners. They were being avidly sought by collectors, and so were too expensive for me to buy. But one day he had a number of copies on a shelf in the hallway. As I walked by them he looked at me and at the shelved Derrydales and said, "You can have the lot for $10 each." That made my day.)

Wood, L. C. *Rafting on the Delaware River*. 1934. Livingston Manor, NY. Livingston Manor Times. illus. index. wrps. 272 pp. (The thrilling story of rafting logs down the Delaware River, with lumbering and rafting data on 42 river and nearby towns.)

CATTARAUGUS COUNTY

CATTARAUGUS COUNTY

Adams, W. (ed.) *Historical Gazetteer & Biographical Memorial of Cattaraugus Co.* Syracuse Oct. 1893. illus. map. 2 vol.

Donovan, M. *Historical Review of Cattaraugus County*. Olean. 1942. illus. 128 pp.

Ellis, F. *History of Cattaraugus County*. Phil. 1878. illus. maps. 512 pp. Reprntd. ca 1976

Hall, L. *West of the Cayuga*. NY. 1940. 88 pp. (sketches of Cattaraugus, Allegany, & adjacent cos.)

Manly, J. (comp.) *Cattaraugus County, Little Valley* 1857. illus. advts. wrps. 136 pp.

Pierce, J. (co. historian) *Cattaraugus County, Sesquicentennial 1808-1958.* ca 1958. illus. advts. wrps.

CATTARAUGUS, Cattaraugus Co.
Anon. *One Hundred Years and More of Cattaraugus - New Albion Happenings*. Cattaraugus Hist. Soc. 1979. illus. 294 pp.

Anon. *The Village of Cattaraugus. Diamond Jubilee. 1882-1957.* illus. wrps. unpaged.

Sager, I. *The Cattaraugus Home Front in World War I*. 1965. wrps. 12 pp. (reprntd from *Cattaraugus Times*.)

DAYTON, Cattaraugus Co.
Schults, C. *Hist. & Biog. History of Township of Dayton, Comprising the Villages of Cottage, Wesley, Markham, Dayton, South Dayton, & Fair Plain*. Buffalo. 1901. illus. 302 pp.

ELKO, Cattaraugus Co.
Pierce, J. *Notes on the Town of Elko*. Allegany. 1954. map. 19 pp. typed mss. at SLA.

ELLICOTTVILLE, Cattaraugus Co.
Charlton, J. *Early Days in Western New York (1899)* 14 pp. typed mss. in BHS.
Northrup, J. *Unusual History of Ellicottville Centennial 1837-1937*. illus. advts. 20 pp.

FRANKLINVILLE, Cattaraugus Co.
Van Hoesen, R. *Franklinville in Pictures & Story*. Frnkvle 1914. illus. map. advts. 184 pp.

FREEDOM, Cattaraugus Co.
Howlett (and others) *150 Years of Freedom 1811-1961*. (1961) illus. wrps. 99 pp.

GOWANDA, Cattaraugus Co.
Anon. *Growing Gowanda ... An Historical Review*. Gowanda. 1940. 64 pp.
Leonard, I. (comp.) *Historical Sketch of Gowanda, Commemorating 50th Anniversary of Its Incorporation*. Aug. 8, 1898. illus. wrps. 116 pp.
Plumb, A. *Address Aug. 9, 1898. In Commemoration of the 50th Anniversary of Incorporation of the Village*. 6 pp.

LEON, Cattaraugus Co.
Dorsey, B. *Facets of Rural Life Before the Auto*. Leon 1949. pub. by author. wrps. 65 pp.
Dorsey, B. *Hist ... of Leon*. Leon 1958. pub. by the author. wrps. lmtd 250 copies. 131 pp.
Luce, G. *Lest We Forget*. (Early settlement of Leon.) Cattaraugus. 1970. pamphlet.

LYNDON, Cattaraugus Co.
Case, J. (and others) *History of Town of Lyndon*. Franklinville. 1928. wrps. 16 pp.
A mss. on Lyndon hist. is in a private collection.

MACHIAS, Cattaraugus Co.
Watson, S. *A Hist. of Machias ... 1827-1977*. 1977. illus. 172 pp.

NEW ALBION, Cattaraugus Co.
Buskist. *The Village of New Albion "Horth's Corners."* Cattaraugus. 1965. 11 pp. leaflet.

OLEAN, Cattaraugus Co.
Anon. *Directory of Olean, With Brief History of the Town*. Olean. 1882. map. 115 pp.
Bradley, K. *Sketches of Olean Rock City; Historic Glimpses of Olean*. 1920. wrps. 54 pp.
Brooks, M. A. *Sketch of Early Settlement of Olean & Its Founders*. Olean. 1898. pvtly. prntd. 32 pp.
Chapin, L. (ed.) *Olean the City of Material Advantages. Its History*. Olean. 1889. 56 pp.

PERRYSBURG, Cattaraugus Co.
A 2-reel tape has been made on Perrysburg history, by Mr. Russell, Perrysburg historian. Is not now in his possession.

PINE VALLEY COMMUNITY, Cattaraugus Co.
(Pine Valley Yorkers, sponsored by E. Oehser.) *Pine Valley*

Community. n.d. map. wrps. 46 pp. (Includes: Cherry Creek, Arkwright, Villenova, Ellington, Charlotte, Dayton, Leon, Connewango, New Markhams, Connewango Val., Balcoms Corners, & Hamlet.)

PORTVILLE, Cattaraugus Co.
Holcomb. H. *Glimpses of 50 Years.* Portville 1931. wrps. 100 pp.

RANDOLPH, Cattaraugus Co.
Latham, C. *Illus. Souvenir of Randolph & East Randolph.* Bradford, PA. 1895. 46 pp.

RICH VALLEY, Cattaraugus Co.
Hall. *Early History of Rich Valley & Snyder Hill.* 1965. 16 pp. leaflet, plus map, and chart of pioneer family intermarriages. (Originally pub. in the *Cattaraugus Times* newspaper.)

S. DAYTON, Cattaraugus Co.
Perry, J. *Village of South Dayton.* Gowanda 1906. booklet.
Sweetland, H. *History of South Dayton.* 1940. (See PINE VALLEY COMMUNITY.)

YORKSHIRE, Cattaraugus Co.
Westover, F. *A Brief History of the Town of Yorkshire* 1957. 39 pp. typed mss. in SLA.

CAYUGA COUNTY

CAYUGA COUNTY
Anon. *Biographical Review of Leading Citizens of Cayuga Co.* Boston. 1894. illus. 2 vol.
Allen, H. *A Story of Cayuga County.* 1958. wrps. 15 pp.
Barnes, W. *Account of the Early History of Central New York. (Cos. of Cayuga, Cortland, Oneida, Onondaga, Oswego, Madison).* Albany. 1875. 37 pp.

Howland, E. *Historical Sketch of Friends in Cayuga County. (1795-1828)* Auburn. 1882. wrps. 44 pp. (Quaker history in co. A note on the title page of the copy I had says, "But two copies of this pamphlet known to exist. One is the Author's copy. This is the other.")
(Snow, B. ed.) *History of Cayuga Co.* Auburn 1908. illus. 598 pp.
Snow, D. *Early Cayuga Days. Folklore & Local History of a NY Co..* Masters' Thesis 1940. State Teachers' Coll. Albany.
Storke & Smith. *History of Cayuga County 1789-1879.* Syracuse. 1879. illus. map. 556 pp. Reprntd. 1978 with index.
Wheeler, C. *Inventors & Inventions of Cayuga Co.* With Suppl. by D. Osborne. Auburn. 1882. illus. wrps. 179 pp.

AUBURN, Cayuga Co.
Allen, H. A. *Chronicle of Early Auburn. 1793-1860.* Auburn 1953. map. wrps. mimeo. (Partially pub. in *Citizen Advertiser* 1950-1953.)
--- *A Chronicle of Auburn 1861 to 1940.* (1941.) Copy in SPL.
--- *Story of Auburn to August, 1935.* n.d. mimeo. 14 pp.
--- *A Chronicle of Auburn from 1793 to 1955, Being a Chronicle of Early Auburn and Chronicle of Auburn Consolidated.* Auburn. 1955. map. wrps. mimeo. 152 pp.
Hall, H. *History of Auburn.* Auburn. 1869. 579 pp.
Monroe, J. *Historical Records of a Hundred and Twenty Years.* Geneva. 1913. illus. 278 pp.

CAYUGA, Cayuga Co.
McIntosh, F. *History of Cayuga Village.* Syracuse. 1927. illus. maps. 112 pp.

FAIRHAVEN, Cayuga Co.
Sant, R. *Fairhaven Folks & Folklore.* 1941. illus. wrps. 145 pp.

FLEMING, Cayuga Co.
Post, A. (comp.) *Historical Sketch of Town of Fleming.* 1923. wrps. 45 pp.

MORAVIA, Cayuga Co.
Gardner, H. Many articles about life in early Moravia, by Gardner, were pub. in Moravia newspapers in 1870s & 1880s.
Luther, L. *Historical Sketches of Early Moravia & St. Matthews' Church.* 1956. 11 pp. typed mss. in NYSHA.
Luther, L. *Moravia and Its Past, and Adjoining Townships.* Indianapolis. 1966. index. illus. 534 pp. (Includes: Montville, Niles, Sempronious, Locke, Genoa, Venice, and Scipio.)
Wright, J. *Historical Sketch of Town of Moravia 1791-1873.* Auburn. 1874. 289 pp. Another ed. covered 1791-1918. Auburn. n.d. illus. 527 pp.

OWASCO, Cayuga Co.
Case, W. *Along Owasco's Waters.* 1950. illus. wrps. 20 pp.

PORT BYRON, Cayuga Co.
Blauvelt, E. *Gram's Story.* NY. 1955. illus. 69 pp.
Kerns, E. *History of Port Byron & Mentz from Indian Tribes to 1922.* (1922) illus. 12 pp.

SENNETT, Cayuga Co.
Smith, E. (comp.) *Along the Road Through Sennett's Past.* 1977. illus. map. 64 pp..

SPRINGPORT. Cayuga Co.
Yawger, R. *The Indian & the Pioneer* Syracuse. 1893. illus. map. 332 pp.

SUMMER HILL, Cayuga Co.
Buckley, E. *Summer Hill.* (1900.) 127 pp.

THROOPSVILLE, Cayuga Co.
Crysdale & Wait (comps.) *Owasco River Valley Facts & Folklore 1793-1965.* Ithaca. 1965. wrps. 167 pp. (Includes Throopsville, Clarksville, Haydenville, Port Byron, Auburn.)

UNION SPRINGS, Cayuga Co.
(Getman, M.) *Centennial Program 1848-1948.* ca 1948. illus. map. advts. 82 pp.

WEEDSPORT, Cayuga Co.
Hopkins, L. *Facts Regarding Weedsport.* Livingston. 1933. pvtly. prntd. illus. 79 pp. ("This book was set up and prntd. by the Livingston Press, operated by patients at Potts Memorial Hospital, Livingston, Columbia, Co., NY.")
Merriman, C. (& others) *Brutus, Macedonia, Weeds Basin, Weeds Port.* (ca 1963.) wrps. 32 pp. (Pub. by Weedsport Central School for 7th grade use.)

CENTRAL NEW YORK

(Adams, I.) *A Narrative of the Life, Travels, and Adventures of Capt. Israel Adams; Who Lived at Liverpool in Onondaga Co., NY: The Man Who, During the Last War, Surprised the British Boats Lying in the Cay of Quoenti; Who Took by Stratagem the Brig Toronto, and Took Her to Sacketts Harbor; and For Whom the British Offered a Reward of 100 (Pounds).* Utica: Printed by D. Bennett. 1847. 36 pp.. pamphlet. (Adams, born in 1776, travelled widely in NY

State engaging in several occupations, and spent some time at sea. He was in the Navy on Lake Ontario and the River St. Lawrence in the War of 1812. He seems to have out-adventured every other known person in the course of human history. This pamphlet was originally pub. in Cortland, NY, in 1843, 28 pp. Sabin does not note the 1843 printing, and the only copy of the 1847 printing he located lacked the title page.)

Ball, L. *Tanning and Currying, in Their Various Branches, From Actual Experience.* Sangerfield (NY). Joseph Tenny. 1827. 29 pp. pamphlet. (The author had over 20 years experience in tanyards and curry shops, evidentally some of them in the Sangerfield area. He writes about: tanning, calf skins, sheep skins, hog skins, recipes, tanning sole leather, and other topics. This was the first American work on leather tanning. The copy I had was well used, and the last 3 pp. were in photocopy. A very rare work, as *American Imprints* and Rink locate only one other known copy. Tenny pub. newspapers at Sangerfield from 1814 into the 1830s.)

---- *Balloting Book, and Other Documents Relating to Military Bounty Lands, in the State of New York.* Albany. 1825. 189 pp. (A major reference on the settling of central NY State by military men after the Revolutionary War: Acts, Laws, Congressional Resolutions, Land Office Minutes, &c. Names of military men, township, lot number, acreage, date of Patent. There is also a list of the 18 Townships in the Military Tract with names of their men and the Lot number. Much other data of interest. I am quite sure this has been reprntd.)

Bancroft, F. *The Life of William H. Seward.* 2 vols. 1900. index. (Seward, the statesman of Auburn, NY, was Governor of NY State, and was Secretary of State under Lincoln. The DAB calls this biog. "sympathetic yet critical ... exceedingly well proportioned." A set I once had contained a mss. letter from the author telling of Seward's love of liquor.)

--- *Barber's Great Western Rail Road and Family Almanac, for 1856.* Homer, Cortland Co., NY. Dixon & Cass, Printers. (Barber had a wholesale and retail Emporium in Homer where he sold groceries, hardware, dry goods, paint, lumber, stoves, and almost everything else a local resident would need to comfortably live in Cortland Co. He had a brillant idea: he acquired a quantity of the *Farmer's Almanac* by David Young, for 1856, and issued by Richard Marsh of NY, and had his own wrapper prntd. and put on and called it *Barber's Great Western ... Almanac.* Three leaves advertise his Emporium, and the front leaf has a time table for the Syracuse and Binghamton Rail Road. It has a small illus. of a train, and a decorative border.)

--- (Bath, NY) *Annual Report of New York State Soldiers and Sailors Home, at Bath, Steuben County, New York, for 1900.* Albany. 1901. 89 pp. (Brief statistical data, but mainly an 86-page inventory of the Home's property. All the way from the buildings, to: the

band's 2 hand grenades, an ashcan at the stable, 4 pictures in the hospital, 2 pterisadiantoides in the floral dept., to 3 rat traps in the main dining hall.)
--- *Bloomville Mirror.* Newspaper pub. in Bloomville, Delaware Co. Simon B. Champion, ed. Small folio. (Bloomville was a very small hamlet, French's *Gazetteer* reporting in 1861 it had a post office and a population of 184. The Civil War years of this newspaper are important because they contain a great many letters from soldiers serving on the battle field with NY State regiments, including the 144th, 124th, 17th, 104th, 89th, and others.)
Bronson, J. & R. *The Domestic Manufacturer's Assistant and Family Directory, in the Arts of Weaving and Dyeing: Comprehending a Plain System of Directions ... Cotton and Woollen Goods: Including Many Useful Tables and Drafts.* Utica. William Williams. 1817. 204 pp. A slip with 9 lines of errata is pasted to the inside of the rear cover. (This work is included here because it is a classic on hand weaving and dyeing, and quite likely was widely used in the central NY area. Nothing appears to be known about the authors except that they were in the weaving and dyeing business since 1800, and their preface is dated: New-Hartford, Oneida Co., NY, July, 1817. The section on dyeing was reprntd. in 1826. The entire book was reprntd. in 1949 in an ed. of 500 copies. It was reprntd. in 1977 by Dover Pub. in paperback, slightly corrected, and with an introduction by Rita J. Adrosko, Curator, Division of Textiles, National Museum of History and Technology.)

Brutcher, C. *Joshua: A Man of the Finger Lakes Region. A True Story Taken From Life.* Copyright by Chas. Brutcher and Melvin J. Rosekans. 1927. illus. 139 pp. (One of the scarcest and most sought after central NY State books, involving the famous Loomis Gang of thieves which terrorized the countryside from the 1840s to the 1860s. A few copies contain a famous two page appendix, which some folks claim contains a veiled reference to a famous NY State family. As with many scarce books, it is claimed that the family bought up and destroyed as many copies as it could find. My copy of *Joshua* was dug out of the cellar of Sam Murray of Wilbraham, MA. Sam was a travelling new book salesman who in his spare time bought huge quantities of old books, pamphlets, and mss., and stored them away. At the same time he built up an extensive reference library. When he retired and went into the business full-time he had an excellent stock, and the book tools for research. His vast stock was crammed into a garage, a two-story barn, his cellar, and into almost every room in the house, and this great collection was a mecca for hordes of travelling booksellers. Many great treasures were discovered here, and it is where I acquired a number of fine NY State books. Sam and his wife, Jo, were the epitome of hospitality. The very first of the many times I went there we had never met, and I don't think Sam had even heard of me. I got there about 10:00 in the morning, and we stopped looking at the pricing books at 2:30 the next morning! As the last book was packed into a box Sam said, "I have an appointment and have to get up at 7:00 o'clock. You can sleep in the little room right here. When you wake up, go in the kitchen and have some breakfast and just be sure the door is shut when you leave." Such hospitality and confidence is rare indeed.)

--- (Budge Murder, Lyons Falls, NY) *A Review of the Case, the People Against Rev. Henry Budge, Indicted for the Murder of His Wife Priscilla Budge (Tried at Oneida, NY, Circuit Court, Aug. and Sep. 1861.)* (An approximately 100-page article in: Transactions of Medical Society of the State of NY for 1862. The Reverend was acquitted of murdering his wife with a knife. I have included this item as being of exceptional interest as it has a series of gruesome plates showing four positions in which a person's throat could be cut. While on the subject of unusual publications, it might be fun to list some of the extraordinary objects that have appeared on booksellers' catalogs: a classic car (a Rolls Royce, as I recall), an island in West Indies, and a NY State dealer once advertised a stuffed timber wolf which he could not resist buying while on a book purchasing trip. Years ago I acquired and advertised a pair of pall bearer's gloves used at Lincoln's funeral.)

--- *The Cardiff Giant Humbug. Complete and Thorough Exposition of the Greatest Deception of the Age. Richly Illustrated With Views and the Giant From the Quarry to the Tomb.* Fort Dodge, Iowa. 1870. wrps. 36 pp. (An interesting piece of ephemera, telling how the block of gypsum was taken from a quarry near Fort Dodge, carved into a giant at Chicago, and transported to NY State and buried and resurrected as the wonder of the age. The last time I saw him he was peacefully reposing at the Farmer's Museum at Cooperstown.)

--- (Cherry Valley Methodists) *Trial and Defence of Mrs. Sally Thompson, On a Complaint of Insubordination to the Rules of the Methodist Episcopal Church, Evil Speaking and Immorality, Held Before a Select Committee of Said Church in Cherry Valley (NY), June 10, 1830, To Which is Annexed an Exposition of Some Facts ... Written by Herself.* Lowell (MA.) 1839. wrps. 24 pp. (Sally was accused of carrying on meetings in the Cherry Valley, NY, area, of lying, and of calling one Brother a snake in the grass and another Brother a spy. She was dismissed from the Methodist Church. An interesting account of prejudice against an early Methodist woman preacher in NY State.)

Clinton, DeWitt. *Account of the Salmo Otsego, or the Otsego Basse. In a Letter to John W. Francis, M.D. ... From ... Governor of the State of New York.* NY. 1822 plate. 6 pp.. pamphlet. (This was the first scientific description of this tasty fish, peculiar to Otsego Lake, at Cooperstown, NY, which Agassiz the noted naturalist, later called "... a distinct fish, not found in any

other waters of the world." The plate was an engraving of the Otsego Basse after a painting by Ezra Ames the eminent Albany artist, and was laid in the pamphlet.)
--- Cortland County Agricultural Warehouse. A. & S. D. Freer. July 1850. Broadside. 12 x 18 inches. (Advertises for sale: farming implements, scythes, forks, rakes, grind stones, ploughs, tin ware ... "and a little less than one mile of stove pipe.")
--- (Cortland, NY, and the KKK) Attention. Food for Thought. For Those Who Have Read the Insult Against the Ku Klux Klan Written and Circulated by Wm. D. Tuttle. Broadside, 8 x 11 inches, ca 1920s. (This broadside was prepared, pub., and circulated by a group of peace-loving citizens of Cortland who believed in fair and square dealing with every cause and none of the citizens "are members of the KKK." The peace-loving citizens were actually a white supremacy group attacking Tuttle for attacking the Klan.)
Cutten, G. & M. The Silversmiths of Utica, With Illustrations of Their Silver and Their Marks. pvtly. prntd. Hamilton, NY. 1936. illus. with five mounted plates. 67 pp. Lmtd. to 257 copies. (Biog. of many silversmiths, goldsmiths, jewelers, and watchmakers who worked in Utica between 1799 and 1860.)
Eddy, A. "Black Jacob," a Monument of Grace. The Life of Jacob Hodges, an African Negro, Who Died in Canandaigua, NY, Feb. 1842. 1842. 94 pp. (Hodges was involved in a murder in Orange Co., NY, but the shot he fired was not fatal. After being sent to Auburn Prison he was pardoned by the Governor. While he was in prison he was converted, and when released he moved to Canandaigua where he lived a long and exemplary life.)
--- Elmira Budget, newspaper, folio, issue of March 25, 1894. (This newspaper, which states "The Budget always leads in news and attractive features," prints in this one issue articles on 4 murders, 2 executions, 7 other crimes, 2 disasters, and mentions a Suicide Club.)
Estlake, A. The Oneida Community. A Record of an Attempt to Carry Out the Principles of Christian Unselfishness and Scientific Race-Improvement, by ... Member of the Oneida Community. London. 1900. 158 pp. (The preface states that the aspects of the Oneida Movement represent, "the ultimate ideal which the human race should strive to attain, and the only ideal which will solve the problems that have agitated mankind ... the most valuable enterprise which has ever been undertaken since the foundation of Christianity.")
Fillmore, Millard. The Early Life of Millard Fillmore. A Personal Reminiscence. Buffalo (NY). The Salisbury Club. 1958. 15 pp. Lmtd. to 250 copies. (An autobiography of Fillmore's first 23 years. For the first 18 years he lived in Cayuga Co. and then the family moved to western NY where he was admitted to the bar of Erie Co. at age 23.)
Freeman, J. The Forgotten Rebel. Gustav Stickley and His Craftsman Mission Furniture. 1966. illus. bib. index. 112 pp.

Lmtd. ed. (Besides a brief biog. of Stickley and a discussion of his work, this also contains an index to the *Craftsman Magazine* pub. by him. Stickley's furniture, made in NY State, is highly collectible.)

Freeman, J. *The Oneida Community ... And Modern Political Socialism by ... Treasurer of the Oneida Community, Ltd.* A small broadsheet (a sheet of paper prntd. on both sides). ca 1909. (A discussion of the wage-profits system, low pay and unemployment: "The working people are practically slaves ... the only people who ... offer with hope and confidence a remedy, are those who proposed the Oneida Community and Bible Method, common ownership.")

--- *Grace Brown's Love Letters. Read in the Herkimer Court House, Nov. 20, 1906, at the Trial of Chester E. Gillette Charged With Her Murder.* Herkimer. (1906.) wrps. illus. 23 pp..

--- *Guide to the Central Lakes. The Steamer Simeon DeWitt Leaves Ithaca ... and Cayuga ... Albany.* Munsell. ca 1840s. 4 pp. folder. (A description of points of interest for the traveller on Cayuga Lake. Included is brief data on the Ithaca and Owego Railroad. A very scarce Munsell item not listed in his *Bibliography*.)

Hazard, T. R. *Eleven Days at Moravia.* 1873. wrps. 45 pp.. (The adventures of Hazard, a dedicated believer in Spiritualism, when he visited the far-famed "spirit house" of Morris Keeler, the noted Spiritualist of Moravia.)

--- *Highways and Byways, or What We Found Behind the Catskills. A July Trip by Rail, Tally-Ho and Steamer. Via Otsego Lake, Cooperstown, Richfield Springs.* Season 1885. map. illus. wrps. 24 pp. (A description of vacation areas west of the Catskills. Probably issued by the West Shore Railway which sold Through Excursion Tickets.)

--- Hiram P. Crozier, New York. Gerrit Smith, Peterboro (NY), Aug. 9, 1849. Broadside, 8 x 13 inches. (Smith, the nationally known abolitionish and reformer of Peterboro, NY, castigates Crozier, a minister, for working in a store which had a liquor department, although Crozier evidentally did not handle the potent stuff. The minister had issued a circular defending his work, and said the liquor department was a subordinate one kept to accomodate, satisfy, and retain customers. Smith replies to Crozier in this broadside by asking, "What, however, if for the purpose of accomodating, satisfying, and retaining their customers, your employers shall add another attraction in their store, and set up a brothel department in it?")

--- (Hops and Politics) *To Whom It May Concern* (a 3 pp.. leaflet), and *To the Farmers of the 24th District* (handbill) issued by David Wilber, and his supporters, for his re-election to Congress. 1888. (Wilber, a hop grower of Oneonta, NY, claims the railroad men are against him because he found it cheaper to use his own teams of horses than to use the railroad. They also had accused him of buying hops from the West. He defends himself, and tells how he favored hop growers

during his previous term in Congress. His opponent, John S. Pindar, of Cobleskill, had served two years in Congress and had acted against the growers. An unusual twist of events occurred: Wilber won, but never attended a session because of ill-health, dying in 1890. Pindar was elected to fill his vacancy.)
--- *Hutchins Improved ... Almanack ... For 1808. by J. N. Hutchins ... NY.* Prntd. and sold by Alexander Ming (successor to Hugh Gaine.) (About this time lands in central NY State for Revolutionary War veterans were in the process of being settled. A feature of this almanack is a section titled, "Routs to and from the Military Lands, in the State of New-York.")
Kellogg, F. (ed.) *Tryphena Ely White's Journal. Being a Record, Written 100 Years Ago, of the Daily Life of a Young Lady of Puritan Heritage. 1805-1905.* Pvtly. prntd. illus. Genealogy Chart. 46 pp. Lmtd. to only 250 copies. (Tryphena, 1784-1816, lived in the town of Camillus, Onondaga Co. The journal begins June 1804 and ends September 20, the same year. It provides an interesting view of life in that place and time.)
Klock, J. N. (ed.) *Literary History of Cossville Literary Society 1868-69.* 1907. Portrait. 266 pp. (This soc. was formed in the Fall of 1868, in Cossville, which was somewhere in Steuben Co. It pub. a small literary paper titled *The Bud of Genius,* of which 20 numbers were issued. The members contributed poetry, humor, and anecdotes. *The Bud* was pub. in book form 35 years later, and prntd. on Klock's press. Cossville must have been a wee bit of a place, or part of a larger town, as it is not listed in French's *Gazeetteer of New York,* 1861.)
--- (Ku Klux Klan) *Official Document No. 12, Syracuse, Aug. 1927.* 2 pp. Mimeographed leaflet. Plus: *Special K-Duo Bulletin, Syracuse, Aug. 1927.* 1 pp. Mimeographed sheet. (These two scarce Klan items contain: notice of a special meeting, news that a Klan parade in Corland nearly provoked a riot, names of men rejected for Klan membership, dates of co. celebrations, other news, organizing dramatic teams, and qualifications for receiving the Second Degree.)
Leonard, W. A. *Stephen Banks Leonard of Owego, Tioga Co..* prntd. for private circulation. 1909. port. illus. 342 pp.. Lmtd. to 200 copies. (Leonard, 1793-1876, U. S. Representative in Congress, newspaper ed., postmaster, and he established the first stage route from Owego to Bath in 1816.)
Marks, M. (ed.) *Memoirs of the Life of David Marks, Minister of the Gospel.* Dover, NH. 2nd ed. 1847. 516 pp. (Marks, a Free Will Baptist minister, travelled widely in central NY. This is an important Mormon item as Marks visited some Mormons at Fayette, NY, in March 1830, and gives his opinion of the Book of Mormon some weeks before the Mormon Church was founded. Item #5278 in Flake's *Mormon Bibliography*.)
--- *Lines Composed on the Visit and Preaching of a Youth Aged Sixteen Years: - viz: DAVID MARKS, from Junius, NY, to Brookfield, NY. During His*

Stay from Dec. 4, 1821, to Feb. 1, 1822, 40 Persons Were Hopefully Converted to the Lord. Broadside poem, decorative border. ca 1822. approx. 6 x 10 inches. (This poem with 14 four-line verses gives the author's thoughts and hopes about Marks. In the 2nd ed. of the life of Marks, 1847, there is a 3-page detailed description of the revival held at Brookfield. This rare broadside does not appear in *American Imprints* or in Sabin.)

--- *A Narrative of the Revival of Religion in the County of Oneida, Particularly in the Bounds of the Presbytery of Oneida, in 1826.* Utica. 1826. 88 pp. (A fine account by town, of this famous revival which brought Charles G. Finney into prominence in the evangelization of central NY State. Includes some data on opposition forces.)

--- *New York, Ontario and Western Railway Timetable.* Norwich, NY. July 25, 1885. 9 x 11 inches. (This was a special timetable to accomodate hop pickers in the Oswego, Oneida, and Morrisville areas.)

--- *Notable Men of Central New York. Syracuse and Vicinity. Utica and Vicinity. Auburn, Oswego, Watertown, Fulton, Rome, Oneida, Little Falls. 19th and 20th Centuries.* 1903. illus. index. 428 pp. (A collection of over 1400 ports. of noteworthy men, with occupation, and an occasional date. Only a few of them were entirely clean-shaven.)

Noyes, John H. *Confession of Religious Experience ... 1849. Part I. Oneida Reserve.* Leonard & Company, Printers. 70 pp. plus 24 pp. appendix. (all pub.) (This was written about a year after Noyes founded the famous Oneida community, and is rare.)

Nutting, Judge. *The History of One Day Out of Seventeen Thousand.* Oswego, NY. 1889. illus. by Caroline S. King. 53 pp. (The judge, born in 1840, tells of his hunting adventures in the area of West Monroe near Oneida Lake. The last paragraph in the book states, "I have told you the history of one day out of seventeen thousand, and, if you are pleased with it, I will tell you about a trout-fishing trip I had the next spring, with my father, along the waters of the 'South Branch of the Little Salmon.'" The book on fishing was never prntd. The book on hunting is listed in Phillips' notable bib. *American Game Mammals and Birds. A Catalogue of Books.*)

Osborne, T. M. *Within Prison Walls. A Narrative of Personal Experience During a Week of Voluntary Confinement in State Prison, Auburn, NY, ... by ... (Thomas Brown, Auburn No. 33,333X).* 1915. 328 pp. (The author was Chairman of the State Commission on Prison Reform, and lived under an assumed name as a prisoner to get a first-hand view of a life of confinement. This is a day-by-day account of events and his thoughts. I did not read the book but one chapter is titled, "A Night in Hell." Dealers cannot possibly read all of the books they sell. Once I asked my barber if he knew where I could store several thousand books. [Barbers do seem to know everything.] He said, "No. Have you read them all?" I replied, "No," and you should have seen the startled look on his face when I said, "But I know what is in most of them." I have a part-time dealer friend who told me he does not sell a book until he has read it. His house is piled high with tottering stacks of books, and I doubt he is a fast enough reader to sell more than three books a week.)

Outland, E. *The "Effingham" Libels on Cooper. A Documentary History of the Libel Suits of James Fennimore Cooper Centering Around the Three Mile Point Controversy and the Novel: Home as Found. 1837-1845.* 1929. index. bib. wrps. 272 pp. (Cooper, the noted novelist of Cooperstown, NY, was involved in numerous lawsuits against the Whig newspapers of NY State.)

--- *Proceedings of the 5th Anniversary of the General Missionary Society of Young People of the Middle District ... Report of Board of Managers.* Catskill. 1820. wrps. 19 pp. (Missionaries visited the settlements in the "waste places" of Delaware, Otsego, Schoharie, and surrounding co., mainly beyond the Catskills. A great many towns are named, some with reports on activities: New Berlin, Unadilla, Milfordville, others. This provides a close look at the state of religion in that rather recently settled area of NY State. Not in Sabin or *American Imprints*.)

--- *Proceedings of the Sangerfield Meeting, Held at the Presbyterian Meeting House in the Village of Waterville, Jan. 14, 1830. With the Address of Elder Nathan N. Whiting on the Subject of Speculative Free Masonry.* Utica: Press of William Williams. 1830. 16 pp.. pamphlet. (Among other things, it was resolved that Free Masonry was opposed to the principles of the Gospel of Christ. This item is not listed in the bib. of the printings of William Williams.)

Provol, W. *The Pack Peddler.* 1937. port. 254 pp. (The true story of the life of a pack peddler's family in the Syracuse area around the turn of the century. Many a thriving business was begun by a man who had started out as a pack peddler.)

--- *Report of Inspectors of Auburn State Prison ... A Statement of the Mode of Punishment, &c.* NY State Assembly. Feb. 1846. 73 pp. (Actually a 54-page catalog of the names of disobedient prisoners, their offence, the date they were whipped and the number of blows. One wonders if the following infractions of the rules were worthy of lashing: singing in the cell, talking from a privy window, giving an ivory toothpick to a newly arrived convict, grimacing at the spectators, baking a cake, grinning darkey fashion, going to bed early, mis-matching a piece of carpet.)

--- *Reward. John Burns ... Highway Robbery ... A great blower ... great admirer of dog and cock fights ... also a fast short distance runner ... William Sullivan, Chief of Police, Ithaca, NY.* 1879. Broadside. Photo attached. (This "wanted" reward broadside has a note in pencil on the margin, "Arrested in Canada. Sentence 5 years in Auburn Prison." Some years ago I did a Book Fair in western NY. The doors opened at 10 a.m., and the first customer came in about 10:30 a.m. Needless to say I sold very little, but I think I had the second highest sales of any dealer there. I do not think I cleared expenses. Anyway, on the way home I stopped at a dealer who said, "I have something here in the drawer that you are going to buy. There is no way you are going to turn it down." "Well," I replied, "Let me see it first before I say yes or no." He pulled out of the drawer a scrapbook full of reward posters similar to the above, from NY and other states. There must have been a hundred of them pasted in. I took them to a friend of mine who is an expert on tricks of the trade with books and paper, to soak off so they could be sold individually. He later told me he spent a week dousing the sheets in water in the kitchen sink, the bath tub, and in pans scattered about his apartment. He did a great job, and I issued a successful catalog of posters of wanted criminals.)

--- *The Rules of the Court of Common Pleas, of Seneca County, Ovid (NY)*. Prntd. by M. Hayes. 1818. wrps. 18 pp. (Hayes prntd. newspapers at Ovid, ca 1816-1830. This work also includes the costs of many items: crier calling action and ringing the bell, first motion fees, swearing witnesses, notice of bail, much else. A very rare work, as *American Bibliography* does not locate any copies.)

--- *Rural Directory of Steuben Co., New York, Farm Journal*. illus. pub. by Wm. Atkinson Co., Phil. 1917. 416 pp. some advts. map. (An alphabetical list of residents: name, town, street, type of work, sometimes acreage owned, if they have a telephone, number of children, if retired. "Names in CAPITALS are those of *Farm Journal* subscribers - always the most intelligent and progressive people in any co.")

Sanger, J. *An Answer to General Jonas Platt's Address to the People of the County of Oneida*. October, 1800. Broadside. 13 x 16 inches. (Details of a controversy between Sanger and Platt over the division of co. lands and location of the Court House. According to an affadavit by a Nathan Smith, regarding a statement by Platt, "... he (Platt) with a degree of warmth, declared that he would pledge his honor and reputation, that what he asserted was true, and that if we did not find it so when we returned home, he would forfeit his ears.")

Seely, L. J. *Flying Pioneers at Hammondsport, NY, ... "The Cradle of Aviation." G. H. Curtiss ... A. G. Bell ... Aerial Experiment Association ... 1904-1914*. 1929. illus. wrps. 55 pp. (History of very early aviation at Hammondsport.)

--- *Slavery and Marriage. A Dialogue*. 1840. 14 pp. pamphlet. (Although not so stated, this was issued by the famous Oneida Community which did not practice monagamous marriage. Included is a 30-line article about the possible poisoning of his wife by a Mr. Lowder of Yates, NY, detailing the outrageous treatment he accorded her in the weeks before her death. This murder is not in McDade's *The Annals of Murder. A Bibliography*.)

Smith, Gerrit. *To the People of the Town of Smithfield.* Peterboro, March 15, 1843. Broadsheet, 8 x 12 inches. (Smith, the noted reformer, congratulates the Smithfield people for refusing to elect excise men who would be willing to license dram-selling. Nonetheless, dram selling continues in the town. "Let no man flatter himself that he is contributing to break up dram-shops, if he spends his leisure hours in them ....")

Smith, S. *Sailing on Skaneateles Lake. 1812-1934.* With 16 illus. 1934. Bib. wrps. 97 pp. (There is a 5-page list of the names of sail boats and their owners, and the years used on the lake. There are also descriptions of 33 boats.)

Spencer, J. *The Twelve Who Came Early.* 1975. illus. maps. bib. index. 130 pp. Lmtd. to 100 copies. (Very early history of the Onondaga Valley of NY.)

Stern, M. *William Williams: Pioneer Printer of Utica, NY. 1787-1850.* 1951. wrps. 22 mimeo. pages.

(Stewart, Mr.) *An Examination of the Opinion Contained in the Report of the Onondaga Commissioners, of the 17th of Feb. 1800, to ... the Governor ... With a View to Its Refutation By a Western Citizen.* Albany. Prntd. for the author. 1800. 24 pp. (How the state of NY handles the frontier lands designated for military veterans. Evans, 37389, identifies the author as a "Mr. Stewart of the Western Country.")

Thomas R. *The Man Who Would Be Perfect. John Humphrey Noyes and the Utopian Impulse.* 1977. port. bib. index. 199 pp. (Noyes, who has been called a "Vermont Cassanova," moved to NY State, founded the famous Oneida Community, and the dust jacket blurb says he "emerges as a man who overcame a tortured personal life and marshalled his inner resources to grapple with a confusing and rapidly changing social world.")

--- *To the Persons Who Derive Title From Myself or My Late Father to Land in Charlotte River and Byrnes Tracts, in the Counties of Delaware, Otsego, and Schoharie ... Peterboro.* May 24, 1844. Gerrit Smith. Broadside, 8 x 12 inches. (In this circulated broadside Smith tries to placate tenants on his lands who had been told by whites disguised as Indians that their titles were no good. He blasts the "Indians" as unfit to investigate land titles and accuses them of stealing his timber. An important broadside, issued at the height of the Anti-Rent troubles in the area. Of all the landlords involved in the troubles of Anti-Rentism, Smith was probably the one that cared the most for his tenants.)

Trolley. *The Great Card Game.* Mfrd. by Snyder Bros. Elmira, NY. ca 1904. Boxed deck of playing cards, with detailed instruction pamphlet for several games. (Issued during the splendid days of trolley travel, the cards have illus. of: Trolleys, Passenger, Motorman, Conductor, Transfer Ticket, and Fare. A number of fine sets of this game, and the original metal printing plates, were found by a book scout in a NJ antique shop, and he sold them to me.)

Truesdell, J. W. *The Bottom Facts Concerning the Science*

of *Spiritualism: Derived From Careful Investigations Covering a Period of 25 Years*. NY. 1883. illus. 231 pp. (The author lived in Syracuse, and was a student of Spiritualism for many years. There are chapters on the Moravia (NY) Medium, and an account of a Seance with Delegates from the Oneida Community. There is also a chapter which only spiritual mediums were to read.)

--- *Utica. The Ideal City. Gem of the Mohawk Valley.* 1909. illus. and descriptive. wrps. 48 pp. (A well-illus. booklet proclaiming the advantages of Utica, with information on many of its businesses. A well-known librarian in NY State once said to me when I mentioned the Adirondacks, "The Adirondacks! The Adirondacks! Everybody is collecting the Adirondacks! They should be collecting Uitca! That's the place!")

Vance, A. T. *The Real David Harum. The Wise Ways and Droll Sayings of One "Dave" Hannum, of Homer, NY. The Original of the Hero of Mr. Westcott's Popular Book.* 1900. port. illus. 123 pp. (Marvellous stories of a Homer, NY, horse trader. E. N. Westcott pub. a novel in 1898 about a horse-trading country banker titled "David Harum." Westcott, himself a banker, used Hannum of Homer as his model. The novel became instantly popular and over the years sold more than a million copies.)

--- *Wayside Telephone Service.* Wayside Telephone and Auto Service Co., New York. ca 1920. illus. wrps. 24 pp. (Someone had a novel idea for making money in the early days of motoring in NY State, and started this service in Oneida Co., NY. Locked phones were placed at one mile intervals along highways, and were available for emergency calls by subscribing drivers who had keys. Motorcycle patrols checked on the phones, and on motorists in trouble.)

Werner, C. J. *A History and Description of the Manufacture and Mining of Salt in New York State.* pub. by the Author. 1917. illus. map. 144 pp. Lmtd. to 100 copies. (A major work by an historian who also was Vice President of the Independent Salt Co.)

--- *Will the People of Oneida County Protect Themselves Against the Criminal and Lawless? Read! Read! Read!.* ca 1888. 4 pp. leaflet. (This item advises Republicans to think before voting for Thomas Wheeler who had been nominated by the Republicans to run for Sheriff of Oneida Co. He had been sentenced to jail for assault and battery. It also claims that for years he had resided at a house of ill fame.)

Williams, J. C. *An Oneida County Printer, William Williams. Printer, Publisher, Editor, With a Bibliography of the Press at Utica ... 1803-1838.* 1906. Illus. 214 pp.. Lmtd. to 180 copies. Reprntd. in 1974. (Fine reference work and bib. on an important printer in central NY State.)

Williams and Cardamone. *Cherry Valley Country.* 1978. illus. bib. 121 pp. (Fine illus. of buildings from Albany to Manlius.)

--- *White's Utica Pottery. Catalog of an Exhibit at the Munson-Williams-Proctor In-*

stitute at Utica. 1969-70. illus. wrps. 20 pp. 89 entries. (Traces the hist. of this famous pottery from the 1830s through 1900.)

CHAUTAUQUA COUNTY

CHAUTAUQUA COUNTY
Anon. *Centennial History of Chautauqua Co.* Jamestown. 1904. illus. maps.
Anderson, A. *The Conquest of Chautauqua, Jamestown & Vicinity in the Pioneer & Later Periods.* Jamestown 1932. illus. Vol. 1 (all pub.) 476 pp.
Anderson, A. *A Pioneer Chautauqua County Family.* January 1936. illus. wrps. 14 pp.
Brown, S. (Gave series of lectures on co. hist. at Jamestown Academy, 1843. Then pub. in newspapers of the co.)
Dilley, B. (ed.) *Biography & Portrait Cyclopedia of Chautauqua Co., With Historical Sketch of the Co. by O. Edson,* Phil. July 1891. illus. 730 pp. (Some copies lack portrait between pp. 209-210)
Doty, Congdon, Thornton. (eds.) *Historical Annals of Southwestern NY.* NY 1940. illus. 3 vol. (Includes Cattaraugus & Allegany Co.)
Downs, Hedley, Fenwick. *History of Chautauqua Co.* NY. 1921. illus. maps. 3 vol.
Edson, O. *History of Chautauqua Co.* Boston 1894. illus. 2 vol.
Another ed. microfilmed by Bell & Howell, Cleveland, Ohio. 1964.
McMahon, H. *Chautauqua Co., A History.* Buffalo 1958. illus. maps. 339 pp.
Merrill, A. *Southern Tier.* Vol. I. 1953. 213 pp. (Includes: Chautauqua, Cattaraugus, Allegany & Steuben Cos.)
Morrison, W. *Chautauqua Co.* 1969. illus. 96 pp. (Reprnt of the text from Child's *Gazetteer and Directory of Chautauqua Co.,* 1873.)
Warren, E. *Sketches of the Hist. of Chautauqua Co.* Jmstwn. 1846. 159 pp. Reprnt. ca 1976.
Another ed. microfilmed by Bell & Howell, Cleveland, Ohio. 1964.
Woodward, J. *Address at Centennial Celebration of First Settlement of Chautauqua Co., June 24, 1902, at Westfield.* Jamestown 1902. 15 pp.
Young, A. *History of Chautauqua Co.* Buffalo 1875. 672 pp. (index by R. M. Nallie, 1948, 117 pp. mimeo. in SLA) (This work has approximately 100 ports. of co. citizens. "The aggregate costs of the portraits exceeds 8,000 dollars...." "I congratulate myself on the termination of my arduous and protracted labors.")
Other ed. microfilmed by Bell & Howell, Cleveland, OH. 1964.

BUSTI, Chautauqua Co.
Peake, L. *History of Busti.* Lakewood. n.d. mimeo. 20 pp.

CASSADAGA, Chautauqua Co.
Anon. *Cassadaga-Lily Dale Sesquicentennial 1809-1959.* illus. wrps. 35 pp.

CHARLOTTE, Chautauqua Co.
Edson, O. *Celebration of 100th Anniv. of Am. Independence at Sinclairville, NY, July 4, 1876. In the 68th Year of the Settlement of Town of Charlotte.* Sinclairville. 1876. 73 pp.

CHAUTAUQUA, Chautauqua Co.
Richmond, R. *Chautauqua, An American Place.* NY 1943. illus. 180 pp.
Warren, R. *Chautauqua Sketches. Fair Point & The Sunday*

School Assembly. Buffalo. 1878. illus. map. 128 pp.

CHERRY CREEK, Chaut. Co.
Schults, C. (ed.) *Historical & Biog. Sketch of Cherry Creek.* Buffalo. 1900. illus. 175 pp.

CLYMER, Chautauqua Co.
Anon. *Hist ... of Clymer.* ca 1930. typed mss. at BHS.
Morrison. *History of Clymer, New York. 1821-1971.* ca 1971. illus. maps. 79 pp.

DUNKIRK, Chautauqua Co.
Anon. *The City of Dunkirk - A Souvenir Number of the Grape Belt.* July 1896. illus. advts. wrps. 76 pp.
Anon. *Historical & Descriptive Review of Dunkirk. From a Matter of Fact Standpoint.* Dunkirk. 1889. illus. 96 pp.
Chard, L. *Out of the Wilderness. Dunkirk's First Century 1805-1905.* Dunkirk. ca 1972. illus. index. 132 pp.

ELLICOTT, Chautauqua Co.
Hazletine, G. *The Early History of the Town of Ellicott. Comp. Largely From The Personal Recollections of the Author.* Jamestown. 1887. 556 pp.

FLUVANNA, Chautauqua Co.
Sherwin, H. *Early History of Fluvanna.* Jamestown. (1926.) illus. 126 pp.

FORESTVILLE, Chautauqua Co.
Gillette, S. *History of Forestville. 1808-1908.* Forestville. 1908.

FREDONIA, Chautauqua Co.
Adams, E. *Tales of Early Fredonia.* Fredonia. 1931. illus. 155 pp.
Davis, P. (ed.) *Frontier to 1825.* State U., Fredonia. May 1959. map. wrps. mimeo. 69 pp.
Swan, C. (ed.) *Historic Fredonia 1825-1875.* State U. Fredonia. May 15, 1960. illus. wrps. mimeo. 99 pp.

FRENCH CREEK, Chautauqua Co.
Peterson, A. *French Creek Twp. Sesquicentennial. 1829-1979.* 1979. illus. map. 44 pp.

HANOVER, Chautauqua Co.
Many hist. articles on Hanover appeared in Silver Creek weekly newspaper.

HARMONY, Chautauqua Co.
Fowler and Nagel. *Hist ... of Harmony Incl. Blockville, Watts Flats, Niobe, Panama.* 1977. illus. map. bib. 256 pp.

IRVING, Chautauqua Co.
(H. W.) *Irving on Lake Erie.* Buffalo. 1837. 47 pp.

JAMESTOWN, Chautauqua Co.
Anon. *Jamestown, Historical & Industrial Review.* (Jamestown ca 1912.) illus. 117 pp.
(Barrett, R. ed.) *Jamestown Past & Present.* Jamestown. 1913. maps. 143 pp.
Hatch, V. (ed.) *Hist. of Jamestown* Jmstown. 1900. illus. 297 pp.

NORTH HARMONY, Chaut. Co.
Darrow, F. *History of Town of North Harmony.* 1953-1955. wrps. 2 vol. (Includes: Ashville, Stedman, Stow.)

POMFRET, Chautauqua Co.
Crocker, E. *Yesterdays in & Around Pomfret. Book I* Fredonia 1960. wrps. 69 pp.
--- *Book II 1961.* 69 pp.
--- *Book III 1962.* 72 pp.
--- *Book IV 1963.* 76 pp.
--- *Book V 1964.* 80 pp.
(Above reprntd. from weekly column in *Fredonia Censor*.)

PORTLAND, Chautauqua Co.
Taylor, H. *Historical Sketches of Town of Portland. Also Pioneer History of Chautauqua Co.* Fredonia. 1873. illus. 446 pp.

RIPLEY, Chautauqua Co.
Anon. *Ripley Sesquicentennial.* 1966. illus. advts. wrps. 88 pp.

SHERMAN, Chautauqua Co.
Anon. *Some Events in the History of Sherman. Pub. in Connection With the Centennial Celebration.* Aug. 1923. illus. 116 pp.
(French Creek Yorkers) *History of Sherman.* (1953) illus. advts. wrps. 64 pp.

SILVER CREEK, Chautauqua Co.
Heaton, G. (ed.) *A Review of Leading Business Houses & Early History of Mercantile Trade in Village of Silver Creek.* Silver Creek 1884. advts. wrps. 32 pp.

STOCKTON, Chautuaqua Co.
Miller, P. *Stockton Cent. Address 1810-1910.* 1910. wrps. 32 pp.

CHEMUNG COUNTY

CHEMUNG COUNTY
Anon. *Biographical Record of Chemung Co.* NY. 1902. illus. 512 pp. (pp. 273-277 misnumbered.)
Anon. *History of Chemung County. 1826-1879.* 1879. 288 pp. Reprntd. ca 1976.
Cheney, T. *Historical Sketch of the Chemung Valley, Watkins* 1868. 59 pp.
Kelsey (& others) *Chemung Co., Its History.* Elmira. 1961. illus. maps. wrps. 108 pp. 2nd. Printing: Jan 1963.
Merrill, A. *Southern Tier Vol. 2 1954.* 212 pp. (Chemung, Tioga, Broome Cos.)
(Sexton, J.) *An Outline History of Tioga & Bradford Cos. in PA.* Chemung, Tioga, Tompkins, & Schuyler Cos. in NY. Elmira 1885. 283 pp. (Written for Elmira Gazette Co.)
Towner, A. *Brief History of Chemung Co.* 1907. 103 pp. (For school use)
--- *Our County & Its People. A History of Valley & County of Chemung.* Syracuse. 1892. illus. 880 pp.

ELMIRA, Chemung Co.
Elmira Centennial. 1864-1964. wrps. illus. maps. 1964. 68 pp.
Galatian, A. (ed.) *History of Elmira, Horseheads, & the Chemung Valley.* Elmira. 1868. illus. advts. 280 pp.
Ottman, W. *A History of the City of Elmira.* Ph.D. Thesis 1900. Cornell U.
Southwick, S. *Views of Elmira.* 1836. 20 pp.
Taylor, E. *A Short History of Elmira.* Elmira. 1937. illus. wrps. 68 pp.

HORSEHEADS, Chemung Co.
Waid, R. *Early History of Horseheads.* 1937. wrps. illus. 32 pp.
Zim. *Foolish History of Horseheads.* ("Not copyrighted but protected by 2 male fists.") 1927. advts. wrps. 96 pp.

CHENANGO COUNTY

CHENANGO COUNTY
Anon. *Book of Biographies of Leading Citizens of Chenango Co.* Buffalo 1898 2 vol.
Anon. *Chenango Co. Hist Facts.* 1923. advts. unpaged.
Clark, H. *History of Chenango Co.* Norwich 1850. illus. 120 pp. lmtd. to 100 copies.
Lynch, C. *History of Chenango Co. & ... Pioneer Life. 1778-1929.* (1929) wrps. 39 pp.

Smith, J. *History of Chenango & Madison Counties.* Syracuse 1880. illus. map. 2 vols. Also issued in 1 vol. Reprntd. ca 1978 with index.

AFTON, Chenango Co.
Hayes, C. *Story of Afton.* Afton (1961) wrps. 44 pp.

BAINBRIDGE, Chenango Co.
Colwell, E. *Hi-ho Jericho, or Items of Interest About Early Bainbridge.* Bainbridge. 1946. 64 pp.

COVENTRY, Chenango Co.
Judd, O. *Hist ... of Coventry.* Oxford. 1904. (Originally a serial in local newspapers.) wrps. 99 pp.

GREENE, Chenango Co.
Cochrane, M. *From Raft to Railroad: History of Town of Greene. 1792-1867.* Ithaca. 1967. index. illus. 357 pp.
Folsom, M. *Echoes of the Past. Annals of Town of Greene. 1867-1967.* 1971. (Book)
Purple & Gulian. *Hist ... of Greene.* Greene 1858. 56 pp. (Reprntd. from *Chenango American* Dec. 1857-Jan. 1858.)

GUILFORD, Chenango Co.
Anon. *Diary of Guilford Resident Tells of Events 100 Years Ago.* (*Oxford Review Times* Dec. 12, 1963.)
Ingersoll, R. *Some Interesting Facts of Guilford as Told by the Late R. C. Ingersoll of That Place.* (*Norwich Sun,* Aug. 5, 1940.)

NEW BERLIN, Chenango Co.
Entwistle, O. *A History of New Berlin to 1907.* Masters' Thesis 1953. Colgate U.
(Fuller, E. & others) *New Berlin Centennial.* Aug 1908. New Berlin 1909. illus. wrps. 84 pp.
Hyde, J. *Historical Sketch of Old New Berlin Being a Second Printing of Some Articles From Ye Pen of Ye Late John Hyde, Esq.* First pub. in 1876. New Berlin. 1907. illus. 108 pp.
Wilber, F. *Early Glimpses of the New Berlin Area.* New Berlin 1964. revised ed. illus. maps. lmtd. 200 copies. 469 pp.

NORTH GUILFORD, Chenango Co.
Palen, I. *North Guilford Pioneers NY 1946.* illus. 156 pp. (Said to be a very lmtd. printing.)

NORWICH, Chenango Co.
Phillips, A. *Annals of Norwich Along the Chenango Canal.* (1964.) illus. wrps. 40 pp.
Shinners, L. (city historian) *Norwich Golden Anniversary. 1914-1964.* illus. wrps. 44 pp.

OXFORD, Chenango Co.
Anon. *1790-1882. Brief Sketch of the First Pioneers & Old Landmarks of Oxford.* Oxford. 1892. wrps. 26 pp.
Galpin, H. (ed.) *Annals of Oxford.* Oxford. 1906. illus. 564 pp. index.
Welch, E. *"Grips" Historical Souvenir of Oxford.* Albany. 1897. illus. 76 pp.

PITCHER, Chenango Co.
A mss. on Pitcher history, dated 1954, is in a pvt. collection.

PRESTON, Chenango Co.
Kallicicki, E. (town historian) *Preston Town History.* 1961 wrps. 20 pp. (Reprntd from *Chenango Union.*)

SHERBURNE, Chenango Co.
(Gomph, J.) *Sherburne Illus. A*

History of the Village of Sherburne. Utica. 1896. illus. 110 pp. (Still available for sale in 1948.)
Hatch, J. *Reminiscences, Anecdotes, & Statistics of Early Settlers & the Olden Time in the Town of Sherburne.* Utica 1862. 104 pp. Reprntd. Sherburne 1948. wrps. 91 pp. (Includes Town Clerk Records for 1795-1799)
Raymond, M. *Souvenir of the Sherburne Centennial.* Tarrytown. 1893. illus. 111 pp..

SMYRNA, Chenango Co.
Munson, G. *Early Years in Smyrna, & Our First Old Home Week.* Norwich 1905. illus. 208 pp.

CLINTON COUNTY

CLINTON COUNTY
Averill, H. *A New Geography & History of Clinton Co.* 1853. 2nd. ed. revised. enlrgd. Plattsburgh. 1880. map. illus. 240 Another ed: 1885. 32 pp.
Averill & Hager. *A New & Concise Geography & Historical Description of Clinton Co., Adapted to the Wants of Business & to the Use of Schools.* Plattsburgh. 1879. map. 25 pp.
Everest, A. (ed.) *Recollections of Clinton Co. & the Battle of Plattsburgh 1800-1840.* Memoirs of early residents from notebooks of Dr. D. S. Kellogg. Plattsburgh. 1964. map. wrps. 75 pp.
Hurd, D. *History of Clinton and Franklin Counties.* Phil. 1880. illus. maps. 2 vol. Reprntd. ca 1980 with indexes.
Stonnes, E. *The Impact of External Contacts; Development of Dependence, The Case of Clinton County, New York. 1820-1970.* 1978. 334 pp.

Wedd, S. *Centennial Oration at Plattsburgh* 1876. 8 pp.
Winans (Ed.) *Clinton County: I Remember When.* illus. ca 1985. 130 pp.

BEEKMANTOWN, Clinton Co.
Shields (ed.) *Beekmantown.* ca 1986. illus. map. 268 pp.
White, P. *Beekmantown, NY. Forest Frontier to Farm Community.* 1979. maps. illus. index. 398 pp.

CHAMPLAIN, Clinton Co.
Taylor, D. *Historical Oration on Champlain Town. Delivered July 4, 1877.* Boston. 1880. wrps. pvtly. reprntd. by Moorsfield Press, Champlain, NY, 1936. Ed. with notes by Hugh McLellan. wrps. 37 pp.. lmtd. 183 copies. (McLellan says Taylor wrote a mss. hist. of Champlain which wasn't pub., and could not be found.)

CHAZY, Clinton Co.
Anon. *Reminiscences of Old Chazy Given by Descendants of Early Settlers.* Aug. 23, 1888. Plattsburgh 1888. 44 pp.. Reprntd. 1968.
Barnett & Martin. *Hist ... of Chazy.* Burlington, VT. 1970 illus. ports., maps. 360 pp.

DANNEMORA, Clinton Co.
Dow, M. (town historian) *History of Dannemora.* 1962. Typed mss. in Dannemora Free Lib.

MOOERS, Clinton Co.
Anon. *Hist. Review ... of Mooers.* ca 1985. 100 pp. illus.

PERU, Clinton Co.
Arnold, S. (comp.) *Rem. & Early Hist. of Old Peru.* 1913. 58 pp.
Sunderland, L. *History of Peru, New York.* 1977. pub. by author. illus. map. 1916 pp.

PLATTSBURGH, Clinton Co.
Anon. *Historical Sketches.* Plattsburgh. ca 1985. illus. 56 pp.
Everest. *Briefly Told.* ca 1984. illus. 64 pp. (History of Plattsburgh, 1784-1984.)
Fitzpatrick, S. *Plattsburgh Once Upon A Time.* 1924. 23 pp.
--- *Spots, Comments & Anecdotes About Plattsburgh History.* 1934. 24 pp.
Palmer, P. *Hist. Sketch of Plattsburgh to Jan. 1, 1876.* Plattsburgh 1877. 83 pp. (From *Plattsburgh Republican* 1871.) Enlrgd. ed. 1893. 102 pp. Reprntd. 1968.
Porter, M. *History of Plattsburgh 1785-1815-1902. The Barracks Anniversary Edition 1814-1964.* ca 1964. illus. 122 pp.
--- *Old Plattsburgh.* Plattsburgh 1944. illus. map. 63 pp.

ROUSES POINT, Clinton Co.
Ross. J. *This Happened Here.* Rouses Point 1955. wrps. unpaged. app.rox. 600 copies prntd. (Series of articles in the *North Countryman*.)

COLONIAL NEW YORK
--- *A Conference Between the Comissaries of Massachusetts-Bay, and the Commissaries of New York; at New Haven in the Colony of Connecticut. 1767.* Boston. Prntd. by Richard Draper. 1768. 27 pp. (An attempt to settle the boundary between the colonies of NY and MA Bay, which failed. This pamphlet contains a journal of the proceedings, history of the boundary, and other matters, and was prntd. to be distributed to members of the MA Legislature. Some copies contain 9 pp. of advts.)
--- *An Account of Her Majesty's Revenue in the Province of New York. 1701-1709. Customs Records of Early Colonial New York.* 1966. folio. map. illus. glossary. index. Over 300 pp. (This is an exceptionally valuable record as it is the earliest itemized accounts of the Port Collector at NY, and the monies collected were used for expenses of the Colony. These are the most detailed records of trade and customs of that period that have survived. A history of the provenance is given. The records are reproduced in facsimile.)
Asher, G. M. *A Bibliographical and Historical Essay on the Dutch Books and Pamphlets Relating to the New Netherlands, and to the Dutch West India Co. ... Also ... the Maps, Charts, Etc., of New Netherland.* Amsterdam (the Netherlands) 1854-1867). Large folding map, 3 illus. 237, 22, and 23 pp. (An unsurpassed reference work for those interested in New Netherlands. It was reprntd. at least twice in the 1960s by N. Israel, in Amsterdam, 1960 and 1966. Justin Winsor, on page 439 of vol. 4 of his *Narrative and Critical History of America,* highly praises Asher's work.)
(Bayard, N.) *An Account of the Commitment, Arraignment, Tryal and Condemnation of Nicholas Bayard, Esq.; For High Treason, In Endeavouring to Subvert the Government of the Province of New York ... by his signing and procuring others to sign Scandalous Libels, call'd Petitions or Addresses to his Late Majesty King William, the Parliament of England, and the Lord Cornbury now Governour of that Province ... Printed at New*

York by Order of his Excellency the Lord Cornbury, and reprinted at London, 1703. small folio. 32 pp. (Bayard, 1644-1707, secretary of the province of NY, was sentenced to be hanged for treason, but the charge was dropped on the appeal of Gov. Cornbury to Queen Anne. This London ed. is a reprnt of the NY ed. by Bradford in 1702. Both printings are very rare, only 3 copies are known of 1702 ed.)

DeRonde, Lambertus. *De Gekruicigde Christus, Als Het Voornaamste Toeleg ... 14 October, 1750. Nieuw-York, Gedrukt by Hendricus De Foreest, in't Jaar, 1751.* 28 pp. (This was the first sermon preached by Rev. DeRonde as the colleague of the Rev. Gualtherus DuBois, in the Dutch Reformed Church in NY. DeRonde's biog. appears in Appleton's *Cyclopedia of American Biography* under: Ronde. Printer DeForeest was an apprentice, and for a short while was a parner of William Bradford, the famous printer.)

Fowler, R. (ed.) *Facsimile of the Laws and Acts of the General Assembly for Their Majesties Province of New York, Etc., Etc., at New York. Printed and Sold by William Bradford, Printer to Their Majesties King William and Queen Mary, 1694. Together With an Historical Introduction, Notes on the Laws, and Appendices, by ... Counsellor-at-Law.* NYC. Grolier Club. 1894. bound in vellum. Lmtd. to 315 copies. (This is a facsimile of the first collection of NY laws which were prntd. by Bradford at NYC at 1694, and it was the first book prntd. in NY. Of especial interest are Fowler's Historical Introduction, and Notes on the Laws; and C. R. Hildebrun's bib. notes on the seven known copies of the original ed. of 1694.)

Harrison, F. *The English and Low-Dutch School-Master, Containing Alphabetical Tables of Most Common Words in English and Dutch.* NY. 1730. 144 pp. Also has a title page in Dutch. 1976 reprnt. (This was the only Dutch-English language guide prntd. in the American colonial period, and only two copies of the original are known to exist. It is not recorded by either Evans or Sabin. It appears in Bristol's *Supplement to Evans* .... The original ed. has never come my way, but I have had the 1976 reprnt.)

Hastings, H. (ed.) *Ecclesiastical Records. State of New York. 1621-1810.* Albany. 1901-1916. 7 vol. illus. index. (This work is arranged under the heads of the respective Governors, and in chronological order. It is an important source of NY hist., especially in colonial days.)

Hough, F. B. *Papers Relating to Pemaquid and Parts Adjacent in the Present State of Maine, Known as Cornwall County, When Under the Colony of New York, Compiled From Official Records in the Office of the Secretary of State, Albany.* 1856. 136 pp. (The first printing of important papers regarding the portion of present ME which was under the jurisdiction of NY in the late 1600s. A representative from ME was sent to the NY General Assembly.)

Jogues, Rev. I. *Novum Belgium: An Account of New Netherland in 1643-1644, by ... of the Society of Jesus. With Fac-*

simile of *His Original Mss.. His Portrait. A Map and Notes by John Glimary Shea.* NY. pvtly. prntd. 1862. Lmtd. to 100 copies. (One of the earliest descriptions of New Netherlands.)
--- *Journal of the Legislative Council of the Colony of New York Begun 9th Day of April 1691 ... Ended 3rd of April 1775.* 2 vol. Albany. 1861. index. total of 2079 pp. (A wealth of research material of absolute necessity in the study of early NY. Much of this work was destroyed by fire, and a set is quite difficult to find.)
--- *Journal of the Votes and Proceedings of the General Assembly of the Colony of New York, From 1766 to 1776, Inclusive.* Albany. Buel, Printer to the State. 1820. Thick folio. (In 1820 the state discovered that only one copy of the original journals were in existence, so it reprntd. them in an ed. of only 50 copies. See Sabin 53720 for the complete and intricate collation of this excessively rare volume. The copy I was fortunate enough to acquire did not contain the six leaves subsequently prntd. and inserted.)

Metz, H. *Colonial Highways of Greater New York, Discussion of the Present Interest of the City Therein.* 1908. Many maps. wrps. 165 pp. (A fine work on the history of the early highways. The maps show the location of the old roads in relation to the streets of 1910.)

Murphy, H. *Anthology of New Netherland, or Translations From the Early Dutch Poets of New York, With Memoirs of Their Lives.* NY. 1865. index. 208 pp. Lmtd. to 125 copies. (The New Netherlands poets of the 1600s were: Jacob Steendam, Henricus Selyns [or Selijns], and Nicasius DeSille. This work is pub. No. 4 of the Bradford Club Series.)

--- *New Amsterdam Gazette. Historical Sketches and Reminiscences of the Dutch Regime of New Amsterdam and the New Netherlands History of the Early Churches. Dutch Progress in Later Years in Holland and America. Views of Holland and Other Illus.* Morris Coster, Ed. and Pub. NY. illus. maps. 8 vol., all pub. 1883-1895. (A wealth of hist. on early New Amsterdam, with some genealogical data.)

O'Callaghan, E. B. (abstractor) *Calendar of New York Colonial Commissions 1680-1770.* NY. 1929. index. 108 pp. Lmtd. to 200 copies. (An important reference work, listing civil and military appointments.)

O'Callaghan, E. B. (ed.) *Documents Relative to the Colonial History of the State of New York Procured in Holland, England, and France by J. R. Brodhead.* Albany. 1856-1887. 15 vols. maps. (This massive and indispensable work is entirely in English. The Dutch and French mss. were translated by O'Callaghan. The hist. of this work is quite interesting. In Feb. 1844 a committee issued a report questioning the value of sending Brodhead to Europe to procure manuscripts relating to the colonial history of NY. "He is still abroad pursuing his researches among the rubbish of European manuscripts." They say the expense is too great, and much of the material is useless and frivolous. In May 1845 another committee issued a report ac-

cepting Brodhead's statement of his work and his expense account because, "A respect for the memorials of the past may be justly considered as one of the marks of an advanced civilization.")
O'Callaghan, E. B. (ed.) *Voyages of the Slavers St. John and Arms, of Amsterdam 1659, 1663; Together With Additional Papers Illustrative of the Slave Trade Under the Dutch. Translated From the Original Manuscript, With Introduction and Index, by ... Albany Munsell.* 1867. 254 pp. lmtd. to 100 copies. (Much on slavery in New Netherlands.)
Seymann, J. *Colonial Charters, Patents and Grants to the Communities Comprising the City of New York.* 1939. maps. bib. 612 pp. lmtd. to 500 copies. (Hist. and text of the charters, patents, and grants.)
Van Der Zee, H. & B. *A Sweet and Alien Land, The Story of Dutch New York.* 1978. illus. maps. bib. index. 560 pp. (A hist. of the unprofitable and troublesome outpost of New Netherland, 1626 to 1664, from a Dutch point of view.)

COLUMBIA COUNTY

COLUMBIA COUNTY

--- *Biographical Review. Sketches of the Leading Citizens of Columbia County, New York.* Boston. Biog. Review Pub. Co. 1894. illus. index. 604 pp. (Biog. vol. were pub. for many co. in the U. S. An agent would scour a co. getting residents to submit their biog. In almost every instance the subject, and no doubt some of his relatives and friends, would subscribe for a copy, thus insuring the pub. enough money to actually issue the book. The brief prntd. Contract for this Columbia Co. "mug book" reads: "I hereby agree to take one copy of your proposed *Biographical Review of Columbia County, New York*, if you should succeed in publishing the same, for which I promise to pay to your order Fifteen Dollars ($15.00) when delivered at my residence or place of business. I base this order on what is promised in your prospectus. I promise to correct, revise or rewrite and return within the time allotted therefor, the copy of my Biography when sent to me for that purpose." This volume does have a long article on the North Family of Shakers at Mount Lebanon; also biographies of Elders Joseph Holden, Calvin Reed, William Anderson, and George W. Clark. There is a portrait of Calvin Reed.)
Collier, F. *Columbia in History.* 1907 wrps. 16 pp.
Ellis, F. *History of Columbia Co.* Phil. 1878. illus. map. 447 pp. Reprntd. 1974. Reprntd. 1985. Lmtd. to 1000 copies.
McNamee, D. *If You Remember.* 2nd ed. Hudson. 1937. illus. 158 pp.
Raymond, W. *Biog. Sketches of the Distinguished Men of Columbia Co.* Albany 1851. 119 pp. ("Columbia Co. has produced more distinguished men, it is believed, than any other co. of equal size & population in this state or in any other state in the Union.")
Thomson, M. *Columbia Co. Past & Present.* 1943. Pub. by Columbia Co. Council for Social Studies for use in 7th Grade. wrps. mimeo. 183 pp.

Williams, M. *Columbia Co. at the End of the Century: A Historical Record of its Foundations.* Hudson. 1900. illus. 2 vol.

ANCRAM, Columbia Co.
(Anon.) *A History of the Roeliff Jansen Area.* Ancram, Copake, Gallatin, Hillsdale. Roeliff Jansen Hist. Soc. Pub. No. 1. 1975. wrps. 87 pp.

AUSTERLITZ, Columbia Co.
(Osborn, C.) *A Brief Historical Sketch of the Settling of Austerlitz Township (1959).* illus. map. wrps. 16 pp. (Map not dated - should be 1875. Mostly about Spencertown.)

CANAAN, Columbia Co.
Anon. *Reflections Canaan, New York.* Bicentennial. 1976. wrps. 64 pp.
Boughton, F. (ed.) *BiCentennial Celebration July 11-12, 1959.* illus. maps. wrps. 47 pp.

CLAVERACK, Columbia Co.
Gebhard, E. *The Parsonage Between Two Manors.* Hudson. 1909.
2nd. ed. 1910. 316 pp.
3rd. ed. 1925. illus. 330 pp.
Porter, E. *Social & Civil Hist ... of Claverack.* (1867). wrps. (Through page 33 it is hist. of the Dutch Reformed Church of Claverack.) 56 pp.
Schram, B. *Claverack Township. History and Heritage.* 1976. wrps. 96 pp.
Webb, F. *Claverack Old & New.* (1892) n.d. illus. wrps. 88 pp. Reprntd. 1973.

CLERMONT, Columbia Co.
Clarkson, T. *A Biographical History of Clermont or Livingston Manor Before & During the War for Independence.* Clermont 1869. illus. 319 pp. Pub. for, and in the hands only, of subscribers. Sabin, 13500, says that only 150 copies were prntd., and that some copies lack the 5 plates.
Hunt, T. *A Hist. Sketch of Town of Clermont.* Hudson. 1928. pvtly. prntd. illus. maps. 149 pp. Reprntd. 1984 with index.

GERMANTOWN, Columbia Co.
Miller, W. *History of 18th. Century Germantown.* 1976. wrps. map. bib. 219 pp.

GHENT, Columbia Co.
(Anon.) *Squampamock, Bicentennial History of Ghent.* 1976. wrps. 121 pp.

GLENCO MILLS, Columbia Co.
Black, H. *A History of Glenco Mills. 1714-1976.* wrps. 24 pp.

GREENPORT, Columbia Co.
James, H. *Greenport, A Town's Progress.* 1961. illus. map. wrps. 18 pp.

HILLSDALE, Columbia Co.
Collin, J. *A History of Hillsdale.* ed. by Prof. H. S. Johnson, AM, ed. of *Hillsdale Herald.* Philmont 1883. 195 pp..

HUDSON, Columbia Co.
Bradbury, *A History of the City of Hudson.* Hudson. 1908. 223 pp.
Industrial Advertising Co. of America (comp.) *Hudson of Today, Its History, Resources, & Institutions.* (Kinderhook.) 1905. illus. wrps. 24 pp.
Miller, S. *Historical Sketches of Hudson.* Hudson. 1862. 120 pp. (Reprntd. in *Columbia Co. at the End of the Century.* See **COLUMBIA COUNTY**, M. Williams. "It is reproduced entirely, with the exception of those pages which would sub-

stantially repeat what is printed in the Hudson history in the body of the book....") (A copy has been found with *Recollections of Hudson* by G. Worth appended; see below.)

Terry, R. *The "Hudsonian", Old Times & New.* Hudson 1895. 264 pp.

(Wait, W.) *City of Hudson Sesquicentennial 1785-1935.* illus. wrps. 32 pp.

(Worth, G.) Pen name (Ignatius Jones) *Recollections of Hudson.* 78 pp. (Appended to 2nd. ed. of his *Recollections of Albany 1850.* See entry ALBANY, ALBANY COUNTY.)

KINDERHOOK, Columbia Co.
Collier, E. *History of Old Kinderhook.* NY. 1914. illus. maps. 572 pp. (Unknown to most people, copies of this book were in stock at the Tuttle Book Co. in Rutland, VT. A part-time dealer in Kinderhook used to buy them through me. I said to him, "Howard, it isn't far to Rutland. You can go over there and buy as many copies as you need." "No," he said, "I would rather buy them through you." Once a year or so I would buy several copies and ship them to him. We both made a few dollars per vol. and were happy. I believe Tuttle sold their last copy several years ago.)

Rathbone. *A Glimpse of Life in the Town of Kinderhook in Foot Stove Days.* Chatham. 1929. illus. 30 pp. Probably less than 50 copies were prntd. (Memories of the 1800s.)

Vanderpoel, A. *Reminiscences of Old Dutch Village.* 19-- 14 pp.

LEBANON SPRINGS, Columbia Co.

Anon. *A Sketch of Lebanon Springs.* Pittsfield, MA. 1871. map. wrps. 31 pp. (pub. by D. Gale, prop. of Columbia Hall.) 2nd. ed. 1872. map. 31 pp.

LIVINGSTON, Columbia Co.
Link, L. *History of Livingston.* 1976. wrps. 32 pp.

NEW LEBANON, Columbia Co.
Anon. *Comprehensive Plan of Town of New Lebanon.* 1965. maps. wrps. mimeo. 32 pp. (Has an hist. sketch.)
Spencer, A. *Historical Sketches of New Lebanon.* ca 1870.

NORTH CHATHAM, Col. Co.
Otten, M. *North Chatham and Malden Bridge Recall the Past.* 1976. wrps. 92 pp..

RAYVILLE, Columbia Co.
Shepherd, C.D. *History of Rayville, New York.* 1937. wrps. illus. with 7 mounted photographs. 76 pp.

SPENCERTOWN, Columbia Co.
Davenport, C. *Recollections of Spencertown.* Sept. 1923. (14-page mss. in private hands, of which several copies have been made.) It has been pub. in *Chatham Courier* newspaper. (Davenport: born in 1843, died in 1924.)

STOCKPORT, Columbia Co.
Lathrop, J. *The Township of Stockport 1919.* (Includes: Columbiaville, Stottville.) 2nd. ed. 1924. wrps. 22 pp.

STUYVESANT, Columbia Co.
Frisbee, P. *Town of Stuyvesant, A Brief History.* 1976. wrps. 36 pp.

VALATIE, Columbia Co.
Hardenbrook, L. *History of*

Valatie. ca 1956. 12 pp. typed mss. at HHK.

Rogati, B. *Hist ... of Valatie.* 1976. wrps. 40 pp.

CORTLAND COUNTY

CORTLAND COUNTY

Anon. *Biog. Sketches of Leading Citizens of Cortland Co.* Buffalo 1898. illus. 511 pp.

Anon. *Cortland Co. 1876-1927.* ca 1927. 47 pp.

Anon. *Cortland Co. Sesquicentennial Celebration 1808-1958.* July 20-26, 1958. illus. advts. 192 pp.

Anon. *Residents of Cortland County.* 1800-1810. pub. by Cortland Co. Hist. Soc. 1972 pamphlet.

Blodgett, B. *Stories of Cortland Co. for Boys & Girls.* 1932. illus. 287 pp. Another ed. Cortland 1952 with additional illus. 307 pp.

Cornish, C. *The Geography & History of Cortland Co., Ann Arbor, Mich.* 1935. illus. maps. 60 pp. (Orig. Masters' Thesis Cornell U. 1929)

Goodwin, H. *Pioneer History of Cortland Co. and The Border Wars of NY.* NY. 1859. illus. 456 pp. (Copyright date is 1855.)

Smith, H. *History of Cortland Co.* Syracuse 1885. illus. map. 552 pp.

Whitmore, F. *100th Anniv. of Cortland Co. 1808-1908.* 100 pp.

CORTLAND, Cortland Co.

Al-Khayat, H. *A Geographic Analysis of Growth of Cortland.* Thesis Syracuse U. June 1959. maps. mimeo. 103 pp.

Kurtz, D. *Past & Present, A Historical & Descriptive Sketch of Cortland.* Binghamton 1883. illus. wrps. 53 pp.

Reusswig, H. *Cortland 1792-1854.* Master Thesis Syracuse U. 1934. 30 pp.

Welch, E. *"Grips" Historical Souvenir of Cortland.* 1899. illus. 234 pp. (Includes Homer & McGraw.)

KEENEY, Cortland Co.

Webster, O. *Keeney Settlement.* 5 pamphlets. 1917-1923-1923-1924-1925. Cortland. pvtly. pub. by author. wrps. 50 to 90 pp. each.

Whitmarsh, M. *Historical Sketches of Keeney Settlement.* Articles in *DeRuyter Gleaner,* 1932-1933.

MARATHON, Cortland Co.

Welch, E. *"Grips" Marathon & Vicinity.* Fayetteville 1901. illus. 87 pp.

TRUXTON, Cortland Co.

Wicks, P. *Truxton Historical Review.* Truxton. (1924.) wrps. 16 pp.

VIRGIL, Cortland Co.

Bouton, N. *Festive Gathering of the Early Settlers & Present Inhabitants of Virgil. Aug. 25, 1853. Embracing a Historic Sketch of the Town.* Cortland. 1855. wrps. 47 pp. Another ed: Dryden 1878. *With Supp.lementary Letters on History of the Town Down to July 4, 1876.* 129 pp. (13 pp. typed index in SPL.)

WILLETT, Cortland Co.

Willet Correspondent. *History of Town & Early Settlers.* Article in *Cortland Democrat* Jan. 1905.

DELAWARE COUNTY

DELAWARE COUNTY

Anon. *Biog. Review of Delaware*

Co. Boston 1895. illus. 724 pp.
(Anon.) *Echoes of the Past in Delaware County.* Compiled by Local Hist. Group of Walton Adult Education School. 1947-1948. wrps. mimeo. bib. map. 141 pp.
(Anon.) *The Spirit of Delaware County, A Look Back from 1976.* wrps. 127 pp.
Davidson, H. *Delaware County. Fur Trade to Farming.* 1976. wrps. 123 pp.
DeVine, J. *Three Centuries in Delaware Co.* NY. 1933. illus. 88 pp.
Gould, J. *History of Delaware Co.* Roxbury 1856. port. map. 426 pp. (This was written at the age of 20 by Jay Gould who later became a famous financier. Many copies were lost by fire: other copies were bought up and destroyed by Gould.) Reprntd. 1977.
Monroe, J. *Chapters in the History of Delaware Co.* Margaretville 1949. maps. index. 132 pp.
Monroe, J. D. *The Anti-Rent War in Delaware County. The Revolt Against the Rent System.* pvtly. prntd. 1940. Bib. 2 illus. 128 pp. Lmtd. to 100 copies. (Written by a lawyer, a major contribution from the anti-renters point of view.)
Munsell, W. (ed) *History of Delaware Co. 1797-1880.* NY. 1880. illus. map of NY State. 363 pp. Reprntd. 1976.
Murray, D. (ed.) *Delaware Co. Centennial History 1797-1897.* Delhi 1898. illus. 604 pp.. Reprntd. ca 1978 with index.
Raitt, J. *Delaware County History.* 1977. Delaware Co. Hist. Society. 24 pp.
Wood, L. *Holt T'Other Way!* 1950. illus. 252 pp. (Folklore & history of Delaware River area, embracing several co.)

BOVINA, Delaware Co.
(Anon.) *Bovina History.* 1820-1970. (1970) mimeo. typed. stapled. 11 pp.

CANNONSVILLE, Delaware Co.
Boyd, L. *Cannonsville 1786-1956.* ca 1956. 44 pp.

DELHI, Delaware Co.
Welch. E. *"Grips" Hist. Souvenir* .... 1897. illus. 62 pp.

FLEISCHMANNS, Delaware Co.
Anon. *History of Fleischmanns.* Article in *Catskill Mt. News,* Margaretville. Aug. 1963.

HANCOCK, Delaware Co.
Wheeler, F. *Pioneer Days* .... 1915. 7 pp. mss. at NYSHA.

MARGARETVILLE, Del. Co.
(Bussy, E.) *History & Stories of Margaretville & Surrounding Area.* (1960) illus. 191 pp.

MIDDLETOWN, Delaware Co.
Sanford, W. *Brief History of Town of Middletown.* Article in *Catskill Mt. News,* Margaretville, Aug. 1963.

PINE LAKE, Delaware Co.
Hamblin, J. *Pine Lake: A History.* 1973. wrps. bib. illus. maps. 44 pp.

ROXBURY, Delaware Co.
More & Griffin. *Hist ... of Roxbury.* Walton 1953. illus. wrps. 281 pp. Revised ed. 1978.

SIDNEY, Delaware Co.
Anon. *Souvenir of Sidney.* 8 pp. plus views. n.d.

SIDNEY PLAINS, Delaware Co.
Anon. *Centennial Jubilee at Sidney Plains.* Ann Arbor, Mich. 1875. illus. 99 pp.

SOUTH KORTRIGHT, Delaware Co.
Galloway, H. (comp) *A Souvenir of So. Kortright.* Hobart 1906. 25 pp.

STAMFORD, Delaware Co.
(Anon.) *Stamford in the Catskills.* Stamford ca 1900. wrps. illus. 26 pp. (Has a brief history.)

STOCKPORT, Delaware Co.
Lotterer, E. *Stockport on the Delaware.* 1964. 71 pp.

WALTON, Delaware Co.
Anon. *History of Walton* (Chicago 1923) 47 pp. (Extracts from articles in *Walton Chronicle.*)
(Anon.) *The Story of Walton 1785-1975.* Walton Hist. Soc. 235 pp.
North, A. *The Founders & Founding of Walton, Preceeding the Adoption of the Federal Constitution.* (Walton.) 1924. illus. map. 51 pp. (4-page typed index in copy at LIHS.)

DUTCHESS COUNTY

DUTCHESS COUNTY
Anon. *Biographical Record of Dutchess Co.* Chicago 1897. illus. 941 pp.
Anon. *Biographical Record of Dutchess & Putnam Cos.* Chicago 1897. illus. 1149 pp.
Anon. *Historical & Genealogical Record of Dutchess & Putnam Cos.* Poughkeepsie. 1912. illus. 476 pp.
Ackert, A. *Dutchess Co. in Colonial Days. Paper Read Before Dutchess Co. Soc. in City of NY Feb. 28, 1898.* ca 1898. wrps. 10 pp.
--- *Dutchess Co. a Paper.* 1899. wrps. 30 pp.
Hasbrouck, F. (ed.) *The Co. of Dutchess.* Poughkeepsie 1909. illus. map. 791 pp. (Item in *Poughkeepsie Sunday Courier,* March 26, 1911, says a supplement was nearly ready, to be pub. by S. A. Matthieu.)
MacCracken, H. *Blithe Dutchess. The Flowering of an American County From 1812.* 1958. Map. Bib. Index. 495 pp. (MacCracken, former President of Vassar College at Poughkeepsie, was up to his mortar board in local history. He gave over 300 talks on the radio about Dutchess Co. "Few populations have been more completely historicized, from seventh-graders to the oldest inhabitants." Most local and county histories are a compilation of dry facts strung together in some sort of order, which only the most avid researcher can happily wade through. Almost anyone interested in history can contentedly read these volumes, as they are written with sparkle, wit, perception, and color.)
--- MacCracken, H. N. *Old Dutchess Forever! The story of an American county, 1609-1812.* NY. 1956. map. bib. index. 503 pp. (The history of Dutchess Co. up to 1812.)
Sherrill, H. *A Review of the Diseases of Dutchess Co. 1809-1825).* NY. 1826. 184 pp.
Smith. *History of Dutchess Co.* Syracuse. 1882. illus. 562 pp. Reprntd. 1980 with index.
Smith, P. *General History of Dutchess Co. 1609-1876.* Pawling 1877. pub. by author. illus. maps. 507 pp. (Typed index by G. Pierce in SLA.) (A very few copies have a folding map inside the rear cover.)
WPA Guide. *Dutchess Co.* Phil. 1937. illus. maps. 166 pp. (A large folding map laid in is lacking from many copies that come on the market.)

AMENIA, Dutchess Co.
Reed, N. *Early History of Amenia.* Amenia 1875. 151 pp. Reprntd. Amenia. 1964. wrps. 108 pp.

ANNANDALE, Dutchess Co.
Lewis, J. *Reminiscences of Annandale.* Lecture at St. Stephen's College. Phil. 1895. wrps. 16 pp. Reprntd. Brooklyn 1909. 32 pp.

ARTHURSBURG, Dutchess Co.
Staats, R. *A Quaker Community of Yesteryear.* 1950. illus. wrps. 20 pp.

BEACON, Dutchess Co.
Forrestal, M. (ed) *Beacon Golden Jubilee.* 1963. illus. advts. wrps. unpaged.
Spaight, F. *Looking Backward 1861-1895.* Fishkill-on-Hudson. 1896. advts. 43 pp.
Westbrook. Cook. Graham. *Fishkill Centennial.* Fishkill Landing 1883. 36 pp. (Beacon was originally called Fishkill Landing.)

CLINTON, Dutchess Co.
(Upton Lake Grange members comps.) *Town of Clinton, an Historical Review.* 1959. mimeo. wrps. 30 pp.

DOVER, Dutchess Co.
Maher, R. *Historic Dover.* Dover Plns. 1908. illus. wrps. 60 pp.

EAST FISHKILL, Dutchess Co.
(Staats, R.) *East Fishkill Centennial Celebration 1849-1949.* advts. wrps. 88 pp. (Includes: Wiccopee, Hopewell, Hopewell Jct., Fishkill Plains, Shennandoah, Gay Head, Clove Branch, Hortontown, Hillside Lake, Pecksville, Fishkill Hook, Stormville, Leetown, Cortlandville.)

Reprntd. *History of Town of East Fishkill 1849-1959.* 1959. maps. advts. 88 pp.

FISHKILL, Dutchess Co.
Anon. Thick Scrapbook at NYSHA has many articles from Fishkill newspapers on Fishkill hist. during ths 1800's. Especially rich in date on the business district. (Comp. by Harold Nestler.)
Bailey, H. *Local Tales & Hist. Sketches.* Fishkl Lndng. 1874. illus. 431 pp. (Fictitious tales and hist. sketches. Includes: Dutchess Co., Poughkeepsie, Pine Plains.)
(Brinckerhoff, T.) *Historical Sketch & Directory of Town of Fishkill.* Fishkill Landing 1866. map. advts. 153 pp.
Skinner, W. *A History of Fishkill, NY, 1683-1873.* 1978 illus. map. bib. index. 93 pp.

HYDE PARK, Dutchess Co.
Anon. *Hyde Park Has an Old Fashioned Fourth.* 1958. illus. advts. wrps. unpaged. (Has brief history.)
Cantin, E. *History of Hyde Park-on-Hudson.* Rhinebeck 1949. illus. map. wrps. 20 pp.
Fredriksen, B. *Our Local Heritage. A Short History of the Town of Hyde Park.* Hyde Park. 1962. illus. map. wrps. 56 pp. Reprinted 1971.
--- *Hyde Park Past & Present 1609-1959.* Hyde Park. 1959. illus. maps. wrps. unpaged.

KIPSBERGEN, Dutchess Co.
Smith, E. *Kipsbergen in Dutchess Co.* Rhinebeck. 1894. wrps. 26 pp. (Rhinebeck area.)

LAGRANGE, Dutchess Co.
Anon. *La Grange, an Historical Review 1959.* illus. map. advts. wrps. 70 pp.

MILLBROOK, Dutchess Co.
Hicks, C. *Millbrook* ca 1933. illus. advts. wrps. 24 pp. (Very brief hist.)

PAWLING, Dutchess Co.
Green, J. *History & Traditions of Pawling.* 1951. wrps. 58 pp. (Quaker Hill series.)
Pearce, N. *Lights & Shadows of Pawling.* Pawling. 1934. wrps. 69 pp. (From *Pawling Pioneer* 1870.)

PINE PLAINS, Dutchess Co.
Anon. *The Gateway to the Land of the Little Nine Partners.* ca 1935. illus. map. advts. wrps. 32 pp. Revised ed. pub. in pamphlet form by Little Nine Partners Hist. Soc., 1973, titled, *Historic Highlights of Pine Plains and Vicinity.*
Cole, H. *A History of Pine Plains.* An article prntd. in the *Pine Plains Register Herald* newspaper 1937, then issued as a booklet. (Possibly the same as above entry.)
Huntting, I. *History of Little Nine Partners of N. E. Precinct, & Pine Plains.* Amenia. 1897. Vol. 1. all pub. 411 pp. (102 pp typed index comp. by G. Pierce, 1921, at SLA.) (Vol. 2 is in existence in mss. form. Huntting may have burned any vol. that did not sell, possibly as many as 200 or 300.) Reprntd. 1974 with index. Lmtd. to 500 copies.)

PLEASANT VALLEY, Dutchess Co.
Anon. *Sesquicentennial of the Post Office of Pleasant Valley 1813-1963.* (1963) souvenir program. advts. wrps. 128 pp. (Back during the depression-era of the 1930s, my folks rented a few rooms in a farm house near Pleasant Valley. One bitter winter morning I spilled some water on the floor; it ran under our four-legged heating stove and froze. Some years ago several of us were talking to an old-timer up near Ticonderoga, in the land of long winters and long underwear. When he said, "I go South every winter to keep warm," someone joshed him with, "You don't go South. You've never been more than 50 miles away from home in your life." He retorted, "Yes, I do. I move out of the North bedroom into the South bedroom.")

POUGHKEEPSIE, Dutchess Co.
Anon. *Poughkeepsie. The Bridge and its Connections.* Souvenir No. of Poughkeepsie *Eagle* newspaper. 1889. illus. maps. wrps. folio. 44 pp.
Platt, E. *The Eagle's History of Poughkeepsie, 1683-1905.* Poughkeepsie. 1905 illus. map. 328 pp. (About 60 copies found, bound, & sold ca 1980.) Reprntd. ca 1987. (Here is a good place to write about John Lindmark, Poughkeepsie's best known bookseller. He had an old school building at the foot of Union Street near the river, and near my uncle's neighborhood grocery store. According to a 1945 newspaper article, he had 300,000 books; and he took good care of them. He sprayed the place with DDT and kept track of the humidity. Alexander Wolcott was one of his customers, and when the Mid-Hudson Bridge was completed Franklin D. Roosevelt said it would bring the world to Lindmark's door sill. [The bridge was formally opened on August 25, 1930, and I

celebrated my 9th birthday by walking over it.] About 1945 Lindmark wanted me to work for him and learn the business, but for some reason which I cannot recall I did not take his offer. It wasn't until 1952, after I had moved to New Jersey, that I began buying and selling books part-time. On rare occasions he would quote to me a book he knew I wanted. I remember one card which read something like, "Unused and Unread. There is no substitute for virginity." Sometime after the bridge was built the entrance system was expanded and Lindmark had to move his huge stock within 12 days. I do not know what happened as I was not living in Poughkeepsie at the time, but I think that some of the books were moved to another building. The story is that thousands of books were put out on the curb and that many treasures were garnered by passersby. Another Poughkeepsie bookseller that deserves mention was a Mr. Logan whom I only knew slightly as I was in his shop once or twice at the most. I read somewhere that he was almost bitten by a rattlesnake while looking at books in a barn in Dutchess Co.)

(Reynolds, H.) *250th Anniv. Celebration 1687-1937.* 1937. illus. wrps. 30 pp.

Reynolds, H. W. *The Records of Christ Church, Poughkeepsie, New York 1755-1910.* Pub. 1911. illus. index. 440 pp. + Vol. 2, pub. in 1921. 399 pp. (A detailed history, with biog., church hist. records; and records of baptisms, households, marriages, deaths, burials, confirmations. Vol. 2 is very rare. In January 1921, Miss Reynolds wrote to a prospective purchaser, "Vol. II of the *Records* is just come from the binder. The ed. consists of only 58 copies most of which are for deposit in standard libraries ... but a few are for sale." I have owned two sets of this major work on Poughkeepsie genealogy, one of which contained the author's letter.)

QUAKER HILL, Dutchess Co.
Allen, M. *North Quaker Hill & Its Traditions.* 1950. 64 pp.
Daniels, H. *Quaker Hill at the Turn of the Century.* 1958. 68 pp.
Stearns, A. *Ancient Homes & Early Days of Quaker Hill.* 1903. 36 pp. 2nd. ed. 1913. illus. map. 44 pp.
Thomas, A. *My Reminsicences of Quaker Hill.* 1965.
Wilson, W. *Quaker Hill, A Sociological Study.* NY. 1907. illus. maps. 168 pp.
--- *Quaker Hill in the 18th Century.* 1905. 68 pp.
--- *Quaker Hill in the 19th Century.* 1903. 36 pp. 2nd. ed. map. 1907.

RHINEBECK, Dutchess Co.
Anon. *Rhinebeck.* (1957) illus. map. wrps. 16 pp.
Lienhard, F. *Reminiscences of Rhinebeck.* Written in 1979. Published in 1984. wrps. 57 pp. (The author's memories of Rhinebeck from 1911 to 1930.)
Morse, H. *Historic Old Rhinebeck.* Rhinebeck. 1908. pub. by author. illus. maps. 448 pp. Reprntd. 1977 with index.
Smith, E. *Documentary History of Rhinebeck.* Rhinebeck. 1881. map. 239 pp. Reprnt. 1974 with index. Lmtd. to 500 copies.

SALT POINT, Dutchess Co.
Buck, C. *Salt Point History & People*. 1963. map. 84 pp typed mss. in POPL.
Burhans, M. *A History of Salt Point & De Lavergnes Store*. Stanfordville. 1964. wrps. 20 pp.

WAPPINGERS FALLS, Dutchess Co.
De Lavergne, C. (comp.) *Directory and History of Wappingers Falls*. 1932. advts. map. wrps. 53 pp.

WASHINGTON, Dutchess Co.
Anon. *Our Town. A Short Documentary on the Town of Washington*. 1959. wrps. 20 pp.

WASHINGTON TOWNSHIP, Dutchess Co.
Coffin, R. *History of the Town of Washington in General, and Specifically Dealing With the Coffin Family*. n.d. unpub. mss.
Diarpino, C. *History of the Town of Washington*. 1976. wrps. illus. bib. 107 pp. (Has special chapters on area Gardens and the Millbrook Hunt Club.)

WHALEY LAKE, Dutchess Co.
Young, R. *History & Traditions of Whaley Lake*. Also: *The Settlers Revolt*, by Hillery. *The Old Quaker Meeting House*, by Hoag. 1954.

ERIE COUNTY

ERIE COUNTY
Anon. *Memorial & Family History of Erie Co*. NY. 1906-1908. illus. 2 vol.
Anon. *Perry Sesquicentennial. Erie Co. Industry, History, & Directory 1813-1963*. Souvenir Magazine. illus. advts. wrps. 50 pp.

Dunn, W. *History of Erie Co. 1870-1970*. 1972. illus. 462 pp.
Horton. Williams. Douglass. *History Northwestern NY*. Erie, Niagara, Wyoming, Genesee, & Orleans Cos. NY. 1947. illus. maps. 3 vols.
Johnson, C. *Centennial History of Erie Co*. Buffalo. 1876. 512 pp. (typed index at SPL.)
White, T. (ed) *Our County & Its People*. Boston. 1898. illus. maps. 2 vol.

ALDEN, Erie Co.
Anon. *History of Town of Alden*. 1971. pamphlet.
Ewell, E. *History of the Town of Alden*. Nov. 1875. 47 pp. mss. in BHS.

AMHERST, Erie Co.
Glover, W. *History of Town of Amherst*. 1971. pamphlet.
Young, S. (ed. town historian) *The Town of Amherst*. Sept. 1955. wrps. 14 pp.

AURORA, Erie Co.
Anon. *150 Years in Aurora*. 1818-1968. pub. by Aurora Hist. Soc. 1968. Book.
Davison, E. *History of Town of Aurora*. 1971. pamphlet.
(Jr. Hist. Soc.) *All Around the Town of Aurora*. 1957. illus. map. 27 pp. (Includes: East Aurora, West Falls, Griffins Mills.)

BLASDELL, Erie Co.
Thompson, E. *The Day Before Yesterday in Blasdell*. 1951. illus. 69 pp.

BOSTON, Erie Co.
Bradley, C. A. *Brief History of the Town of Boston*. 1966. illus. wrps. 33 pp.
Bradley, C. *History of Town of Boston*. 1971. pamphlet.

BRANT, Erie Co.
Anon. *Quarto Centennial of the Town of Brant. 1839-1964.* (1964.) 46 pp.
Weller, E. *History of Town of Brant.* 1972. pamphlet.

BUFFALO, Erie Co.
Anon. *A Directory for the Village of Buffalo ... To Which is Added a Sketch of the History of ths Village from 1801 to 1828.* Pub. by L. Cary. Buffalo 1828. folding map. 55 pp. (First Buffalo directory.)
Anon. *History of the City of Buffalo.* Pub. by *Buffalo Evening News* 1908. illus. 247 pp.
Anon. *Men of Buffalo.* Chicago 1902. (416 pp. of ports.)
(Ball, S.) *Buffalo in 1825: Containing Historical & Statistical Sketches.* Buffalo. 1825. folding map. 14 pp. (First hist. of Buffalo)
Becker, S. *Sketches of Early Buffalo & The Niagara Region.* 1904. 168 pp.
Bingham, R. *The Cradle of the Queen City. History of Buffalo to the Incorporation of the City.* Buffalo. 1931. illus. maps. 504 pp.
Devoy, J. *History of the City of Buffalo & Niagara Falls.* Buffalo. 1896. illus. 363 pp.
Hawes, L. *Buffalo 50 Years Ago.* Buffalo. 1886. 10 pp.
Hill, H. *Municipality of Buffalo. A History 1720-1923.* NY. 1923. illus. maps. 4 vols.
Ketchum, W. *An Authentic & Comprehensive History of Buffalo.* Buffalo. 1865. 2 vols.
Larned, J. *A History of Buffalo ... With Sketches of the City of Rochester ... & the City of Utica.* NY. 1911. illus. 2 vols.
Severance, F. (ed.) *Picture Book of Earlier Buffalo (Views of the City From 1820 to 1870)* 1912. 507 pp. (Vol. 16 of BHS Proceedings.)
Smith, H. *Hist ... of Buffalo & Erie Co.* Syracuse. 1884. illus. 2 vols. (149 pp. mimeo. index, by R. McNallie, 1950, in SPL.) Reprntd. ca 1976
Snow, J. *Early Recollections of Buffalo.* 1908. 39 pp.
Welch, S. *Recoll. of Buffalo During the Decade from 1830 to 1840, or Fifty Years Since.* Buffalo. 1891. 423 pp.

CHEEKTOWAGA, Erie Co.
Baker, D. *History of Cheektowaga.* U. of Buffalo. June 1951. maps. 115 pp. typed mss. at BPL.
Reinstein, J. *History of Town of Cheektowage.* 1971. pamphlet.
Reinstein, J. *Town of Cheektowaga Historical Atlas.* 1955. Lmtd. to 100 copies. wrps. 163 pp. (Additional pp. were prntd. & added to each atlas.)
Reukauf, C. *Cheektowaga Cavalcade. The First Hundred Years. 1839-1939.* Cheektowaga. 1939. illus. maps. wrps. 84 pp.

CLARENCE, Erie Co.
(Baker, O.) *Clarence Sesquicentennial 1808-1958.* illus. advts. wrps. unpaged.
Baker, O. *History of Town of Clarence.* 1971. pamphlet.
Glovack, J. *Survey of Clarence & Its Educational System.* U. of Buffalo. June 1952. maps. 68 pp. typed mss. in BPL.

COLDEN, Erie Co.
Girl Scouts - Troop I, Colden. *Notes on Early History of Colden.* (1936.) Broadside 10 x 11 inches.
Weller, E. *History of Town of Colden.* 1972. pamphlet.

COLLINS, Erie Co.
Painter, L. (town historian) *The Collins Story.* June 1, 1962. il-

lus. map. 160 pp.
Spencer, L. *History of Town of Collins.* 1971. pamphlet.

CONCORD, Erie Co.
Anon. *Sesquicentennial Booklet. Towns of Concord, Springville.* (Springville.) July 1, 1962. illus. 64 pp.
Briggs, E. *History of the Original Town of Concord, Being the Present Towns of Concord, Collins, North Collins & Sardinia.* Rochester. 1883. illus. map. 977 pp.
Geiger, L. *History of Town of Concord.* 1971. pamphlet.

EAST AURORA, Erie Co.
Anon. *Pictorial & Historical Review of East Aurora & Vicinity.* (East Aurora.) 1940. illus. 84 pp.
Dirlam & Simmons. *Sinners This is East Aurora. The Story of Elbert Hubbard & the Roycroft Shops.* NY. 1964. illus. 263 pp.
(Smith, L.) *Historic Highlights of East Aurora & Vicinity.* East Aurora. 1940. illus. unpaged.

EBENEZER, Erie Co.
Lankes, F. *The Ebenezer Community of True Inspiration.* Gardenville. 1949. illus. map. 100 pp. pub. by author for distribution at the pharmacy of Julius Bednarz. (See **WEST SENECA**, entries by Anon. and the first two titles by Lankes.)
Metz, C. *Reminiscences 1842-1855.* 12 pp. typescript carbon copy trans. from the German by N. R. Reamer at CU.

EDEN, Erie Co.
Anderson, D. *An Informal History of Eden.* (Vol. 1) Eden 1946. illus. advts. wrps. 72 pp.
--- *(Vol. 2)* 1971. pamphlet.
--- *(Vol. 3)* 1977. illus. 88 pp. index to 3-vol. set. 1977. 39 pp.

Warren, A. *Paper on Town of Eden.* April 23, 1864. 5 pp. mss. in BHS.

ELMA, Erie Co.
Briggs. *History of Town of Elma.* 1971. pamphlet.
Jackman, W. *History of Town of Elma 1620-1901.* Buffalo. 1902. 331 pp.
Sigman, F. (ed. town hist.) *The Centuries in Elma.* Buffalo. (1956.) illus. maps. 336 pp.

EVANS, Erie Co.
Barker, P. *Early History of Town of Evans.* 1869-1870. 16 pp. mss. in BHS.
Cook, D. (town historian) *Faces & Places.* illus. articles in the *Evans Journal.*
Cook, D. *History of Town of Evans.* 1972. pamphlet.

GRAND ISLAND, Erie Co.
Klingel, M. *History of Town of Grand Island.* 1972. pamphlet.
Macleod, R. *Cinderella Island.* 1950. maps. wrps. 52 pp.

HAMBURG, Erie Co.
Anon. *Hamburg Sesquicentennial 1812-1962.* illus. map. advts. unpaged.
Sipprell, M. *History of Town of Hamburg.* 1971. pamphlet.

HOLLAND, Erie Co.
Brown, R. *History of Town of Holland.* 1971. pamphlet.

KENMORE, Erie Co.
Parkhurst, F. *History of Kenmore.* Kenmore. 1926. illus. 96 pp.

LACKAWANNA, Erie Co.
Anon. *Lackawanna Golden Jubilee Commemorating 50 Years of Progress.* 1959. illus. advts. wrps. 75 pp.
Weller, E. *History of Town of Lackawanna.* 1971. pamphlet.

LANCASTER, Erie Co.
Anon. *A History of Lancaster as Told by Lancaster's Community Newspaper.* 1978. Lancaster Hist. Soc. 186 pp. (Reproductions of pp. from 3 Lancaster newspapers 1878-1978).
Bissell, E. *Early Town History of Town of Lancaster.* 44 pp. carbon copy of hist. articles copied from *Lancaster Enterprise* 1953-1954 in NYSHA.
Mikula, E. *History of Town of Lancaster.* 1971. pamphlet.

MARILLA, Erie Co.
Neumann, C. *History of Town of Marilla.* 1971. pamphlet.
Smith, L. *History of Town of Marilla 1823-1937.* illus. advts. wrps. unpaged.

NEWSTEAD, Erie Co.
Weller, E. *History of Town of Newstead.* 1917. pamphlet.

NORTH COLLINS, Erie Co.
Weller, E. *History of Town of North Collins.* 1971. pamphlet.
Weller, E. *North Collins Remembers: A Comprehensive History of North Collins & Vicinity.* Gowanda. 1941. illus. 42 pp.

ORCHARD PARK, Erie Co.
Printy, J. *History of Town of Orchard Park.* 1971. pamphlet.

SARDINIA, Erie Co.
Weller, E. *History of Town of Sardinia.* 1972. pamphlet.

SLOAN, Erie Co.
(Barry, T., village hist.) *Village of Sloan History.* 1966. 24 pp.

SOUTH WALES, Erie Co.
(Smith, L. ed.) *History of South Wales.* Community Fair 1939. illus. advts. wrps. 20 pp.

SPRINGVILLE, Erie Co.
(Smith, L. ed.) *Springville History* 1939. illus. unpaged.

TONAWANDA, Erie Co.
Parkhurst, F. *History of Town of Tonawanda 1805-1930.* (Kenmore.) 1930. illus. map. 126 pp.
Percy, J. *Tonawanda, The Way It Was, 1805-1903.* 1978. illus. map. index. 130 pp.
Stewart, J. *History of Town of Tonawanda.* 1971. pamphlet.

WALES, Erie Co.
Weller, E. *History of Town of Wales.* 1971. pamphlet.

WEST SENECA, Erie Co.
Anon. *West Seneca 1851-1951.* Orig. Known as Ebenezer. Buffalo. 1951. 96 pp. (See **EBENEZER**, titles by Lankes and Metz.)
Lankes, F. *An Outline History of West Seneca.* West Seneca 1962. wrps. 21 pp.
Lankes, F. *Changing Scenes of West Seneca.* West Seneca. 1959. wrps. 20 pp.
Lankes, F. *Gone Are the Days.* Miscellany of local events. West Seneca. 1972. pamphlet.
Lankes, F. *The Ebenezer Society.* 1963. illus. wrps. 141 pp. (Hist. of settlement by Community of True Inspiration in West Seneca & Elma, Erie Co. Group believed in Bible as explained by their mediums.)
Seller, E. *Hist. ... of West Seneca.* 1972. pamphlet.

WILLIAMSVILLE, Erie Co.
Anon. *Williamsville Sesquicentennial 1800-1950.* ca 1950. illus. advts. wrps. 106 pp.

ESSEX COUNTY

ESSEX COUNTY

Anon. *Biog. Review. Leading Citizens of Essex & Clinton Cos.* Boston. 1896. illus. 543 pp.

Cook, F. *Home Sketches of Essex Co.* 1858. 139 pp. 443

Smith, H. *History of Essex Co.* Syracuse. 1885. illus. 2 vols.

Watson, W. *A General View and Agricultural Survey of the County of Essex.* 247 pp. (In: Transactions of the NY State Agricultural Soc. 1853.) Much hist. 34-page suppl. appeared in Soc. Transactions in 1854.

Watson, W. *Military & Civil History of Essex Co.* Albany. 1869. illus. maps. 504 pp.

CROWN POINT, Essex Co.

Barker, E. *Crown Point, New York, in the Civil War.* 1962. 133 pp.

Lonergan, C. *Historic Crown Point. The Story of the Forts & The Village.* Boston. 1942. 79 pp.

Spaulding, S. *History of Crown Point from 1800 to 1874.* Port Henry 1874. 42 pp.

ELIZABETHTOWN, Essex Co.

Brown, G. *Pleasant Valley. A History of Elizabethtown.* Elizabethtown. 1905. illus. map. 474 pp.

ESSEX, Essex Co.

Anon. *Essex, New York, Champlain's Historic Harbor.* (1969.) wrps. illus. maps. Essex Free Library. 76 pp.

Noble, H. *A Sketch of the History of the Town of Essex.* Champlain. 1940. pvtly. prntd. lmtd. 142 copies. 19 pp.

Trost and DeLong. *A History Celebrating the 150th Anniversary of Town of Essex. 1805-1955.* 1955. illus. 64 pp.

INDIAN PASS, Essex Co.

Street, A. B. *The Indian Pass.* NY. 1869. 201 pp. (A classic on Adirondack hiking, which seldom comes on the market. Reprntd. in recent years. The DAB says that Street wrote 2 other books on the Adiondacks which apparently were never pub. Some years ago my son and I hiked into Indian Pass from the Adirondack Loj (short for Lodge) at Heart Lake in September. While eating our lunch on a boulder overlooking the chasm we saw an event of nature which few have probably seen at that spot: hundreds of Monarch Butterflies migrating southward, their fragile wings fluttering in the wind currents in that narrow pass. Reprntd. 1975.)

KEESEVILLE, Essex Co.

Kings Daughters (comp.) *Old Keeseville Tales.* Port Henry. 1900. 99 pp.

LAKE PLACID, Essex Co.

Hayes, A. *Lake Placid, Its Early History from Civil War to Present.* 1946. illus. wrps. 52 pp. (Author was guide & building contractor.)

MINERVA, Essex Co.

Anon. *History of a Town in Essex Co. 1817-1967.* 1967. Minerva Hist. Soc. illus. wrps. 111 pp.

NEWCOMB, Essex Co.

Fennessy L. *History of Newcomb.* 1977. illus. map. bib. 105 pp.

PORT HENRY, Essex Co.

Warner & Hall. *History of Port Henry.* Rutland, VT. 1931. illus. 182 pp.

SARANAC LAKE, Essex Co.

(Many years ago my son and I

fell out of a canoe in Saranac Lake, hollered for help, and were rescued by a priest from Tupper Lake.)
Dora and Keough. *A Past to Remember. A Future to Mold.* Saranac Lake. 1977. wrps. illus. 96 pp.
Raymond, H. *Story of Saranac, A Chapter in Adirondack Hist.* NY. 1909 illus. 78 pp.

SCHROON LAKE, Essex Co.
Leavitt, P. (comp.) *Scaroon.* 1977. Schroon-North Hudson Hist. Soc. 12 pp.

TAHAWUS, Essex Co.
Shaw, G. *Tahawus, Newcomb, & Long Lake.* 1955. illus. maps. unpaged.

TICONDEROGA, Essex Co.
Anon. *Historic Ticonderoga* (1933) wrps. map. 28 pp.
Bascom, F. (ed) *Letters of a Ti Farmer 1851-1885.* Ithaca. 1946. 134 pp.
Cook, J. *Centennial Address. Ticonderoga 1764-1864.* 1864. 106 pp.
Cook, J. *Home Sketches of Ticonderoga.* Keeseville. 1858. (The author was 19 years old, and pub. under the name of Flavius J. Cook.)
--- *A Historical Address. The First Centennial of the Settlement of Ticonderoga.* Ticonderoga. 1909. illus. 109 pp.
Johnson, E. *Streetroad, Its History & Its People. Facts, Folks, Fancies.* (Formerly called Ti Street.) Ithaca. 1956. illus. mimeo. 64 pp.
Lape, J. (ed.) *Ticonderoga Patches and Patterns From its Past.* FirstvVol. Tcndrg. Hist. Soc. 1959. illus. map. 343 pp.
Stoddard, S. *Ticonderoga Past & Present.* Albany 1873. 78 pp.

WESTPORT, Essex Co.
Glenn, M. *The Story of Three Towns: Westport, Essex, and Willsboro, New York.* pub. by author. 1978. illus. map. 354 pp.
Royce, C. *Bessboro: History of Westport* 1902. map. 611 pp. (mimeo. supplement by H. Odell, 1940, in SPL - 7 pp. plus 1/2 pp. typed data)

WILLSBORO, Essex Co.
Watson, W. *Pioneer History of Champlain Valley. Being an Account of the Settlement of the Town of Willsboro, by Wm. Gilliland.* Albany. 1863. lmtd. 200 copies. 231 pp. (27 copies on large paper.)

FRANKLIN COUNTY

FRANKLIN COUNTY
Ives, H. *Recollections of the Adirondacks.* 1915. 124 pp.
Seaver, F. *Historical Sketches of Franklin Co.* Albany. 1918. 819 pp.

ALTAMONT, Franklin Co.
Simmons, L. (comp.) *Highlights of a Half Century of Progress in A Friendly Town.* 1952. illus. advts. wrps. 70 pp.

BANGOR, Franklin Co.
Smith, R. *Those Were the Days. A History of Bangor.* Malone. 1977. maps. illus. bib. errata slip. wrps. 99 pp.

BURKE, Franklin Co.
Anon. *Reflections. A Brief History of Burke, 1797-1976.* Burke Bicentennial Commission. 1977. illus. bib. 47 pp.

FORT COVINGTON, Franklin Co.
Donovan, H. *Fort Covington & Her Neighbors, a History of 3 Towns (Ft. Covington, Bombay,*

Westville). 1963. illus. map. 447 pp.
McCartney, W. *Fifty Years & Country Doctor.* 1938. 575 pp.

LAKE TITUS, Franklin Co.
Daily F. *Lake Titus Potpourri.* 1977. illus. 34 pp.

MALONE, Franklin Co.
(Forkey, D.) *Malone Sesquicentennial 1802-1952.* illus. advts. wrps. 162 pp.

MOIRA, Franklin Co.
Reed, W. *Moira Area: Life on the Border 60 Years Ago.* Fall River, MA. 1882. wrps. 120 pp.
Saxton, K. *Life's Book of Recollections, 1825-1975.* Gale Road Settlers. pub. by author. 1977. illus. map. 87 pp.

OWL'S HEAD, Franklin Co.
Fitch, M. *History of Ragged Lake.* Providence, RI. 1934. mimeo. bib. index. 214 pp. Lmtd. to 45 copies. A supplement was issued later.

PAUL SMITHS, Franklin Co.
Collins, G. *The Brighton Story. Being the History of Paul Smiths, Gabriels, and Rainbow Lake.* 1977. map. bib. illus. 202 pp.

WESTVILLE, Franklin Co.
Stockwell, O. *Mini Sketches of Westville, 1977.* pub. by author. 116 pp.

FULTON COUNTY

FULTON COUNTY
Cook, A. (comp.) *Hist. Sketch of Fulton Co.* 1940. 52 pp.
Frothingham, W. *History of Fulton Co.* Syracuse. 1892. illus. index. 800 pp.
Palmer, R. *Historical Fulton.* 1964. illus. wrps. 12 pp.

BROADALBIN, Fulton Co.
Cloutier, I. *History of Broadalbin 1700-1838.* Masters' Thesis, 1951, State Teachers' College, Albany.
Honeywell, R. *Broadalbin in History.* Amsterdam 1907. illus. 24 pp.

GLOVERSVILLE, Fulton Co.
Hart, L. *History of Gloversville, Yesterday & Today.* 1940. 10 pp.
Sprague, H. *Gloversville, Or, The Model Village. A Poem With an Appendix Containing a Succinct History of the Same.* Gloversville. 1859. 131 pp. (Has numerous biog. sketches and some genealogical notes.)

JOHNSTOWN, Fulton Co.
McMartin, D. *Johnstown, or Wit & Humor in an Old American Village.* n.d. 2nd. ed. Sept. 17, 1914. With additional chapters, wrps. 32 pp.
O'Neil, E. (comp) *Historical Events of the City of Johnstown 1755-1931.* ca 1931. 30 pp.

PERTH, Fulton Co.
Zierak, S. *Perth Memories and Reflections. 1838-1976.* 1977. illus. map. bib. 186 pp.

SACONDAGA, Fulton Co.
Becker, H. *Historical Notes on the Sacondaga Valley.* 1958. maps. mimeo. 33 pp.

STRATFORD, Fulton Co.
Hist. articles have appeared in *Leader-Herald, Glovers-ville,* & *Little Falls Times,* Little Falls.

GENESEE COUNTY

GENESEE COUNTY
Anon. *Sesquicentennial of Genesee Co. 1802-1952.* Batavia. 1952.

illus. maps. advts. 119 pp.
Beers, F. (ed) *Gazetteer & Biographical Record of Genesee Co. 1788-1890.* Syracuse. 1890. illus. map. 660 pp. plus 199 pp. business directory. Reprntd. 1977 with index.
Hungerford, E. *The Genesee Country.* 1945. illus. 22 pp.
Kennedy, J. *The Genesee Country.* Batavia. 1895. illus. 230 pp.
North, S. (ed.) *Our County & Its People.* Boston. 1899. illus. 731 pp.
Rial & Westervelt. *Century History of the Genesee County Fair. 1839-1939.* 1939. 69 pp.
(Williamson, C.) *Description of the Genesee Country* Albany. 1798. maps. 37 pp.
Second ed. ... NY. 1799. map. 63 pp.
Reprntd. as a supplement to John Payne's *New and Complete System of Universal Geography.* NY. 1799.
Another ed. ... (Candadigua?) prntd. for author. 1804. 24 pp.
Another ed. ... NY. 1804. prntd. for the author. 1804. 16 pp.
Another ed. ... Baltimore. 1804.
Re-written and reprntd. at Frederick Town (MD) 1804, titled: *A View of the Present Situation of the Western Parts of State of New York.* 23 pp.
Reprntd. in Vol. 2 of the *Documentary History of the State of New York.* 1849.
Reprntd. Rochester, NY, 1892. Lmtd. to 300 copies.
(On a few of the ed. the pseudonym of Robert Munro, was used. Pamphlet has had a complicated printing hist., and no doubt there were other ed.)

BATAVIA, Genesee Co.
Aderman, W. (ed.) *A Source Book for 7th Year Social Studies.* Batavia Public Schools. (1944.) mimeo. wrps. 128 pp.

(Sketches of: Alexander, Bethany, Pembroke, Darien, Pavilion, Elba, LeRoy, Oakfield, Alabama, Stafford, Bergen.)
Seaver, W. *A Historical Sketch of Village of Batavia.* Batavia. 1849. wrps. 56 pp.
Williams, C. *Outline History of Batavia.* Batavia. DAR. 1934. illus. wrps. 17 pp.

BETHANY, Genesee Co.
Anon. *History of Town of Bethany, Sesquicentennial.* 1962. illus. 76 pp.

BYRON, Genesee Co.
Merrill, A. *The Pioneer Story of Asa Merrill.* NY. 1872. wrps. 23 pp.

CORFU, Genesee Co.
Fuller, P. *History of Village of Corfu & School District.* 1946. illus. map. 22 pp. typed mss.

LEROY, Genesee Co.
Schmidt, C. *The Le Roy Settlement* ca 1960. mimeo. 8 pp.

OAKFIELD, Genesee Co.
Anon. Special Newspaper Issue. *Rochester Post Express.* Dec. 19, 1896.

PAVILION, Genesee Co.
Broughton, J. (ed.) *The Pavilion Community of New York State 1800-1941.* LeRoy 1941. illus. 155 pp.

GREENE COUNTY

GREENE COUNTY
Beecher, R. *Out to Greenville and Beyond, Historical Sketches of Greene County.* 1977. wrps. 144 pp.
Beers. *History of Greene Co.* NY. 1884. illus. maps. 462 pp. Reprntd. 1969.

Chadwick, G. *The Old Times Corner.* 1932. 125 pp. (reprnt of articles in *Catskill Examiner.* November 1929 to December.
Chase, E. *Local History Gleanings.* 1910. wrps. 22 pp. (Mostly legal and political hist., with data on 5 murders.)
Gallt, F. *Dear Old Greene Co.* Catskill 1915. illus. maps. advts. 580 pp. Another ed.: Catskill illus. 1922.
Ross and Kozacek. *Greene County, New York. '76 Bicentennial Overview, Beginnings and Background.* 1976. wrps. bib. index. illus. 200 pp.
Smith, M. *Greene Co. A Short History.* 1963. illus. map. wrps. 18 pp. Second ed. 1964. Revised ed. 1968, 22 pp.
Vedder, J. *History of Greene Co. 1651-1800.* 1927. Vol. I (all pub.) illus. wrps. (Also includes chronology of important events of 1925-6-7.) 2nd. ed. (1928) pvtly. prntd., illus., wrps. 207 pp. Unbound sheets were found and bound in 1966.

ATHENS, Greene Co.
(Anon.) *Athens, Its People and Industry. 1776-1976.* wrps. 242 pp.
Loomis, K. *Athens Sesquicentennial 1805-1955.* 1955. wrps. advts. illus. 30 pp.

CATSKILL, Greene Co.
Hill, H. *Recollections of an Octogenarian.* Boston. 1884. 195 pp.
Pinckney, J. *Reminiscences of Catskill.* Catskill. 1868. wrps. 79 pp. Reprntd. 1981 with addition of 8-page name index.
Vedder, J. *Historic Catskill.* 1922. illus. 98 pp.

COXSACKIE, Greene Co.
(Anon.) *Coxsackie on the Hudson 1776-1976.* Hoot of the Owl. 1976. wrps. 47 pp.
Van Bergen, R. *Ye Olden Time, As Compiled From the Coxsackie News of 1889.* 1935. wrps. 118 pp.

DURHAM, Greene Co.
(Anon.) *Town of Durham, Bicentennial Booklet.* 1976. wrps. 42 pp.

GREENVILLE, Greene Co.
Anon. *Memorial Celebration. Aug. 23-24, 1871.* 60 pp.

HALCOTT, Greene Co.
(Anon.) *Halcott Valley.* 1851-1976. wrps. 16 pp.

JEWETT, Greene Co.
Hitchcock, E. *History of Town of Jewett.* 1976. wrps. 54 pp.

NEW BALTIMORE, Greene Co.
Ackerman, E. (Ed.) *Heritage of New Baltimore.* 1976. wrps. 232 pp.

WINDHAM, Greene Co.
Prout, H. *Old Times in Windham.* Cornwallville. 1970 map. index. 178 pp. (Prout, 1810-1879, grew up in Windham.) Originally pub. in the *Windham Journal* newspaper 1869-1870.)

HAMILTON COUNTY

HAMILTON COUNTY
Aber & King, *History of Hamilton Co.* Lake Pleasant. 1965. illus. maps. indexes. 1209 pp. 515
--- *Tales From An Adirondack Co.* Prospect. 1961. illus. 208 pp.

BLUE MOUNTAIN LAKE, Hamilton Co.
Hochschild, H. *An Adirondack Resort in the 19th Century,*

Blue Mountain Lake. 1870-1900. Stage Coaches & Luxury Hotels. 1962. 106 illus. 3 maps. 112 pp. (Rev. of portion of author's *Township 34.*) See **TOWNSHIP 34.**)

INDIAN LAKE, Hamilton Co.
Articles on Indian Lake hist. have been pub. in *Indian Lake Bulletin*, at North Creek.

LONG LAKE, Hamilton Co.
Becker, H. *History of South Pond & Origin of Long Lake Township.* Rexford 1963. Over 90 maps and illus. mimeo. lmtd. 100 copies. 274 pp.
--- (ed.) *Inca-Pah-Co: Long Lake.* Rexford. 1962. unpaged.
--- *Some Early Long Lake Documents* (1957) illus. maps. mimeo. (Reprints of writings about Long Lake.) Between 17 and 50 copies were issued.
Emerson, L. (ed. by H. Becker) *Early Life at Long Lake.* 1956. wrps. mimeo. lmtd ed. 63 pp.
Todd, J. *Long Lake.* 1845. Ed. by J. Brace, Jr. 100 pp. A mimeo ed of 35 pp. made in 1955. Reprt with intro by Warder H. Cadbury, 1983. illus. 128 pp.

SPECULATOR, Hamilton Co.
Stanyon, M. P. *The Quiet Years.* 1965. illus. by M. S. Colvin. 112 pp. Lmtd. to 400 copies. (Life in Speculator, NY, 1888 to ca 1940.)

TOWNSHIP 34, Hamilton Co.
Hochschild, H. *Township 34, A History With Digression of an Adirondack Township in Hamilton Co.* NY. 1952. pvtly. prntd. illus. maps. lmtd. 600 copies. 614 pp. (Portions of this book were revised & reprntd. in 1962. See **BLUE MOUNTAIN LAKE.**) (Book received award of merit & the citation "a remarkable local history" from American Assn. for State & Local Hist.) Prntd. as giveaway, it is rumored that a cache of new copies remained hidden for some years. Supplement issued. A copy has been noted with a 24-page addendum to Chapter 13, the pages being numbered 170A through 170X.

HERKIMER COUNTY

HERKIMER COUNTY
Anon. *Herkimer Co. Commemorative Brochure.* Herkimer. 1954. illus. 77 pp.
Beers, F. (ed.) *History of Herkimer Co. 1791-1879.* NY. 1879. illus. maps. 289 pp. Reprntd. 1980.
Benton, N. *History of Herkimer Co.* Albany. 1856. illus. maps. 497 pp. 1000 copies prntd.
Hardin, G. (ed.; asstd. by F. Willard) *History of Herkimer Co.* Syracuse. 1893. illus. maps. 825 pp.
Nellis, C. *Early Cheese Making in Herkimer Co.* (NY.) ca 1940s? 14 typed pp. (The author was a cheesemaker, and knew many of the early cheese makers and buyers.)

BIG MOOSE LAKE, Herkimer Co.
Whited, K. *Big Moose Lake, An Historical Sketch.* n.d. map. wrps. 16 pp.

FAIRFIELD, Herkimer Co.
Raynore, J. *Historical Events of the Early Settlers of Fairfield, White Creek, & Vicinity.* Newport. 1909. 44 pp.

HERKIMER, Herkimer Co.
Anon. *Herkimer Flood. Also A Historical Sketch of the Village.* 1910. illus. 32 pp.
Draheim, H. *History of Village of*

Herkimer. *Sesquicentennial Celebration 1807-1957.* Little Falls. 1957. illus. map. wrps. 44 pp.

Murray, T. (comp.) *Panorama & History of Herkimer 1725-1900. Original Sketches by A. Zintzmaster & D. Devondorf.* Herkimer. 1900. illus. wrps. 108 pp.

ILION, Herkimer Co.
Anon. *Ilion 1852-1952.* 1952. illus. map. advts. 160 pp.
Anon. *Souvenir of Ilion. Historical Sketch.* (Ilion. 1904.) illus. 66 pp.
Schulz, W. *Ilion. The Town Remington Made.* 1977. bib. 192 pp. (Remington Arms Co. influence on Ilion.)

LITTLE FALLS, Herkimer Co.
Anon. *Centennial Review. Little Falls. 1811-1911.* illus. wrps. 96 pp.
Cooney, E. (ed. city historian) *Little Falls Sesquicentennial 1811-1961.* illus. maps. wrps. 140 pp.

NEWPORT, Herkimer Co.
Johnson G. (& others) *History of Town of Newport 1806-1906.* Newport. (1906.) illus. 80 pp.

NORWAY, Herkimer Co.
Anon. *Norway Tidings* 4 pp. monthly publ., mostly Norway hist. Vol. 1, #1 - Jan. 1887. Last issue Vol. 4, #12 - Dec. 1890. Plus Centennial No. Sept. ? 1897. 12 pp.

OLD FORGE, Herkimer Co.
Grady, J. *The Adirondacks. Fulton Chain. Big Moose Region. The Story of a Wilderness.* Little Falls. 1933. illus. map. 320 pp.
Thistlethwaite, W. *The Romance of Old Forge.* wrps. 8 pp.

(reprntd. from *Utica Daily Express* Dec. 8, 1915.)

POLAND, Herkimer Co.
Anon. *Poland Sesquicentennial 1955.* illus. advts. wrps. 58 pp.

SCHUYLER, Herkimer Co.
Klock, E. *Reminiscences of Town of Schuyler.* 1930. 354 pp. carbon copy of typed mss. in SLA.

WEST WINFIELD, Herkimer Co.
Smith, T. *Along West Winfield's Streets.* Article in *West Winfield Star.* 1964.

HUDSON VALLEY

(Abbatt, Wm.) *A Catalog of the Famous Abbatt Reprints.* NY. Decker. ca 1935. wrps. 31 pp. Also prntd. by W.F. Humphreys Press, Geneva, NY. ca 1935. (William Abbatt, 1851-1935, of Tarrytown, NY, was ed. of the *Magazine of History.* In conjunction with the magazine he issued "Extra Numbers" which were reprints of rare items of Americana. They can actually be considered new ed. as notes were added to each, and illus. to many. Sixty-four copies, or less, were prntd. of each title, and as there were 55 subscribers, only a handful were available to the public. Peter Decker & Co. of NYC had acquired a few copies of a number of the titles and issued this "Complete List of the Abbatt Reprints." In a few instances they list the number of copies available, and many entries are marked "All gone." There are a number of annotations. One hundred and ninety-nine titles are listed, of which 52 are Lincolnia. A small handful of Abbatt reprints have found their way to me, but it is years since I have even seen a copy for sale. Only a very few of the items in the catalog are of NY State interest, but there are some on Revolutionary War activity in the Quebec area. I have found that people interested in the Revolutionary War in NY State are also eager to acquire material on parallel events in Canada because of the close connection between the two countries. Also, Abbatt wrote, or edited, several works on Revolution in NY.)

Adams, C. *Memoir of Washington Irving.* NY. 1870. 299 pp. (The author notes that Edward Everett the famous orator once wrote, "The American father who can afford it and does not buy a copy [of 'Tour on the Prairies'] does not deserve that his sons should prefer his fireside to the bar-room ....")

Akerly, S. *An Essay on the Geology of the Hudson River, and the Adjacent Regions ... Sandy Hook ... Towards the Catskill Mountains.* NY. 1820. 69 pp. Has a fine folding plate from Long Branch, NJ, along the west shore of the Hudson River to above Newburgh.

--- (Albany) *Directory to the Trades in Albany, for the Year 1853.* Albany. J. Munsell. 1853. wrps. 62 pp. (An extensive listing of Albany tradesmen and their addresses, including: bill sticker, crier of lost children, junk shops, map writer, outdoor meat stall, missionary, wood measurer.)

--- *Albany Lumber Trade. Its History and Extent.* 1872. wrps. 42 pp. (Hist. sketches of approximately 40 lumber companies in Albany, NY.)

--- (Albany Malt Houses) *Report of Trial of the Cause of John Taylor vs. Edward C. Delavan, Prosecuted for an Alleged Libel; Tried at Albany Circuit, April, 1840. And Mr. Delavans Correspondence With the Ex. Committee of the Albany City Temperance Society.* Albany. 1840. wrps. 48 pp. (Delavan was a wine-merchant turned temperance advocate, and Taylor owned a malt house. Taylor prosecuted Delavan for libel when the latter accused him of using stagnant water for malting, and lost. This is a very detailed account of the trial proceedings. A most interesting map shows the locations of: the Malt House, slaughter houses, dead hog, remains of a dead horse, a privy, heaps of manure, mouths of 3 sewers, and a number of churches.)

Anderson, S. *Ulster County's Old Timbered Crossings. Past and Present.* (1965.) maps. illus. wrps. index. 53 pp. (This has over 35 photos of covered bridges with brief data, two photos of bridge builders' tools, and other photos of interest.)

Anon. *Account Book of a Country Store Keeper in the 18th Century at Poughkeepsie. Records in Dutch and English.* 1911. 122 pp. wrps. (A very detailed record covering the years 1737-1746. An excellent source for prices paid in the early 1700s. It also contains copies of some deeds, a list of marriages, and other data.)

--- *Anti-Rent Song. Tune: "The Little Pig's Tail."* Broadside, 6 x 9 inches. 10 verses, 9 lines to a verse. ca 1846. (This broadside urges the election of John Young as

Governor of NY State, and names other pro Anti-Renters who should be elected to the Senate, Congress, Sheriff, and County Clerk. Young, who had previously sided with the rebellious farmers, was elected by a wide margin, and immediately pardoned 14 imprisoned anti-renters.)

--- *The Aristocracy Unmasked. Chancellor Kent and Judge Spencer in Favor of Disfranchising 75,000 Freeman.* Broadside, 12 x 17 inches, issued by the Albany Republican General Committee. ca 1821. (At the Constitutional Convention of 1812 at Albany, the greatest debates were on suffrage: Who were those eligible to vote? Kent, who for a time had lived on the edge of financial disaster, is reported to have said that giving voting rights to the poor "has been regarded with terror by the wise men of every age," and "There is a tendency in the poor to covet and share the plunder of the rich." This broadside includes an extract from the speech of Martin Van Buren which opposes the arguments of Kent and Spencer, and reports that "Judge Spencer's aristocratic proposition was rejected by a vote of 100 to 19.")

--- *Attention R. P. I. ... The undersigned ... on the arrival of the Boat from Castleton ... they will be on hand with their efficient Overland Wheel-barrow Express, to convey those who are unable to navigate, to their residences. Hues and Parrish, Late of the Institute.* Small handbill, ca 1870s. (R. P. I. is: Rensselaer Polytechnic Institute of Troy.)

--- *Autobiography of Frederick Nelson Du Bois.* 1940. wrps. 87 mimeo. pp. (Du Bois, 1829-1915, born near Catskill, NY, went into the silver business in Buffalo and then in Chicago. In 1862 he took his family by wagon to the Colorado gold fields. Returning east he went into the woodworking business in NYC, and built houses on Washington Heights. Eventually he found time to spend his summers at Catskill. He wrote his autobiography in the early 1900s, and in 1940, it was typed from the original mss. and a few mimeo. copies were made for the family.)

Bailey, W. W. *My Boyhood at West Point, by ... (Late of Co. D., 10th Rhode Island Infantry.).* 1891. 38 pp. wrps. Lmtd. to 250 copies. (Bailey was born at West Point in 1843, where his father was a Professor. He tells of a Cadet at the Point who complained to the head waiter that he had found a small mouse in his food. The waiter responded, "You cannot expect us, for the terms, to furnish rats!")

Baldwin, S. E. *Life and Letters of Simeon Baldwin.* 1919. port. illus. index. 503 pp. (Baldwin, 1761-1851, a CT jurist, had been a Schoolmaster at Albany, NY 1782-83. There are 94 pages on his sojurn in the capital district, with many excerpts from his interesting Journal. "...I am obliged to perform military Duty as the Legislature of the State of New York seem never to have thought the promotion of Literature an object worthy of their attention..." Many libraries and collectors in NY State concentrate on books that are devoted in their entirety to

the state. It is important to realize that many books with only a chapter or two on New York given keen insights into the state by shrewd observers.)
--- *The Beautiful Hudson by Searchlight.* Issued by the Peoples' Evening Line Steamers. NY. 1905. wrps. illus. 24 pp. (Evening trips were taken by ship on the Hudson in which a searchlight was used to illuminate points of interest. There are fine scenic views, and some interior views of the ship.)
--- *The Bee.* Albany. William Augustus Munsell (ed.) 1844-1845. (This was a 4-page small newspaper written, edited, and set in type by the son of Joel Munsell the noted Albany printer. Nine issues were sporadically prntd. between March 9, 1844, and April 1845. William Augustus was only 8 years old when he put out the first issue. Among the pub. articles were anecdotes, accounts of his trips to other towns, and his great grandfather's memories of his service in the Revolutionary War.)
Benton, Charles. *Four Days on the Webutuck River.* Amenia, NY. Pvtly. prntd. July 1925. wrps. Lmtd. to 200 copies. (A description of a four-day boat trip on the Webutuck, or Ten Mile River, in Dutchess Co., in 1860. The introduction was written by Sinclair Lewis.)
Best, H. *Border Iron.* 1945. illus. with drawings. 219 pp. (Fiction of the Ancram Iron mine area about 1740. It includes the famous Livingston family, and the border squabble with MA)
Black, M. (Intro.) *Ammi Phillips: Portrait Painter 1788-1865.* NY. Museum of American Folk Art. 1969. illus. bib. map on rear of the dust jacket. 56 pp. (Phillips was a portrait painter along the NY-CT-MA border. He was "the best, the most prolific, and the most inventive American country portrait painter of the 19th century." There are 80 illus. of his work, three in color. Listed are 309 of his ports., in most cases giving the approximate date and the residence of the sitter. His work is highly regarded, and has been bringing extremely high prices at auction. According to some reports his present popularity has caused some unsigned portraits to be attributed to him. This was the first book pub. by the Museum of American Folk Art, and is becoming quite scarce.)
--- *(Boston Corners, Columbia Co.) Report ... On the Annexation of District of Boston Corner in Massachusetts to the State of New York.* NY Assembly, March 1849. 2 pp. (Boston Corner was an enclave with nine freeholders cut off from the parent state of Massachusetts by the high ridge of the Taghkanic Mountains. Because of its isolation it became a haven for criminals, and was the scene of outlawed prize fights, including the famous bout between John Morrissey and "Yankee" Sullivan. In 1853 MA agreed to give up this thousand acre tract, it was confirmed by the U. S. Congress in 1855, and in 1857 the annexation was completed. A great many items of interest can be gleaned by scanning through the NY State Assembly and Senate reports.)
Boyd J. *Horatio Gates Spafford. Inventor, Author, Promoter of*

Democracy. 1942. Reprntd. from *Proceedings of American Antiquarian Society.* wrps. 74 pp. (Spafford, 1778-1832, lived in the Albany area for many years, and was a remarkable man who deserves to be better known. Boyd provides a great deal of information that is of utmost importance in understanding one of the best informed men of NY State. Spafford's most influential works were his gazetteers of NY State, pub. in 1813 and 1824.)

--- *Boyds Poughkeepsie and Fishkill Landing Directory, With a Business Directory and Gazetteer of Dutchess County, 1864-64.* Comp. by Andrew Boyd. 237 pp. including some advt. pps. (This work even lists the country store owners and hotels in many of the hamlets with which the county was peppered at that time.)

--- *Boyd's Susquehanna Railroad Directory and Gazetteer. Business Directory of the Counties (Excepting Albany) Through Which the A. & S. RR Passes; With Business Directory of Albany and Troy Patrons to the Work.* Albany. 1869. Numerous advts., some with illus. 168 pp. (The Albany and Susquehanna Railroad ran from Albany to Binghamton, and later became part of the Delaware and Hudson RR system. About 40 towns are listed in the Table of Contents.)

Brown, H. C. *The Lordly Hudson.* NY. Scribner. 1937. Many full-page plates of which 15 are in fine color. Lmtd. to 920 copies of which 874 were for sale. (This finely produced book is the corner-stone of any Hudson River collection. It was pub. near the end of the Great Depression when money was still scarce. Tim Trace, one of the great and best known dealers in the decorative arts, told me in 1977 that this book was remaindered, only about 40 copies being originally sold. At that time he bought about 35 copies at $8.00 each. Now that money is more plentiful than fine books, this superb vol. commands a handsome price when it can be found.)

--- *Carrier Addresses.* For many years newspapers distributed Carrier Addresses to their patrons on New Year's Day. This practice began as early as the 1750s and lasted into the 20th century. Usually prntd. as broadside poetry with decorative border, the Addresses were sometimes put up in pamphlet form, and occasionally pub. in the newspaper's columns. Sometimes the poetry is sentimental, sometimes it reviews events of the past year, and usually is political in election years. (Sometime ago I was in a well-stocked bookshop in NJ that normally has very little in my lines of interest. There, on top of a radiator, was a large scrapbook full of clippings from Albany, NY, newspapers, priced at ten dollars. I flipped through it twice, and on the second flip-through I spotted a Carriers Address. That alone was worth more than ten bucks, so with a two dollar dealer's discount, I carted it home for eight dollars. A page-by-page exploration of the scrapbook uncovered about a dozen more Carrier Addresses from Albany and Schenectady newspapers. [On occasion scrapbooks reveal hidden gems, and a careful search is sometimes rewarding.] Here are a few excerpts from the verses: Our paper isn't being prntd. today because, "The pressmen altogether, have hired a splendid carriage, To give their girls an airing, and press them into marriage. So quaff your wine, and eat your pies, and cast away all sorrow, For though we disappear today, we'll meet you all to-morrow." "Jackson, Van Buren, both their country's pride; Who have and will the nation's vessel guide ... Anticipation flies on rapid wing - Canals and Rail-roads added comforts bring: Soon new improvements to the present join'd, Shall make our State the marvel of mankind." To encourage tips to the Carrier, one Address ends, "Remember him ... Who at your threshold oft has brought, and brings Fame's dusty roll of Coblers, Clowns, and Kings.")

--- *Catalog of the Officers and Students of Spencertown Academy, Columbia Co., NY.* Hudson. 1853. wrps. 12 pp. (The President of this Academy was Timothy Woodbridge, the noted blind pastor. This pamphlet lists: officers, faculty, students names and home towns, tuition, and discipline. The students were forbidden to visit groceries for the purpose of pleasure of entertainment.)

Christman, H. *Tin Horns and Calico. A Decisive Episode in the Emergence of Democracy.* 1945. illus. map. bib. index. 377 pp. (A colorful hist. of the Anti-Rent War which was waged between renters and landlords in the Hudson Valley in the mid-1800s. The landlords "controlled the destinies of 300,000 people and ruled in amost kingly splendor over nearly 2,000,000 acres." This war led directly to the passage of the federal Homestead Act of 1862. A collector could spend many enjoyable years gathering the prntd. and manuscript materials of this Hudson Valley conflict which affected thousands of people, and dismayed politicians and large landholders.)

Cohen, D. S. *They Walk These Hills: A Study of Social Solidarity.* University Microfilms. Ann Arbor, MI. 1973. wrps. index. bib. 308 pp. probably only a few copies were made. (This is a doctoral dissertation on the Ramapo Mountain people who live along the NY-NJ border in the towns of Hillburn, NY, and Ringwood, NJ. Originally known as the Jackson Whites, they are now called the Ramapough Indians. Cohen gathered material among them for one year, and wrote a doctoral dissertation. This work contains a great deal more information, especially folkloric, than appears in the book he wrote for publication titled *The Ramapo Mountain People.*)

Cohen, D. S. *The Ramapo Mountain People.* Rutgers Univ. Press. New Brunswick, NJ. 1974. illus. maps. tables. bib. index. 285 pp. (This popular work has gone through several printings.)

Colton, J. H. *Guide Book to West Point and Vicinity ... Descriptive, Historical, Statistical ... 1844.* folding map. 112 pp. (What to see at the Point, hist., courses of study, opinions about the Academy, several trips in the vicinity. It

has an excellent and detailed map: roads, streams, many buildings, Revolutionary War redoubts, monuments, hills, site of the Revolutionary War chain across the Hudson River, ferries to the opposite shore.)
--- *Constitution and By-Laws of the Cornwall Democratic Club.* ca 1860. broadside 9 x 9 inches. (Informs the members they are to work to "present the bright example of a community so thoroughly cleansed of abolitionists and other political niggerheads, that the entire combination of malcontents cannot raise a sufficient force to represent the fag end of a broken-down party ....")
Cooper, M. *Some Old Letters and Bits of History.* NY. pvtly. prntd. 1901. 54 pp. Lmtd. to 200 copies. (These NYC and Hudson Valley letters, dated 1796-1814, were found in a Long Island attic. There is frequent mention of voyages on the Hudson River. Even today there are such collections of letters, and mss., hidden away in attics, cellars, barns, bureaus, or even propping up a rickety bookcase. Every so often a treasure-trove is rediscovered, and comes on the market.)
--- (Croton Aqueduct) *Completion of the Croton Aqueduct Celebrated.* NY. October 4th, 1842. (A prntd. silk bookmark, pub. by W. L. Ormsby, 142 Nassau Street. Letters engraved by a machine just invented by W. L. Ormsby: time ... 8 letters per minute. This has a vignette of an Indian and a white man, a hist. of the aqueduct, and a list of the members of the Common Council of NYC.)
--- *Descriptive Circular, of the Columbia Springs, Stockport, New York,* Chas. B. Nash, Prop. Hudson. 1855. illus. wrps. 23 pp. (Although used as early as 1805 these medicinal springs were first commercialized in 1855, and came complete with a tree house for adults. Someone said the water from one of the springs tasted like "the risings of a gun barrel.")

Devyr, T. A. *The Odd Book of the 19th Century ... Chiefly Land Reform, For the Last Fifty Years.* NY. Pub. by the author. 1882. 431 pp. (Devyr, an Irish revolutionary, was the spark that organized the Hudson Valley farmers against the Landlords in the Anti-Rent troubles of the 1840s. He spoke at their rallies and worked closely with them. This book gives some data on that famous struggle, and gives a good insight into the man and his passion for reform. There is much on Devyr in Christman's notable book *Tin Horns and Calico*, and Christman used a copy of *The Odd Book* in his research.)

Dugdale, R. *The Jukes, a study in crime, pauperism, disease, and heredity.* 1877. Folding charts. index. 121 pp. (During an investigation of a NY State co. prison in 1874, a family pre-disposed to crime and immorality was found. I believe I read somewhere that the family was from the hill country of the lower Hudson Valley, and to protect their identity they were given the name of "Jukes". Dugdale, a social economist, made a thorough study of the family and wrote this major study. It went through 3 ed. in 1877, and a new ed. was issued in 1884.)

(Dunn, N.) *Autobiographical Sketch of the Life of Nathaniel Dunn.* NY. Jan. 12, 1884. Born in Poland, ME, Jan. 29, 1800, died NY Oct. 17, 1889. Copied from original mss. Typed and duplicated 1939. 80 pp. Lmtd. to 30 copies. (Dunn was in the acid and lumbering business in the Hudson Valley, taught school in the NYC area, lectured widely, and was an inventor and a Mesmerist.)

Duryea. *The Story of Samuel and Margaret Sloan.* 1927. illus. 175 pp. Lmtd. to 100 copies for circulation in the family. (Sloan became president of the Hudson River Railroad in 1855, and president of the Delaware, Lackawanna, and Western Railroad in 1869. In later life he lived at Garrison, NY.)

(Dutchess Co.) *Book of the Supervisors of Dutchess Co., New York, 1718-1722.* Old miscellaneous records of Dutchess Co. 2nd. *Book of Supervisors and Assessors, 1723-1729.* Old miscellaneous records of Dutchess Co. *3rd Book of Supervisors, 1729-1748.* 3 vols. wrps. Poughkeepsie. Pub. by Vassar Bros. Institute 1908-1911. (A wealth of data on early Dutchess Co: assessments, records of meetings, court records, animal brands, wills, roads, Great Nine Partners Patent, apprentices contracts, official salaries, paying a coroner for viewing a dead body, painting a constable's staff, lock and key for a record chest, much much else.)

Estabrook, A. *The Jukes in 1915.* Pub. by the Carnegie Institution. 1916. Tables. Diagrams. 85 pp. (This work continues the study of the Jukes up to 1915. This family cost the state of NY taxpayers over two million dollars in prison and relief expenses.)

Edison Machine Works. (An album of 24 plates of photographs issued by the company in 1892, with a total of 118 illus: officers, exterior views, many interior views, machinery. In 1886 the company moved from NYC to Schenectady, setting up shop in old locomotive works buildings. In its new and expanded location, the company grew rapidly.)

To the Electors of the County of Rennsselaer. Ca 1828. wrps. 12 pp. (An anti-Jackson diatribe, by an unknown writer, at the time Old Hickory was condidate for the U. S. presidency. It states that a man in Troy openly avowed he "would support Gen. Jackson ... if certain that it would be the ruin of our country." The writer attacks Jackson on many points. He asks, "What might be expected from his irascible temper, his lawless ambition, his fierce and vindictive spirit, when clothes with ... immense power...?" This elusive pamphlet is not recorded in *American Imprints*, Sabin, or Wise and Cronins bib. of Jackson.)

Ellis, W. J. *The History of My Life.* Poughkeepsie. 1912. wrps. 39 pp. (Ellis, the son of slaves, was a travelling singer, a horse racer, a lecturer on the Zodiac, and he organized the Queen City Band, and the Queen City Orchestra of Poughkeepsie.)

Fast, Howard. *Peekskill: USA. A Personal Experience.* Pub. by the Civil Rights Congress. 1951. Illus. 127 pp. (A very detailed account of the violence that occured in August and September, 1949, when Paul Robeson, the noted black singer, gave concerts in the Peekskill area.)

Fly, J. C. (Pub.) *Kingston Merchants' City Directory for 1875.* 186 pp. + some advts. pp., with a few more illus. (Kingston had a Human Hair Dealer, and more saloons than clergymen. There is a record of a Human Hair dealer in NYC who had a girl kidnapped and her tresses cut off.)

Forester, Frank. *The Warwick Woodlands.* Introductory chapters by Harry Worcester Smith. Warwick Valley Dispatch Press. 1921. Illus. 213 pp. Lmtd. to 100 copies. (This book, considered by many to be Herbert's finest, was first published in 1845, and went through several ed. This ed. of 100 copies was prntd. for Smith and signed by him, and has information on and illus. of the celebration of Forester Day at Warwick on Oct. 23, 1920. Just prior to this, also in 1921, there was an ed. of 50 copies prntd. for presentation and review.)

Fowler, H. (ed.) *Mary M. Chase and Her Writings.* Boston. 1855. 336 pp. (Mary Chase, born in Chatham, NY, in 1822, wrote poetry, taught in a Female Academy, and died in 1852. This work has a brief biog. of her, her poems, and excerpts from her letters, many of which were written from Chatham.)

Garret Smith's Reply to Colored Citizens of Albany. Peterboro (NY). March 13, 1846. 3 pp. leaflet. (Smith, a noted Abolitionist, replies to a letter from a black committee of Albany that wants the right of suffrage for their people. He gives his views on slavery and suffrage, and chides the blacks who apparently had been influenced by unscrupulous politicians, "If today, the right of suffrage were restored to the colored men of this state, tomorrow would see them enrolled in proslavery parties....")

Gibbs, R. *Diary of Theron Zadock Gibbs, written during 1850, 1851, 1852, and part of 1853. With a brief biographical sketch.* 1925. port. illus. index. 244 pp. (Gibbs, 1826-1896, lived in eastern Washington Co., and there are references to: Hartford, Granville, Fort Ann, Adamsville, Union Village, Hebron, Glens Falls. He taught school part time, and later became a doctor in Fort Ann. This is a fine record of life in eastern Washington Co.)

Gilman, W. (comp.) *The Story of the Ferry, being an account of the ferry, between Dobbs Ferry, Westchester Co., New York, and Snedens Landing, Rockland Co., New York, on the Hudson River, established about the year 1698.* Pub. May 30, 1903. wrps. 14 pp. (Only 5 copies were made: 4 for libraries, and one for some chap who was interested in the subject. That chap's copy was probably disposed of by a disinterested relative or executor as a copy appeared on the market in February, 1974.)

Gray and Savage. *Ale: in prose and verse.* New York. 1866. Illus. 97 pp. (Information on the Brewery of John Taylor and Sons, of Albany, NY, with a biographical sketch of the founder. There is a fine illus.

of the Brewery buildings at Albany, and some interior views.)

Griffen, C. & S. *Natives and Newcomers. The ordering of opportunity in mid-19th century Poughkeepsie.* 1978. Hist. notes. tables. index. 291 pp. (A very detailed study of "The careers of all workers in each occupation - the entire labor force in this city with an 1870 population of 20,000 - are traced over 3 decades.")

Hand Book for the Dutchess and Columbia Railroad. With descriptive sketches and complete Business Directory of each place on the road. Newburgh. 1871. wrps. 170 pp. (This railroad went from Plum Point near the present Beacon, NY, to the CT boundary near Salisbury. It was routed through Fishkill, Hopewell, Billings Gap, Millbrook, Bangall, Pine Plains, Millerton, and many points in-between. Includes a brief history of the D & C RR.)

Harrington, H. *The Responsibilities of American Citizenship: a sermon preached on occasion of the "Anti-Rent" disturbances.* Dec. 22, 1844. 1845. 23 pp. (Harrington, a Unitarian minister of Albany, preached this pro-landlord sermon during the time of Anti-Rent actions in Columbia Co. He declared, "There is something essentially wrong in the impelling spirit of a mob.")

Hassett, w. *Off the Record with F. D. R. 1942-1945.* NY. 1958. illus. index. 366 pp. (An insight into the private, unknown life of President Franklin D. Roosevelt during the World War II years. He spent some time at his home in Hyde Park, NY, and there is mention of nearby places: Highland, Poughkeepsie, the Nelson House Hotel in Poughkeepsie, Val Kill Cottage, the Vanderbilt Mansion.)

(Haydock, G.) *Incidents in the Life of George Haydock, ex-professional wood-sawyer of Hudson.* Hudson. Columbia Washingtonian Print. 1846. wrps. 48 pp. (Haydock, born in 1805, lived in NYC, Schoharie Co., but spent most of his life in Hudson. He was a professional drunkard, and belonged to the Garret Soc., which was a drinking club in Hudson, one of its rules being that rum bills had to be paid before bread bills. This is a lengthy account of his drinking adventures and mishaps. Eventually he reformed when Temperance workers came to Hudson, and then travelled widely preaching abstinence.)

(Hill, L. B.) *Benjamin Franlin Lewis. 1842-1828. The man and his business.* ca 1936. Illus. 122 pp. (This is a biog. of Lewis who was involved in the pub. business from the 1870s into the 1920s. Much of the book is a hist. of the Lewis Pub. Co. which issued a great many works on co. and state hist., including NY. They also pub. genealogical and biog. books. About 1904 they switched, to a great extent, from single vol. ed. to multi-volume ed., one or two vol. being hist. and the balance of the set biog. or genealogical. The Lewis Co. worked closely with the American Hist. Soc., the Directors of both being practically identical, and after 1912 the American Hist. Soc. issued many of the works of the Lewis Co. Many people

63

bought the hist. vol., but would only buy the biog. vol. that included themselves, their ancestors or relatives. It is very difficult to determine exactly how many vol. were in each set the company pub. For instance, Hazleton's *The Boroughs of Brooklyn and Queens, and Counties of Nassau and Suffolk*, 1925, were issued in at least 7 vol. Vol. 5 and 7 are lacking from a great many known sets. A very useful reference book would be a bib. of sets giving the correct number of vol.)

Hine, C. G. *History and Legend, Fact, Fancy, and Romance of the Old Mine Road*. Kingston, NY, to the Mine Holes of Pahaquarry (NJ) Hines Annual. 1908. wrps. 176 pp. plus index. lmtd. ed. (The Old Mine Road, still in existence for most of the way, is one of the oldest roads in the U. S. of considerable length, and was probably built in the mid-1600s. Hine's informative book on this highway is found with and without illus. Reprntd. in 1963 with an introduction by Henry Charlton Beck containing a considerable amount of information about Hine and his scarce pub.)

Hine, C. G. *The House That Tom Built. Showing why, how, when and where this house was erected ... construction ... inpartial notes on the architect; an opinion of the furnace man..suggestions for those about to select a home*. Hines Annual 1910. Illus. with tipped-in photos. Approximately 40 pp. lmtd. printing. (A discussion of a house built on Staten Island by Thomas Avery Hine, an architect. The copy I had of this rather scarce work was autographed by Tom.)

Hine, C. G. *The New York and Albany Post Road from King's Bridge to "The Ferry at Crawlier, over against Albany", being an account of a jaunt on foot made at sundry convenient times between May and November, 1905*. Hines Annual, 1905. Book I. 89 pp. lmtd. printing. (Hine collected a variety of information on his walk up the east side of the Hudson River. This work was also prntd. in a popular ed. which turns up from time to time.)

Hine, C. G. *The West Bank of the Hudson River. Albany to Tappan. Notes on its history, legends ... gathered by a wayfaring man who may now and then have erred therein*. Hines Annual. 1907. Illus. Index. 174 pp. Lmtd. to 52 copies. (The only time I have ever had a copy of this rare work was back in 1971.)

Hoyt, E. *The Goulds. A social history*. 1969. Illus. Index. 346 pp. (A study of how Jay Gould acquired his vast fortune, and how his descendants spent it. Not one has gone on welfare. At the time he was making his infamous finicial deals, he lived at his home name "Lyndhurst" on the southern edge of Tarrytown. That home is now open to the public as a museum, and concerts are held on its lawn in the summer.)

Hudson Fulton Celebration Souvenir Handkerchief. 1909. (A large cloth handerchief, approximately 18x18 inches. Illus: Henry Hudson, Robert Fulton, the Clermont, the Half Moon, the State of Liberty.)

The Hudson Highlands. William Thompson Howell Memorial.

1933-1934. 2 vol. Illus. Lmtd. to 200 sets. (In my opinion this is the most informative work on the Hudson Highlands and their residents in the early 1900s. Howell, and his companions, usually dressed in ties, vests, and suitcoats (!), and carrying a heavy camera, a backpack, and buckets of food, would tramp up and down the mountains, sometimes going more than 20 miles a day. [I have hiked many of their trails, wearing more comfortable clothes, and with no encumbrances, and can only easily manage 5 to 8 miles.] The set has more than 50 illus. of scenery, a few ancient buildings, and a number of Highland inhabitants. These books are full of Highland lore, and should be on the shelf of anyone interested in these tumbled and rocky hills. One bit of folklore not included by Howell is a tale I heard from the east side of the Hudson near the village of Garrison. A locally renowned hunter once saw some bear tracks in the snow when that creature was supposed to be hibernating. He excitedly ran to his house, got his gun, and followed the tracks until he came to a woman hanging clothes on a line in her bare feet. Anyway, the set was reprntd. in 1982 by the Walking News, Inc. of NYC, and issued in one vol. in wrps. Its value is enhanced by the addition of comprehensive indexes. Within one hour of the George Washington Bridge in NYC it is possible to be tramping on the rugged and rocky trails of the Hudson Highland and not see another person all day. If you are very, very fortunate you may catch a glimpse of an endangered timber rattlesnake or a wandering black bear. I have never seen either one in all of the miles I have hiked there, but I do know of people who have.)

The Hudson River Portfolio was pub. in the 1820s, and had 20 plates engraved by John Hill after water colors by W. G. Wall, and were in fine hand-colored aquatint. (The NY Hist. Soc., NYC, in 1961, pub. an 87-page illus. pamphlet by R. J. Koke *A Checklist of the American Engravings of John Hill* which goes into great detail about the pub. of this very rare portfolio. None of the original prints from this work have ever come my way. In the 1920s several of the plates were reprntd., and a few of them have found a temporary home in my stock. Also, in the 1920s Wagar's Coffee Shop, of Albany, reissued the prints in black and white, and in the smaller format of 7x10 inches.)

The Hudson River Steamer: Mary Powell. 1895. Illus. wrps. 65 pp. (A guide book pub. for passengers on this famous Hudson River steamer, the "Queen" of the waters. When people talk of the river excursion ships of by-gone days the one that usually comes to mind first is the *Mary Powell*. Besides a time table, fare schedule, and map, this pamphlet has information on over 160 hotels and boarding houses giving: location, name of owner, miles from the steamer landing, and prices.)

Hudson River Telephone Directory. May 1907. wrps. 310 pp. (This fine item lists all the Hudson Valley telephone numbers from the hundreds of subscribers in Albany to the 1 subscriber in Blue Stores, to the 4 Shaker telephones at Mount Lebanon. Early telephone directories are an excellent source for the names of residents and the town they lived in. The first directory was issued in New Haven, CT, in 1878. Some of the early ones pub. locally were a few names prntd. on stiff cardboard or paper.)

Hufeland, O. *A Check List of Books, Maps, Pictures, and Other Printed Matter Relating to the Counties of Westchester and Bronx.* White Plains. NY. 1929. index. 320 pp. (A town-by-town listing, with some annotations. This work is so comprehensive it even includes a contract for transplanting trees at the Kensico Reservoir. There is a total of 2520 entries.)

Hunt, W. S. *Frank Forester (Henry William Herbert) A Tragedy in Exile.* Newark, NJ. Carteret Book Club. 1933. port. 2 illus. bib. Chronology of Herbert's writings. Index, errata pp. with 1 entry. (Herbert, 1807-1858, wrote many books on field sports under the name of "Frank Forester". One of his most famous books was *The Warwick Woodlands*, an account of his adventures at Warwick, NY. The errata page in the Hunt book is only found in a few copies as over half of the books were distributed before the slip was prntd. Lmtd. to only 200 copies. Years ago there was a dealer, named Kinsey McColl, who had a shop in Haverstraw, and who later lived in Tuxedo. He turned up some fine items in that southeastern NY State area, and one time I bought from him an autographed copy of *Sporting Scenes and Sundry Sketches: being the miscellaneous writings of J. Cypress, Jr.*, ed. by Frank Forester. 1842. 2 vols. illus. This was the first work in which Herbert's pseudonym of "Frank Forester" appeared. Autographed books by Herbert rarely come on the market. One day I got a card from Kinsey saying he and his wife were taking their camper and moving out west. I haven't heard from him since.)

Ingraham, J. H. *The Gipsy of the Highlands, or, The Jew and the Heir. Being the adventures of Duncan Powell and Paul Tatnall.* Boston. 1843. 31 pp. (An anti-Semitic novel set in the Highlands of the Hudson. Ingraham was a popular writer, grinding out an amazing number of short novels. It is said that one year he produced 20 of them. According to Wright's *American Fiction 1774-1850*, he wrote two fictional accounts of Arnold's treason.)

(Irving, Washington). *Colored Engravings of American Scenery.* Proposals for publishing to subscribers only, a connected series of forty atmospheric or hist. views of American scenery, from water color drawings by Geo. Harvey, A.N.A. A 4-page advertising flyer. 1841. (Harvey lived at Hastings-on-the-Hudson, and helped Irving design his home "Sunnyside". When he proposed his American views he prevailed upon Irving to edit the work. The above prospectus was issued, listing the titles of the 40 views, and the location where made. There were not enough subscribers and only 4 views were ever pub. See Blanck's *Bibliography of American Literature*, vol. 5, p. 46, for a description of this work.)

Irving, Washington. *The Legend of Sleepy Hollow*. Drawings by Arthur I. Keller. Indianpolis. Bobbs-Merrill Co. Oct. 1906. 92 pp. (There are 14 full-page illus., plus an illus. at the top of each page, and illus. on the binding and end papers. Keller, gloriously born on the Fourth of July in 1867, was a major illustrator winning many awards. The DAB says, "He delighted in getting his local color or historical settings accurate to the minutest detail....")

Irving, Washington. *Rip Van Winkle, a posthumous writing of Diedrich Knickerbocker*. With introduction by Mark Van Doren. NY. Limited Editions Club. Illus. reproduced from engravings by Felix Darley. 1930. 58 pp. Signed by F. G. Goudy. (Prntd. in Kaatskill Type, especially designed and cut by Frederic W. Goudy, Marlborough-on-Hudson, NY. A classic of NY State literature, with a type designed by a foremost type designer, and issued by a major literary club. The Limited Editions Club of NY issued a great many finely produced books of outstanding literature, and many of the vol. were either signed by the artist or book designer. From 1500 to 2000 copies were printed of each title, and there are avid collectors of the entire set. They reprnted. at least 3 of James Fennimore Cooper's classics, and possibly other titles of NY State interest. A number of years ago I stopped at the shop of an antique dealer who I was told also had some books. He was not home, but as I had a feeling I should be sure to see him I went to get a bite to eat, and returned to his place. To my relief he was in, but said I had only 15 minutes as he was on his way to Cape Cod for a vacation. With no time to do any serious looking at the cluttered shelves, I spent a few moments talking with him. "By the way," he said, "are you interested in the Limited Editions Club? There is a man near here with a lot of them for sale. I'll send you over." I didn't know a thing about them, but figured I had better go take a look as I had nothing else to do. I went over and scanned the extensive collection, and was completely confused and overwhelmed by what I saw: I had no idea what they were worth. So I said to the amiable owner, "Look, I'm not sure if I can use these or not. I will let you know in the morning, if it is OK with you." He said it was, but also told me how much he wanted for the lot. I immediately drove well over an hour to see another dealer who I hoped knew the value of these fine printings. He did. "About how many books are there? Are these 5 titles in the lot?", he asked, and rattled off the names. I told him the approximate number of vol., and said, "Yes, those 5 titles are there." Before I could take a breath he shot back, "I will take them", and he gave me the figure he would pay. His offer was worth a month's pay to me, and the next morning I rescued those now more

beautiful Limited Editions. My car was dragging with its load as I bumped into his driveway before noon. He looked amazed and said, "I never thought I would see you again after I told you what they were worth." In all the years since that time, I have never seen another lot like it.)
John Burroughs in Remembrance. (1921). wrps. 24 pp. (Issued at the time of the services in memory of Burroughs, the noted Hudson Valley naturalist, at Riverby, West Park-on-the-Hudson, April 2, 1921. It includes poetry by various authors, and there are two selections from Burroughs' writings. It has a mounted photograph of Burroughs at his home in Riverby, and a mounted photo of a sculpture of Burroughs by C. Pietro, sculptor.)

Johnson, A. G. *A Chapter of History, or the Progress of Judicial Ursurpation.* Troy. 1863. 63 pp. (A legal hist. of the famous Van Rensselaer Manor lands, which were involved in the Anti-Rent Wars. Johnson, a Whig lawyer, is frequently mentioned and quoted in Christman's *Tin Horns and Calico.* Johnson's final word, "If the ballot box does not answer, then as a last resort, every man can stand on his own threshold and defend his own home.")

Johnson, F. M. *The Romantic Legend of Jules Bourglay, the Old Leather Man.* 1977. Meriden, CT. The Bayberry Hill Press. illus. map. bib. 65 pp. Lmtd. to about 100 copies. (Bourglay, a mysterious Frenchman, dressed in leather and wandered a set route between the lower Connecticut River and the Hudson River in the latter 1800s. He appeared in the same village with startling regularity every 34 days. This book is a fictionalized account based on facts and documents. It has four different mounted illus. of Bourglay, and illus. of his kit bag and tobacco pouch. A great many newspaper and magazine articles have been written about the Old Leather Man. A commercial photograph of him, taken by L. B. Gorham, a Mt. Kisco, NY, photographer, was issued with the compliments of F. W. Gorham, a druggist in Katonah, NY. The Johnson book was reprntd., also in 1977, in an ed. of about 50 copies.)

(Johnstown, NY) *The Writings of a Pretended Prophet, (in six letters) who assumed the title of "A Faithful Servant of Jesus Christ", officially commissioned by Almighty God to demand and receive of Abraham Morhouse, Esq. of Johnstown, (New York), two thousand pounds; with terrible denunciations in case of refusal. To which is added, his recantation; or four letters, written by the prophet, after his detection.* Second Vermont Ed. (Rutland.) July 1816. 12 pp. (Several ed. were prntd. of this work. Sabin, 105630, quotes from another source, "The original was prntd. [in 1796] by Mr. [Jacob] Dockstader in Johnstown [New York] where the transaction took place." I know absolutely nothing about this book, but it does have an intriguing title.)

Kent, E. *The Isle of Long Ago. Sporting Days.* 1933. NYC. Scribner. 194 pp. (The author's hunting and fishing adventures in the late 1800s and early 1900s in southern Dutchess Co., and in the Tuxedo area of Orange Co. to which he had moved. This is one of the very few sources of information on sporting in these areas. One of the selling points of this book is that it contains an etching by the famous M. J. Schadlach, an important wildlife artist.)

Kim, S. *The Manor of Cortlandt and its Tenants. 1697-1783.* Ann Arbor, MI. University Microfilms. 1966. 287 pp. (A college thesis on: the lordship of the manor, relations between tenants and proprietors, economic and social welfare of the tenants, relation of tenants to social and political events. Probably only a few copies were prntd.)

(Knapp, S. L.) *The Picturesque Beauties of the Hudson River and its Vicinity; illus. in a series of views, from original drawings, taken expressly for this work, and engraved on steel by distinquished artists. With historical and descriptive illus.* NY. J. Disturnell. 1835-6. wrps. Parts I and II. Total of 28 pp. and 8 views. ("Part I, is offered as a Specimen.... If duly encouraged Part II, will appear on the first of Sept. next.... The work when complete will consist of 12 parts...." Sabin, 33520, says, "Of this fine work Parts I and II only were issued. The panic of 1857 [1837] caused its discontinuance." The 8 views are of the NY-NJ area from the Palisades south.)

Letters from Old-Time Vassar. Written by a student in 1869-70. Pub. 1915. 149 pp. (An un-named student writes of life at Vassar College in Poughkeepsie: it is rumored that the riding master killed a man in a duel in Germany; the parlor looks disreputable with shells and orange skins on the floor; she prays immediately after she eats and before colic sets in; describes trips taken. All in all, a delightful book by a careful and discerning student.)

Lewis, J. *The Hudson River.* 1964. 272 pp. (Lewis, a water colorist, illus. this book with 110 of his paintings, 18 of them being tipped in color plates. The rest are sepia plates. There are views of scenery, buildings, bridges, people, streams, and other points of interest from Lake Tear in the Clouds on the south slope of Mount Marcy to NYC. This is an unusual contribution to Hudson River art.)

Lieber, F. (Ed.) *Letters to a Gentleman in Germany, written after a trip from Philadelphia to Niagara.* 1834. 356 pp. (This book was re-issued the next year under the title, *The Stranger in America, or Letters to a Gentleman in Germany....* The writer comments on his trip up the Hudson to Niagara: politics, women, customs, etc., comparing it all with what he has seen in earlier years in Europe. Larned says his comments are fair and his judgements correct. He may have been the first European to dscover the first American T-shirts. Here is what he wrote, "On ... steamboats, between New York and Albany ... there is generally a man with a case of types, offering them for sale to passengers, who are desirous of printing their names, with indeliable ink, on their wearing apparel."

Livingston, E. B. *The Livingstons of Livingston Manor. Being the history of that branch ... which settled in the English Province of New York ... also including an account of Robert Livingston of Albany, "The Nephew", a settler in the same province, and his principal descendants.* 1910. illus. map. bib. index. 590 pp. + large folding genealogical chart. lmtd. to 275 copies. (A major reference work on one of the earliest and most important Hudson Valley families. The Livingstons owned vast lands in southern Columbia Co. on which tenants resided, and much of the Catskill Mountain region. It is said that one of the Livingstons could stand on his porch overlooking the Hudson River and the distant Catskills and declare that he owned all that he could see. There is a story in Columbia Co. folklore that the landlord Livingston took one of his tenants, and the tenant's little boy, to the top of a hill near Ghent and told him he could have all the land that he could see. The little boy was hopping around in delight and telling his father how wonderful the landlord was. The Dutch tenant farmer shook the happy lad and said, "Shut up, you little fool! How are we going to pay all the taxes?")

Livingston, R. R. *Essay on Sheep: their varieties ... account of the Merinos ... raising a flock in the U. S. ...* NY. 1809. 186 pp. (Robert R. Livingston, of Clermont in Columbia Co., and U. S. Minister to France, was a pioneer in the importation of Merino Sheep into the U. S. This book, which went through several ed., was the first important work on the Merinos pub. in America.)

McGrath, E. F. *I was Condemned to the Chair. Sing Sing Death House Prisoner No. 60021. Recommitted for 20 years to life as No. 61550.* Introd. by G. W. Kirchwey, former warden of Sing Sing Prison. 1934. 312 pp. (Author spent his time in prisons at Sing Sing, Dannemora, and Comstock. The warden writes that this book is "a vivid and colorful account of a long prison experience forged in the heat of revolt against its wilful indignities and shameful corruption and we have also the pitiful record of twenty months spent in the death-house at Sing Sing, with its cumulative horrors.")

A Man of Sixty. Five Lessons for Young Men. Albany. 1837. 198 pp. (The author, evidently a resident of the Albany area, apparently wanted to reform the city. He writes against the theatre, circus, race ground, and intemperance. The Albany of 45 years ago "had no Theatres, no Circuses; no places for loungers and laziness; and ... consequently no vagabonds.")

Maynadier, G. *The First American Novelist?* 1940. Port. 79 pp. (Charlotte Ramsay Lennox, 1720-1804, spent about the first 15 years of her life in the Albany, NY, area where her father was an army officer. In her teens she was sent to England and never returned. She wrote a number of novels. Two of them are partially set in the Hudson Valley, mainly Albany: *Life of Harriot Stuart* pub. in 1751, and *Euphemia* pub. in 1790.

Maynadier discusses her life and work, and says that in *Harriot Stuart* "for the first time in English fiction American scenes were presented by one who knew them firsthand.")

Mayo, A. D. *Symbols of the Capitol; or civilization in New York.* 1859. 368 pp. (A study of civilization as symbolized by the institutions in Albany: society, labor, gold dollar, law, crime, women, churches, the rural cemetery. The author was well acquainted with civilization in Albany as he was the minister at the Division Street Unitarian Church from 1856 to 1863.)

Mel and Gene. *The Log of Spendthrift II. Being the records of her fourth cruise. Shoved off Sept. 1, 1930 - returned Sept. 7, 1930.* Prntd. and bound by William Edwin Rudge the noted pub. of fine works. ca 1930. Illus. with 2 smll mounted photos and 1 cartoon. 7 pp. of text. Lmtd. to 17 copies. (A small boat cruise on the Hudson River from Haverstraw to Crumb Elbow. They struck Duck Rock near West Point, and had repairs made at Newburgh. Would you believe, I have had two copies of this impossible to find work.)

Mershon, S. L. (Mershon made a special study of English land grants and shore rights in the NYC and lower Hudson Valley areas. His four works most often seen are the following:) *The Major and the Queen, or, a royal grant to a gallant soldier.* 1915. Illus. Map. Index. 98 pp. (Major Lancaster Symes and the early history of Staten Island.) *English Crown Grants.* 1918 266 pp. (A legal study of the early land grants of Staten Island, including data on: Riparian Rights, Public Bathing Places, Fish, Title Guarantees, Quit Rents.) *The Power of the Crown in the Valley of the Hudson.* 1925. Maps. Illus. 209 pp. (A detailed study on land titles and shore front boundaries. *Shore Front Rights in the State of New York.* 1929. Folding map. 98 pp. (An hist. study of the ownership of shores and underwater lands, especially on Long Island and Staten Island.)

Milbert, J. G. *Itineraire Pittoresque du Fleuve Hudson et des Parties Laterales de l'Amerique du Nord.* Paris. 1828-29. 2 vols., plus map and folder of 54 plates. (Much of the text and many of the plates of this major work are of NY State interest as the author spent most of his time going up the Hudson Valley to Lake George and then along the Mohawk to Niagara. He drew some of the first pictures of frontier communities, and his accounts constitute the first prntd. record of some localities. The two vols. have been found bound together. Sabin says, "Twenty-five copies of the atlas were issued as proof impression on India paper before the letters." Howe's *USiana* states that some sets contain only 53 plates. The plates apparently were issued both in black-and-white and color. A 3-page prospectus was issued. This work went through at least two more printings in the 1830s. Complete sets rarely come on the market as many of the finer prints have been removed and framed. The strikes of the

71

later ed. are not as sharp as the impressions of the first printing. In 1837 Roux De Rochelle, who was French Minister to the U. S. 1829-1831, wrote a book titled *Etats-Unis D'Amerique*, which went through several ed. In this work he used a number of the Milbert prints, some of which he varied slightly. He also used some drawings by Milbert which did not appear in the *Itinerary*. The original prints were folio size; the De Rochelle printing reduces them to approximately 8x5 inches. There also was a printing made in Italy which reduced the prints even further. In 1968, the Gregg Press, of Ridgewood, NJ, reprntd. the prints in full size. These recent reprints have frequently been framed, and it takes a good eye to tell the difference between them and an original. Before buying any Milbert print you should examine it unframed. Most of my early Milbert Prints of the Hudson River came from Rocky Gardiner of Stamford, CT. Rocky was from NY State and stored quantities of material at the old homestead in Hadley, NY. From time to time he would drive up there and load up his big station wagon to replenish his house and storage building in CT. He had been in the antiques and book business from about the age of 14, and had soaked up an enormous amount of knowledge of his chosen profession. He could rattle off accurate information on almost any subject and was widely respected by major museums and dealers. Some of his acquisitions went to such places as Sturbridge, Williamsburgh, Winterthur, Shelburne, and even the American Museum in England. But much of it went to average dealers like myself who stopped by for a few hours to dig through huge piles of mostly unsorted books, pamphlets, mss., maps, atlases, stero views, broadsides, and prints. Some of this stuff was even stored in rare chests and desks that would eventually end up in a major museum. Rocky had a good eye for unusual material, and said that he bought something almost every day. Someone once said he could go downtown for a haircut and come home with a box full of manuscripts. Countless times I visited Rocky, usually arriving about 10 a.m., and leaving about midnight. Many fine NY items came my way from him. Nothing was priced, and after dinner at his home or in a nearby fine restaurant, we would sit down at a round antique table in the dining room and go through the huge piles of material I had dug out. We did not always agree on the prices, and I usually happily acquired about two-thirds of my choices. Rocky would usually give a brief lecture on almost every item, and from time to time he would pick up a book, lean towards me, and peering at me over his half-glasses, say, "Where did you find this? I haven't seen it in several years. Do you know what makes this book important? It is the last paragraph on page 163." The he would open up the book and read, and invariably he was right. After he did that a few times I concluded he was a genius. His love for his profession was profoundly shown the last time I saw him before he passed away. I had picked up a few unpriced books at his house, and went to see him in the hospital. I walked in and said, "Hi, Rock! Here are a few books you have to price for me." He roused his weak and tired body, opened his eyes, and partially sat up in bed with a smile on his face. He was back in business again!)

Moore, Pliny. *Journal of Drink.* 1774. Champlain (NY). Pvtly. prntd. at the Moorsfield Press. 1929. wrps. 12 pp. Lmtd. to 86 copies. (Moore, 1759-1822, of Spencertown, kept a record of the liquor he drank at home, and on a trip to Sheffield and Great Barrington, MA, to consult a Dr. Whiting. The entries are dated April 14 through July 19, 1774, and frequently mention where and with whom he drank the "Spiritual Liquors." He began as a drummer boy in the Revolutionary War, and later was the first white settler of the Champlain, NY area. Evidentally he reformed his drinking habits, as he was later a Judge, and was President of the Clinton County, NY, Bible Soc. His port. and a number of facts about him appear in Tuttle's *Three Centuries in the Champlain Valley,* 1909.)

Mt. Beacon. Folder of 16 photogravures of Mt. Beacon resort, and surrounding points of interest. ca early 1900s. (Includes illus. of black walnut tree, near Fishkill, used as a whipping tree during Revolutionary War. It blew down some years ago in a storm, and a few years ago my uncle made a case for a grandfather clock from its wood.)

Munsell, Joel. *A Chronology of Paper and Paper Making.* 1856. 61 pp. Prntd. for presentation only. (Albany's man of many interests, Joel Munsell, wrote this first major American work on the subject. It went through 5 ed. by 1876, and all of them are very scarce. This first ed. of 1856 is unusual in that one page is prntd. on Japanese paper procured by Lt. Fry of the U.S. Expedition to Japan, being part of a present made by one of the officers of the Japanese government. Another page is prntd. on straw paper made by a John Thorp who seems to have lived near Utica, NY. Munsell writes that Thorp did not have the means to manufacture it for market. Another page is prntd. on straw paper made by a Mr. Ames of Springfield, MA. Each ed. of the *Chronology* had added information, the 1876 ed. having 218 pages. The 1870 printing states that an issue of the *Syracuse Standard* newspaper was prntd. on paper made from the wrappings of Egyptian mummies. Dard Hunter's *Papermaking* discusses Munsell's claim, and tells about paper made at Broadalbin, NY, from mummy cloth.)

Munsell's Guide to the Hudson River by Railroad and Steamboat. Staten Island to Troy ... For the Convenience of the Business Man and Traveller. Albany. ca 1859. Hudson River Time Table, dated May 9, 1859. 8 maps. index. wrps. 56 pp. (Interestingly, this guide, in opposition to most others like it, starts from Troy and goes south. Although not noted in the book, this was compiled by F. B. Hough.

This was the first ed., and it was repub. in several subsequent years.)
National Progressive Party Song Sheet of Roosevelt-Strauss Ratification. Madison Square Garden. Nov. 1, 1912. (A song book with 10 songs, 2 of them about Theodore Roosevelt. It includes Roosevelt's platform, and a brief sketch of his runningmate, Hiram W. Johnson. At this time Roosevelt was candidate for U. S. President, and Strauss was candidate for Governor of NY.)
The New Steam Boat Rip Van Winkle, Capt. S. Schuyler. Evening Line for New York. 1848. No Monopoly. Small advertising broadside, 4 x 6 inches, with small woodcut of *Rip Van Winkle* by Forbes and Pease.

Partridge, B. *An Imperial saga. The Roosevelt Family in America.* 1936. illus. charts. bib. index. (An amazing collection of facts for the Roosevelt family trivia lover. In here you will discover which Roosevelt refused an audience with the Pope, which one sued a newspaper for libel and collected 6 cents, and which one was married to the tune of "Wearing of the Green.")

Pelliana (Pell of Pelham) 1635-1919. Vol. 1 Nos. 1 thru 3. Published 1934-36. Pvtly. prntd. illus. maps. wrps. Total of 164 pages. (Information on the Pells of Westchester Co. It also has 18 pages of the diary of Joshua Pell III, an Officer of the British Army in America 1776-1777, who served in Champlain Valley.)

Pepper, C. Jr. *Manor of Rensselaerwyck, by ... Counsel-lor at Law.* Pub. by the Albany and Rensselaer Anti-Rent Associations. Albany. Munsell. 1846. wrps. 34 pp. (Although 1500 copies of this pamphlet were prntd., it rarely comes on the market. I can recall having only had 1 copy in well over 30 years. The author unsuccessfully tried to start a law suit over the title of the manor by cutting down a tree in the proprietor's own woodlot.)

Perry and Pell. *Hell's Acres. A Historical Novel of the Wild East in the 50s.* Pub. 1938. map. 400 pp. (Horse thieves and prize fights at Boston Corners, NY, where the NY, MA, and CT borders meet. This Columbia Co. novel has become very scarce and much sought after. The fortunate discoverer of this vol. will probably have to settle for a less than perfect copy as it was not very well bound.)

Phelps, H. P. *Players of a Century. A Record of the Albany Stage. Including Notices of Prominent Actors Who Have Appeared in America.* Albany. 1880 2nd. ed. index. 424 pp. ("The history of the Albany stage is, in a great measure, the history of the theatre in America.")

Philalethes (Pseud.) *The Importance of Revivals as Exhibited in the Late Convention at New-Lebanon, Considered in a Brief Review of the Proceedings of That Body.* Ithaca, NY. 1827. wrps. 19 pp. (Finney, the decidedly different NY State revivalist, used some unusual methods in his meetings which were opposed by other fire and brimstone preachers. A meeting held at New Lebanon in 1827 to mend the breach was attended by Finney and his supporters, and by his opponents. It is generally conceded that the convention ended with no clear-cut victory for either side, but Cross, in his book on enthusiastic religion in western NY, *The Burned Over District*, declares that the end result was a victory for Finney.)

Pope, F. L. *The Western Boundary of Massachusetts: A Study of Indian and Colonial History.* Pittsfield, MA. 1886. map. wrps. 62pp. pvtly. prntd. (A study of the complicated history of this highly disputed boundary. Much involved were the colony of NY, the Livingstons, the Van Rensselaers, and the early anti-Renters.)

Price, J. H. *Miscellany, in Verse and Prose.* Albany. 1813. 168 pp. Dedicated to DeWitt Clinton. (The author wrote many of these poems while studying for a law career. He apparently lived in the Troy area as he mentions the *Northern Budget* newspaper, the Baptist Meeting House in Troy, and the Republican Electors of Rensselaer Co. There is a sentimental 2-1/2 page poem titled, "Elegy On a Dead Mouse Found in a Trap." His reason for writing the poem, "Mice should have elegies as well as Kings.")

Proceedings at Presentation of Mementos of President and Mrs. Roosevelt, and Fala, to the F. O. R. Library, Hyde Park, New York, ... May 1947. 44 mimeo. pages. (This is a short list of the few people attending the ceremony, and the text of the brief speeches. Probably only a few copies were made.)

Ransom, J. M. *Vanishing Ironworks of the Ramapos.* Rutgers University Press. New Brusnwick, NJ, 1966. maps. illus. bib. index. 382 pp. (This is a very valuable study of the iron mines of Orange and Rockland Cos., in NY, and of the mines across the border in northern NJ. There are many evidences of mining operations in the Harriman-Bear Mountain State Park: mine holes, slag heaps, furnace ruins, and wood roads used by the ore wagons. One of the old furnaces can be seen on the east side of the NY State Thruway at Harriman, NY. Hiking trails go to or near many of the mining sites. This excellent book is getting difficult to find, and when found is expensive.)

Raymond, C. *Memories of a Child of Vassar.* 1940. port. 73 pp. (Life at Vassar College in the late 1800s.)

Reynolds, H. W. *Dutch Houses in the Hudson Valley Before 1776.* 1929. Folding map. 150 Plates. index. 467 pp. (The great authority on this most important field of Hudson Valley hist. The introduction was written by Franklin D. Roosevelt, whose interest in the subject began when he saw a delightful old Dutchess Co. house demolished. This book has been reprntd. in paperback by Dover Publications of NY.)

Reynolds, H. W. *Dutchess County Doorways, and Other Examples of Period Work in Wood 1730-1830.* 1931. map. illus. index. 280 pp. plus 204 plates.

Rice, H. C. *Le Cultivateur American Etude Sur L'Oeuvre De Saint John De Crevecoeur.* Paris. 1933. illus. map. Bib. index. 263 pp. (A good study, entirely in French, of De

Crevecoeur, a Frenchman who had a farm in Orange Co., NY, prior to the Revolutionary War.)

Rice, N. S. *Albany Silver. 1652-1825. Exhibit of Albany, NY, Silver.* Albany Institute of Art and Hist. 1964. map. bib. errata slip. Many illus. 81 pp. (Detailed descriptions of items exhibited; with brief biog. of the Albany silversmiths.)

Ringwald, D. C. *Hudson River Day Line, The Story of a Great American Steamboat Co.* 1965. illus. maps. bib.. index. 228 pp.

Ringwald, D. C. *Steamboats for Rondout. Passenger Service Between New York and Rondout Creek, 1829 Through 1863.* 1981. illus. maps. bib. index.

Risch, J. *The History of the Daniel Gray Fishing Club of White Plains, NY. Organized January 27, 1898.* 1941. illus. map. wrps. 37 pp. (A hist. of the club and its conservation work. "Lord give us Grace to catch a fish so big that even we, when telling of it, may never need to lie.")

Rockland County Distance Table. 1854. wrps. 20 pp. (This pamphlet was issued by R. F. O'Connor to accompany his large wall map of the co. Very detailed distances recorded. Example: From the junction of the roads (on the hook road), 40 rods N.E. of Peter Garabrands house to the junction of the roads on the State road (35 rods S.E. of the Toll Gate), is one and a quarter mile and 49 rods.")

Roe, E. P. (Roe, 1838-1888, Orange Co., NY, novelist, whose avocation was horticulture, wrote 17 best-selling novels, and 5 books on gardening. Here is a list of several of his novels with a Hudson Valley setting:) *From Jest to Earnest.* 1875. *Opening a Chestnut Burr.* 1874. (This was his second novel, and DAB says he wrote it "to determine whether the amazing sale of the first was an accident....) *Natures Serial Story.* 1885. *Near to Nature's Heart.* 1876 (Revolutionary War setting.)

Roosevelt & Brough. *An Untold Story. The Roosevelts of Hyde Park.* 1973. illus. index. 318 pp. (Elliott Roosevelt had read so much inaccurate writing about his parents, F. D. R. and Eleanor, that he wrote this book to set the record straight.)

Roseberry, C. *Steamboats and Steamboat Men.* 1966. illus. bib. index. 192 pp. (Hist. of the Hudson River steamboats which were "the fleetest, handsomest, and most exciting in the world.")

Rules and Regulations, Adopted by the True Assistant Society of Hatters in New-York: And Ordered to be Printed For Their Government (NY, 1795) wrps. 14 pp. (This was one the earliest unions in the U. S. and probably the first one in NYC. Besides all of the other benefits listed they agreed to aid sick members and their families, but "... in case the member deceased, died with an infectious disorder ... the Society shall not be called to attend the funeral." This unique pamphlet is listed, and illus., in: *A Society's Chief Joys. An Exhibition from the Collections of the American Antiquarian Society,* Worcester, MA, 1969.)

Rules for the Practice of the Court

of *Common Pleas for the County of Ulster, Adopted July 7, 1803.* Kingston. Prntd. by Buel and Mitchell. wrps. 30 pp. (Very detailed rules, and lengthy list of court fees. Buell and Mitchell were noted NY State printers, and Buell later served as a judge in the Ulster County Court. Not listed in Sabin or *American Bibliography*.)

Sampson, Davenport & Co. Pubs. *The Albany Directory, for 1875. General Directory of Citizens. Business Directory.* June 1, 1875. 444 pp. (The publishers warn, "With regard to complaints, we desire to say: GREAT CAUTION should be exercised before censuring the book...." A feature of this *Directory* are the numerous fine illus. advts..)

Schenectady and Catskill Railroad. ca 1850s. 2 pp. leaflet. (This was a proposed railroad, one of the advantages being that a direct line between the 2 towns would avoid the 29 canal locks, and the obstructions in the Hudson River. There is a list of officers.)

The School House at Pine Tree Corner, North Salem, NY. 1784-1916. Teaching and Administrative Practices in a One-Room Rural School, in Westchester Co. 1976. maps. illus. bib. index. wrps. 180 pp. (Includes much biog. data, and detailed discussions of a very specialized subject.)

Schophon ... To Deacon Darius Howland and the Rest of the Lying Busybodies Who Have Had to Pay for Their Slanderous Tittle Tattle, Greeting:.... C. A. Hollenbeck, Athens (NY). 1870. Broadside, 6 x 9 inches. (A scurrilous broadside expressing Hollenbeck's belief that his personal enemy, George Lea, is in Hell for various criminal acts committed in NY State, and for having done the author out of his share of War of 1812 prize money.)

Schuyler, G. W. *Colonial New York, Philip Schuyler and His Family.* NY. 2 vols. index. 1885. (Philip Schuyler, 1733-1804, of Albany, was an officer in the French and Indian and Revolutionary Wars, and a large landholder. There are many references to the other important families in the area: Bleecker, Bogardus, Lansing, Livingston, Low, Staats, Ten Broeck, Van Rensselaer.)

Scott, R. *The Last Dying Request and Advice of Robert Scott, Late Pastor and Teacher in the General Baptist Church, Rhinebeck Flatts Sept. 25, 1834.* Kingston. Prntd. by A. L. Stewart, at the Republican Office. 1834. wrps. 12 pp. (An unusual pamphlet, containing an Address by Scott to be read in the meeting house immediately after his burial, and directions for the conduct of his relatives and his place of burial.)

Smith, C. A. (ed.) *Forest Voices. Translated From the German of Putlitz.* Albany. Munsell. 1866. 102 pp. (Prose and poetry from Germany translated into English. The engraved frontispiece is an illus. of: Tivoli Falls. On the Grounds of Gen. Stephen Van Rensselaer. Drawn from Nature by James Eights, Engraved by V. Balch.)

(Smith, Gerrit). *The West Point Mob.* March 1871. Broadside. 8 x 31 inches. (Smith, nationally famous abolitionist of Peterboro, NY, comments on a recent mob scene at the military academy at West Point, and of a colored cadet he says, "The pro-slavery caste-spirit, which reigns at West Point, forbids all social intercourse with him ... let this West Point school so prolific of tyrants and ruffians be suppressed...." A good insight into racial discord at the U. S. Military Academy a few years after the Civil War ended.)

Smith and Forman's New York Sheet Almanac, For the Year 1812. Broadside 15 x 17 inches. (Sheet almanacks are among the rarest of almanacs. Drake's *Almanacs of the U. S.* lists approximately 66 sheet almanacs issued or advertised between 1800 and 1825. He located a total of 11 copies representing only 8 of the 66 almanacs. He did not locate a copy of the Smith and Forman for 1812, but notes that it was advertised in *Hutchins Revived Almanac* for 1812. The copy I owned was acquired from a private home and was slightly defective.)

Specifications for Electric Locomotives Proposed for the New York Central and Hudson River Railroad Co. ... Leased and Operated Lines. Electrical Dept. Submitted by General Electric Corp. Schenectady, NY. 1903. 78 prntd. pages, plus many diagrams, charts, and illus. (A highly technical work. Probably only a lmtd. number were prntd. for the few interested people involved in the building and buying of these locomotives.)

Spurr, Norman. *To the Farmers of Dutchess Co.* Dutchess Steam Print. ca 1872. wrps. 19 pp. (Spurr tries to persuade Dutchess Co. farmers to plant clover, as he is a professional clover seed producer in a nearby county. He also gives advice on fruit raising, timber cutting, and butter churning.)

Squire, Dr. A. O. *Observations Made at Electrocutions of 114 Men at Sing Sing Prison, by ...* Chief Physician at Sing Sing Prison. 1923. wrps. 8 pp. (Technical data on volts, electrode placement, resistance, autopsy findings.)

Stokes, O. *Letters and Memories of Susan and Anna Bartlett Warner.* 1925. Ilus. index. 229 pp. (The Warner sisters were noted novelists during the last half of the 1800s. They lived on Constitution Island near West Point, and at the ancestral home at Canaan, NY. During part of the summer, tours can be taken to Constitution Island from West Point. Reservations are suggested.)

The Story of Banner Man Island. Pub. by Francis Bannerman Sons. NY. 1962. illus. maps. wrps. 47 pp. (There are many fine illus. of the Castle on this famous island in the Hudson near West Point. I do not recall if it is mentioned in this pamphlet or not, but the island was once named Pollopel for Polly Pell. One winter she fell through the ice, was rescued by a young farmer, and was married to him on the spot by a minister who was present.)

(Strang, J.) *The Confession of Jesse Strang, Who Was Executed at Albany, August 21, 1827, for the Murder of John Whipple.* Albany. Prntd. for the pub. 1827. wrps. 24 pp. (This was an unusual case in that the murder had been planned for months, and Strang even served on the coroner's jury which judged the death a murder by persons unknown! See McDades *Annals of Murder* for a good summary of the case.)

Sturcke, A. *Hikes, by ... Member of Adirondack and Green Mountain Clubs.* NY. 1926. wrps. 148 pp. (Descriptions of hikes taken in 1924 and 1925 in the NYC area, the Hudson Highlands, and the Catskills.)

Sullivan, F. J. *Sing Sing. Capital Punishment, and "Honest-Graft."* 1927. 110 pp. (The author, a member of the NY Bar, lists the terrible conditions at the Sing Sing Prison. She urges its closing and the transfer of its inmates to the new facility at Wingdale in Dutchess Co. I heard a bit of pure folklore many years ago on how Sing Sing got its name. A lonely and musically inclined prisoner looked out of his barred window one day and saw a feathered creature happily hopping about. He said, "Sing sing, little birdie, sing.)

Sutherland, J. *Deduction of the Title to the Manor of Livingston ... Confirming the Title.* Hudson. 1850. wrps. 44 pp. (A collection of documents, prior to 1800, confirming the title to the Manor, compiled by Josiah Sutherland an attorney for the Livingstons. He also served in the 32nd. U. S. Congress.)

(Swalm, L.) *Life of the Unfortunate Levi B. Swalm, Embellished With His Likeness, Written by Himself.* NY. Prntd. for the pub. 1858. wrps. 24 pp. (Swalm, of Orange County, NY, tells a tear-jerking story of his travels, and of his mental, physical, and monetary trials. Years ago I owned a copy of this uncommon pamphlet, and sold it to Roger Butterfield the well-known dealer in Hartwick, NY. [Roger had been on the editoral staff of *Life* Magazine, and when he retired to the old homestead he went into the book business and handled many fine items; our Levi B. Swalm pamphlet not being one of the finer ones.] Anyway, a couple of years later I saw that he still had it and I bought it back. A few months later I put it on my NY State catalog, and Roger promptly called me and ordered it, "I had a copy of that once. It's a good one and I would like to have another copy." I did not want to lose a sale so I shipped it off to him without telling him he had recently sold it to me. A couple of years later I was rummaging through Roger's stock of pamphlets, and lo and behold there was Levi's likeness staring up at me. I bought him back, and I have no idea where he is now. Of one thing I am sure, Roger did not buy him back.)

Talbot, A. *Power Along the Hudson. The Storm King Case and the Birth of Environmentalism.* 1972. map. bib. index. 244 pp. (The story of the defeat of the Con. Edison Power Co. in its bid to build a reservoir and power station at Storm King in the Hudson Highlands. This case is considered the beginning of Environmentalism in the U. S. on a national scale.)

To the Anti-Renters of Columbia County! (by) An Anti-Renter. October 27, 1846. Broadside 9 x 11 inches. (Unknown author asks Anti-Renters not to support Silas Camp who was nominated at the Democratic District Convention as candidate for Congress. He details Camp's activities, and adds, "Mr. Camp is not an Anti-Renter at heart, and only professes to be such, for the purpose of cheating them out of their votes." Broadside had some effect as Camp did not become a Congressman.)

The Trial, and Life, and Confessions of John F. Van Patten, Who Was Indicted, Tried, and Convicted of the Murder of Mrs. Maria Schermerhorn, on the 4th. of Oct. Last, and Sentenced to be Executed on 25th. Feb. 1825. NY. 1825. wrps. 16 pp. (This murder occurred in Rotterdam, NY. There is an illus. of a hanging on the title page. See McDade 1020.)

(Tribunus Populi). *A Reply to a Letter From a Gentleman in New York, to His Friend in Brunswick.* (NY 1750). 8 pp. (Written in regard to the NY-NJ boundary line. Sabin 69681, and Evans 6618, locate no copies. Shipton Mooney's *Index of American Imprints* locates a copy at the Henry E. Huntington Library in CA.)

A Troutbeck Letter-Book (1861-1867) Being Unpublished Letters to Myron Benton From Emerson, Sophia Thoreau, Moncure Conway, and Others. Amenia, NY. 1925. Lmtd. to 200 copies. (Benton was a Dutchess Co., NY, poet admired by many of his literary contemporaries. MacCracken in his *Blithe Dutchess* says that the last letter Henry Thoreau wrote was to Myron Benton.)

Troy Directory for Year 1839-40: Names of Residents, Their Professions and Occupations, and List of City Officers. Pub. by Tuttle, Belcher, and Burton. 225 River Street, Up Stairs. 136 pp. (There are over 4500 entries. Among the great variety of trades listed are: bootcrimper, lumber piler, medicamentum beer establishment, ornamental painter.)

(Turner, A. A.) *Villas on the Hudson. A Collection of Photolithographs of 31 Country Residences.* NY. 1860. 3 pp. (A collection of 31 colored plates of lower Hudson valley villas in the 1850s, with 21 floor plans. Each plate gives the owner's name, and town. In most instances the names of the architect is listed on the plan. Each plan is approximately 13 x 18 inches. Complete sets of these fine views of villas seldom come on the market. Only a partial set has ever come my way.)

Van Deusen, Delia. *Murder Bicarb.* 1940. Diagram. 310 pp. (A murder mystery set in the Retired Citizen's Home on Allen Street in Hudson, NY. It includes a plan of the basement floor and of the ground floor of the Home. The authoress of this Columbia Co. mystery novel whets our interest in the very first paragraph by stating, "All the crises came in the wrong places, and the one person who did any detecting did it almost too late." Only 1 copy of this has come my way.)

Van Loon, L. *Crumbs From an Old Dutch Closet. The Dutch Dialect of Old New York.* The Hague (Holland). 1938. wrps. glossary. 47 pp. (A study of the old Hudson-Mohawk Dutch dialect. Years ago I worked with an old Dutchman in a factory in Poughkeepsie. Every so often he would mention a "blauser" snake, which he described as having "a head like a pannycake." I could not find a description of a "blauser" anywhere. Finally, while looking through one of the vol. on the *Natural History of New York* pub. in the 1840s, I found that "blauser" was an old Hudson Valley Dutch word for puff adder.)

Van Norman, I. *Minnewaska. A Legend of Lake Mohonk, Sequel to Longfellow's Hiawatha. And Other Lyrical Poems.* 1897. Has several illus. of the Lake Mohonk area. 243 pp. (If you like marvellous scenery, and the Victorian era, you are missing out on one of life's greatest experiences if you have not visited the Lake Mohonk Mountain House. I found this book in the 1940s in a bookshop down in Australia. Incidentally, it was in an Australian zoo where I first saw a Canadian Goose.)

Vann, J. *Annals of an Adventurous Life, Being a Plain, Unvarnished and Abolutely Truthful Statement of Many Remarkable Occurrences.* Goshen. (NY) 1901. port. wrps. 40 pp. (The author, born in 1807, spent most of his life in the wilderness of Orange and Sullivan Cos. He practiced medicine, hunted bears and panthers, had adventures with snakes, had conversations with Angels, boated on the Delaware and Hudson Canal, guarded lumbermen from ferocious beasts, and seems to have had an improbable adventure almost every minute. The book ends with 1885. Marvellously wild tales, a great contribution to regional folklore.)

Van Wyck, F. *Select Patents of New York Towns.* 1938. illus. 180 pp. Lmtd. to 125 copies. (An in-depth study of the incorporation of towns, and the granting of exclusive fishing rights. Includes Flushing, Westchester, Rochester and Marbletown in Ulster Co., and Brooklyn. It was reprntd. in the same year, in an enlarged and corrected ed. of 190 pps., lmtd. to 75 copies.)

Varney, J. M. *The Life and Career of Oscar F. Beckwith, From the Cradle to the Grave. One of the Most Noted Criminals Ever Born in Columbia County.* Hillsdale, NY. 1890. wrps. 25 pp. (Beckwith had a cabin on Varney Mountain on the eastern edge of Austerlitz, where he is said to have panned for gold. He also was a thief and a passer of counterfeit bills. He induced a man named Vandercook to become his partner in the gold venture, but he soon murdered him, chopped his body up, burned some in a stove, and evidentally ate his heart and liver. When he suspected that he was suspected he fled to Canada. Years later he was discovered, extradicted to Columbia Co., and after a lengthy trial, and conviction, was hung at Hudson in 1888. Numerous accounts of this unappetizing crime have appeared in books and newspapers. In the spring of 1958 a number of severed human bones were found at the site of Beckwith's cabin. The pamphlet prntd. at Hillsdale is very rare. Many years ago I was offered a copy by a man in Chatham for $100.00. Foolishly, I turned it down. Several years later I saw him again, and asked him if he still had it. "No," he said, "I don't have it anymore. I gave it away to a young chap who really wanted it." I have never found another. Back in the 1930s I was in a blue berry pickers cabin in Austerlitz, and talking with John Pinnie who was the gardener for Edna St. Vincent Millay the noted poet who lived just a short way down the road. After we discussed the Beckwith. affair, John echoed the sentiment of the neighborhood when he wiped his brow with the back of his hand and said, "Phew! I'm glad he's gone!" In 1962 Vantage Press, of NY, pub. a book by David Buckman (pseud.) titled *The Mountain Tulip Legend*. It appears to be partially based on the Beckwith story. I found a new copy of this 170 page novel for sale in a public auto garage in Austerlitz soon after publication. I did not particularly like it so disposed myself of it soon after reading it through. Now I am told by local book dealers it is a collector's item, and I can't find a copy.)

Vassar College Song Book. Published for the Alumnae Association of Vassar College by G. Schirmer, NY. 1900. wrps. 165 pp. (Besides the words and music of such staid songs as "Alma Mater," and "Faculty Song," it also contains "We Know It All," and "I Was a Rhizopod.")

Vassar, T. E. *Uncle John Vassar, or the Fight of Faith*. 1879. port. 258 pp. (Uncle John, a brewery worker in Poughkeepsie, became converted, and soon was employed by the American Tract Soc. as a colporteur. While working with soldiers he was captured by the Confederates just before the battle of Gettysburg. Appleton says his captors released him almost immediately "to escape his importunate exhortations and prayers." An illus. ed. was issued with 9 plates.)

Uncle John Vassar in the Army and Among the Freedmen. NY. American Tract Soc. 1867. wrps. illus. 94 pp.

Views in Tuxedo Park. Pub. by George Dart, Tuxedo, NY. ca 1890s? 32 full page views of: drives, homes, churches, the lake, the clubs. Each pp. 6-1/2 x 5-1/4 inches. illus. on front wrapper. (Tuxedo Park is a wealthy private residential area in the town of Tuxedo in Orange Co. This item is included to bring out the point that books and folders of views should be collected and preserved. Very often publications such as these have local illustrations that are available nowhere else.)

Vote Yourself a Farm. Broadsheet. ca 1840s. Available at the office of "Young America" in NYC, and at the office of the "Anti-Renter" in Albany. (The issuers of this hand-out urge citizens to form a true American political party and vote for making the Public Lands available free of charge to actual settlers. On the verso of the sheet is a proposed plan of a six mile square township, and of a proposed village for each township. Much of the outcry for free public land was brought on by the Anti-Rent troubles in eastern NY State.)

Wetherbee and Taylor. *Legend of the Bushwhacker Basket*. Sanbornton, NH. 1986. wrps. illus. map. 64 pp. (For years there were tales of a reclusive group of basket makers known as Bushwhackers, who lived in the area of West Taghkanic in lower Columbia Co. Carl Carmer visited them and calls them the Pondshiners in his book on the Hudson River published in 1939. This excellent work about the Bushwhacker Basket goes into detail about the history and lives of these people, and about the baskets that some of them still make and sell. These excellent baskets are unlike those made anywhere else. This book clears up many misconceptions about these people and their craft.)

Wiles, R. (Ed.) *The Livingston Legacy. Three Centuries of American History.* Bard College. 1987. maps. illus. 444 pp. wrps. (The pub. results of the Livingston Manor Tercentenary Symposium held at Bard College in June 1986. Over 20 very informative papers were given on the Livingston family covering a wide range of subjects: land policy, slavery, archaeology at Clermont, the American Revolution, iron mining, music, biog., Livingston lands in the Catskills, and the breakup of the Manor. There are many hist. notes. This is a major contribution to our knowledge of the influential Livingston family whose Manor of 160,000 acres was in southern Columbia Co. According to the introduction, "Few American families have stirred as much controversy and admiration, veneration and even hatred, as the Livingstons of New York." Hopefully someone will compile an index to aid in the use of this important work.)

Williams, H. *The Gray man.* Pvtly. Prntd.. Salem, NY. 1911. port. mounted illus. 36 pp. (A brief biog. of General John Williams, Member of the Provincial Congress from NY, Army surgeon, and noted gardener of Salem. Lmtd. to 125 copies.)

Willis, N. P. &c. *Forest, Rock, and Stream. A Series of Twenty Steel Line-Engravings by W. H. Bartlett and Others. With Descriptive Text....* Boston. 1887. 84 pages. (There are 20 full-page engravings of Hudson Valley scenes from New York harbor to Mt. Ida near Troy. At least 18 of them are by W. H. Bartlett the famous engraver whose work is avidly collected.)

Wilson's Illustrated Guide to the Hudson River. NY. H. Wilson. 1848. maps. There is 1 illus. in the text plus some illus. advts. 112 pp. (From NYC to Corinth in the southern Adirondacks. There is a NYC street directory, and rates of fare for hackney coaches, carriages, and cabs. The first ed. of this notable guide.)

Winkler, J. *John D. A Portrait in Oils.* 1929. 256 pp. (Although forests have been felled to chronicle the career of John D. Rockefeller, this is the first serious effort to pierce the mystery of the world's mightiest resident. John D. was noted for giving away dimes. Some copies of this book have a dime glued to the front cover. The coin shows through a dime-sized hole in the dust jacket showing Rockefeller giving a dime to his golf caddy. On many copies the dime has been removed, and presumably spent.)

Woodbridge, Timothy. *Autobiography of a Blind Minister, Including Sketches of the Men and Events of His Time.* 1856. port. 312 pp. (Woodbridge, 1784-1862, a blind Presbyterian clergyman, and grandson of the famous Jonathan Edwards, served for many years in Spencertown and Green River in Columbia Co. He was well-liked and it is said that when he left Green River to accept a call to Spencertown about 8 miles away, the value of real estate declined in the former town. Biog. and autobiog. of ministers have a tendency to be neglected, but they often contain facts on local people and events that are available nowhere else.)

Yonkers Military Academy. Yonkers, NY. Established 1852. Benjamin Mason, Principal. ca 1860. illus. wrps. 26 pp. (This pamphlet gives information on the Academy: purpose, method of teaching, courses of study, military drill, rules, co-operation of parents, fees. The student body was lmtd. to fifty students. Their military drill was strict, "All voluntariness of action ceases, and the person becomes a machine....")

Zacarra and Edwards. *The Ironmaking Industry, Dover Furnace, Dover Plains, New York.* 1972. map. diagrams. 14 pp. mimeo. Lmtd. to 50 copies. (Includes data on charcoal making.)

The Zodiac. A Monthly Periodical, Devoted to Science, Literature, and the Arts. Pub. by E. Perry, Albany, NY. From the Steam Press of Packard and Van Benthuysen. Vol. 1 No. 1 - Vol. 2 No. 7. Complete. (July 1835-Jan. 1837.) (Of utmost importance are the articles by James Eights, M.D., an extraordinary Albany naturalist whom the noted James Hall called the best informed man in natural science he ever knew. Besides being on the Antarctic expedition under Capt. Fanning in 1828, Eights aided Lardner Vanuxem in his geologic surveys in NY State. A brief account of his life appears in the *Scientific Monthly* for Feb. 1916. Eights wrote at least 12 articles for the *Zodiac* on entomology, natural history, and geology. He was also an artist and is best known in that line for his views of Albany as it was in 1805, first pub. ca 1850. I have never had a complete set of the *Zodiac*, but I once had a long run that included the 4-page preliminary advertising prospectus prntd. on blue paper, and a 4-page pamphlet of testimonials prntd. on green paper and put out after the 8th. issue.)

INDIANS

Adams, S. *The Long House of the Iroquois. Why the Five Nations Possessing a Rectangular Type of Lodge Like the Shape of Their Ancient Realm in Up-State New York, Called Themselves "Ho-De-No-Sau-Nee" (People of the Long House.)* Skaneateles, NY. Pub. by the author. 1944. Many illus. of area scenes. 175 pp. (Only 500 copies of this book were prntd., of which 285 were offered for sale.)

Alden, Rev. T. *An Account of Sundry Missions Performed Among the Senecas and Munsees.* NY. 1827. port.

180 pp. (There is a great deal of material in this book on Cornplanter, a chief of the Senecas, who has been called the first temperance lecturer in the U. S.; and there is a short vocabulary of the Seneca dialect.)

(Bevier, J. H.) *The Indians: or, Narratives of Massacres and Depredations on the Frontier, in Wawasink and Its Vicinity, During the American Revolution.* Rondout, NY. 1846. 79 pp. (This is a rare and important narrative of the Rondout valley area southwest of Kingston. Sabin does not locate a copy. It has been reprntd..)

Birch, J. J. *The Saint of the Wilderness. St. Isaac Jogues, S.J.* (Soc. of Jesus.) 1936. port. illus. map on dust jacket. 236 pp. (The biography of the Jesuit Father Jogues, martyred at Osseruenon on the Mohawk in 1646 by the Indians. The Shrine of Our Lady of Martyrs at Auriesville, is on the site of the Indian village where Jogues was killed. Birch says that his grandfather, when a baby, was stolen by the Mohawks.)

Blatchford, S. *An Address, Delivered to the Oneida Indians, Sept. 24, 1810, by ... Together With the Reply, by Christian, a Chief of Said Nation.* Albany. 1810. 11 pp. pamphlet. (Rev. Blatchford, a Presbyterian minister from Lansingburgh, urges the Oneidas to be Christians, study English, be industrious, and stop drinking. He warns them, "Your nation is not now what it once was." Christian, the second Chief of the Oneidas, was influenced by Blatchford's speech. He thanked him for his kind words, and adds that he wants a tavern in his settlement removed.)

Bond, R. P. *Queen Anne's American Kings.* 1974. ed. illus. Extensive hist. notes. index. 148 pp. (A detailed hist. of the visit to London in 1710 by 4 Iroquois sachems from the province of NY. They were taken from the wilderness of the New World to the royal court of Great Britain "to impress England with the urgency of Indian affairs...." There have been other ed. of this work.)

Boyd, J. P. (notes by) *Indian Treaties Printed by Benjamin Franklin 1736-1762.* With Introd. by Carl Van Doren, and Historical and Bibliographical notes by Julian P. Boyd. 1938. maps. index. 340 pp. Lmtd. to 500 copies. (Reprints of 13 Treaties prntd. by Franklin. Boyd provides a 70-page essay on Indian affairs in Pennsylvania. A glossary and other important data are added. Although at first glance this seems to be entirely about Pennsylvania there are a great many references in the index to NY: Albany, Canasatego the Onondaga Chief, Cayuga Indians, the Iroquois, Sir William Johnson, Kinderuntie the Seneca Chief, Thomas King an Oneida Chief, Little Abraham a Mohawk Sachem, Minisink Indians, Mohawk Indians, New York, Karaghtadie a Mohawk Chief, Oneida Indians, Onondaqa Indians, Scarouady an Oneida Chief, Seneca Indians, Shikellamy an Oneida Chief, Tagashata a Seneca Chief, and Tokaaio a Cayuga Chief.)

(Brown, T.) *A Plain Narrative of the Uncommon Sufferings and*

Remarkable Deliverance of Thomas Brown of Charlestown, in New England; Who Returned to His Father's House Beginning of January 1760, After Having Been Absent 3 Years and About 8 Months. William Abbatt. NY. 1908. 17 pp. Lmtd. to 64 or less copies. (Brown, a member of Rogers Rangers, was captured by the Indians near Lake Champlain in 1757. His narrative was first pub. in 1760. Vail's Voice of the Old Frontier calls this one of the rarest and most exciting of the Indian captivity stories. Howes' USiana calls it "Sickeningly rare, terrifically thrilling.")

Brush, E. H. Iroquois Past and Present. Including Brief Sketches of Red Jacket, Cornplanter, and Mary Jemison, by E. D. Strickland. 1901. wrps. illus. 104 pp. (Important for contemporary photos of Indians and homes on NY State reservations.)

Bruyas, Rev. J. Radical Words of the Mohawk Language, With Their Derivitives.... NY. 1862. wrps. 123 pp. (Father Bruyas was a Jesuit missionary to the Indians on the Mohawk River in the late 1600s, and was regarded as a master of the Mohawk language. This is probably the oldest grammatical or lexicographical treatise on the Mohawk tongue; it is in Mohawk, Latin, and French. See Pilling's Bibliography of the Iroquoian Languages for a discussion of this work and of Bruyas. Appleton's Cyclopedia of American Biography says, "In 1700 he was instrumental in securing a treaty of peace with the Five Nations, which lasted more than half a century.")

Burke, C. The Indian and His River. Being a Book of Iroquois Indian Songs and Legends, and of the River Genesee. (Poetry) Authentic Iroquoian Decorations and Illustrations by Jack Bieber. 1933. Foreword by Arthur C. Parker, the noted anthropologist who was one-quarter Seneca Indian and who was born on the Cattaraugus Reservation at Iroquois, NY. 45 pp. Lmtd. to 300 copies.

The Burning Village, and Other Indian Stories. By the Editor of "The Youth's Casket." Buffalo. Phinney. 1859 illus. with several full-page woodcuts. 63 pp. (A childrens' book with several NY State Indian stories. The frontispiece is of the famous burning of Cherry Valley by the Indians in November 1778.)

Clark, Joseph. Travels Among the Indians: 1797. 1968. index. 43 pp. Lmtd. to 100 copies. (Clark, 1745-1833, a Quaker, travelled from PA to NYC, and then up the Hudson River and through the Mohawk Valley to visit the Oneida, Stockbridge, and Tuscarora Indians in the Oneida area. The purpose of his trip was to see about the welfare of the Indians, especially the young women. This is the first printing of his diary.)

Clarke, T. W. Eleazar Williams. Half-Breed Indian or King of France? 1935. illus. Bib. 62 pp. Only a very few copies of this work were made by typewriter and distributed to several selected libraries. (This is a discussion of whether Eleazar Williams, a missionary to the Indians of Oneida Castle, was actually the Lost Dauphin of France.

The young Dauphin of France disappeared in the 1790s, and many books and articles have been written, pro and con, on whether he came to the United States and became a missionary to the Indians. Pilling's *Bibliography of the Iorquoian Languages*, 1888, lists a number of works by Williams in the Indian tongue.)

Tyler, A. J. *I Who Should Command All*. 1937. port. illus. 64 pp. (This book promulgates the view that John James Audubon, the naturalist, was actually the Lost Dauphin.)

Colden, C. *The History of the Five Indian Nations Depending on the Province of New-York in America*. NY. Wm. Bradford. 1727. 119 pp. (This was the first hist. of the Iroquois Confederation. The 1727 first printing is exceedingly rare, and a copy has never come my way. I have had the first English ed. prntd. in London in 1747, and a number of the other printings.)

Cook, F. (ed.) *Journals of the Military Expedition of Maj. Gen. John Sullivann Against the Six Nations of Indians in 1779, With Records of Centennial Celebrations*. 1887. illus. maps. 581 pp. (This is a major reference work on this noted expedition as it contains the journals of 26 officers with Sullivan. There are brief biog. of many officers, and much other hist. data.)

Cornplanter, Jesse. *Iroquois Indian Games and Dances. Drawn by Jesse Cornplanter, Seneca Indian Boy*. wrps. 15 drawings depicting Iroquois Indian life, including games, dances, and festivals. Copyrighted by Frederick Starr in 1903. Prntd. in red on orange paper. (This was probably a small printing. Some copies came into the possession of John Skinner, a bookseller of Lake George. He occasionally put up a copy at a NYC auction. I have not seen a copy for sale for many years.)

Curtin, J. *Seneca Indian Myths*. NY. 1923. glossary. 516 pp. (Curtin collected these 90 different myths on the Seneca Indian Reservation near Versailles, NY, in the 1880s.)

Curtin and Hewitt. *Seneca Fiction, Legends, and Myths*. BAE. 1910-11. index. 819 pp. (This material was collected by Curtin in the 1880's on the Cattaraugus Reservation near Versailles, NY, and by Hewitt on the same reservation in 1896. This was the first serious attempt to record the folklore of the Seneca Indians.)

Cusick, D. *Sketches of Ancient History of the Six Nations....* Lockport, NY. 1848. 3rd. ed. illus. wrps. 35 pp. (Cusick was a native Tuscarora Indian historian and doctor. Pilling's *Bibliography of the Iroquoian Languages* says the preface of the first ed. was dated June 10, 1825, and describes several other ed.)

Davis, S. *Shekomeko: or, The Moravians in Dutchess co.* 1858. wrps. 29 pp. (Hist. of the Moravian Mission to the Indians of eastern Dutchess Co. in the 1740s.)

Dawes, E. (ed.) *Journal of General Rufus Putnam Kept in Northern New York During Four Campaigns of the Old French and Indian War 1757-1760*. Albany. Munsell. 1886. port. index. Many annotations. 115 pp. Lmtd. to 100 copies. (An account of Putnam's daily life during 4 campaigns.)

Dencke, C. F. *Nek Nechenenawachgissitschik Bambilak Naga Geschiechauchsitpanna Johannessan Elekhangup. Gischitak Elleniechsink, Untschi C. F. Denke.* NY. Prntd. for the American Bible Soc. 1818. 21 pp. (The Three Epistles of the Apostle John, translanted into Delaware Indian language by C. F. Dencke, a Moravian missionary working among that tribe. Prntd. in English and in Delaware. North's *The Book of a Thousand Tongues* says this Bible portion was the first translation of any part of the Scriptures into the Delaware Indian language, and the first publication by the American Bible Soc. for the American Indian. North was General Secretary of the ABS.)

Donaldson, T. *Indians. The Six Nations of New York. Cayugas, Mohawks (St. Regis), Oneidas, Onondagas, Senecas, Tuscaroras.* Extra Census Bulletin. 11th. Census of the U. S. by Thomas Donaldson, Expert Special Agent. Washington, D. C. 1892. index. maps. 89 pp. (This was the first detailed census of the Six Nations, and ten months were spent on the project. There are many illus. of important living Indians.)

(Duncan, J. M.) *A Sabbath Among the Tuscarora Indians.* Glasgow (Scotland). 1819. 69 pp. (The author visited the Tuscaroras in the fall of 1818 near Niagara. He defends the Indians, and says that the treatment they have received from the whites "has been such as might well lead us to be ashamed of the color we bear." This work was reprnted. in 1821.)

Flexner, J. T. *Lord of the Mohawks, a Biography of Sir William Johnson.* 1979. port. illus. maps. bib. index. 400 pp. (This is a revised ed. of Flexner's *Mohawk Baronet,* pub. in 1959.)

Gray, E. *Old Ninety-Nines Cave.* 1909. Illus. with photographs of local scenes and people. 314 pp. (Ulster Co. fiction based on the tradition of "Old Ninety-Nine", said to have been the last of the Delaware Indians in the Rondout Valley.)

Gridley, L. *Luke Gridley's Diary of 1757. While in Service in the French and Indian War.* 1907. Acorn Club. Hartford. wrps. 64 pp. Lmtd. to 102 copies. (Gridley was a private from Farmington, CT, and spent most of his time at Fort Edward. This is an excellent view of camp life.)

Griffis, W. E. *Sir William Johnson and the Six Nations.* 1891. index. 227 pp. (Author concentrates on Johnson's earlier life, and lightly goes over his later years.)

Harris, G. *The Indian Bread Root of the Senecas.* Waterloo, (NY). 1890. wrps. 6 pp. (A discussion of arum triphyllum, better known as jack-in-the-pulip, as a food for Indians and for early settlers. There is also some data on other wild plants that can be used for food.)

Hathaway, B. *The League of the Iroquois, and Other Legends. From the Indian Muse.* Chicago. 1882. Port. 319 pp. (Hathaway, a Cayuga Co. poet, spent several winters doing research for his poems based on Iroquois traditions. He wrote many of them on barrel heads while he was working as a cooper.)

Hawley, C. *Early Chapters of Cayuga History: Jesuit Missions in Goi-O-Gouen, 1656-1684. Also an Account of The Sulpitian Mission Among the Emigrant Cayugas, About Quinte Bay, in 1668.* Introd. by John Gilmary Shea. Auburn, NY. 1879. wrps. Folding map. 106 pp. (Hawley who was a Presbyterian minister in Auburn, was also President of the Cayuga Co. Hist. Association.)

Hawley, C. *Early Chapters of Seneca History: Jesuit Missions in Sonnontouan, 1565-1684.* Auburn, NY. 1884. map. wrps. 89 pp. Lmtd. to 250 copies.

Heusser, A. H. *Homes and Haunts of the Indians.* Paterson, NJ. index. 110 pp. (A discussion of Indian occupation of area along NY-NJ border, and relics found there.)

Hough, F. B. *Journals of Major Robert Rogers: Containing An Account of the Several Excursions He Made Under the Generals Who Commanded Upon the Continent of North America, During the Late War; ... With an Introduction and notes, and an Appendix Containing Numerous Documents and Papers Relating to the Doings of Major Rogers While Commanding at Michilimackinack, in 1767; and His Conduct in the Early Part of the Revolutionary War.* Albany. Munsell. 1883. Folding map. index. 297 pp. Lmtd. to 100 copies. (A valuable work on French and Indian war activity in the Lake George-Lake Champlain Valley, enhanced with numerous hist. footnotes by Hough.)

Indian Medals: Sir William Johnson's Indian Testimonial. On the occasion of the visit of the Walpole Soc. to the NY Hist. Soc., 1946, there were made from the original copperplate owned by the N. Y. H. S. 50 impressions of Johnson's Indian *Testimonial*, engraved by Henry Dawkins, of Philadelphia, 1770. Lmtd. to 50 copies. (This *Testimonial* was to accompany the presentation of Royal Medals to the Indians for their attachment to the King's interests. In 1946 only 50 copies of this document were made from the original copperplate. It has a small but nice illus. of a medal being given to an Indian.)

(Johnson, Sir William) *An Account of Conferences Held, and Treaties Made, Between Maj. Gen. Sir Wm. Johnson, Bart., and the Chief Sachems and Warriours of the ... Indian Nations in North America, at Their Meetings on Different Occasions at Fort Johnson in the County of Albany, in the Colony of New York, In the Years 1755 and 1756.* London. 1756. 77 pp. Reprntd. in 1930 in an ed. of 200 copies. (Johnson attempted to keep the Six Nations from attacking the settlements on the frontiers of Virginia and Pennsylvania.)

(Kirkland, S.) *The Journal of Samuel Kirkland. Nov. 1764-Feb. 1765.* Clinton, NY. Alexander Hamilton Private Press. 1966. 20 pp. Lmtd. to 150 copies. (Kirkland, a friend of Joseph Brant, made a missionary journey to the Seneca Indians at Canadasaga in 1764-65, and later became a missionary among the Oneida Indians. This is the first printing of this portion of Kirkland's *Journal*. It is also the first book prntd. by this press.)

McDowell, W. (ed.) *Colonial Records of South Carolina. Documents Relating to Indian Affairs.* May 21, 1750-Aug. 7, 1754. pub. 1958. index. 592 pp. (Surprisingly, there are many references in the index to NY: Albany, Gov. George Clinton, Five Nations, Sir William Johnson, Mohawks, NY, and the Six Nations. A very successful book dealer once gave me a hint which has often come in handy: "If a book looks interesting always check the index. A quick run through the index will give you an outline of the book, and will give an indication of its importance.")

Manley, H. (ed.) *Quakers at Cattaraugus Reservation in 1839. Three Letters by Dr. George T. Truman.* ca 1950. wrps. 14 pp. (These letters, according to the introduction, "cast considerable light on the habits and manners of the Senecas and on reservation conditions.")

Milet, Pierre. *Relation de sa Captivite parmi les Onneiouts en 1690-1. Par le R. P. Pierre de la Compagnie de Jesus.* Nouvelle-York: Presse Cramoisy de Jean-Marie Shea. M.DCCC.LXIV 56 pp. (Father Milet was a captive among the Oneida Indians for nearly two years. This observant Jesuit gives us one of the earliest accounts of the Five Nations. This work was reprntd. at NY in 1888 in a pamphlet of 18 pp. It was reprntd. at Chicago in 1897 in an ed. of 75 copies, with hist. notes, index, and bib.)

(Mohawk Indian Speller). *Ne Neh Yonaderihhonnyen Ni Tha Ka Nyen Kehhaka Kawen Nondaghkohn Teke Nih Skarighware Nok Royanen Ra De Ren Nayengh D Ye Ry Wennyh...I Sho No Jowa ne.* NY. Prntd. at the Conference Office. J. Collord. 1829. wrps. 32 pp. (A small book containing: the alphabet, words, Lord's Prayer, Apostle's Creed, Ten Commandments, and Prayers.)

Muster Rolls of the New York Provincial Troops. 1755-1764. NYHS. 1891. index. 621 pp. (A fine research tool on NY men who served in the French and Indian War, giving: name, age, date of enlistment, birthplace, trade, and militia company. The index contains over 8000 names. The appendix contains the text of provincial acts, proclamations, a list of deserters, a list of commissions, and other relevant matter.)

Nammack, G. *Fraud, Politics, and the Dispossession of the Indians. The Iroquois Land Frontier in the Colonial Period.* 1969. maps. illus. bib. index. 128 pp. (4 cases of land fraud in NY State are detailed: Kayaderosseras Grant, Philipse Patent, Conojohary Patent, Mohawk Flatts Grant.)

Narrative of an Attempt Made by the French of Canada Upon the Mohaques Country. 1903. 14 pp. (Account of the important Frontenac Expedition from Canada against the Iroquois in which Schenectady was attacked in 1690. Originally prntd. in NY in 1693; one of the first books prntd. there.)

O'Callaghan, E. B. *A Brief and True Narrative of the Hostile Conduct of the Barbarous Natives Toward the Dutch Nation.* Translated by.... Albany. Munsell. 1863. 4B pp. (This is a petition sent from New Netherlands to the homeland in the 1650s detailing trouble with the Indians, and asking for military aid. According to Field, entry no. 1147, there were only 50 copies prntd.. There was no copy in O'Callaghan's library when it was sold at auction in 1882.)

Our Own Book of Every Day Wants ... Probable Presidential Candidates in 1888 ... Home Cook Book ... A Manual for Farmers ... Family Physician ... Sullivan's Indian Campaign in 1779. For Subscribers of the Weekly Gazette and Free Press. Pub. by the Gazette Co. Elmira, NY. ca 1887. 319 pp. (The pub. of this wide-ranging book managed to find 24 pages on which to tell of Sullivan's Expedition against the Indians of central and western NY. The cook book section will give you an idea of the diet of the residents of the Southern Tier in the 1880s.)

(Placid, P.) *The Contrast; or The Evils of War, And The Blessing of Christianity Exemplified in the Life and Adventures of Paul Placid.* London. (ca 1810?) 83 pp. (Young Placid was a camp follower with General Burgoyne, and was at Ticonderoga and Fort Edward. He was taken prisoner by the Mohawk Indians, and later adopted into the tribe. Not in Cole, Plum, Field, or Sabin. Ayers calls this fictitious.)

Powers, M. *Stories the Iroquois Tell Their Children.* 1917. illus. 216 pp. (Author was adopted into Snipe Clan of the Senecas, named Yeh Sen Noh Wehs, and collected folk tales from 6 Tribes of the Iroquois.)

Pratt, Peter P. *Oneida Iroquois Glass Trade. Bead Sequence 1585-1745.* 1961. 20 pp. + 4 pps. in full color. (Invaluable in the identification of beads.)

Priest, J. *A True Narrative of the Life of David Ogden Among the Indians, In the Time of the Revolution. And of the Slavery and Sufferings He Endured ... Account of His Almost Miraculous Escape After Several Years Bondage.* 1929. wrps. 38 pp. (Ogden was captured by Indians near Fort Stanwix, NY, during the Revolutionary War, and taken to Fort Niagara. He was later taken to Oswego from which he escaped. The book was originally prntd. in Lansingburgh (NY) in 1840, and has gone through several ed.)

Quinlan, J. E. *Tom Quick, the Indian Slayer: and the Pioneers of Minisink and Wawarsink.* Monticello, NY. 1851. 264 pp. (Tom was a famous hunter of Indians in the Port Jervis area during colonial days. This book was reprntd. in 1894 and 1912; and Child's *Gazetteer of Sullivan County*, 1872, has 18 pages on Quick. Several other books have also been written about him. Many years ago I heard a tale about Tom which I have not found recorded anywhere. Tom was surprised and captured by some Indians on top of a high mountain. The jubilant warriors found a nearby barrel, put Tom in it, hammered the head on, and then happily ran down the mountain to tell their friends. While Tom was trying to figure a way out a mountain lion walked by. Tom reached out through the bunghole, grabbed the lion's tail, and pulled it inside the barrel. The startled lion screeched, and ran down the hill. The barrel hit a tree, split open, and Tom escaped. Now, isn't that a TAIL worth preserving?)

Reaman, G. *The Trail of the Iroquois Indians. How the Iroquois Nation Saved Canada for the British Empire.* NY. 1967. illus. maps. index. 138 pp. (Author stimulates your thinking: "had it not been for Sir William Johnson and the Six Nations Indians during the French war in America of 1755-63 the North American continent would probably now be French-speaking.")

Redfield, T. *Report of the Claim of the Iroquois Indians Upon the State of Vermont, for Their "Hunting Ground."* Montpelier (VT). 1854. wrps. 40 pp. (This is a detailed study of the legality of the claims for compensation by the Iroquois Indians for their ancient hunting grounds in the state of VT.)

Remington, Frederic. *A Rogers Ranger in the French and Indian War. 1757-1759.* ca 1897. 5 illus. by Remington, wrps. 12 pp. (This was an article on the Champlain Valley which appeared in *Harpers Magazine* in 1897. Remington had approximately 100 copies reprntd. in pamphlet form to give away to his friends. It is considered by some to be his rarest work. He apparently did not have that many friends, as it is evident he gave the left over copies to the museum store at Fort Ticonderoga. One or more copies have been located with a rubber stamp inscription, which, as I recall, reads, "Printed for Fort Ticonderoga." Back in the late 1960s I acquired a copy at a houses sale for twenty-five cents, and soon sold it for two dollars. Not long afterwards at the NYC Book Fair I saw an expensive copy in a specially made folding case at the booth of Goodspeed's Book Shop. I said to the chap in attendance, "How come this costs so much? I just sold a copy for two bucks." He gently told me about its rarity. I mulled this interesting situation for a few days, and ended up by buying the Goodspeed copy. I also bought back the copy I had originally sold. I had sold it to a dealer in Western Americana who was glad to sell it back to me, as he said, "Sure, you can have it back. It doesn't amount to much. I was going to throw it in with some odds and ends of Remington and Russell stuff I have." These two copies sold rather quickly, one which was the final purchase to complete a Remington collection. Another copy came my way up in the Mohawk Valley a year or so later, and I have not seen a copy since.)

Remington, Frederick, *Joshua Goodenoughs Old Letter.* (This is an 11-page article with 5 illus. in *Harpers New Monthly Magazine.* Nov. 1897. Reprntd. as *A Rogers Ranger* .... in pamphlet form. See previous entry.)

Renz, L. M. *A History of the Thomas Indian School 1855-1948.* 1948. tables. bib. wrps. 77 pp. Mimeo. (This was a state institution for orphan and destitute Indian children on the Cattaraugus Reservation at Iroquois, NY. Includes a nice photograph of the class of 1947.)

Report of the Special Committee Appointed by the Assemby of 1888 to Investigate the Indian Problem of the State. Feb.

1889. index. 410 pp. (This committee of 5 men made a thorough investigation of the social, moral, and industrial conditions; land titles; and treaties; by personally inspecting the Indian reservations and taking testimonies. They list thier recommendations for the improvement of the Indians in this report. Included are the texts of a great many treaties and land grants from the 1700s to 1845.)

Rogers, Rev. Wm. *Journal of a Brigade Chaplain in the Campaign of 1779 Against the Six Nations Under Command of Maj. Gen. John Sullivan.* 1879. maps. 136 pp. (Rogers, from RI, was a Brigade Chaplain in the PA Line. There is a brief biog. sketch of Rogers, and an hist. introduction.)

Sanborn, J. W. *("O-yo-ga-weh," Clear Sky) Legends, Customs, and Social Life of the Seneca Indians of Western New York.* Gowanda, NY. 1878. 76 pp.

(Sanders, D. C.) *A History of the Indian Wars With the First Settlers of the U. S. Particularly in New England.* Montpelier, VT. 1812. 319 pp. (Although this is mainly New England, this work does have some mention of NY State Indians, and has another NY State connection which will be seen soon. It was written by the President of the University of VT, and pub. anonymously and without a preface, and was highly criticised in a magazine review. The chagrined author, or pub., suppressed the book so completely that Field's *Indian Bibliography* states, "its very existence was unknown to the most zealous collectors." It is said that this is one of the best written of Indian histories. The NY State connection is this: It was reprntd. in Rochester in 1828, by Edwin Scrantom. He did not like the chapter on "The Morals of the Indians" and omitted it from his reprnt. The work was again reprntd. in Rochester in 1893, in an ed. of only 200 copies, also omitting the chapter that had offended Scrantom. In 1953 a small pamphlet reprntd. the lost chapter, with a lengthy inntroduction by Betty Bandel, in an ed. of 99 copies. It was prntd., page by page, on a home made press, at Burlington, VT. The 3 ed. of the book, and the 1953 pamphlet, are all rare.)

Schrabisch, M. *Mountain Haunts of the Coastal Aigonquin.* 1919. wrps. 16 pp. Reprntd. in pamphlet form from the *American Anthropolgist*. (Schrabisch mostly writes on the Indian rock shelters in the Catskill and Shawangunk Mountains. While he was investigating the sites during World War I, he was arrested as a German spy and clapped into the Ulster Co. jail. He later said that it raised his dander. Heusser in his *Homes and Haunts of the Indians*, declares that Schrabisch was the first person to bring to public attention the fact that the Indians frequented sheltering ledges of rock. He excavated a number of them to prove his point.)

Seaver, J. E. *A Narrative of the Life of Mrs. Mary Jemison, Who Was Taken by the Indians in the Year 1755. And Has Continued to Reside Amongst Them to the Present Time* ...

Carefully Taken From Her Own Words. Nov. 29, 1823. Canandaigua (NY). J. D. Bemis & Co. 1824. 189 pp. (This is one of the best narratives by the first white woman to see the Ohio River. The catalog of the Braislin Library, 1927, calls this book, "Extremely rare, and for many years unknown to bibliographers and collectors." Also see Ayer 248. In 1762 she moved with the Indians to the river valley south of Rochester, and she is known in western NY as the "White Woman of the Genesee." The book has gone through a great many ed.; some of the later ones giving a bib. of the previous printings. The first ed. of 1824 is very rare.)

(Seneca Indians) *Documents and Official Reports, Illustrating the Cases Which Led to the Revolution in the Government of the Seneca Indians, in the Year 1848, and to the Recognition of Their Representative Republican Constitution, By the Authorities of the U. S. and of the State of New York.* Baltimore. 1857. wrps. 92 pp. (In the early 1800s some Seneca Chiefs signed over to the Ogden Land Co. all of their lands in the state of NY. Other Senecas, concerned over the loss of those lands, formed a new government called the Republic of the Seneca Nation. This is a very detailed study of this revolution, and the recognition of the Republic by the federal and state governments: problems, letters, eloquent speeches, reports, memorial.)

(Senecas) *The Case of the Seneca Indians in the State of New York Illustrated by Facts.* Phil. 1840. 256 pp. Plus: *A Further Illustration of the Case of the Senecas Indians ... in a Review of a Pamphlet Entitled "An Appeal to the Christian Community, &c. by Nathaniel T. Strong, a Chief of the Seneca Tribe."* Prntd. by direction of ... Yearly Meeting of Friends. Phil. 1841. wrps. 84 pp. (These 2 works provide a great deal of information on the Seneca Indian land dealings in western NY, mainly with the famous Ogden Land Co. Included are copies of documents and letters and a census.)

Shea, J. G. *A French-Onondaga Dictionary, From a Manuscript of the 17th. Century.* NY. Prntd. by Munsell and Rowland, Albany. 103 pp. 1860. lmtd. to 160 copies. (Apparently the work of one of the Jesuit Fathers who was a missionary to the Indians of NY in the 1600s, the original mss. was found in the famous Mazarin Library in Paris.)

Simms, J. R. *Trappers of New York, or a Biography of Nicholas Stoner and Nathaniel Foster; Together With Anecdotes of Other Celebrated Hunters, and Some Account of Sir William Johnson, and His Style of Living.* Albany. Munsell. 1850. illus. 287 pp. (Several ed. have been prntd. by Munsell, and others. In 1871 a notable printing was issued by Munsell: a large tinted paper ed. of 297 pp. with an index, and extra ports. and plates. Lmtd. to 50 copies.)

Snyder, C. M. (ed.) *Red and White on the New York Frontier. A Struggle for Survival. Insights From the Papers of Erastus Granger, Indian Agent, 1807-1819.* 1978. map. illus.

96 pp. (During this time the Indians of NY State were struggling with the impact of advancing settlement, and the pressure for removal to the west. Erastus Granger, an early postmaster at Buffalo, was the U. S. Agent for the Indian reservations in NY State in the early 1800s.)

Stephens, A. "Maleska". *The Ladies' Companion*. A Monthly Magazine. NY. Vol. X. Nov. 1838-Apr. 1839. bound vol. (This is a famous tale, set in the Catskill Mountains, of the marriage of an Indian princess to a white man. "Maleska" appears in 3 installments in this vol. It is its first printing. It was reprntd. in an expanded version in 1860 by Beadle & Co. of NY, as the very first of its famous dime novel series. Many collectors seem to be unaware that it was first prntd. in the *Ladies' Companion* magazine.)

Stockton, E. L. Jr. *The Influence of the Moravians Upon the Leather-Stocking Tales*. Transactions of the Moravian Hist. Soc. 1964. bib. wrps. 191 pp. (Discusses the Moravian influence upon the writings of James Fennimore Cooper: Cooper's Moravian Indians, the Moravian Doctrine and Cooper's use of religion, Moravian principles in Cooper's social criticism.)

Tooker, W. W. *Some Indian Fishing Stations Upon Long Island. With Historical and Ethnological notes*. 1901. 62 pp. Lmtd. to 250 copies.

Trelease, A. W. *Indian Affairs in Colonial New York: The 17th. Century*. 1960. illus. maps. bib. index. 379 pp.

Tschoop: The Converted Indian Chief. American Sunday School Union. Phil. 1842. wrps. 36 pp. (Tschoop was the greatest drunkard among the Indians at Shekomeko in eastern Dutchess Co. He was converted under the teaching of the Moravian missionaries there in the 1740s, and became a distinguished teacher.)

(Voegelin, Lilly, &c.) *Walam Olum or Red Score. The Migration Legend of the Lenni Lenape or Delaware Indians. A New Translation, Interpreted by Linguistic, Historical, Archaeological, Ethnological, and Physical Anthropological Studies*. Indianapolis. Indiana Hist. Soc. 1954. map. bib. index. 379 pp. (This is the most important work on this famous chronicle of the Delaware Indians, which relates the tribal story from the Creation through the migration from Asia into North America and eastward across the continent. The *Walum Olum* was studied for 20 years before this book was pub. The book is very scarce, and seldom comes on the market. A dealer in Indiana did acquire some copies, but he let them out very sparingly.)

Vrooman, J. J. *Forts and Firesides of the Mohawk Country. Stories and Pictures of Landmarks of the Pre-Revolutionary War Period....* 1951 ed. map. illus. index. bib. (This book, which has much on Indian affairs, and has gone through a number of ed., is required reading for Mohawk Valley enthusiasts. It also has the distinction of being a great help to me on one occasion. I had driven about 150 miles to look at a collection of religious books, which at that time I was successfully buying and selling. When I checked through some of the books I found that the owner had been a serious theological student and had heavily underlined many of them. I thanked the owner for letting me look at the library, told him I could not sell them because of the underlining, and started for the door. As I went through the living room I saw a copy of the Vrooman book almost hidden on the lower shelf of a two-tiered coffee table, pointed to it and said, "I could use that book." My genial host said, "I can't sell that book. It belongs to a lady down the road. I borrowed it to read. By the way, she is settling an estate there, you might want to stop and see her. You can return the book for me, too." I did just that. I stated my mission of returning the book, and said I understood she was settling an estate. She invited me in, and I saw that the wall was lined with an excellent collection of NY State books. When I evinced an interest in purchasing them she said, "I have to get rid of these things but I can't sell them yet. Wait a minute, let me call the lawyer." She called the lawyer, he gave his permission, and I acquired enough good books to make my long trip worth while.)

(Wright, A.) *Gaa Nah Shoh Ne Oe O Waah Sa O Nyoh Gwah Na Wen Ni Yuh. Ho Nont Gah Deh Ho Di Ya Donyoh. Do Syo Wa* (Seneca Mission Press.) 1843. 136 pp. (A Seneca Indian hymn book, words only, compiled by Asher Wright who was a missionary on the Buffalo and Cattaraugus reservations from 1831 to 1875. The preface, in English, briefly explains Wright's method of writing Seneca, and the index is also in English. The rest of the book is entirely in Seneca.)

Yawger, R. N. *The Indian and the Pioneer, an Historical Study.* Syracuse. 2 vols. 1893. illus. maps. (A valuable study of the Six Nations: home life, fasts, feasts, oratory, Jesuit missions, pioneer life.)

JEFFERSON COUNTY

JEFFERSON COUNTY
Anon. *Centennial Historical Souvenir of Jefferson Co.* Jefferson Co. National Bank. (1916) 49 pp.

Clarke, T. *Emigres in the Wilderness.* 1941. 232 pp.

Coughlin, J. (comp) *Jefferson Co. Centennial 1905.* Watertown 1905. illus. 440 pp.

(Durant & Pierce) *History of Jefferson Co.* Phil. 1878. illus. map. 593 pp.

Emerson, E. *Our County & Its People.* Boston. 1898. illus. map. 1250 pp.

Gould, E. *Jefferson Co. Sesquicentennial Progress & Historical Almanac. 1805-1955.* wrps. 40 pp.

Haddock, J. *Growth of a Century as Illus. in the History of Jefferson Co. 1793-1894.* Phil. 1894.
2nd. ed. Albany 1895. illus. maps. 842 pp. (An updating of the work by Hough. See also Hough, F. below.)

Horton, W. (ed.) *Geographical Gazetteer of Jefferson Co. 1684-1890.* Syracuse 1890. illus. map. 2 vols.

Hough, F. *History of Jefferson Co.* Albany 1854. illus. map. 601 pp. Reprntd. 1976.

Landon, H. *An Elementary History*

of Northern New York. Watertown. 1932. wrps. illus. 76 pp.
Landon, H. The North Country. Jefferson, St. Lawrence, Oswego, Lewis, & Franklin Cos. Indianapolis. 1932. illus. map. 3 vols.
Lansing, R. Jefferson Co. Prior to 1797. 1905. wrps. 74 pp. 554
Oakes, R. Genealogical & Family History - Phenomenal Growth. NY 1905. illus. 2 vols.

ALEXANDRIA BAY, Jefferson Co.
Anon. Alexandria Bay. ca 1905. 32 pp. mss. in JCHS.

ANTWERP, Jefferson Co.
Anon. Antwerp, the First 100 Years 1853-1953. illus. advts. wrps. 80 pp.
Anon. Antwerp. ca 1905. 8 pp. typed mss. in JCHS.

BROWNVILLE, Jefferson Co.
Anon. Brownville's Sesquicentennial. War of 1812. August 11, 1962. illus. advts. 26 pp. (Very brief hist. of early Brownville.)
Field, B. Address on Early History of Brownville. June 10, 1928. 5 pp. typed mss. in WPL.
Massey, F. Historical Sketch of Town of Brownville 1805-1905. n.d. mimeo. 15 pp.

BURRVILLE, Jefferson Co.
Tolman, W. Burrville. ca 1905. 6 pp. typed mss. in JCHS.

CAPE VINCENT, Jefferson Co.
Casler, N. Cape Vincent & Its History. Watertown. 1906. illus. 240 pp.
Pratt, E. An Historical Sketch of Town of Cape Vincent. Cape Vincent. 1876. 48 pp.

CARTHAGE, Jefferson Co.
Anon. Carthage & Black River Valley - A History. Centennial Celebration May 24-26, 1941. illus. advts. 27 pp.
Brownell, C. They Called Me Chuckie. 1943. illus. 208 pp. (Life in the 1880-1900 era.)
Welsh, W. A. Brief Historical Sketch of Carthage Based on Mss. of Floyd J. Rich. Carthage May 1941. illus. wrps. 24 pp. (prntd. on bleached toweling, kraft paper covers) 2nd. printing. 1948. 3rd. printing. 1955.

CHAMPION, Jefferson Co.
Hewitt, G. Champion. ca 1905. 26 pp. typed mss. in JCHS.
Wiley, S. Ten Decades of Town of Champion ... 1776-1876. 1978. pub. by author. 11 pp.

CLAYTON, Jefferson Co.
Garand, P. Historical Survey of Village of Clayton. Clayton. 1902. illus. 216 pp.

DEPAUVILLE, Jefferson Co.
Gillet, W. Depauville. ca 1905. 14 pp. typed mss. in JCHS.

DEXTER, Jefferson Co.
Evans, M. Dexter 1855-1955. ca 1955. illus. map. advts. wrps. 40 pp.

GRENELL ISLAND, Jefferson Co.
Pratt & Mann. The Story of Grenell. Watertown. 1946. illus. map. 108 pp.

HENDERSON, Jefferson Co.
Kruger, H. (ed) A History of Henderson 1800-1950. 7th Grade Social Studies. Nov. 1, 1950. illus. map. mimeo. 13 pp.
Robinson, T. Stories of Andrustown. 1917. 23 pp.

LORRAINE, Jefferson Co.
Anon. Lorraine. ca 1905. 5 pp. typed mss. in JCHS.
Lyman, H. Memories of an Old

Homestead, Oswego. 1900. illus. 181 pp.

LYME, Jefferson Co.
Knapp, H. & C. *Lyme.* ca 1905. 51 pp. typed mss. in JCHS.

PAMELIA, Jefferson Co.
Fulton, E. *Pamelia.* ca 1905. 10 pp. mss. in JCHS.

PENET SQUARE, Jefferson Co.
Near, I. *The History of Penet Square. And Life, Character & Operations of Peter Penet ...* Hornell. 1906. 15 pp.

PHILADELPHIA, Jefferson Co.
LaRue, J. *Philadelphia.* ca 1905. 9 pp. mss. in JCHS.

RODMAN, Jefferson Co.
Heath, H. *Rodman.* ca 1905. 18 pp. typed mss. in JCHS.

SACKETS HARBOR, Jeff. Co.
Anon. *Historical Facts Regarding Sackets Harbor & Madison Barracks With Sidelights on the War of 1812.* Watertown. 1917. wrps. 40 pp.
Heiner, G. *From Saints to Red Legs.* Watertown. 1938. illus. 80 pp.
Stoodley, R. *History of Sackets Harbor Museum & Madison Barracks.* Sackets Harbor. ca 1936.
2nd. ed. Watertown. 1946. illus. 16 pp.

THERESA, Jefferson Co.
Fayel, J. *Theresa.* ca 1905. 21 pp. mss. in JCHS.

THOUSAND ISLANDS, Jeff. Co.
Anon. *Dark Island, Corn Island, Marsh Island, Ice Island.* ca 1920. about 25 pp. (Written for Dark Island owner, Miss M. Bourne, heir to Singer Sewing Machine fortune. Leather bound on special double folded hand-made paper. Lmtd. to 50 copies.)
Anon. *The 1000 Islands of the St. Lawrence River from Kingston & Cape Vincent to Morristown & Brockville, with Their Recorded History.* Alexandria Bay. 1895. illus. map. 416 pp.
Coughlin, R. *St. Lawrence River & 1000 Islands. History & Legend.* Watertown. ca 1940. map. wrps. 63 pp.
Hough, F. *The 1000 Islands.* Syracuse. 1880. maps.
Johnston, H. *The 1000 Islands With Des. of Scenery & Hist. Quotations of Events.* Boston. (1937.) illus. maps. 142 pp.
White, J. *Place Names in the 1000 Islands.* Ottawa, Canada. 1910. wrps. 7 pp.

WATERTOWN, Jefferson Co.
Anon. *Watertown and Its Environs Past and Present.* Social Studies Dept. Watertown Junior-High School. 1940. wrps. 71 pp.
Fitch, J. (comp.) *A Short Account of The Settlement of Watertown.* Watertown. 1840. 17 pp. typed copy at WPAL.
Landon, J. *150 Years of Watertown.* Watertown. 1950. illus. wrps. 71 pp.
Monroe, J. *Through Eleven Decades of History.* Watertown 1800-1912. Watertown. 1912. illus. 261 pp.
(Skinner, C.) *Watertown. History of Its Settlement & Progress.* Watertown. 1876. illus. maps. advts. 128 pp. (Much information on local businesses, as well as brief data on other towns in the co. "The rigor of the winter months ... is as beneficial ... as the delightful, semi-tropical summer season.")

WILNA, Jefferson Co.
Merrill, F. *Wilna.* ca 1905. 15 pp. typed mss. in JCHS.

KINGS COUNTY

KINGS COUNTY
Bergen, T. *Register of the Early Settlers of Kings Co.* NY. 1881. 452 pp.
Custer, E. (comp.) *A Synoptical History of the Towns of Kings Co. From 1525 to Modern Times.* NY. 1911. 36 pp.
Stiles, H. (ed.) *The Civil & Political History of the County of Kings & The City of Brooklyn ... 1683-1884.* NY (1884) illus. map. 2 vols.

BAY RIDGE, Kings Co.
Anon. *The Community in Which You Live. Highlights & Sidelights of the Story of Bay Ridge.* 1950. wrps. 50 pp.
Glen, G. *Old Bay Ridge.* Brooklyn. 1962. illus. maps. wrps. 14 pp.

BROOKLYN, Kings Co.
Armbruster, E. *The Eastern District of Brooklyn.* NY. 1912. illus. map. index. 205 pp.
--- *Brooklyn's Eastern District.* Brooklyn 1942. illus. maps. 400 pp.
--- *The Olympia Settlement in Early Brooklyn.* NY. 1929. 35 pp.
--- *Bruijkleen Colonie (Borough of Brooklyn) 1638-1918.* NY. ca 1918. pub. by author, map. wrps. 12 pp. lmtd. to 200 copies.
Bailey, J. *Historical Sketch of City of Brooklyn & Its Surrounding Neighborhood: Williamsburg, Bushwick, Flatbush, Flatlands, New Utrecht, & Gravesend.* Brooklyn. 1840. pub. by author. 72 pp.
Callender, J. *Yesterdays on Brooklyn Heights.* 1927. illus. 296 pp.
Furman, G. *Notes, Geographical & Historical Relating to the Town of Brooklyn in Kings Co.* 1824. 116 pp. Reprntd. 1865. 607 Reprntd. 1968.
Hazleton, H. *The Boroughs of Brooklyn & Queens, and Counties of Nassau & Suffolk 1609-1924.* NY 1925. illus. 7 vols. (Vol. 7 is biog., and is dated 1925). (Vol. 5 is rare, and lacking in many sets.
Hoffman, J. *The Bay Ridge Chronicles.* 1977. illus. 123 pp.
Howard, H. (ed) *The Eagle & Brooklyn: The Record of the Progress of the Brooklyn Daily Eagle ... With the History of the City of Brooklyn.* Brooklyn. 1893. nearly 1300 illus.
Lomas & Peace. *The Wealthy Men & Women of Brooklyn & Williamsburgh ... With Estimated Possessions of 10,000 & Upward.* Brooklyn. 1847. wrps. 50 pp. (alphabetically arranged with some biog. data)
Ment, D. *The Shaping of a City. A Brief History of Brooklyn.* 1979. illus. map. bib. 103 pp.
Ostrander, S. *History of the City of Brooklyn & Kings Co.* (ed. by A. Black) Brooklyn. 1894. lmtd. 500 copies. 2 vols.
Stiles, H. *A History of the City of Brooklyn, Including the Old Town & Village of Brooklyn, the Town of Bushwick, & Village & City of Williamsburgh.* Brooklyn. 1867-1870. illus. maps. 3 vols.
Van Wyck, F. *Keskachauge, or the First White Settlement on Long Island.* NY. 1924. maps, illus., index. Errata sheet and pasted in slip. 778 pp. (Said to have been suppressed.)
Weld, R. *Brooklyn Village 1816-1834.* NY 1938. illus. maps. 362 pp.

BUSHWICK, Kings Co.
Stiles & Stearns. *History of the Town of Bushwick, & of Town, Village, & City of Williamsburgh.* Brooklyn. 1884. wrps. illus. folio. 37 pp. lmtd. to 40 copies. (Reprntd. from Stiles *History of Kings Co.*)

CONEY ISLAND, Kings Co.
Armbruster, E. *Coney Island.* NY 1924. lmtd. ed. 14 pp.
McCullough, E. *Good Old Coney Island.* NY. 1957. illus. 344 pp.
Pilat & Ranson. *Sodom by the Sea. An Affectionate History of Coney Island.* 1941. illus. maps. 334 pp.

FLATBUSH, Kings Co.
Fisher, E. *Flatbush Past & Present.* Brooklyn. 1901. illus. 95 pp.
Snyder, J. *Tales of Old Flatbush.* 1945. illus. 231 pp.
Strong, R. *History of Town of Flatbush.* Brooklyn 1884. wrps. 46 pp. lmtd. to 50 copies. (Reprntd. from Stiles *History of Kings Co.*)
Strong, T. *History of Town of Flatbush.* NY. 1842. map. illus. 178 pp.
Another ed: 1908. illus. map. 188 pp.
Vanderbilt, G. *Social History of Flatbush & Manners & Customs of Dutch Settlers in Kings Co.* 1881. 351 pp.

FLATLANDS, Kings Co.
DuBois, A. *History of Town of Flatlands.* Brooklyn. 1884. lmtd. to 30 copies. Reprntd. from Stiles *Hist. of Kings Co.*)

GREATER RIDGEWOOD, Kings Co.
Schubel, G. *Illus. History of Greater Ridgewood.* 1913. Vol. 1 (all pub.) 276 pp.

GREENPOINT, Kings Co.
Felter, W. *Historic Greenpoint, A Brief Account of Beginning & Development of the Northerly Section of Boro of Brooklyn, City of NY, Locally Known as Green Point.* (Brooklyn. 1918) illus. 61 pp.
Harding, V. (comp) *Memorable Green Point.* 1944. 69 pp.

MANHATTAN BEACH, Kings Co.
Anon. *The Story of Manhattan Beach. A Practical & Picturesque Delineation of Its History, Development, & Attractions, Also an Account of Coney Island.* NY. 1879. 61 pp.

NEW LOTS, Kings Co.
Hamilton, W. *History of Town of New Lots.* Brooklyn. 1884. wrps. 22 pp. Lmtd. to 30 copies. (Reprntd. from Stiles *History of Kings Co.*)
Landesman, A. *A History of New Lots, Boooklyn to 1887: Including the Villages of East New York, Cypress Hills and Brownsville.* 1977. 268 pp.

NEW UTRECHT, Kings Co.
Anon. *New Utrecht.* Pub. by *Brooklyn Eagle.* n.d. 48 pp.
Bangs, R. *Reminiscences of Old New Utrecht & Gowanus.* Brooklyn. (1912.) 194 pp.
Bergen, T. *History of Town of New Utrecht.* Brooklyn. 1884. wrps. lmtd. 30 copies.

SEA GATE, Kings Co.
Williams, J. *Place Names.* Brooklyn 1965. Brooklyn College thesis on microfilm in LIHS.

WILLIAMSBURG, Kings Co.
Jewell, I. *Historic Williamsburg.* 1926. pvtly. prntd. illus. maps. 44 pp.

Reynolds, S. *History of Williamsburg.* 1852. 137 pp. (reprntd. from Reynolds *Williamsburg City Directory.* 1852)

LEWIS COUNTY

LEWIS COUNTY

Bowen, G. (ed.) *History of Lewis Co. 1880-1965.* Boonville. 1970. illus. map. 563 pp. (This is a continuation of F. Hough's *History of Lewis Co.*, 1883, at the suggestion of his granddaughter when she was County Historian.)

Drew, H. *Tales From Little Lewis* Lyons Falls. 1961. illus. wrps. 56 pp.

Hough, F. *History of Lewis Co.* Albany. 1860. illus. maps. 319 pp. 1325 copies prntd. (There were also 25 copies prntd. on fine paper for private distribution.)

--- *History of Lewis Co.* 1883. illus. 643 pp.

--- *Lewis County Remarks.* Sept. 12, 1872. Sheet folded in envelope in BHS.

BEAVER FALLS, Lewis Co.

Van Arnam, L. *Beaver Falls Cavalcade 1794-1979.* 1979. pub. by author. 222 pp.

CASTORLAND, Lewis Co.

Stephens, W. *Notes of the Voyage ... Towards "Castorland". 1794-1795.* Lowville. Dec. 1, 1868. wrps. lmtd. to 65 copies. 8 pp. (Summary of lectures given by Dr. Franklin B. Hough on the Castorland Settlement. Reprntd. with additions from the *Lewis Co. Democrat.*)

HIGHMARKET, Lewis Co.

Conway, M. *Highmarket "As You Were" - Two Hundred Years of Tug Hill.* 1977. 153 pp. Reprntd. 1978.

LOWVILLE, Lewis Co.

Anon. *Centennial History of Village Lowville.* By the Historical Committee. (1954) map. 100 pp.

Breen, W. *Lowville, Yesterday, Today & Tomorrow. History & Directory of Both Town & Village.* Lowville. 1902. illus. 224 pp.

LYONS FALLS, Lewis Co.

Fisher, C. *History of Lyons Falls.* Boonville. 1918. illus. wrps. 30 pp.

PORT LEYDEN, Lewis Co.

Wilcox, A. *Port Leyden and Vicinity.* 1977. illus. 91 pp.

WATSON, Lewis Co.

(Stephens, W.) *Historical Notes of the Settlement on No. 4, Brown's Tract, in Watson, Lewis Co. With Notices of the Early Settlers.* Utica. 1864. wrps. lmtd. 300 copies 27 pp. (Reprntd. in Donaldson's *History of the Adirondacks.* Approx 100 copies were illus. with photo of Orrin Fenton, early resort owner at No. 4. Copy at SLA has the photo.)

LIVINGSTON COUNTY

LIVINGSTON COUNTY

Anon. *Biog. Reviews of Leading Citizens of Livingston & Madison Cos.* Boston. 1895. illus. 2 vols.

Ashton, J. *Open-Country Holdings in Northern Livingston Co.* Masters' Thesis, Cornell U. 1951.

Doty, L. L. *History of Livingston Co.* Albany. 1867. 3 pp.

Doty, L. L. *History of Livingston Co.* Geneseo. 1876. illus. 685 pp.

Doty, L. R. *History of Livingston Co.* Jackson, MI. 1905. illus.

map. 1016 pp. (This hist. was written by the son of L. L. Doty, who wrote *A History of Livingston Co.*, 1867.)
Smith & Cale. *History of Livingston Co.* Syracuse. 1881. illus. 490 pp.

AVON, Livingston Co.
Brooks, C. *The Story of Avon.* Avon 1931. 27 pp.
Johnson (Ed) *The Pines Letters (1953-1954).* illus. 112 pp. (Includes material on the Mormons. Apparently a very lmtd. ed.)
Preston, M. *Avon, Heart of the Genesee Country.* Avon. 1958. illus. map. wrps. 80 pp.

CALEDONIA, Livingston Co.
Leathersich, D. *Old Days in Caledonia Beginning in 1838.* Caledonia 1906. illus. wrps. 18 pp. (Reminiscences beginning in 1838. Reprntd. from *Caledonia, Era of 1906*)
MacLaren, W. *Early History of Caledonia.* ca 1929. 67 pp. typed mss. in RPL.

CONESUS, Livingston Co.
Boyd, W. *History of Town of Conesus.* Conesus 1887. illus. 177 pp. (Author was a job printer and a farmer, and prntd. this work on his own press.) Reprntd. 1977 with index.

CROCKETT'S CORNERS, Livingston Co.
Hitchcock, S. *The Story of Crockett's Corners.* Livonia 1939. 28 pp.

DANSVILLE, Livingston Co.
Anon. *Dansville Centennial Brochure.* 1946.
Bunnell, A. (ed.) Quick, F. (comp) *Dansville 1789-1902. Hist., Biog., Descriptive.* 1902. illus. map. 267 pp.

Bunnell, A. (ed.) & Quick, F. (comp.) *Dansville (NY) Historical, Biographical, Descriptive. 1789-1902.* Dansville, 1902. illus. map. 540 pp. (This is an expanded ed. of the preceding entry, pub. in the same year. No doubt you can rely upon the information in this work, as the honest ed. states, "I would not conceal the fact that Dansville has had its seamy side ...".)
Clark, J. *Miniature of Danville Village.* Dansville. 1844. 72 pp.
DeLong, H. *Boyhood Reminiscences 1855-1865.* Dansville. 1913. illus. 67 pp.
Sedgwick, H. *Historical Sketch of Dansville.* Dansville. 1882. wrps. 35 pp.

GENESEO, Livingston Co.
Anon. *Geneseo's Centennial 1790-1890.* wrps. 24 pp. (reprntd. from *Livingston Republican* Sept. 18, 1890)
Folsom, G. *Reminiscences of Geneseo & the Genesee Valley.* Geneseo. 1868. wrps. 35 pp.
Ward, F. *"Excelsior" Geneseo.* 1848-1878. wrps. 24 pp.
Ward, F. *Geneseo, Livingston Co., N.Y. 1848-1888, by ... a Forty Years Resident.* Geneseo. 1889. wrps. 29 pp.
---*Village Memories of 20 Years, or Geneseo Between 1848 & 1869.* Geneseo. 1869. 26 pp.

HEMLOCK LAKE, Livingston Co.
Waite, D. *O-Neh-Da Te-Car-Ne-O-Di: or Up and Down the Hemlock.* Canadice. 1883. wrps. 112 pp.

MT. MORRIS, Livingston Co.
Chichester, D. *The Past of Mt. Morris.* Geneseo 1855. wrps. 21 pp.

Parsons & Rockfellow (comps) *Centennial Celebration Mt. Morris. Also Letters of Reminiscences, Biographical Sketches, Directories of Churches.* 1794-1894. Mt. Morris. 1894. illus. 208 pp.

NUNDA, Livingston Co.
Anon. *Nundarama: Sesquicentennial Souvenir 1808-1958.*
Hand, H. (ed) *Centennial History of Town of Nunda 1808-1908.* Rochester. 1908. illus. map. 636 pp.
(Hand, H.) *The Keskequa Trail, by the Bard of the Keskequa Valley.* Nunda. 1908. illus. 34 pp.

SPRINGWATER, Livingston Co.
Wallbridge, O. *Early History of Springwater.* Springwater. 1887. wrps. 91 pp.
Reprntd. with index in 1966. 99 pp.

YORK, Livingston Co.
Root, M. *History of Town of York.* Caledonia. 1940. illus. 205 pp.

LONG ISLAND

LONG ISLAND
Boyton, P. *A Heroic Priest. Memoir of Joseph Francis Brophy, DD. Apostle of Coney Island.* 1910. illus. 134 pp. (A biog. of a famous Coney Island priest in the early 1900s, who worked under trying circumstances and once had to use an ice box for an altar.)
--- *Brentwood Park, L.I., and Its Relation to New York.* Brentwood Realty Co. Owners. ca early 1920s. Illus. Maps. wrps. 24 pp. (Promotional pub. to lure residents from NYC. It warns them not to move westward, "New Jersey is too remote. It is almost foreign, for it is outside of ... NY.")

Cotter, O. *See What You Drink. Read, and Drink No More. Adulterations of Liquors, with Descriptions of the Poisons Used in Their Manufacture, by ... a Reformed Liquor Dealer.* Brooklyn, NY. 1874. Has a plate with 6 illus. of deteriorated stomach interiors. 45 pp. (As an example of adulteration of liquor, a Prof. Lee of NYC said, "A cheap Maderia is made here by extracting the oils from common whiskey, and by passing it through carbon.")
Davis, G. *The South Side Sportsmen's Club of Long Island.* NY. 1909. map. illus. wrps. pvtly. prntd. Lmtd. to 105 copies.
Edwards & Rattray. *"Whale Off!" The Story of American Shore Whaling.* 1932. 21 Reproductions from photographs and a map. Bib. of nautical and local terms used. 285 pp. (The hist. of small-boat whaling off the Long Island shore, 1640-1918.)
Field, F. *The Green House as a Winter Garden, a Manual. With a List of Suitable Plants and Their Mode of Culture. With a Preface by W. C. Bryant.* NY. 1869. Diagrams. (Interestingly, this book was written at the suggestion of William Cullen Bryant, the noted poet and NYC ed., who had a green-house at his Long Island home "under the care of one who needed just such a plain and succinct hand-book of directions." The following comment has nothing to do with books, but I have often wondered how Bryant, who wrote such beautiful nature poetry, could have moved from his beloved New England to work in NYC. I recall the first time I visited Plymouth, Ver-

mont, the home village of President Calvin Coolidge. The first thought that came to my mind as I stepped out of the car and saw the pastoral beauty of that lovely setting was, "How in the world could Coolidge leave here and go to Washington?")

Ford, P. L. *The Honorable Peter Stirling, and What People Thought of Him.* NY. Henry Holt & Co. 1894. 417 pp. (An important novel which the DAB says is "a study of political life based partly on observations made during an unsuccessful attempt to enter politics in the first ward in Brooklyn." The first state of the first ed. has "Sterling" for "Stirling" on the front cover.)

Fullerton, E. *The Lure of the Land. A Call to Long Island.* 1906. Issued by the Long Island Railroad Co. illus. map. 160 pp. (Attempt by the LIRR to lure people to move to Long Island so they would have to use the RR to go back to work in NYC. The RR Co. had an experimental market-garden, and a dairy plot, in a scrub oak section on the island.)

Hine, C. G. *The Log of the Totem.* pvtly. prntd. 1913. illus. with mounted photos. wrps. (Account of yacht trip from Long Island Sound to Staten Island. This must have been a very lmtd. ed. as the author hoped to sell enough copies to buy his wife a pair of shoes. In 1907 the same author wrote a 104 pp. hist. of Cedar Neck on Martha's Vineyard of which hopefully only a few copies were printed: "This edition is limited to such copies as can be given away. Each and every copy being numbered 1.")

Hummel, C. F. *With Hammer in Hand. The Dominy Craftsmen of East Hampton, New York.* 1968. illus. bib. index. 424 pp. (The hist. of the famous Dominy family which made clocks and furniture between 1760 and 1840. A meticulous work.)

Jagger, W. *To The People of Suffolk Co. (New York).* prntd. for the author. June 1837. 4 pp. pamphlet. (Jagger, of the Riverhead area, reports he has distributed 10,000 temperance tracts in the co. He also states that he did his best to defeat Martin Van Buren in the election, and reports that the opposition party called him "desperate and dishonorable.")

Knapp, E. *We Knapps Thought It Was Nice.* 1940. illus. 211 pp. pvtly. prntd. Lmtd. to 200 copies. (A very interesting account of life on the south shore of Long Island in the last half of the 1800s: horses, proficiency with beanshooters, lighting, the first automobile, much on bird hunting, and much on horse racing. Apparently a genteel life style.)

Larremore, T. & A. *The Marion Press. A survey and a Check List Published by the Queens Borough Public Library.* 1943. illus. index. 271 pp. Lmtd. to 228 copies. (The Marion Press was started by Frank E. Hopkins in 1896 in his attic in Jamaica, L.I. Lehmann-Haupt in his *The Book in America* says the Press "became a forerunner of the many private presses that sprang up in America in the early 1900s ...." The text of this book was hand-set, and most of it was printed on the 'Marion' Washington hand-press, and it was hand bound.)

--- The Quality of the "Wild Lands" of Long Island Examined, and Detailed Evidences Given of Their Value ... With as Reasonable Conjecture Why They Have Not Been Improved. NY. 1860. wrps. 16 pp. (An attempt to promote market gardening along the new Long Island railroad.)

Shaw, Osborn. History of Storms and Gales on Long Island. 1939. 27 pp. Lmtd. to 500 copies. (Includes a dramatic account of the famous Hurricane of 1938 by Dorothy Quick, an eye-witness.)

Syrett, H. C. The City of Brooklyn, 1865-1898. A Political History. 1944. map. bib. index. 293 pp. ("Municipal government from 1865 to 1900 is a neglected phase of American history ... it is the story of countless blunders, lack of planning, and widespread corruption.")

Underhill, D. & F. The Underhill Burying Ground. Locust Valley, Long Island, New York, Deeded by the Matinecock Indians Feb. 20, 1667. NY. 1926. map. illus. diagram. 79 pp. lmtd. to 500 copies. (Hist. data and other information on the 238 grave sites in the cemetery.)

Van Wyck, F. Long Island Colonial Patents. Boston. 1935. illus. 175 pp. Lmtd. to 100 copies. (A transcript of the Patents of Easthampton, Flatlands, Hempstead, Smithtown, Southhold; and of 2 Manhattan patents. There is also some data on fisheries.)

MADISON COUNTY

MADISON COUNTY
Anon. Biog. Review ... Leading Citizens of Madison Co. Boston. 1894. illus. 700 pp.

Hammond, L. Hist. Madison Co. Syracuse. 1872. illus. 775 pp.

Lehman, K. (ed.) Madison Co. Today. Oneida Castle. 1943. illus. 216 pp.

Smith, J. (ed.) Our County & Its People. Boston. 1899. illus. maps. 2 vols.

BROOKFIELD, Madison Co.
Tanney, D. Brookfield. Gateway to Madison Co. 1971. Brookfield. pamphlet.

Tanney, D. (Ed.) Remembered Years. 1977. 263 pp.

CANASTOTA, Madison Co.
Adams, J. et al Onions, Tomahawks, & Spoons. Interesting Glimpses Into Local History of Canastota, Oneida, Sherill, Vernon, & the Surrounding Region. 1960. wrps. 112 pp.

CAZENOVIA, Madison Co.
Atwell, C. Cazenovia Past & Present. A Descriptive & Historical Record. (Orlando, Fla.) 1928. illus. 64 pp.

Grills, R. Cazenovia. The Story of an Upland Community. 1977. illus. map. 119 pp.

Monroe, J. Cazenovia. Looking Backward Through 118 Years. 1911. illus. 102 pp.

Webber, K. Nature's Masterpiece. Cazenovia. ca 1949. illus. wrps. unpaged.

DERUYTER, Madison Co.
Welch, E. "Grips" De Ruyter & Vicinity. DeRuyter. 1900. illus. 64 pp.

Wood, W. History of DeRuyter & Vicinity. 1964. illus. wrps. 152 pp.

EATON, Madison Co.
Anon. Eaton in the Bicentennial Year. 1977 illus. map.

McCartan, C. *Hist Geography of Eaton, NY.* 1977. 24 pp. type mss. at Colgate Univ.

EATONBROOK VALLEY, Madison Co.
Isbell, L. *History & Pictures of West Eaton, Pierceville, Eaton.* Hamilton. 1970. wrps. illus. maps. 30 pp.

ERIEVILLE, Madison Co.
Isbell L. *History & Pictures.* Hamilton. 1971. wrps. illus. map. 24 pp.

HAMILTON, Madison Co.
Anon. *Progressive Hamilton.* Utica. 1896. illus. wrps. 110 pp.
Anon. *This Was Hamilton in the 1860's.* Sept. 1957. wrps. 14 pp. (Reprod. of photos taken in the 1860's.)

LEBANON, Madison Co.
Dunham, M. *Lebanon. A Footprint on the Sands of Time.* 1977. pub. by author. illus. bib. 41 pp.

LENOX, Madison Co.
Smith, M. *Sketches of Old Town of Lenox and Madison County.* 1977. illus. 96 pp.

LINCOLN, Madison Co.
Case and Smith. *Town of Lincoln.* 1977. illus. map. 112 pp.

NEW WOODSTOCK, Madison Co.
Ellsworth & Richmond. *New Woodstock & Vicinity. Past & Present.* Cazenovia. 1901. illus. 141 pp.

QUAKER BASIN, Madison Co.
Breed, H. *History of Quaker Basin, Quaker Hill & the Eastern Part of the Township of DeRuyter & Muller Hill. 1800-1900.* DeRuyter. 1931.

wrps. 46 pp.

SMITHFIELD, Madison Co.
Anon. *Benefaction of Wm. Evans, Esq., to the Town of Smithfield.* Syracuse. 1858. wrps. 36 pp.

SULLIVAN, Madison Co.
Nichols, C. *Sullivan in History. Interesting People & Events, Contributing to the Development of the Township.* Chittenango. 1939. illus. maps. wrps. 95 pp.

WAMPSVILLE, Madison Co.
Russell, G. *Wampsville, Historical Sketch.* Oneida. 1909. illus. wrps. lmtd. 200 copies. 57 pp.

MAPS

An Improved Map of the Hudson River. Pub. by Daniel Lowber. Drawn and lithographed expressly for the Travellers Guide. ca early 1800s. 5 x 34 inches. (This map was issued separately in a plain red folder, and shows the area from NYC to Waterford indicating the towns and streams along the shore plus some hills with their elevations.)

Atlas of the Entire City of New York, by G. W. Bromley & Co. Civil Engineers. Pub. by G. W. Bromley and E. Robinson. 1879. folio. 41 plates. (Major and very detailed work showing: locations of public buildings, factories, property lines, fire hydrants, steam railroads, street railways, original watercourses, original farm lines, ward lines, size of water mains, monuments, piers.)

Bevan and Iron. *Historical, Descriptive, and Illustrated Atlas of the Cities, Towns, and*

Villages on the Lines of the Hudson River and New York Central Railroads With Views of Factories and Works of Principal Business Firms. NY. 1862. 2 maps. Many illus. 152 pp. (A fine work on NY State commercial interests at the beginning of the Civil War, covering the towns from NYC to Buffalo along the railroads. Many fine engravings by Waters and Son, of NYC, of factories and commercial buildings. There are also some interior views of factories, and many advts.)

Bien, J. R. *Atlas of the State of New York, From Original Surveys and Various Local Surveys.* New York. J. Bien & Co. 1895. folio. 37 maps. (This work is of great value to local and co. hist. as it shows the boundaries of the Ancient Patents, and, where applicable, the tracts and lots. On each of the maps is printed, "The land lines are shown by full black lines of different strength, showing the Patents and their subdivisions into Townships, Tracts and Lots. The names of the Patents and the numbers of the Lots are in red." Also shown are the townships, towns, hamlets, railroads, hills, roads, streams, and lakes, as they were in 1895.)

Burr, David H. *An Atlas of the State of New York. Containing a Map of the State and of the Several Counties. Projected and Drawn by a Uniform Scale From Documents Deposited in the Public Offices of the State and Other Original and Authentic Information Under Superintendance and Direction of Simeon deWitt, Surveyor General.* NY. 1829. folio. Hand-colored maps. (The GREAT atlas of NY State, with fine, detailed, and decorative maps. Complete vol. are difficult to find as many of these handsome maps have been framed for display. This work was reprntd. several times in the 1830s and 1840s, and in different formats. Some of the individual maps have been reprinted in recent years. In February, 1829, the NY State Senate issued a 3 pp. pamphlet titled: *Report From the Surveyor-General, Relative to the Publication, &c. of a Map and Atlas of this State.* This information about the first printing of the Burr *Atlas* details its size, appropriations, cost of engraving, role of the town supervisors throughout the state, and other data. I once purchased a very rare and entirely different Burr *Atlas of New York State*, pub. at NY in 1838. It had a folding map of the state. The co. maps were small with very little detail. There were a number of city maps. As far as I could gather by asking around there were only 2 other dealers who had ever seen that particular format and as they were close friends they may have seen the same copy. I bought it from a very well-known leading dealer who is still very active in the business, for $130.00, and cataloged it at $165.00 to make a quick turnover. So many orders came in for it, I knew I had made a mistake. [It did give me comfort to know that the leading dealer had made a mistake, too.] I've seen 1 other copy offered for sale since then, and it was priced at $1250.00)

Colles, Christopher. *A Survey of*

the Roads of the United States of America. (NY.) 1789. 83 maps. (This was the first American road guide. See Phillips *A List of Maps of America*, pages 867-868, for a complete list of the contents of this atlas, and for a reprnt. of the proposals for pub. this survey. The atlas includes maps of both sides of the Hudson River from NYC to Albany. At the famous Streeter sale in 1969 a copy sold for $3500.00. In 1974 I spotted a copy at Sessler's bookshop in Philadelphia which Mabel Zahn had priced at $3000.00. I knew a young chap who wanted a copy, and frequented Sessler's but had missed this one. A short while later I phoned him and said I could get him a Colles for $4000.00. He agreed, and we set a date for the exchange. I called Mabel, reserved the book, and went down with a check. She didn't know me very well, and apparently was leery of my check, as she asked for cash. I said, "Mabel, I don't carry that amount of money. It isn't safe." So she reluctantly took the check. I immediately took the book to my customer, who checked it for completeness, and then cheerfully said, "I don't have the money. You will have to wait till my father comes home. He will be here soon." When his father arrived he told him he had just bought the atlas, and how much it cost. His father put his hand in his pocket, pulled out a wad of bills, and counted out $4000.00. I re-counted the money, put it in my briefcase, and drove 2-1/2 hours straight back to my bank without stopping for anything. The price of this rare work has gone up considerably. In 1983 a wormed (i.e., eaten by book worms) copy sold at auction for $8000.00)

Colles, C. *A Survey of the Roads of the U. S. A..* 1789. Edited by W. W. Ristow. 1961. port. illus. maps. index. 227 pp. (A reprint of the earliest American road guide, with a 117 pp. section on Colles and his times.)

Haskell, D. C. (ed.) *Manhattan Maps. A Co-operative List.* 1931. NY Public LIbrary. index. wrps. 128 pp. 1994 items cataloged. (A compréhensive bib. of maps in the Library of Congress, NY Public Library, NY Hist. Soc., American Geographical Soc., and some city departments.)

List of Maps of Sewer Systems and Sewage Disposal Works. NY State Board of Health. 1898. (The State Board of Health issued folders of maps with their Annual Reports. I have had several folders of the maps from around the turn of the century. These are important maps showing, in most instances, the route of the sewer lines; location of manholes, lampholes, and flush tanks; and proposed new lines. There are also diagrams of disposal facilities. What is surprising is how many small NY State towns had sewer systems in the 1890s. [A number of towns in the highly populated area of metropolitan northeastern NJ relied on individual septic tanks until about 25 years ago.] Some of the NY state towns do not have maps of their systems, and actually do not know exactly where the lines are. Some years ago I flushed out some of these maps, made up a catalog, and sent it to the specific towns involved. I sold some to municipalties that were overjoyed to find out where their waste water was flowing. I feel safe in saying it was the one and only catalog ever issued on sewer maps.)

Map of the Hudson River, From New York to Albany, With Historical and Descriptive Notes. Pub. by P. Desobry, NYC. R. Tyrell, Printer. 10 x 29 inches, printed on one side. Not dated, but Phillip's *List of Maps of America*, gives it the date of 1833. (The map is down the middle with descriptive notes on both sides. There is a section on "Winter Travelling on the Hudson" which says that stage coaches rode on the ice; and describes how the steamboat *Commerce* pushed through the ice to Poughkeepsie and back in January 1830.)

Map of Morris Purchase or West Geneseo ... Land Purchased by the Holland Land Company ... Also a Sketch of Part of Upper Canada by Joseph and B. Ellicott. 1800. To the Holland Land Co. Their General Agents Theophilus Cazenove and Paul Busti Esquires This Map in Respectfully Inscribed by the Authors. 1804. Approximately 21 x 27 inches. (Probably the most important map of western NY when Buffalo was still known as New Amsterdam, and when land companies were luring settlers to this new frontier. Shows: boundary lines, streams, wagon roads, salt springs, a saw mill, Indian reservations, Indian villages, Indian paths. Joseph Ellicott surveyd the Holland Purchase which was over three million acres, and for many years he was the Company's agent with an office at Batavia. Even though he was a hot-tempered Quaker he was lenient with the settlers.)

A Map of Tottin and Crosfields purchase and the waters Adjacent in the State of New-York. East and West line 10 Mile North of Crown Point. Or Jessups Patent. Scale 12 Miles to an inch. 8 x 10 inches. n.d. but ca 1770s or 1780s. (One of the earliest maps of this patent, it shows the area from Plattsburgh to Albany, and Skenesboro [Whitehall] to Canada Creek: township boundaries and numbers, streams, lakes, towns, roads, forts.)

Maps and Atlases For Sale by J. B. Beers & Co., 36 Yesey Street, NY. (1880.) 16 pp. small pamphlet. (A catalog of atlases, wall maps, pocket maps, and co. maps prntd. and pub. by Beers. The last 4 pp. are lined so they can be used by the company to write letters to customers. An excerpt from one of their letters, "We have no sheets of *Warren Co. Atlas*. We usually print to make complete books and bind all." Among the 241 items listed, there are 41 NY State atlases, 10 NY State wall maps, 9 NY state pocket maps, and 6 NY State co. hist. Title and price only, no other description. Although not noted in this catalog, this company also rented odometers.)

Mathews-Northrup. *Up-To-Date Map of New York.* 1899. 21 miles to an inch. Approximately 20 x 16 inches. lightly colored. (This is a jig-saw puzzle map of the state of NY. Do you know where the following towns are: Millers Place, Bird, Volusia, Sholes, Denley, Oulcout, Long Year? You might not be able to find them on a modern road map but you can find them on this 19th. century map.) (NYC Map) A complete set of 48 wooden cartographic cubes that can be assembled in 6 different ways, to reveal 6 different 19th. century maps. Each block measures 1-3/4 inch per side, making a complete layout approximately 10 x 13 inches. There is no imprint, but ca 1860s? The 6 maps that can be made are: (1) Map of North America showing its political divisions and recent Polar discoveries. (2) Map of the U. S. West Territories (3) Co. map of Kentucky and Tennessee (4) Plan of NYC. (5) Plan of Washington (6) East and Canada.)

The New York Wilderness. Hamilton County and Adjoining Territory. 1879. Compiled by B. C. Butler. J. A. Cooper, Del. Lithographed by Weed, Parsons and Co. Albany. Folio. Linen backed. Folded into a cloth folder. (This is one of the more desireable maps of the Hamilton Co. area, showing: streams, townships, tracts, purchases, towns.)

Panorama of the Hudson River From New York to Albany. Drawn From Nature and Engraved by William Wade. NY: William Wade. Phil. William Croome. 1845. Prntd. by Burton. 12 foot long by 6 inches wide. (This is the most desireable and sought-after map of the Hudson River. It gives a view of both shorelines from the middle of the river exactly as they were seen from shipboard in 1844: many buildings, lighthouses, hills, islands, ships in the river, creek names, kilns, quarries, boat houses, locations of the Revolutionary War chains that spanned the river, and much more. It was reprinted in 1846 with the title *Wade and Croome's Panorama of the Hudson River from New York to Albany*, and contained a 32 page descriptive pamphlet plus an errata sheet; and was pub. by J. Disturnell of NY. Its popularity was so great that Disturnell issued it again in 1847, extending the map a short ways north of Albany and titling it: *Wade and Croome's Panorama of the Hudson River from New York to Waterford.* This issue contained a 38-page pamphlet. Scale 1 mile to 1 inch. Both black and white and colored copies were printed.)

Wharves, Piers, and Slips Belonging to the Corporation of the City of New York. 1868. 2 vols. Approximately 130 maps. (One vol. covers the North [or Hudson] River, and the other vol. the East River. There is data on each wharf, pier, or slip. The information varies with each plan: present value, cost of repairs, value after repairs, depth of water at low tide.)

Traveller's Guide of the Hudson River. Pub. by H. B. Kirkham, for the Prop., and For Sale on All the Steamboats and at the Principal Hotels in the U. S. Price One Shilling. ca 1850. Map. Broadside, approximately 9 x 26 inches. (Actually a map of the Hudson River from Staten Island to

Glens Falls, with descriptions of towns on both sides of the map. A printed note on the bottom margin states, "On the other side the traveller will find the principal Hotels in the U. S. ...." The other side is blank. I have only had 1 copy of this, and it appeared to have originally been in a small folder.)

Radcliff, W. *Sight-Seeing Map of the Hudson River. Points of Interest Visible from the Hudson River Boats, Trains, and Airplanes.* 1929. wrps. 20 pp. (Many points of interest are indicated from Albany to the Statue of Liberty; and there is an illus. of the proposed bridge from NYC to Fort Lee, New Jersey - now known as the George Washington Bridge.)

MARTIN VAN BUREN

--- *A Word in Season, or Review of the Political Life and Opinions of Martin VanBuren ... Dedicated to the Tippecanoe Clubs of the Union, by a Harrison Democrat.* Washington. 1840. 3rd. edition. 48 pp. pamphlet. (An anti-VanBuren publication, accusing him of double dealing, disingenuousness [see Webster]; and of being an apostate Whig, a Tory, and a traitor. A fine day can be spent in the village of Kinderhook, NY, VanBuren's home town. The federal government has done an excellent job in restoring and furnishing "Lindenwald", VanBuren's home and it is well worth a visit and guided tour; the Van Alen homestead nearby is open to the public seasonally; in the center of town is the House of History museum, and around the corner is the museum of the Columbia Co. Hist. Soc. There are several places to have lunch in the area. On one of my catalogs I recommended a place for dinner in PA; shortly afterward it changed owners.)

Alexander, H. *The American Talleyrand. Career and Contemporaries of Martin VanBuren, 8th President.* 1935. illus. bib. 430 pp. (A note on the front of the dust jacket of this book states that VanBuren founded dirty politics in the United States, indicating that this is an anti-VanBuren work. The author later writes that Matty, who rose to the U. S. Presidency from being pot-boy in his father's tavern in Kinderhook, "lacks immortality even as he lacked ... sufficient courage or conviction to champion any cause for its own sake ...." A one-page cast of characters in the book lists, among others, John Quincy Adams as a nudist, DeWitt Clinton as a ditch digger, William Henry Harrison as a clodhopper, Edward Livingston as a refugee, Washington Irving as a gentle skeptic, and Thurlow Weed as the Nemesis.)

--- *American, Extra. Biographical Sketch of the Life of Martin VanBuren, by a Gentleman of New York.* May 1832. 16 pp. pamphlet. (A pro-VanBuren pub. Not listed in Miles, or Wise and Cronin.)

Bancroft, G. *Martin VanBuren to the End of His Public Career.* 1889. 239 pp. (VanBuren read the mss. of this book before its pub. and declared that it was authentic. It must have taken Bancroft a long time to decide to pub. this work, as

Matty Van of Kinderhook died in 1862.)

--- *Biography of Martin VanBuren.* (1832) 15 pp. pamphlet. (A pro-VanBuren work issued by the Albany *Argus* newspaper as an Extra at the time of his nomination for the Vice-Presidency of the U. S.)

--- *The Bunker Hill Club.* (newspaper) Penn Yan, NY. Bennett and Reed. April 24, 1840 - Jan. 8, 1841. 4 pp. each issue. (A pro-VanBuren campaign paper issued when he was running against Harrison. At one time I had 18 miscellaneous issues. Not listed in the Union List of Serials.)

Butler, W.A. *Martin VanBuren: Lawyer, Stateman and Man.* NY. 1862. 47 pp. (An appraisal of Van Buren shortly after he died by a noted lawyer and author who attended his funeral, and who saw there rustic beauties, matronly women, and hale men.)

--- *The Contrast: or, Plain Reasons Why William Henry Harrison Should Be Elected President ... and Why Martin VanBuren Should Not be Re-Elected. By an Old Democrat.* NY. J. P. Giffing. 1840. 16 pp. pamphlet. (VanBuren "... delights in popular tumults and excitements ... is in favor of the increase of the salaries of public officers ..." There are two fine full-page wood cuts of the candidates titled: "VanBuren and Ruin." "Harrison and Prosperity.")

--- *Democratic Republican General Committee, Tammany Hall, NYC.* Oct. 24, 1832. 1 pp. printed letter signed in type by the Committee of Correspondence. (This prntd. form letter advocated the election of Van Buren as Vice President of the U. S. and was sent throughout NY State to gather support for the Republicans. The Committee "are desirous of procuring from you such information in relation to the approaching election as in your opinion may be interesting, and which may tend to advance the interest of the Republican party ..." The copy I owned had been sent to Jacob Settle who was the Post Master at Bern in Albany Co.)

--- *Deutsche Burger der Bereinigten Staaten. "Die VanBuren, oder Tammany-Partei."* Broadside, 9 x 12 inches. 1837. (This political broadside, in German, dated 6 November 1837, 11th Ward NYC, mentions: Van Buren, Tammany Party, Navy Yard, Shinplasters, and Whig.)

--- *Extra Globe*, newspaper, pub. by Blair and Rives, Washington, D. C. May 16, 1840 through Oct 26, 1840. Total of 26 issues, comprising 416 pages, plus an extra issue dated Jan. 29, 1841, giving the results of the Presidential election. (An important pro-VanBuren newspaper pub. only during the famous Log Cabin and Hard Cider campaign of 1840.)

--- *Fire of the Flint.* Ed. by Killey and Lossing. Poughkeepsie, NY. Sep. 12, 1840 thru Oct. 31, 1840. (All pub.) (This was a 4page newspaper, with a total run of 8 issues, that supported VanBuren in his bid for re-election to the U. S. Presidency. A purely political newspaper that ceased publication the Saturday before the polls opened. One of the editors was Benson J. Lossing the famous historian and engraver. Several of his engravings appear in this paper. Not listed in the Union List of Serials.)

--- *The Free Soil Almanac for 1849. Freemen's Ticket: VanBuren and Adams.* Rochester, NY. D. M. Dewey, Arcade Hall. Shepard and Reed, printers. (This rare almanac includes brief biog. of the political lives of VanBuren of Kinderhook, and Charles Francis Adams, the famous diplomat from MA. There are ports. of the candidates, and some Free Soil Campaign Songs. This Party lasted only a few years, and this may have been the only almanac they issued. Drake locates only two copies.)

--- *The Harrison Almanac.* 1841. NY. J. P. Giffing. illus. 18 leaves. (This interesting work contains the words of two political campaign songs mentioning VanBuren. It also says that he uses dishes of gold at dinner parties, and adds that the voters will give "The Little Mischief Maker his passport to Kinderhook." VanBuren seems to have taken the campaign darts thrown at him in good humor. It is said that he hung anti-VanBuren cartoons on the walls of his study.)

--- *Letters Addressed to Martin VanBuren, Esq., Secretary of State: Correcting Many Important Errors in a Late Biography of that Gentleman. By Corrector.* NY. Prntd. October first, AD 1830. 15 pp. pamphlet. (A scathing attack upon the political integrity of VanBuren: "... you daily corrupt the very sources of power, and endanger the existence of the Union." This is a violent reply to an account of VanBuren that had quite recently appeared in newspaper and pamphlet form.) Mackenzie, W. L. *The Life and Times of Martin VanBuren: The Correspondence of His Friends, Family, and Pupils ....* 1846. index. 308 pp. (The author, a noted Canadian journalist, spent a year in the Rochester, NY, jail for his part in the Candaian Insurrection of 1837. Larned's *Literature of American History* says this is a scrappy work in which the author's "animosity toward VanBuren is marked.")

--- *To Protestants of Every Denomination Throughout the United States.* ca 1836. 12 pp. pamphlet. (A vehement, unsigned anti-VanBuren political tract, pub. at the time he was running for President. It accuses him of intriguing with the Pope in Rome to secure for himself the Catholic vote in the U. S. It also claims that Governor Clinton of NY, on his deathbed, said of Van Buren, "If it be necessary to secure his ends, he will dig up and sell the bones of his mother!" Not in Sabin or in Wise and Cronin.)

--- *The Shorter Catechism of Negro Equality.* ca 1864. Broadside, approximately 5 1/2 x 10 inches. (This was issued at the time General George McClellan was nominated as Democratic candidate for U. S. President. It discusses the Democratic party and negro equality, and lists the rights given to negoes over many years. "All these things are done by Democrats, and yet they deny being in favor of negro equality, and charge it upon the Republicans." This is of VAN BUREN interest as it mentions that he presided over the Convention that gave the negroes the right of suffrage in NY. It states that Richard M. Johnson [Vice President under VanBuren] had married a negro. "If President VanBuren had died, and Richard M. Johnson had become President, who would have become the Democratic mistress of the White House? This negro woman." A fine example of discord on racial equality between the two major political parties during the Civil War.)

MONROE COUNTY

MONROE COUNTY
Hanford, F. *The Origin of the Names of Places in Monroe Co.* Scottsville 1911. wrps. lmtd. 200 copies. 54 pp.
Lee, F. (co. historian) *The Founding of Monroe Co.* 1958. maps. wrps. 6 pp.
Lee, F. *Pleasant Valley. An Early Hist of Monroe Co. & Region. 1650-1850.* NY. 1970. maps. illus. index. 321 pp.
(McIntosh, W.) *History of Monroe Co. 1788-1877.* Phil. 1877. illus. maps. 320 pp. (Index pub. by Monroe Co. Historians Office in 1966). Reprntd. ca 1976.
Osgood, H. *The Struggle for Monroe Co.* Rochester 1892. 4 pp.
Peck, W. (& others) *Landmarks of Monroe Co.* Boston 1895. illus. 2 vols.
Thompson & Husted. *Preface to Tomorrow: Monroe Co. History Briefly Told and Illus.* 1971. wrps. map. illus. unpaged.
Turner, O. *History of the Pioneer Settlements of Phelps & Gorham's Purchase ... Co. of Monroe, Ontario, Livingston, Yates, Steuben, Most of Wayne, and Allegany & Parts of Orleans, Genesee & Wyoming. To which is Added a Supplement or Extension of the Pioneer History of Monroe Co.* Rochester. 1851. 624 pp.
Another ed. *To Which is Added a Supplement, or Continuation of the Pioneer History of Ontario, Wayne, Livingston, Yates & Allegany.* Rochester. 1852. 588 pp.

BRIGHTON, Monroe Co.
Cumpston, D. (town historian) *Brighton, A Town With an Interesting Past & Promising Future.* Sept. 1952. mimeo. 27 pp.
Brighton Town Historian. *This is My Home; a Chronological Story of Brighton.* 1956. typed mss. in BMLR.
--- *History of the Town of Brighton.* 1946. 2 vols. typed mss. in BMLR.
Williams, H. (ed.) *Sesquicentennial History of Town of Brighton 1814-1964.* (1964) illus. maps. wrps. 56 pp.

BROCKPORT, Monroe Co.
Martin, C. *The Story of Brockport 1829-1929.* Brockport. 1929. illus. wrps. 90 pp.
Smith and Husted (eds.) *We Remember Brockport. Reminiscences of 19th Century Village History.* 1979. wrps. illus. maps. 32 pp.

CASTLE TOWN, Monroe Co.
Cober, R. *Castle Town. An Historiette of Southwest Rochester.* 1935. illus. advts. wrps. 48 pp.

CHILI, Monroe Co.
Moore, C. *Chili Chapters. A Condensation of Chili's Hist. Based Primarily on Town Records.* Chili. 1972. map. 64 pp.
Moore, C. *Hidden Strands From*

the Fabric of Early Chili. 1977. pub. by author. illus. map. 151 pp.

CLARKSON, Monroe Co.
Ladue, D. *History of Early Clarkson.* 1953. illus. typed mss. in BRPL.
Tuttle, R. *Town of Clarkson. Sesquicentennial.* 1969. Brockport. pamphlet.

CLIFTON, Monroe Co.
Emens, H. *Hist of Clifton.* 1963. typed mss. in CPLR.

EAST ROCHESTER, Monroe Co.
Anon. *50th Anniv. of Village of East Rochester 1897-1947.* Special Anniv. No. of *East Rochester Herald* May 30, 1947.
Saunders, L. *History of East Rochester.* 1970. A mss.

FAIRPORT, Monroe Co.
Anon. *Souvenir Book of Fairport. Being a Historical Review of Interesting Events, Compiled From Early Records.* Fairport. 1908. illus. advts. wrps. 63 pp.

GATES, Monroe Co.
Anon. *From the Wilderness. Town of Gates Sesquicentennial 1813-1963.* illus. map. wrps. unpaged.

GLEN HAVEN, Monroe Co.
Anon. *Echoes From Glen Haven. Rochester's Family Summer Resort.* 1892. advts. wrps. 56 pp.

GREECE, Monroe Co.
Anon. *The Town of Greece.* ca 1964. wrps. 10 pp.

HENRIETTA, Monroe Co.
Henrietta Town Historian. *History of Town of Henrietta. 1790-1835.* May 1961. typed mss. in Henrietta Pub. Library.
Kalsbeck, E. *Henrietta Heritage.* 1977. pub. by author. illus. map. 356 pp.

HILTON, Monroe Co.
Husted, S. *Capsul Hist of Hilton & Parma.* 1959. mimeo.
--- *Pioneer Days of Hilton, Parma & Ogden. 1809-1959.* Albany. 1959. illus. map. advts. 126 pp.
Keller, E. (village hist.) *The Hilton Story. 1805-1959.* Hilton. (1959.) map. wrps. 62 pp.

HONEOYE FALLS, Monroe Co.
Cooney and Powell. *Hist ... of Honeoye Falls & Mendon.* 1977. illus. map. 76 pp.
Maloney, D. (village historian) *Honeoye, Its Beginning.* Honeoye Falls. Feb. 1963. wrps. 52 pp.

IRONDEQUOIT, Monroe Co.
Anon. *Irondequoit Centennial Album 1839-1939.* Rochester. 1939. 79 pp.
West, M. (town historian) *Irondequoit Story. 1839-1957.* (1957.) illus. maps. 150 pp.

KING'S LANDING, Monroe Co.
Slocum, H. *King's Landing (1797-1830) A History of the First White Settlement West of the Genesee River.* Rochester. 1948. illus. maps. 24 pp.

MENDON, Monroe Co.
(Krieger, A.) *Celebrating 150 Years of Living in the Town of Mendon & Village of Honeoye Falls 1813-1963.* Honeoye Falls. Aug. 1963. illus. advts. wrps. 43 pp.

NORTHAMPTON, Monroe Co.
Wright, A. *Old Northampton in Western New York.* map. 424 pp. (Title page lacking in

copy at SLA.)

OGDEN, Monroe Co.
Rich, A. (comp.) *Ogden Centennial. Pioneer Reminiscences. 1802-1902.* Rochester. ca 1902. 103 pp.

PARMA, Monroe Co.
Husted, S. *Parma, NY: The Hub of the Universe. Old Parma Families Remember Their Yesteryears.* 1984. index. 138 pp.

PENFIELD, Monroe Co.
Brahler, V. *I Remember When ... Penfield as told to Brahler.* 1961. illus. wrps. 41 pp.
Thompson, K. (town historian) *Penfield's Past 1810-1960.* Rochester. 1960. illus. maps. 213 pp.
Thompson, K. (town historian) *Penfield's Past Supplement, 1960-1976.* 1977. 31 pp.

PERINTON, Monroe Co.
Davis, E. *Geographic Influences in History of Town of Perinton.* 1939. typed mss. in FPL.
Merriman, M. *Early Days in Perinton.* 1964. illus. with photos. typed mss. in RPL.
--- *The Early Settlers of Perinton. 1790-1830.* Fairport. 1951. unpaged.
Watts, H. *Perinton Heritage. Sesquicentennial 1812-1962.* ca 1962. illus. map. advts. wrps. unpaged. (Including Fairport.)

PITTSFORD, Monroe Co.
Hart, I. *History of Pittsford.* Pittsford. 1972. pamphlet.
Hart, I. *Reminiscences of Pittsford, 1900-1913.* Pittsford. 1973. pamphlet.
(Pugsley, F.) *Pittsford Sesquicentennial 1789-1939.* Pittsford. (1939.) wrps. 16 pp.
Town Historian. *Historical Facts Pertaining to Pittsford.* comp. Oct. 1939. Reprntd. Nov. 1946 732
--- *History of Pittsford.* 1959. typed mss. in PPL.

ROCHESTER, Monroe Co.
Anon. *Biog. Record City of Rochester & Monroe Co. NY.* 1902. illus. 481 pp.
Anon. *History of City of Rochester.* 1895. illus. 276 pp.
Anon. *In Rochester 100 Years Ago & Now. 1831-1931.* pub. by Rochester Savings Bank. 1931. illus. 46 pp.
(Am. Guide Series) *Rochester & Monroe Co.* Rochester. 1937. illus. map. 460 pp.
Atwater, M. *Moses Atwater of Canandaigua, New York, to Samuel J. Andrews of Derby, Conn. A Packet of Letters Relating to the Early History of Rochester. 1812-14.* 1914. 30 pp.
Bragdon, G. (ed) *Notable Men of Rochester & Vicinity 19th & 20th Centuries.* Rochester. 1902. 373 pp. (Mostly ports.)
Brownyard, M. *The Diary of Mary Jane Brownyard.* (1964) map. mimeo. unpaged. (Errata & addenda in pen written in copy at NYSHA)
Elwood, G. *Some Earlier Public Amusements of Rochester.* Rochester. 1894. 62 pp.
Foreman, E. (ed. city historian) *Centennial History of Rochester.* Rochester. 1931-1934. illus. maps. 4 vols.
(Hawley, J.) *A Directory for Village of Rochester to Which is Added a Sketch of the History of the Village.* Rochester. 1827. 142 pp. (The first directory and hist. of Rochester.)
(Hawley, J.) *Rochester in 1827.* map. Rochester. 1828. 155 pp.
--- *Industries of the City of Rochester ... Past History, Progress ... Industrial Ad-*

vantages ... Comprehensive Sketches of Representative Enterprises ... 1888. illus. map. wrps. 280 pp. (Descriptions of innumerable companies.)

Johnson, P. *A Shopkeeper's Millennium. Society and Revivals in Rochester, New York. 1815-1837.* 1978. maps. tables. index. 210 pp. (A fresh approach to Rochester as a growing frontier city.)

Kelsey, J. *Lives & Reminiscences of Pioneers of Rochester & Western NY.* Rochester. 1854. map. 117 pp.

Lowe, E.B. *Rochester Industry and Trade Unionism.* ca 1920. 83 pp. (Hist. of trade unionism in Rochester, strikes, lockouts, anti-union shops.)

McKelvey, B. *An Emerging Metropolis. 1925-1961.* Rochester. 1961. illus. 404 pp.

McKelvey, B. *Rochester on the Genesee. The Growth of a City.* Syracuse. 1973. 292 pp.

McKelvey, B. *A Panoramic View of Rochester.* 1979. illus. map. bib. index. 264 pp.

--- *Rochester, The Flower City. 1855-1890.* Harvard U. Press. 1949. illus. maps. 407 pp.

--- *Rochester, Quest for Quality.* H.U.P. 1956. illus. map. 432 pp.

--- *Rochester, The Water Power City.* H.U.P. 1945. illus. map. 383 pp.

Merrill, A. *Rochester Sketchbook.* 1946. 182 pp. (reprntd. from the *Democrat & Chronicle*)

O'Reilly, H. *Rochester in 1835. Brief Sketches of the Present Condition of the City of Rochester.* Rochester. 1835. 14 pp. (One reference states 16 pp.)

O'Reilly, H. *Settlement in the West. Sketches of Rochester; With Incidental Notices of Western New York.* Rochester. 1838. illus. map. 416 pp. (Author's name sometimes spelled O'Rielly.)

Osgood, H. *Rochester, Its Founders & Its Founding.* Rochester. 1894. 8 pp.

Parker, J. *Rochester, A Story Historical.* Rochester. 1884. illus. 412 pp.

Peck, W. *History of Rochester & Monroe Co.* NY. 1908. illus. 2 vols.

--- *Semicentennial History of City of Rochester.* Syracuse. 1884. 736 pp. (The first 15 chapters are a reprnt. of: Harris, G. "Aboriginal Occupation of the Lower Genesee Country." Rochester. 1844. 96 pp.)

Rosenberg, S.E. *The Jewish Community in Rochester 1843-1925.* 1954. Hist. notes. glossary. bib. index. 325 pp. (A study of the hist. evolution of an immigrant Jewish community settled in a provincial American city.)

Strong, A. *Reminiscences of Early Rochester.* Rochester. 1916. wrps. 18 pp.

Ward, F. *Early Rochester.* 1860. 48 pp. (Vol. 1 of the Hist. Collections of the Jr. Pioneer Assn. of Rochester & Monroe Co.)

RUSH, Monroe Co.

Hallock, B. (town hist.) *Rush in Early Wars.* 1962. wrps. 39 pp.

--- *Your Folks & Mine. Rush Memories & Anecdotes of and About the People of Rush.* Rush. 1963. map. wrps. 75 pp.

--- *The Town of Rush 1818-1949.* 1949. typed mss. in RPL.

SCOTTSVILLE, Monroe Co.

Slocum, G. *The First Houses in Scottsville.* Scottsville. 1904. lmtd. 100 copies. wrps. 13 pp.

SWEDEN, Monroe Co.
Dobson, H. *Town of Sweden, Sesquicentennial 1814-1964.* ca 1964. illus. map. 114 pp.

WEBSTER, Monroe Co.
Anon. *A Hist. of Webster for 7th Graders.* typed mss. in WEPL.
Dunn, E. *Webster ... Through the Years.* 1971. book.
Town Historian. *50 Years of Progress: Village of Webster.* 1955. pamphlet.

WHEATLAND, Monroe Co.
Garbutt, P. *The Pioneers of Wheatland.* Scottsville. 1903. wrps. lmtd. 100 copies 17 pp.
--- *The Supervisors of Wheatland.* Scottsville. 1916. wrps. 25 pp.
McGinnis, E. *Pictorial Wheatland.* 1971. 2 pamphlets.
Schmidt, C. *History of Town of Wheatland, Scottsville, Mumford, Garbutt, Belcoda, Beulah, Wheatland Center.* Rochester. 1953. illus. maps. 296 pp.
Slocum, G. *Wheatland, A Brief Sketch of Its History.* Scottsville. 1908. illus. lmtd. 350 copies. 138 pp.

WHITE CITY, Monroe Co.
Dengler, D. *The Rise & Fall of White City, Windsor Beach, & Summerville.* 1945. typed mss. in IPLR.

MONTGOMERY COUNTY

MONTGOMERY COUNTY
Barkley, W. *A Descriptive Geography of Montgomery Co. With Hist Explanations & Notes.* 1892. advts. wrps. 63 pp.
Beers, F. (ed.) *History of Montgomery & Fulton Cos. 1772-1878.* NY. 1878. illus. map. 252 pp. Reprntd. 1979.
Frothingham, W. (ed.) *History of Montgomery Co.* Syracuse. 1892. illus. 809 pp.
Perry & Wilcox. *History of Montgomery Co. Buildings 1772-1836-1936.* 87 pp. carbon copy mss. (Listed in book dealer's catalog)

AMSTERDAM, Montgomery Co.
Kellogg, S. *From Boyhood to Manhood: Father, Peradventure You May Care to Know My Name: Spencer Kellogg.* pvtly. prntd. Buffalo. 1914. illus. 213 pp. Lmtd. to 100 copies. (Life in the Amsterdam area during the last half of the 1800s.)

AURIESVILLE, Montgomery Co.
Donlon, H. *The Story of Auricsville, "Land of Crosses,"* Worcester, Mass. 1932. 176 pp.

CANAJOHARIE, Montgomery Co.
Anon. *Canajoharie & The Sullivan - Clinton Expedition.* 1929. illus. maps. 127 pp. (Includes a hist. of Canajoharie.)
Bush, H. Wrote a series of hist. articles for the *Canajoharie Courier-Ft. Plain Standard* in 1938.

FONDA, Montgomery Co.
Crane, M. *Historical Sketch of the Village of Fonda 1850-1950.* 1950. illus. map. advts. wrps. 128 pp.

FORT PLAIN, Montgomery Co.
Greene, N. *Fort Plain - Nelliston History 1580-1947.* Ft. Plain. 1947. illus. 111 pp.
--- *The Story of Old Fort Plain & the Middle Mohawk Valley. 1609-1914.* Ft. Plain. 1915. maps. 399 pp.

ST. JOHNSVILLE, Montgomery Co.
Anon. *Centennial of St. Johnsville. 1857-1957.* Aug. 1957. pamphlet.

MUNSELL'S HISTORICAL SERIES

This series is so important it deserves a special section in this book. It began as a collection of 9 titles pub. in 10 vol. between 1857 and 1861. Beginning in 1882 other titles were added to the series, and by 1895 there was a total of 23 vol. in the set. Rarely does this work come on the market as a complete set. I occasionally acquire odd vol., but only once did I get the first 10 vol. at one time. A dealer told me he hoped to buy some Munsell titles, but as such pronouncements seldom bear fruit I did not return to his shop for some time. When I finally went back there on the floor were the first 10 vol. of the Munsell Historical Series. He said he had them for a week, nobody wanted them, and I could have the lot for $ 100.00 I gave him a check, scooped up the books, and almost knocked him over as I fled through the door.

(In this section are listed the first 9 titles in 10 vol. See Edelstein's *Joel Munsell: Printer and Antiquarian* for a detailed account of the printing of this important series.)

Commissary Wilson's Orderly Book. Expedition of the British and Provincial Army, under Maj. Gen. Jeffrey Amherst, Against Ticonderoga and Crown Point, 1759. 1857. Map. 220 pp. Lmtd. to 100 copies. (Annotated by Dr. E. B. O'Callaghan.) (General J. Watts de Peyster, of Tivoli, NY, owned the original orderly book, and O'Callaghan advised Munsell to print it. For some unknown reason DePeyster refused to let O'Callaghan's name appear anywhere in the book. Actually 120 copies were prntd., plus 6 on large paper. Sixty copies went to DePeyster for private distribution, twenty copies went to O'Callaghan, leaving 46 copies to be sold to the public.)

A Narrative of the Causes Which Led to Philip's Indian War, of 1675 and 1676, by John Easton of Rhode Island; With Other Documents Concerning This Event in the Office of the Secretary of State of New York. 1858. map. index. 207 pp. Introd. and notes by F. B. Hough. Approximately 120 copies printed. (Although mentioned by Cotton Mather many years earlier, these papers had been considered lost until Hough found them in the Office of the NY Secretary of State. Long Island is frequently mentioned in this work. I once owned a copy which had a note written on the front flyleaf, dated 1859, "..but 100 copies were printed of this size, and 5 copies on large paper. There were 12 or 15 additional small paper copies printed, which Dr. Hough received in part compensation for his Editorial services.")

Orderly Book of the Northern Army, at Ticonderoga and Mt. Independence, From Oct. 17th, 1776 to Jan. 8th. 1777, with Biographical and Explanatory Notes, and an Appendix. 1859. port. map. index. 224 pp. (This work was annotated by the pub.) Lmtd. to 140 copies.

Diary of the Siege of Detroit in the War With Pontiac. Also a Narrative of the Principal Events of the Siege, By Major Robert Rogers; A Plan for Conducting Indian Affairs, by Colonel Bradstreet; and Other Authentick Documents, Never

Before Printed. 1860. index. 304 pp. Lmtd. to 136 copies. (Ed. with notes by F. B. Hough. Many references to: Sir William Johnson, Albany, Delaware Indians, Mohawk Indians, NY, Niagara, Seneca Indians.)

Obstructions to the Navigation of Hudson's River; Embracing the Minutes of the Secret Committee Appointed by the Provincial Convention of New York, July 16, 1776, and Other Original Documents Relating to the Subject; Together With Papers Relating to the Beacons. 1860. map. diagrams. index. 210 pps. Lmtd. to 125 copies. (A major source of information about the chains put across the Hudson River to prevent the British fleet from sailing up-river. Book was compiled by E. M. Ruttenber, and the hist. notes were written by Munsell.)

The Loyal Verses of Joseph Stansbury and Doctor Jonathan Odell; Relating to the American Revolution. 1860. index. 199 pp. Lmtd. to 150 copies. Ed. by Winthrop Sargent. (Stansbury and Odell were the most influential Loyalist poets of the American Revolution, and both were involved in the Arnold-Andre affair. There is frequent mention of NY.)

Orderly Book of Lieut. Gen. John Burgoyne, From His Entry Into the State of New York Until His Surrender at Saratoga, 16th. Oct. 1777, From the Original Manuscript Deposited at Washington's Headquarters, Newburgh, NY. 1860. ports. map. plate. index. 221 pp. Lmtd. to 210 copies. Ed. by E. B. O'Callaghan.

Early Voyages Up and down the Mississipi, By Cavelier, St. Cosme, Le Seur, Gravier, and Guignas. 1861. index. 191 pp. Lmtd. to 100 copies plus a few copies on large paper. Intro. and notes by J. G. Shea.

Proceedings of the Commissioners of Indian Affairs Appointed by Law for the Extinguishment of Indian Titles in the State of New York. Published From the Original Manuscript. 1861. 2 vol. maps. index. Limited to 210 sets. Introduction and notes by F. B. Hough. (This was the first printing of these negotiations. A most important and comprehensive work on the dealings of the white man with the Indian in NY State. I once had Hough's own copy with marginal notes on some pages. Also included was a preliminary map made by Hough which was used for one of the printed maps. Laid in was the official permission to pub. the mss., and a preliminary description of the proposed book. There also were 3 pages of notes taken by Hough when he interviewed Dr. John Bay, of Albany, in 1861, concerning the Leasee Co. Bay names those he remembered as being members of the Company - most of them from Columbia Co. This work is so important that within 18 years of its pub. it was selling for $400.00 per set.)

NASSAU COUNTY

NASSAU COUNTY

Bailey, L. (ed.) *Long Island, A History of Two Great Co.* NY. 1949. 3 vols.

Darlington, O. *Glimpses of Nassau Co. History.* Mineola. 1949. illus. 22 pp.

Hodges, A. *Nassau Co. The Netherlands of the New World.* Rckvle. Ctr. 1940. illus. 82 pp.
Merritt, J. *The Historical Importance of Nassau Co.* Address Before NYSHA Sept. 28, 1939. Farmingdale. (1939.) 18 pp. (Water Witch ed. 1 of 90 copies on rag paper in SLA.)
Smits, E. *Creation of Nassau Co. 1899.* 1960. 27 pp.

BALDWIN, Nassau Co.
(WPA GUIDE) *Hick's Neck, The Story of Baldwin, L.I.* 1939. illus. map. 61 pp.

BETHPAGE, Nassau Co.
Gibbs, I. & A. *Bethpage Bygones.* 1962. illus. map. wrps. 54 pp.
Hunt, T. *Bethpage. The Years of Development: 1840-1910.* Bethpage. 1972. pamphlet.

EAST MEADOW, Nassau Co.
Clarke, M. *East Meadow, Its History Our Heritage. 1658-1952.* Little Neck. 1952. illus. map. 28 pp.

EAST NORWICH, Nassau Co.
Downing, R. *A Brief History of East Norwich.* Syosset. 1960. illus. wrps. 20 pp.

EAST ROCKAWAY, Nassau Co.
Anon. *Incorporated Village of East Rockaway. 50th Aniv. Celebration.* 1950. 16 pp.

EAST WILLISTON, Nassau Co.
Meyer, N. *East Williston History 1663-1970.* 1970. Book. (See E. WILLISTON, Suffolk Co.)

FAR ROCKAWAY, Nassau Co.
Smith, V. *Far Rockaway in Reminiscenes.* Jamaica. 1936. illus. 32 pp.

FARMINGDALE, Nassau Co.
Anon. *Founders' Day. 235th Anniv. Oct. 11-13, 1930.* Farmingdale. 1930. 63 pp.

FLORAL PARK, Nassau Co.
Anon. *Floral Park Golden Anniv. 1908-1958.* (Floral Park, 1958.) illus. 35 pp.
Purcell, E. *Across the Years, the Story of Floral Park.* 1958. 160 pp. ("An Almanac pub. in 1925 by the Floral Park Police Assn. Relief Fund yielded much of the early hist. of organizations.")

FREEPORT, Nassau Co.
Anon. *Historic Freeport. 70th Anniv.* 1962. wrps. 46 pp.

GARDEN CITY, Nassau Co.
Smith, M. *History of Garden City.* 1953. illus. maps. 144 pp.

GLEN COVE, Nassau Co.
Merritt, J. *One Long Island Neck of Land. Dosoris, East & West Islands.* 1943. 19 pp. typed mss. in NYSHA.
Scudder, H. *Glen Cove, An Address May 25, 1868.* Glen Gove. 1868. 195 pp.

GREAT NECK, Nassau Co.
Spear, D. & G. *The Book of Great Neck.* Great Neck. 1936. 152 pp.

HEMPSTEAD, Nassau Co.
Anon. *Hempstead Yesterday & Today.* 1959. Pub. by League of Women Voters. 30 pp.
Marshall, B. *Colonial Hempstead.* Lynbrook 1937. illus. maps. 392 pp. (Includes No. Heampstead. Ed. very lmtd.) 2nd. ed. *Port Washington.* 1962. with corrections. 392 pp.
Moore, C. *Early History of Hempstead.* NY. 1879. 14 pp. (Reprntd. from *NY Genealogical & Biog. Record.* Jan. 1879.)

Onderdonck, H. *Annals of Hempstead 1643-1832.* Hempstead. 1878. 107 pp.

HEWLETT Nassau Co.
Anon. *Historical Article on Hewlett in South Shore Record.* Oct. 30, 1958.

HICKSVILLE, Nassau Co.
Anon. *Hicksville Story 1648-1948.* 1948. 52 pp.

INWOOD, Nassau Co.
(WPA GUIDE) *The Story of the Five Towns: Inwood, Lawrence, Cedarhurst, Woodmere, & Hewlett.* (Rckvle Cnt.) 1941. illus. wrps. 70 pp.

ISLAND PARK, Nassau Co.
Anon. *Silver Anniv. 1926-1951. Incorporated Village of Island Park.* Island Park. 1951. 26 pp.

LOCUST VALLEY, Nassau Co.
Frost, J. *The Frost Genealogy 1912.* (Chapt. I is titled: "Old Matinecock".)

MALVERNE, Nassau Co.
VanAllen, G. (village historian) *The Rise of Malverne.* 1955. illus. wrps. 8 pp. (Reprntd. from *Long Island Forum*, March 1955)

MATINECOCK, Nassau Co.
Cocks, G. *Old Matinecock.* Locust Valley. 1910. 27 pp.

MERRICK, Nassau Co.
Anon. *Memories of the Merricks.* 1977. Pub. by Hist. Soc. of the Merricks. illus. map. 64 pp.
Hoffman, L. *History is Adventure. Merrick Our Special Town & One of the Oldest Settlements in America.* n.d. 75 pp.
Kent, C. *A Historical Sketch of Merrick. 1643-1900.* Merrick. 1900. wrps. index. 79 pp.

NORTH HEMPSTEAD, Nassau Co.
Anon. *Town of North Hempstead.* 1977. bib. 90 pp. (Hist. essays by North Hempstead high school students.)
Mann, H. *A Brief Account of the Indians in the Township of North Hempstead, & Their Dealings With the White Settlers.* Great Neck. 1924. wrps. 32 pp. 2nd. ed. 1949.

OYSTER BAY, Nassau Co.
Irvin, F. *Historic Oyster Bay.* 1926. illus. 12 pp.
2nd. ed. revised. enlrgd. Oyster Bay. 1953. 24 pp.
--- *Oyster Bay in History.* ca 1963. 176 pp.
Smith, V. *The Village of Oyster Bay 1653-1700.* Garden City. 1953. pvtly. prntd. maps. 104 pp.
Weekes, A. *Life in an Oyster Bay Farmhouse Before the Rev War. Illustrated by Extracts from the Diary of Mrs. Joseph Cooper.* NY. 1918. 30 pp.

PLAINVIEW, Nassau Co.
Eisner, J. *The Plainview - Old Bethpage Community.* 1966. 18 pp.

PORT WASHINGTON, Nassau Co.
Merriman, C. *Tales of Sint Sink.* Port Washington. 1935. illus. maps. 258 pp.

ROCKAWAY, Nassau Co.
Bellot, A. *History of the Rockaways 1685-1917, In the Rockaway Peninsula, Comprising the Villages of Hewlett, Woodmere, Cedarhurst, Lawrence, Inwood, Far Rockaway, Arverne, Rockaway Beach, Belle Harbor, Nesponsit & Rockaway Point.* Far Rockaway. 1918. illus. maps. 110 pp.

Far Rockaway High School Students. *History of the Rockaways.* 1932. illus. 56 pp.

ROCKVILLE CENTRE, Nassau Co.
Xulver, F. *History of Rockville Centre.* (article in the *Long Island News and the Owl*, March 20, 1937.)

ROSLYN, Nassau Co.
Gerry, P. & R. *Old Roslyn.* 1954. illus. map. advts. 40 pp. (Architecture of Roslyn buildings.)
Moger, R. *Our Town, Roslyn. A Brief History of the Roslyn Area, to Serve the Staff in Guiding Their Students on Trips Around Roslyn.* Roslyn Pub. Schools. 1960. illus.
--- *Roslyn Then & Now. A Brief Illus. History of the Roslyn Area.* Roslyn. 1965. 185 pp.
Skillman, F. *Some Notes Relating to Roslyn.* Roslyn. 1892-1894. 20 pp. mss. in LIHS.

SEA CLIFF, Nassau Co.
Anon. *Sea Cliff Diamond Jubilee 1883-1958.* S. Clf. 1958. 62 pp.
Ransom, C. *Gaslight & Gingerbread. A Photo Recoll of Old Sea Cliff.* 1971. Book.

WANTAGH, Nassau Co.
Forbush, W. *Wantagh, Jerusalem, & Ridgewood 1644-1892.* Wantagh. 1892. 16 pp.
Smith, J. A. *Story of Wantagh Before Electricity* (1958.) mimeo. 24 pp.

NEW YORK COUNTY

NEW YORK COUNTY
Field, M. *City Architecture; or, designs for dwelling houses, stores, hotels, etc., in 20 plates, with descriptions, and an essay on the principles of design.* NY. 1854. 75 pp. (Written especially to improve the architecture of NYC, using designs and adaptations of the street architecture of Rome, Florence, and Venice.)

GOVERNOR'S ISLAND, New York Co. (in New York Bay)
Anon. *Three Centuries Under 3 Flags. The Story of Governor's Island from 1637.* NY. 1951. illus. map. wrps. 110 pp.
Bellamy, B. *Governor's Island.* NY. 1897.
DePuy, Col. *Governor's Island. 1637-1937.* NY. 1937. 64 pp.
Smith, Chaplain. *Governor's Island. Its Military Hist Under Three Flags. 1637-1922.* NY. 1923. illus. maps. 243 pp.

HARLEM, New York Co.
Caldwell, A. *A Lecture: The History of Harlem 1589-1674.* 1882. 49 pp. + 11 pp. of advts.
Riker, J. *Harlem, Its Origin & Early Annals.* NY. 1881. (In a letter written Dec. 9, 1887, Riker said he only had 5 copies left.) 636 pp.
2nd. ed. 1904. illus. maps. 908 pp. (Revised from author's notes & enlrgd. by H. Toler.)
Toler & Nutting. *New Harlem Past & Present.* 1903. illus. maps. 338 pp.

KINGS BRIDGE, New York Co.
Edsall, T. *History of Town of Kings Bridge, Now Part of the 24th Ward*, NYC. 1887. pvtly. prntd. illus. map. lmtd. 53 copies. 102 pp.

NEW YORK CITY, New York Co.
Abbott and McCausland. *Changing New York.* Photographs by B. Abbott. Text by E. McCausland. 1939. 208 pp. (There are 97 full page plates with descriptions, and locations, of

NYC scenes. Many of these scenes can no longer be seen, among them: a roast corn man, rope store, Provincetown Playhouse, Third Avenue Car Barns, and a horse drawn wagon peddling tinware.)

Allen, F. L. *Metropolis, An American City in Photographs. Assembled by A. Rogers. With Running Comment by Allen. E.M. Weyer, Photographer.* 1934. 2nd ed. Index of pictures. (A collection of 215 fascinating photos of NYC, including: views, buildings, horse drawn wagons, slums, the homeless, markets, stock exchange, a dead gangster. For some years now I have refused to drive into the big cities that I used to go into on rare occasions, namely NY, Boston, and Philadelphia. About the biggest city I will now tool into is Albany; I would much rather travel the narrow rural roads. Cars and cows are more compatible than cars and cars. Anyway, a few years ago I was told by a NYC dealer that I would soon get a call about a major collection of Americana for sale in the city. At that time my book-buying fund was flat broke, I could not even have purchased a subway token. When the call came I was relieved to say that I could not come, even though I secretly was anxious to see the lot. I gave the caller the names of two or three other dealers to call. The very next day I got a large amount of accounts receivable in the mail, which made me wish I hadn't felt so relieved the day before. A few days later I called the chap back, found that he had not gotten around to calling the other dealers and told him I did not drive into the city but would appreciate it if he would bring a few boxes to my house. He did and I was astonished at the quality I saw. I made a deal with him: I would go look at the books in the city if he did all of the driving and used his car. We made two trips, loading up his car both times, and in retrospect I wish I had bought two more car loads. The apartment the books were in was in what was once a handsome building which had fallen on disastrous times. There were four or five locks on the door, and a heavy metal grill had been fastened to the inside of the door to thwart would-be burglars. A noteworthy collection of 100,000 pieces of Am. sheet music, with a music reference library, lined the walls. It covered the entire sweep from the earliest days to more modern times. The chap I was doing business with could have gone into the sheet music business with a grand flourish but I believe he had to sell it as a lot as he was settling an estate.)

--- *American Champion.* Newspaper. NYC. Vol. 1 No. 3. Jan. 21, 1847. 4 pp. folio. William S. Tisdale, ed. A.B. Flower, Pub. (A pro-American and pro-Labor newspaper, which advocated a tax on emigrants to protect American industry. Not in Gregory, Mott, or Union List of Serials.)

Anon. *Reminiscences of City of NY & Vicinity.* NY. 1855. lmtd. 50 copies. 350 pp. (reprnt. of articles from *Manual of City of NY.*)

Archdeacon, T. *New York City, 1664-1710: Conquest and Change.* 1976. maps, charts, tables. 224 pp.

Barker J. *Court of General Sessions.* (NY.) June 6, 1822. wrps. 50 pp. (Jacob Barker was accused of challenging a Naval lieutenant to a duel, and this is his speech to the court asking for a new trial or for an arrest of judgment. Barker, 1779-1871, of Quaker background, was a noted NYC merchant, lawyer, and financier. He was pugnacious, stormy, and almost always in the middle of a dispute. This important dueling item is only briefly mentioned by Sabin, 3392, and is not listed in *American Imprints.*)

--- *The Bazar Book of Decorum. Care of the Person, Manners, Etiquette, Ceremonials.* NY. Harper & Bro. 1870 index. 278 pp. (This work covers a great many topics of interest to the up-and-coming youth of NYC. Some of the more interesting subjects are: nasal beauty, sweating feet, winking, mutilated courtesy, evils of late parties, and luxury of woe.)

Belden, E. P. *New York: Past, Present, Future ... History of the City ... Description of Present Condition ... Estimate of Future Increase.* 3rd ed. 1850. Folded map. 19 plates of views. 141 pp. + *New York As It Is: Being the Counterpart of the Metropolis of America.* 1849. 24 pp. [This is about a model of NYC being exhibited in various cities.] + *The American Advertiser, Designed for the Cards and Advts. of Mercantile and Manufacturing Establishments.* 3rd. ed. 1850. 203 pp. with several advts. to each pp. There are some illus. and a 4-page prospectus for the book. (All of this bound into one vol.)

Beastall, W. *A Useful Guide, for Grocers, Distillers, Hotel and Tavern-Keepers, and Wine and Spirit Dealers, of Every Denomination; Being a Complete Directory for Making and Managing All Kinds of Wines and Spiritous Liquors ... Recipes.* NY. pub. by the author. 1829. index. 340 pp. (This work also has information on curing meat and fish, and on preserving fruits and vegetables. No doubt a number of NYC tavern-keepers and spirit dealers acquired a copy of this work when it came off the press. A copy I once had may have been carried in the back pocket of a moonshiner - there was a bullet hole through the back cover and about 20 pages.)

Barnes, D. M. *The Draft Riots in New York. July, 1863. The Metropolitan Police: Their Services During Riot Week. Their Honorable Record.* 1863. index. 118 pp. (A precinct by precinct description of this madness in which thousands of New Yorkers, mainly poor and foreign-born, rioted against the unfairness of the federal military draft, some of them shouting "Hurrah for Jeff Davis!" Many lives were lost and property damage was extensive.)

--- *Bibliography of the Writings and Speeches of Gabriel Wells.* pub. by Charles F. Heartman. 1939. wrps. Port. 24 pp. (Wells was a noted NYC bookseller and philosopher, who also lectured and wrote on a wide variety of subjects; everything from divorce to capitalism to an appeal to common sense. Less than 200 copies were prntd. for friends of Gabriel Wells as a Yuletide Gift.)

Blair, H. W. *The Temperance Movement: Conflict Between Man and Alcohol.* 1888. illus. 4 color plates. many tables. index. 583 pp. (A study of the effect of alcohol on the body, remedies, prohibition, temperance reform, data on organizations, and recommendations. A feature of this book is the folding map of NYC of the area from 114th Street to the Battery, showing the location of over 9000 places licensed to sell liquor.)

Bolton, R. *Washington Heights, Manhattan, Its Eventful Past.* 1924. 345 pp.

Bonner, W. T. *New York. The Worlds Metropolis. 1623-4 --- 1823-4. A Presentation of the Greater City at the Beginning of its Second Quarter Century of Amalgamated Government and the 300th Anniversary of Its Founding.* Pub. by NYC Directory, R. L. Polk & Co. 1924. illus. maps. bib. index. 953 pp. (A vast amount of information: hist., professions, wealth, real estate, manufacturing, transportation, biog., much more. There are over 6,000 entries in the index. A metal seal, two inches in diameter, showing a Dutch settler and an Indian looking from the Battery at a city of tall buildings, is imbedded in the front cover.)

Booth, M. *History of City of NY.* NY. 1859. illus. 846 pp.

Reprntd. NY. 1860. 850 pp.

Reprntd. NY. 1866.

Reprntd. NY. 1867. 2 vols. There also was an 1867 ed. of 892 pp., lmtd. to only 100 copies.

Reprntd. NY. 1880. illus. 915 pp.

Braynard, F. *The Tall Ships. Official OP Sail '76 Portfolio.* Sabine Press. NY. 1976. (On July 4, 1976, over 200 sailing vessels from 30 nations paraded into NY harbor. It was truly a grand display. We went by train down to the Hoboken, NJ, docks where we had to pay a fee to watch the great Tall Ships proudly sail up the North River. The train was so crowded with sardine-packed sightseers that the conductors gave up trying to collect fares. Frank Braynard, General Manager of OP Sail, was also an artist, and this portfolio contains 20 lithographs from his drawings, plus data on each of the 20 ships depicted. Each plate is 11 x 14 inches.)

Bruce, H. A. *Above the Clouds and Old New York. An Historical Sketch of the Site, and a Description of the Many Wonders of the Woolworth Building.* 1913. Illus. - some in color. wrps 30 pp. (When completed, this famous NYC landmark was the highest inhabitable building in the world.)

--- *Care of the Sick, and Recipes for Sick People.* 1875. Distributed to its Policy-Holders by the Mutual Life Insurance Co. of NY. index. wrps. 72 pp. (This was an early attempt by a NYC Insurance Co. to keep its customers from collecting life insurance before they had paid a considerable amount in premiums. Do you remember insurance men coming around every month with a thick customer register to collect premiums of 25 or 50 cents, or even a dollar?)

Carman, H. J. *The Street Surface Railway Franchises of New York City.* 1919. index. bib. maps. wrps. 259 pp. (Written at the time of the great agitation for the municipal ownership of the many street surface

railways of Manhattan. Contains hist. of nearly 30 independent Manhattan railways.)
--- *Catalogue of Fancy and Humorous Books ... Handsomely Illustrated With Plates.* Henry Stephens, 85 Nassau St., NY. Broadside, 6 x 9 inches, ca 1860s. (An early example of risque titles, *The Amours of a Quaker. Intrigues and Amours of Aaron Burr.* Plus 78 other titles. If the purchaser wanted the books wrapped up so no one would know what he was carrying, the bookseller offered a special service: "We do them up in a manner to defy detection.")
--- *Catalog of Genteel Household Furniture, For Sale by Auction, by Henry H. Lees & Co. ... April 29, 1853 ... At No. 231 East 10th Street, Near 1st Avenue.* wrps. 8 pp. (Room by room listing of 127 pieces of furniture for sale, including the front basement, basement hall, and 3rd story hall. A fine inventory of NYC home in 1853.)
--- *Catalog of the New York Museum of Anatomy, 618 Broadway, NY. Drs. Jordan and Beck. Open Daily, for Gentlemen Only, From 10 AM to 10 PM.* 1870. wrps. 47 pp. (If you think there are wonders at the NYC museums of today, you should have seen what they had in this museum in 1870. Among the over 2000 items exhibited were such beauties as: the skull of Robert Burns, the fearful effects of tight lacing, Martha Jones who lived to be 115, Eve and the apple, diseased ribs, Burke who killed an Italian boy for his teeth, a lamb with a poodle dog's head.)
Chaplin, J. Duncan Dunbar. *Life of the Late Pastor of the McDougal Street Baptist Church, New York.* 3rd ed. 1866. Port. 312 pp. (Dunbar, ca 1791-1864, spent many years preaching at McDougal Street. An old time New Yorker once told me a story about a horse who dropped dead of the heat on that street. The policeman on the beat who had to write out a report could not spell McDougal so he dragged the horse over to Wall Street. Speaking of telling stories, Ben Tighe of Athol, MA, was an old-time respected dealer and a great story-teller. Several years ago another bookseller told me that after he had heard Ben tell the same story several times within a short period of time he said, "Ben, you told me that story just last week." "That's OK," Ben replied, "I want to hear it again myself.")
--- *Charles DeBehr.* Broadway, NYC, July 1828. 16 pp. (This is an early catalog of French and Italian books for sale by DeBehr.)
--- *Copy of a Memorial from the Trustees of the College of Physicians and Surgeons of the City of New York, to the Regents of the University.* Albany. Feb. 1828. small folio broadside. (The college is objecting to the incorporation of a new medical school in NYC, stating that they are already contending with medical schools in Baltimore, New Haven, Dartmouth, and other places. They also infer that there would not be enough corpses for anatomical studies.)
Cozzens, I. *A Geological History of Manhattan or New York Island, Together With a Map of the Island, and a Suite of Sec-*

tions, Tables, and Columns, for the Study of Geology. NY. 1843. 9 colored plates. 114 pp. (Includes a catalog of minerals; and has a list of subscribers, including Henry Schoolcraft and John J. Audubon. There is also some data on RI and Niagara Falls. This work is briefly discussed in Merrill's *The First One Hundred Years of American Geology*, 1924.)

Crapsey, E. *The Nether Side of New York; or, the Vice, Crime, and Poverty of the Great Metropolis.* 1872. 185 pp. (Among other topics this book discusses: professional criminals, harbor thieves, private detectives, why thieves prosper, fences, faro gamblers, tenement life, outcast children, haunts of vice. The author, a journalist, spent four years gathering material for this detailed work. He dealt with "these repulsive subjects, in the hope that I might furnish a basis of fact for the operations of the social reformers of the future.")

Davies, J. *Phrenology Fad and Science. A 19th Century American Crusade.* 1955. illus. bib. index. 203 pp. (A study of the popularity of phrenology in the U. S. in the 1800s. There is much on the Fowler brothers, Orson and Lorenzo, of Cohocton, NY, who opened a phrenological establishment in NYC. Here they studied the bumps on thousands of human heads, and wrote reports on the subjects' mental abilities and character traits. From the reports still in existence, it seems they rarely wrote an unfavorable one. They also published books, periodicals, and almanacs. Orson built an octagon house at Fishkill, and he "liked to ride the railroad because he believed it charged him with electricity.")

Disbrow, L. *Disbrows Expose of Water Boring. Practice Versus Theory.* 1831. wrps. 8 pp. (Disbrow, a NYC well driller, calls to task the faculty of the Lyceum of Natural Hist. for daring to assert that there was no ready supply of good water to be found beneath the rock of Manhattan Island. He says he has drilled wells beneath the rock, found pure water, and gives the location of two of them. He also says the shallow wells he bored behind the City Hall were called mineral by the Lyceum men. "The cause is apparent when we see so much urine spilt in that neighborhood. But the gentlemen say that urine sweetens the water.")

Disturnell, J. *Guide to the City of New York; Containing an Alphabetical List of Streets, &c. Accompanied by a Correct Map.* NY. Pub. by J. Disturnell. 1836. 16 pp. one illus. Folding map. Plus: *Guide to the Environs of the City of New York, Containing a Description of all the Places of Resort in the Vicinity of New York Accompanied by a Correct Map.* NY. Disturnell. 1836. 16 pp. Folding map. Plus: *The Hudson River Guide; Containing a Description of All the Landings and Principal Places on the Hudson River, as Far as Navigable; Stage, Canal, and Railroad Routes. Accompanied by a Correct Map.* pp. 226-240. Folding map. (These three items were bound in one small vol., with cover title: *New York City Guide, Environs, and Hudson River*

Guide. 1836. Not in Sabin in this form.)

Duer, Wm. A. *Reminiscences of an Old Yorker, by the Late ... President of Columbia College.* NY. Albany. Munsell. 1867. index. 102 pp. Lmtd. to 35 copies. (These reminiscences were originally pub. in the *American Mail*, a NYC weekly newspaper which lasted only from June 5 to Aug. 21, 1847. Duer recalls his very early life in the city. One copy of this exceptionally rare book has come my way. Someone once took this work and made it into two vol. by extra-illus. it with prints from the early 1800s. Somehow this special set got separated and I acquired vol. 2. In it was an original letter from Egbert Benson, noted NY State Revolutionary War leader, dated 1798, in which he complained about his ill health. I checked the DAB and found out that he lived for 35 more years.)

Duffy, J. *A History of Public Health in New York City 1625-1866.* 1968. tables. bib. index. maps. illus. 619 pp. (An engrossing study of the sanitary and health problems of a major city which was swept by epidemics, almost overwhelmed with rubbish in the early 1800s, and was exceedingly dirty by 1861.)

Duncan, W. *The Amazing Madame Jumel.* 1935. Bib. 321 pp. (A biog. of the charming but unscrupulous Madame Jumel who became one of the wealthiest women in America, lived in the famous Jumel Mansion in NYC, and married Aaron Burr to her sorrow.)

--- *East River Bridge.* (This is an 11 panel view book, pub. by Wittemann, NYC, 1884, with views of this famous NYC bridge. Captions are in English and German on 10 of the panels. There is also a list of the souvenir view albums pub. by Witteman.)

Ellington, Geo. (Pseud.) *The Women of New York or the Under-World of the Great City ... Women of Fashion ... of Pleasure, Actresses and Ballet Girls, Saloon Girls, Pickpockets, and Shoplifters, Artist's Female Models, Women-of-the-Town, &c. &c. &c.* 1869. Many illus. 650 pp. (An expose of the female under-world of NYC.) Reprntd. in 1972.

Ellis, E. R. *The Epic of New York City, A Narrative History from 1524 to the Present.* 1966. bib. index. 640 pp. (An entertaining hist. Did you know that at one time New Yorkers planned to saw off Manhattan Island? That in 1862 one-tenth of all New Yorkers had police records?)

Everitt, C. P. *The Adventures of a Treasure Hunter. A Rare Bookman in Search of American History.* 1952. 224 pp. (Everitt was one of the great NYC dealers in Americana, and he worked in and had several shops, one of them being "opposite Gregory's Bar on upper Lexington Avenue." This book is delightfully full of his experiences in buying and selling, and in his memories of other dealers. The story is told that Charlie was a nut for the Grand Circuit horse races, and the NYC chislers would go to his shop right after his return. To recoup money he would sell his stock at cost or less. One day Charlie bet all of his money on a 20 to 1 shot on a tip from the horse's book-collecting owner, and won. As soon as he returned home he attended an under-advertised sale of choice Americana and out-bid all of the chislers. Bill Kelleher, of Cliffside Park, NJ, a specialist in western Americana, was another NYC bookseller of note. I visited him a number of times and now wish I had written down all of the stories he told me. Here is a story that someone else told me about Bill: During the Great Depression of the 1930s he would take an armload of books and peddle them about the city. One day a wealthy chap, possibly a bootlegger, got a hold of Bill and said he wanted to buy some really big books to fill up some shelves he was having built in his home. So Bill spent his money and lugged some huge tomes up to the new library, only to find the owner watching as the carpenter was finishing building average size shelves. Bill said, "You said you wanted big books and I spent all my money on these big ones and now you have small shelves. What do you want me to do?" The buyer said, "You have to make them fit somehow. Here is your money." The carpenter asked, "Do you care how we do it?" The owner said, "No," and went out. Bill later said, "I was flabbergasted. That carpenter took an electric saw and cut the books in half.")

Fish. *The New York Privateers 1756-1763*. 1945. illus. index. 100 pp. Lmtd. to 400 copies. (Includes a list of ships taking out privateer's licenses in NY 1756-1763.)

Fiske, S. *Off-Hand Portraits of Prominent New Yorkers*. 1884. 356 pp. (Brief descriptions of 58 noted New Yorkers, including: Bennett, Dana, Edison, Field, Gould, Morton, Reid, Roebling, Schurz, Tilden, Vanderbilt. Of Whitelaw Reid he writes, "When he recently lectured upon Journalism it was at once evident how little he knew of his chosen profession.")

Flagg, J. *Flagg's Flats*. 1909. 280 pp. (An apartment owner's troubles with the NYC police. Among the characters in the book are Teddy Roosevelt, George Ade, Oscar Hammerstein, and William Gaynor. Originally circulated in typewritten form, Flagg's friends urged him not to pub. it as it might cost him his life. He tried to find a pub. but could not, and finally pub. it himself in 1909. It went through three ed. in 1910, and as he was still alive he put out another ed. in 1911.)

Francis, J. *Old NY or Reminiscences of the Past 60 Years*. NY. 1858. index. 384 pp.

Francis, John W. *Old New York: or Reminiscences of the Past Sixty Years. With a Memoir of the Author by H. T. Tuckerman*. NY. 1865. 2 vol. Large paper ed. lmtd. to 100 copies for subscribers. [There were several ed. of this work 1857-1866. See *USiana*.] (The copy I had was the famous 2-vol. set extended to 6 vol. by Charles C. Moreau, a noted NYC bibliophile. He extra-illus. this set with 729 ports. and views, many of them from the late 1700s and early 1800s. A number of them were of high rarity or unusual local interest. According to Tredwell's *A Monograph on Privately Illustrated Books*, Brooklyn,

1882, Moreau, an insurance man, extra-illus. about 160 books. That must be some sort of a record for grangerizing. The importance of this particular set is affirmed by the fact that it was offered for sale by John E. Scopes, the noted Albany bookseller, in the 1920s for $500. And that was a lot of money in those days. Scopes deserves some recognition here. He was a rare book dealer in Albany for many years, and lived to be very old. During that time he acquired a great many rarities, one of the reasons being he was right in the center of hist.: Albany, one of the most important state capitols in the U. S. was also one of the earliest settled places in North America. It was a crossroads of hist. and emigration. Charlie Everitt, the noted NYC bookseller, said that when Scopes was living he was one of the dozen best Americana bookdealers in the world. Scopes issued mimeo. catalogs, but I have not yet been able to find any of them. Recently I acquired his prntd. catalog No. 88, undated, 16 pp., containing 118 entries, many with informative annotations. Occasionally, years ago, I would find a clipping from one of his catalogs laid in a book. His catalogs must have been full of bib. data available nowhere else. He also was a yachtsman, and during the Hudson-Fulton celebration in 1909 he was Chairman of the Albany Naval Parades Committee. A biog. of Scopes would be a great addition to the literature about celebrated American booksellers. Not too long before he died I visited Scopes in his home and shop near the capitol. He told me he had a warehouse full of material that he would sell for what he had it insured for. I did not ask him what his asking price was because at that time I was about flat broke and had no storage place. Now, I wish I had.)

Francis, John W. *Reminiscences of Printers, Authors, and Booksellers, In New York.* 1865. (On October 20, 1865, W. J. Widdleton, pub., 17 Mercer St., NYC, issued a prntd. flyer announcing the coming pub. of the above title. "This volume will be printed in a superior manner, uniform in size with the author's 'Old New York.' It will contain, besides the original paper of Dr. Francis bearing the above title, sketches from his pen of Washington Irving, Fenimore Cooper, Philip Freneau, and other persons eminent in literature. It will be illus. by an entirely new port., expressly engraved for the work, and a facsimile of the author's mss. The subscription list for this book, of which only a hundred copies will be prntd. in any form, is now open." As far as I know, this book never came off the press.)

Frankel and Dublin. *Heights and Weights of New York City Children, 14 to 16 Years of Age. A Study of Measurements of Boys and Girls Granted Employment Certificates.* NY. Metropolitan Life Insurance Co. 1916. wrps. tables. graphs. 53 pp. (This investigation studied over 10,000 children. The pub. results were to be used to insure that only normally developed applicants received certificates. Highly

statistical, with some emphasis given to nationality.)
--- *Friars Club. 107 West 45th St., New York City. George M. Cohan, the Abbot.* (An 8 pp. folder, ca 1920s?, listing the menu for a dinner dance, the honored guest being John Ringling, the circus magnate. The Friars Song, musicated by Victor Herbert, was sung. Illus. with humourous drawings, one showing Ringling watching an Elephant drink a barrel of Castor Oil.)
--- *The Gem, or Fashionable Business Directory, for the City of New York.* 1844. NY. George Shidell. index. 108 pp. (Business advts., usually several to a page, of which a few are illus.; also poetry. The first and only ed. of this rare work. The *National Union Catalog* locates only one copy, and Spear's *American Directories Through 1860* locates only one other copy.)
--- *General Orders No. 43. War Dept., Washington, D. C.* Feb. 13, 1863. 35 pp. pamphlet. (Justus McKinstry, of NY, and a West Point graduate, was a Union General in the Civil War. As Quartermaster he was accused of dishonesty and neglect of duty, and court-martialed. Sixty-one specificiations were listed against him, and, upon conviction, he was dismissed from the service. He later used his talents as a NYC stockbroker.)
--- (George Washington Bridge.) *Roebling Cables for the Hudson River Bridge. Problems ... Requirements ... Research ... Manufacture ... Plan Installation ... Cable Spinning.* Ed. by F. W. Skinner, Consulting Engineer. ca 1930. wrps. illus. 157 pp. (Many fine illus. of this bridge under construction.)
--- (George Washington and NYC) *Addresses of the City of New York to George Washington, With His Replies.* NY. 1867. Port. wrps. 14 pp. lmtd. to 75 copies. (On four occasions, when Washington visited NYC, the city greeted him with an Address; and he replied to each one. This work contains the four Addresses and Replies.)
--- *Gerit Smith and the Vigilant Association of the City of New York.* 1860. 29 pp. pamphlet. (Smith, noted abolitionist from Peterboro, NY, accuses the Vigilant Assn. of libel, and holds them responsible "for calling in effect upon the people both of the North and South to detest and abhor him." This group was formed by a group of wealthy NYC businessmen who were afraid of losing southern trade. According to Mushkat's history, *Tammany, the Evolution of a Political Machine 1789-1865*, someone once called this Assn. "A kid glove, scented, silk stocking, poodle-headed, degenerate aristocracy.")
Gilder, R. *The Battery; The Story of the Adventurers, Artists, Statesmen, Grafters, Songsters, Mariners, Pirates, Guzzlers, Indians, Thieves, Stuffed-Shirts, Turn-coats, Millionaires, Inventors, Poets, Heroes, Soldiers, Harlots, Bootlicks, Nobles, Nonentities, Burghers, Martyrs, & Murderers Who Played Their Parts During Full Four Centuries on Manhattan Island's Tip.* Boston. 1936. illus. 304 pp.
--- *A Guide to New York City's Strange Sections.* 1926. Little Blue Book Series. wrps. 64 pp. (A guide to Little Africa, New

Jerusalem, Millionaires Hive, Middle Ages in NYC, and other interesting areas.)

Hall, C. R. *A Scientist in the Early Republic. Samuel Lathan Mitchill, 1764-1831.* NY. 1934. port. bib. index. 162 pp. (Mitchill, of NYC, physician, author, U. S. Congressman, scientist, and Professor, has been called a "living encyclopedia" with a "chaos of knowledge." This biog. lists 49 learned societies of which he was a member, and he no doubt belonged to a number of others.)

--- *Harbor News Association.* 1849. Broadside. 10 x 15 inches. (Printing of an agreement between the six major NYC newspapers to hire small boats and four men to visit ships at the Narrows and in the East River to gather marine intelligence, the news to be shared by the six papers. A copy I had was signed in ink by James G. Bennett, and J. Watson Webb, and representatives from the four other papers.)

Hardie, J. *An Account of the Malignant Fever, Lately Prevalent in the City of New York.* NY. 1799. wrps. 148 pp. (A detailed account of the famous yellow fever epidemic that devastated the population of NYC, listing the names of the dead. It also lists the donations received from outside of the city for the relief of the people; i.e., "The inhabitants of Fishkill, one load potatoes, six fowls, eight cabbages, and one roll of butter." Hardie, the author, ca 1750-1832, was a tutor at Columbia College, but he became poor and dissipated and finally found employment with the board of health of the city. In spite of his dissipation he lived to be about 80 years old and wrote a number of books.)

--- *Harry Hills Dance Hall on the Bowery. While Painted Wantons Ply Their Vile Wiles Upon Chaste Sailors, Ingenuous Billposters, Innocent Printers, Godly Hackdrivers, and Immaculate Barbers, Two Great Brutes Battle With Bare Knuckles in the Most Sanguinary of all Ring Encounters ...* ca early 1900s. (This is a print, approximately 14 x 8 inches, showing two men boxing in the middle of a dance floor. I do not know where this came from, but I had to buy it because of its title. Other dealers, collectors, and libraries were intrigued by it also, because when I cataloged it I got a hall full of orders for it.)

Heartman, C. F. *Twenty-Five Years in the Auction Business, and What Now? Reminiscences and Opinions.* NY. prvtly. prntd. June 1938. wrps. 2 illus. 28 pp. Lmtd. to 400 copies. (Charles F. Heartman, an immigrant German, came to the U. S. in 1911, and soon went into the bookselling, publishing, and auction business. Although he lived in several places from Rutland, VT, to New Orleans, he worked mainly in NYC. He uncovered untold numbers of rarities, issued over 280 auction catalogs in 20 years, over 20 catalogs of books for sale, pub. two or more magazines, and his famous Heartman's Hist. Series consisted of at least 44 numbers all of which were lmtd. In 1936 he wrote and prvtly. pub., *Twenty-Five Years in the Book Business.*

Reminiscences and Opinions. 2 illus. 31 pp. Lmtd. to 300 copies.)
--- (Heartman, C. F.) Weiss, H. B. *The Bibliographical, Editorial and Other Activities of Charles F. Heartman, With an Annotated Bibliography.* Pvtly. prntd. Christmas, 1938. wrps. 24 pp. Lmtd. to 300 copies. (There is a four-page sketch of Heartman's activities; the balance is a bib. of his pub., not including his auction or book catalogs. Weiss, himself, was no slouch. He was an Entomologist, worked for the state of NJ, and wrote as an avocation, mainly on entomological and hist. subjects. The pub. bib. of his writings, covering the years 1912 to 1964, listing books, pamphlets, and periodical articles, includes 793 items! And he was probably still writing.)
--- Henry Rich. *Missing. Reward. 1882. Red flannel underwear, laced shoes, wears a truss. Alive or Dead, and no questions asked. Mrs. H. Rich, 252 East 53rd St., NY.* Broadside with a photo of Rich prntd. on the paper. Printed by the Police Gazette Steam Pictorial Print, NY.
Hicks, A. *Life, Trial, Confession and Execution of ... the Pirate and Murdered, Executed on Bedloes Island, New York, Bay, 13 July 1860, for Murder of Capt. Burr. Full Account of His Piracies, Murders ... Nearly 100 Murders!* NY. 1860. Illus. wrps. 68 pp. (Hicks murdered the Captain, and others on an oyster sloop in lower NY Bay. McDade. 473.)
(Hutchins, J. N.) *An Almanack for 1753.* by John Nathan Hutchins. NY. Hugh Gaine 1752. (This was the first book prntd. by Hugh Gaine the famous NYC printer and bookseller. Charles F. Heartman, a NYC bookseller discovered a copy of this almanac in a collection of items he had purchased from Harry Stone, another NYC dealer, and determined that it was the only known copy. He pub. it in 1913 as Heartman's Hist. Series No. Four, and sold the original the same year at auction for $150.00.)
(Hutchins, J. N.) *Hutchins Improved: ... Almanack ... 1786.* by John Nathan Hutchins. NY. H. Gaine. (Includes data on how to tell the age of a horse by its teeth, and has woodcuts of a set of horses' teeth. To cure the Chin-Cough in humans, "Take a spoonful of wood-lice, and bruise 'em, and mix them with breast-milk ....")
--- *The Illustrated Water-Cure and Health Almanac, for 1850.* Fowler & Wells. illus. 48 pp. (One article in this almanac is against inoculation, and another article says you should take a cold bath on the days you eat buckwheat cakes.)
Ireland, J. N. *Records of the New York Stage From 1750 to 1860.* 2 vols. 1866-67. index. (Packed full of information for the serious researcher on the hist. of plays and players in NYC. This work was reprntd. in 1968.)
--- *Isaac Carow, No. 222, Pearl-Street. New-York, Has for Sale at Very Reduced Prices, a complete Assortment of Hardware, &c.&c.&c. Among Which Are the Following Aricles ... Orders from any part of the United States or West*

Indies, punctually and carefully executed ... Broadside. ca 1810. 10 x 14 inches. (Carow was a prominent NYC merchant in the early 1800s. This broadside has 87 lines listing hardware and other items for sale: blistered steel, guns, twine, knives, backgammon games, saddlery, violin strings, spectacles, soap, "and a great variety of British, German, and American Goods, too numerous for detail." Not in Romaine, Sabin, or Evans.)

(Judah, S. B. H.) *Gotham and the Gothamites. A Medley.* NY. Pub. for the author, and sold by S. King. 1823. 94 pp. (Judah, a failed NYC dramatist, wrote this libelous satire on New Yorkers, adding footnotes to footnotes. Although pub. anonymously, the author and pub. were known and thrown in jail. Sabin says the book was suppressed, but *American Imprints* locates 23 copies.)

Kielty, B. *The Sidewalks of New York.* 1923. wrps. maps. illus. with drawings. 124 pp. (A book about NYC for tourists, which was pub. for the 5 Bowman Hotels in the city. One chapter is titled "Cherry Trees and Crime.")

Klein, H. *Sacrificed. The Story of Police Lieutenant Charles Becker.* 1927. 432 pp. (Herman Rosenthal, a gambler, was murdered in 1912 in front of the Hotel Metropole in NYC. Becker, a police officer, was electrocuted in Sing Sing Prison in 1915 for the killing, going to the chair saying, "I am sacrificed for my friends." Author writes, "It is a tale of gamblers, gunmen, and police graft in NYC, with politics and politicians thrown in.")

Lamb, M. J. *History of the City of New York, Its Origin, Rise and Progress.* NY. 1877-1881. 2 vol. illus. (This highly acclaimed work won her wide recognition. During her life time she was elected to 26 historical and other societies. In 1896 it was expanded with the aid of Mrs. B. Harrison, and pub. in 3 vol. It has since been reprntd.)

Landauer, B. *My City "Tis of Thee. New York City on Sheet-Music Covers ... Selections From Music Collection of Bella C. Landauer at New York Historical Society.* 1951. 25 pp. plus 80 illus.

Lankevich and Furer. *A Brief History of the City of New York.* 1983. 334 pp.

--- Lawrence & Andrews (comps.) *Catalogue of the Engravings Issued by the Society of Iconophiles of the City of New York 1894-1908.* NY. 1908. illus. index. 87 pp. Lmtd. to 125 copies on special O.W. hand-made paper, and 12 on imperial Japan paper. (This soc. was formed in 1894, never had more than 10 active members, but did much to preserve illus. of hist. sites of NYC. It also endeavoured to keep alive the art of hand engraving on copper. Among the artists it used were: Edwin Davis French, Joseph Pennell, C. F. W. Mielatz, Sidney L. Smith, Francis S. King, and Water A. Aikman. From time to time they issued series of views of NYC in folders, usually limited to 104 sets or less. On one occasion they reached a grand total of 132 impressions for one printing. By 1930 they had issued a total of 199 plates in folders. At first the excess number of pub.

were sold through two booksellers: J. O. Wright & Co. and Dodd Mead & Co. To facilitate the distribution of the extra copies it was decided in May of 1905 to admit 50 associate or subscribing members chosen by the active members.)

Leonard, J. *History of City of New York 1609-1909.* 1910. illus. maps. index. 954 pp.

Leuchs, F. *The Early German Theatre in New York. 1840-1872.* NY. 1928. bib. index. 298 pp. (A very detailed work listing plays, actors, and German-American journalistic pub.)

Linn, Wm. D.D. *The Blessings of America, A Sermon in Middle Dutch Church. July 4, 1791. At the Request of the Tammany Society.* NY. T. Greenleaf. 1791. wrps. 30 pp. Lmtd. to 600 copies. (Prntd. at the expense of the Tammany Soc., this was an important sermon as it was an early appeal for the oppressed peoples of Europe to come to America, "Here is an asylum for you, our brethren of the Old World ... Forsake your hard taskmakers. Refuse to dig an ungrateful soil which will not yield you bread. Haste you to the fertile plains of America. She opens wide her arms to embrace millions." I will leave it to your imagination whether this sermon was effective or not.)

Lossing, B. *History of NYC.* NY. 1884. illus. maps. 2 vol.

Lowi, T. J. *At the Pleasure of the Mayor. A Study of Appointment Politics in New York City, 1898-1958.* Dec. 1960. bib. many charts. 259 pp. (An in-depth study of political appointments in NYC: political framework, representation, career ladders, recruitment, continuity, reform. Probably only a few copies were issued.)

Lyman, S. *The Story of NY.* NY 1964. illus. map. 282 pp.

Macatamney, H. *Cradle Days of New York. (1609-1825).* NY. 1909. illus. 230 pp. (Originally pub. in the *New York Tribune* under the title "Little Old New York.")

(McKim, C. ed.) *The Salles Letters 1825-1850.* 1957. wrps. illus. index. 236 pp. lmtd. to 100 copies. (Letters of the Salles family of France and NY. Laurent Salles was a noted NYC businessman. Barrett's *Old Merchants of New York* says that Salles was a voracious eater and the more his boarding house charged him for food the more he would eat. They finally asked him to leave.)

McWatters, G. S. *Knots Untied; or, Ways and By-Ways in the Hidden Life of American Detectives, by ... Late of the Metropolitan Police, New York. Marvellous Experiences Among All Classes of Society ... Criminals ... Swindlers ... Thieves, Lottery Agents ... Necromancers ... &c.* Hartford (CT.) 1871. illus. 665 pp. (Among the scams noted are the: Gambler's Wax Finger, counterfeiting, genealogical swindlers, bogus lotteries, sorcery, forgery, and others.)

Martin, E. W. *Secrets of the Great City ... Virtues, Vices, Mysteries, Miseries, Crimes of NYC.* 1868. illus. folding plates. 552 pp. (This book discusses the city's secrets, among them: the Police, street musicians, fashionable shopping, hotel life, poor girls, street walkers, wickedest man in NY, wickedest woman in NY, baby farming, gift enterprises.)

Mathews, J. *Recollections of Persons and Events, Chiefly in the City of New York, Being Selections From His Journal.* NY. 1865. index. 368 pp. (The author personally knew many noted men of early NYC, including: Robert Fulton, Aaron Burr, Governor Clinton, Chancellor Kent.)

Maverick, A. *Henry J. Raymond and the New York Press, for 30 Years. Progress of American Journalism From 1840 to 1870.* 1870 portrait, illus. appendix. index. 501 pp. (Raymond, 1820-1869, ed. and politician born at Lima, NY, became a noted newspaper ed. in NYC. This is an excellent biog. of Raymond, with much light on the NYC newspaper business. Elected to the NY State Assembly in 1849 this young chap "leaped into prominence in the week he took his seat," according to the DAB.)

(Medical Society) *Report of the Committee of the Medical Society of the City and County of New York, Appointed to Investigate the Subject of a Secret Medical Association.* NY. 1831. 12 pp. pamphlet. (The report names the members of the Secret Soc., and says they interfere with the public good. It adds "patients who fall into their hands, may be reduced to such an extremity as to render a consultation necessary.")

Mitchill, S. L. *Catalogue of the Organic Remains, and Other Geological and Mineralogical Articles, Contained in the Collection Presented to the New York Lyceum of Natural History, by ... One of the Members.* NY. 1826. wrps. 40 pp. (Mitchill, a wide-rnaging collector and scientist, who has been called "a chaos of knowledge," presented about 400 items to the Lyceum, and compiled the above catalog. One of the specimens was, "The fatty matter into which a woman was converted, after lying in the grave 33 years.")

(Mitchill, S. L.) *The Picture of New York; or the Travellers' Guide, Through the Commercial Metropolis of the U.S. by a Gentleman Residing in This City.* NY. 1807. 223 pp. (The first guide book to NYC. It has been said that this work inspired Washington Irving to write his "Knickerbocker History" of NY, but that assertion appears to be open to disputation. The preface of the book says it was pub. without maps or plates, but in some copies are found a "Plan of the City of New York ... From Actual Survey by William Bridges, City Surveyor ... Engraved by Peter Maverick.")

Moscow, H. (comp.) *The Street Book: An Encyclopedia of Manhattan's Street Names and Their Origins.* 1978. illus. bib. 276 pp.

Still, B. *Mirror for Gotham.* NY 1956. illus. 417 pp.

Stokes, I. *The Iconography of Manhattan Island. 1498-1909. Compiled from Original Sources and Illustrated by Photo Intaglio Reproductions of Important Maps, Plans, Views, and Documents in Public and Private Collections.* NY. R. H. Dodd. 1915-1928. 6 vol. Lmtd. to 360 sets on Japanese vellum. (Highly prized for its pictorial content and maps, this set rarely comes on the market. During the past several years it has brought more than $2,000.00 at auction. It was reprntd. by Arno Press, NY, in 1967, and I believe it was remaindered. I was not sensible enough to pick up a set at the time, and the first four vol. I acquired a few years ago are practically useless without the index vol. The complete reprntd. set sold at auction in 1986 for $900.00. Over the years I have had several vol. of the original ed., but only one complete set. That set I bought at Tuttles Antiquarian Books in Rutland, VT, several years ago, and actually had it sold before I bought it.) Reprntd. NYC. 1967.

--- *Neighbors on the Block. Life in Single Room Occupancy Hotels. Photographs by Laurence Salzmann.* Pub. by the NY State Council on the Arts. 1971. This is a portfolio of 40 photos, taken on the upper West side of NYC, representing a "microcosm of failure and despair."

--- New York City. *Norton's Handbook of New York City, Containing 44 Engravings of the Most Celebrated Public Buildings in the City.* Pub. by Albert Norton. 1859. map. wrps. 32 pp. (There is data on some of the buildings, also a few advts. A description is given of Otis A. Bullard's famous Panorama of NYC, which was painted on 18,000 feet of canvas, and exhibited throughout NY State, and in several out-of-state cities. Included is a brief biog. of Bullard who was born at Howard, in Steuben Co., NY.)

--- *The New York Ladies Southern Association, 1866-1867.* Pub. by a chapter of the United Daughters of the Confederacy in NYC. 1926. wrps. 113 pp. (An account of the relief furnished by citizens of NYC to the devastated regions of the south right after the Civil War.)

O'Connor, R. *Gould's Millions.* 1962. illus. bib. index. 335 pp. (The story of Jay Gould's famous $100,000,000 raid on the American economy, which left him hated, feared, and friendless. This NY State Napoleonic genius has been called "the Skunk of Wall Street," and "the worst man on earth since the beginning of the Christian era." By the time he was 20 years old he had worked on several co. maps and pub. a hist. of Delaware Co., NY. The DAB says that at the age of 21 he was "undersized, keen-witted, unscrupulous.")

--- *New York Supreme Court. Sarah Ann Angell vs. Edwin Gould, et al. Plaintiffs Depositions. Supreme Court, NY County. Sarah Ann Angell, Plaintiff, against Edwin Gould, et al, Defendants. Pleadings. Defendants Depositions.* ca 1898. 1357 pp. (Sarah claimed she had married Jay Gould in 1853 at Champlain, NY, that they lived together for about three months before he deserted her, that she had a daughter, and that she is entitled to dower in the real estate that Jay left to his son Edwin by his "second" wife. Edwin said that Sarah was never married to his father. This was a very intricate case, with depositions being taken in MA, Wyoming, and MI. There are excerpts from many letters written by Jay, and there is a great deal of data on his map making and surveying. Included is the diary of J. W. Champlin, who spent three months surveying the area of the upper Delaware River. [See the DAB for Champlin.] Also, there is a lengthy testimony from the sister of Jay. This is a most important source of information on the early life of Jay Gould, as his life is traced from early childhood to some years subsequent to the alleged marriage in great detail. Incidentally, after all the legal proceedings, Sarah recanted her allegations.)

--- *Ode for the Celebration of the French Revolution in the City of New-York, November 25, 1830. Written at the Request of the Printers of New-York, by Samuel Woodworth, Printer.* Stereotyped by James Conner, Franklin Buildings. broadside, 7 x 11 inches. Seven 8-line verses, with a 4-line chorus. (Note printed at the bottom margin of the broadside: "The foregoing Ode was printed on a moveable stage, on the 25th. of Nov. 1830, and distributed to the citizens, during the procession in honor of the triumph of liberal principles in France. It was afterwards sung, on a platform erected for that purpose, in the center of Washington Square, by all the vocalists of the Park Theatre, accompanied by the whole orchestra of that establishment.")

--- *Opening Ceremonies of the New York and Brooklyn Bridge.* May 24, 1883. 122 pp. (This work contains wonderful orations at the opening of this famous bridge. Abram S. Hewitt, noted politician, and later the mayor of NYC, stated, "A large portion of our vices and crimes are created either by law, or its maladministration.")

Patten, J. *Lives of the Clergy of New York, and Brooklyn ... 200 Biographies of Eminent Living Men in All Denominations ... Illustrated With Portraits on Steel.* 1874. 635 pp. (The author talked to almost every one of the clergymen, and went to hear them preach, to "prepare myself for writing the personal descriptions and criticisms ....")

Patterson, M. S. (Comp.) *View of Old New York. Catalogue of the William Sloane Collection.* 1968. prvtly. prntd. index. bib. wrps. 80 pp, plus 31 pp. of illus. of views. (This work contains descriptions of 43 engravings, aquatints, and lithographs; 14 oils and watercolors; plus 4 prints, in the Museum of the City of NY.)

Pelletreau, W. S. *Early New York Houses, With Historical and Genealogical Notes.* NY. 1900. in 10 parts. *Photographs of Old Houses and Original Illustrations by C. G. Moller, Jr.* index. 243 pp. Lmtd. to 300 copies. Also 25 copies on Japan Paper, signed and numbered by the pub.

--- *The People's Democratic Guide.* NY. James Webster, Pub. Agent. Vol. 1 thru No. 12 (Nov. 1841 - Oct. 1842) index. 376 pp. all pub. (Because of "The nefarious manner in which the producing and working classes have been cheated out of their votes and rights by the Federal Whigs," several competent persons in NYC undertook to edit and compile a periodical to be devoted to the cause of democracy.)

--- *Report of the Board of Managers of the Free Produce Association of Friends, of New York Yearly Meeting.* 1852. wrps. 12 pp. (The Quakers had a store in NYC in which they would not handle any item produced by slave labor. The pamphlet lists the members, and gives an account of the problems of the store.)

--- *Report of the Mayor's Push-Cart Commission.* NYC. 1906. illus. maps. tables. 233 pp. (A major study of NYC push cart peddlers, detailing: problems, existing evils, nationality of the peddlers and their poverty, licenses, extortion of shopkeepers, goods sold.)

--- *Reward! Frank Austin Roy, M.D.D.D.S. Missing ... 1887. Practicing Dentisty. Reserved, Bashful. Double row of flat warts under chin. The Doctor is a very close student, and it is feared has wandered away under a temporary derangement of mind from over application to his profession.* William Murray, Supt. Police, 30 Mulberry St., NYC. broadside.

Rockwell, A. D. *Rambling Recollections. An Autobiography.* 1920. illus. index. 332 pp. (Rockwell, 1840-1933, was a NYC physician, and a Prof. in the NY Post Graduate Medical School. Besides being one of the first to develop the use of electricity in medical therapeutics, he also invented the electric chair and witnessed some of the earliest executions in the state. His autobiog. gives personal sketches of many people, including: Teddy Roosevelt, Vanderbilt, Tweed, William Astor.)

Rowson, S. H. *Charlotte Temple. A Tale of Truth. Reprinted From the Rare First American Edition (1794). Over 1200 Errors in Later Editions Being Corrected, and the Preface Restored. With Historical and Biographical Introduction, Bibliography, Etc.,* by F.W. Halsey. 1905. maps. illus. index. 150 pp. (Halsey's work is a major contribution to the hist. of Susanna Rowson's novel which was the first American best seller book of fiction. She set it partially in NY. It is said that it has gone through more than 200 ed.)

Rubin & Brown. eds. *Walt Whitman of the New York Aurora. Editor at Twenty-Two.* 1950. index. 148 pp. (Whitman was ed. of the *New York Aurora* for a short time in 1842, and he wrote most of its copy. This book presents more than 80 articles and 2 poems from the paper. None of these articles, which were mostly on NYC and NYC politics, had appeared in any biog. of Whitman or in collections of his writings.)

Sampson, W. *Is a Whale a Fish? An Accurate Report of Case of James Maurice Against Samuel Judd, Tried in ... City of NY.* 30-31 Dec. 1818. NY. 1819. 79 pp. (A case involving three casks of fish oil which had not been gauged, inspected, or branded, contrary to the law. One of the witnesses called to the stand was a Capt. Preserved Fish. No doubt this is the famous Fish whose name has been preserved in the DAB.)

--- *"Seeing New York." Automobiles. Four Separate Routes.* 1905. A 3-panel folder advertising auto tours of NYC. "The first (pioneer) company to inaugurate the sight-seeing business in the U. S."

American Sight-Seeing Car and Coach Co. (Lists some of the attractions to be seen: a tree planted by Li Hung Chang, offices of Hetty Green, and a Sanitarium for Birds. The Company also conducted a Yacht trip around Manhattan Island. There is an illus. of their coach and yacht. See Kane's "Famous First Facts" for a Brooklyn Company that had a sight-seeing bus built in 1900.)

--- *A Sketch of Events in the Life of George Law. Published in Advance of His Biography.* NY. 1855. port. 96 pp. (Law, 1806-1881, born at present Shushan, NY, became a contractor on the Croton Water Works, owned ships sailing to CA, and owned the Staten Island Ferry. Most of his life was lived in NYC. Politically he was affiliated with the Know-Nothing Party, and this campaign biog. was written anonymously at the time some supported him for that party's U. S. presidential nomination. Instead, Fillmore received the party's support in 1856. The proposed biog. referred to was never pub.)

Smith, S. *The City That Was.* 1911. illus. diagrams. 211 pp. (This book details the incredibly vile sanitary conditions in the tenement districts of NYC in the 1860s. On the basis of his investigations, Smith, a pioneer in public health, drafted a Metropolitan Health Law, which was passed in 1866, and which "became the basis of civic sanitation in the U. S. .....")

--- *Social Etiquette of New York.* NY. 1892. ed. 268 pp. (A fascinating description of social forms and usages as practiced by the superior families of NYC during the Gay Nineties: introductions, chaperons, visiting cards, parties, dinners, weddings, extended visits, much else.)

Stafford, M. *The Life of James Fisk, Jr. A Full and Accurate Narrative of His Career ... Great Enterprises ....Assassination.* NY. pub. by the author. 1872. illus. 325 pp. + an appendix of 16 pp. "Enjoined Love Letters." (Fisk, 1834-1872, of NYC, rose from being a circus ticket-seller to being a jolly and pleasure-loving capitalist and speculator. He was involved in the Erie Railroad scandal, bought a Colonelcy in the NY Milita, and was murdered.)

Steele, Z. *Angel in Top Hat.* 1942. port. illus. bib. 319 pp. (The biog. of Henry Bergh, the founder of the ASPCA of NYC. He was a colorful character who was known to have used a whip on a driver who had whipped his horse. He also aided in forming a soc. for the prevention of cruelty to children.)

Stephen, H. *Branch's Anaconda.* Vol. 1 No. 1. NY. 1862. (This is a small 4 pp. newspaper. In the lead article Branch tells of two men named Smith and Lovell who were superintendants in the NYC Street Dept., and who fled to the South at the start of the Civil War and became Confederate Generals! He wonders why ex-Mayor Tiemann, their former boss, is strangely quiet. He also states, "New York has some precious Judges. I know three whose crimes should consign them to a dungeon for life, and one who should be sent to the scaffold." Only a few issues of this paper were published. Branch also produced three other very short-lived papers, 1858-1866: the Alligator, Resurrection, and Union. See the Union List of Serials.)

Stevens, H. *Recollections of Mr. James Lenox of New York and the Formation of His Library.* London. 1886. ports. 211 pp. (One of the most delightful books ever written by an antiquarian bookseller. It is actually a recounting of the exploits of Stevens, who, along the way, supplied many Americana rarities to the Lenox Library of NYC. The Lenox Library is now part of the NY Public Library.)

Stokes, I. N. Phelps. *New York Past and Present. Its History and Landmarks 1524-1939. One Hundred Views Reproduced and Described from Old Prints, Etc., and Modern Photographs.* 1939. map. 96 pp. (The copy I had contained an inserted prntd. leaf by Geo. A. Zabriskie stating, "I obtained from Mr. Stokes a number of sheets, hot off the press, to bind up for my friends.")

Stone, W. *History of NYC.* NY. 1868. 252 pp.

Reprntd. NY. 1876. Titled: *Centennial History of NYC.*

--- *History of NYC to the Present Day.* NY. 1872. 896 pp.

Strong, J. R. (ed.) *Letters of George W. Strong.* 1922. port., 264 pp. Letterpress ed. lmtd. to 60 copies for private distribution. (Strong, 1783-1855, was an eminent NYC lawyer who trained many young men in the profession, including the son of Chancellor Kent. These are letters to and from Strong, 1805-1841, giving a good look at the life and thought of a NYC lawyer.)

Thomas, J. *The Mills Hotels, With Some Account of Workingmen's Hotels in Europe and America.* 1899. illus. wrps. 34 pp. (Mostly data on the two Mills' Hotels in NYC, which were built because the average boarding house was shamefully inadequate, and most workingmen were respectable. "When the Hotel was first opened, it was predicted that bathing would have to be made compulsory, but this rule ... is unnecessary ....")

Thorpe, Col. T. B. *Reminiscences of Charles L. Elliott, Artist (1868).* 11 pp. pamphlet. (Elliott, 1812-1868, born at Scipio, NY, became an itinerant port. painter. Later he opened a studio in NYC, and according to the DAB became widely acclaimed. He was once advised to go see the Butchers at the Fulton Fish Market as they are the "finest looking of any class of our citizens." Thorpe, the author, was also an artist of note [see the DAB]. He gives his personal memories of his recently deceased friend, Elliott, especially regarding his work in NYC.)

Ulmann, A. *Landmark History of NY.* NY. 1901. 285 pp.

--- Another ed. 1909. 279 pp.

--- *A Landmark History of NY, Including a Guide to Commemorative Sites & Monuments.* NY. 1939. illus. maps. 440 pp.

Valentine, D. *History of City of NY.* NY. 1853. illus. maps. 404 pp. (Believed by some historians to have been written by W. I. Paulding)

Valentine, D. T. *Manuals of the Corporation of the City of New York.* 1841-1870. (Valentine, who gradually went from being a grocery clerk to becoming clerk of the Common Council of NYC, compiled and issued a series of annual vol. popularly known as "Valentine's Manuals." One was pub. every year from 1841 till 1870, skipping only the year 1867. They were packed full of NYC history, and most of them were liberally supplied with maps and illus. There were a great many fine colored plates. The yearly books were so popular that the DAB says they became almost a necessity for New Yorkers. The maps and plates were popular, too, and many were removed from the vol. I have had a number of the manuals and very rarely has one been complete. They had to be sold as "breakers" for others to remove the remaining plates for sale. Framed, the colored prints usually command a good price. Only once did I have a complete run 1841 through 1870, and that set was intact, and it was a doubly impressive acquisition as it was finely bound. I bought that gem from Tuttle's Antiquarian Books in Rutland, VT, several years ago. For collectors of the manuals it is essential to have an index to use them adequately for reference, and to collate the maps and plates. In 1900 Otto Hufeland, a Westchester Co. historian, compiled an hist. index to the manuals containing 2325 entries, which was pub. in an ed. of 250 copies. In 1906 R. H. Lawrence, President of the Grolier Club, compiled an index to the illus., maps, and facsimilies of the manuals, which was pub. in an ed. of 250 copies. These two works very seldom come on the market. In 1981 Harbor Hill Books, Harrison, NY, reprntd. both of them in one vol. Every owner of the manuals needs this reference work to adequately use and appreciate his collection.)

Vanderpoel, A. E. (ed.) *Personal Memoirs of Edwin A. Ely, Ed. by His Nephew.* 1926. illus. 517 pp. lmtd. to 200 copies. (Ely, born in 1836, was prominent in the leather business in NYC. This book contains much interesting data on the city. Among many other things, it states that John Wilkes Booth went to a shooting gallery at 600 Broadway and used a photograph of Abraham Lincoln as a target during pistol practice.)

Van Pelt, D. *Leslie's History of the Greater New York.* NY. 1898. illus. 3 vols.

--- *Views of Early New York, With Illustrative Sketches. Prepared for the New York Chapter of the Colonial Order of the Acorn.* NY. 1904. prvtly. prntd. illus. 142 pp. lmtd. to 213 copies. (The six fine copper plates in this work were done by Edwin Davis French from the original prints. For the biog. of French the noted copper engraver, see the DAB.)

Waring, G. E. *Earth-Closets: How to Make Them and How to Use Them.* 1868. diagrams. wrps. 45 pp. (Waring, 1833-1898, was drainage engineer of Central Park in NYC, installed a sewer system in Memphis, TN, and was street-cleaning commissioner of NYC. He was appalled at the primitive sanitation facilities he saw, and called outdoor privies "temples of defame and graves of decency." So he wrote this descriptive work on Earth

143

Closets which could be used indoors. This pamphlet has good instructions for constructing and locating this ingenious device. One of his instructions for users is "Rise from the seat quickly.")

--- Charles L. Woodward was an old-time NYC bookseller of the late 1800s, and from his shop at 78 Nassau Street he issued catalogs and advertising flyers. One of his employees, Wilberforce Eames, later became a famous bibliographer and librarian. (Now it is a recognized fact that there is a phenomenon known as "auction fever" which strikes bidders so hard they will pay more for a book at an auction house than they would in a bookshop. An old NY book dealer, now retired, told me, "I was at an auction and saw this guy bid on a book. He was outbid by someone else. After the auction was over, I went over and offered him a better copy of the same book for half the price and he turned it down." In July 1890 Woodward put out an advertising circular addressing this strange turn of affairs, "My experience, and that of some other dealers with whom I have compared notes, has convinced us that there are a good many buyers ... who will never pay us a dollar for a book they can buy at auction for two.")

Woodward, Charles L. *Catalogue of an Attractive and Valuable Selection of Books and Pamphlets Relating Mainly to America ... Revolutionary War ... Indians ... For Sale by Charles L. Woodward, 78 Nassau St., NY.* ca late 1800s. 51 pp. (In several places in the catalog Woodward comments on high auction prices for books which he sells more cheaply, on customers who misplace books on shelves, and states at the beginning, "Each book on my shelves is marked in plain figures, and my most distant customer may buy it by letter, as cheap as the meanest screw that ever entered a book shop.")

Whitson, S. *New York City 100 Years Ago.* 1977. illus. 40 pp.

Wilkenfeld, B. *The Social and Economic Structure of the City of New York. 1695-1796.* 1978. bib. 264 pp.

Wilson, J. (ed.) *Memorial History of City of New York. to 1892.* NY. 1892. maps. 4 vols.

--- *World's Cattle Show. Entrance in 42nd Street.* (NYC). broadside, 6 x 9 inches, ca mid-1800s. (An announcement of a tent exhibition of Monster Cattle. Eleven specimens are listed with brief descriptions. Among their names were: Jenny Lind, DeWitt Clinton, Henry Clay, Silas Wright. For 25 cents you could feast your eyes on these beauties for 10 minutes.)

RIVERDALE, New York Co.
Kane, M. *Yesterday in Riverdale.* Spuyten Duyvil. 1947. map. wrps. 42 pp.

WEST FARMS, New York Co.
Wray, S. *The Old Village of West Farms, Now in NYC.* ca 1953. maps. 230 pp. typed mss. in WCHS.

NIAGARA COUNTY

NIAGARA COUNTY
Anon. *Souvenir History of Niagara Co.* Lockport. 1902. illus. 228 pp.

Aiken, J. (& others) *Outpost of Empires. A Short History of Niagara Co.* Phoenix, NY. 1961. illus. maps. 153 pp.
Pechuman, L. *Niagara Co. & Its Towns.* (A series of 18 maps.) Lockport. July 1959. wrps.
Pool, W. *Landmarks of Niagara Co.* Syracuse. 1897. illus. 447 pp.
Porter, P. *Old Niagara Co. Shore in Battle of Lake Erie.* Niagara Falls. 1913. illus. maps. wrps. 16 pp.
Reed, R. *Niagara County in the Civil War.* 1966.
(Turner & others) *History of Niagara Co.* NY. 1873. illus. 397 pp.
Wiley & Garner. *Biog. & Portrait Cyclopedia of Niagara Co.* Phil. 1892. illus. 640 pp.
Williams, E. *Niagara Co. A Concise Record of Her Progress & People. 1821-1921.* Chicago. 1921. illus. 2 vols.

LEWISTON, Niagara Co.
Anon. *Lewiston & Auburn Directory Together With a History of Lewiston & Auburn.* Lewiston. 186-? 179 pp.
Bruni, S. *Lewiston Centennial.* 1971. Book.
Hawes. Lewiston. *Past, Present, Future.* 1887? wrps. 15 pp.
Kimball, H. *A Homely Approach to Lewiston 1800-1954.* March 1954. wrps. 64 pp.
Robson, M. *Under the Mountain.* Buffalo. 1958. illus. maps. 142 pp.
Rosseel, F. *A Back Number Town.* Buffalo. 1891. illus. 28 pp.

LOCKPORT, Niagara Co.
Benziger, G. *An Early History of Lockport.* U. of Buffalo. Feb. 1949. 51 pp. typed mss. in BPL.
Kaiser, C. *The Streets of Lockport With Notes on Early History of the City.* 1948. 2nd. ed. 1949. 20 pp.
Lacy, I. & A. *Dusty Lockport Pages.* Lockport. Jan. 1952. wrps. 36 pp.
Nicholls, H. *The Twilight of My Native Town.* Lockport. March 1956. wrps. 24 pp.

NEWFANE, Niagara Co.
Newell, R. *History of Newfane.* Lockport. 1950. wrps. 16 pp.

NIAGARA, Niagara Co.
Anon. *Reminiscences of Niagara By Several of the Oldest Residents.* n.d. 61 pp. (Reprnt. of Niag. Hist. Soc. Pub. No. 11)
Holley, G. *Niagara, Its History & Geology.* Toronto. 1872. 165 pp.
Also: NY. 1872. 165 pp.
Johnson, R. *Niagara: Its History, Incidents, Poetry.* Washington D.C. 1898. illus. 85 pp.
Porter, A. *Reminiscences of Niagara from 1806 to 1872, By An Old Resident.* Niagara Falls. 1872. pvtly. circulated. (Dow, *Anthology & Bibliography of N. F.* says, "There seems to have been several editions of this article.")
--- *Historical Sketch of Niagara 1673-1876.* n.d. 51 pp.
Porter, P. *Goat Island.* 1900. illus. maps. lmtd. 85 copies. 54 pp.
Vinal, T. *Niagara Portage from Past to Present.* Buffalo. 1949. illus. map. 157 pp.
Williams, E. *Niagara, Queen of Wonders* Boston. 1916. illus. 188 pp.
Williams, M. *Brief History of Niagara Falls.* 1972. 41 pp.

NIAGARA FRONTIER, Niagara Co.
Marshall, O. *The Niagara Frontier. Sketches of Its Early Hist.*

& Indian, French, & English Local Names. Buffalo. 1866. prntd. for pvt. circulation. Reprntd. 1881.

Wilner, M. *Niagara Frontier, A Narrative & Documentary History.* Chicago. 1931. illus. maps. 4 vols. (Narrative portion expanded from story of Buffalo, pub. in daily installments in *Buffalo Evening News* 1929-1930.)

NORTH TONAWANDA, Niagara Co.
Anon. *North Tonawanda Centennial Magazine 1865-1965*, pub. by Tonawanda News.
Saliba, G. *History of North Tonawanda*. Warner, H. *Historical Data of North Tonawanda*. Root, E. *Romantic History of North Tonawanda*. unpub. mss. in North Tonawanda Public Library.

ROYALTON, Niagara Co.
Winner, J. (comp) *Yesterday in Royalton*. Lockport. April 1957. map. wrps. 52 pp.

SOMERSET, Niagara Co.
Porter, R. *The Story of Somerset*. Lockport. July 1960. illus. wrps. 42 pp.

WILSON, Niagara Co.
Anon. *Wilson Centennial 1858-1958*. illus. wrps. unpaged.

YOUNGSTOWN, Niagara Co.
Howard, E. & V. *History of Youngstown*. Lockport. June 15, 1951. wrps. 20 pp. 2nd. ed. 1951.

NORTHERN NEW YORK

Abbott, Mrs. E. *Personal Sketches and Recollections*. 1861. 359 pp. (The authoress was born in Watertown, NY, in 1821, and had a career as a teacher, and as a travelling bookseller. The book contains much on life in the Jefferson Co. area. There were probably very few lady booksellers in that day, travelling or otherwise.)

Abbott, Henry. "Birch Bark Books." (Abbott wrote a series of privately printed "Birch Bark" books about the Adirondack Mountains, which he issued as Christmas greetings from 1914 to 1932. All are illus., and are very scarce. There is a complete title list in Plum's *Adirondack bibliography*. Plum also wrote an article for the July-August 1952 issue of *Ad-i-ron-dack* Magazine about these small and elusive vol. Not too many years ago they were reprinted in a one-vol. format.)

(Adirondack Photographs) H. M. Beach was a photographer from Remsen, NY, (also Lowville,) about 1911-1912. He published huge photos of Adirondack views: 10 inches by 30 to 40 inches long, with title, and a thick black border. The actual picture is about 6-1/2 x 26 or more inches long. They must be quite scarce as in all the years I have been in business only 9 of them have come my way.

Armstrong, Rev. L. *The Temperance Reformation of this 19th. Century, the Fulfillment of Divine Prophecy. A Sermon.* NY. 1845. 16 pp. (Prntd. with the sermon is the Constitution of the Temperance Soc. of Moreau and Northumberland in Saratoga Co., 1808, which was the first union temperance society in the U. S. There is also some information on the founding of the soc. whose members were allowed to drink on the advice of a physician and at public dinners. Rev. Armstrong was a Presbyterian minister & founding member.)

Bacheller, I. *Silas Strong, Emperor of the Woods.* NY. Harper. 1906. 340 pp. bound in 3/4 crushed morocco. (An excellent novel written at Lake Placid. Bacheller said that he wrote it to "show from the woodman's viewpoint the play of great forces which have been tearing down his home and turning it into the flesh and bone of cities....")

Benton, R. *The Vermont Settlers and the New York Land Speculators.* Minneapolis. 1894. Prvtly. prntd. "Distributed With Compliments of the Author." 188 pp. (A discussion of the famous quarrel over the lands in VT claimed by NY in the 1700s.)

Bethke, R. *Adirondack Voices. Woodsmen and Woods Lore.* 1981. index. illus. map. 148 pp. (A fine collection of folklore, gathered in the 1970s in St. Lawrence Co. from woodsmen. It includes some songs with music.)

Briggs, A. Jr. *The Novels of Harold Frederic.* 1969. bib. index. 234 pp. (Frederic, 1856-1898, a journalist and novelist born in Utica, NY, wrote 10 novels, many of them set in the Mohawk Valley. This is a critical discussion of his works of fiction.)

Brown, A. *The Elgin Botanic Garden, Its Later History and Relation to Columbia College, The New Hampshire Grants and the Treaty With Vermont in 1790.* 1908. index. 57 pp. (The author provides much data on the dispute over the NY-VT boundary line.)

Bufford, J. H. (Adirondack Prints.) Bufford, of NYC, was an outstanding lithographer, one of the best in America. In 1838-39 he issued a folder of Adirondack views, which had first appeared in Ebenezer Emmons Geological Survey which was pub. as NY Assembly Document No. 200 in 1838. (These separately pub. views, and maps, seldom come on the market. Once I acquired 8 loose views. Another time I found a bound folder with 14 plates, 10 of them pertaining to the Adirondacks. This folder I pulled out from under my foot on the floor of a disintegrating house filled, helter-skelter, with books, pamphlets, mss., and prints, on every conceivable subject under the sun. An informative and illustrated article on Bufford, by David Tatham, was printed in the Proceedings of the American Antiquarian Soc. of Worcester, MA, in 1976, and was reprnted. in pamphlet form.)

Burke, M. B. *A Random Scoot, Memoirs by.* 1983. port. 81 pp. (Memories of the St. Lawrence Valley in the early 1900s. The title is taken from Old Mountain Phelps, the famous Adirondack Mountain guide, whose expression for a haphazard walk through the woods was a "random scoot." Donaldson's *The Adirondacks* devotes an entire chapter to Phelps, and has his port.)

(Burt, C. H.?) *The Opening of the Adirondacks. With a map and illustrations.* NY. 1865. Folding map. 8 full page illus. 82 pp. (Plum 35, states, "Munson credits authorship to C. H. Burt." William Munson was a noted collector of

147

Adirondackiana. Cole locates only 1 copy of this work.)

Card, H. *The Collector's Remington. Notes on Books by Him; Books illustrated by Him; and Books Which Gossip About Him.* Woonsocket, RI. 1946. wrps. 8 pp. Lmtd. to 100 copies. (Frederic Remington, the noted illus., was born in Canton, NY. Although he is justly famous for his western art, he also did some work on northern NY. This item was rapidly snapped up by the numerous Remington collectors, and a copy rarely comes on the market.)

Card, H. *The Collector's Remington. A Series II. The Story of His Bronzes, with a Complete Descriptive List.* Woonsocket, RI. 1946. wrps. 10 pp. (Jeff Dykes in his *Fifty Great Western Illustrators*, 1975, item #1368 under Remington, says this was lmtd. to 100 copies. In his article on Remington rarities in the April 1966 issue of the *American Book Collector*, Dykes says Card was one of the Remington scholars who met in the old Mannados Bookshop in NYC.)

Chaumont, V. Leray de. *Avis Aux Emigrants.* 1st Novembre, 1848. Broadside, 9 x 9 inches. (The Chaumont family was greatly responsible for the settling of the vast area north and west of the Adirondacks. Written in French, this broadside was evidently for the information of prospective French settlers coming into the area. It has information on travelling to New Bremen, Lewis Co., from NYC, via Albany and Rome. It lists the fare, and the name of the land agent at Carthage. This broadside has also been found printed in German.)

(Coffin, N. W.) *The Forest Arcadia of Northern New York, Embracing a View of Its Mineral, Agricultural, and Timber Resources.* Boston. 1864. 224 pp. (This is one of the scarcest books on the Adirondacks, and was pub. anonymously. Years ago I had the first prntd. copy of this book, it had been presented by the author to his wife.)

Conway, M. *Highmarket "As You Were." Two Hundred Years of Tug Hill.* Pub. by the author. 1977. map. illus. 153 pp. (Facts, fables, and fancies of the little known Highmarket area of the remote Tug Hill Plateau between Lake Ontario and the Adirondacks. It is the largest roadless area on the map of NY state outside of the Adirondacks.)

Cook, M. *The Wilderness Cure.* 1881. 153 pp. (A very good book on camping in the Adirondacks for tuberculosis sufferers. Earlier in 1881 Cook had written a magazine article about regaining health in the woods. It aroused such interest that he expanded the magazine article into a full sized book.)

Coolidge, G. *The French Occupation of the Champlain Valley From 1609 to 1759.* Montpelier, VT. VT Hist. Soc. 1938. maps. wrps. 170 pp. (The first major study of this subject.)

Daniel Claus Narrative of His Relations With Sir William Johnson and Experiences in the Lake George Fight. (1755) 1904. wrps. 40 pp. (Claus was in the Indian Department, and was a son-in-law of Sir William Johnson. Pound's

Johnson of the Mohawks gives considerable data on Claus and gives the reason why he wrote his *Narrative*. Encyclopedias and dictionaries have been compiled on the Revolutionary and Civil Wars. As far as I know no major such work has been done on the French and Indian War or the War of 1812. Give it some thought: maybe you, the reader, would like to tackle it.)

Directory of the Village of Whitehall. 1892-93. wrps. 52 pp. (In this first general directory of Whitehall the publishers suggest that the town spend some money for street signs. "Many residents do not know the name of the street upon which they live.")

Dornburgh, H. *Why the Wilderness is Called Adirondack*. Glens Falls, NY. 1885. wrps. 14 pp. (This elusive work includes a detailed hist. of the Adirondack Iron Works. Dornburgh had worked for the company for many years. Over 20 years ago this pamphlet was bringing $35.00 on the open market. One day I got a catalog from a New England dealer with a copy listed for $1.00. Immediately I ordered it and when it came there was a note attached to the invoice, "I have more of these if you can use them." I grabbed the phone to order more, and the delighted chap on the other end informed me, "They are all gone. A guy from Albany came over and took all I had left. I had found 60 copies." A year or more later I visited this dealer and found a copy of Dornburgh on top of a pile of books. "Oh yes," he said, "I found that stray copy from the lot I bought. That one will cost you 5 bucks." The pamphlet has been reprinted in recent years.)

Einhorn, Arthur. *Franklin B. Hough: An Incipient Anthropologist of the Early 19th. Century.* 1974. (This is a 13 pp. study of Hough's anthropological contributions in: *American Anthropology. The Early Years.* Proceedings of the American Ethnological Soc. 1974.)

Everest, A. *Rum Across the Border. The Prohibition Era in Northern New York.* 1978. illus. map. 172 pp. (An account of rum-running in the Rouse's Point-Plattsburgh area during the 1920s and early 1930s. Much of the material was gathered through interviews with law enforcement officers, attorneys, bootleggers, and spectators. The author even tells of some border officers who resigned from law enforcement and went into bootlegging.)

Everest, A. S. *British Objectives at the Battle of Plattsburgh.* 1960. Moorsfield Press. Champlain, NY. wrps. bib. 21 pp. Lmtd. to 500 copies. (A variant view of this important War of 1812 battle on land and lake at Plattsburgh in which the Americans were victorious. In commenting on the total war, the writer concludes, "Under the circumstances this war cannot conceivably be considered a triumph of American arms.")

Farnham, C. W. *Bar Bills at Crown Point: Some 1761 Law Suits Against Rhode Island Soldiers.* 1960. wrps. 8 pp. (Cornelius Culnon of Albany, merchant, supplied the RI soldiers, and when he was not paid he filed suits against them. This work lists the names of the culprits, their home town, and civilian occupation.)

Field, M. *Hard Times. Another Stimulating Cause.* A long handbill, ca late 1870s. (Field, a Congressman from MI, was born at Watertown, NY, and educated at the Victor, NY, Academy. In this handout he rails against the use of fractional paper currency. He goes into great detail writing of Lincoln, a Syndicate ring, the NY Stock Exchange, taxation, bondholders, and says of Congress, "it is in reality a British bond-holders parliament.")

(Ford, W. C. ed.) *General Orders of 1757, Issued by the Earl of Loudoun and Phineas Lyman in the Campaign Against the French.* NY. 1899. index. 144 pp. (A full transcript of the mss. orderly book kept by the regiment of General Phineas Lyman, of Connecticut, May-November 1757. Almost every entry is from Fort Edward. This work provides, for the serious researcher, excellent source material on camp activities, duties, and discipline. Only 250 copies were prntd. Reprntd. 1970.)

Fouquet, L. (comp.) *Lake Champlain, Lake George! the Adirondacks, Lake Memphremagog, and Mount Mansfield!* Burlington, VT. 1867. Comp. by ... of Plattsburgh, NY. maps. illus. some advts. Time tables. wrps. 62 pp. (No doubt issued for benefit of Fouquet's Hotel at Plattsburgh, NY, D. L. Fouquet & Son, Props. Cole locates 1 copy of this *Guide*.)

Fox, W. *Forest Fires of 1903.* NY Forest, Fish, and Game Commission. wrps. 19D4. illus. 55 pp. (Almost entirely on fires in the Adirondacks. It lists the causes of the fires; one was started by someone smoking out a hedgehog.)

Granger, M. E. *A Guide to Schroon Lake, Essex Co., NY.* Warrensburg. ca 1880. wrps. 24 pp. (This is a guide, in verse, to the hotels in the Schroon Lake area. It has a directory of hotels and cottages. It also includes routes to Schroon Lake giving times of departure, arrival, and fare. "Splendid stages owned and run by Mr. Fremont Prouty. Mr. Prouty is an excellent driver and obliging withal." Not listed in Cone, Cole, or Donaldson. It first appears in the 1973 supplement to Plum's *Adirondack Bibliography*.)

Haddock, J. *Routes Pursued by the Excursion Steamers Upon the St. Lawrence River From Clayton and Ganaoque to Westminster Park and Alexandria Bay.* 1895. Advts. illus. wrps. 96 pp. (cover title: *The Rambler*.) (Information for summer visitors: history, descriptive lists of islands, seasonal post offices, and other data of interest. Among the advice given is "don't stop to gossip on the gang plank." I had a copy that included a 12-page supplement with time tables.)

Hall, H. *The History of Vermont, From Its Discovery to Its Admission Into the Union in 1791.* Albany, Munsell. 1868. map. index. 522 pp. (This is the best history of VT before 1791, and it concentrates on the controversy over the NY-VT boundary.)

Hall, R. *History Was Made Where You Live.* A series of 13 radio broadcasts. WGY (Schenectady) 1938. wrps. 224 pp. (Hist. data on the area between Troy and Ticonderoga.)

Hanna, A. *A Bibliography of the Writings of Irving Bacheller.* Rollins College Bulletin. 1939. wrps. map. index. 48 pp. (This was pub. in September 1939 in honor of the 80th. birthday of Bacheller, a northern NY novelist, essayist, and the founder of the first newspaper syndicate in America. Several of his novels were set in the "Land of Frozen Flame" [as Carl Carmer called the North Country] and a few of his works were written at an Adirondack camp. His best known work is *Eben Holden: A Tale of the North Country*, of which hundreds of thousands of copies have been sold. In 1901 a special edition of 250 copies with additional material was issued in honor of the author. Bacheller occasionally wrote brief poems on the flyleaves of his books.)

Headley, J. *Confederate Operations in Canada and New York.* 1906. illus. 480 pp. (A pro-Southern book about the operations on the northern border of the U. S. by Confederate soldiers. Although a raid was made into St. Albans, VT, it appears that only tentative plans were made to attack Fort Montgomery at Rouses's Point, NY. VandeWater in his *Lake Champlain and Lake George* tells how this raid into NY was foiled by a parade and quantites of bourbon.)

Hill, W. *A Brief History of the Printing Press in Washington, Saratoga, and Warren Counties ... NY.* Fort Edward, NY. 1930. Prntd. by Tory Press, Rutland, VT. 117 pp. Lmtd. to 54 copies. (This useful work also includes a check list of printings before 1825, very brief data on paper mills, and a list of books relating to that area of the state. This almost-impossible-to-find book was reprntd. by Harbor Hill Books, Harrison, NY, in 1973.)

Hosmer and Bruce. *Plan for Township 40, Totten and Crossfield Purchase, Hamilton Co., NY.* State Forest Preserve. Washington, D. C. 1901. wrps. illus. maps. 64 pp. (An important work on Adirondack lumbering in the Raquette Lake area.)

Hough, R. B. *The American Woods, Exhibited by Actual Specimens and With Copious Explanatory Text.* Lowville, NY. 1888 - additional vol. were printed in succeeding years. (Hough had a factory at Lowville, NY, where he made novelties out of wood. He invented a machine that could make extremely thin slices of wood which aided him in producing his famous "American Woods." Each vol. of the "Woods" consisted of 25 cards with 3 sections of wood each, representing 25 species. These were stereoptican cards, 6 x 9 inches, to be used before an audience with a magic lantern. Each card has 3 thin wood panels showing: transverse, radial, and tangential to study the minute structure of the wood, heart and sap-wood. They are sufficiently thin to allow the transmission of light thus showing the tints and structure of the wood. A discriptive pamphlet accompanied each vol., and the special binding needed to hold the pamphlet and 25 loose cards was designed by Hough. This work earned gold medals and prizes. Hough illus. his stationery with both sides of the medal he won at the Paris Exposition of 1889. Begun in 1888, by 1907 ten vol. of the "Woods" had been issued. Work slowed down and a 1924 advt. states "13 have been issued, two remaining parts, designed to complete the series, being now in preparation, the whole covering practically all of the important woods of the U. S. and Canada." I do not know if the series was ever completed as Hough died in Sept. 1924. Occasional vol. from this set appear on the market from time to time, but long runs are seldom found.)

Hubbard, Elbert. *Health and Recreation in the North Woods. A Little Journey to Billy Bean's Beanery.* 1913. wrps. 15 pp. (The noted Elbert Hubbard of the Roycroft Press of East Aurora, NY, issued this as an advt. for the Inn of the North Woods, at Wanakena in the Adirondacks. This elusive and ephemeral piece is not listed in Plum or Cole.)

Hudowalski, G. *The Adirondack High Peaks and the Forty-Sixers.* 1970. illus. index. 357 pp. (Natural hist. and other data on the 46 High Peaks. There is a list of nearly 600 climbers who conquered them all. One very well known Forty-Sixer once said to me, "I have often wondered why I did it.")

In Memoriam Walter Abbott Wood. (1893). portrait. 64 pp. (Wood, 1815-1892, was an internationally known inventor, and manufacturer of agricultural machinery, and had a large factory at Hoosick Falls. His machinery won more than 1200 prizes. This vol. of biog. data, eulogies, and newspaper extracts was largely compiled by his wife, but she was called to glory before the book was completed. Laid in this book is a 2-page folder titled "In Memoriam. Mrs. Walter A. Wood.")

Interbrook Lodge. M. E. Luck, Prop. ca early 1900s. wrps. illus. of the surrounding scenery. 24 pp. (Details the advantages of this peerless resort for vacationers. The only disadvantage seemed to be, "A small charge is made for use of the bathroom.")

(Iron ore) *Description of the Iron Mountain of New York, on Lake Champlain.* Albany. 1869. wrps. 12 pp. (A description of the iron ore property on the Lewis Patent: veins, quality, advantages, reports, and opinions. Not in Cone. Cole only locates 1 copy. It did not appear in Plum until the *Supplement*, item #8676.)

Journal of Joseph Smith, of Groton (CT) June-Sept. 1758. 6 pp. + *Diary of Ebenezer Dibble, Ensign in the CT Troops, June-Nov. 1759, and May-Aug. 1762.* 17 pp. (These 2 articles on the French and Indian War in NY colony involve activity at Lake George, Fort Edward, Ticonderoga, and other nearby areas. They may escape notice in NY State as they are printed in the Papers and Addresses of the Soc. of Colonial Wars in the State of CT ca 1903.)

Juckett, M. *My Canaling Days. 1897-1907.* Granville (NY). 1959. illus. 15 pp. (The authoress worked on the Champlain Canal, and boated to NYC. Includes a list of the canalers she knew.)

(Kane, J.) *Walter Hunt, American Inventor.* 1935. wrps. illus. 75 pp. (Hunt, 1796-1859, of Martinsburg in Lewis Co., and NYC, is credited with many inventions, including a lock-stitch sewing machine before Elias Howe, and a shoe which enabled acrobats to walk on the ceiling! The *National Cyclopedia of American Biography* lists over 20 of his major patents.)

Kinchen, O. *The Rise and Fall of the Patriot Hunters.* 1956. illus. bib. index. 150pp. (A study of the Patriots War, called the Rebellion of 1837 in Canada. This was an armed conflict between militant and moderate groups in Upper and Lower Canada. Sympathizers from the U. S. formed a Patriot Army and carried out raids on Upper Canada. There are many references to northern NY. It was said that Governor Marcy of NY, and Martin Van Buren were either members or sympathizers of the Hunters. This is a surprisingly scarce book.)

(Lake George) *Horicon Lodge.* 1899. wrps. illus. 12 pp. (A description of this noted and accomodating hotel, with its terms for vacationers. This obliging hotel would help you find other lodgings if you did not like theirs! In my many experiences with hotels and motels I felt they would not appreciate it if I asked them to recommend a better and cheaper place to stay.)

Loescher, B. G. *The History of Rogers Rangers. Vol. 1. The Beginnings Jan. 1755-April 6, 1758.* San Francisco. Pub. by the author. 1946. maps. With 3 colored plates by Helene Loescher. 43B pp. Lmtd. to 1500 copies. The 3 colored plates were also pub. separately, unfolded, for framing. (The author made much use of the Loudoun mss. at the Huntington Library in San Marino, CA, one of the great libraries of Americana in America.)

Loescher, B. G. *Genesis. Rogers Rangers. The First Green Berets. The Corps. The Revivals. April 6, 175B-Dec. 24, 1783.* With maps and Uniform Plate. 1969. index. 311 pp. Lmtd. to 750 copies. (In between the 2 above vol. Loescher pub. another on Rogers Rangers but I have never seen it. In spite of the relatively large number of copies pub., this work rarely comes on the market. Not in Plum. Cole locates only 1 complete set, and an odd volume.)

Longstreth, T. M. *The Lake Placid Country. A Tramper's Guide to 60 Walks and Climbs.* Pub. by the Lake Placid Club. 1922. maps. index. wrps. 76 pp. + 12 pp. of advts.

Lucas, F. W. *Appendiculae Historicae; or, Shreds of History Hung on a Horn.* London. prntd. for the author. 1891. maps. bib. index. 216 pp. (A most important book on the French and Indian War, 1755-1760. with considerable reference to NY State, and with much important topographical detail.)

Lyon, Caleb. *Narrative and Recollections of Van Diemans' Land, During a Three Years'*

Captivity of Stephen S. Wright ... An Account of the Battle of Prescott. NY. 1844. 80 pp. (A very rare pamphlet on the Patriots' War, in which Canada was invaded by Americans near Ogdensburg, NY. Some of the invaders were captured and sent into exile to Van Diemans' Land, a British penal colony in Australia. A copy sold at auction in 1976 for $2,200.00. The 1844 ed. is the one always referred to, but Sabin, 42847, notes an 1843 printing. About 1970 approximately 10 copies were photostated on good quality bond paper, at Watertown, NY, and advertised at $25.00 each.)

(M'Alpine, J.) *Genuine Narratives and Concise Memoirs of Some of the Most Interesting Exploits and Singular Adventures of ... a Native Highlander, From Time of His Emigration From Scotland to America. 1773 Till Dec. 1779.* Greenock (Scotland). 1780. 63 pp. (M'Alpine settled in northeastern NY State, had trouble with the Green Mountain Boys, was imprisoned but escaped, served with Burgoyne, and later lived on Long Island. He returned to England in 1779. Several ed. of the book were pub. The only one I have had is the 1883 reprint of 67 pp., also made at Greenock, of the 1780 ed.)

Mante, T. *The History of the Late War in North America, and the Islands of the West Indies, Including the Campaigns of 1763 and 1764 Against His Majesty's Indian Enemies, by ... Assistant Engineer During Siege of the Havanna, and Major of a Brigade in the Campaign of 1764.* London. 1772. 18 maps and Plates. 543 pp. (This is considered the best contemporary account of this war, and there is much on northern NY and Quebec. I have never been fortunate enough to acquire a copy of the original ed., but have had several copies of the excellent 1970 reprnt. The reprnt, I believe, was remaindered, but a copy seldom comes on the market. A dealer I knew in CT managed to get a carton full but would only sell 1 or 2 at a time.)

Manvill, Mrs. P. *Lucinda; or the Mountain Mourner. Being Recent Facts, in a Series of Letters, From Mrs. Manvill, in the State of New York, to Her Sister in Pennsylvania. Second Edition - With Additions.* Ballston Spa (NY). 1810. 168 pp. (These letters were written from the Kayaderosseras Mountains. First prntd. at Johnstown in 1807, there was a 3rd. ed. prntd. at Ballston Spa in 1817, and Munsell of Albany reprntd. the 3rd. ed. in 1852. Incidentally, have you noticed going north on the Northway south of Saratoga, that the so-named creek is spelled: Kayderosseras on the signboard, and going south on the Northway it is spelled: Kayaderosseras?)

Marshall, M. H. *An Echo of the Battle of Plattsburgh.* Moorsfield Press. Champlain, NY. 1929. 3 illus. 14 pp. Limited to 156 copies printed for the Saranac Chapter Daughters of the American Revolution. (The story of this famous battle as told by Mrs. Marshall as she heard it from her father and grandmother.)

Mathiasen, M. *Sommer I Adirondack Bjergene.* Milo'ske

Boghandels Forlag, Odense (Danmark). 1911. Title page is in color. illus. with 3 drawings. 135 pp. (Entirely in Danish except for a 2-page poem titled "A Little Poem Dedicated to Camp Danmark", by Eckardt V. Eskesen. Plum 1036. Not in Cole.)

Millionaire Shot Dead From Ambush in the Adirondacks! O. P. Dexter ... Slain ... Reward. Broadside, 5 x 9 inches, advertising the story of this murder in the *Utica Saturday Globe* (1903). (According to Donaldson's *Adirondacks* the murderer was never caught, even though the children of the area knew who he was.)

Milne, A. *The Woman That Lives Without Eating. Being An Authentic Narrative of Mrs. Simeon Hayes, of Chester, Warren Co., NY.* Glens Falls. 1858. wrps. 47 pp. (This medical marvel lived without partaking of any solid nourishment since 1856 and retained her usual amount of flesh. This extraordinary event was attested to by 5 physicians.)

The Moorsfield Antiquarian. A Quarterly Magazine of American History. Pub. by the Moorsfield Press, Champlain, NY. May 1937-Feb. 1939. 8 vol. index. All pub. Hugh McLellan, ed. and pub. (A great deal of material from unpub. mss. was prntd. in this magazine. Besides local material there are articles on John Jacob Astor, Lincoln, and the West. The prospectus includes a list of the 19 pub. of the Press from 1919 to 1936, all but one of them lmtd. to 25 to 183 copies each.)

Murray, D. *Franklin B. Hough, M.D., Ph.D.* 1886. (This is a 20 pp. biog. of Hough in the *Proceedings of the 23rd. Convocation of the University of the State of NY. Held July 7-9,1885.* Albany. 1886. Also in the *Proceedings* is a 27-page bib. of the writings of Hough, by J. H. Hickcox. Hough, 1822-1885, was a forester and physician of Lewis Co., NY, who found time to do a great deal of historical research and writing.)

New York Land Patents, 1688-1786. Covering Land Now Included in the State of Vermont (Not Including Military Patents.) State Papers of VT. 1947. index. 537 pp. (Transcripts of the text of a great many land patents, chronologically arranged, with a detailed index. An excellent reference for those interested in the NY-VT land disputes east of the present border.)

Newhouse, S. *The Trapper's Guide for Capturing Furbearing Animals, and Curing Their Skins.* Pub. by the Oneida Community, Kenwood, Madison Co., NY. Ed. by John Humphrey Noyes. 1893 ed. port. illus. 126 pp. (Newhouse did much of his trapping on the Brown Tract in the Adirondacks, and in the Oneida Lake region. Work includes 10-page Trap Catalog.)

The Northern Adirondacks. Issued by the Northern Adirondack Railroad Co. 1889. Folding map. illus. wrps. 64 pp. (This was distributed to promote the Northern Adirondack Railroad Co. It provides descriptions of area towns, lists of hotels and boarding houses, excursion routes, fares, advertisements, and other data of interest to vacationers. John Hurd, the president of the railroad, was a reckless speculator, and the importance of these rails into the wilderness can be surmised from what Donaldson says of him in his *Adirondacks*: "He built his railway by gradually extending it to nowhere in particular, and then creating a semblance of somewhere.")

Paul Smiths Adirondack Park. Ten Lakes, Twenty-three Miles of Waterway, 30,000 Acres of Land. Folder, ca early 1900s, with 7 illus. Listing activities available for vacationers.

The Pensioner. (This is a 12-page religious tract, about a pensioner who lived on the east side of Lake George about 10 miles from the outlet. He had lost all of his family but one daughter, and she was lost in a storm on the lake while the writer was visiting him. No author, pub., or date is given, but this rare work was found in a vol. of bound pamphlets pub. in Dublin, Ireland in the 1820s. Not in Plum or Cole.)

Perkins, G. *Journeys to the Adirondacks For the Years 1879-1882-1883-1885. Exact Copies of the Diaries of...President of the Hollywood Club 1902-1916.* wrps. 1956. 20 pp. Prvtly. prntd. Lmtd. to 200 copies. (Plum 10054)

Phelps, O. S. *The Growth of a Tree From Its Germ or Seed.* ca 1880? wrps. 26 pp. (Written by Old Mountain Phelps, the famous Adirondack guide, this first appeared in the *Plattsburgh Republican* newspaper in 1877. It was later printed in pamphlet form. The copy I acquired had 26 pages. Both Plum and Cole note only 20 pages, and they both located only one copy - that one at the Keene Valley Public Library.)

Piercefield Paper Co. ca early 1900s. wrps. 10 pp. (A description of this plant on the Racquette River: production, facilities, estimate of value.)

The Practical Application of Economic Theories in the Factories of Alfred Dolge and Son illustrating the Feasibility of a Labor Insurance and Pension System. Dolgeville. 1896. illus. Tables. wrps. 244 pp. (Dolge, 1848-1922, started extensive piano felt and sounding board factories in Herkimer Co., and introduced insurance, pensions, and earning-sharing plans. He stated that capitalists enrich themselves at the expense of labor, and labor should get its rightful proportion of the earnings of business. This pronounced view caused a great furor in capitalist circles. See the *National Cyclopedia of American Biography*, Vol. 1, page 309, for a detailed description of the benefits Dolge gave his employees.)

Prime, W. (ed.) *Samuel Irenaeus Prime. Autobiography and Memorials.* 1888. port. index. 385 pp. (Prime, 1812-1885, was raised in Cambridge, Washington Co., NY; was a Presbyterian clergyman; and was ed. of the *New York Observer* in NYC for many years. There are nearly 150 pages on his early life in Cambridge.)

Ray, F. M. (ed.) *The Journal of Dr. Caleb Rea, Written During the Expedition Against Ticonderoga in 175B.* Salem, Mass. Essex Institute. 1881. wrps. 71 pp. (Rea, 1727-1760, was a regimental surgeon, and died of small pox in January 1760.

156

His journal was begun on May 29, 1758, the day he set out from Danvers, MA, to go on the expedition to "Ticonderogue". Plum 118.)

Redford Glass Co. (This is a sheet of 6 pieces of scrip dated 183... (date was filled in when script was used.) Approximately 12 x 8 inches. "On demand Twelve Cents will be paid to the bearer, in Goods, at the Store of the Redford Glass Co. Redford...." There are 2 three cent scrips, 1 five cent scrip, 1 six cent scrip, 1 ten cent scrip, and 1 twelve cent scrip. There was an extensive manufactory of crown glass at Redford from about 1832 to 1852. See page 240 of French's *Gazetteer* for further information.)

Redmond, D. *The Leather Glove Industry in the U. S.* 1913. wrps. 97 pp. (Actually a study of the glove manufacturing industry in Gloversville. Sir William Johnson imported glove makers from Scotland as early as the 1760s.)

Rich, H. *A Dream of the Adirondacks and Other Poems.* NY. 1884. 171 pp. (The authorness was born in a log cabin in 1827 in Jefferson Co., NY, ran away to school on a frosty morning at the age of 4, and became the first woman suffragette in northern NY.)

Roberts, K. *Northwest Passage.* Leipzig (Germany). Pub. by the Albatross. 1939. Prntd. boards with cloth backstrip and paper label. 479 pp. (A popular hist. novel of Robert Rogers and his Rangers, partially set in the Champlain Valley. This is the ed. printed in Nazi Germany, and is probably scarce in the U. S. as it was issued just a short time before the outbreak of World War II. It is not listed in the *National Union Catalog* or its supplement.)

Rogers, F. *Reveries of an Undertaker.* 1899. port. wrps. 122 pp. (Rogers, who also wrote *Folk Stories of the Northern Border*, writes of his adventures as a funeral director in northern NY. The book contains a full page advt. for Germa Wheaten, a health food manufactured by Snell and Makepeace of Theresa, NY. The advertisers are so bold as to happily declare at the top of the ad, "It is Injuring the Undertakers.")

Rogers, M. *A Battle Fought on Snow Shoes. Rogers Rock, Lake George. March 13, 1758. by ... Great-Great-Granddaughter of Major Robert Rogers.* Pub. by the author. 1917. portrait. wrps. 66 pp.

(Rogers, Robert) *Rare Americana. Books and Pamphlets ... Orderly Books Relating to the French and Indian War ... Autograph Letters by Robert Rogers ... Auction. Charles F. Heartman. June 11, 1932.* Metuchen, NJ. wrps. 55 pp. (An historically important collection, with extensive excerpts from Rogers' letters to his wife written over a period of 20 years: 1759 to 1779.)

Roosevelt, Theodore, and Minot, H. D. *The Summer Birds of the Adirondacks in Franklin Co., NY.* 1877. 4 pp. (Roosevelt made his observations of birds, mainly in the St. Regis Lakes country, in 1874, 1875, and 1877. This was his first separate pub. It has been reprntd. several times. The 1925 printing, lmtd. to 200 copies, includes his "Notes on Some of the Birds of Oyster

Bay, Long Island," pub. in broadside form in 1879.)

Ross, O. J. (comp.) *The Steamboats of Lake Champlain 1809 to 1930. Delaware and Hudson Railroad, Board of Directors. Inspection of Lines June 6-8, 1930.* pub. 1930. illus. maps. index. 184 pp. (An important work on Lake Champlain steamboats, with numerous illus. of steamboat broadsides.)

Ross, O. J. *The Steamboats of Lake George, 1817-1932.* Pub. 1932. illus. maps. 174 pp.

Santway, I. A. *A Brief Sketch of the Life of John Brown the Martyr-Emancipator ... Buried at Lake Placid.* 1934. illus. with 4 mounted photos. 18 pp. (Some of the information in this work came from Lyman Eppes, a colored man who was living in Lake Placid in the 1930s and who knew Brown. He sang "Blow Ye The Trumpet, Blow" at Brown's funeral.)

(Saranac Lake) *Walton, Starks and Co. Hardware Dealers. illustrated Catalog.* Saranac Lake, NY. 1898. illus. 102 pp. (A fine reference showing the type of items used in the Adirondacks in their heyday when swells from the city invaded the mountains. A few of the hundreds of items: kitchenware, oil cans, sap spouts, pails, insect bellows, fireplace hardware, lanterns, fly traps, baskets, laundry appliances.)

Slade, W. (comp.) *Vermont State Papers; Being A Collection of Records and Documents ... Establishment of Government By the People of Vermont ... With the Journal of the Council of Safety.* Middlebury (VT). 1823. index. 568 pp. (A major source for correspondence and legal proceedings over the NY-VT border dispute which raged before and through the Revolutionary War.)

The Smallest Perfect Locomotive in the World. This is a mounted photograph, ca late 1800s. 5-1/2 x 2-3/4 inches. (This is a photo of a locomotive and tender built by Henry Case of Gloversville, NY. It took him 3-1/2 years of actual labor to complete the project. On the verso of the photo is a very detailed description of the set which was 12 inches long, weighed 2 pounds and 2-1/2 ounces, and had 2,836 parts. It actually worked, and the engineer and fireman could put their heads out of the window.)

Smith, H. P. *The Modern Babes in the Woods, or Summerings in the Wilderness. To Which Is Added a Reliable and Descriptive Guide to the Adirondacks, by E. R. Wallace.* 1872. illus. (This was the first guide book entirely on the Adirondacks, and it went through several enlarged ed. Donaldson in his hist. of the Adirondacks states that he was not able to find a copy with the above 2 titles bound together, even though the Smith book lists the Wallace *Guide* on its title page. He did find them bound separately.)

Splendid Red Coaches. For Extras and Parties of Pleasure ... To Run Between Albany, Ballston, Saratoga Springs ... Lebanon Springs ... Young and Walbridge, Props. Albany. May 1830. (This is a small time-table ticket, with a nice illus. of a stage coach and horses, giving departure times for points in NY and New England in the summer. It is a small ticket 2-1/2 x 3-1/2 inches.)

Squirrel Hunt! Fort Edward Against Kingsbury. Captains: Lyman A. Cox, Fort Edward. Geo. W. Warren, Kingsbury. Broadside, approx. 5 x 8 inches, ca mid-1800s? (Actually a list of game to be hunted, with points credited for each. Thirty eight species of animals and birds are listed. The lowest points are 5 for a striped squirrel, and the highest points are 300 for a panther. This broadside was distributed to generate interest in this sport.)

(Staton, F.) *The Rebellion of 1837-38. A bibliography of the Sources of Information in the Public Reference Library of the City of Toronto, Canada.* 1924. wrps. 81 pp. (A bib. of books, pamphlets, newspapers, and periodicals on the attempt of some Canadians, with the help of many sympathetic Americans, to liberate Canada from British domination. This conflict is better known on the U. S. side of the border as the "Patriots War", and some of the activity took place in northern NY. A good hist. account is Kinchen's *The Rise and Fall of the Patriot Hunters.*)

Stephens, W. P. *Canoe and Boat Building. A Complete Manual for Amateurs ... Comprehensive Directions for Construction of Canoes, Rowing and Sailing Boats and Hunting Craft, by... Canoeing Editor of Forest and Stream.* NY. 1889. 4th. ed. Many diagrams. index. 263 pp. + folder of 50 detailed and folded plates. (Although this is not a NY State book, the author was a member of the NY Canoe Club, and there is occasional mention of craft built in the state. Its rarity is told in the following incident: Some years ago I had a copy of the 1891 ed. with the folder of 50 plates, and advertised it for $10.00. I was inundated with orders. Later Marcia Smith, librarian at the Adirondack Museum, at Blue Mountain Lake, told me the Museum Library had the only other known copy with plates, and a man had come all the way from CA to see it.)

Stevens, G. *The Flora of the Adirondacks.* Albany. Munsell. 1868. wrps. 18 pp. (This was reprntd. from the Transactions of the Albany Institute, and is mostly on Essex Co. It is well to note here that many pamphlets are actually reprints of articles that originally appeared in professional journals or in magazines. In some cases the authors had copies run off to pass out to friends. A case in point is Frederic Remington's work on Roger's Rangers. In many cases there is no indication in the pamphlet that it is a reprnt. from another pub.)

Stickler, J. *The Adirondacks as a Health Resort.* 1886. 198 pp. (This is the most detailed and comprehensive work on early health seekers in that area.)

Stobo, R. *Memoirs of Major Robert Stobo, of the Virginia Regiment.* Pittsburgh. 1854. Folding plan. 92 pp. (Stobo, 1727-1770, an officer in the French and Indian War, was captured by the French but escaped from prison at Quebec and fled to the British forces then in control at Louisbourg. He then took part in the English expedition against Quebec. This elusive and widely travelling chap returned to England, came back to NY in 1760, bought land on Lake Champlain in 1767, and returned to England the next year. Somewhere along the way he was in the West Indies. The last we hear of him is in a letter written to Sir William Johnson by James Rivington of NY, dated Sept. 24, 1770, "Capt. Stobo has shot himself dead.")

Stoddard, S. R. *The Adirondacks: illustrated.* Albany. 1874. illus. maps. Some advts. 204 pp. (This is the first of Stoddard's famous books on the Adirondacks. It includes a partial list of photos and stereo views also issued by him. The earliest copies of this work do not have a map in the rear pocket. Stoddard states on the thanks page that a map of the Adirondacks promised by Verplanck Colvin was not yet ready. Colvin evidently hurried up his project as some later copies of this ed. do have the map.)

Stoddard, S. R. *Camp Life. 12 Photogravures From Original Photographs by S. R. Stoddard.* Boston. ca 1890. (A thin book with 12 plates. There are 2 illus. on 6 of the plates, and one illus. on the other 6 plates. Not in Cole or Plum.)

Stoddard, S. R. *Picturesque American Resorts, Phototype Views of Lake George, the Adirondacks, and the Hudson River Valley.* Glens Falls. 1892. Small folio 42 Plates, several illus. on most plates. Descriptive text on facing pages. (Almost entirely on northern NY. Apparently not in Cole or Plum.)

To the Democratic Electors of the County of Lewis, Who, With the Undersigned Supported the Election of Gen. Jackson and Martin Van Buren. Lowville. 1840. 14 pp. pamphlet. (This political item actually urges the voters to withold their votes from Van Buren and elect Gen. Harrison for President. Includes the names of 160 Lewis Co. citizens.)

To the Electors of the Western District. Fellow Citizens! The outrageous attack on the Liberties of the People, discolosed in the following documents, demands the serious reflection of every free-born citizen and friend to American Freedom ... Western District Committee. April 14, 1813. Broadside, 11 x 12 inches. (The 7 members of the Committee report that Col. Pike, U. S. Commandant at Sackets Harbor, had ordered the arrest of all persons at Massena who were involved in treasonable acts, and had them brought by foot to Sackets Harbor to be court-martialed. "This deponent was informed that among said persons seized were all the town officers of Massena...." The Committee members decry "this military tyranny ... Our Rulers are following the footsteps of the King of Great Britain, and his measures in 1775." They give their opinion that the accused should be tried by jury. Evidently voting for public office was soon to take place as they add, "Your elections will speak your sentiments on this subject. It is at the polls where your rulers are to be taught that you yet love liberty...." Interestingly, this arrest of all the town officials of Massena by the U. S. Army during the War of 1812 is not noted in Hough's *History of St. Lawrence County*.)

Tuttle, G. (ed.) *Three Centuries in the Champlain Valley. Historical Facts and Incidents.* 1909. illus. index. 4B5 pp. (A day-by-day listing of historical facts; i.e., January 1st has facts for 11 different years 1766-1894. This valuable reference work is enhanced by an exhaustive index.)

Victory Mountain Park. 1919. illus. map. wrps. 44 pp. (This pamphlet was issued by the Association for the Protection of the Adirondacks. Although no author is given, Donaldson says it was written by the Secretary of Assn. Dr. Edward H. Hall. This work outlines a plan to purchase Mount'marcy and adjacent lands and make a park to commemorate the victory of World War I. It includes an appeal for funds.)

Waddell, W. *Northern New York. A Paper Read Before the American Geographical and Statistical Society, Nov. 2, 1854.* NY. Putnam. 1855. wrps. map. 48 pp. (One of the rarest of Adirondack items. Cole locates only 1 copy. The only copy I ever had contained 8 engraved plates which appeared to have been inserted at a later date.)

Wallace, E. *Descriptive Guide to the Adirondacks, (Land of the Thousand Lakes).* 1895 ed. illus. maps. index. 522 pp. (This work includes a special index listing 10 hermits. I wonder how delighted they were with that type of publicity?)

Wallace, E. *Specimen Pages of Wallace's Guide to the Adirondacks, &c. Terms for Advertising.* Syracuse, NY. Waverly Pub. Co. ca 1876. wrps. illus. approx. 60 pp. (The pub. of this well-known *Guide* issued this pamphlet for prospective advertisers in future eds. It shows various styles of advertisements with prices.)

Walworth, H. *Four Eras in the History of Travelling Between Montreal and New York, From 1793 to 1892.* Plattsburgh, NY. 1892. wrps. 8 pp. (Mainly extracts from travellers' journals, and directions for travellers, dated 1793, 1809, 1853, and 1891. The compiler predicts that by 1992 most long journeys will be through the air, and that it would take 4 hours to fly from NYC to Montreal. Considering the extensive ground delays at the airports his prediction is probably right on target.)

Whipple, G. *Fifty Years of Conservation in New York State 1885-1935.* ca 1935. illus. Tables. wrps. 199 pp. (Surveys, fires, trespass, reforestation, wild life, Aidrondack guide, much else. Plum 2068.)

(Whiteman, J.?) *Lake George Camp and Canoe Chats. Gossip on Canoes, Camps, Religion, Social Manners, Medicine and Law, Gastronomy, Politics, and Marriage.* NY. ca 1887? illus. 134 pp. (A man named Newcomb sued the author and pub., alleging that he had found a cryptogram in the book, using the first letter of the first word of each chapter, that libelled his wife. He also found another cryptogram in the book that was anti-his wife. Anyway, you can read more about it in Hill's *Brief History of the Printing Press in Washington, Co....*)

Wightman. *Summers in the Adirondacks. 1902-1911.* Pub.

by the author 1917-1921. illus. 203 pp. (This book is probably scarce as the author also set the type, cut the paper, took the photos, and bound the book. He wrote the text at the seashore, in the woods, and even in his automobile.)

Woodbury, Rev. G. *Colportage Wagon Work or How the Adirondack Colporter Missionary Does His Work.* American Baptist Pub. Soc. ca early 1900s. 3 illus. wrps. 8 pp. (Plum 9429, not in Cole. A rare bit of Adirondack ephemera, and on a subject on which little research has been done. At this point I cannot resist telling you of Rev. Timothy Dewey who was a Methodist circuit rider in northern NY in the early 1800s. He had 10 children whom he named: Anna Diadema, Philander Seabury, Franklin Jefferson, Armenius Philadelpnus, Almira Melpomena, Marcus Bonaparte, Pleiades Arastarcus, Victor Mellenus, Octavia Ammonia, and Encyclopedia Britannica.)

(Woodworth, John) *The Battle of Plattsburgh: A Poem, in Three Cantos, by an American Youth.* Montpelier (VT). 1819. 46 pp. pamphlet. (Woodworth's father fought in this battle.)

(Woolsey, M.) *Letters of Melancthon Taylor Woolsey, Colonel, New York Provincial Troops in the French and Indian War.* Champlain (NY). Moorsfield Press. 1927. wrps. 21 pp. Lmtd. to 150 copies. (Woolsey was Colonel of the 2nd. Battalion of the NY Regiment, and went with his troops to the Mohawk River in May 1758. He wrote letters to his wife and brother, from Albany, Nestigauni, Fort Edward, Lake George, and Schenectady, giving his impressions of what he saw: camp life, and military activity. He died in September of dysentery.)

The World's Most Hygenic Water. Adirondack Ozonia. 100,000 to 1 Pure Natural Medicinal Spring Water. Pub. by H. I. Cutting, Potsdam, NY. ca 1906. wrps. 44 pp. (The owner bottled the water from a spring on the north bank of the west branch of the St. Regis River in St. Lawrence Co., NY. He thoughtfully presumed that mid-westerners would also like his pure Adirondack Ozonia so he opened a branch office in Indianapolis.)

ONEIDA COUNTY

ONEIDA COUNTY

Bashant, N. (Ed.) *History of Oneida County.* 1977. pub. by Oneida Co. Dept. of Planning. illus. map. bib. index. 256 pp. (Chapters written by local historians.)

Bashant, N. (ed.) *History of Oneida County Commemorating the Bicentennial of Our National Independence.* 1978.

Brown, D. *Oneida Co.* (1953) wrps. mimeo. 16 pp.

Canfield & Clark. *Things Worth Knowing About Oneida Co.* Utica. 1909. illus. 148 pp.

Cookingham, H. *History of Oneida Co. From 1700 to the Present.* Chicago. 1912. illus. maps. 2 vols.

Durant, S. *History of Oneida Co.* Philadelphia. 1878. illus. maps. 678 pp.

Galpin, W. *Central NY, An Inland Empire. Oneida, Madison, Onondaga, Cayuga, Tompkins, Cortland, Chenango Counties.* NY. 1941. illus. 4 vols.

Jones, P. *Annals & Recollections of Oneida Co.* Rome. 1851. pub. by author. 893 pp.

O'Callaghan, E. (comp) *Papers Relating to the Oneida Country & Mohawk Valley 1756-57.* n.d. maps. wrps. 26 pp. (An extract from *Documentary Hist. of State of NY.* Vol. 1 1849)

Tracey, W. *Notices of Men & Events Connected With the Early History of Oneida Co.* Utica. 1838. wrps. 45 pp.

Wager, D. *Our County & Its People.* Boston. 1896. illus. maps. 1267 pp.

AUGUSTA, Onedia Co.
(Anon.) *The Colonels Hat: A History of the Township of Augusta.* 1977. Augusta Bicent. Comm. illus. map. 145 pp.

BARNEVELD, Oneida Co.
Fuller, J. (ed.) *The Holland Patent Central School Area: Barneveld, Camroden, East Floyd, Floyd, Frenchville, Hinckley, Holland Patent, North Western, Prospect, South Trenton, Steuben, Stittville, Trenton Falls, Westernville.* By students at Holland Patent Central School. 1949. illus. wrps. 24 pp.

BOONVILLE, Oneida Co.
Best, T. *Boonville & Its Neighbors.* 1961. illus. maps. bib. 195 pp.

Ryder, R. (comp.) *You Have Always Wanted to Know.* 1978. illus. 40 pp. (Chronological list of events.)

BRIDGEWTER, Oneida Co.
Porter, E. (comp.) *Historical Sketches of Bridgewater.* Oxford. 1914. illus. 115 pp.

CAMDEN, Oneida Co.
Pike, E. *Pioneer History of Camden.* Utica. 1897. illus. 559 pp.

Welch, E. *"Grips" Historical Souvenir of Camden.* Camden. 1902. illus. 149 pp.

CLINTON, Oneida Co.
Anon. *Clinton, NY & Vicinity.* 1912. illus. maps. wrps. 42 pp. (Comp. by high school students.)

Stanley, E. *A Half Century in the Life of Clinton. 1915-1965.* 1966. 76 pp.

Williams, O. *Early History of Clinton.* Clinton. 1848. wrps. 28 pp.

CLINTON SQUARE, Oneida Co.
Dever, M. *History of Clinton Square.* Clinton. 1961. illus. wrps. 45 pp.

DEERFIELD, Oneida Co.
Folts, A. *Our Deerfield Heritage. 1798-1976.* 1977. illus. 60 pp.

FLOYD, Oneida Co.
Evans, E. *Floyd. 180 Years.* 1977. illus. map. wrps. 72 pp.

JEWELL, Oneida Co.
Anon. *History of Jewell.* no date. 3 pp. typed mss. about 15 copies made.

KIRKLAND, Oneida Co.
Gridley, A. *History of Town of Kirkland.* NY. 1874. illus. map. index. 232 pp.

MARCY, Oneida Co.
Anon. *Town of Marcy Centennial.* 1932. advts. 32 pp.

Brown, T. *Old Home Day & Centennial Celebration, Marcy, Aug. 27, 1943.* illus. advts. wrps. unpaged. (Includes Stittville.)

MARSHALL, Oneida Co.
Anon. *Town of Marshall. Bicentennial History and Directory.*

1977. Marshall Town Board. illus. map. 20 pp.

NEW HARTFORD, Oneida Co.
Prescott, C. (& others) *New Hartford Centennial.* Utica. 1889. illus. 200 pp.

ONEIDA CASTLE, Oneida Co.
(Rathbone, T. village historian) *Brief History of Oneida Castle & the Oneida Indians.* 1930. illus. map. 40 pp.

ONEIDA COMMUNITY, Oneida Co.
Eastlake, A. *The Oneida Community.* 1900. 158 pp.
Edmonds, W. *The First Hundred Years.* 1948. illus. 75 pp.
Jacoby, J. *Two Mystic Communities in America.* 1975 ed. 104 pp. (Included are 50 pages on the Oneida Community. It is highly anti-John Humphrey Noyes. It says of him, "One could wish for him ... that for a time ... he had found himself a member of a ball-and-chain gang, or been shanghaied to China.")

PARIS, Oneida Co.
Rogers, H. *History of Town of Paris and the Valley of the Sauquoit.* Utica. 1881. illus. 404 pp.
Rogers, H. *History of Town of Paris and Valley of the Saquoit.* 1977. illus. 398 pp.

PETERBORO, Oneida Co.
Ernenwein, R. *The Borough of Peter.* 1970. illus. wrps. 150 pp.

PROSPECT, Oneida Co.
Thomas, H. *The Life of a Village. A History of Prospect.* Prospect. 1950. illus. map. 151 pp.

REMSEN, Oneida Co.
Roberts, F. *A Narrative History of Remsen & Parts of Steuben & Trenton) 1789-1898.* Syracuse. 1914. illus. prvtly. distributed. lmtd. to 250 copies. 398 pp. (Remsen was the largest Welsh settlement in the U. S.) Reprntd. with index, ca 1970s?

ROME, Oneida Co.
Marcosson, I. *Industrial Main Street. The Story of Rome the Copper City.* 1953. illus. index. 211 pp.
(McNamara, T.) *The Twin Cities of the North - Otherwise Rome & Saratoga. A Brief Historical Sketch. 1777-1927.* ca 1927. 68 pp.
Scott, J. *Rome a Short Hist.* Rome. 1945. illus. wrps. 35 pp.
Staley, G. *A Century of Hardware Service 1847-1947. Being a Hist of Rome & the Part Taken by the Wardwell Hardware Co.* (1947.) illus. 30 pp.
Wager, D. (ed.) *Our City & Its People.* Rome. Boston. 1896. illus. map. 300 pp.

SHERILL, Oneida Co.
Robertson, C. *Golden Anniv. of Sherill.* 1966. illus. map. advts. wrps. 125 pp.

SOUTH TRENTON, Oneida Co.
Anon. *South Trenton. Where Memory Abounds and History Resounds.* illus. map. 88 pp.

TRENTON, Oneida Co.
Seymour, J. *Trenton, Its First Settlement. Centennial Address. July 4, 1876.* Utica. 1877. wrps. 149 pp.

TRENTON FALLS, Oneida Co.
Pitcher, C. *The Golden Era of Trenton Falls.* Utica. 1915. illus. 103 pp.

Thomas, H. *Trenton Falls, Yesterday & Today.* Prospect 1951. illus. 177 pp.

UTICA, Oneida Co.

Anon. *A Bibliography of the History and Life of Utica.* Utica Public Library. 1932.
Anon. *Old Home Week Souvenir. Aug. 3-10, 1914.* Utica. 1914. illus. advts. wrps. 50 pp.
Anon. *Outline History of Utica & Vicinity.* Utica. 1900. illus. 201 pp. (By New Century Club.)
Anon. *Semicentennial of City of Utica.* Oneida Hist. Soc. Utica. 1882. 196 pp.
Anon. *The Tale of the Treasure Chest. Being Somewhat the Story of Old Ft. Schuyler & Its People.* First National Bank. Utica. 1926. illus. map. 45 pp.
Bagg, M. (ed) *Memorial History of Utica.* Syracuse. 1892. illus. maps. 2 vols. Also issued in a 1 vol. ed.
--- *Pioneers of Utica ... to 1825.* Utica. 1877. illus. 665 pp.
(Clark, L.) *Utica Centennial Souvenir 1832-1932.* 1932. illus. wrps. 28 pp.
Clarke, T. *Utica For A Century & a Half.* Utica. 1952. illus. bib. index. 332 pp.
(Devereaux, L. ed) *Utica & Its Savings Bank 1839-1939.* ca 1939. illus. map. 46 pp.
Miller, B. *A Sketch of Old Utica.* Utica 1895. illus. 63 pp. 2nd. ed. 1913. 92 pp.
Another ed.: Utica. 1919. illus. 91 pp.

VERNON, Oneida Co.

Anon. *Our American Heritage. Vernon Our Community. 1963-1964.* 2 vols. (By Monday Club.)
Peal, B. *A Glimpse Into the History of Vernon.* 1959. 42 pp.

VERONA, Oneida Co.

Ernewein, R. *Verona Town History.* 1970. Book.

WATERVILLE, Oneida Co.

(Anon.) *Waterville, N.Y. Centennial History 1871-1971.* Sherburne. 1971. pub. by Waterville Centennial Inc. wrps. illus. maps. 72 pp.
Anderson, W. *Social Change in a Central New York Rural Community.* 1954. Pamphlet pub. by Cornell University Agricultural Experiment Station. map. illus. (An economic survey with a brief history.) 56 pp.

WESTMORELAND, Oneida Co.

Anon. *Westmoreland. 200 Years.* 1977. Westmoreland Bicentennial Committee. illus. 231 pp.

WHITESBORO, Oneida Co.

Anon. *A Few Stray Leaves in the History of Whitesboro, by a Villager.* Utica. 1884. wrps. 56 pp.
Rohman, D. *Here's Whitesboro, An Informal History (1784-1949)* NY. 1949. illus. map. 110 pp.

ONONDAGA COUNTY

ONONDAGA COUNTY

Bannan, T. *Pioneer Irish of Onondaga Co. (About 1776-1847)* NY. 1911. 333 pp.
Beauchamp, W. *Onondaga in the Revolution. Some Errors in Current History Corrected.* Syracuse. Nov. 1897. 4 pp.
--- (ed.) *Revolutionary Soldiers Resident or Dying in Onondaga Co. With Supplementary List of Possible Veterans. Based on a Pension List of Franklin H. Chase.* Syracuse. 1913. 307 pp. Reprntd. with index ca 1990 by Heritage Books, Inc.
Benedict, G. *Resources of Onon-*

daga Co. Historical Sketches. Syracuse. 1883. 216 pp.

Bruce, D. *Onondaga's Centennial.* Boston. 1896. illus. maps. 2 vols.

Clark, J. *Onondaga, or Reminiscences of Earlier & Later Times.* 1849. map. illus. 2 vols. (51 pp. typed index, ca 1934, in SLA.)

Clayton, W. *History of Onondaga Co. 1615-1878.* Syracuse. 1878. illus. maps. 430 pp.

Geddes. *Survey of Onondaga.* In: Transactions of the NY State Agricultural Society for 1859. Albany. 1860. map. illus. 132 pp.

Hall & Patterson (comps.) *History of Onondaga Co. 1794-1867.* Syracuse. 1867. advts. wrps. 60 pp.

(Hasbrouck, M.) *Early Onondaga in Letters to Young Students, by "An Old Lady."* Syracuse. 1942. 66 pp.

Mulford, H. *Onondaga Co. Centennial Address, May 27, 1894.* Syracuse 1894. 28 pp.

Northrup, A. *The Formative Period Some Intellectual & Moral Influences in the History of Onondaga Co.* Syracuse. May 1896. 8 pp.

Slocum, R. *In Old Onondaga Valley.* Syrcus. Jan. 1897. 12 pp.

Smith, C. *Pioneer Times in the Onondaga Country.* Syracuse. 1904. illus. 415 pp. (Orig. pub. in Syracuse *Sunday Herald* 1899.)

Teall, S. *Onondaga's Part in the Civil War.* Syracuse. 1915. wrps. 88 pp.

BALDWINSVILLE, Onondaga Co.
Hall, E. (comp.) *History of Baldwinsville.* Baldwinsville 1936. pvtly. prntd. 94 pp.

CAMILLUS, Onondaga Co.
(Maxwell, M.) *Among the Hills of Camillus. The Story of a Small Town.* 1952. illus. map. 137 pp.

(White, T.) *Tryphena Ely White's Journal, Being a Record Written 100 Years Ago.* NY. 1904. illus. lmtd. 250 copies. 46 pp.

CICERO, Onondaga Co.
Sheller, A. *A Vanished World.* Syracuse. 1964. 365 pp. (Cicero childhood, late 1800's.)

CLINTON SQUARE, Onondaga Co.
Brewster, A. *Memories of Clinton Square & Other Tales of Syracuse.* Syracuse. 1951. 239 pp.

DEWITT, Onondaga Co.
Anon. *History & Directory.* 1943. illus. advts. 40 pp.

FAYETTEVILLE, Onondaga Co.
(Anon.) *Celebrating Completion of Last Link of the Genesee Turnpike Between Albany and Buffalo.* 1921. wrps. illus. advts. (Hist. of Fayetteville.) 63 pp.

Anguish, L. *History of Fayetteville-Manlius Area.* 1966. illus. wrps. 96 pp.

LAFAYETTE, Onondaga Co.
Dodge. *Cross Roads Town. A Photo-Biography of the Town of Lafayette, NY.* 1981. (400+ photos, documents, maps, sketches, cem. transcriptions, and road tax lists for 1828.)

LIVERPOOL, Onondaga Co.
Schaefer, J. *Random Reminiscences of Liverpool in the Nineties.* Syracuse. 1957. wrps. 21 pp.

LYSANDER, Onondaga Co.
(Palmer, L. comp.) *Historical*

Review of Town of Lysander. ca 1947. wrps. 24 pp. (Prntd. serially in Baldwinsville Messenger 1941-1946.)

MANLIUS, Onondaga Co.
Durston, H. *History of Manlius.* Manlius. 1935-1938. illus. 144 pp.
Swarthout, L. *Village of Manlius. A Brief History.* Cittenango. 1970. pamphlet.
Van Schaack, H. *A History of Manlius Village.* Fayetteville. 1873. Revised & enlrgd. ed. Fayetteville. 1873. 82 pp. (Author had compiled 3 scrapbooks on newspaper clippings on Onondaga Co. hist.)

MARCELLUS, Onondaga Co.
Heffernak, K. *Nine Mile Country. The History of the Town of Marcellus.* 1878. illus. map. bib. 299 pp.
Parsons, I. *Centennial History of Marcellus.* Marcellus. 1878. 108 pp.

POMPEY, Onondaga Co.
Anon. *Re-Union of the Sons & Daughters of the Old Town of Pompey, Held at the Pompey Hill. June 29, 1871. Also Hist of Town. Biog. Sketches of its Early Inhabitants.* Syracuse. 1875. illus. 432 pp. (66 pp. mimeo. index by Van Brocklin, 1960, in SLA.)
Shoebridge, S. *Pompey. Our Town in Profile.* 1977. 2 vols.

SKANEATELES, Onondaga Co.
Beauchamp, W. *Notes of Other Days in Skaneateles.* Written for the *Skan. Democrat* in 1876. Syracuse. 1914. 82 pp.
--- *Notes of Other Days in Skaneateles. Reminiscenes of Syracuse & Supplement to Revolutionary Soldiers of Onondaga Co.* Syracuse. 1914. 217 pp. (See ONONDAGA COUNTY, W. Beauchamp's *Revolutionary Soldiers....*)
Leslie, E. (comp.) *History of Skaneateles & Vicinity 1781-1881.* Auburn. 1882. illus. 142 pp.
Another ed. Auburn. 1896.
Another ed. NY 1901. illus. 483 pp.
Another ed. NY. 1902. 477 pp.
Wells, L. *The Skaneateles Communal Experiment 1843-1846.* 1953. wrps. 17 pp.

SOLVAY, Onondaga Co.
(Cordonnier, V.) *Solvay.* Phoenix. 1959. revised ed. illus. 73 pp. (Orig. issued in mimeo. form.)

SOUTH ONONDAGA, Onondaga Co.
Newman, W. *South Onondaga & Vicinity 1834-1904.* Syracuse. 1904. illus. maps. 108 pp.

SPAFFORD, Onondaga Co.
Collins, G. *History of Spafford.* Syracuse. 1917. illus. 2-vol.-in-1.

SYRACUSE, Onondaga Co.
Baker, A. *Old Syracuse 1654-1899.* 1941. 182 pp.
Beauchamp, W. *Past & Present of Syracuse & Onondaga Co.* NY. 1908. illus. 2 vols.
Bruce, D. (ed) *Memorial History of Syracuse.* Syracuse. 1891. illus. map. 894 pp.
Chase, F. *Syracuse & Its Environs.* NY. 1924. illus. 3 vols.
Cheney, T. *Reminiscences of Syracuse.* Syracuse. 1857. 103 pp. (Originally pub. in Syracuse *Daily Standard* newspaper.)
Faigle, E. *Syracuse, A Study in Urban Geography (1936)* unpub. dissertation. maps. photos. 100 pp. (In NYSHA.)

Fellows & Roseboom. *Road to Yesterday.* 1948. pictorial wrappers. 100 pp. plus bib.
Hand, M. *Syracuse From A Forest to a City.* Syracuse. 1889. 203 pp.
Powell, E. *Gone Are the Days.* Boston 1938. 293 pp. (Memories of late 1800's.)
--- *The Social Evil in Syracuse. Report of an Investigation of the Moral Condition of the City Conducted by a Committee of 18 Citizens.* 1913. tables. 127 pp. (A detailed study of prostitution, including case histories. "Citizens have come and gone ... but the madams of Syracuse have endured.")
Smith, C. *Syracuse Village & City History of the Half Century of its Cityhood.* Syracuse. Oct. 1897. 16 pp.
Smith, H. *Syracuse & Its Surroundings.* Syracuse. 1878. 148 pp. (Approximately 100 mounted stereo views with viewer attached to front cover. Variant views in each vol.) Lmtd. to 200 copies.
Strong, G. *Early Landmarks of Syracuse.* Syracuse. 1894. 393 pp.

VAN BUREN, Onondaga Co.
Scisco, L. *Early History of Town of Van Buren.* (Baldwinsville. 1895.) wrps. 63 pp. (Reprnt. of articles in *Baldwinsville Gazette* 1895. typed index in copy at SLA. Mss. notes made by author in copy at NYPL.)

ONTARIO COUNTY

ONTARIO COUNTY
Aldrich, L. (comp.) *Hist. of Ontario Co.* Syracuse. 1893. illus. 2 vols. Also issued in 1 vol.
DeVoll, J. *Political Geography of Ontario Oc. 1789-1969.*

Museum. Canandaigua. 1969. A mss.
Fisher, J. *Pictorial History of Ontario Co.* 1972. pamphlet. (Emphasis on founding the co.)
(McIntosh, W.) *History of Ontario Co. 1788-1876.* Phil. 1876. illus. map. 276 pp. Reprntd. ca 1976.
Milliken, C. *A History of Ontario Co. & Its People.* NY. 1911. illus. maps. 2 vol.

CANADICE, Ontario Co.
Waite, B. *History of Town of Canadice. 1808-1908.* Springwater. n.d. 150 pp.

CANANDAIGUA, Ontario Co.
Caplise, J. *History of Canandaigua.* Canandaigua. 1907. illus. 187 pp.
Clarke, C. *Village Life in America. 1852-1872. As Told in the Diary of a Schoolgirl.* NY. 1912.
New, enlrgd. ed. NY. 1913. 225 pp.
Granger, J. *History of Canandaigua. Address Centennial Celebration. July 4, 1876.* Canandaigua. 1876. 16 pp.
--- *History of Early Canandaigua.* Canandaigua. 1905. 25 pp.
Milliken, C. *Canandaigua.* "The Old Town." n.d. 16 pp. (Very small pamphlet.)
(Porter, A.) *Recollections of Canandaigua 1812-1816.* Revived in 1876. n.d. wrps. 12 pp.
(Richards, C.) *Diary of Caroline Cowles Richards 1852-1872.* Canandaigua. 1908. 39 pp.

CLIFTON SPRINGS, Ontario Co.
Gifford, F. *The Early History of the Village of Clifton Springs.* 1984. 64 pp. (Clifton Springs was originally named Sulphur Springs.)

FARMINGTON, Ontario Co.
Katkamier, A. (comp) *History of the Town of Farmington.* Farmington. 1897. advts. wrps. 80 pp.

GENEVA, Ontario Co.
(Adams, F. & others) *Geneva Sesquicentennial.* Aug. 1957. illus. maps. wrps. 60 pp.
Adams & Breed. *Historic Geneva.* Geneva. 1929. illus. maps. wrps. 32 pp.
Brigham, A. *Geneva, Seneca Falls, & Waterloo Directory for 1862-63, With History of the Towns.* Geneva. ca 1863. 270 pp.
Brumberg, G. *The Making of an Upstate Community: Geneva, New York. 1750-1920.* 1976. maps. 128 pp. Reprntd. in 1981.
Brumberg, G. *Geneva, NY: A Community Study, 1786-1860.* 1977. bib. 173 pp.
Conover G. *A Hundred Years Ago When Kanadesaga Was Named Geneva.* ca 1892. Broadside 4 x 14 inches. (Reprntd. from *Saturday Review*)
--- *Early History of Geneva.* Geneva. 1877. 8 pp. (Especially strong on importance of preserving original lines, this was written for delivery at the annual tax meeting on proposition to raise $700.00 for making a map of the village.)
--- *Early History of Geneva.* (Formerly Called Kanadesaga.) 1880. wrps. 60 pp. lmtd. to 300 copies? (Reprntd. from *Geneva Courier* newspaper of March 1879. Copy at UR has marginal notes.)
--- *Echoes of Seneca Lake, or Reminiscences of an Centenarian.* ca 1880. wrps. 12 pp.
Monroe, J. A. *Century & A Quarter of History. Geneva From 1787 to 1912.* Geneva. 1912. illus. 234 pp.
Smith, W. *An Elegant But Salubrious Village. A Portrait of Geneva.* Geneva. 1931. illus. 146 pp. (Has erratum note on front fold of dust jacket.)
(Taylor, F.) *Geneva on Seneca Lake.* Geneva Chamber of Commerce. 1902. illus. wrps. 108 pp.

HONEOYE, Ontario Co.
Morse, E. *Centennial Address at Honeoye.* 1889. pamphlet.

HYDESVILLE, Ontario Co.
Cadwallader, M. *Hydesville in History.* Chicago. 1917. illus. 62 pp.

MANCHESTER, Ontario Co.
Van Duyne, A. *Manchester Through the Years.* Houghton. 1971. pamphlet.

NAPLES, Ontario Co.
Pottle, E. *Naples 1789-1889.* Address July 4, 1889. 1954. mimeo. 14 pp.

OAKS CORNERS, Ontario Co.
Oaks, M. *The Corners.* Trumansburg. 1958. illus. wrps. 79 pp.

PHELPS, Ontario Co.
Bannister, C. *Town of Phelps, Its History.* Vienna. 1852. wrps. 16 pp.
Ridley, H. *When Phelps Was Young.* Phelps 1939. 135 pp. (I once had a copy of this book which included a wooden certificate, value of "two wooden nickels." This "money" could be used in any store in Phelps during its sesqui-centennial, until noon August 12, 1839. When I lived in Monticello, NY, in the late 1930s, they had a celebration in which wooden

money could be used within the town for a specified time. I think I still have a piece of it around somewhere.

PITTSTOWN, Ontario Co.
Pitts, H. *The Pittstown Centennial.* 1896. pamphlet.

RICHMOND, Ontario Co.
Blackmer, C. *History of Our Town.* 1929. pamphlet.

SENECA FALLS, Ontario Co.
Lum, D. *The Seneca Falls of David B. Lum. 1806-1875.* 1970. 22 pp.

VICTOR, Ontario Co.
Childs, R. *History of Victor 1656-1898.* Canandaigua. 1898. illus. 43 pp.
Van Denbergh, J. *History of Victor, 1669-1900.* Albany. 1943. 52 pp. (This is photostat copy of a scrapbook of newspaper clippings from *Victor Herald* Jan. 5-July 20, 1900. It is a revision of the author's hist. of Victor orig. pub. in *Ontario Co. Times,* beginning in May 1874.)

ORANGE COUNTY

ORANGE COUNTY
(Anon.) *Orange County, A History.* pub. by National Bank of Orange Co. Goshen. 1922. wrps. 24 pp.
Anon. *Orange Co. Art Work.* illus. of Orange Co. views. (Has hist. sketch.) 1893. 94 pp.
Anon. *Orange Co. Biog.* Phil. 1881. illus. 820 pp.
Anon. *Portrait & Biog. Record of Orange Co.* NY. 1895. 1547 pp. (See **ORANGE COUNTY**, Anon. *Portrait & Biog. Record of Rockland & Orange Cos.*)
Akers, D. *Outposts of History in Orange Co.* Washingtonville. 1937. lmtd. 250 copies.
2nd. ed. March 1937. lmtd. 500 copies. 114 pp.
Denniston, G. *Survey of Orange Co. Its Early History & Settlement, Source of Title to Land.* Albany. 1863. 100 pp. (Reprntd. from Transactions NY State Agriculture Soc.)
Eager, S. *Outline History of Orange Co.* Newburgh. 1846-47. 652 pp. (Index by L. Eastabrook, Rutland, VT. 1940. 48 pp. Some years ago I saw a prntd. index made in the late 1800's. A cache of 90 copies said to have been found in 1972 is believed to be a false rumor.) Reprntd. in 1969.
Gardiner, E. *Orange Co. Brieflet.* 1904. 40 pp.
Headley, R. *History of Orange Co.* Middletown. 1908. illus. 997 pp.
Lautenschlaeger, M. *The Origin of Orange County, New York. And a List of Its People, 1883 to 1847.* 56 pp. (Lists over 3000 early residents.)
Moffat, A. *Orange Co.* Washingtonville. 1928. illus. 87 pp.
Ruttenber, E. *History of the Co. of Orange.* Newburgh. 1875. illus. map. 424 pp.
Ruttenber & Clark. *History of Orange Co.* Phil. 1881. illus. map. 920 pp. Reprntd. 1980.
Seese, M. *Old Orange Houses.* Vol. 1 Middletown. 1941. illus. 106 pp.
--- Vol. II. Middletown. 1943. illus. 115 pp. (Hist. data and photographs of over 200 Orange Co. houses.)

BALMVILLE, Orange Co.
Barclay, D. *Balmville to 1860.* Newburgh. 1900. 19 pp.

CHESTER, Orange Co.
Durland, F. *Early Chester & Its Settlement.* ca 1937. 14 pp.

Levy, S. *Chester, New York. A History.* 1947. 122 pp.

CORNWALL, Orange Co.
Beach, L. *Cornwall on the Hudson.* Newbrugh. 1873. illus. 200 pp.
Dempsey, Fulton, & O'Neill. *Cornwall, New York, Images from the Past. 1788-1920.* 1989, 148 pp. many illus.
Wright, A. *The Standard Guide of Cornwall.* ca 1892. wrps. illus. advts. 63 pp.

DEERPARK, Orange Co.
Gumaer, P. *History of Deerpark.* Port Jervis. 1890. 204 pp. Reprntd. ca late 1970s.

FOREST ROAD, Orange Co.
Hasbrouck, K. *History of Forest Road.* 1949. illus. maps. wrps. 11 pp.

GOSHEN, Orange Co.
Anon. *Goshen, The Spirit of '64. The Story of Goshen on its 250th Anniv.* 1964. illus. advts. wrps. 134 pp.
Coleman, R. *Biog. Sketches & Reminiscences.* Newburgh. 1909. wrps. illus. 95 pp.
--- *Some Traditions of Goshen and Its People and Some Recollections of Farm Life in Orange Co. Sixty Years Ago.* 1909. wrps. 86 pp.
Sharts, E. *Cradle of the Trotter. A Goshen Turf History.* 1946. index. illus. 235 pp. (Hist. of horse racing at Goshen track. Harriman family is prominent in book. Many famous horses whirled racing carts around this supreme track. Fine racing museum nearby.)
Sharts, E. *Cradle of the Trotter.* 1947 ed. illus. indexes. 247 pp.
--- *History of Goshen.* 1943. illus. 20 pp.

--- *Land O'Goshen. Then & Now.* 1960. 147 pp.

GREENVILLE, Orange Co.
Anon. *Greenville Centennial 1853-1953.* Hist. Program Souvenir. 88 pp.

GREENWOOD LAKE, Orange Co.
Mss. on Greenwood Lake hist is in a pvt. collection.

LEPTONDALE, Orange Co.
Hasbrouk, K. *History of Leptondale.* 1948. illus. map. wrps. 12 pp.

LITTLE BRITAIN, Orange Co.
Niven, A. *Centennial Memorial ... Little Britain ... 100th Anniv.* A. R. Presby. Ch. 1859. 251 pp.
Wallace, A. *Rev. Robert H. Wallace & The Little Britain Country.* 1923. 161 typed pp. with 39 original photgraphs pasted in. Bound. 3 or 4 copies were made.

MIDDLETOWN, Orange Co.
Anon. *50 Years. Commemorating the 50th Anniv. of Middletown as a City.* Middletown. 1938. illus. maps. 39 pp. (Also pub. in a DeLuxe Ed. of 300 copies.)
Dougherty, E. *Middletown Theaters and a Few Grocery Stores. 1852-1978.* 1978. illus. 40 pp. pub. by Hist. Soc. of Middletown and Walkill Precinct.
Williams, F. *Middletown, A Biog.* Middletown. 1928. illus. 201 pp.

MINISINK, Orange Co.
Anon. *Bicentennial Celebration of the 200th Anniv. of the Settlement of Minisink Valley.* July 22, 1890. Port Jervis. ca 1890. 28 pp.

Anon. *Tom Quick the Indian Slayer, & the Pioneers of Minisink & Warwarsink.* Monticello. 1851. pub. by Devoe & Quinlan. 264 pp.

Stickney, C. *History of Minisink Region, Which Included Present Towns of Minisink, Deerpark, Mt. Hope, Greensville, Waywayanda, in Orange Co.* Middletown. 1867. 211 pp. Reprntd. 1970 with index.

Twichell, H. *History of Minisink Country.* 1912. wrps. illus. 207 pp.

MONROE, Orange Co.
Freeland, D. *Chronicles of Monroe in Olden Times.* NY. 1898. map. 249 pp. Reprntd. in 1977.

MONTGOMERY, Orange Co.
(Locke) *Sesquicentennial Celebration 1809-1959.* 1960. illus. map. advts. 80 pp.

NEW WINDSOR, Orange Co.
Anon. *New Windsor Centennial.* 1883. Newburgh. 1883. 41 pp.
(Bates, C. town historian) *Town of New Windsor. Bicentennial Celebration 1763-1963.* illus. map. wrps. 36 pp.
Ruttenber, E. *History of Town of New Windsor (to 1870).* Newburgh. 1911. illus. map. 213 pp. (Pub. after author died.)

NEWBURGH, Orange Co.
Anon. *250th Celebration.* Newburgh 1709-1959. illus. advts. wrps. unpaged.
Corning, A. *Newburgh 75 Years a City.* 1940. illus. map. 50 pp. (For many years Corning wrote a local hist. column for the Newburgh newspaper.)
Monell, J. *Historical Sketches. Washington's Headquarters. Newburgh & Adjacent Localities.* Newburgh. 1872. illus. 98 pp.
Nutt, J. (comp) *Newburgh ... Historical Descriptive, Biog.* Newburgh. 1891. illus. maps. 335 pp.
Ruttenber, E. *History of Town of Newburgh.* Newburgh. 1859. illus. 335 PP.
--- *History of Town of Newburgh 1825-1907.* ca 1907. map. illus. 340 pp.

PEENPACK, Orange Co.
Ogden, L. *The Journal of the Records of Peter E. Gumaer: 1771-1869.* ca 1980? (Has much on Peenpack.)

PORT JERVIS, Orange Co.
Anon. *History of Port Jervis, NY, Area Early 1820s to 1982.* Illus. 144 pp. illus. compiled by the Port Jervis Heritage Commission.
Angell, P. *Fifty Years on the Frontier With the Dutch Congregation at Maghaghkamik 1737-1937.* Port Jervis. 1937. wrps. 46 pp.
Raynor & Color. *Where the Rivers Meet - Port Jervis Golden Jubilee.* 1957. 40 pp.

QUARRY HILL, Orange Co.
Patterson, M. *The Pioneers of Quarry Hill, Rio, Orange Co.* NY. ca 1980?

TUXEDO, Orange Co.
(Astor, W.) *Historical Names of the Tuxedo Region.* NY. 1888. map. 7 pp.
Crofut, D. *Life in Tuxedo Village Circa 1900-1910.* 1979. 13 pp.
Kent, E. *The Story of Tuxedo Park.* Rhinebeck. 1937. pvtly. prntd. 30 pp.
Rushmore, G. *The World With A Fence Around It ... Tuxedo Park the Early Days.* NY. 1957. illus. 232 pp. ("An insiders

account of the early days ... the exclusive playground and home of upper-crust society which shared with Newport and Southampton a reputation for high living and higher spending." Among those who lived or visited there were the Astors, Harrimans, Lorillards, Morgans, Bakers, Mark Twain, and royalty. Twain stayed at the home of the author's father, and told why his taste in cigars was perverted and he could not smoke a good one. This book contains the first printing of two letters written by Twain.)

WARWICK, Orange Co.
Hornby, E. *Under Old Rooftrees.* Jersey City, NJ. 1908. 271 pp.
Hull, R. *People of the Valleys. History of Valleys of Town of Warwick, NY. 1700-f1976.* Florida, NY. 1975. wrps. illus. index. 179 pp.

WEST POINT, Orange Co.
Anon. *The Hudson Highlands 1780-1880.* NY. 1883. imprntd. for Henry Cranston. wrps. 32 pp.
Boynton, E. *Hist of West Point.* NY. 1863. maps. 408 pp. (100 copies on large paper.)
Another ed. London. 1864.
Another ed. NY. 1866.
Another ed. NY. 1871.
Forman, S. *West Point.* 1950. 230 pp.
Park, R. A. *Sketch of History & Topography of West Point.* Phil. 1840. 140 pp.

WOODBURY, Orange Co.
McWhorter, E. *History of Woodbury.* 1948. illus. 131 pp. (Mainly worksheets in Rushmore Memorial Library, Highland Mills.)

ORLEANS COUNTY

ORLEANS COUNTY
Anon. *Hist Album of Orleans Co. 1824-1879.* NY. 1879. illus. map. 320 pp. Reprtd 1979.
Signor, I (& others) *Landmarks of Orleans Co.* Syracuse. 1894. illus. 999 pp.
Thomas, A. *Pioneer History of Orleans Co.* Albion. 1871. illus. 463 pp. Reprntd. in 1977 with index.

ALBION, Orleans Co.
Thomas, A. *Sketches of the Village of Albion.* Albion. 1853. wrps. advts. 40 pp.

CLARENDON, Orleans Co.
Copeland, D. *History of Clarendon From 1810-1888.* Buffalo. 1889. 382 pp.

GAINES, Orleans Co.
Anon. *Sketch of Village & Town of Gaines.* Albion. 1909. wrps. 34 pp.
(Pratt, J.) *Sesquicentennial of Town of Gaines. 1809-1959.* (Albion. Aug. 15, 1959) wrps. illus. 28 pp. lmtd. to 1000 copies.

KENDALL, Orleans Co.
Canuteson, R. *A Little More Light on the Kendall Colony.* Northfield, Minn. 1954. map. wrps. 20 pp. (Reprntd. from: Norwegian-American Studies & Records XVIII.)

MEDINA, Orleans Co.
White, Co. *Medina Past and Present.* 1982. map. illus. wrps. advts. 100 pp.

OSWEGO COUNTY

OSWEGO COUNTY
Churchill, J. (& others) *Landmarks of Oswego Co.* Syracuse. 1895.

illus. maps 1200 pp.
Faust, R. *The Story of Oswego Co. With Notes About the Several Towns in the Co.* Oswego. 1934. illus. 107 pp. Revised & enlrgd. ed. 1948
(Johnson, C.) *History of Oswego Co.* Phil. 1877. illus. maps. 449 pp.
Salisbury, S. (Ed.) *Bicentennial Journal.* pub. by Oswego Co. Hist. Soc. 1977. illus. map. 239 pp.
Snyder, C. *Oswego Co. in the Civil War.* 1962. 110 pp.
Tyler, R. *Oswego Co. 50 Years Ago. Address Aug. 21, 1879.* Fulton. 1880. 18 pp.

BREWERTON, Oswego Co.
(Anon.) *Brewerton, NY.* USA. 1973. illus. index. map.

FULTON, Oswego Co.
Anon. *Fulton ... An Illus. Sketch of Local History From the Birch Bark Canoe to the Automobile.* Friendship. 1901. illus. maps. wrps. 78 pp.

HANNIBAL, Oswego Co.
Sturge, G. *Hannibal Historical Highlights.* Hannibal. 1949. illus. 280 pp.
--- *Hannibal Centennial Edition 1860-1960.* 1960. illus. advts. wrps. 43 pp.

MEXICO, Oswego Co.
Burgess, A. *The Old Pratham Church With Incidents in the Early History of Mexico, New York.* Syracuse. 1877. wrps. 56 pp.
Simpson, E. *Mexico, Mother of Towns. Fragments of Local History (1792-1949).* Buffalo. 1949. illus. maps. 551 pp. Said to be lmtd. to 200 copies to be given away. Reprntd. wrps. ca early 1980s?
Welch, E. *"Grips" Historical Souvenir of Mexico.* Syracuse. 1904. illus. 92 pp.

ONEIDA LAKE, Oswego Co.
Landgraff, H. *Oneida Lake. An Historical Sketch.* 1926. wrps. index. 66 pp.

OSWEGO, Oswego Co.
Anon. *Oswego, An Historical Sketch of This Beautiful City.* Rochester. 1897. 28 pp. (Reprntd. from Rochester *Post Express* Nov. 27, 1897.)
Clark, G. *Oswego, an Historical Address.* 1896. wrps. 26 pp. Reprntd. 1913
Gimelli, L. *A History of Oswego 1727-1848.* Masters' Thesis, NYU, 1954.
Slosek, A. *Oswego. Hamlet, 1796-1828.* 1978. map. illus. 300 pp. typescript.

PHOENIX, Oswego Co.
Sauers, E. *The Story of Schroeppel, Being a History of Phoenix.* Phoenix. May 1, 1958. illus. maps. 86 pp.
Welch, E. *"Grips" Historical Souvenir of Phoenix & Vicinity.* Pulaski. 1904. illus. 92 pp.

PULASKI, Oswego Co.
Austin & Huntington. *Early Pulaski History (1924)* wrps. 10 pp. lmtd. ed.
Welch, E. *"Grips" Historical Souvenir of Pulaski & Vicinity.* 1902. illus. 75 pp. Reprntd., ca 1980s?

SANDY CREEK, Oswego Co.
Davies, T. *Centennial Souvenir History of Sandy Creek.* Sandy Creek. 1925. illus. 112 pp.

OTSEGO COUNTY

OTSEGO COUNTY
Anon. *Otsego Co. Biog. Review.*

Boston. 1893. illus. 857 pp.
Bacon, E. *Otsego Co. Geographical & Historical From Earliest Settlements to Present.* Oneonta. 1902. illus. maps. 85 pp.
Beardsley, L. *Reminiscences ... Early Settlements of Otsego Co.* NY. 1852. illus. 575 pp.
Butterfield, R. *In Old Otsego. A New York Co. Views its Past.* Cooperstown. 1959. wrps. bib. 57 pp.
Cooper, J. *Legends & Traditions of a Northern Co.* NY. 1921. lmtd. 600 copies. 263 pp.
Cooper, W. *A Guide in the Wilderness, or the History of the First Settlements in the Western Cos. of NY, with Useful Instructions to Future Settlers.* Dublin, Ireland. 1810. 71 pp. (Howes *USiana* reports only 5 known copies.)
Reprntd. Rochester. 1897. lmtd. 300 copies. 41 pp.
Reprntd. Cooperstown. April 1936. 49 pp.
Reprntd. Cooperstown. 1949. wrps. 49 pp. lmtd. to 2000 copies.
Hurd, D. (ed.) *History of Otsego Co.* Phil. 1878. 378 pp. Reprntd. in 1978 with index.
Neal, J. *Otsego Bits and Pieces.* Laurens. 1968. 32 pp.
(Peck, J.) *The Political Wars of Otsego; or, Downfall of Jacobinism & Despotism. Being a Collection of Pieces, Lately Pub. in the Otsego Herald. By the Author of the Plough Jogger.* Cooperstown. 1796. prntd. for the author. wrps. list of subscribers. 126 pp.

BUTTERNUT VALLEY, Otsego Co.
Ecob, K. *A History of the Butternut Valley.* pub. by Butternut Val. Garden Club. 1965. 8 pp.

CHERRY VALLEY, Otsego Co.
(Campbell & Seward) *Centennial Celebration July 4, 1840.* NY. 1840. 60 pp.
(Rock, E.) *Christmas Eve in Cherry Valley.* 1835. wrps. 8 pp. (Used as a Christmas card in 1948.)
Sawyer, J. *History of Cherry Valley 1740-1898.* Cherry Valley. 1898. 156 pp. (Typed index of names, by M. Wetzel, Jan. 1965, in NYSHA.)
(Schwartz) *Recollections of "Aunty-Grandma" Cornelia Beekman Schwartz, As Told to Her Nephew, Abraham Beekman Cox in 1932 ... at Cherry Valley.* Cherry Valley. ca 1932. wrps. 51 pp.
Streeter, H. *Historic Cherry Valley.* Cherry Valley. 1926. illus. map. 48 pp.
Reprntd. 1927. (Some copies have 4 pp. supplement dated 1928.)
Swinnerton, H. *Story of Cherry Valley.* Cherry Valley. n.d. 22 pp.

COOPERSTOWN, Otsego Co.
Anon. *Cooperstown Centennial Celebration 1907.* Cooperstown. 1907. illus. 180 pp.
Arnold, I. (ed. by S. Shaw) *A Brief History of Cooperstown.* 1886. 240 pp.
Birdsall, R. *The Story of Cooperstown.* 1917. illus. maps. 425 pp. (There were 2 printings of the first ed. of 1917. The first printing had a chapter on the "Railroad War" which was ommitted from the 2nd. & later ed., presumably at the request of a prominent Copperstown family.) Reprntd. many times.
Browning, C. *Full Harvest.* Phil. 1932. illus. 301 pp. (Recollections of Cooperstown.)

(Cooper, J.) *The Chronicles of Cooperstown.* Cooperstown. 1838. 100 pp. (Included in *Livermore's History* in 1862.) (See also **COOPERSTOWN**, Livermore, S.)

--- *Reminiscences of Mid-Victorian Cooperstown & Sketch of William Cooper.* Cooperstown. 1936. 57 pp. (Reprnt. of articles in Cooperstown newspapers 1935-1936.)

--- *Chronicles of Cooperstown.* Shaw, S. *History of Cooperstown 1839-1886.* Littell, W. *History of Cooperstown 1886-1929.* (These 3 items pub. in 1 vol. Cooperstown. 1929. 259 pp.) (See also **COOPERSTOWN**, Soraker & Carpenter.)

Dunn, J. *Social Cooperstown 1814-1815.* (1956) wrps. 5 pp. (Reprntd. from *Freeman's Journal.* March 14, 1956.)

Jones, L. *Cooperstown (1769-1949).* Cooperstown. (1949.) illus. 86 pp. 4th ed. 1965.

Kesse, G. *A Few Omitted Leaves in the History of Cooperstown.* ca 1908. wrps. 13 pp. (reprntd. from *Freeman's Journal*, Sept. 10, 17, 24, & Oct. 1, 1908.)

Livermore, S. *A Condensed History of Cooperstown.* Albany. 1862. 276 pp. (See also **COOPERSTOWN**, Cooper, J.) Lmtd. to 600 copies.

Loesch, F. *Gleams From the Glimmerglass.* Cooperstown. 1943. illus. 37 pp. Reprntd. 1947. illus. 38 pp.

Phinney, E. *Reminiscences of the Village of Cooperstown.* Cooperstown. 1891. wrps. 28 pp.

Russell, M. (comp.) *Centennial Year Book 1791-1891.* Cooperstown. 1891. illus. advts. wrps. 50 pp.

Spraker & Carpenter. *Supplement to a History of Cooperstown, by Cooper, Shaw, Littel.* Aug. 1, 1929-Dec. 31, 1962. Cooperstown. 1963. wrps. 125 pp. (See also --- *Chronicles of Cooperstown* above.) Works by Cooper, Shaw, Littel, Carpenter, and Spraker were reprntd. in a number of complicated combinations and with variant supplements.

EAST UNADILLA, Otsego Co.
Merriman, R. *East Unadilla.* Mss. printers copy.

EDMESTON, Otsego Co.
Edwards, E. Articles on hist. of Edmeston in *New Berlin Gazette.* New Berlin. 1955 & 1961.

Nonemacher, B. (comp.) *Edmeston, Echoes of the Past.* 1978. illus. map. 200 pp.

GILBERTSVILLE, Otsego Co.
Ecob, H. (comp.) *Reminiscences of Early Days 1747-1867.* 1927. illus. 68 pp.

Francke, K. *Gilbertsville Long Ago.* 1937. wrps. 28 pp.

HARTWICK, Otsego Co.
Weeks, P. *History of Hartwick (Village & Town).* Hartwick. 1934. illus. 89 pp.

MARYLAND, Otsego Co.
Hotchkin, A. *A Concise History of Town of Maryland, Also History of the First Settlement of Village of Schenevus.* Schenevus. 1876. advts. 66 pp.

Larson, H. *Hist. ... of Maryland.* (1941) 30 pp. typed mss. in NYSHA. (Typed from articles in *Schenevus Monitor* Aug. 14, 1941. through Oct. 16, 1941.)

MIDDLEFIELD, Otseg Co.
(Staats, E. town historian) *Town*

of Middlefield. *Some Hist Notes Gathered Here & There.* 1961. maps. wrps. 73 pp.
--- *A Few Omitted Items from First History of Middlefield.* 1964. wrps. 31 pp.

MILFORD, Otsego Co.
McRorie, W. *History of Milford.* Address Jan. 24, 1956. mimeo. 6 pp.
Stevens, E. *Early History of Town of Milford & Other Parts of Otsego Co.* ca 1903. 95 pp. typed mss. copies from orig. in Huntington Lib., Oneonta, in NYSHA. (Index by M. Wetzel, Jan. 1966, in NYSHA.) (Stevens: "Several efforts have been made by different individuals to write a history of the town of Milford, and all are very imperfect and erroneous.")

MORRIS, Otsego Co.
Foote, J. *Morris, New York. 1773-1923.* 1970. wrps. illus. 119 pp.
(Ladies Soc. of Universalist Ch.) *Historic Morris.* Morris. 1904. illus. wrps. unpaged.

ONEONTA, Otsego Co.
Campbell, D. *A History of Oneonta.* Oneonta. 1906. illus. 190 pp.
--- *Sketch of History of Oneonta.* Oneonta. 1883. wrps. 67 pp.
Huntington, W. *Oneonta Memories & Sundry Personal Recollections of the Author.* San Francisco. 1891. illus. 219 pp.
(Jackson, F.) *Oneonta Centennial 1848-1948.* Plus *Oneonta Diary 1743-1948.* Oneonta. 1948. wrps. 48 pp.
Jackson & Gibbs. *Oneonta Golden Anniv. 1908-1958.* Oneonta. 1948. wrps. 14 pp.
Moore, E. *In Old Oneonta.* Vol. 1 1962. 97 pp.
Vol. 2 1963. 97 pp.
Vol. 3 1964. 97 pp.
Vol. 4 1965. 97 pp.
Welch, E. *"Grips" Historical Souvenir of Oneonta & Vicinity.* Albany. 1896. illus. 85 pp.

OTEGO, Otsego Co.
Blakely, S. *A History of Otego.* Cooperstown. (1907.) map. bib. 152 pp. Reprntd. in 1976, in an ed. of about 1000 copies, for benefit of relocating the public library. Laid in is a reprntd. folding map of Otego dated 1900. The book became out-of-print on April 7, 1980, when a dealer bought the last copies from the library.
Myers, H. *A Bicentennial History of Otego.* 1977. illus. map. bib. 207 pp.

RICHFIELD, Otsego Co.
Hughes, G. (ed) *The Town of Richfield.* Richfield Springs. 1961. illus. map. wrps. 144 pp.
Ward, H. *Annals of Richfield.* Utica 1898. 102 pp.
Winne, E. *The Town of Richfield.* Collection of local history articles. 1961. illus. 144 pp. (Emphasis is post-1898.)

RICHFIELD SPRINGS, Otsego Co.
Bailey, W. *Richfield Springs & Vicinity. Hist., Biog., Descriptive.* NY. 1874. illus. 227 pp.

SPRINGFIELD, Otsego Co.
Gray, K. *The History of Springfield.* East Springfield. 1935. map. 251 pp. (Preface: "Springfield has never had a printed history.") (Index by R. Spraker, 1961, prnted. wrps.)

UNADILLA, Otsego Co.
Anon. *History of Unadilla 1855-1930.* 75th Anniv. No. of *Un-*

adilla Times. advts. wrps. 32 pp. (The author: "... was never a resident of the town or had relatives among its people. As a boy he for a time attended the old academy ....")

Anon. *The Ontio in the Land of the Six Nations.* Unadilla. 1904. illus. wrps. 20 pp.

Halsey, G. *The Pioneers of Unadilla Village 1784-1840, by Francis Whiting Halsey, & Reminiscences of Village Life & of Panama & Calif. From 1840 to 1850, by Gaines Leonard Halsey, a Physician in Unadilla for 50 Years.* Unadilla. 1902. illus. map. Lmtd. 650 copies. 340 pp. ("The surviving author has presented 600 copies of these memorials to the vestry of St. Matthew's Church in Unadilla with a view to their sale.")

(Hunt, W. ed.) *The Village Beautiful. Local History of Unadilla in the Last 50 Years.* (Project of Rotary Club.) Unadil. 1957. illus. map. 255 pp.

Morse, R. *Unadilla in its First Century.* (ca 1965.) illus. wrps. 18 pp.

WESTFORD, Otsego Co.
Westford Union School. *A Century and a Half in Westford.* 1938. maps. mimeo. 120 pp.

WORCESTER, Otsego Co.
Anon. *Worcester Sesquicentennial Celebration 1797-1947.* ca 1947. advts. wrps. 4 pp.

(Doig, A.) *Town of Worcester History.* Cooperstown. (Dec. 1953.) illus. wrps. 156 pp. (12 pp. typed errata & addenda by I. Shafer in copy at NYSHA.)

PUTNAM COUNTY

PUTNAM COUNTY
Anon. *Putnam Co. Almanac & Guide.* 1958. maps. wrps. 64 pp. (Has hist. sketch.)

Anon. *Putnam Co. History the Last 100 Years.* 1957. mimeo. wrps. approx. 100 pp.

(Anon.) *Putnam County Workshop.* (Articles by various authors on Putnam Co. hist., mainly prior to 1873.) 1954. maps. wrps. 45 pp. mimeo.

Anon. *Today in History. Almanac of Putnam County.* 1977. map. bib. 164 p. (Brewster National Honor Soc. Local hist. articles written by high school students.)

Blake, W. *History of Putnam Co.* NY. 1849. 368 pp. Reprntd. in 1970.

Hillery, H. *Putnam Co. in the Civil War.* 1961. illus. unpaged.

Pelletreau, W. *History of Putnam Co.* Phil. 1886. illus. maps. 771 pp. Reprntd. 1975.

BREWSTER, Putnam Co.
Howe, A. (ed) *Brewster Through the Years 1848-1948.* Hist. & folklore. (1948.) illus. 156 pp. map.

COLD SPRING, Putnam Co.
Adams, O. *Historical Reminiscences of Cold Spring, Nelsonville, & Vicinity.* 1955. 82 pp.

Dunseith, F. *Cold Spring History. (Before 1896).* Feb. 1, 1961. 26 pp. typed mss. in PCHS.

Floyd-Jones, E. *The Origin & Development of Cold Spring-on-Hudson. 1846-1946. A Centennial History.* illus. wrps. 26 pp.

(Wilson, M.) *Thirty Years of Early History of Cold Spring & Vicinity by One Who Has Been A Resident Since 1819.* Cold Spring. 1886. wrps. 48 pp. (3 typed pp. index, ca 1966. inserted in some copies.)

GARRISON'S LANDING, Putnam Co.
Saunders, J. *Garrison's Landing.* July 1966. illus. folio size. wrps. 12 pp.

LAKE MAHOPAC, Putnam Co.
Warren, U. *Lake Mahopac. Preservation in Picture & Story ... in 1906 With Historical Sketches.* n.d. illus. 183 pp.

NELSONVILLE, Putnam Co.
Adams, Jaycox, DeLanoy. *Cent. History of Nelsonville* (1955.) illus. advts. wrps. 28 pp.

PHILLIPSTOWN, Putnam Co.
Gerwig, H. *Historic Phillipstown in the Highlands of the Hudson.* Cold Spring. ca 1966. wrps. 8 pp.

QUEENS COUNTY

QUEENS COUNTY
Anon. *History of Queens Co. 1683-1882.* NY. 1882. map. 576 pp. (Many copies lack port. of Henry S. DeBevoise, pp. 281.)
Anon. *Portrait & Biog. Record of Queens Co.* NY. 1896. 1204 pp.
Onderdonck, H. *Documents & Letters Intended to Illustrate the Rev Incidents of Queens Co. With Connecting Narratives, Explanatory Notes & Additions.* NY. 1846. 264 pp.
Same. 2nd. Series. Hempstead 1884. 70 pp.
--- *Queens Co. in Olden Times: Being a Supplement to the Several Histories Thereof.* Jamaica. 1865. 122 pp.

FLUSHING, Queens Co.
Lawson, H. *Olde Flushing.* 1952. illus. 207 pp.
Mandeville, Rev. *Flushing Past & Present.* Flushing. 1860. illus. 180 pp.

Trebor, H. *Colonial Flushing. A Brief History.* Flushing. 1945. wrps. 64 pp.
Waller, H. *History of Town of Flushing.* Flushing. 1399. 287 pp.

JAMAICA, Queens Co.
Armbruster, E. *Historical Data Relating to Places & Families of Jamaica.* n.d. 3 pks. of mss. in LIHS.

LITTLE NECK, Queens Co.
Meissner (Ed.) *The History of Little Neck.* 1952. wrps. illus. 89 pp.
Riley, L. *The Chronicle of Little Neck & Douglaston.* NY. 1936. 26 pp.

LONG ISLAND CITY, Queens Co.
(Kelsey, J.) *History of Long Island City.* NY. 1896. illus. map. 202 pp.

NEWTOWN, Queens Co.
Armbruster, E. *Long Island Landmarks (Newtown, Including Long Island City).* lmtd. to 300 copies. 1923.
Riker, J. *The Annals of Newtown.* NY. 1852. illus. maps. 437 pp. (In a letter dated Nov. 1, 1887, Riker wrote that he had a few unbound copies on hand, and added that a few of them had the extra port. which had appeared in only a few of the previous copies.) Reprntd. in 1982.

SPRINGFIELD, Queens Co.
Eardeley, W. *History of Springfield, Town of Jamaica.* Brooklyn. 1914.

REFERENCE BOOKS

The successful collecting, and buying and selling of books demands a good reference library.

Money spent on research tools is well spent. If you are near a good public library, or a university library open to the townspeople, you could use that facility, but in the long run it probably is more economical to have your sources right at hand. Would you want to drive 3 miles in a blinding blizzard to find out the name of the coxswain of the barge that took the fleeing traitor Benedict Arnold to the British ship the *Vulture*? (His name was James Larvey. I just looked it up at home in Lossing's *Field Book of the American Revolution*.) You should buy all the reference works you can in your chosen field of interest. Many dealers have working libraries that are almost as large as their stock for sale. Mine is approaching that point. Although I use an extensive range of books for research, I find the general reference works listed here to be of great value in researching the hist. and people of NY State.

Adams, J. T. (ed.) *Dictionary of American History*. NY. Chas. Scribner's Sons. 1940. 5 vols. + index. (An unrivalled source of information, brought together by the collaboration of more than 1100 leading historical scholars. In 1961 a supplemental vol. was issued. All in all, approximately 7000 topics are covered. About 1962 a one-vol. ed. was pub., titled *Concise Dictionary of American History*. This single vol. is handy for everything from an explanation of the implied powers of the Constitution, to a brief definition of the Dutch word Burgher.)

Appletons' Cyclopedia of American Biography. Ed. by J. G. Wilson and J. Fiske. NY. 1886-1889. illus. 6 vol. Reprntd. 1898. A supplemental vol. was pub. in 1900. (Approximately 20,000 short biog. are given in this very useful work. A major feature are the numerous facsimilies of autograph signatures which are "for the most part from the collection of some six thousand American autographs in the possession of the senior editor." They are frequently used for comparison when trying to authenticate an original signature. Sometimes when another dealer is buying autograph material from me he will say, "Let's see if this guy's signature is in Appleton." As I hand him the required vol. I silently hope they compare so that I don't lose a sale.)

Biographical Directory of the American Congress 1774-1971. pub. 1971. 1972 pp. (Pub. many years ago, this work contains a vast amount of material, and has been updated and reprntd. from time to time. It has the biog. of every person from NY State who ever served in the U. S. Congress. It must be used carefully, though. It gives a good biog. of a long-time and powerful representative from another state, including the date of his death, but does not record that he went to prison for padding his Congressional payroll.)

Boatner, M. M. III. *Encyclopedia of the American Revolution*. 1966. bib. index of maps. 1287 pp. (An essential reference with nearly 2000 entries.)

Boatner, M. M. III. *Landmarks of the American Revolution. A Guide to Locating and Knowing What Happened at the Sites of*

Independence. 1975. maps. illus. index. 608 pp. (The number of NY sites involved in the Revolutionary War is indicated by the fact that they take up 110 pages in this valuable book, more than any other state.)

Brigham, C. S. *History and Bibliography of American Newspapers 1690-1820.* Worcester, MA. American Antiquarian Soc. 1947. 2 vol. indexes. (Besides brief hist. of each newspaper, locations of files and dates available are given. There are 230 pages devoted to NYC and State.)

(Clinton, G.) *The Public Papers of George Clinton.* 10 vol. 1899. index. maps. illus. (An indispensable source work on the Revolutionary War in NY State.)

Cole, G. G. (ed. & comp.) *Historical Material Relating to Northern New York. A Union Catalog.* Canton, NY. North Country Reference & Research Resources Council. Revised ed. 1976. index. 452 pp. (This is a union catalog of prntd. hist. materials pertaining to northern NY found in 114 libraries and institutions in the 8 counties represented in the North Country Council. There are 4407 numbered entries with 1 or more locations given for each item.)

Dictionary of American Biography. Charles Scribners, NY, 1936. 10 vol. + supplements. (No doubt this is the most used work of its type, containing over 14,000 scholarly biog. of important Americans. Every entry has a bib. listing other sources of biog. data. This mammoth set was pub. in various years, beginning about 192B, and issued in either 10 or 20 vol. plus supplements.)

Donaldson, A. L. *A History of the Adirondacks.* 2 vol. NY. 1921. illus. maps. bib. index. (Donaldson amassed a library of over 800 vol. on the Adirondacks, and wrote his classic history over a period of 10 years. Among those who aided him with information were Peter F. Schofield and Frank S. Gardner, both of whom were leaders in the long fight to preserve the forests. He sent them his preliminary chapter on Legislative Control, and they sent back several pages of suggestions and revisions. Seven hundred and eighty-eight copies of the book were sold within 4 months of pub., which delighted Donaldson as he only expected 500 copies to sell in such a short time. His collection of Adirondack books went to the Saranac Public Library. Whenever I think of the Adirondacks, I think of Bob Paulson, a NJ antiquarian book dealer, and here is the reason why: Many years before I went into the antiquarian book-business full time, I had a career delivering milk house to house in northern NJ. One day on my lunch break I stopped at a bookshop in Englewood. I walked in and said to the chap behind the desk, "Do you have any sleepers in here?", meaning: are there any unrecognized and underpriced good books. He looked at me and at the milk truck and probably thought to himself, "What does this milk-jockey know about books?", and replied, "I hope not." That fellow was Bob Paulson, we became good friends, and he was one of several dealers who urged me to go into the business fulltime. Bob loved the Adirondacks, spent much time there, knew many of the old timers, and liked to hike the abandoned railroad tracks. He also knew and frequently visited Rockwell Kent the noted author and artist who lived in northern NY. Over the years Bob acquired many Adirondack books, and he was an expert on Kent's works. He was an excellent book dealer, widely known, and well liked.)

Edelstein, D. *Joel Munsell, Printer and Antiquarian.* 1950 bib. index. 421 pp. (A major biog. of Albany's most famous printer, with special emphasis on his printing and pub. career. It is full of necessary information for the collector of Munsell imprints. Some folks have said that this book is dry reading, but I have found it quite interesting. I keep a copy on my reference shelf to check up on the authors and books published by Munsell.)

Evans, C. *American Bibliography. A Chronological bibliography of All Books, Pamphlets, and Periodical Publications Printed in the United States of America From the Genesis of Printing in 1639.* Chicago. 1903-1934. 12 vol. Prvtly. prntd. for the author. (Evans died in 1935, after having gotten through the "M" series in 1799. A 13th vol., ed. by C. K. Shipton, carried the entries through 1800, and was pub. by the American Antiquarian Soc. in 1955. The 13 vol. had a total of 39,162 entries. In 1969 the AAS pub. a 2-vol. set *National Index of American Imprints Through 1800. The Short-Title Evans*, by Shipton & Mooney, which contained more than 10,000 additional titles. In addition, in 1970 the Bibliographical Society of America pub. a 2-vol. set by R. P. Bristol titled *Supplement to Charles Evans' American Bibliography.* These 3 works are indispensable references listing many NY State and colony imprints. The 13 vol. of the Evans were prntd. by tne Mini-Print Corp. of Metuchen, NJ, in 1967, in a one-vol. ed.)

Evers, Alf. *The Catskills From Wilderness to Woodstock.* 1972. maps. illus. Hist. notes. bib. index. 821 pp. (One of the great regional books of NY State. Packed full of information in short, easy to read chapters. Evers even quotes an old-timer as saying that when President Grant visited the Overlook Mountain House he was so drunk, "They had to pour him in bed." This is one of the most enjoyable books I have ever read, and I use it frequently as a reference book on Catskill Mountain history. Evers has also written more than 50 childrens' books. And you may want to try to find them.)

Flick, A. C. (ed.) *History of the State of New York.* 10 vol. NY. 1933-1937. (The best reference on the hist. of the state. It was reprnted. by Kennikat Press, of Port Washington, NY, in 1962. In my experience, the reprint turns up less frequently than the original ed. Flick was the state historian of NY, and when in his office one day in Albany I heard him say, "There ought to be a law against books without an index." A plus for this set is that each vol. is separately indexed, making the book complete in itself. Vol. 10 has an index for the entire set. I will let you in on a secret, though: I once came across a book that Dr. Flick wrote that had no index.)

French, J. H. *Gazetteer of the State of New York ... a Complete History and Description of Every County, City, Town, Village and Locality ... Illustrated by Original Steel Engravings, and Accompanied by a New map of the State.* 1859. index. 739 pp. some advts. (One of the most referred to reference books on NY State. It went through at least 10 ed. A comprehensive name index, with approximately 16,000 entries, was compiled by Frank Place, and pub. in 1962, and reprntd. in 1969. That index adds greatly to the value of the gazetteer, which also has been repub. The title page mentions a "map" but there is no map in the book. It was a huge wall map on rollers, and was to be sold with the book. Those 2 items seldom stayed together: the book is very common, and the map rarely comes on the market. Many copies of the *Gazetteer* have come my way, but only 2 of the roller maps. Once I had a map which had been linen backed and folded.)

Gephart, R. M. (comp.) *Revolutionary America 1763-1789. A bibliography.* Lib. of Congress. 1984. 2 vols. index. (This is the most comprehensive work on the subject, and is a catalog of the prntd. primary and secondary works in the Library of Congress. There are more than 20,000 titles listed 1n 14,810 numbered entries. Numerous annotations add to the great value of this work.)

Gregory, W. (ed.) *American Newspapers 1821-1936, A Union List of Files Available in the U. S. and Canada.* 1937. 791 pp. Reprntd. 1967. (There are 60 pages of listings of locations of NY State and City newspaper files. It even includes the dates available at each location. It is true that in some instances only microfilms can be seen. In order to save space some depositories have had their newspaper collections microfilmed and then disposed of the bulky volumes. Many papers prntd. on woodpulp, which Process began about 1850, had to be microfilmed because they were rapidly falling apart and could no longer be used by researchers.)

Groce & Wallace. *Dictionary of Artists in America 1564-1860.* 1957. bib. 759 pp. Reprntd. several times. (Brief biog. data on over 10,000 American artists, many of whom lived and worked in NY.)

Hamilton, M. *The Country Printer. New York State 1785-1830.* NY. 1936. bib. index. 360 pp. (An indispensable hist. of early NY State printing, with brief biog. data on a great many printers, ed., and pub. This book has been reprntd.)

Hedrick, U. P. *A History of Agriculture in the State of New York.* 1933. illus. bib. index. 462 pp. (A distinguished book reprntd. in 1966 in paperback, with a lengthy introduction by Paul W. Gates, Prof. of Hist. at Cornell University. This reprint omits some of the illus. found in the original ed.)

Heitman, F. B. (comp.) *Historical Register of Officers of the Continental Army During the War of the Revolution, April 1775, to Dec. 1783.* New, revised, and enlarged ed. 1914. 692 pp. (An essential reference with records of 14,000 officers. There is also a section on French officers, a calendar for the years 1775-1783, and a list of battles, plus other useful data. It was reprntd. in 1973.)

Hodge, F. W. (ed.) *Handbook of American Indians North of Mexico.* 2 vols. 1907-1910. map. illus. bib. (The standard encyclopedia on American Indians, it is so detailed it even lists the sub-tribes of the Wappinger confederacy of the lower Hudson Valley. It has been reprntd. several times.)

Hough, F. B. *Gazetteer of the State of New York.* Albany. 1872. Map Illus. index. 745 pp. (The scarcest of the later NY state gazetteers. Hough actually did much of the work on the famous French's *Gazetteer* pub. in 1860. This 1872 work under his name is a wholly rewritten version of the 1860 pub. Altho printing was started and dated 1872, there were considerable delays in completing the volume. The salesman's sample book for canvassing for subscriptions contained a portrait of Hough which was not to appear in the *Gazetteer*, and a copy I once owned was dated 1873.)

Howes, W. *USiana. (1650-1950) A Selective Bibliography in Which are Described 11,620 Uncommon and Significant Books Relating to the Continental Portion of the U. S.* Revised and enlarged ed. 1962. (First pub. in 1954, it sold out rapidly; the revised ed. of 1962 had to be reprntd.; and it was re-issued about 1980. In 1981 the Jenkins Co. of Austin, Texas, pub. a catalog of books for sale titled *A Full Howes*, consisting of nearly 3000 items that had appeared in *USiana*. Included in the Jenkins catalog was a chronological finding list for U. S. government documents in Howes, and corrections to some errors in Howes. There are a number of NY related entries in *USiana*.)

Klein, M. M. (comp.) *New York in the American Revolution. A Bibliography.* 1974. index. 197 pp. (There are 1089 entries, many with annotations. Divided into chapters by subject headings: Politics, Campaigns, Loyalists, Economy, Indians, &c., each chapter is begun with an essay-ette.)

Larned, J. N. (ed.) *The Literature of American History. A Bibliographical Guide.* 1902. index. 588 pp. Repub. in 1966. (There are 4145 annotated entries, describing important books in all fields of American hist. Larned, director of the Buffalo, NY, Library, edited this excellent reference work without fee or reward for his labors.)

List of Prints, Books, Manuscripts, Etc. Relating to Henry Hudson, The Hudson River, Robert Fulton, and Steam Navigation. Exhibited in the Lenox Branch, New York Public Library, On the Occasion of the Hudson-Fulton Celebration, September, 1909. Pub. 1909. wrps. 86 pp. (One of the most useful references of its type. There are 24 pp. of biog., co. and town hist., and books about the river. The most important section contains descriptive listings of over 745 prints. There is also a brief section on maps and plans.)

McDade, T. *The Annals of Murder. A Bibliography of Books and Pamphlets on American Murders From Colonial Times to 1900.* 1961. illus. index. 360 pp. (A number of the 1126 entries refer to NY State.)

The Month. Goodspeeds Book Shop. Boston, MA. October 1929 through June 1969. (For nearly 40 years Goodspeed's pub. a well-illus. and annotated catalog of books for sale. An index to the set was issued in 1959, and another index was put out in 1969 covering the intervening years. It is especially valuable for its annotations and hist. explanations. A complete set is difficult to compile. Sam Dauber, one of the old time NYC booksellers, told me it was one of the most useful reference works he had and he advised me to get a set. It took me several years to acquire a complete run, and I had to get a photocopy of the first issue. It is amazing how many NY State items Goodspeeds handled over the years.)

Munsell, J. *Bibliotheca Munselliana. Catalog of the Books and Pamphlets Issued from the Press of Joel Munsell ... 1828 to 1870.* 1872. index. 191 pp. Somewhat over 20 copies were prntd. (Munsell the celebrated Albany printer, and man of many interests, apparently was the first American pub. to issue a bib. of the issues of his press. In this useful work he often lists the number of copies prntd., and was very frank in his comments, "Of the 500 copies prntd., most of them were used for wrapping paper." Edelstein's informative biog. of Munsell devotes several pages to this book. I have never had the original ed. of 1872, but a number of copies of the 1969 reprint have come my way.)

National Cyclopedia of American Biography. 1893 + illus. James T. White Co. (This is the greatest concentration of biographies of notable Americans that I know of. There are many thousands of entries, and you can find information here available nowhere else. Well over 50 vol. were issued, the company ceasing pub. not many years ago. An index vol. was put out at various times, the one I have came out in 1969 and covers vol. 1 thru 51. This large, heavy set takes up a lot of room, and it is difficult to gather together a complete run. I have vol. 1 through 25 in my reference library, lacking vol. 23 and 24. For several years I have searched for them without success. Fortunately, the index has seldom referred me to those 2 particular tomes. The most useful for the antiquarian are the earlier vols. as they contain many personages from the beginnings of America, and there are many facsimile signatures. The later vol. contain more recent worthies.)

O'Callaghan, E. B. (ed.) *Documentary History of the State of New York.* Albany. 1849-51. 4 vols. illus. maps. index in each vol. (A great repository of material relating to colonial NY. It contains plates and a number of fine maps. Most of the sets

I have seen are incomplete, as some of the pictorial and cartographic material has been removed for framing. I have spent hours sitting on the dusty floors of book shops collating sets of this work to see if they were complete. I have become so tired of that chore that for the time being I have stopped purchasing that set. NY State Assembly Document No. 136, dated April 6, 1854, goes into detail about the pub. of this very useful set. Although these books should have been sold as a unit, the printer reported that there were 26,422 copies of vol. 1, 27,000 copies of vol. 2, 24,678 copies of vol. 3, and 10,137 copies of vol. 4! There were 3000 copies prntd. of each vol. of the quarto ed. It was reported that the Secretary of State had a hard time finding places to send this mammoth printing. He said, "I shall, in all cases, give preference to associations of laboring men, though I may have enough to distribute among those of a different class." He eventually sent sets to a great variety of newspaper ed., institutions, and individuals, some of them in other states. Some sets also ended up in France, Bohemia, and Egypt. I can just imagine an Egyptian antiquarian bookseller finding a set of this in a bazaar in Cairo and saying to himself, "What in the world can I do with this?")

Peters, H. T. *America On Stone ... A Chronicle of American Lithography.* Garden City, NY. 1935. 18 colored plates, and 136 black and white plates. 415 pp. lmtd. to 751 copies. bib. (An alphabetical list of American printmakers, with data on each one. A great many worked in NY. Reprntd. in 1976 by Arno Press. At this time Arno also reprntd. Peters' other great works: *California on Stone,* and his 2-vol. *Currier and Ives.*)

Phillips, P. L. *A List of maps of America in the Library of Congress.* 1901. 1137 pp. (A comprehensive list of maps in the Library of Congress as of November 1897. Many hundreds of the maps are of NY State and City interest. Besides separately prntd. maps this work also includes maps found in atlases, books, and magazines. This major reference was reprntd. in 1967 by Theatrum Orbis Terrarum Ltd. in Amsterdam, the Netherlands.)

Pilling, J. C. (comp.) *Bibliography of the Iroquoian Languages.* 1888. illus. of some title pages. 208 pp. Chronological index. (A detailed listing of Indian language pub. 1545-1888, and of some other works about Indian languages. There are many annotations, and occasional biog. data about some of the authors. Mainly works in the tongue of the NY State Indians: Mohawk, Onondaga, Oneida, Seneca, Tuskarora, and Cuygua; although there are some in Huron, Cherokee, and Wyandot.)

Pilling, J. C. (comp.) *Bibliography of the Algonquian Languages.* 1891. illus. of some title pages, and a few other pages. 614 pp. Chronological index. (Some references to the Delaware Indians who inhabited part of southeast NY.)

Plum, D. A. (ed.) *Adirondack Bibliography. A List of Books,*

Pamphlets, and Periodical Articles Published Through the Year 1955. Gabriels, NY. Adirondack Mt. Club. 1958. map. index. bib. 354 pp. 7539 numbered items. A supplement carrying the work from 1956 to 1965, was pub. by the Adirondack Museum, Blue Mt. Lake, NY, in 1973. 198 pp. carrying the numbered items from 7540 through 10641. The index in the supplement covers both vol. (The "bible" for collectors of Adirondackiana.)

Richmond, M. L. *Shaker Literature. A Bibliography.* 2 vols. 1977. index. (There are over 4000 entries in this comprehensive work. That is a lot of items by and about a religious sect that had a total of approximately 20,000 members during its two centuries of existence. There were several Shaker communities in NY State.)

Roberts, R. B. *New York's Forts in the Revolution.* 1980. illus. diagrams. maps. glossary. bib. index. 521 pp. (The first attempt to catalog and give the hist. of every known fortification in NY State during the Revolution. A comprehensive work which no student of those times can afford to be without. In 1981 it was brought to Robert's attention that a Conrad Widrig in his application for a pension in 1837 stated he was at the battle at Fort Mike in the Mohawk Valley. Roberts did further research and found that New Petersburg Fort at East Schuyler in Herkimer Co. had also been called Fort Mike, probably prior to 1777. Incidentally, at that battle 11 men successfully repelled an attack by over 200 British, Indians, and Tories.)

Sabin, J. *A Dictionary of Books Relating to America.* 1868-1929. (A comprehensive, detailed, bib. of over 100,000 books relating to American hist. and social life. Sabin died before its completion, and the work was carried on by Wilberforce Eames and R. W. G. Vail. The last vol., no. 29, came out in 1929. The set I have was pub. by N. Israel, Amsterdam (the Netherlands) in 1961-62 bound in 15 vol. A very useful addition *Author-Title Index* compiled by J. E. Molnar, was issued in 1974 in 3 vol. by the Scarecrow Press, Metuchen, NJ. Sabin's complete *Dictionary* was also issued in Readex Microprint card form with a 12 power eye magnifier. It takes up a lot less space than the standard prntd. set, but is a bit more difficult to use.)

Sabine, L. *The American Loyalists, or Biographical Sketches of Adherents to the British Crown in the War of the Revolution.* Boston. 1847. 733 pp. (It is amazing how many Tories were in or from NY. The set I constantly use for reference is the enlarged ed. issued in 2 vol. in 1864.) Reprntd. 1966.

(Scoville, J. A.) *The Old Merchants of New York City, by Walter Barrett, Clerk.* NY. 1885 ed. 5 vols. indexes. (Packed full of short, factual sentences, this set is very difficult to read for enjoyment. But as a source of information about hundreds upon hundreds of obscure NYC merchants it is invaluable. I use it frequently in research. This work started out as a column in the

New York Leader newspaper, but became so popular the author was forced to issue it in book form. The first ed. came out in 5 vol. 1863-1869, and has been reprntd. several times. The 1872 ed. had a map and 11 plates. Scoville was himself a NYC merchant for a time, then became a journalist and a novelist. For a time he was private secretary to John C. Calhoun, and during the Civil War he was extremely sympathetic to the South.)

Shaw & Shoemaker. *American Bibliography. 1958-1988.* Scarecrow Press, Metuchen, NJ. (This is an attempt to locate and record every book pub. in the U. S. beginning in 1801, with locations of 1 or more copies. To date the work has been completed through 1839, with a total of 109,607 entries. It has had various editors and assistants, and in 1820 the title was changed to *American Imprints.* Along the way various helpful indexes have beenr issued. It is invaluable for knowing where a specific copy of a work can be seen; and, as it gives the number of pages of each book, it can help you determine if a copy you might have is complete. The entire set as of now consists of 39 vol., plus several vol. of indexes.)

Spafford, H. G. *A Gazetteer of the State of New York 1813.* Albany. Map. 336 pp. (This was the first gazetteer of the state, and is an excellent reference on the towns and counties of the early 1800s. Spafford had copies prntd. and apparently had them bound up as orders came in. If he had the money he had plates bound in; if he was short of money, which was quite often, he had the book bound without plates. The plates most commonly seen are the View of Lake George, and General View of the Falls of Niagara. Over the years a dozen or more copies have come my way. The most unusual one had 4 plates. Besides the Lake George and Niagara engravings, there was an illustration of the Protestant-Dutch Church in Albany, and A View of the Fort and Harbor of Oswego From Lake Ontario Representing the Attack by the British on the 6th. of May 1814. Boyd's life of Spafford goes into great detail about this work, but does not mention the lack of, or variation in the number of plates.)

Spafford, H. G. *A Gazetteer of the State of New York.* Albany. 1824. With a aap and profiles of the canals. 620 pp. (Because of the vast amount of new data, this book can rightfully be called a new work, and not a second ed. of the 1813 pub. In his preface, Spafford tells how he accumulated all of the material incorporated into this very useful work for the present-day historian. Reprntd. in 1981 by Heart of the Lake Pub., Interlaken, NY, with an added preface by Warren F. Broaderick, Public Records Analyst of the NY State Archives.)

Spear, D. N. *Bibliography of American Directories Through 1860.* Worcester, MA, American Antiquarian Soc. 1961. 389 pp. (An alphabetical listing of 1647 directories found in the Library of the AAS and a number of other libraries. One or more locations are given for each entry. There are listings for more than 23 NY cities. All the way from the 1 directory for Geneva to the more than 150 for NYC. Although this work ends with 1860, it may be well to add here that directories contaning personal names are especially valuable as much of the U. S. census for 1890 was destroyed.)

Sullivan, J. &c. (eds.) *The Papers of Sir William Johnson.* Albany. 1921-1965. 13 vol. + index vol. illus. maps. (A treasure trove of the correspondence to and from Sir William Johnson, British superintendent of Indian affairs on the Mohawk River, covering 1738 to 1774. There is a vast amount of material for the serious researcher to get happily lost in. Not appearing in this set are the Johnson documents pub. in the *Documentary History of New York*, or *Documents Relative to the Colonial History of New York*.)

Werner, E. A. *Civil List and Constitutional History of the Colony and State of New York.* Albany. 1889. illus. index. 757 pp. (A major reference work with hist. data, and lists of the names of state and co. officials from colonial times to almost the date of pub. The index in this vol. has approximately 20,000 names. It was pub. in various years, and is one of the more useful vol. for hist. researchers.)

Who Was Who in America. 1897-1942. Biographies of the Non-Living With Dates of Death Appended. Chicago. The Marquis Co. 1942. 1396 pp. (This covers a period of time for which few other handy references are available.)

Whitford, N. *History of the Canal System of State of New York. Histories of the Canals of the U. S. and Canada.* 1906. 2 vol. illus. maps. (Of major importance is the 188-page bib. of NY canals and the biog. of canal engineers.)

RENSSELAER COUNTY

RENSSELAER COUNTY

Anderson, G. *Landmarks of Rensselaer Co.* Syracuse. 1897. illus. 2 vol.

Crait & Crait. *Our Yesterdays, A History of Rensselaer Co.* Troy. 1948. maps. mimeo. 120 pp.

Sylvester, N. *History of Rensselaer Co.* Phil. 1880. illus. maps. 564 pp.

Weise, A. *History of the 17 Towns in Rensselaer Co. From the Colonization of the Manor of Rensselaer to the Present.* Troy. 1880. index. 158 pp. (Pub. in *Troy Daily Times*.)

WPA GUIDE. *A Souvenir of the Founding of Rensselaer Co. 1791.* (Troy. 1941.) illus. wrps. 31 pp.

BERLIN, Rensselaer Co.

Hull, N. *Reminiscences in the Settling of the Valley of the Little Hoosick. Town of Berlin.* Troy. 1858. wrps. 33 pp.

BRAINARD, Rensselaer Co.

Thomson, F. *A Hist. of the Hamlet of Brainard 1743-1978.* ca 1978. illus. map. wrps. 28 pp.

CASTLETON, Rensselaer Co.

Ton, E. *History of Castleton-on-Hudson.* 1949. wrps. 53 pp. ("There have been no great men born here ....")

GRAFTON, Rensselaer Co.

Bennett, R. *The Grafton Hills of Home.* ca 1975.

LANSINGBURGH, Rensselaer Co.
Anon. *Lansingburgh, NY. 1771-1971.* pub. by Lansingburgh Hist. Soc. 48 pp.
Lord, J. *Lansingburgh 1771-1971.* 1971. 48 pp.
Moore, H. *Pictorial Reminiscences & Brief History of Lansingburgh.* 1957. illus. advts. wrps. 99 pp. (Part of the city of Troy.)
Weise, A. *History of Lansingburgh. 1670-1877.* Troy. 1877. wrps. 44 pp.

RENSSELAER, Rensselaer Co.
Fraser, J. *Bath-on-the-Hudson. Early Years.* 1974. illus. maps. wrps. 28 pp.

SAND LAKE, Rensselaer Co.
Carpenter, M. *Reviews & Reminiscenses. A Brief Hist. ... of Sand Lake.* (1979.) wrps. illus. 26 pp. A 10-page supplement was also issued in 1979.
Hayner, M. *A Story of Sand Lake.* 1965. mimeo. 10 pp.

STEPHENTOWN, Rensselaer Co.
Bayba, A. (comp.) *Stephentown Historical Album #2.* 1979. 52 pp. (Hist. essays by school children.)

TROY, Rensselaer Co.
Buel, D. *Troy for 50 Years.* Troy. 1841. 35 pp.
Goddard, A. *The Trojan Sketch Book.* Troy. 1846. illus. 180 pp.
Hayner, R. *Troy & Rensselaer Co.* NY. 1925. illus. 3 vols.
Rezneck, S. *Profiles of the Past of Troy.* 1970. Book.
Weise, A. *City of Troy & Vicinity.* Troy. 1886. map. illus. 376 pp.
--- *Hist. ... of Troy.* Troy. 1876. illus. maps. 400 pp.
--- *Troy's 100 Years, 1789-1889.* Troy. 1891. illus. 453 pp.

Woodworth, J. *Reminiscences of Troy. 1790-1807.* Albany. 1853. wrps. 39 pp. (A small ed. for private distribution.) 2nd. ed. with notes. Albany. 1860. lmtd. 200 copies. 112 pp.

REVOLUTIONARY WAR

Advertisement to the Publick. By Order of the Committee, Isaac Low, Chairman. New-York, July 9, 1770. Broadside, 8 x 12 inches. (Low, Chairman of the Committee of Inspection of NYC, announces that the majority of the inhabitants of the city favor the importation of all goods except "Tea, or any other Article whatsoever, which now is, or may hereafter be subject to Duty for the Purpose of raising a Revenue in America...." In 1775 Low made a violent speech against the King, but he later became a Tory and stayed in NYC during the war. In 1783 he moved to England. The usually solemn John Adams once exclaimed that Low's wife was "a beauty." This broadside is not listed in Evans or Bristol.)

An Ordinance of the Convention of the State of New York, Organizing and Establishing the Government Agreed to by the Said Convention. Fish-Kill: Prntd. by Samuel Loudon. 1777. wrps. 12 pp. (The very first Constitution of NY State was adopted in April 1777. A temporary government was needed until the Govenor and Legislature could be elected, so the Convention at Kingston, on May 8, 1777, appointed a Council of Safety of 15 men to conduct the government of the state. This is the first printing naming the leaders of the newly formed state and the oath they are to administer to the new Governor upon his taking office. It also names co. judges, sheriffs, and clerks; and lists the duties of the sheriffs in regard to elections.)

Andre-related etchings by William H. Wallace, ca 1890s: Front of the Joshua Hett Smith House 1890; Beverly Robinson House; Seventy-Six Stone House Rear; Treason House Haverstraw; Inside 76 Stone House Tappan; DeWint House at Tappan; Seventy-Six Stone House at Tappan; Washington Room in DeWint House. (A pencilled note on the Joshua Hett Smith House etching, states, "A few copies of this set of plates printed." See Groce-Wallace' *Dictionary of Artists in America*. It was only by being contrary to my mode of operation that I obtained this set of rare etchings. Almost all of the items that I handle come from other dealers; I rarely buy from private parties. But one winter day I got a call to look at a collection some distance away, and for no particularly good reason I said, "OK I will come down. How do I get there?" It was a non-descript house that I arrived at, and the interior looked like the proverbial Collyer brothers domicile. In that horrendous clutter I discovered these etchings. Also an extra-illus. history of the city of NY, and a host of other great items. I made a second trip there several days later, and altogether got 2 car trunk loads from that treasure trove.)

Andre's Journal. *An Authentic Record of the Movements and Engagements of the British Army in America From June 1777 to November 1778 as Recorded From Day to Day by Major John Andre*. Ed. by Henry Cabot Lodge. Issued by the Bibliophile Society. Boston. 1903. With facsimile reproductions of original maps and plans drawn by John Andre. index. 2 vol. lmtd. to 487 sets. Boston. 1903. (A magnificent printing of this important journal, with the engraved portrait of Andre signed by the engraver, W. F. Hopson; the title page signed by the engraver, E. D. French; and an etching of Andre signed by the etcher, W. H. W. Bicknell. Quite often the white vellum bindings are somewhat soiled, and slightly warped. If the vellum is not heavily soiled, I have been able to clean it up very well by rubbing lightly with COLD WATER and a rag.)

Andre, Maj. John. *The Frantick Lover*. NY. Blue Ox Press. Nov. 1941. 8 pp. pamphlet. (The first printing of a poem by Major Andre from the original mss. Howard M. Peckham, in the foreword, states that it relates the defeat of a British officer by a Provincial, and that the girl involved presumably was a hospitable damsel of NY.)

Andrews, W. L. *An Essay on the Portraiture of the American Revolutionary War Being an Account of a Number of the Engraved Portraits Connected Therewith, Remarkable for Their Rarity or Otherwise Interesting. Appendix Containing Lists of Portraits of Revolutionary Characters to be Found in Various English and American Publications of the*

18th. and Early Part of the 19th. Century. Illustrated With Reproductions by the Photogravure Process of 20 of the Original Engravings. NY. 1896. index. 100 pp. lmtd. to 185 copies on hand made paper, and 15 on Imperial Japan Paper.

(Armstrong, J.) *Hints to Young Generals. By An Old Soldier.* Kingston. (NY.) J. Buel. (1812). diagrams. 71 pp. (Written by John Armstrong, an officer in the Revolutionary War, who was present at the surrender of Burgoyne. He was the composer of the famous "Newburgh Letters" of 1783, which listed the grievances the army officers held against Congress. He married the sister of Chancellor Robert R. Livingston, was a U. S. Senator, Minister to France, U. S. Secretary of War, and wrote biog. and a book on agriculture. For a number of years he lived at Red Hook, NY. Martin Van Buren, who only lived about 35 miles from Armstrong, said of him, "His disposition was eminently pugnacious." There is a long biog. of Armstrong in the DAB.)

Baldwin, T. *The Revolutionary Journal of Col. Jeduthan Baldwin 1775-1778, Edited With a Memoir and Notes.* Bangor, (ME). Prntd. for the De Burians. 1906. illus. 164 pps. lmtd. to 200 copies. (There is much on Baldwin's service in the Lake George Champlain area. The first few pages of the *Journal* are from his service in the same area in 1755-1756.)

Bannerman, F. *History of the Great Iron Chain, Laid Across the Hudson River at West Point in 1778, by Order of ... Washington. On Exhibition at Military War Museum.* NY. ca early 1900s. 2 small illus. wrps. 8 pp. (Bannerman sold hist. military goods at his establishment in NYC. He also owned Bannerman's Island in the Hudson River below the city of Beacon. The island is now part of a state park. He acquired some links from the Hudson River chain, and turned some of them into desk weights and hammer heads. You can get a good view of Bannerman's Island by parking your car on route 9W northbound about a mile south of Mountain Road, Cornwall. A marked trail, hilly and rocky in sections, can be followed to the top of Storm King Mountain. From that point there is an excellent view of the northern Hudson Highlands and the island. You should get a hiking map to be sure you follow the right trail.)

Barbe-Marbois. *Complot D'Arnold Et De Sir Henry Clinton Contre Les Etats-Unis D'amerique Et Contre Le General Washington. Septembre 17BO.* Paris. 1816. map of West Point, and engraved port. of Arnold and Washington. 184 pp. (A very early prntd. discussion, in French, of Arnold's treason by the Secretary of the French Legation at Philadelphia at the time of Arnold's defection. Parts of this work were translated into English and published in the *American Register*, Phil., 1817. It was reprntd. in 1831.)

Barck, O. T. *New York City During the War for Independence, With Special Reference to the Period of British Oc-*

192

cupation. 1931. map. bib. index. 267 pp. (Emphasizes the social and economic existence of the average citizen's life in the city.)

Barnum, H. L. *The Spy Unmasked, or, Memoirs of Enoch Crosby, Alias Harvey Birch ... (Taken from his own lips, in short-hand)*. NY. 1828. port. illus. map. 206 pp. (Crosby was a patriot spy in the Hudson Valley during the Revolutionary War. There has been much controversy about the claim that he was the pattern for Havey Birch the hero of Cooper's novel *The Spy*. At least 9 ed. of *The Spy Unmasked* were pub. before 1890, and at least 3 of them were versions for children. It also was pub. by the Whitman Pub. Company, in 1936, in their Big Little book series; and I believe a comic strip based on *The Spy* appeared in a NJ newspaper in the 1930s. The *Weekly Times* newspaper of Fishkill, NY, reprntd. the 1828 ed. in 1886, and up until about 1940 some unbound copies were in the safe-room of Herman Dean the village historian. He gave me a copy about that time. He died soon after, and I was never able to find out what became of the rest of the ed. However, the most intriguing question is: "Who was H. L. Barnum?" All that Herman Dean could come up with were speculations that he was a Captain from CT, a surveyor, and a dandy with the ladies. Prof. James H. Pickering, a Cooper specialist, delved into the mystery of Barnum and came up with some interesting facts and conjectures, especially about his rather wide-spread pub. activities. He appeared on the scene in 1824 and disappeared in 1836, pub. an agricultural magazine and numerous books in the interval. Pickering's findings are given in the introduction to the 1975 facsimile reprint of the first ed. of Barnum's book on Enoch Crosby.)

(Becker, John P.) *The Sexagenary, or Reminiscences of the American Revolution*. Albany. 1833. index. 203 pp. (One of the very few accounts written by a resident eye-witness to the Revolutionary War events in the upper Hudson Valley. Although the book is almost without exception attributed to S. DeWitt Bloodgood, it was actually written by Becker. Bloodgood was the ed. Brandow in his *The Story of Old Saratoga* devotes 3 pages to this book and its authorship. The 1833 ed. was suppressed and is now very rare. It was reprntd. in 1866 by Munsell in an ed. of 350 copies.)

Bennett, E. *The Female Spy; or, Treason in the Camp: A Story of the Revolution*. ca 1875. Cincinnati: pub. by U. P. James. wrps. 112 pp. Plus: *Rosalie Du Pont; or, Treason in the Camp*. ca 1875. wrps. 112 pp. (Fiction about the Arnold-Andre episode. *Rosalie Du Pont* is a sequel. See Blanck's *Bibliography of American Literature*.)

By His Excellency George Clinton, Esquire. Governor of the State of New York, General and Commander in Chief of All The Militia, And Admiral of the Navy of the Said State. Proclamation ... Poughkeepsie, 17 April 1783. (Probably prntd. by John Holt, the state printer at Poughkeepsie.

Governor Clinton announces that Cessation of Arms has been declared with his Britannic Majesty, and that this proclamation should be read to the public and to the militia. Very Rare: not in Evans, Shipton-Mooney, Bristol, or Sabin.)

Bixby, W. *Two Letters. Anthony Wayne and Lake George. Letter From Gen. Anthony Wayne to Gen. Schuyler, Ticonderoga, March 23, 1777. (&) Washington's Announcement of Arnold's Treason. Letter From George Washington to the Judge Advocate General Sept. 26, 1780.* Pvtly. prntd. 1922. small folio. lmtd. to 250 copies. (Prints facsimiles of the two letters. Wayne writes of his problems with the troops at Ticonderoga, and tells of Indian captivities and skirmishes nearby. Washington briefly mentions that Arnold had gone to NY. These 2 letters were from the holdings of Bixby, a noted mss. collector.)

Blake, W. *Brief Account of the Life and Patriotic Services of Jonathan Mix of New Haven (CT). Being an Autobiographical Memoir, Edited From the Original Manuscript.* 1886. 98 pp. (Mix, 1753-1817, served in the Revolutionary War on Long Island, was on the Canadian Expedition, was in the company that raided Rivington's press in NYC, he was later captured and confined on the infamous Jersey prison ship at NY. In 1809 he moved from CT to NYC. This work is not in Gephart.)

Bushnell, C. I. (ed.) *The Destructive Operation of Foul Air, Tainted Provisions, Bad Water, and Personal Filthiness Upon Human Constitution ...*
Unparalleled Cruelty of the British to American Captives at New York During the Revolutionary War, on Board Their Prison and Hospital Ships, in a Communication to Dr. Mitchill, Sept. 4, 1807. Also a Letter to the Tammany Society by Capt. Alexander Coffin, Jun. One of the Surviving Officers. NY. 1865. port. illus. wrps. 28 pp. lmtd. to only 30 copies. (The best account of sanitary conditions on board the infamous Jersey prison ship in NY harbor.)

A Card, Number 1. A Member of the Church of England, and a Son of Liberty, Presents His Compliments to Those Gentlemen, Who Are For an Immediate and Untimely Importation of Goods. From Great Britain ... New York, June 16, 1770. A Card, Number 2 ... New York, June 20, 1770. Broadside 8 x 10 inches. (Evans *American Bibliography* 11594.) (Beginning in 1765 the colonists attempted to win political rights by refusing to import goods from Britain. The Nonimportation Agreements between the colonists alarmed the mother country and concessions were made. This broadside was issued in 1770 at the time many of the NYC merchants were wavering in their devotion to the agreement. I got this treasure some years ago from an old-time, well known dealer who handed me a thick vol. of the Proceedings of the Sons of the American Revolution in the state of NY, pub. in the 1890s. "You might be interested in this," he said. I casually flipped through it and replied, "What's with this? I see it around all of the time, and never bother to pick it up." "Go through it carefully," he countered. I did. Interleaved by a collector, and carefully folded, were about 25 broadsides prntd. between 1770 and 1809. I walked out of that shop with one of the most important purchases of my career. I have often wondered if that unknown collector realized what a great treasure he had created. Several of those broadsides are included in this present work.)

Chambers, Capt. Wm. *Atlas of Lake Champlain 1779-1780.* Bennington and Montpelier, VT. 1984. 31 pp. of illus. text: introductory essay by J. K. Graffagnino, hist. notes, glossary. Plus 31 atlas charts. folio. (Chambers, Commander of the British Fleet on Lake Champlain from 1778 to 1783, compiled a mss. *Book of Directions Necessary for all Commanders of Vessels Employed on Lake Champlain.* They were the first charts and sailing directions for this lake which played a major part in the defense of NY during the American Revolution. This is the first pub. of this atlas, and was made from the mss. copy owned by the VT Hist. Soc.)

Clark, D. *Index to Maps of the American Revolution in Books and Periodicals. Illus. The Revolutionary War and Other Events of the Period. 1763-1789.* pub. 1974. index. 301 pp. (There is a 35-page listing of NY interest.)

(Coghlan, Mrs.) *Memoirs of Mrs. Coghlan, Daughter of the Late Major Moncrieffe, Written by Herself ... Being Interspersed With Anecdotes of the late American and Present War ....* 2 vol. London. 1794. Also pub. the same year in Dublin and Cork. NY, 1795. (Margaret Moncrieffe, daughter of a British officer and a cousin of the American General Mongtomery, was staying at General Putnam's house in NYC in 1776. Major Aaron Burr, on the staff of Putnam, fell in love with this 14-year-old lass. When it was learned that they possibly wanted to get married she was whisked away to the British forces. Sabin declares, "Margaret Coghlan was seduced by Col. Burr, and afterwards led an abandoned life in NY and Europe." Gore Vidal, in his acclaimed novel *Burr*, says she became the lover of Charles James Fox a British statesman. These memoirs were repub. in 1864 in NYC by T. H. Morrell, in an ed. of 100 copies, plus 20 copies on large paper. A preface was written for the NY 1795 ed. but it was suppressed, and is not found in most known copies. It does appear in the 1864 printing. The only copies of this work I have owned are 2 copies of the regular 1864 reprint, and 1 copy of the very lmtd. large paper ed. The latter was extra-illus. with 84 full-page plates. Tredwell's *Privately Illustrated Books, a Plea for Bibliomania*, 1892, the ed. lmtd. to 250 copies prntd. on hand-made paper, states that a Mr. Toedteberg, of Brooklyn, had extra-illus. a copy of the large paper ed. with 200 ports.)

Conkling, H. *Le Chevalier de la Luzerne.* 1908. port. illus. 63 pp. (Luzerne was the French Minister in America during the American Revolution, and became very influential in American affairs. Included in this work is the story of the unsuccessful attempt of Benedict Arnold to borrow money from the Chevalier to meet the claims of his creditors. Lake Luzerne in the Adirondacks was named after this Frenchman.)

Coxe, McGrane. *The Sterling Furnace and the West Point Chain.* Prvtly. prntd.. 1906. wrps. map. illus. 54 pp. (The Sterling Furnace, just west of Tuxedo Park, NY, made part of the famous West Point Chain. Jim Ransom's excellent book *Vanishing Ironworks of the Ramapos*, has a chapter on the chains across the Hudson, and mentions Coxe and his pamphlet. Ransom also mentions the possibility of some chains used for other purposes being sold fraudulently as from the historic chains stretched across the Hudson River during the Revolutionary War.)

Cresswell, D. *The American Revolution in Drawings and Prints. A Checklist of 1765-1790 Graphics in the Library of Congress.* 1975. indexes. 455 pp. (921 items are cataloged. There are hundreds of illus. with annotations and several are in color. There are numerous references to NY State.)

Dawson, H. B. *The Assault on Stony Point, by General Anthony Wayne, July 16, 1779.* Morisania, NY. 1863. map. 18 facsimiles of autograph letters. index. 156 pp. lmtd. to 250 copies. (The appendix of this work contains numerous copies of orders, letters, and despatches.)

Dawson, H. B. *Major General Israel Putnam. A Correspondence On This Subject With the Editor of the "Hartford Daily Post."* Prvtly. prntd. 1860. 169 pp. lmtd. to 250 copies, of which 117 were destroyed by fire. (This work discusses Putnam's responsibility for the defeat of the American army at the Battle of Long Island.)

Dawson, H. B. *The Sons of Liberty in New York.* Prntd. as mss. for private circulation. 1859. 118 pp. (Organized to denounce British tyranny before the Revolution, Dawson calls the Sons of Liberty the only genuinely revolutionary element in the population, and he carries their activities down to Jan. 19, 1770.)

Decker, M. *Brink of Revolution. New York in Crisis. 1765-1776.* 1964. illus. maps. bib. index. 290 pp. (A study of the turbulence in NYC just prior to the Revolutionary War.)

Decker. M. *Ten Days of Infamy. An Illustrated Memoir of the Arnold-Andre Conspiracy.* 1969. illus. map. bib. index. 138 pp. (Many of the photographs in the book were taken in 1897 when the sites were much the same as they were during the treason in 1780.)

Decker, M. *Benedict Arnold, Son of the Havens.* Tarrytown, NY. Wm. Abbatt. 1932. maps. illus. bib. index. 534 pp. A very lmtd. ed. (In 1961 the book was reprntd. by the Antiquarian Press of NY, and lmtd. to 750 copies.)

DeCosta, B. *Notes on the History of Fort George, During the Colonial and Revolutionary Periods, With Contemporaneous Documents.* NY. Sabin. 1871. maps. index. wrps. 78 pp. (Fort George was near the head of Lake George. This work includes the Orderly Book of James McGee, kept at Fort George in July and August of 1776, copied from the original mss. in the NY State Library.)

Diamant, L. *Chaining the Hudson. The Fight for the River in the American Revolution.* 1989. illus. maps. bib. notes. index. 233 pp. (A comprehensive history of the great chains placed across the Hudson River from the area of the present George Washington Bridge to just south of Newburgh, to prevent the British fleet from sailing up the river. A very valuable contribution is his chapter titled "The Great Chain Hoax", in which he discusses the fact that many of the links on display purporting to be from the Hudson River chains were actually made in England in the mid-1800s. This chapter is so important it has been separately indexed.)

Edmonds, W. D. *Drums Along the Mohawk. An Educational Edition by H. Brewer.* 1954. Illust. with stills from the motion picture. map. 542 pp. (This ed. was issued specifically for use in schools, with suggestions for questions, discussions, themes, and an examination.)

Efner (trans.) *Warfare in the Mohawk Valley. Transcriptions From the Pennsylvania Gazette. 1780-1783.* wrps. 14 pp. mimeo. Probably only a few copies were made. (These are important excerpts from a Philadelphia newspaper on military activities in the Mohawk Valley, some in considerable detail.)

Fales, E. Jr. (ed.) *Arsenal of the Revolution*, 1975. illus. maps. wrps. 96 pp. Many advts. Newspaper format pub. by the Lakeville (CT) *Journal and the News.* (Many interesting articles on the hist. of northwestern CT in the Revolution, and the neighboring areas of Dutchess and Columbia Co. in NY State into which cannon, cattle, and food were shipped.)

Figliomeni, M. *The Flickering Flame. Treachery and Loyalty in the Mid-Hudson During the American Revolution.* 1976. illus. map. bib. index. 226 pp. (This is a "narrative of the wily speculators, crafty counterfeiters, and treacherous agents who caused confusion and distress" in Orange, Rockland, Ulster, and Dutchess Co. during the Revolutionary War.)

Fishkill Monument Dedication. Oct. 14, 1897. Pub. by J. E. & R. E. Dean, Fishkill. illus. 18 pp. (This monument erected just north of the Wharton House on Route 9 south of Fishkill village, in memory of the Revolutionary War veterans buried nearby. Fishkill was a major depot during the Revolutionary War, it is mentioned in countless books and documents, almost every important officer in the American forces passed through the town. Unfortunately over the years precious little has been done to preserve its great heritage. A shopping mall now occupies the old Army camp ground across the Post Road from the Wharton House. The Wharton House was a headquarters during the Revolution, and is now a museum. In the nearby village can be seen the Reformed Dutch Church which was used as a prison in the Revolution, and the Trinity

Church which was used as a hospital and a meeting place for the NY Legislature. Back in the early 1930s, one of the local residents involved with the Dutch Reformed Church in Fishkill gave me a guided tour of that historic edifice. Not given to thinking about architectural destruction at that young age, I asked him if I could take a sliver of wood from the church as a souvenir. He glared at me and said, "Of course not! If everyone who came in here did that, the church would soon fall down!")

Flexner, J. T. *The Traitor and the Spy. Benedict Arnold and John Andre.* 1953. Historical notes. index. 431 pp. (One of the standard works on the affair. Some copies contain a 25-page separately prntd. pamphlet of bib.)

(Fisher, E.) *Elijah Fisher's Journal While in the War for Independence and Continued for Two Years After He Came to Maine. 1775-1784.* Augusta (ME). 1880. wrps. 29pp. (Elijah spent considerable time in NY State. Here is an example of his marvellously written entries, "The guard left Piekskill and Crossed at Kings farrey Marched on to Col. Hazes and Encampt after Marching two and three is five miles.")

Ford, P. L. (ed.) *The Journals of Hugh Gaine, Printer.* 2 vol. NY. 1902. port. illus. lmtd. to 380 sets. (Gaine was a Tory printer in NYC during the Revolutionary War, and his *Journals* contain much of interest on life at that time. This work also contains an exhaustive bib. of Gaine's printing from 1752 to 1801.)

Foster, J. *The Story of a Private Soldier in the Revolution.* 1902. wrps. 13 pp. (Moses Fellows, of NH, went with Arnold on his expedition to Quebec; he also was at Ticonderoga, Fort Edward, Saratoga, and on Sullivan's expedition.)

French, A. *The Taking of Ticonderoga in 1775: The British Story. A Study of Captors and Captives ... Based Upon Material Hitherto Unpublished.* 1928. bib. 90 pp. lmtd. to 500 copies. (French was able to study the reports, and other letters, sent by the captured British officers to General Gage the British Commander-in-chief.)

Greene, G. W. *Nathanael Greene, an Examination of Some Statements Concerning Maj. Gen. Greene in the 9th. Volume of Bancroft's History.* Boston. 1866. 86 pp. (George Bancroft's monumental hist. of the U. S. first appeared in 1834-1875, and went through many ed. Vol. IX stirred up a hornet's nest, as he brought out accusations against several of our Revolutionary War heroes. A "Grandfathers' War" erupted when grandsons wrote pamphlets defending their Revolutionary War grandfathers. Nye's *George Bancroft, Brahmin Rebel*, 1944, goes into detail about this minor fire-fight. Bancroft claimed that General Greene was responsible for the loss of Fort Washington on Manhattan Island in Nov. 1776. Greene is defended by his grandson in the above pamphlet. Here are the titles of 2 more defensive pub.: Amory, T. C. *General John Sullivan. A Vindication of His Character as Soldier and Patriot.* 1867. 52 pp. [Bancroft had called Sullivan incompetent.] And Schuyler, G. L. *Correspondence and Remarks upon Bancroft's History of the Northern Campaign of 1777, and The Character of Maj. Gen. Philip Schuyler.* NY. 1867. 47 pp. Only 200 copies were prntd., plus 2 copies on tinted paper. [The author, who incidentally, married successively two granddaughters of Alexander Hamilton, defends Gen. Schuyler against Bancroft's charge that the General's cowardice caused the precipitous evacuation of Fort Ticonderoga in the summer of 1777.])

Hadden, James M. *Hadden's Journal and Orderly Books. A Journal Kept in Canada and Upon Burgoyne's Campaign in 1776 and 1777, by Lieut. James M. Hadden, Roy. Art., and Orders Kept by Him and Issued by Sir Guy Carleton, Lieut. Gen. John Burgoyne, and Maj. Gen. Wm. Phillips, in 1776, 1777, and 1778. With Notes by Horatio Rogers.* Albany. Munsell. 1884. index. maps. 581 pp. (A major source work on the Burgoyne expedition in NY State. Reprntd. in 1972.)

(Hamilton, A.) *The Fate of Major Andre. A Letter from Alexander Hamilton to John Laurens.* NY. Charles F. Heartman Hist. Series No. Eighteen. 1916. port. 22 pp. lmtd. to 120 copies. Accompanied by a portfolio titled, *Collection of Prints Illustrating The Fate of Major Andre*, containing 20 reproductions. (Hamilton wrote this letter shortly after Andre's execution at Tappan, NY, in 1780. It was prntd. in the *Pennsylvania Packet* newspaper, Philadelphia, on Oct. 14, 1780, and reprntd. in the *Pennsylvania Journal* on Oct. 18th. It also appears in his biog. pub. in 1834. The original letter has disappeared, and only 2 contemporaries copies are known. I found one of the contemporary copies, unsigned and not in Hamilton's hand, at a book and paper fair along with a first ed. of the proceedings of Andre's trial pub. at Phil. in 1780, and the second ed. of Miss Seward's Monody on Major Andre prntd. in Phil. These 3 items, bound into one vol., are now in a major collection of Andreana. Andre was interred on what is now known as Andre's Hill in Tappan, NY, but in 1821, at the demand of the British government his body was removed and shipped to England. John Trumbull, the noted artist of the Revolution, designed a small coffin for Andre's remains, and a young cabinet maker's apprentice built a larger case to hold the coffin. He it was who placed the remains in the coffin, and then in the case, and prepared it for shipment. Much later, to his consternation, he found that one bone was left over: a great toe. It eventually became a conversation piece, and he made a small coffin for it. A newspaper article said in 1971 it was in the possession of a NJ family living near the Tappan border. When the body reached Westminster Abbey in London for internment the small chest with the bones was buried in Andre's final resting place, and the larger case made by the apprentice was stored away and forgotten. Within the past year or so the case was re-discovered by

Robert Maguire an Andre expert while on a visit to the Abbey.)

Harte, C. R. *The River Obstructions of the Revolutionary War.* 1946. wrps. illus. maps. bib. 53 pp. (This is an excellent work on the famous chains stretched across the river to prevent British ships from passing through the Hudson Highlands. It is a reprint from an article in the Report of CT Soc. of Civil Engineers. Chains were installed at several sites along the river, and many of the hist. museums in the lower Hudson Valley have several links on display. There are so many of these links still in existence that I have often wondered if any are prvtly. owned by collectors. Fort Putnam, at West Point, is open at stated times, and on display is an excellent map of the Hudson Highland area. An audio lecture on military action in the region points out the location of the chains. One of the grandest views in the northern highlands is from Fort Putnam.)

Hillard, E. B. *The Last Men of the Revolution. A Photograph of Each from LIfe, Together With Views of Their Homes Printed in Colors. Accompanied by Brief Biographical Sketches of the Men.* Hartford, CT. 1864. 64 pp. (During the Civil War a Rev. Hillard visited the six still living veterans of the Revolutionary War. All of them were over 100 years old, and 4 of them lived in NY State towns: Edinburgh, Syracuse, Clarendon, and Adam's Basin. He photographed each of them, and made sketches of the exteriors of their homes. The charm and importance of the book lies in the photographs of these aged men: it is our only photographic link with the Revolution. This work was reprntd. in 1968 with an introduction by Archibald MacLeish the noted poet, playwright, and assistant secretary of state. He writes about the life and character of Rev. Hillard, who was his grandfather.)

Hornor, J. W. Jr. *Obstructions of the Hudson River During the Revolution.* Metuchen, NJ. Prntd. for Charles F. Heartman. 1927. maps. illus. Hist. notes. 27 pp. lmtd. to 60 copies.

Hough, F. B. *Notices of Peter Penet, and of His Operations Among the Oneida Indians, Including a Plan Prepared by Him for the Government of That Tribe.* Lowville, NY. 1866. index. 36 pp. Prntd. for the author by Munsell in Albany. lmtd. to 50 copies. (An adventurous Frenchman, Penet has been called the Confidence Man of the Revolution. He contracted with Congress to supply arms from France which he could not deliver, and later sold lands at Oneida Lake which he did not own.)

Hough, F. B. (introd. & notes) *The Order Book of Capt. Leonard Bleeker, Major of Brigade ... Expedition Under Gen. James Clinton, Against the Indian Settlements of Western New York.* 1779. NY. 1865. index. 138 pp. lmtd. to 250 copies. (A valuable contribution to the hist. of the Mohawk Valley and Otsego Co.)

Hough, F. B. (introd.) *Proceedings of a Convention of Delegates From Several of the*

New England States, Held at Boston, Aug. 3-9, 1780, to Advise on Affairs Necessary to Promote the Most Vigorous Prosecution of the War ... Edited From an Original Manuscript ... in New York State Library. Albany. Munsell. 1867. wrps. index. 80 pp. Has a chart of Continental currency depreciation. lmtd. to 100 copies. (To illus. the condition of public affairs at this time there are copies of letters from Orangetown, Tappan, Poughkeepsie, and the Robinson House opposite West Point.)

(Hunt, L. L.) *Biographical Notes Concerning General Richard Montgomery, Together With Hitherto Unpublished Letters.* 1876. wrps. 31 pp. (Montgomery, son-in-law of Robert R. Livingston, served in the French and Indian Wars and the Revolution, and was killed at Quebec in 1775.)

(Jay, John) *An Address of the Convention of the Representatives of the State of New York to Their Constituents.* Fishkill, (NY). Prntd. by S. Loudon, 1776. 19 pp. (The name in type at the end of the address is that of Abraham Ten Broeck, President of the NY Convention. The copy I had once belonged to James Kent the noted lawyer and close friend of John Jay. In a contemporary hand on the verso of the title page is, "This admirable Address is said to be the Composition of Chief Justice Jay." Evans, Shipton and Mooney, and Sabin do not credit Jay for the *Address*. Sabin, 53480, lists several reprints. Years ago I had an avid collector of Hudson Valley Revolutinary War material. He probably had one of the best and most valuable libraries on that subject in private hands. He suddenly died, and I heard through the grapevine that some problems arose and the settlement of the estate dragged on for some time. To the detriment of scholarship his fine collection was dispersed. In 1976 I was in a NYC bookshop, and saw the Kent copy of the Jay *Address* priced at $750.00. I immediately developed a case of sticker price shock. But that night I called my customer and described the pamphlet, adding, "The price is $750.00. That's too high; I don't think it's worth it. But I thought you should know about it anyway." He shot back over the wire, "I'll take it!" I ordered the item from the NYC dealer, and sent it on to the collector, my profit being the 10% dealer discount given me.)

Johnson, P. D. *Claudius, the Cowboy of Ramapo Valley, A Story of Revolutionary Times in Southern New York.* 1894. 206 pp. (Claudius and his gang raided the Ramapo Valley area during the Revolutionary War. He finally was captured on Long Island and hung at Goshen. The cave where his gang hid is in the highlands east of Tuxedo. You can hike into this wild area via marked trail from the Tuxedo railroad station. This book has gone through several ed.)

Journals of the Provincial Congress, Provincial Convention, Committee of Safety, and Council of Safety of State of New York, 1775-76-77. Albany. 2 vol. indexes. 1842. lmtd. to 250 sets. (Vol. 1 contains the journals; Vol. 2

contains the correspondence. This is a fine reference work. The compilers were so pleased with their work that they designated that a set be sent to the State Library of each state in the union.)

Kelby, W. (comp.) *Orderly Book of the 3 Battalions of Loyalists. Commanded by Brig. Gen. Oliver DeLancey. 1776-1778. To Which is Appended a List of New York Loyalists in the City of New York During the War of the Revolution.* 1917. index. 147 pp. lmtd. to 200 copies. Reprntd. in 1972. (These battalions mostly served on Long Island.)

Lancaster, B. (foreword) *From Cambridge to Champlain. March 18 to May 5, 1776.* A mss diary. Prvtly. prntd.. 1957. 30 pp. lmtd. to 250 copies. (A diary of an unknown soldier who went from Cambridge, MA, to Champlain, NY, via NYC, Fort Montgomery, Half Moon, Fort Edward, Ticonderoga. Some years ago several copies came my way in a short space of time, and I had a difficult time selling them in spite of their scarcity. I finally sold them, and haven't seen or heard of a copy since.)

Lossing, B. J. *Pictorial Field-Book of the Revolution ... 1850-1852* (This major and useful work was first pub. in 30 parts in 1850-1852. It was then pub. in 2 vol., and has been reprntd. many times since. There is much material on NY State. A 20-page unfavorable critique appeared in the *American Whig Review* magazine in Sept. 1852, which ends with, "does not contain a single original thought which the world will not willingly let die." A 4-page circular, ca 1856, advertising a revised ed. and describing its advantages, adds, "the young read the pages ... with the same avidity as those of a romance." Included are comments on Lossing's work by a number of notables including Millard Fillmore, Jared Sparks, Washington Irving, and George-Bancroft.)

Lucanera, V. M. *The Role of Orangetown (NY) in the Revolution.* New City, NY. Rockland Co. Public Librarians' Assn. 1972. wrps. maps. diagram. bib. index. 108 pp. (After a very brief history of this area of southeastern Rockland Co., the book concentrates on events of the Revolutionary War: campaigns, Baylor Massacre over the line in NJ, Arnold-Andre Affair.)

Major Andre's Arrest and Execution. Air: Dog and Gun. Broadside ballad, words only, prntd. by H. DeMarsan, NYC, 1860. 6 x 9 inches. (This has a colorful border not in keeping with the subject of the song: a colored man playing a banjo, a man drinking out of a cup, a traveller with a small handbag, and a man who seems to be filling a pipe.)

Manifesto and Proclamation. To the Members of Congress, The Members of the General Assemblies, or Conventions of the Several Colonies ... and all others, free Inhabitants of the said Colonies ... by the Earl of Carlisle, Sir Henry Clinton, and William Eden, Esq. Commissioners Appointed by his Majesty ... to treat, consult, and agree upon the Means of quieting the Disorders now subsisting in certain of the

Colonies ... New York 3 October 1778. Broadside 14 x 19 inches, prntd. by James Rivington. (A most important and rare broadside issued by the British Peace Commission vowing to continue the war with increased vigor if the colonists did not accept peace. The Continental Congress retorted by ordering the arrest of anyone found in possession of the broadside.)

(Mann, H.) *The Female Review; or, Memoirs of an American Young Lady...Being a Continental Soldier for Nearly 3 Years...by a Citizen of Mass.* Dedham. 1797. port. 263 pp. (Deborah Sampson, dressed as a man, joined the army. She spent considerable time in the West Point area, and was at Fort Ticonderoga; all of the while going under the name of Robert Shurtleff. She was discovered when another lady became infatuated with her, and she was honorably discharged. This work was reprntd. in Boston in 1866 in an ed. of 285 copies, with copious notes correcting errors and presenting additional information. Bbatner says that this rather horse-faced woman gave lectures in later life about her war adventures, and may have been the first female lecturer in the U. S.)

Martin, J. P. *A Narrative of Some of the Adventures, Dangers and Sufferings of a Revolutionary Soldier; Interspersed With Anecdotes of Incidents That Occurred Within His Own Observation. Written by Himself.* Hallowell, (ME). 1830. 213 pp. (The most graphic, and detailed, account of service in the Revolution written by a Continental soldier who served throughout the war. Much of his time was spent in the Hudson Valley. It was reprntd. in 1962, with a map, index, and 305 pp.)

Mather, F. G. *The Refugees of 1776 from Long Island to Connecticut.* 1913. illus. maps. index. 1204 pp. (This is an indispensable work with much biog. and genealogical material, with nearly 20,0D0 names in the index. A feature of this work of value to autograph and mss. collectors are the facsimile illus. of 559 autographs.)

Millis, W. *A Spy Under the Common Law of War.* 1925. wrps. 24 pp. (Almost entirely about Major Andre.)

(Moody, J.) *Lieut. James Moody's Narrative of His Exertions and Sufferings in the Cause of Government, Since 1776; Authenticated by Proper Certificates.* London. 1783. 2nd. ed. 65 pp. (Moody, 1744-1809, considered the most famous spy in the British service during the American Revolution, was active in NJ and the NYC area. In 1780 he was captured and sent to several prisons in the Hudson Valley. He ended up at West Point where he was confined in a horrid dungeon on orders of Benedict Arnold, which, interestingly enough, was just before Arnold defected to the British! Moody escaped on a stormy night, and continued his activities for the British until more than a year later when he went to England at the suggestion of General Sir Henry Clinton. Many years ago a copy of this pamphlet came on the market with several mss. notes by Moody. In one of them he says that

Clinton's "Intentions seldom lasted longer than the day." This *Narrative*, with an introduction and notes by C. I. Bushnell, and illus., was prvtly. re-prntd. in NY in 1865, in an ed. of 100 copies.)

Neilson, C. *An Original, Compiled, and Corrected Account of Burgoyne's Campaign.* Albany. Munsell. 1844. map. 292 pp. Reprntd. in 1926. (Neilson lived near the battle site, and wrote the book to answer inquiries, and to aid in selling his property. Sales of the book were slow, and he eventually went bankrupt.)

New York. Sir, By Virtue of the Authority Vested in us by Certain Resolutions of the Congress of the Colony of New York ... In the Year 1776 ... We ... Summon You to Appear Before Us .... Broadside 8 x 9 inches. (Prntd. by Samuel Loudon at Fishkill.) (This was the offical prntd. summons issued to Loyalists under the Act of Attainder.)

On the Death of General Washington ... Who Died December 14th, 1799 And A Much Approved Song on the Capture of General Burgoyne. Broadside, approximately 17 x 21 inches. ca 1800. (These 2 poems, plus 4 other poems, are prntd. side by side on a single sheet. While doing research on this unusual item I was told by another dealer that there was a printer in ME in the early 1800s who ran off double broadsides. They were made to be separated down the middle into two broadsides. The one listed here apparently is one of the very few that remained intact. Actually, very few of the two halves have been located. I sold it to another dealer in 1980 and he cataloged it the same year for $950.00.)

Onderdonck, H. Jr. *Documents and Letters Intended to Illustrate the Revolutionary Incidents of Queens Co.* 1846. map. index. 264 pp.

Onderdonck, H. Jr. *Revolutionary Incidents of Suffolk and Kings Counties; With an Account of the Battle of Long Island, and the British Prisons and Prison Ships at New York.* 1849. map. index. 268 pp. (These 2 books have been reprntd. 2 or more times. Harriet Stryker-Rodda compiled a comprehensive index of over 6500 entries for the 1846 and 1849 printings, as the indexes in the books are highly inadequate. This new index was prvtly. prntd. in 1974 in pamphlet form, 68 pp.)

(O'Rielly, H.) *Notices of Sullivan's Campaign, in the Revolutionary Warfare in Western New York ....* Rochester. 1842. 192 pp. Reprntd. in 1970.

(Paine, Thomas) *A Dialogue Between the Ghost of General Montgomery Just Arrive From the Elysian Fields, and an American Delegate, In a Wood Near Philadelphia.* NY. 1865. 16 pp. lmtd. to 100 copies. (The *Dialogue*, first prntd. in Philadelphia in 1776, was on the grand subject of American independency. Montgomery, whose home was on the Hudson River in northern Dutchess Co., and who had married into the famous Livingston family, was killed in the attack on Quebec on the last day of 1775.)

Palmer, D. R. *The River and the Rock. History of Fortress West Point, 1775-1783.* 1969.

maps. illus. bib. index. 395 pp. (A definitive history.)

Paltsits, V. H. (ed.) *Minutes of the Commissioners for Detecting and Defeating Conspiracies in the State of New York.* Albany Co. Sessions. 1778-1781. 3 vols. 1909-10. illus. Extensive index. (A major reference for those interested in the attempt to search out and control the Loyalists of the Albany area. Included is a hist. of tne Commission, and a description of its function.)

Patrick, L. S. *Washington's Headquarters and the Revolutionary Army at Fredericksburgh, in the State of New York. Sept. 19 - Nov. 28, 1778.* Quaker Hill, NY. 1907. illus. wrps. 69 pp. This has been reprntd.. (A detailed study. Fredericksburgh was in the present Pawling area of Dutchess Co. The author was a descendant of the noted Col. Henry Ludington of the Dutchess Co. militia.)

Ranlet, P. *The New York Loyalists.* 1986. illus. Tables. maps. Hist. notes. bib. index. 303 pp. (The author "disputes the time-honored view that NY had an unusually high proportion of Loyalists.")

Raymond, M. (comp.) *Souvenir of the Revolutionary Soldiers Monument Dedication at Tarrytown, NY. Oct. 19, 1894.* Tarrytown. 1894. illus. 210 pp. (This actually contains a great deal of Westchester Co. Revolutionary War hist., genealogy, and some lists of Revolutionary War soldiers.)

Raynor, &c. *History of the Town of Cheshire, Berkshire County, Mass.* 1885. 214 pp. plus index. (Unknown to most historians, Chapter 2 of this book has some data on the activities of Cheshire men during the Revolutionary War at Bennington, and Stone Arabia in the Mohawk Valley. Some ofthese men later returned to settle in NY State.)

Read, D. B. *The Life and Times of Gen. John Graves Simcoe, Commander of the Queens Rangers During the Revolutionary War, and First Governor of Upper Canada...With Some Account of Major Andre and Capt. Brant.* Toronto. 1890. port. illus. 305 pp. (The first biog. of Simcoe whose Rangers were very active in the NY-NJ area during the Revolution.)

Riedesel, Mrs. General. *Letters and Journals Relating to the War of the American Revolution, and the Capture of the German Troops at Saratoga. Translated From the Original German by William L. Stone.* Albany. Munsell. 1867. port. illus. index. 235 pp. lmtd. to 275 copies. Reprntd. 1968.

Rivington's New York Gazetteer: Or, Connecticut, Hudsons River, New Jersey, and Quebec Weekly Advertiser. Printed at his Open and Uninfluenced Press. NY. April 20, 1775. 4 pp. small folio newspaper. (This important issue prints a petition from the General Assembly of the colony of NY to the British king. Rivington also prints a woodcut of himself hanging in effigy! He notes that he was hung in effigy by some of the lower class citizens of New Brunswick, in NJ. Before the end of the year he closed this newspaper and fled to England.)

Roberts, J. A. *New York in the Revolution as Colony and State.* Albany. 1897. illus.

map. 261 pp. (This is actually a printing of the muster rolls of NY State men who served in the Revolution, containing the names of 41,633 men. This is the first and lmtd. ed. which contains the 8 famous illus. by R. A. Grider. These drawings did not appear in the subsequent ed. of this work. Grider is said to nave been an art teacher in the Canajoharie, NY, school system. At one time I owned 2 of his original wash drawings used in the Roberts book.)

Rogan, R. *Benedict Arnold, Our First Marine. His Contemporaries and the Story of His Life.* 1931. port. illus. 210 pp. Prvtly. prntd. for distribution among the author's friends. (This is a sympathetic view of Arnold, which makes this book unusual.)

Sabine, W. *Suppressed History of General Nathaniel Woodhull, President of the New York Congress and Convention in 1776.* 1954. maps. bib. index. 225 pp. (A detailed study of the events in the life of General Woodhull, and a discussion of his mysterious death. There is much on Long Island in the early part of the Revolutionary War.)

Proceedings of a General Court Martial Held at White Plains ... NY ... by Order of ... Washington ... For the Trial of Maj. Gen. St. Clair, Aug. 25, 1778. Maj. Gen. Lincoln, Pres. Phil. 1778. map. 52 pp. (St. Clair was ordered to defend Ticonderoga in 1777, but later evacuated the fort. He was completely exonerated at the court martial but the DAB says, "he was not, for the rest of the war, placed in a position to render conspicuous service." The *Proceedings* were reprntd. in the 1880 vol. of the *Collections* of the NYHS.)

Salsig, D. *Parole: Quebec; Countersign: Ticonderoga. Second New Jersey Regimental Orderly Book 1776. Edited and Annotated.* 1980. maps. illus. bib. index. 310 pp. (This regiment whose only previous combat had been throwing snow balls at each other, served under Benedict Arnold in his attempt to capture Quebec. They were forced to retreat to Ticonderoga. There is much information on their ill-fated adventures in NY State.)

Sargent, W. *The Life of Major John Andre, Adjutant-General of the British Army in America.* NY. Appleton. 1871. map. 2 port. index. 478 pp. (Considered by many to be the best biog. of Andre.)

Scott, J. *Fort Stanwix (Fort Schuyler) and Oriskany. Repulse of St. Legers British Invasion of 1777..in Chronological Order and Details. Contemporary Reports, Letters, Diaries* 1927. illus. maps. bib. (Some copies contain a 7-page appendix; and some copies have a 7-page index which includes a list of illus., maps, diagrams, and corrections.)

(Sigsby, Wm.) *Life and Adventures of Timothy Murphy the Benefactor of Schoharie.* Prntd. by W. H. Gallup, Schoharie, C. H. January 1839. wrps. 32 pp. (A copy I once had contained a note on the margin of one page recommending that the reader also read the *History of Scoharie County and Border Wars* by Simms.)

Simms, J. R. *The Frontiersmen of New York ... Customs of the Indians ... Border Strife in Two Wars ... Thrilling Stories Never Before Published.* Albany. 1882. 2 vol. illus. maps. (Simms amassed an amazing amount of material on the NY frontier. Unknown to many people interested in the Hudson Valley there are 50 pages on the chain obstructions stretched across the Hudson to prevent the British fleet from going up-river.)

Smith, J. H. *An Authentic Narrative of the Causes Which Led to the Death of Major Andre ... To Which is Added a Monody on the Death of Maj. Andre, by Miss Seward.* London. 1808. port. map. Plate of monument of Maj. Andre. 358 pp. + 2 advt. pp. (The first ed. of this most important work. Joshua Hett Smith, who lived in Haverstraw in Orange Co., was involved in the Arnold-Andre affair, and Sabin says he wrote this book to "justify his own character against the charge of being involved in the Arnold treason." Some writers believe he was innocently involved, but it has been said that neither the American or British officials were ever convinced of his true allegiance. Richard Koke in his book *Accomplice in Treason. Joshua Hett Smith and the Arnold Conspiracy*, pub. in 1973, gives more facts for believers in either his innocence or guilt to cogitate on.)

Snell, C. *A Report on the Strength of the British Army Under Lt. Gen. John Burgoyne, July 1, to Oct. 17, 1777, and on the Organization of the British Army on Sept. 19, and Oct. 7, 1777.* 1951. wrps. 100 pp. (Statistcal account of Burgoyne's Army at Saratoga; including the names of many officers.)

Sobel, R. *For Want of a Nail ... If Burgoyne Had Won at Saratoga.* 1973. bib. index. 441 pp. (Informed hist. speculation.)

Stone, William L. (ed.) *Ballads and Poems Relating to the Burgoyne Campaign.* Albany. Munsell. 1893. index. 359 pp. (This is an extensive collection, with numerous hist. footnotes by Stone. There is also much other data on Burgoyne and Saratoga. Reprntd. in 1970.)

Stone, William L. (translator). *Letters of Brunswick and Hessian Officers During the American Revolution.* Albany. Munsell. 1891. index. 258 pp. (A good source on military activity and life in NY State as many of these letters were written by Hessian Officers with Burgoyne. Reprntd. in 1970.)

Stone, William L. (Ed.) *Orderly Book of Sir John Johnson During the Oriskany Campaign, 1776-1777.* Albany. Munsell. 1882. port. illus. map. index. 273 pp. Annotated by Stone. Includes a biog. of John Johnson by John Watts De Peyster, and a discussion of the Loyalists by T. B. Myers. (The Myers essay was pub. separately in pamphlet form in: 1882; 123 pps. DePeyster's biography of Johnson was separately pub. in 1882 under the title *The Life and Misfortunes and Military Career of Brig. Gen. Sir John Johnson, Bart.*, with map, and 168 pp.)

Sullivan, E. *Benedict Arnold, Military Racketeer.* 1932.

port. bib. 306 pp. (A highly anti-Arnold work. According to the introduction, "Nearly everyone ... during the Revolution was sorry when Arnold arrived and glad when he departed." Even Aaron Burr, who does not appear to have been an angel, said of Arnold, "he is utterly unprincipled." I must add that the author does say Arnold was "the most brilliant personal leader in the Revolutionary War." I once had a copy of this book which Arnold's enemies must have read and tossed about, as the binding was wondrously worn and unattractive.)

Sullivan & Flick (eds.) *Minutes of the Albany Committee of Correspondence 1775-1778. Minutes of the Schenectady Commiteee 1775-1779.* 2 vols. 1923-1925. index. (These committees were involved in many areas in keeping the war going: troop training, detection of Loyalists, regulation of taverns, money, law and order, food rationing, much else.)

Sullivan-Clinton Campaign in 1779. Chronology and Selected Documents. 1929. illus. bib. maps. index. wrps. 216 pp. (An excellent reference.)

Swiggett, H. *War Out of Niagara. Walter Butler and the Tory Rangers.* 1933. illus. bib. map. index. 309 pp. (Actually a study and defense of Walter Butler. According to the preface he was, "The typical, proud, restless, unhappy, luckless figure of romance who threw away his life for a lost cause." Reprntd. in 1963.)

Trumbull, J. H. *The Origin of the Expedition Against Ticonderoga in 1775.* Hartford. 1869. wrps. 15 pp. Only 50 copies were prntd.

Vail, R. W. G. (ed.) *The Revolutionary Diary of Lieut. Obadiah Gore, Jr.* 1929. illus. map. wrps. 34 pp. (Gore was on the famous Sullivan-Clinton Expedition against the Indians in central NY State, and kept a diary from July 31, 1779 to Sept. 19, 1779. Enhanced by numerous hist. footnotes.)

Voyage of the First Hessian Army from Portsmouth to New York. 1776. NY. Charles F. Heartman Hist. Series No. Three. Jan. 1915. 31 pp. ("The following Historical Sketch is a translation from the German of A. Pfister. It was published some 50 years ago in a German periodical and is interesting enough to be reprntd. in English as it contains hitherto very little known details of this voyage. At the end will be found an Extract from the Diary of the German Poet and Adventurer, J. G. Seume, a Hessian Soldier and Participator on the Voyage.")

Washington, I. and P. *Carleton's Raid.* 1977. maps. bib. index. 103 pp. (A detailed account of British officer Major Carleton's raid in October 1778 along the shores of Lake Champlain to destroy supplies ano take rebel prisoners. "Three weeks later the expedition returned to Canada with 39 prisoners and the report that it had destroyed 4 months provisions for 12,000 men.")

Westbrook, M. *Rachel Du Mont; A Brave Little Maid of the Revolution. A True Story of the Burning of Kingston, NY. By the British, 1776. For Girls and Boys, and Older People.* Originally written for private distribution. 4th. and illus. ed. Albany. Munsell. 1890. 96 pp. (Illus. with woodcuts.

The frontispiece is an engraved port. of Rachel. Several of the illus. are by H. Rosa who was the daughter of Benson J. Lossing, the noted author and artist.)
Whereas An Act Was Passed Last Session of Parliament, For Repealing the Act Imposing a Duty On ... New York, June 12, 1770. Broadside, 7 x 6-1/2 inches. (In this statement, the subscribers, evidentally NYC merchants, say they are willing to import all duty-free commodities from England, but are waiting for the concurrence of Phil. and Boston.)
Whereas a Meeting of the Inhabitants Was Called Yesterday, Without the Knowledge of the Committee Appointed to Inspect Into the Importation of Goods...New York, May 21st, 1770. Broadside 8 x 10 inches. (The inspection committee of 18 men complains that this irregular meeting cancels their effectiveness, and requests the inhabitants of the city to meet and appoint another committee.)
Wilshin, F. *Preliminary Report on the Source Material of the Burgoyne Campaign of 1777.* 1940. wrps. 81 pp. (This bib. contains 305 entries, and much other pertinent material. It was reprntd. in 1976.)
Wilson, D. *The Life of Jane McCrea, With an Account of Burgoyne's Expedition in 1777.* NY. 1853. 155 pp. (On the last page is an advertisement, "The Subscriber, being censured through the public prints for cutting down the famous Jane McCrea Tree, and importuned by his friends, presents to the public elegant Canes and Boxes manufactured from this world-renowned tree....")

Yoshpe, H. *The Disposition of Loyalist Estates in the Southern District of the State of New York.* 1939. illus. maps. bib. index. 226 pp.

RICHMOND COUNTY

RICHMOND COUNTY, (Staten Island)
Bayles, R. (ed.) *History of Richmond Co.* NY. 1887. illus. maps. 741 pp.
Clute, J. *Annals of Staten Island.* NY. 1877. 464 pp.
Dubois & Smith. *Staten Island Patroons.* 1961. 34 pp.
Hampton, V. *Staten Island's Claim to Fame.* 1925. 187 pp.
Hine, C. *History & Legend of Howard Ave. & the Serpentine Road, Grymes Hill, S.I. From Real Estate Records & Long Memories.* 1914. pvtly. prntd. illus. map. 80 pp.
Hine & Davis. *Legends, Stories, & Folklore of Old Staten Island. Part I North Shore.* 1925. 140 pp.
Johnson, W. (1877-1957) *T.J. Grows Up on S.I.* ca 1957. mimeo. 31 pp.
Johnston, J. *Staten Island During The Am Revolution.* Masters' Thesis NYU. 1949.
Kolff, C. *Early History of Staten Island.* 1918. 32 pp.
Leng & Davis. *Staten Island & Its People. 1609-1929.* NY. 1930. illus. maps. 4 vols.
Morris, I. *Morris's Memorial History of Staten Island.* 1898. illus. 2 vols.
Steinmeyer, H. *Staten Island 1524-1898.* 1950. 134 pp.
Tysen, R. *Lecture on History of Staten Island.* Tompkinsville Lyceum. Apr. 12, 1842. Staten Island. 1842. 13 pp.

CLIFTON, Richmond Co.
Anon. *Description of Clifton, S.I.*

at *The Narrows*. NY. 1838. 24 pp.

NORTHFIELD, Richmond Co.
Clute, J. *Account of Centennial Celebration in Northfield*. 4th July 1876. Hist. sketch. NY. 1876. 23 pp.

RICHMOND, Richmond Co.
Anon. *The Historic Village of Richmond Town & Vicinity*. 1937. illus. map. brochure 2nd. printing 1946.
Davis, W. *Richmond Abut a Hundred Years Ago*. 1979. 17 pp. (Richmond in 1848, reprntd. from the January 1938 issue of the *Staten Island Historian*.)

ROCKLAND COUNTY

ROCKLAND COUNTY
Anon. *A Brief School History of Rockland Co*. by Pupils, Teachers, Friends of Rockland Co. Pub. Schools. New City. 1941. mimeo. 43 pp.
Anon. *Portrait & Biog. Record of Rockland & Orange Cos*. NY. 1895. illus. 1547 pp. (See also **ORANGE COUNTY**, Anon. *Portrait & Biog. Record of Orange Co*.)
Anderson, J. *Rocklandia. 300 Years of Rockland County*. Unpub. mss. in a private collection.
Baker, N. *The Way It Was in Northern Rockland*. 1973. illus. 72 pp.
Bedell, C. *Now And Then And Long Ago in Rockland Co*. Suffern 1941. pvtly. prntd. maps. 368 pp. Reprntd. in 1950.
Cole, D. *History of Rockland Co. 1686-1884*. NY 1884. maps. illus. 344 pp. Reprntd. in 1969.
Conover, A. *Historic Rockland Co*. ca 1936. A booklet.
Green, F. *The History of Rockland Co*. NY. 1886. maps. 450 pp. Reprntd. in 1969.
Hasselbarth, W. *The History of Rockland Co*. (pub. in Rockland Co. *Journal* March 1855 thru Feb. 1856) Microfilmed by Bell & Howell, Cleveland, Ohio. 1964. 234 pp.
Selivanova, N. *Rockland Co. A Historical Sketch*. n.d. (prior to 1950) 16 pp. typed mss. in NKPL.
Suffern, Jr. High School. *Ramapo & Rockland in the Homespun Age 1800-1860*. n.d. 40 pp.
Talman, W. *How Things Began in Rockland County and Places Nearby*. 1977. Rockland Co. Hist. Soc. illus. index. 320 pp. (Mostly social hist.)
Tompkins, A. (ed.) *Historical Record of Rockland Co*. Nyack. 1902. illus. 775 pp.
Upper Nyack. PTA. *A Guide Thru Rockland Co*. revised. enlrgd. ed. 1965. wrps. 59 pp. (brief history)

GRAND-VIEW-ON-HUDSON, Rockland Co.
Mathias, F. (ed.) *A Brief History of Grand-View-on-Hudson*. 1959. mimeo. 30 pp.

HAVERSTRAW, Rockland Co.
Anon. *Haverstraw*. 20 pp. typed mss. of extracts from *City & Country Magazine 1878-1887*, in NKPL.
Farley, J. *Haverstraw, My Home Town*. 1935. wrps. 11 pp. (Mostly hist. of Post Office.)
Freeman, A. *Thirty Years in Haverstraw*. Address Jan. 1. 1875. 29 pp. typed mss. dated 1920 in NYPL
McCabe, A. *Americas Bicentennial*. Haverstraw. 1977. ed. by D. DeNoyelles. illus. map. 136 pp.
Penfold, S. (county historian) *The Beginnings of the Village of*

Haverstraw. Centennial souvenir 1854-1954. wrps. 12 pp.

NEW CITY, Rockland Co.
Baker, N. *The Way It Was. Informal History of New City. (1890-1970).* 1973. illus. 48 pp.

NYACK, Rockland Co.
Anon. *Old Nyack. An Illustrated Sketch.* pub. by Nyack Natl. Bank. 1928. wrps. illus. map. 64 pp.
Coates, L. *Old Nyack. Interview With L. W. Coates, Sept. 26, 1914 Thru Nov. 28, 1914.* 10 pp. typed mss. in NKPL.
Nordstrom, C. *Of Shoes, Ships, & Sealing Wax. 1671-1893.* 1957. maps. 345 pp. typed mss. in NKPL.
(Oblenis, C.) *Reminiscences by C. M. O.* pub. in Rockland Co. *Journal* 1886-1887. 39 pp. mss. copied in 1938, in NKPL.

PALISADES, Rockland Co.
Gilman, W. (& others) *Essays on History of Palisades. 1876-1916.* 96 pp. typed mss. in Palisades Pub. Lib.

PEARL RIVER, Rockland Co.
Knight, R. *History of Pearl River, NY.* Typewritten mss. in a private collection.

PIERMONT, Rockland Co.
Faulds, C. *The Piermont Study. Aspects of History.* Suffern. 1970. pamphlet.

RAMAPO WORKS, Rockland Co.
Pierson, E. *The Ramapo Pass, Including the Village of Ramapo Works, Founded by the Pierson Brothers in 1795 ... and Other Historical Particulars. Written by ... 1915.* Ed. by H. P. Mapes 1955. pub. 1955. wrps.

mimeo. (Probably only a few copies prntd.) 185 pp.

SOUTH NYACK, Rockland Co.
(Christie, J. probably by) *The History of South Nyack.* ca 1880. 18 pp. mss. in NKPL.

SPRING VALLEY, Rockland Co.
Penfold, S. *The First 100 Years of Spring Valley. 1842-1942.* Tallman 1944. wrps. 26 pp. A lmtd. ed. with list of names of the 177 subscribers.

STONY POINT, Rockland Co.
Kiefer, W. (ed.) *Stony Point Illus. An Account of the Early Settlement.* NY 1888. illus. 166 pp.

SUFFERN, Rockland Co.
Anon. *Suffern: 200 Years. 1773-1973.* Bicentennial Committee. wrps. illus. maps. bib. 86 pp.
Penfold, S. *Suffern Historical Researches.* Parts I-V. Suffern Post. 1950. In broadside form.
Penfold, S. *Romantic Suffern to 1896.* Tallman. 1955. 106 pp.
--- *Suffern's Contribution to the Founding of Rockland Co.* 1948. wrps. 32 pp.
Watts, G. (village historian) *A Short Hist of Suffern & the Ramapaugh Area, With Emphasis on Rev Days & Ways.* ca 1966. mimeo. 15 pp.

TAPPAN, Rockland Co.
Talman, W. B. & others. *Tappan. 300 Years. 1686-1986.* Tappan Hist. Soc. maps. illus. 200 pp.

UPPER NYACK, Rockland Co.
Anon. *A History of Upper Nyack.* Issued by Upper Nyack Democratic Committee. Nanuet. ca 1960. wrps. map. illus. 16 pp.

WEST NYACK, Rockland Co.
Scott, J. *Short History of West Nyack Area.* 1964. map. mimeo. 21 pp.

ST. LAWRENCE COUNTY

ST. LAWRENCE COUNTY
Blankman, E. *Geography of St. Lawrence Co.* Canton 1898. illus. map. 126 pp. (Includes hist.)
Curtis, G. *Our County & Its People.* Syracuse. 1894. illus. maps. 2 vols.
(Durant & Pierce) *History of St. Lawrence Co.* Phil. 1878. illus. map. 550 pp. Reprntd. in 1981 with index.
Hough, F. *History of St. Lawrence & Franklin Cos.* Albany. 1853. illus. maps. 719 pp. Ltd to 1500 copies; plus 25 copies on fine paper with add. illus. Reprntd. in 1970.
(Smithers, N.) *St. Lawrence is Our Co.* Canton. 1961. map. 47 pp. (Brief hist.)
Webster, C. *St. Lawrence Co. Past & Present.* (Watertown.) 1945. wrps. 64 pp.

BLACK LAKE, St. Lawrence Co.
(Biondi, M. town historian) *Black Lake.* Hammond. ca 1954. illus. advts. wrps. 50 pp.
Payne, F. *Souvenir of Black Lake.* (Gouverneur.) 1917. wrps. 16 pp.

CANTON, St. Lawrence Co.
Hensley, P. *An 18th Century World Not Quite Lost ... Social & Economic Structure of [Canton], 1810-1880.* 1979. 278 pp.

CRANBERRY LAKE, St. Lawrence Co.
Fowler, A. *Cranberry Lack 1845-1959. An Adirondack Miscellany.* 1959. map. 160 pp.

Fowler, A. (ed.) *Cranberry Lake. From Wilderness to Adirondack Park.* 1968. illus. 256 pp.

DE KALB, St. Lawrence Co.
Anon. *De Kalb Sesquicentennial 1806-1956.* illus. 27 pp.

GOUVERNEUR, St. Lawrence Co.
Anon. *Gouverneur Sesquicentennial History 1805-1955.* illus. maps. wrps. 128 pp.
Corbin, J. *Centennial Souvenir of History of Gouverneur, Rossie, Fowler, Hammond, Edwards, and De Kalb.* Watertown. 1905. illus. 384 pp.
Gleason and Nulty. *Gouverneur, a History. 1805-1890.* 1977. illus. index. 88 pp.
Parker, C. *Gouverneur, Its Past & Present.* Gouverneur. 1890. wrps. 65 pp.
Webster, C. *History of Gouverneur Reprinted From Tribune-Press.* Issues of 9-4-35 to 6-24-36. 1936. wrps.

HAMMOND, St. Lawrence Co.
Allen, A. *History of Hammond,* articles in *Hammond Advertiser,* 1905-1906. (Allen died before completing the hist., & the *Advertiser* is no longer pub.)

HEUVELTON, St. Lawrence Co.
A mss. on Heuvelton hist. is in a private collection.
Smithers, C. *History of Heuvelton & Vicinity f1806-1956.* Ed. & brought up to date by P. Boyesen. 1971. Book.

HOPKINTON, St. Lawrence Co.
Sanford, C. *Early History of Hopkinton. History of East Village.* (Nicholville.) Boston. 1903. illus. map. lmtd. ed. 604 pp.

MASSENA, St. Lawrence Co.
Dumans, E. *History of Massena -*

the Orphan Town. 1977. illus. 210 pp.
Prince, L. (ed) *The Story of Massena. 1802-1952.* Massena. 1952. illus. maps. wrps. 57 pp.

NORWOOD, St. Lawrence Co.
Chase, L. *The Story of Norwood. Century of Progress 1872-1972.* Norwood. 1972. illus. wrps. 64 pp.

OGDENSBURG, St. Lawrence Co.
(DAR. Sew-kat-si Chapt. ed.) *Reminiscences of Ogdensburgh 1749-1907.* NY. 1907. illus. 183 pp.
Fell, H. *Homes in the Making. Story of Early Ogdensburg.* ca 1930. Reprntd. from articles in the *Republican Journal* newspaper January 1930. wrps. 13 pp.
Garand, P. *History of City of Ogdensburg.* Ogdensburg. 1927. illus. maps. 469 pp.

OSWEGATCHIE, St. Lawrence Co.
Bonsted, C. *Oral Historical Interview with William Joseph Griffin.* Oswegatchie, NY. May 19-20, 1958. Forest Hist. Foundation, Inc. (Griffin was born in 1863.) 26 pp. typed mss. in SLA.

PITCAIRN, St. Lawrence Co.
Anon. *Sourvenir: Town of Pitcairn Celebrating 100 Years.* June 20, 1936. wrps. 32 pp. (Brief hist.)

POTSDAM, St. Lawrence Co.
Chapman, M. *Early History of Potsdam.* Potsdam. 1956. wrps. 23 pp.
Keller & Little. *Potsdam & the Civil War.* 1961. illus. wrps. 60 pp.
Leete, C. (town historian) *The Early History of Potsdam.* Talk at West Potsdam June 1, 1928. wrps. 11 pp. (reprntd. from Potsdam *Herald Reporter*)

ROSSIE, St. Lawrence Co.
(Tait, J.) *Early History of Ox Bow & the Scotch Settlement 1820-1921.* 1921. wrps. 23 pp.

RUSSELL, St. Lawrence Co.
Manning, D. *Russell 1807-1957.* ca 1957. illus wrps. 27 pp.

STAR LAKE, St. Lawrence Co.
Anon. *Star Lake, NY, Centennial. 1878-1978.* 1978.

SYLVIA LAKE, St. Lawrence Co.
Anon. *History of Sylvia Lake Since 1800.* (Gouverneur. 1956.) wrps. lmtd. 300 copies. 32 pp. (Actually hist. of a lake, not a town.)

SARATOGA COUNTY

SARATOGA COUNTY
Anderson, G. *Our County & Its People.* Boston. 1899. illus. 2 vols.
Booth, J. *History of Saratoga County.* Ed. by Dunn and Sweeney. 1977. 209 pp. (First printing of Booth's mss. written in 1858).
Kinns, H. *Historical Data Relating to Saratoga County and Its Town. 1791-1964.* 1964. 84 pp.
Scott, G. *Saratoga Co. An Historical Address.* Ballston Spa. 1876. 47 pp.
Sylvester, N. *History of Saratoga Co.* Phil. 1878. illus. maps. 514 pp. (index by H. Ritchie, 1950, mimeo. 151 pp.) Reprntd. in 1979 with index.
--- *History of Saratoga Co. With Biog. Sketches* (prepared by Wiley & Garner.) Richmond, IN. 1893. 635 pp.
Vanderwerker, J. *Early Days in*

Eastern Saratoga Co. Schuylerville. 1938. illus. wrps. 23 pp.

BATCHELLERVILLE, Saratoga Co.
Gordon, W. *Scattering Memories of a Sacondaga Home 1850-1870*. 1960. port. wrps. 97 pp. With a preface by Howard I. Becker, the noted author on the Adirondacks. Lmtd. to 100 copies. (An important contribution about life in the Sacandaga Valley.)

BACON HILL, Saratoga Co.
Vanderwerker, J. *Reminiscences of Bacon Hill & Vicinity*. 1928. illus. wrps. 30 pp. (Reprntd. from the *Saratogian* newspaper, 1928.)

BALLSTON SPA, Saratoga Co.
Anon. *Year of History. Ballston Spa. 1609-1959*. 45 pp.
Grose, E. *Centennial History of the Village of Ballston Spa, Ballston, & Milton*. Ballston Spa. 1907. illus. 258 pp. (Includes unpub. hist. by the late John C. Booth.)

BATCHELLERVILLE, Saratoga Co.
Gordon, W. *Scattering Memories of a Sacondaga Home 1850-1870*. (1960) wrps. mimeo. lmtd. about 100 copies. 97 pp.

CHARLTON, Saratoga Co.
Cavert, W. *Farming & Community Life in Charlton Circa 1900*. (1919.) mimeo. 12 pp.
Taylor, Packard, Van Epps. *Stories & Pictures of Charlton*. Middle Grove. 1959. 46 illus. 122 pp. 1000 copies prntd.

CLIFTON PARK, Saratoga Co.
Becker, H. *Early Town Roads of Clifton Park*. (1959.) maps. mimeo. wrps. 58 pp.

Becker, H. (Ed.) *1790-1850 Town Census of Clifton Park, Half Moon, Waterford and Niskayuna ... 10,000 Names*. ca 1950s. (A printing of the census of these two years. Maps of each town are included, showing the house and the name of the occupant at the time the census was taken. Only 50 copies were prntd.)

CORINTH, Saratoga Co.
Shorey, M. *The Early History of Corinth, Once Known as Jessup's Landing*. Corinth. 1959. illus. maps. wrps. 71 pp.

GANSEVOORT, Saratoga Co.
Vanderwerker, J. *Early Days in Gansevoort & Vicinity*. 1938. 23 pp.

MECHANICVILLE, Saratoga Co.
Sheehan, H. *Mechanicville Centennial 1859-1959*. illus. advts. wrps. 76 pp.

MOREAU, Saratoga Co.
Winch, D. *Introd. to Local History: Upper Hudson, Moreau, Northumberland, Wilton*. 1954. illus. maps. 131 pp.

NORTHUMBERLAND, Saratoga Co.
Vanderwerker, J. *Early Days in the Vicinity of Northumberland & Bacon Hill*. Schuylerville. 1938. illus. 21 pp.

ROUND LAKE, Saratoga Co.
Weise, A. *History of Round Lake*. NY. 1887. 103 pp.

SARATOGA, Saratoga Co.
Allen, R. *Handbook of Saratoga & Strangers Guide*. NY. 1859. illus. 131 pp.
Bradley, H. *Such Was Saratoga*. NY. 1939. 386 pp.
Brandow, J. *The Story of Old*

Saratoga. Albany. 1900. illus. maps. 396 pp. 2nd. ed. Albany. 1919. illus. map. 528 pp.

Britten, E. *Chronicles of Saratoga.* Saratoga Springs. 1959. illus. pvtly. prntd. 620 pp.

Britten, W. *Chronicles of Saratoga.* 1947. illus. 351 pp.

Bullard, E. *History of Saratoga & the Burgoyne Campaign of 1777. Address July 4, 1876.* Ballston Spa. 1876. wrps. 22 pp. (Includes G. Scott's *Saratoga Co. An Historical Address* and N. Sylvester's *Saratoga & Kay-ad-ros-se-ra. Historical Address July 4, 1876* in some bound copies.)

Durkee, C. (comp.) *Reminiscences of Saratoga.* 1928. illus. 316 pp.

Heimer, M. *Fabulous Bawd, The Story of Saratoga.* 1932. illus. 244 pp. (... "Dedicated to the horses, who, alone in Saratoga over the years have remained honest.")

Ingraham, P. *Saratoga Winter & Summer.* 1885. illus. 120 pp.

Sears, R. *A Poem on the Mineral Waters of Ballston & Saratoga, With Notes Illustrating the History of the Springs & Adjacent Country.* Ballston Spa. 1819. 108 pp. (Local hist. in verse & prose of Saratoga Springs.)

Smith, J. *Reminiscences of Saratoga or Twelve Seasons at the "States."* 1897. illus. 326 pp.

Stone, W. *Reminiscences of Saratoga & Ballston.* NY. 1875. 451 pp.

Another ed. NY. 1880. illus.

Another ed. NY. 1890. illus. 448 pp.

Sylvester, N. *Saratoga & Kay-ad-ros-se-ra. Historical Address July 4, 1876.* Troy. 1876. 52 pp.

Tuck, G. *History of Saratoga Springs.* Unpub. mss. 15 pp. in Hist. Soc. of Saratoga Springs Museum.

Waller, G. *Saratoga. Saga of an Impious Era.* Englewood Cliffs, NJ. 1966. illus. 392 pp.

Wickham, R. *A Saratoga Boyhood.* (Syracuse.) 1948. illus. map. 243 pp. (1880-1890 era.)

SCHUYLERVILLE, Saratoga Co.

Adams, J. *Schuylerville Old & New.* Ft. Edward. 1899. illus. 36 pp.

Allen, C. (comp) *Schuylerville, the Historical Village.* Official Souvenir Book. Saratoga Springs. 1912. illus. 116 pp.

SOUTH GLENS FALLS, Saratoga Co.

Soper, E. *History of So. Glens Falls & Town of Moreau.* Masters' Thesis, State Teachers' College, Albany, 1943.

WATERFORD, Saratoga Co.

Hammersley, S. *History of Waterford.* 1957. pvtly. pub. illus. maps. 400 pp.

Waterford Study Club (comp.) *The Old Town by the Ford. 1794-1912.* 1912. wrps. lmtd. to 100 copies. 23 pp.

SCHENECTADY COUNTY

SCHENECTADY COUNTY

Greene, N. (ed) *History of the Mohawk Valley, Gateway to the West (1614-1925) Covering Schenectady, Schoharie, Montgomery, Fulton, Herkimer, and Oneida Cos.* Chicago. 1925. illus. 4 vols.

Howell, G. (ed.) *History of the Co. of Schenectady. 1662-1886.* NY. 1886. illus. 218 pp.

Van Santvoord, C. (comp.) *History*

of Co. of Schenectady. Schenectady. 1887. map. 54 pp.
Yates, A. Schenectady Co., Its History to the Close of the 19th Century. NY. 1902. illus. 721 pp.

DUANESBURG, Schenectady Co.
Foote, C. Footprints of Duanesburg & the Schoharie Valley. 1969. Book.

GLENVILLE, Schenectady Co.
Van Epps, P. (town historian) Contributions to the History of Glenville. (1935) mimeo. 160 pp.
--- The Schenectady Patent of 1684 & The Common Land of Glenville. Glenville. 1948. illus. wrps. 15 pp.

SCHENECTADY, Schenectady Co.
Anon. "Grips" Gazette. Vol. I. No. 5 Jan. 1894. 8 pp. (Special issue on Schenectady.)
Bennett, C. Many Mohawk Moons. 1938. illus. maps. 30 pp.
Birch, J. The Markers Speak. An Informal History of the Schenectady Area. Schenectady. 1962. illus. maps. 179 pp.
Conde, E. The Beautiful Land, A History of Schenectady & Adjacent Areas. ed. by J. Joyce. ca 1965. mimeo. 282 pp.
(Conde, E. & others) Schenectady & the Great Western Gateway. Schenectady. 1926. illus. wrps. 68 pp.
Hanson, W. Schenectady During The Revolution. (Brattleboro, VT.) 1916. 304 pp. (Sketches of all men who served in the war.)
Monroe, J. Schenectady, Ancient & Modern. Geneva. 1914. illus. maps. 285 pp.

Pearson, J. A History of the Schenectady Patent in the Dutch & English Times. ed. by J. MacMurray. Albany. 1883. illus. maps. index. 466 pp. Lmtd. to 350 copies; plus 50 copies on large paper with added illus. (This is an enlarged ed. of Pearson's Contributions to the Genealogies ... of the First Settlers ... of Schenectady, pub. in Albany 1873). The 1873 ed. was reprntd. in 1982.
Roberts, G. Old Schenectady. Schenectady. (1904.) illus. maps. 296 pp.
Sanders, J. Early History of Schenectady. Albany. 1879. index. 346 pp.
Toll, D. Narrative, Embracing the History of Two or Three of the First Settlers & Their Families of Schenectady ... Visits ... Recreations ... Tea Parties. Schenectady. 1847. 57 pp.
Veldran, B. History of Schenectady. Masters' Thesis, State Teachers' College, Albany, 1934.
Westover, M. Schenectady Past & Present. Strasburg, VA. 1931. illus. map. 73 pp.

SCOTIA, Schenectady Co.
Van Epps, P. Story of the Maalwyck, Its Settlers .... Glenville 1937. 14 pp. typed mss. in SLA.
Williams & Palermo. The Story of Scotia. Scotia. 1943. illus. mimeo. 194 pp.

SCHOHARIE COUNTY

SCHOHARIE COUNTY
Brown, J. Brief Sketch of the First Settlement of the Co. of Schoharie by the Germans. Schoharie. 1823. 23 pp. (Howes USiana: "Rarest NY co. hist.") 2nd. ed. Cobleskill. 1891. 52 pp.

(Pub. by G. W. Bellinger, ed. of the *Index* newspaper, and presented at Christmas to its readers. The *Index* had a circulation of 2600 copies per week.)
Reprntd. 1940. wrps. 19 pp.
Reprntd. 1975. wrps. 24 pp.
Bulson, D. *To-Wos-Scho-Hor: The Land of the Unforgotten Indian*. 1961. illus. maps. 35 pp.
James, F. *Folks & Places Along the Schoharie. 1888-1945*. 1945. mimeo. 88 pp.
2nd. ed. 1946. mimeo. 88 pp.
Noyes, M. (ed.) *A History of Schoharie Co*. Richmondville. 1957. 130 pp. illus. maps.
Enlarged ed. Richmondville. 1964. illus. maps. 184 pp.
Roscoe, W. *History of Schoharie Co. 1713-1882*. Syracuse. 1882. illus. maps. 470 pp.
Microfilmed by Bell & Howell, Cleveland, OH. 1964.
Sias, S. *A Summary of Schoharie Co*. Middleburg. 1904. illus. maps. 154 pp. (For school use.)
Simms, J. *Frontiersmen of NY*. Albany 1882-1883. 2 vols. ("Really a 2nd. ed. of Simms' *History of Schoharie Co*." See below.)
--- *History of Schoharie Co. & Border Wars of NY*. Albany. 1845. illus. 672 pp. 2000 copies prntd. (Sold by the author.) Reprntd. ca 1974.
Taylor, E. *Schoharie Co. in Legend & History*. Schoharie. 1946. illus. map. wrps. 34 pp. (Includes "Timothy Murphy" by H. Eddy, State Archivist of NC.)
Vrooman, E. *Schoharie Valley Lore*. ca 1920. 77 pp.
Warner, G. *Military Records of Schoharie Co. in Four Wars*. Albany 1891. 428 pp. (The tragic hist. of this book is told in Carl Carmer's book, *Listen for a Lonesome Drum*.)

BARNERVILLE, Schoharie Co.
Rickard, C. *Annals of Barnerville*. Cobleskill. 1932. wrps. 15 pp.

BLENHEIM, Schoharie Co.
(Bliss, H. town historian) *Hist ... of Blenheim 1797-1959*. illus. map. wrps. 190 pp.

BLENHEIM HILL, Schoharie Co.
Mayham, A. C. *The Anti-Rent War on Blenheim Hill, An Episode of the 40s. History of the Struggle Between Landlord and Tenant Growing Out of the Patroon System in the Eastern Part of New York*. Jefferson, NY. 1906. illus. map. 89 pp. (Hist. of anti-rent activities in Schoharie Co.)
Pollard, R. *Sketches of Blenheim Hill*. 1927. illus. pamphlet.

CENTRAL BRIDGE, Schoharie Co.
Anon. *Over the Bridge to Yesteryear*. Central Bridge. 1978. pub. by the Eccentric Club. 60 pp.

CHARLOTTEVILLE, Schoharie Co.
Lamont, T. *A Brief Account of the Life at Charlotteville of Thomas William Lamont and of His Family*. 1915. 135 pp. (Much on life in a small Schoharie Co. town in the 1800s. Charlotteville had about 40 houses in 1860.)

COBLESKILL, Schoharie Co.
Fake, K. (town historian) *Official History of Town of Cobleskill*. Cobleskill. 1937. illus. 197 pp.
Ryder, E. *Civil War Days in Cobleskill*. 1930. wrps. 8 pp (repub. from *Cobleskill Times*)
--- *Reminiscences &*

Remembrances of Main St. Cobleskill 1855-1875. 1929. 8 pp.

Welch, E. *"Grips" Hist. Souvenir of Cobleskill.* 1895. 48 pp.

CONESVILLE, Schoharie Co.
Mattice, B. *They Walked These Hills Before Me. An Early History.* 1980. 221 pp.

ESPERANCE, Schoharie Co.
Montayne, F. (town historian) *Village of Esperance.* Delanson. 1944. wrps. 34 pp.

JEFFERSON, Schoharie Co.
Anon. *History of Town of Jefferson, Sesquicentennial 1803-1953.* 24 pp.
Bailey, M. *History of Town of Jefferson.* 1976. wrps. maps. illus. 187 pp.
Hubbell, R. Articles by Dr. Hubbell on Jefferson hist. pub. in the *Jefferson Standard* newspaper ca 1920-1923. (In 1909, Hubbell proposed writing & pub. hist. of Jefferson in illus. book of about 200 pages. Project never carried out.)
Keyser, L. *The Early History of the Town of Jefferson.* Ca 1950. wrps. 43 pp.

MIDDLEBURG, Schoharie Co.
(Andrew, B. & others) *Bridging the Years 1712-1962.* ca 1962. illus. maps. wrps. 131 pp.
Beekman, Judge. *Historical Address, Aug. 1912.* wrps. 17 pp.
Welch, E. *"Grips" Historical Souvenir of Middleburg.* Albany. 1894. illus. 46 pp.

SEWARD, Schoharie Co.
(Van Schaick, J.) *Address Delivered at the Centennial Celebration of the Seward Massacre in 1780, Oct. 18, 1880.* Cobleskill. 1880. wrps. 33 pp.

SHARON SPRINGS, Schoharie Co.
Durlach and Blumin. *The Short Season of Sharon Springs.* ca 1980s? 128 pp. (The rise, decline, and survival of an unusual town.)

SCHUYLER COUNTY

SCHUYLER COUNTY
Anon. *Biog. Record of Schuyler Co. NY.* 1903. illus. 546 pp.
(Anon.) *Schuyler County History.* 1879. 226 pp. Reprntd. ca 1976.
Bell, B. *Little Tales From Little Schuyler.* Watkins Glen. 1962. wrps. 89 pp.
Corbett, J. (asst. ed.) *Historical & Biog. Reminiscences of Schuyler, by a Local Historian.* Pub. in *Watkins Express* beginning in 1889. (These articles were later reprntd. in book form, n.d., copy at Cornell U. Lib. ends with p. 120, but appears to have been longer.)
Upson, R. *The Early Development of Four Finger Lake Cos. Being the Settlement and Agricultural History of Schuyler, Seneca, Tompkins, & Yates Cos. 1790-1870.* Masters' Thesis, Cornell U. 1938.

CATHARINE, Schuyler Co.
Cleaver, M. (comp.) *History of Town of Catharine.* Rutland, VT. 1945. illus. maps. 686 pp.

ODESSA, Schuyler Co.
Hausner, K. *History of Odessa.* Broadside history originally prntd. in the *Watkins Express* newspaper, July 12, 1916. Written by a high school student. 6x20 inches. Distributed with the compliments of Assemblyman H. J. Mitchell.)

SENECA COUNTY

SENECA COUNTY

Anon. *Centennial Anniv. of Seneca Co.* Seneca Falls. 1904. 80 pp. (2nd annual report of Seneca Falls Hist. Soc.)

Anon. *History of Seneca Co. 1786-1876.* Phil. 1876. illus. map. 170 pp. Reprntd. in 1976 with separate index and supplement. "Additions have been made of many old views from the Village Wall-Maps of Ovid, Seneca Falls and Waterloo pub. by J. H. French in the 1850s."

Anon. *Portrait & Biog. Record of Seneca & Schuyler Cos.* NY. 1895. illus. 508 pp.

Hawley, C. *Early Chapters of Seneca History ... Jesuit Missions in Sonnontouan. 1656-1684.* Auburn. 1884. 152 pp.

(Spafford, H.) *An Early History of Seneca Co.* 1813. pub. ca 1976. wrps. illus. 20 pp. (From H. G. Spafford's work of 1813.)

Watrous, H. *The County Between the Lakes. A Public History of Seneca Co.* NY. Waterloo. 1983. illus. index. 386 pp.

AURORA, Seneca Co.

Hollcroft, T. *A Brief History of Town of Aurora.* 1977. map. illus. bib. 76 pp.

FAYETTE, Seneca Co.

Willers, D. *Centennial Historical Sketch of Town of Fayette.* Geneva. 1900. 157 pp. Reprntd. in 1983 with added illus.

JUNIUS, Seneca Co.

Anon. *1000th Anniv. of Town of Junius 1803-1903.* Seneca Falls Hist. Soc. 1903. wrps. 76 pp.

Lutz, E. *History of Town of Junius 1803-1921.* Geneva. 1921. illus. 41 pp.

LODI, Seneca Co.

Donohoe, M. (ed.) *A Survey of the Village of Lodi, Seneca Co, NY.* 1979. Lodi Hist. Soc. illus. map. 134 pp.

OVID, Seneca Co.

Morrison, W. (Comp.) *Town & Village of Ovid, Seneca Co. NY. An Early History.* 1980. maps. illus. 338 pp. (Covers 1789-1889). "Unprecendented in the annals of local history publications is the magnitude of handsome illus. contained in this tome."

ROMULUS, Seneca Co.

(Willers, D. ed.) *Centennial Celebration of Official Organization of Town of Romulus. June 13, 1894.* Geneva. 1894. 142 pp.

Willers, D. *Historical Address, June 13, 1894.* Geneva. 1894. 69 pp.

SENECA FALLS, Seneca Co.

Anon. *As We Were: The Life and Times of The Early 20th Century in Seneca Falls, NY.* Vol. 2. 1979. Seneca Falls Hist. Soc. illus. map. 48 pp.

(Gulder, A. & others) *Seneca Falls.* illus. 78 pp. (Title page lacking in copy at BPL.)

Welch, E. *"Grips" Historical Souvenir of Seneca Falls.* Syracuse. 1904. illus. 144 pp.

SHELDRAKE, Seneca Co.

Robinson, E. *Sheldrake 1789-1962. A History.* wrps. illus. maps. pub. 1962. 39 pp.

WATERLOO, Seneca Co.

Becker, J. *A History of Village of Waterloo (1792-1949).* Waterloo. 1949. illus. maps. 576 pp.

Welch, E. *"Grips Historical Souvenir of Waterloo.* Syracuse. 1903. illus. 104 pp.

(SHAKERS)

(Bates, Barnabas) *Peculiarities of the Shakers, Described in a Series of Letters From Lebanon Springs ... 1832 ... Origin, Worship, Doctrines, of the Shaker's Society. By a Visiter.* NY. 1832. 116 pp. (This is such a sympathetic account that the New Lebanon Shaker society told Bates they would take a dozen copies of the book if he ever reprntd. it.)

Brainard, D. C. *Rural Register and Almanac for 1877. From ... Mount Lebanon, NY. For the Southern and Middle States.* Albany. Weed, Parsons and Co. Printers. 1877. 63 pp. (Richmond entry no. 261 locates only the 1876 ed., and only 1 location for it. There is, I believe, an 1875 printing in existence.)

Brown, Thomas. *An Account of the People Called Shakers: Their Faith, Doctrines, and Practice, Exemplified in the Life, Conversations, and Experience of the Author During the Time He Belonged to the Society ... by ... of Cornwall, Orange Co., New York.* Troy. 1812. 372 pp. (One of the earliest, if not the earliest, book written by an apostate Shaker.)

Card. *A Tribute of Thanks to Our Neighbors ... Committee. Jonathan Wood. Edward Fowler. Peter H. Long.* New Lebanon, May 10th, 1852. Broadside with decorative border. 5 x 6 inches. (Some rather isolated Shaker buildings caught fire on May 9th. during church services. Worshippers in a nearby church abandoned the sermon they were hearing to put out the fire. The very next day the Shakers issued this excessively rare broadside to thank their neighbors for their efforts, especially to the females.)

Catalogue. *Auction of Shaker Antiques at Darrow School, New Lebanon, New York. August 5, 1961.* 17 pp. 690 lots listed. (Perhaps the most important sale of Shaker antiques, up to that time.)

Honeywood, St. John. *Poems by...With Some Pieces of Prose.* NY. 1801. 159 pp. (Honeywood was a lawyer and newspaper editor who lived for some years at Salem, NY. This work includes an 8 page chapter on the Shakers at Niskayuna. "The Magistrates ... have behaved with wisdom in taking no notice of them; neglected, they will sink to nothing; persecuted, they will certainly increase." Richmond 2274.)

Remains of Joseph A. H. Sampson. Who Died at New-Lebanon 12 mo. 14, 1825, Aged 20 Years. Published by Request of his Friends. For the Benefit of Youth. Rochester, NY. Prntd. by E. F. Marshall, for Proctor Sampson, of New Lebanon. 1827. 54 pp. (Mostly poetry. It also includes an account of the death of Polly Lawrence at the Shaker settlement at Portbay, (Sodus) Wayne Co., NY. This no doubt was prntd. at the expense of Proctor Sampson who was a man of means when he joined the Shakers. He bought land for the Order, and contributed liberally to the publication of Shaker literature.)

Shaker Almanac. 1884. Illus. 32 pp. (One of the scarcest of the Shaker almanacs. It has 3 illus. of Mount Lebanon, NY. Interestingly, the back wrapper has one of the earliest illus. of the Statue of Liberty "Being erected on Bedloes Island, NY, Harbor." There is a 3/4-page article on the sculptor and the statue which "when finished ... will be the wonder of the world.")

Shakers' Descriptive and Illustrated Annual Catalogue and Amateur's Guide to the Flower and Vegetable Garden. William Anderson, Mount Lebanon, NY. Mount Lebanon: Washington Jones, Book and Job Printer. 1882. Illus. wrps. Priced. 84 pp. (Cover title states: Printing Press of the United Soc. of Shakers ... Eighteenth Ed. Anderson was the head gardener at Mount Lebanon. This was one of the last of the major Shaker Seed catalogs as the seed business was on the decline at this time.)

Shaker Dwelling Sale. Darrow School, New Lebanon, NY. 1972 wrps. Illus. Floor plans. 36 pp. (The Darrow School was forced to sell the North family dwelling and its remaining contents, and issued this fine catalog to those interested in submitting written offers. There are fine interior illus., and brief descriptions of 182 items. Here is a good place to permanently record a story told to me by a lady who worked at the North family many years ago. It was told to her by Martha, one of the hired help, and is about Sister C who joined the Shakers when very young and must have been a limb of mischief. Here it is in my informant's words, "After Sister C's death the others found among her things a small piece of colored glass and wondered what was it and why it had been kept. Martha knew but had sense enough not to tell them. She told me the story. It seems that long ago, some years or more, when the Shakers were much more numerous and had many young people and even children in their care that a famous lecturer was to speak at the Lebanon Valley Church. I don't know the subject of his speech, but as the Shakers were invited to it, it may have concerned them or some phase of their religion. Well, after due consideration, the Elders and Eldressess decided to attend but not to allow any of the young people to go. They might hear or see some thing not proper for them. There were a few partially independent ones who decided to go without the consent of their Elders. Sister C was one and very likely a leader. They coaxed one young Brother (he was living when I worked there) to harness his team. This is the team he usually worked. As soon as the Elders had gone down the main road, the young fry took a sneak to the barn. The team was hooked to the sleigh in short order and (minus bells) they raced down a short cut and arrived at the church just after the service had begun. Of course they dared not enter so they drove up close to a window but could hear nothing. Then Sister C spied a crack in the window and by careful work removed the little corner of glass. This allowed the sleighful of young culprits to see and hear quite well, by turns at least. When they thought the meeting was nearly over, they left. Ran the horses back up the lane (and its up, too, I know that road) put the horses in, unharnessed, and blanketed them, then hurried into their own beds. The Elders suspected something for Sister C said that they went throught all the rooms with lights and looked closely at each sleeping (?) young person, but nothing ever more ever came of it, and that was where she got the colored glass.)

(Smith, J. E. A.) *Taghconic; or Letters and Legends about our Summer Home.* By Godfrey Greylock [pseud.] Boston. 1852. 228 pp. (Smith crossed the border into NY State and attended a Shaker meeting at New Lebanon. He devoted one chapter to this impressive event in his life, and calls New Lebanon "the rural Vatican which claims a more despotic sway over the minds of men than ever Roman Pontiff assumed." Apparently, the Shakers, or their supporters, did not appreciate his views, as this chapter does not appear in subsequent ed. of the book.)

Symonds, J. *Thomas Brown and the Angels. A Study in Enthusiasm.* London. 1961. Illus. map. bib. index. 175 pp. (Brown, a Methodist, turned Quaker, joined the Shakers at Niskayuna near Albany in 1799. There is much on Brown at Niskayuna, some references to his trip to New Lebanon, and some information on the tiny and short-lived Shaker community, at Cornwall, NY.)

Youngs, Isaac N. *A Short Abridgement Of The Rules of Music. With Lessons For Exercise, and a few Observations; For new Beginners.* Prntd. at New Lebanon; 1843. Blue wrappers. Leather backstrip. 40 pps. (Youngs apologizes in the introduction, "This little abridgement is intended only for present necessity, and for the lack of type and time to accomplish the work, it is very deficient and imperfect." Edward Deming Andrews, the noted collector and authority on the Shakers, believed this work was prntd. on a small hand-press by Youngs. It was reprntd. ln 1846. Both ed. are very rare. Over the years I have had several copies of the 1846 printing, but only 1 of the 1843. Most of these came from Tim Trace, the well-known and highly respected dealer of Peekskill, NY. A man of many talents and much knowledge, Tim was an engineer, good cook, consultant to major museums, specialist in decorative arts, expert on Shaker literature, and a fountain of stories about books and dealers. He lived about an hour from me, and I would visit him several times a year. I would always come home with some treasures: an early manuscript on steamboat experiments on the Delaware River, a box of Shaker literature, and once a collection of a number of ed. of the famous Williams' *Indian Captivity.* I don't believe anyone ever left Tim's house without hearing at least 4 or 5 book related stories told with gusto. Tim passed away several years ago, but he is still remembered with affection whenever several booksellers gather together and talk about books and dealers.)

(STATE WIDE)

Beach, S. A. *The Apples of New*

York. 2 vols. 1905. Illus. Bib. Hundreds of varieties are briefly described in this fine work. There are 78 halftone and 133 colored plates. It was reprntd. In 1912 and 1913. Thousands of sets were reserved for legislators, but about 1910 a scandal errupted when it was discovered that many of those sets had ended up in the hands of bookdealers. Recently three of us dealers were discussing this set, and one remarked that he once sold an odd volume for 25 cents to get it out of his way. At the present time it is highly priced in book shops and brings even a higher price at local auctions. Whenever I see a high-priced set I refuse to buy it. I look at it and say to myself, "It can't be worth that much. They prntd. and distributed 29,000 sets of this thing." That is a lot of sets. The pub. history of this work is to be found in the introduction of Hedrick' *A History of Agriculture in the State of New York*. 1966 Reprint.)

Benson, Egbert. *Memoir, Read Before the Historical Society of State of New York. December 31, 1816*. NY. 1817. 72 pp. (Benson, a noted NY State jurist during the Revolutionary War, spoke on NY State place names. He took several copies of his prntd. address, and made marginal notes and inserted mss. pages. Each copy had different mss. notes which made them individually unique. One of them came my way with comments on boundary lines, and banking laws; a Long Island Indian legend; description of the execution of an Indian captive by a squaw near Albany; and some comments on his attendance with Alexander Hamilton, and others, at a pre-U. S. Constitutional Convention at Annapolis, Maryland, in Sept. 1786. I sold that for $225.00 in 1971. Over the years several ed. of this pamphlet were prntd. Sabin says that the Hist. Soc. objected to Its printing at the time it was delivered. The story of my acquisition of this pamphlet gives some insight into the legendary independence of antiquarian booksellers. I had heard about 2 fellows who had their stock in a barn, and were careful about who they let in. One day when I was about an hour and a half away I phoned to see if I could stop in, and told them what I was interested in. They said, "No, we probably don't have anything for you. Don't come today. Sometime if you are going by give us another ring." Immediately I drove over, and knocked on the door. They were startled to see me, and I said, "I'm Harold Nestler. I phoned you awhile ago. I was going right by and so stopped in." One of them said, "We told you to call first. Now that you are here you can come in for a little while." In less than two hours, I bought several hundred dollars worth of books, including the Benson pamphlet with mss. notes. When I left they said, "Come back anytime. We'll be glad to see you. Just be sure to phone first." We became good friends and I purchased a number of important items from them. In contrast to that story is the one told of a dealer who had visited another dealer five or six times, spending 200 to

600 dollars in about two hours on each visit. In addition, he had been the means whereby that dealer had acquired a large lot of finely printed books. Then one day "the roof fell in": when he got to the dealer's house he was met with, "I will give you only an hour. You come here and spend practically nothing, and waste my time." The chap was so shocked he could not say a word in defense of himself, and stared at him in disbelief. For an hour he worked furiously, and spent between 300 and 400 dollars. After that he phoned the dealer two or three times but was never allowed to visit or spend money there again.)

Burt, O. (ed.) *American Murder Ballads and Their Stories.* 1958. index. Some music. 272 pp. (The author's happy mother used to sing tragic songs to lull her children to sleep. The front cover is decorated with an illus. of 3 people hanging from a gallows. According to the index, some of these murders occurred in NY State.)

A Census of the Electors and Inhabitants in the State of New York, Taken in the Year 1790. Prntd. by Childs and Swaine, Printers to the State. (1791) Broadside, 9-1/2 x 18 inches. (The first census of NY State. Evans 23614.)

Census of the State of New York for 1845. Albany. 1846. folio. (A huge book filled with a tremendous amount of statistical data. It is the largest book in size and weight that I have ever handled: 13 x 19 inches x 3 inches thick. Other notable NY State census vol. that have come my way were for 1835, 1855, and 1875. None of them contain personal names. In 1865 a 56-page pamphlet of "Instructions for Taking the Census" was issued.)

Clark, L. G. (ed.) *The Literary Remains of the Late Willis Gaylord Clark. Including the Ollapodiana Papers, the Spirit of Life, and a Selection From His Various Prose and Poetical Writings.* NY. 1844. 480 pp. (L. G. Clark, the ed. was the twin brother of Willis Gaylord Clark. They were from Otisco, NY, and were major literary figures among America's minor authors. There are some literary vignettes of travels in the Mohawk Valley, the Kaatskills, and the Niagara area. Their biog. are in the DAB.)

Clinton and Economy, Versus Tompkins and Taxation. A Few Words to the Sober Sense of the People! Published by Order of the Republican Committee. Folio broadside. Cayuga *Republican-Extra* (Auburn, NY. 1820.) (This political poster was issued during a venomous campaign in which Daniel D. Tompkins, former Governor of NY and now Vice President of the U. S., was running against incumbent DeWitt Clinton. It details how Tompkins was a spendthrift while Governor and details how thrifty Clinton reduced his own salary and the salaries of many government officials. "If you want to turn out Clinton and put in Tompkins, then look well to your money, your purse, and your taxes, and prepare for the tax-gatherer." Not in *American Imprints.*)

Dillon, J. J. *Several Decades of Milk. A History of New York's Diary Industry.* 1941. Tables.

index. 340 pp. (A comprehensive hist. of a major NY State industry. NY's rural roads have more cattle crossings than many other states. This book discusses: the first dairy organizations, freight rates, united dairymen, strikes, milk laws, dealer's schemes. I once knew a milkman who told a lady who complained that the Grade A milk was watery, "Ma'am, the cow's back must have leaked when it rained.")

Documents of the New York Sabbath Committee. 1857-1867. Bound volume of over 40 pamphlets issued by the Committee about the relationship between the Sabbath and Railroads, news crying, liquor, theatres, the military. (This was an important organization whose work resulted in 2 major legal decisions, and whose pub. were also distributed in Europe. Several of the pamphlets in this collection are in German to reach the Germans among whom there was an anti-Sunday movement.)

Douglas, E. *Gazetteer of the Mountains of New York State.* Washington, D. C. 1927. wrps. 36 mimeo. pp. (An alphabeticaly listing of 1530 named NY State elevations with: name, county, latitude, longitude, elevation,; and, if a mile or more in length, the length is given.)

Finney, C. G. *The Character, Claims, and Practical Workings of Freemasonry.* 1869. 272 pp. (An anti-Masonic work by NY state's most famous Evangelist. Finney had been Secretary of the Masonic Lodge of Adams, NY, but resigned after his conversion to Christianity. When William Morgan pub. his famous anti-Masonic book Finney said it was a true expose.)

Gazetteer and Business Directory. Handbill, ca late 1860s. 6 x 8 inches. (Hamilton Child of Syracuse, NY, pub. gazetteers and business directories of many NY co., and some New England co., from the 1860s to the 1880s. They contain: hist. matter, advts., descriptions of towns, village directories, list of county officers, postal rates, much else. Occasionally he included such useful information as: a recipe for brilliant white wash, how to get a horse out of a fire, how to measure a haystack. Each gazetteer had a map, at least some of which were made by the Weed, Parsons Co. of Albany. These works should be on the "want list" of everyone interested in a particular co. as they contain a wide variety of material available nowhere else. The handbill referred to above lists the contents of his gazetteers. At the top is a place for the Canvassing Agent for Child to write in the name of the Co., and at the bottom is a blank space for the Agent to write in his name. No doubt these were used as advts. and order forms by the Agents.)

Gorham, B. W. *Camp Meeting Manual, A Practical Book for the Camp Ground.* Boston. 1854. illus. 168 pp. (Gorham, a minister from Binghamton, NY, wrote this manual on how to build and conduct camp meetings. It includes a diagram of a plan for a camp ground, showing: platform, altar, and seats. Camp meetings have been held all over NY state, but are now dying out. The famous Chautauqua

225

movement, with its cottages, is an outgrowth of the camp meeting movement of the 1800s. The word "camp-meeting" has been sometimes applied to tent meetings. One of the wealthy and well-known Thorne families of the Millbrook area of Dutchess Co. for many years had a huge tent put up on their front lawn. People drove there from many miles around to hear the great Bible teachers and hellfire and brimstone evangelists of the 1930s. I recall going there a number of times, and on several occasions heard the famous Billy Sunday.)

Halsey, R. *Pictures of Early New York on Dark Blue Stafford Shire Pottery.* NY. 1899. Many illus. index. 329 pp. Lmtd. to 298 copies. (Many illus. of NYC and State were used on this collectible pottery, including the Hudson Highlands, the Erie Canal, and the Catskills.)

Harper's New York and Erie Rail Road Guide Book. Description of Scenery, Rivers, Towns, Villages. With 136 Engravings by Lossing and Barritt. NY. 1851. 174 pp. (A description of this famous route from Piermont on the Hudson River to Dunkirk on Lake Erie.)

The Historical Magazine, and Notes and Queries Concerning the Antiquities, History, and Biography of America. Vols. 1 thru 10: Jan. 1857-Dec. 1866. Second Series Vol. 1 thru 10: Jan. 1867-Aug. 1871. Third Series Vols. 1 thru 3: Jan. 1872-Apr. 1875. There were several extra numbers, and a total of 23 volumes. (Founded in Boston in 1857, this major magazine moved to NY the next year. Among its ed. was Henry B. Dawson, of Morissania, NY, and a number of noted historians were among its contributors. As the set is seldom found complete it is fortunate that each vol. was indexed. It had an erratic pub. hist., and at least 3 times pub. was suspended for several months. This periodical contains a great deal of information on NY State, and has material available nowhere else. Only one long run, not quite complete, has been acquired by me, and it went to a retired major airline pilot who was studying for a degree in American history.)

(Hoffman, C. F. [ed.] *The New York Book of Poetry.* NY. Dearborn. 1837. 253 pp. (A vol. of poems, many with a NY State setting, by residents of NY State including Irving, Paulding, Bleecker, Street, and Stone. Blanck's *Bibliography of American Literature* says it also contains the "earliest located formal book pub. of "A Visit from St. Nicholas" pp. 217-219." [This delightful poem, better known to us as "The Night Before Christmas" by Clement C. Moore, was first pub. anonymously in the Troy *Sentinel* newspaper on Dec. 23, 1823.] The BAL also quotes the *American Monthly Magazine*, NY, Jan. 1837, "Never before, we believe, has Moore's 'A Visit...' appeared under the name of the real author.")

Holley, O. L. (ed.) *The New York State Register, for 1845; Containing an Almanac for 1845-47. With Political, Statistical, and Other Information. Complete List of County Officers, Attorneys, &c.* Pub. by J. Disturnell, NY. 1845. 660 pp.

(This is a bottomless pit of data: population, election returns, post offices, banks, canals, census data, newspapers, steamboats, railroads, even the amount of flour manufactured by mills in Rochester. This highly statistical work was pub. for at least several years.)

Illustrated Catalogue Of the "Four Track Series". Pub. by the Passenger Department. NY Central and Hudson River RR. Revised ed. 1896. wrps. Illus. 32 pp. (A catalog of the famous "Four Track Series" of pamphlets issued by the NYC & HR RR. They were pub. for the information of prospective vacationers, and covered such topics as: Suburban Homes North of the Harlem, the Adirondacks, Lakes of Central NY, Niagara Falls, Thousand Islands, the Catskills, NY as a Winter Resort, Block Signals, definitions of railroad terms. Eighteen different titles are listed, plus 8 etchings, and a wall map. These pamphlets are quite scarce, and several of them I have never seen.)

Jenkinson, I. *Jefferson and Burr*. 1898. wrps. 55 pp. (Actually a pro-Burr tract, with data on Burr's political influence in NY State and the formation of a Clinton party against him.)

Kaiser, L. *A Checklist of the Post Offices of New York State to 1850. With the Names of the First Postmasters*. 1965. index. wrps. Lmtd. to 100 copies. (A county-by-county work, with very brief data on each co., alphabetical list of the post offices in the co. with date established, and name of the first Postmaster.)

(Knapp, J.) *Autobiography of Elder Jacob Knapp. With an Introductory Essay by R. Jeffrey*. NY. 1868. 341 pp. (Knapp, 1799-1874, a Baptist evangelist from Otsego Co., travelled widely in NY State, drawing huge crowds. Sometimes the police had to be called to prevent riots during and after his compelling preaching. This book is quite scarce. In fact, in 1887 Appleton's *Cyclopedia of Biography* declared it had never been prntd.)

Lee, C. *A Catalogue of the Medicinal Plants, Indigenous and Exotic, Growing in the State of New York. With a Brief Account of Their Composition and Medical Properties*. NY. 1848. index. wrps. 64 pp. (Lee, 1801-1872, was Prof. of Materia Medica in Geneva (NY) Medical College, and the University of Buffalo. He wrote or ed. books on physiology, geology, and forensic medicine. The DAB says this work on medicinal plants is his best known, and that he had 1500 specimens in his own herbarium.)

Lossing, B. J. *Pictorial Field-Book of the War of 1812*. 1868. Maps. illus. (This work was first pub. in 12 parts, and then issued in one vol. of 1084 pages. It is an excellent reference, and there is much on NY State.)

(Lotteries) *Report of the Lottery Committee ... and an Act to Limit the Continuance of Lotteries*. NY State Assembly. March 21, 1822. 4 pp. (After pub. some data on the state's lottery losses, the perceptive committee adds, "losses are much more likely to occur in such a concern, managed by the state, than they would be if it were managed by those immediately interested in its success.")

Mather, J. *Geography of New York State.* 1847. Maps. 432 pp. (This is a county-by-county description, with a small map of each co. showing township locations and streams. A large map was issued separately.)

Mercantile Agency Reference Book ... Corrected Up to Jan. 1886. Pub. by R. G. Dun & Co. NY. 1886. Map. 1314 pps. + 25-page list of NY State banks. (A town by town listing of NY State [not including NYC] naming each tradesman in the town, giving his estimated value and credit rating. All the way from the wealthy merchants of the major cities to poor John Ryan a wagon maker of Attlebury (population 20) who was worth less than 500 dollars and given no credit rating at all. This work was a forerunner of the famous Dun and Bradstreet Reports.)

(Missionary work) *A Narrative of the Missions to the New Settlements According to the Appointment of the General Association of ... Connecticut.* New Haven. 1794. 17 pp. Plus: *A Continuation of the Narrative of the Missions to the New Settlements ... New Haven.* 1795. 23 pp. (These 2 companion items give a good picture of religious conditions on the NY frontier shortly after the Revolutionary War, and when that area was being quite rapidly settled. The Congregational Church of CT sent missionaries to the new settlements in northern and western NY to gather and organize churches, and to ordain ministers. They went north to Crown Point and west to the Genesee Valley. Their itineraries are listed, and reports given. They found little religious instruction, one settlemant not having heard a sermon for nearly 2 years. Included is a letter from Baron Von Steuben, and others, thanking the Association for sending missionaries to their "infant settlement in the wilderness.")

Mott, E. *Between the Ocean and the Lakes. The Story of Erie.* 1899. Maps. Illus. 511 and 157 pp. (This is the scarcest and preferred ed. of this thorough work on the hist. of the Erie Railroad which ran from the lower Hudson River through southern NY State to Lake Erie. It contains a 157 pp. biog. section not found in the other ed., and has 25 full-page port. not found in the others. This work went thru at least 3 ed.: 1899, 1901, 1908.)

Natural History of New York. 30 vol. illus. maps. colored plates. Albany. 1842-1894. (This great work was ed. by such notables in their field as: James DeKay, zoology; John Torrey, botany; Lewis C. Beck. mineralogy; Ebenezer Emmons, agriculture; W. W. Mather, geology; James Hall, paleontology; and many others. There are many fine plates, diagrams, and maps. A complete set is very difficult to find or to put together by picking up odd vol. here and there. The most expensive book of the series is the 1844 work with 141 full-page color plates of birds, colored by J. W. Hill. It will cost several hundred dollars when found. It is frequently stated that only 300 vol. of the Birds were hand-colored. The NY State Museum Bulletin No. 322 lists no limitation, and so many copies have turned up, none of them being black and white, it seems to be the concensus among dealers that the entire printing of the Birds was colored. Sabin describes this set in considerable detail.)

New York Mercantile Union Business Directory ... To Which is Appended a Short Advertising Register ... for 1850-51. NY. 1850. 2 folding maps. index. 431 pp. (An excellent reference as this is an exhaustive list of trades with names and addresses of the tradesmen. Over 1100 trades are noted, including: Artificial Flower Importer, Seal Engravers, Historical Painters, Leech Dealers, Quill Manufacturers, Guitar Teachers.)

Peace, Liberty, and Commerce ... Let the Peace Candidates, Van Rensselaer and Huntington, be the Watch Word. Albany. April 13th., 1813. Broadside, 8 x 12 inches. (Issued by the anti-War Federalists this broadside urges the nomination of the Peace Candidates for the offices of Governor and Lt. Governor of NY State. "...are not our towns at the mercy of the enemy ... The war will be without end ... enormous TAXES will grind the POOR to dust ... Fellow Citizens - Save your country ... The advocates for blood ... are fattening upon office and salary, while the country is driven to destruction...." The Peace Candidates lost and the War of 1812 continued for nearly 2 more years.)

Pell, F. *A Review of the Administration and Civil Police of the State of New York, From the Year 1807 to the Year 1819.* NY. 1819. wrps. 184 pp. (Pell seems to have been in politics in NYC and an officer in the State Militia. This pamphlet is in the form of a letter to a member of Congress, Pell giving his views on the administration of the state, and heartily supports DeWitt Clinton as Governor. He discourses on a wide range of subjects: criminal law, banks, the militia, finances, fiscal reform, the Grand Canal, political discord. From his pen, on occasion, issued rhetoric supreme. Here is an example, "In the present constitution of every thing human, wisdom cannot dispense blessings without animating putridity: but the foetidness of the one is not abated by the purity and sweetness of the other. The same sun which imparts glow and fragrance to the rosebud, gives animation and fatness to the maggot; but the reptile is not less nauseous, because it glistens in rotteness amid smiles and sun-shine." In all likelihood the reading public could not digest his writing and tossed this work out as soon as possible. *American Bibliography* locates only 2 other copies.)

Ratner, L. *Anti-Masonry, the Crusade and the Party.* 1969. 100 pp. (A hist. of anti-Masonry, with frequent reference to: William Morgan, Thurlow Weed, William H. Seward, Jabez Hammond.)

Report of the Regents of the University on the Boundaries of the State of New York. 2 vols. NY Senate. 1874 and 1884. index. (The major work on the boundaries of NY State, much of the material heretofor being available only in mss. form in the state archives. These are actually copies of documents relating to the boundaries: 1614-1881.)

Roberts, K. & J. *Planemakers and Other Edge Tool Enterprises in New York State in the 19th. Century.* 1971. illus. tables. Bib. 230 pp. (A comprehensive work.)

Scnneider, D. *The History of Public Welfare in New York State 1609-1866.* Chicago. 1938. illus. bib. index. 395 pp.

Spafford, H. G. *A Pocket Guide for the Tourist and Traveller, Along the Line of the Canals, and the Interior Commerce of the State of New York.* NY. Swords. Index. 1824. 72 pp. (Spafford travelled about 1500 miles compiling facts for guide, but apparently he was short of money or did not expect it to sell well as he states in the preface that only a small number of copies were prntd.. It contains a great deal of data, including: tolls, mileages, and names of the Canal Collectors. On the last page in the book he says he is going to send copies to captains of canal packets and steam boats and others he met on his travels with the request they notify him of any errors or ommissions they may discover. They evidentally found some and notified him, as a second ed. of 89 pages with corrections and additions was pub. at Troy, NY, by W. S. Parker, in 1825.)

(Stark, Cordelia ?) *The Female Wanderer. A Very Interesting Tale. Founded on Fact, Written by Herself.* Boston (MA). Pub. by Leonard Deming. 1829. wrps. 36 pp. (A wild tale of a female from near Saratoga who posed for 2 years as a man, wandering about NY State from Buffalo to NYC, and finally shipping out as a sailor. Deming, a pub. and bookseller, advertises in this improbable work that Hairdressing and Shaving were also available at his establishment. (Wright's *American Fiction*, lists a number of ed. of this work beginning in 1824, with a comment on the name of the author.)

Toby. *The American Tours of Messrs. Brown, Jones, and Robinson, Becoming the History of What They Saw and Did in the United States, Canada, and Cuba.* NY. Appleton. 1872. (Actually 74 plates, mostly humorous, each with a brief descriptive line of text. At least 40 of the plates are of NY State interest: Crossing Broadway, West Point, Climbing in the Kaatskills, Drinking Congress Water at Saratoga, Cave of the Winds, Lake George. These are delightful illus.

Transactions of the American Agricultural Association. NY. 1846. Part I. 60 pp. (This association was founded in 1845, and Luther Bradish was its President. There are a series of articles on: meteorology, crop rotation, hop culture, manures, wheat culture in western NY, timber diseases. Hops were becoming an important crop in NY State at this time. There was a Luther Bradish who was Lt.-Gov. of NY State. The biog. sketches of him in the DAB, Appleton, and NCAB do not mention his interest in agriculture. According to the Union List of Serials this was only part pub.)

The Traveller's Pocket Directory and Stranger's Guide: Exhibiting Distances on the Principal Canal and Stage Routes in the State of New York ... Descriptions of the Railroads Now Building ... List of Broken Banks ... Rates of Toll on the Canals ... Variety of Other Matter. Schenectady. Prntd. by S. Wilson for the pub. 1831. 69 pp. + 33 pp. of advts., some with illus. of Schenectady establishments.

VanDeWater, F. *Grey Riders. The Story of the New York State Troopers.* 1922. Illus. 370 pp.

Walworth, J. *History of New York, In Words of One Syllable.* 1881. illus. 186 pp. Colorful, illus. binding.

Washington (pseud.) *To the People of the United States on the Choice of a President.* Boston. Prntd. for the author. 1812. 28 pp. pamphlet. (An anti-DeWitt Clinton tract when he was running against James Madison for the U. S. presidency. The unknown author says of Clinton, "...friends he has none ... there is not a parasite in his livery that believes his own declarations....")

Whipple, G. *Freak Trees of the State of New York.* 1926. Syracuse. NY State College of Forestry. wrps. 17 pp. (There are 38 illus. of unusually shaped trees.)

Whittemore, H. *Fulfillment of Three Remarkable Prophecies in the History of the Great Empire State, Relating to the Development of Steamboat Navigation ... and Railroad Transportation 1808-1908.* 1909. Illus. 80 pp. (Steamboat and railroad hist. of NY State.)

Wilde, E. *The Civic Ancestry of New York - City and State.* NY. Pub. by the author. 1913. 3 Color plates. 80 pp. Lmtd. to 210 copies. (Actually a hist. of the Arms, Seals, and Medals of the city and state of NY.)

Williams, J. (ed.) *First Annual Industrial Directory of New York State.* 1912. index. 826 pp. (Descriptions of all towns with a population of over a thousand. There is very brief data on thousands of factories, and a vast number of tables.)

Williamson, J. *The American Hotel. An Anecdotal History.* 1930. Illus. index. 324 pp. (There are occasional references to hotels in NYC and State. Did you know that Crosby's Hotel in Albany was the scene of a romance between its chambermaid and the Mayor of Mexico City? They were married and she acquired much polish.)

Wittmeyer, Rev. A. (Ed.) *Registers of the Births, Marriages, Deaths of the "Eglise Francoise a la Nouvelle York", from 1688 to 1804.* NY. 1886. Collections of the Huguenot Soc. of America. Illus. Vol. 1 (all pub.) 431 pp. + a 42 pp. Index. Lmtd. to 500 copies.

(Wood, G. B.) *Journal of Dr. George B. Wood, of Pennsylvania. Aug. 1817-July 1829.* Pub. in 1939 as a Christmas gift. (Wood, 1797-1879, was a most prominent physician and medical Professor whose aristocratic diaposition prevented him from riding in a street car. See DAB. There are 12 pages on his trip through NY State in 1827 travelling to NYC, Long Island, Kauterskill Falls, and the Mohawk Valley. And there are 2 pp. on his trip in 1829 up the River to Hudson, and then through Lebanon to Pittsfield, MA. Probably only a few copies were prntd.)

Woodruff, R. *I worked on the Erie.* ca 1956. wrps. 140 pp. mimeo. (The author worked on the Erie Railroad for 48 years, becoming General Superintendant and Vice President. He tells of the joys and sorrows of running this famous line. I would guess that not too many copies were pub.)

Ye Sons of Patriots Gone, A Patriotic Song, Written, Composed, and Respectfully Dedicated, to the Democratic Republicans, by an Amateur. NY: Thos. Birch, Music Engraver, Printer and Pub., Wholesale and Retail. ca 1830. (This is a 2-page piece of sheet music, with white lettering and music on a green background. It has 6 verses and a chorus urging people to go to the Ballot Box to vote for Liberty and Laws. The Democratic Republicans were forced in the late 1820s to support Andrew Jackson, in 1832 they backed Jackson and Martin Van Buren on the national ticket; and they were the forerunners of the Democratic Party.)

STEUBEN COUNTY

STEUBEN COUNTY

Bull, W. *Incidents in the Early Settlement of Steuben Co. & Its Vicinity.* Jan. 1865. 6 pp. mss. in BHS.

Clayton, W. *History of Steuben Co.* Phil. 1879. illus. map. 2 vols. Reprntd. in 1976 in one vol., with 100 pp. Index.

Denniston, G. *Survey of Steuben Co. History ... 1789 to Present.* In: Transactions of the NY State Agricultural Society for 1861. Albany. 1862. map. 114 pp.

Hakes, H. (ed.) *Landmarks of Steuben Co.* Syracuse. 1896. illus. 909 pp.

McMaster, G. *History of Settlement of Steuben Co.* Bath. 1853. advts. 303 pp. Reprntd. 1893. Lmtd. to 300 copies. 207 pp. Reprntd. ca 1976.

Near, I. *History of Steuben Co.* Chicago. 1911. illus. 2 vols.

Pawling, G. *Over My Shoulder. A Backward Look at Life in a Steuben County Rural Community Before the 20th Century Changes.* Cameron Mills, NY. 1969. pub. by the author. wrps. 198 pp. Lmtd. ed. (Life in southern Steuben Co.)

Roberts, M. *Gazetteer of Steuben Co.* Syracuse. 1891. maps. 946 pp.

Stuart, W. *Who's Who in Steuben Co ... Steuben's Place in History.* Dansville. 1935. 294 pp.

Stuart, W. *Stories of the Kanisteo Valley.* 1920. illus. wrps. 208 pp. Lmtd. to 60 copies. (Repub. from the *Canisteo Chronicle* newspaper. The author later wrote, "It cannot be said that the advent of the volume produced any excitement....") 2nd ed. 1929. 146 pp. Lmtd. to 235 copies. (This work sold with amazing rapidity.) 3rd ed. Dansville, 1935. 261 pp. (Above 3 books, with same titles, are actually 3 different books.) This 3rd. ed. has a chapter on the little-known anti-rent troubles in Steuben Co.

Thrall, W. *Pioneer History & Atlas of Steuben Co.* Addison. 1942. maps. wrps. 98 pp.

BATH, Steuben Co.

Hull, N. (ed.) *Official Records of*

Centennial Celebration at Bath. June 4-7, 1893. Bath. 1893. maps. 280 pp.
Rogers, S. Centennial Celebration of Settlement of Town of Bath. 1893. 39 pp.
Smith, L. Half a Century of Village Development: The Social & Economic Development of Bath, Geneva, & Canandaigua. NY. 1736-1836. Masters' Thesis. Cornell U. 1948.

BOWLBY, Steuben Co.
Van Housen, I. A History of the Bowlby District. Bath. 1940. illus. 192 pp.

BRADFORD, Steuben Co.
Oliver, J. A Short History of Town of Bradford. Buffalo. 1947. 8 pp. typed mss. in BHS.

COHOCTON, Steuben Co.
Field & Waugh. History of Cohocton. Cohocton. 1916. 69 pp.
Folts, J. History of Town of Cohocton. Cohocton. 1965. illus. maps. 129 pp.

CORNING, Steuben Co.
Dimitroff and Janes. History of Corning - Painted Post area ... 200 Years in Painted Post Country. Pub. by Corning area Bicentennial Dec. 1977. illus. maps. index. bib. 384 pp. lmtd. to 2000 copies all of which were sold by Feb. 1978.
Mulford, U. Pioneer Days & Later Times in Corning, & Vicinity. 1789-1920. (1922) pub. by author. 528 pp.

HAMMONDSPORT, Steuben Co.
Anon. Hammondsport. ca 1920. illus. map. 19 pp.
Swarthout, L. A History of Hammondsport to 1962. Corning. 1971. pamphlet.

HORNELL, Steuben Co.
Near, I. Early History of Hornellsville. Hornell. 1890. 29 pp.

PAINTED POST, Steuben Co.
Anon. Indian Monument Dedication. Painted Post. May 28-30, 1950. illus. map. advts. wrps. unpaged
Erwin, C. Hist. ... of Painted Post, & of ... Erwin 1779-1874. Painted Post. 1874. 73 pp.
Reprntd. Painted Post. 1917. wrps. 85 pp.

PRATTSBURG, Steuben Co.
Van Valkenburgh, F. Grandpapa's Letters to His Children, Being the Story of a Boy's Life in a Country Village. 1835-1847. Norwalk, CT. 1958. pvtly. prntd. 95 pp.

TROUPSBURG, Steuben Co.
Bliss, M. (ed.) Hist of Troupsburg. 1977. Troupsburg. Bicent. Comm. 102 pp.

WAYLAND, Steuben Co.
Anon. Our Heritage. Wayland Area (North Cohocton, Atlanta, Perkinsville, Loon Lake, and Patchinville.) 1976. illus. map. index. 167 pp.
Jervis, C. A History of the Village of Wayland. 1901. illus. advts. wrps. 177 pp.

WOODHULL, Steuben Co.
Hollis, E. Early History of Woodhull, NY, and Family Records. 1913. wrps. index. advts. 54 pp.

SUFFOLK COUNTY

SUFFOLK COUNTY
Anon. Portrait & Biog. Record of Suffolk Co. NY. 1896. illus. 1039 pp.

Bayles, R. *Historical & Descriptive Sketches of Suffolk Co.* Port Jefferson. 1874. 433 pp. Reprntd. Port Washington. 1962. 424 pp.

Carse, R. *Centennial History of Suffolk County.* 1885.

(Cooper, J. & others) *History of Suffolk Co.* NY. 1882. illus. map. 488 pp.

Howell, N. *Know Suffolk, the Sunrise Co.* 1952. illus. 181 pp.

McDermott, C. *Suffolk Co.* NY. 1965. illus. 86 pp.

Nicholl, H. *Early History of Suffolk Co.* Brooklyn. 1866. 18 pp.

Titus, S. (ed) *History of Suffolk Co., Address at Riverhead Nov. 15, 1883.* Babylon. 1885. 125 pp.

Whitaker, E. & C. *Bicentennial. A History of Suffolk Co. Comprising the Addresses Delivered at the Celebrations ... Riverhead Nov. 15, 1883.* Babylon. 1885. 125 pp.

Wood, S. *Sketch of the Early Settlements of Long Island.* 1824. 66 pp. lmtd. to 250 copies. 2nd ed. 1826. 112 pp. Lmtd. to 200 copies. 3rd ed. 1828. Lmtd. to 100 copies. (One copy of this ed. has been located with pages 18-19 and 22-23 blank.) Reprntd. with life of Author, by Spooner, 1865. Reprntd. 1968

AMAGANSETT, Suffolk Co.
Field, L. *Amagansett Lore & Legend.* Amagansett. 1948. illus. maps. 125 pp.

AMITYVILLE, Suffolk Co.
Hemans, M. *Amityville, Past & Present.* 30 pp. typed mss. in Amityville Pub. Lib.

ASHAROKEN, Suffolk Co.
Brooks, E. *Short History of Asharoken.* 1953. 20 pp.

BABYLON, Suffolk Co.
Field, B. *Babylon Reminiscences. Sketch of the Author by J. Cooper. Historical Sketch of Babylon, by J. Eaton.* Babylon. 1911. illus. 80 pp.

Smith, R. *Brief History of Town of Babylon.* 1978. 12 pp.

BAYSHORE, Suffolk Co.
Ames, C. *250 Years in Bayshore & Bright Waters. 1708-1958.* ca 1958. advts. wrps. 40 pp.

Tuttle, E. *A Brief History of Bayshore.* ca 1963. mimeo. 96 pp.

BELLPORT, Suffolk Co.
Bigelow, S. *Bellport and Brookhaven, A Saga of the Sibling Hamlets at Old Purchase South.* 1979. illus. map. bib. index. 126 pp. (Covers 1700-1820).

BRENTWOOD, Suffolk Co.
Dyson, V. *A Century of Brentwood.* June 1950. illus. 300 pp. (Contains much data on the settlement of Modern Times, a little known quasi-free love community.)

--- *Supplement & Index to a Century of Brentwood.* 1953. wrps. 161 pp.

Linton, E. *Fifty Years After At Brentwood. 1855-May 30, 1905.* Brooklyn. ca 1905. illus. 8 pp.

BRIDGEHAMPTON, Suffolk Co.
Adams, J. *Memorials of Old Bridgehampton.* Bridgehampton. 1916. 399 pp. Reprntd. 1962. Port Washington. 399 pp. Lmtd. to 300 copies.

Clowes, E. *Wayfarings.* 1953. 346 pp.

Halsey, W. *Sketches From Local History.* 1935. many maps. 189 pp.

Hedges, H. *Centennial & Histori-*

cal Address Delivered at Bridge-Hampton, L.I. July 4, 1876. Sag Harbor. 1876. 24 pp.

BROOKHAVEN, Suffolk Co.
Bayles, T. *Historical Sketches of Brookhaven Town.* 1946.
Bayles, T. *Brookhaven Villages of 1874.* Brookhaven Bicentennial Commission. 1975. 12 pp.
Smith, E. *Brookhaven 1665-1876.* Hist. sketch. (1876.) 10 pp.

CENTRAL ISLIP, Suffolk Co.
Dyson, V. *The History of Central Islip.* 1954. illus. map. advts. 104 pp.

COLD SPRING HARBOR, Suffolk Co.
Anon. *Cold Spring Harbor Soundings.* 1953. 85 pp.
Valentine & Newman. *Main St. Cold Spring Harbor.* 1960. 28 pp.

CORAM, Suffolk Co.
Anon. *An Ancient Settlement. Historical Article in Suffolk Every Sunday, April 10, 1932.*

COW NECK, Suffolk Co.
Dodge, R. *Tristram Dodge & His Descendants in America, With History & Description ... of Block Island, & Cow Neck, Long Island, NY.* 1886. 233 pp.

CUTCHOGUE, Suffolk Co.
Jefferson, W. *Cutchogue, Southold's First Colony, NY.* 1940. illus. Lmtd. to 500 copies. 166 pp.

DEER PARK, Suffolk Co.
Dyson, V. *Deer Park & Wyandanch History.* 1957. illus. map. advts. 133 pp.

EAST HAMPTON, Suffolk Co.
Beecher, L. *A Sermon Containing a General History of Town of East Hampton.* Sag Harbor. 1806. 40 pp. Reprntd. Lyons, Iowa. 1886. 24 pp.
Gardiner, D. *Chronicles of Town of East Hampton.* NY. 1871. Lmtd. to 100 copies. 121 pp. (orig. pub. in the *Corrector*, ca 1840.)
Hedges, H. *History of Town of East Hampton.* Sag Harbor. 1897. 344 pp.
--- *The 200th Anniv. of Settlement of East Hampton.* Sag Harbor. 1850. 101 pp.
Miller, M. *An East Hampton Childhood.* 1938. wrps. illus. 44 pp. (Miller was born in 1849.)
Rattray, J. *East Hampton History With Genealogies.* 1953. 619 pp.
Rattray, J. *Up & Down Main Street. An Informal History.* 1968. map. 152 pp.
--- *Three Centuries in East Hampton.* 1937. 44 pp.
Seabury, S. *275 Years of East Hampton.* East Hampton. 1926. illus. 140 pp. (Also issued in a Deluxe Ed. of 100 copies boxed.)

EAST WILLISTON, Suffolk Co.
Meyer, N. *East Williston History, 1663-1978.* 1978. illus. map. bib. index. 68 pp. (See also **EAST WILLISTON**, Nassau Co.)

EATON'S NECK, Suffolk Co.
Voyse, M. *History of Eaton's Neck.* 1955. 42 pp. 3rd. printing 1958.

FIRE ISLAND, Suffolk Co.
Hildreth, E. *Between Bay & Ocean.* NY. 1960. illus. 92 pp.
Shaw, E. *Legends of Fire Island Beach & the South Side.* NY. 1895. illus. 121 pp.

FISHER'S ISLAND, Suffolk Co.
Ferguson, H. *Fishers Island 1614-1925*. 1925. pvtly. prntd. illus. 104 pp. (The Ferguson family owned the island.) Reprntd. in 1974.

GARDINER'S ISLAND, Suffolk Co.
Payne, R. *The Island.* NY. 1958. illus. map. 248 pp. 1478
Rattray, J. *Gardiner's Island ... A Collection of Historical Highlights.* 1958. illus. 50 pp.

HAUPPAUGE, Suffolk Co.
Wood, S. *A History of Hauppauge.* NY. 1920. ed. by C. Werner. Lmtd. to 100 copies. 92 pp.

HEAD OF THE HARBOR, Suffolk Co.
Van Liew, B. (Comp.) *Fifty Years. 1928-1978, Head of the Harbor, Suffolk Co.* NY. 1978. illus. map. bib. index. 78 pp.

HUNTINGTON, Suffolk Co.
Gould & Klaber. *Colonial Huntington. 1653-1800.* 1953. 92 pp.
Hall, M. *The Heart of Huntington.* 1958. mimeo. maps. 18 pp.
Johnston, G. *Detailed History of the Original Township of Huntington.* 1926.
Lott, R. (town historian) *Huntington Tap Roots.* 1960. 52 pp.
Pelletreau, W. *Silas Wood's Sketch of the Town of Huntington, From its First Settlement to the End of the Revolution ... Ed. with Genealogical Notes by Pelletreau.* NY. 1898. Lmtd. 215 copies 63 pp.
Platt, H. *Old Times in Huntington.* Hntngton. 1876. 83 pp.
(Sammis, R.) *Huntington-Babylon Town History.* (Huntington.) 1937. 296 pp.

Wood, Silas. *A Brief Statement of the Claim ... of Huntington to Cap-Tree Island, Oak Island & Grass Island ... in the South Bay.* Brooklyn. 1816. 16 pp.
--- *A Sketch of the Geography of...Huntington, With Brief Hist of Its First Settlement & Condition to End of the Rev.* Wash., D. C. 1824. 30 pp. A lmtd. ed. (Wood was Congressman. Many copies lost when fire burned neighbor's home.) Rprtd 1898. Ed. With genealogical notes by W. Pelletreau. index. 63 pp. lmtd. to 215 copies.

ISLIP, Suffolk Co.
Weeks, G. (town historian) *Some of the Town of Islip's Early History.* 1955. Lmtd. 350 copies. 160 pp.

LAKE RONKONKOMA, Suffolk Co.
Watts, L. *Historical Footprints at Lake Ronkonkoma.* 1963.

LLOYD HARBOR, Suffolk Co.
Alexander, I. *A History of the Incorporated Village of Lloyd Harbor. 1926-1976.* 1977. illus. map. 88 pp.

MATTITUCK, Suffolk Co.
Craven, C. *A History of Mattituck.* 1906. pub. for author. illus. map. 400 pp.

MIDDLE ISLAND, Suffolk Co.
Bayles, T. *Bygone Days in Middle Island, Coram, Yaphank, Middle Island.* 1947. 12 pp.

MILLER PLACE, Suffolk Co.
Gass, M. *History of Miller Place.* 1971. 70 pp.

MONTAUK, Suffolk Co.
Ayres, J. *Legends of Montauk*

With Historical Appendix. Hartford. 1849. 127 pp. (Mostly poetry.)
Rattray, J. *Montauk, Three Centuries of Romance, Sport, Adventure.* East Hampton. 1938. illus. 95 pp.
--- *Ship Ashore! A Record of Maritime Disasters off Montauk. 1640-1955.* 1955. 256 pp.

NORTHPORT, Suffolk Co.
Hendrie, C. *Historical Vignettes of Great Cow Harbor.* Northport. 1969. pamphlet.

ORIENT, Suffolk Co.
Anon. *Historical Review: Word & Picture Journey Into Orient Past.* 1959. illus. map. 39 pp.
Griffin, A. *Griffin's Journal. First Settlers of Southold. First Proprietors of Orient.* 1857. 312 pp.

PATCHOGUE, Suffolk Co.
Anon. *The Argus Business & Residential Directory of Patchogue, With Historical Sketch.* Patchogue. 1904.
Reeve, B. *Reminiscences of Patchogue at Centennial Celebration July 4, 1876.* Rvrhd. 1906. pvtly. prntd. 7 pp.

PECONIC, Suffolk Co.
Newell, R. *A Rose of the Nineties.* (1962.) illus. 115 pp.

PORT JEFFERSON, Suffolk Co.
Welles and Proios. *Port Jefferson: History of a Village.* 1977. illus. map. index. 84 pp. (Much on shipbuilding.)

QUOGUE, Suffolk Co.
Post, R. *Notes on Quogue 1659-1959.* 1959. illus. 88 pp.

RIVERHEAD, Suffolk Co.
Hallock, L. *Riverhead the Town of Many Ports.* ca 1963. mimeo. 5 pp.
Meier, E. *The Riverhead Story. 1792-1967.* 52 pp.
Miller, G. *History of Town of River Head, Read at Centennial Celebration. July 4, 1876.* 8 pp.

SAG HARBOR, Suffolk Co.
Anon. *Sag Harbor in the Land of the Sunrise Trail 1707-1927.* 1927. 52 pp.
Sleight, H. *Sag Harbor in Earlier Days. A Series of Historical Sketches of the Harbor & Hampton Port.* Sag Harbor. 1930. index. 293 pp. Lmtd. to 200 copies.
Hedges, H. *Early Sag Harbor.* Sag Harbor. 1902. 51 pp.
Willey, N. *The Story of Sag Harbor.* Sag Harbor. 1939. illus. 20 pp.
2nd printing. 1945.
3rd printing. 1949.
4th printing. 1954.

SALTAIRE, Suffolk Co.
Dobie, R. *History of Incorporated Village of Saltaire, Fire Island.* 1952. mimeo. 58 pp.

SAYVILLE, Suffolk Co.
Edwards, C. *A History of Early Sayville.* Sayville. 1935. illus. map. wrps. 40 pp.

SETAUKET, Suffolk Co.
Adkins, E. *Setauket, The First 300 Years. 1655-1955.* 1955. 108 pp.

SHELTER ISLAND, Suffolk Co.
Anon. *Shelter Island 300th Anniv. Celebration 1652-1952.* 1952. 35 pp.
Duvall, R. *History of Shelter Island. 1652-1932.* Staten Island Heights. 1932. 229 pp.
2nd. ed. with supplement 1932-1952 by J. Schladermundt.

Staten Island Heights. 1952. illus. map. 304 pp.

Horsford, C. *The Manor of Shelter Island*. NY. 1934. illus. 27 pp.

Mallman, J. *Historical Papers on Shelter Island, & Its Presbyterian Church With Genealogical Tables.* NY. 1899. illus. 332 pp.

Wortis, H. *A Woman Named Matilda and Other True Accounts of Old Shelter Island.* 1978. illus. map. bib. 79 pp. (Reprint of 6 articles from the Long Island Forum.)

SMITHTOWN, Suffolk Co.

Smith, J. *The History of Smithtown.* 1961. illus. map. 40 pp. (Reprntd. from Cooper's *History of Suffolk Co. 1882.*)

SOUTHAMPTON, Suffolk Co.

Adams, J. *History of Town of Southampton (East of Canoe Place).* Bridgehampton. 1918. 424 pp.

Reprntd. Port Washington. 1962. 110 pp. of illus. Lmtd. to 300 copies. 424 pp.

Halsey, A. *In Old Southampton.* 1940. index. illus. 144 pp. Another ed: 1952.

Howell, G. *Early History of Southampton.* NY. 1866. 318 pp. (Has genealogies.)
2nd. ed. revised, corrected, enlarged. Albany. 1887. 473 pp.
--- *When Southampton & Southold on Long Island Were Settled.* Albany. 1882. 14 pp.

Manley, H. *No Mans Land.* 1953. 8 pp.

Pelletreau, W. *Centennial Celebration at Southampton July 4, 1876.* Sag Harbor. 1876.

SOUTHOLD, Suffolk Co.

Anon. *Celebration for the 250th Anniv. of the Formation of the Town & Church of Southold.* Southold. 1890. 220 pp.

Case, A. *Historical Sketch of Southold Read July 4, 1876.* Revised & corrected. Greenpoint. 1876. 16 pp.
Reprntd. Southold. 1931.

Currie-Bell, A. *Old Southold Town's Tercentenary 1640-1940.* 1940. 161 pp.

Hedges, P. *An Address Delivered Before the Suffolk Co. Historical Soc. Oct. 1, 1889. (On the Claim of Southold to Priority of Settlement over Southampton).* Sag Harbor. 1889. 14 pp.

Howell, G. *Settlement of Southold.* Babylon. 1894. 4 pp.

(Jefferson, W.) *Southold Town 1636-1939. Oldest English Settlement in State of N.Y.* ca 1939. 103 pp.

Whitaker, E. *History of Southold.* Southold. 1881. 354 pp.
--- *Whitaker's Southold: Being a ... Reproduction of the Hist of Southold, L.I., Its First Century,* by Rev. Whitaker. ed by Rev. C. Craven. Princeton, NJ. 1931. illus. 194 pp.

STONY BROOK, Suffolk Co.

Lapham, E. *Stony Brook Secrets.* NY. 1942. illus. 146 pp.

WADING RIVER, Suffolk Co.

Anon. *Wading River. 1671-1971.* 1971.

Meier, E. *The Wading River, Pauguaconsuk.* Riverhead. 1955. 50 pp.

WATER MILL, Suffolk Co.

Halsey, A. *Harvest of Water Mill History.* 1978. wrps. 62 pp.

WEST ISLIP, Suffolk Co.

Wilcox, G. & J. *First History of West Islip.* 1976. 161 pp.

WESTHAMPTON BEACH, Suffolk Co.

Rogers, B. *Historical Sketch of Incorporated Village of Wes-*

thampton Beach 1640-1951. Islip. (1953.) illus. map. index. 151 pp.

YAPHANK, Suffolk Co.
Homan, L. *Yaphank As It Is & Was & Will Be ... An Impartial Description of the Advantages & Disadvantages Enjoyed & Suffered by Its Citizens.* NY. 1875. illus. 220 pp.

SULLIVAN COUNTY

SULLIVAN COUNTY
Child, H. *Gazetteer & Business Directory of Sullivan Co.* 1872. map. 350 pp. (Has a large section on co. hist. Includes an 18 pp. condensation of Quinlan's biog. of Tom Quick, the Indian fighter) Reprntd. in 1975.
Feldman, B. (ed) *Brass Buttons & Leather Boots. Sullivan Co. & the Civil War.* Nov. 1963. illus. maps. 84 pp.
(Heidt, W.) *Frances J. Knapp's 103 Years, A Brief History of the Development of Sullivan Co.* 1956. wrps. 36 pp. (Not her memories, but a recounting of what took place in the co. during her lifetime: 1837-1839.)
Quinlan, J. *History of Sullivan Co.* Liberty. 1873. 700 pp. (It has been said there were also 20 or less copies bound in fine leather.)
Reprntd. ca 1966.
Reprntd. in 1975.

BLOOMINGBURGH, Sullivan Co.
Lloyd, J. P. *Bloomingburgh Memories.* 1976. illus. with 24 full-page drawings by the author. Map of Bloomingburgh is dated 1908. 70 pp. (The author's memories of Bloomingburgh in the early 1900s. There is some brief data on many people, including Spiketooth Decker, and a German in World War I who flew the American flag when he was sober and the German flag when he had been drinking. Among the customs he saw disappear were openly bought votes and dog-dropping collectors. Although it does not state so, I would assume this was a lmtd. ed., pub. and sold by the author.)

CALLICOON, Sullivan Co.
Graham, J. *The Calicoon Historian.* Hancock. 1892. wrps. advts. 64 pp.
Hicks, C. *History of Town of Callicoon.* 1942. illus. 49 pp.

COCHECTON, Sullivan Co.
Cochecton Bicentennial Committee. *The Cochecton Papers, Being a Miscellaneous Collection of Documents (both new and old), Histories, Recollections. Map and Pictures. All Relating to the Township of Cochecton.* 1977. wrps. 104 pp.
Sinnett, C. *Pioneer Days at Cochecton.* Copied from Original Nathan Skinner Records. Fertile, Minn. (1924) 29 pp. typed mss. in NYPL. Prntd. in booklet form ca 1970.

FREMONT, Sullivan Co.
Hick, C. *The Town of Fremont.* 1954. 14 pp. (Reprint of articles in *Sullivan Co. Democrat.*)

HARTWOOD, Sullivan Co.
Campbell, C. *Traditions of Hartwood.* 1930. illus. 155 pp.

LIBERTY, Sullivan Co.
(Pinney, E. & others) *Liberty. Cent. Addresses 1907.* 20 pp.

LONG EDDY, Sullivan Co.
Meyers, A. *Douglas, the Delaware Valley City. 1867-1878.* Long Eddy. 1969. wrps. 24 pp.

MONTICELLO, Sullivan Co.
Curley, E. *Old Monticello.* Monticello. 1930. illus. 192 pp. (Memories of the author.) Reprntd. in 1978.

NARROWSBURG, Sullivan Co.
Skinner, J. *Historical Sketch of Narrowsburg & Vicinity.* 1932. wrps. 50 pp. (Mostly reprints of articles in *Delaware Valley News*)

TUSTEN, Sullivan Co.
Anon. *Tusten Centennial.* 1953. 60 pp.
Meyers, A. *And They Called it Tusten.* 1967. wrps. 65 pp.

WURTSBORO Sullivan Co.
Anon. *Wurtsboro, Sullivan Co. & Mamakating Park.* Issued by Board of Trade and the Mamakating Park, Wurtsboro, ca 1890-1900. wrps. 62 pp. of early illus., one page of hist.

TIOGA COUNTY

TIOGA COUNTY
Kingman, L. (ed.) *Our County & Its People.* Elmira. 1897. illus. 2 vols.
Peirce & Hurd. *History of Tioga, Chemung, Tompkins, & Schuyler Cos.* Phil. 1879. illus. maps. 2 vols. (Index by N. Sheldon, 1965, mimeo., in SPL)

NEWARK VALLEY, Tioga Co.
Purple, G. *As We Remember the Village of Newark Valley From 1880 to 1937.* ca 1937. illus. unpaged.
Settle, L. *Our Native Town.* NY. 1913. illus. 48 pp.

OWEGO, Tioga Co.
Kingman, L. (ed.) *Owego Sketches by Owego Authors.* Owego. 1904. illus. 126 pp.
--- *Owego, Some Account of the Early Settlement.* Owego. 1907. illus. lmtd to 50 copies. 673 pp.

SPENCER, Tioga Co.
Estelle ... (comp.) *Spencer, How It Was Named. Some of its History ... Masonic History.* 1962. wrps. mimeo. 24 pp.
Ferris, F. *Some Spencer History.* Ithaca. 1958. wrps. 113 pp.

WAVERLY, Tioga Co.
Albertson, C. *History of Waverly & Vicinity.* Waverly. 1943. 319 pp. (Orig. pub. weekly in Waverly *Sun-Record.*)

TOMPKINS COUNTY

TOMPKINS COUNTY
(Anon.) *Tompkins County History.* 1879. 288 pp. Reprntd. ca 1976.
Bell, B. *Glance Backward.* 1970. pub. by the author. wrps. illus. 89 pp. (Hist. of the co.)
Day, C. (comp.) *Report of the Semi-Centennial Jubilee & Reunion of the Half Century Club of Tompkins Co., Sept. 8, 1881, With Historical & Biog. Sketches ... Also a Full List of Residents of the Co. Over 70 Years of Age.* Ithaca. 1881. 132 pp.
Lee, H. *History of Railroads in Tompkins Co.* Ithaca. 1947. illus. maps. wrps. 48 pp.
Mara and Sachse. *The Spirit of Enterprise. 19th Century in Tompkins County.* 1977. bib. 20 pp.
Morris, W. (co. historian) *Early Explorers & Travelers in Tompkins Co.* Ithaca. 1961. wrps. 68 pp.

--- Old Indian Trails in Tompkins Co. Ithaca. 1944. illus. maps. wrps. 32 pp.
--- Origin of Place Names in Tompkins Co. Ithaca. 1951. illus. maps. 56 pp.
Selkreg, J. Landmarks of Tompkins Co. Syracuse. 1894. illus. maps. 276 pp.
Walrath, F. A History of the Agriculture of Tompkins Co. Ph.D. Thesis, Cornell U. 1927.

CAROLINE, Tompkins Co.
Heidt, W. Jr. Forests to Farm in Caroline. Ithaca. 1965. illus. maps. 58 pp.

CAYUGA BRIDGE, Tompkins Co.
Wells, J. Cayuga Bridge. Ithaca. 1961. 18 pp.

DRYDEN, Tompkins Co.
Ameri, N. Twenty-Five Years of Change in the Business Side of Farming 1927-1952. Masters' Thesis, Cornell U. 1953.
Goodrich, G. (ed.) Centennial History of Town of Dryden, 1797-1898. 1898. illus. map. 272 pp.
Kensler, G. A Sociological Analysis of Village of Dryden, With An Historical Interpretation. Masters' Thesis, Cornell U. 1927.
(Rumsey, H.) History of Dryden From 1797-1857, by the Old Man in the Clouds. Transcribed by B. Clark, town of Dryden historian. 1961. wrps. 19 pp. (Reprntd. from articles pub. in Rumsey's Companion, 1857, believed to have been written by H. Rumsey.)

ELLIS HOLLOW, Tompkins Co.
Pritchard, Z. Ellis Hollow Lore ... Pioneer Days, Yesteryear, & Today. Ithaca. 1962. map. wrps. 54 pp.

FREEVILLE, Tompkins Co.
Genung, A. Historical Sketch of Village of Freeville. 1943. lmtd. to five typed copies. 153 pp. (copy in DeWitt Hist. Soc., Ithaca.)

GROTON, Tompkins Co.
Baldwin, M. Historical Sketch of the Town of Groton. Groton. 1868. advts. wrps. 40 pp. Reprntd. Groton 1923, titled The Beginnings of Groton, minus some statistics. Includes Reminiscences of Capt. W. E. Mount which was reprntd. from Grip's Historical Souvenir 1899. (See below.)
Welch, E. Grip's Historical Souvenir of Groton & Vicinity. Albany. 1899. illus. 58 pp.

ITHACA, Tompkins Co.
Abt, H. Ithaca. Ithaca. 1926. illus. map. 251 pp.
Goodwin, H. Ithica As It Was and As It Is. Ithaca. 1853. 64 pp.
King, H. Early History of Ithica (sic.), A Lecture of April 5, 1847. Ithaca. 1847. 21 pp. (Only a few copies were prntd., and some of them were destroyed in a printing office fire.)
Kurtz, M. Ithaca & Its Resources. Historical & Descriptive of the Forest City. Ithaca. 1883. illus. 122 pp.

LANSING, Tompkins Co.
Parish, I. (town historian) It Happened in Lansing. 1964. 78 pp.
Parish, I. This Too Happened in Lansing. Ithaca. 1967. wrps. map. 78 pp.

LANSING TOWNSHIP, Tompkins Co.
Hoecher, R. A Study of the Farm Mortgage History in Lansing Township, Tompkins Co.

1860-1938. Masters' Thesis, Cornell U. 1939.

LUDLOWVILLE, Tompkins Co.
Conlon, J. *Silently They Stand.* Ithaca. 1966. 26 pp.

TRUMANSBURG, Tompkins Co.
Free Press (comp.) *History of Trumansburg.* 1890. illus. 116 pp.
Martin, C. *Trumansburg, NY.* 1972. pamphlet.
Sears, L. *A History of Trumansburg, NY. 1792-1967.* pvtly. prntd. 1968. wrps. maps. illus. 186 pp.

ULYSSES, Tompkins Co.
(Thomas, A.) *Notes from the Diary of Abner H. Thomas, Town of Ulysses. 1863-64-65.* Transcribed by His Daughter, E. A. Thomas 1948. Ithaca. 1960. wrps. 46 pp.

TRYON COUNTY

(Tryon Co. no longer exists. Originally it covered a very large area west of Albany.)
Anon. *150th. Anniv. of Tryon Co.* Souvenir Program. 1922. illus. wrps. 40 pp.
Campbell, W. *Annals of Tryon Co., or The Border Warfare of NY During the Revolution.* NY. 1831. map. illus. 269 pp.
2nd. ed. NY. 1849. Titled: *The Border Warfare of NY.* map. 396 pp.
Reprntd. Cherry Valley. 1880. 312 pp.
Reprntd. NY. 1924. map. 257 pp.

ULSTER COUNTY

ULSTER COUNTY
Alliteraricus. *Mother Goose History of Ulster County, and Anniversary Songs. 1658-1908.* 1908. wrps. 22 pp. (Nonsense poems about almost every town in the co. Sample: "There once was a man of Katrine, Who sat on a can of benzine. He happened to scratch a lucifer match, And, since then, he hasn't been seen.")
Anon. *Biog. Record of Ulster Co.* Chicago. 1896. illus. 1330 pp.
Brink, B. M. (ed. & pub.) *Olde Ulster. An Historical and Genealogical Magazine.* Kingston. 1905-1914. (This was a monthly magazine pub. from Jan. 1905 through Dec. 1914, featuring Ulster Co. hist. and genealogy.)
Clearwater, A. (ed) *History of Ulster Co.* Kingston. 1907. illus. index. 712 pp. (The author still had copies for sale in 1930.)
Plank, W. *Banners & Bugles, Ulster Co. in the Civil War.* Newburgh. 1963. illus. maps. 164 pp.
Sylvester, N. *History of Ulster Co.* Phil. 1880. illus. 2 vols. Reprntd. in one vol. in 1977.
Van Buren, A. *History of Ulster Co. Under the Dominion of the Dutch.* Kingston. 1923. 146 pp.
Zimm, L. (ed) *Southeastern NY: Ulster, Dutchess, Orange, Rockland, Putnam Cos.* NY. 1946. illus. three vols.

ALDER LAKE, Ulster Co.
Gerrow, J. *Alder Lake.* Liberty. 1953. lmtd. to 400 copies. 138 pp.

BIG INDIAN, Ulster Co.
Aley, L. *The Valley, Facts and Legends on Big Indian and Oliverea.* 1973. wrps. 37 pp.

CLINTONDALE, Ulster Co.
Mitchell, P. *History of Village of Clintondale.* 1894. illus. advts. wrps. 48 pp.

Van Siclen & Hurd. *History of Village of Clintondale.* Sept. 1959. illus. maps. wrps. 48 pp.

ELLENVILLE, Ulster Co.
Anon. *Early Ellenville Industries (Including Napanoch).* n.d. mimeo. 11 pp.
Anon. *Sesquicentennial of Ellenville 1805-1955.* illus. advts. 46 pp.
Charles, C. *Ellenville, A History for Young People.* 1976. wrps. 16 pp.
Sanderson, D. *Ellenville Days & Ways Until 1897.* 1968 pub. by author. illus. map on dust jacket. 166 pp.

ESOPUS, Ulster Co.
Polhemus, M. (Ed.) *Town of Esopus Story 3000 BC - 1978 AD.* 1979. illus. map. index. 456 pp.

GARDINER, Ulster Co.
Hasbrouck, K. (town historian) *History of Town of Gardiner 1853-1953.* 1953. illus. map. wrps. 68 pp. Reprntd. in 1978. 65 pp.

HURLEY, Ulster Co.
Anon. *Historic Town of Hurley.* n.d. illus. map. 12 pp. folder ("This is the first of three issues depicting Hurley's houses of history.")
--- 2nd. issue. ca 1959. 12 pp.
Anon. *Hurley's 300th Anniv. 1661-1961.* illus. map. wrps. 20 pp.

KINGSTON, Ulster Co.
DeWitt, W. (city historian) *Peoples Hist of Kingston, Rondout, & Vicinity (1820-1943).* 1943. illus. 445 pp. (Brings Schoonmaker's hist. up to date. See below.)
Forsyth, M. *The Beginnings of New York, Old Kingston, the First State Capitol.* Boston. 1909. 67 pp.
Fowler, E. *The Founding & Early Development of Kingston ... With Description & Views of Old Houses Standing at the Time Kingston Was Burned by British, Oct. 16, 1777.* (Kingston.) 1924. illus. 47 pp.
Fried, M. *Early History of Kingston and Ulster Co.* NY. 1975. 206 pp. maps.
Hendricks, H. *The City of Kingston ... A History.* Kingston. (1902.) Issued gratuitously. 70 pp.
Hickey, A. *The Story of Kingston 1609-1952.* NY. 1952. illus. bib. index. 233 pp.
Schoonmaker, A. *The History of Kingston ... to 1820.* NY. 1888. illus. map. index. 558 pp.

LLOYD, Ulster Co.
Sherwood, W. *History ... of Lloyd 1953.* wrps. illus. map. 180 pp. (Sherwood wrote longer hist. - never pub.)

MARBLETOWN, Ulster Co.
Anon. *Marbletown Album 1669-1977.* 1977. Stone Ridge Library. 107 pp.

MARLBORO, Ulster Co.
Bensel, A. *History ... of Marlborough.* 1857. 12 pp. (9 pp. of amusing nonsense; 3 pp. of precinct records 1772-1779.)
Cochrane, C. *History of Town of Marlboro From its First Settlement in 1712 by Capt. Wm. Bond to 1887.* Poughkeepsie. 1887. illus. map. 202 pp.
Plank, W. *History of Town of Marlboro. 350th. Anniversary.* wrps. advts. map. 48 pp. lmtd. to 1000 copies. (Includes Milton & Lattingtown.)
Woolsey, C. *History of Town of Marlboro.* Albany. 1908. illus. maps. 471 pp.

MODENA, Ulster Co.
Hasbrouck, K. *History of Modena.* 1949. illus. map. wrps. 19 pp.

NEW HURLEY, Ulster Co.
Hasbrouck, K. *History of New Hurley, The Flint, Plains Road, Sherwood Corners, St. Elmo.* 1949. illus. map. wrps. 25 pp.

NEW PALTZ, Ulster Co.
Anon. *The Paltz Patent.* ca 1950. wrps. 8 pp.
DuBois, C. (comp.) *The Story of the Paltz.* 1936. pvtly. prntd. illus. 55 pp.
Elting, I. *Dutch Village Communities on the Hudson River.* Baltimore. 1886. 68 pp. (vol. 4 of John Hopkins Univ. Studies in Hist. & Political Science. Much on New Paltz.)
Hasbrouck & Heidgerd. *Historic New Paltz.* New Paltz. 1959. maps. wrps. mimeo. 100 pp.
Hasbrouck, K. *New Paltz. Brief History of the Village.* New Paltz. 1950. illus. wrps. 43 pp.
Lefevre, R. *History of New Paltz & Its Old Families (1678-1820).* 1903. 593 pp.
Appendix to the *History of New Paltz* by Lefevre. n.d. illus. index. 208 pp. (This was pub. separately after the first ed. was issued, and it was incorporated into the 2nd. ed.)
2nd ed. Albany. 1909. Reprntd. in 1973.
7th Grade, New Paltz Central School. 1961. *New Paltz 1677-1961.* wrps. illus. maps. bib. 60 pp.

OLIVE, Ulster Co.
Sickler, V. *History of Town of Olive. 1812-1973.* wrps. 48 pp.
Sickler, V. *Town of Olive Through the Years. Part 1.* 1976. wrps. 96 pp.
Sickler, V. *The Town of Olive Through the Years. Part 2.* 1979. pub. by the author. 60 pp. (Also has data on the towns of Shokan and Ashokan.)

PINE HILL, Ulster Co.
Smith, N. *Pine Hill.* 1976. wrps. 64 pp.

ROSENDALE, Ulster Co.
Gilchrist, A. *Footsteps Across Cement, A Hist. of the Township of Rosendale.* 1976. 174 pp.
Rosendale Township Assn. *Rosendale.* 1934. illus. map. advts. wrps. 40 pp.

SAUGERTIES, Ulster Co.
Barritt & Jernegan. *The Pearl. Saugerties. Vol. 1 No. 1 through Vol. 1 No. 12 (1875).* 8 pp. each issue. Map showing probably every house in the village up to 1876. Each issue has three photographs of local scenes, taken expressly for this work. Approximately 250 copies of each issue were pub. (Much Saugerties hist.)
Brink, B. *The Early History of Saugerties 1660-1825.* Kingston. 1902. illus. 365 pp.

SHANDAKEN, Ulster Co.
Anon. *Shandaken Bicentennial.* 1976. wrps. 36 pp.

SHAWANGUNK, Ulster Co.
Hasbrouck, K. *History of Township of Shawangunk.* 1955. illus. maps. wrps. 76 pp.

STONE RIDGE, Ulster Co.
--- *A History of Stone Ridge* was written in mss. form but has been lost.

WALKILL, Ulster Co.
Anon. *Souvenir of "The Liveliest Spot on Earth".* Walkill, NY. 1922. wrps. illus. 27 pp.

WAWARSING, Ulster Co.
Bevier, A. *The Indians, or Narrative of Massacres & Depredations on the Frontier.* Rondout. 1846. 79 pp. Reprntd. ca 1970s.
Terwilliger. *Wawarsing, Where the Streams Wind. Historical Glimpses of the Town.* 1977. 350 pp.

WOODSTOCK, Ulster Co.
LeGallienne, R. *Woodstock, An Essay. With Reproductions of Work by Woodstock Artists.* 1923. advts. wrps. 40 pp.
Rose, W. *The Vanishing Village.* NY. (1963.) 350 pp. Reprntd. in 1970.
Smith, A. *Woodstock History & Hearsay.* 1959. illus. map. index. 209 pp.
Smith, A. *It Happened in Woodstock.* 1972. 165 pp. (This is an abridged & updated version of entry *Woodstock History and Hearsay*.

WARREN COUNTY

WARREN COUNTY
Brown, W. (ed.) *History of Warren Co.* 1963. illus. map. 302 pp.
Mason, H. *Backward Glances. Reminiscences of Warren Co.* 1963. illus. Vol. 1. 138 pp.
Vol. 2. 1964. illus. 146 pp.
Vol. 3. 1965. illus. 111 pp.
(Above 3 vols. based on articles in Glens Falls newspapers)
Smith, H. *History of Warren Co.* Syracuse. 1885. illus. map. 702 pp.
WPA GUIDE. *Warren Co. A History & Guide.* (Glens Falls.) 1942. illus. map. 275 pp.

ADIRONDACK, Warren Co.
Masten, A. *The Story of Adirondack.* 1923. map. pvtly. prntd. illus. lmtd. to 125 copies. 199 pp. Rprntd. Syracuse in 1968, with new illus. and introduction.

GLENS FALLS, Warren Co.
Anon. *Bridging the Years. 1763-1978.* Glens Falls, NY. 1978. Glens Falls Hist. Association. map. 239 pp.
Holden, J. *Glens Falls, The "Empire City" & Past & Place in History.* Glens Falls. 1908. illus. 48 pp.
Hyde, L. *History of Glens Falls.* Glens Falls. 1936. illus. pvtly. prntd. lmtd. to 300 copies. 347 pp. (Ed. by W. Hill after Hyde died in 1934.)
Van Dusen, R. *Glimpses of the Past.* 1970. pamphlet.

LUZERNE, Warren Co.
Anon. *A Peep at Luzerne.* Albany. 1877. wrps. 22 pp.
Butler, B. *From Home Spun to Calico.* Albany. 1877. 52 pp.

QUEENSBURY, Warren Co.
Holden, A. *History of Town of Queensbury.* Albany. 1874. illus. 519 pp.

SILVER BAY, Warren Co.
King, C. *Ondia-ta-Doc-Te ... Being a History of Lake George With Special Reference to Silver Bay At Sabbath Day Point.* Hudson Falls. 1935. illus. maps. 67 pp.
Worman ... *The Silver Bay Story 1902-1952.* 1952. illus. 133 pp.

WASHINGTON COUNTY

WASHINGTON COUNTY
Anon. *History & Biog. of Washington Co. & the Town of Queensbury.* Richmond, IN. 1894. illus. 436 pp. Also pub. 1894 with Chicago imprint.
Corey, A. *Gazetteer of County of*

Washington. Schuylerville. 1850. maps. 264 pp.

Fitch, A. *Historical, Topographical, & Agricultural Survey of Co. of Washington, 1848.* 97 pp. (In: Transactions of the NY State Agricultural Soc. 1848. This brings the co. hist. down to just prior to the Revolutionary War.) The hist. was continued in the Transactions of the Soc. for 1849. maps. 191 pp.

Gill, I. *History of Washington Co. History of the Argyle Patent.* Greenwich 1956. 87 pp. (Probably a continuation of Hill's works on Washington Co. See following entries under Hill.)

Hill, W. *A Brief History of the Printing Press in Washington, Saratoga, & Warren Cos. with Checklist of Their Publications Prior to 1825.* Rutland, VT. 1930. pvtly. prntd. Lmtd. to 54 copies. 117 pp. Supplement prntd. in Addenda Part 2 Old Ft. Edward. See **FORT EDWARD**.)

--- (comp) *History of Washington Co.* Ft. Edward. 1932. Unnumbered vol. pvtly prntd. Lmtd. to 125 copies. 298 pp.

Vol. 1 Brooklyn. 1954. lmtd. 200 copies.

Vol. 2 Brooklyn. 1955. lmtd. 200 copies.

Vol. 3 Brooklyn. 1956. lmtd. 200 copies.

Johnson, C. *History of Washington Co.* Phil. 1878. illus. map. 504 pp. Rprntd. in 1979.

Stone, W. *Washington Co.* NY. 1901. illus. 870 pp.

ARGYLE, Washington Co.
MacMorris, M. *Argyle, Then, Now, Forever.* (1964) illus. map. 104 pp.

McWhorter, E. *History &*
Reminiscences of the Village of Argyle 1738-1938. Hudson Falls. ca 1938. wrps. 12 pp.

CAMBRIDGE, Washington Co.
Anon. *Old Home Week.* Cambridge. Sept. 1916. illus. 167 pp.

Moscrip, A. *Old Cambridge District.* 1969. 123 pp. (Includes Cambridge, Jackson, & White Creek. The author states that Ethan Allen's capture of Fort Ticonderoga in 1775 involved "less risk than a raid on a chicken house.")

Smart & Noble (comp.) *Proceedings of the Centennial Anniv. of Old Town of Cambridge.* Cambridge. 1874. 111 pp.

COSSAYUNA, Washington Co.
Gill, I. *History & Directory of Cossayuna & Vicinity.* 1957. wrps. illus. maps. advts. 68 pp.

EASTON, Washington Co.
Easton Book Club. *Some Chapters in the History of the Town of Easton.* Greenwich? 1959. wrps. 160 pp.

FORT EDWARD, Washington Co.
Bascom, R. *Fort Edward Book ... Some Historical Sketches.* Ft. Edward. 1903. 274 pp.

Brislin, A. *Narratives of Old Fort Edward.* 1962. illus. wrps. 40 pp.

Hill, W. *Fort Edward, The End of the 19th Century, and Later as I Remember.* Brooklyn. 1944-1956. pvtly. prntd. Lmtd. 100 copies. (Many typographical errors. Author gave book away as gifts to friends.)

--- *Old Fort Edward Before 1800.* Glens Falls. 1929. illus. map. Lmtd. 500 copies. 383 pp.

--- *Addenda Old Fort Edward Before 1800.* Ft. Edward. 1956.

wrps. pvtly. prntd. Lmtd. 200 copies. 80 pp.
--- Addenda Part 2. *Old Fort Edward Before 1800.* Ft. Edward. 1957. pvtly. prntd. 99 pp.

GREENWICH, Washington Co.
Gill, I. *The Greenwich Community of 1850.* 1953. wrps. Lmtd. to 200 copies. 65 pp. (Includes Greenwich, Easton, and parts of neighboring towns.)
Sharpe, L. *History of Greenwich 1809-1909.* Greenwich. 1909. illus. wrps. 58 pp.
Tefft, G. *The Story of Union Village as Gathered From the Files of the Greenwich Journal.* Rprntd. from articles appearing in the *Journal* newspaper from Feb. 12, 1941 through May 28, 1941. Greenwich 1942-1943. 2 vols. (Originally known as Whipple City, Union Village was later re-named Greenwich.)
Thurston, E. *History of Town of Greenwich to 1876.* Salem 1876. illus. 95 pp.

HARTFORD, Washington Co.
Brayton, I. (town historian) *The Story of Hartford.* Glens Falls. 1929. illus. map. 212 pp.
Miller, S. *History of Hartford.* 1896. 156 pp.

HUDSON FALLS, Washington Co.
Sawyer, W. *Some Facts Concerning Our Local History.* Hudson Falls. 1930. illus. map. 62 pp.

SALEM, Washington Co.
Anon. *The Salem Book. Records of the Past & Glimpses of the Present.* Salem 1896. illus. 250 pp. (A copy has been seen with a note pasted to inside front cover, "One of the corrected copies of the *Salem Book*.")

Fitch, A. *Early History of Town of Salem (1761 to End of Revolutionary War).* Salem. 1927. wrps. 20 pp. (Rprntd. from *Salem Press* Oct-Nov. 1927)

SHUSHAN, Washington Co.
Brown, A. (comp.) *Shushan Old Home Day. Yesterday and Today.* 1977. illus. map. 36 pp. (From the construction of the covered bridge in 1858 to the present.)

WHITE CREEK, Washington Co.
Jones, P. *Our Yesteryears. A Narrative History of White Creek.* (1959.) illus. maps. 96 pp.

WHITEHALL, Washington Co.
Kellogg, L. *A Sketch of the History of Whitehall. Discourse June 27, 1847.* Whitehall. 1847. 16 pp.
Wilson, D. *Life in Whitehall During the Ship Fever Times.* Whitehall. 1849. Written by a Citizen. 57 pp. (Although this is a novel, it contains much history; many characters represent real people; and buildings and streets are mentioned by the names they had in 1847.)
Reprinted in 1900. Whitehall. illus. advts. 76 pp.

WAYNE COUNTY

WAYNE COUNTY
Bacon, R. & C. *Hoffman Foundation Essays.* (11 competition essays by High School Students on Wayne Co.) 1971. A mss.
Clark, L. *Military History of Wayne Co.* Sodus 1883. 920 pp.
Cowles, G. (& others) *Landmarks of Wayne Co.* Syracuse. 1895. illus. maps. 820 pp.

DAR. *Historical Sketch of Wayne Co.* ca 1940. illus. 137 pp.
Jacobs, S. *Wayne County. The Aesthetic Heritage of a Rural Area.* Wayne Co. Hist. Soc. 1979. map. bib. 288 pp.
(McIntosh, W.) *History of Wayne Co. 1789-1877.* Phil. 1877. illus. maps. 216 pp. Rprntd. ca 1976.
Morrison. *History of Wayne Co.* NY. Clyde 1970. illus. map. "A concise, illus. hist. taken partially from various earlier county histories and Child's *Gazetteer.*"

ARCADIA, Wayne Co.
Jackson, C. (comp.) *Annals of Arcadia.* 1978. illus. map. 73 pp. (Rprnt. of articles pub. in the *Newark Courier-Gazette.*)
Lyon, C. *In the Penumbra: Effects of the Depression on Arcadia.* NY. 1978. illus. bib. 59 pp. typescript. (Hist. of the Great Depression in Arcadia, compiled by a high school senior.)

CLYDE, Wayne Co.
DeLisio, D. *On the Corner of Caroline and Lock Streets, Clyde.* NY. 1978. illus. bib. 55 pp. typescript. (A study of the buildings on the corner of Caroline and Lock Streets in Clyde, 1834-1978, by a high school senior.)
Morrison, A. & W. *History of Clyde 1722-1955.* Williamson. 1955. illus. wrps. 48 pp.
Welch, E. *"Grips" Historical Souvenir of Clyde.* Syracuse. 1905. illus. 68 pp.

LYONS, Wayne Co.
Welch, E. *"Grips" Historical Souvenir of Lyons.* Lyons. 1904. illus. 108 pp.

MACEDON, Wayne Co.
Eldredge, M. (comp.) *Pioneers of Macedon.* Macedon Center 1912. 190 pp. (Has full page list of articles on Macedon history that were ommitted for lack of space and funds.) Reprntd. with additions in 1976. index. bib. maps. 310 pp. Lmtd. to 200 copies.

MARENGO, Wayne Co.
Chalker, C. *Marengo, Town of the Past.* Wayne Co. Museum. Lyons. 1969. A Mss.

MARION, Wayne Co.
Curtis, V. *History of Town of Marion 1795-1937.* Marion. 1937. wrps. 32 pp.

NEWARK, Wayne Co.
Jackson, C. *Newark 100 Years. 1853-1953.* Newark Dec. 1953. illus. wrps. 64 pp. (First pub. in the Newark *Courier-Gazette* newspaper.)
Russell, I. *Old Time Days in Newark.* Newark. 1902. illus. 64 pp.
Stroup, I. *Around the Town in By-Gone Days. Newark & Town of Arcadia 1791-1853.* (1957) illus. map. wrps. 40 pp. (Reprntd. from articles in Newark *Courier Gazette.*)

ONTARIO, Wayne Co.
Anon. *History of Town of Ontario 1804-1957.* Williamson. 1957. illus. 131 pp.
Scully, V. (ed.) *History of Town of Ontario. 1807-1971.* Empire State Weeklies. Webster. ca. 1971.

PALMYRA, Wayne Co.
Anon. *A Memorial of the Celebration at Palmyra of the Centennial July 4, 1876.* Rochester. 1876.
Anon. *Palmyra, Canal Town.* Palmyra 1971. pamphlet.
Anon. *The First Settlement, An*

Early History of Palmyra. A Review of Rev. Mr. Eaton's Thanksgiving Sermon ... Embracing Some Incidents & Anecdotes Hither to Unpublished. 1858. wrps. 10 pp. (See also Eaton, H. below.)

Bean, W. *ABC History of Palmyra, & the Beginnings of Mormonism.* Palmyra. 1938. illus. 94 pp.

Benjamin, A. *History of Palmyra 1789-1865.* 1964. illus. advts. wrps. unpaged. (Orig. written as Masters' Thesis, U. of Rochester, 1942)

Cook, T. *Palmyra & Vicinity.* Palmyra 1930. illus. 310 pp. (Cook wrote this hist. with a quill pen, and read proofs and made corrections in his 93rd year.) 2nd. printing. 1976. 3rd. printing. 1977. 4th. printing. 1980. index. Lmtd. to 50 copies.

Eaton, H. *Early History of Palmyra. Thanksgiving Sermon Nov. 26, 1858.* Rochester. 1858. 26 pp.

Smith, P. *Americana in Drumlin Square.* ca 1962. 33 pp. typed mss. in SLA.

Women's Soc. Western Presby. Ch. (comp.) *Palmyra.* 1907. illus. wrps. 80 pp.

PULTNEYVILLE, Wayne Co.
Anon. *Pultneyville. Post Office Sesquicentennial 1807-1957. A Brief History & Facts Concerning Pultneyville & Its Vibrant, Living People.* Lebanon, IN. 1957. map. wrps. 51 pp.

RED CREEK, Wayne Co.
Frost, G. *Red Creek: Once Upon a Time.* 1978. pub. by author. illus. 119 pp.

ROSE, Wayne Co.
Roe, A. *Neighborhood Sketches, Rose, Wayne Co., With Glimpses of the Adjacent Towns, Butler, Wolcott, Huron, Sodus, Lyons, Savannah.* Worcester, MA. 1893. illus. map. 443 pp. (The author visited every home in Rose.) Reprntd. in 1975. Lmtd. to 250 copies.

SODUS, Wayne Co.
Green, W. *History, Reminiscences, Anecdotes, Legends of Great Sodus Bay, Sodus Point, Sloop Landing, Sodus Village, Pultneyville, Maxwell, & the Environing Regions.* Rochester. 1945. illus. 309 pp. Reprinted 1947.

SODUS POINT, Wayne Co.
Clark, A. *Pioneer History of Sodus Point.* Lyons. 1915. 32 pp.

WILLIAMSON, Wayne Co.
American Legion Post 394 (comp.) *A Directory & Brief History of Town of Williamson.* Williamson. 1928. map. 100 pp.

WOLCOTT, Wayne Co.
Brown, E. *Chronicles of Old Wolcott.* 1954.
(Brown, E. & others) *Town of Wolcott 1810-1960. Sesquicentennial Celebration (Comprising Towns of Huron, Butler, Wolcott, & Rose. Also Red Creek, So. Butler, No. Wolcott.)* ca 1960. advts. wrps. unpaged. (Mentions *No. Wolcott of Yesteryear* by B. Reynolds)
Rotary Club Wolcott. *Historical Highlights of Village of Wolcott.* n.d.
Wadsworth, J. *Wolcott, NY, Old and New. History of the Original Town, and the Four Present Townships, Butler, Huron, Rose, Wolcott ... and Genealogic Sketches of the*

Pioneer Families. 1975. illus. index. 1478 pp. (Wadsworth died in 1944, and his niece, Mrs. Clement H. Wadsworth, revised and completed the mss. up to 1963.)
Welch, E. *"Grips" Historical Souvenir of Wolcott.* Lyons. 1905. illus. 84 pp.

WESTCHESTER COUNTY

WESTCHESTER COUNTY

Anon. *Biog. History of Westchester Co.* Chicago. 1899. illus. 2 vols.
Anon. *This is Westchester.* 1954. illus. maps. 240 pp.
Bolton, R. *A History of the Co. of Westchester.* 1848. illus. maps. 2 vols.
--- *The History of the Several Towns, Manors, & Patents of the Co. of Westchester ... ed. by C. Bolton.* 1881. 2 vols. (Actually a revised ed. of the entry above.) 3rd. ed. NY. 1905. Lmtd. 240 copies, 2 vols.
Cornell, A. *Some of the Beginnings of Westchester Co. History.* 1890. illus. maps. 38 pp.
Couzens, M. (comp.) *Index of Grantees of Lands Sold By Commissioners of Forfeitures ... Situate in the Manor of Phillipsburg ... 1880.* 54 pp.
Cushman, E. *Glimpses of Co. History.* (Tarrytown.) 1931. illus. map. 135 pp.
Cushman & Nichols. *Historic Westchester 1683-1933.* Tarrytown. 1933. illus. map. wrps. 135 pp.
Dawson, H. *Westchester Co. During the American Revolution.* Rye. 1886. illus. map. Lmtd. 250 copies. 281 pp.
French, A. (ed.) *History of Westchester Co., New York, 1925-1927.* illus. maps. 5 vols.

Griffin, E. *Westchester Co. & Its People.* NY. 1946. illus. 3 vols.
Hansen, H. *North of Manhattan. Persons & Places in Old Westchester.* 1884. Another ed. 1950. illus. with photos by Samuel Chamberlain. 181 pp.
Hoffman, R. *Historic Highlights of Westchester.* 1969. wrps. illus. 40 pp.
Hufeland, O. *Westchester Co. During the American Revolution. 1775-1783.* 1926. maps. 473 pp.
Hultz, H. *Incidents from Westchester Hist.* 1934. 34 pp.
Pelletreau, W. *Early Wills of Westchester Co. 1664-1784 With Genealogical & Historical Notes.* NY. 1898. 488 pp.
Pryer, C. *Legends, Traditions & Superstitions of Westchester Co.* NY. 1890. prntd. for pvt. distribution. 74 pp.
Scharf, J. *History of Westchester Co. (Including Morrisania, Kings Bridge, & West Farms Which Have Been Annexed to NYC)* Phil. 1886. map. 2 vols.
Sherman, A. *Westchester Co. & The Town of Rye.* Rye. 1909. 32 pp.
Shonnard & Spooner. *History of Westchester Co. to 1900.* NY. 1900. illus. map. 638 pp. Reprntd. in 1982 with minor corrections.
Weigold, M. (Ed.) *Westchester Co. The Past Hundred Years. 1883-1983.* illus. 384 pp. Sponsored by the Westchester Co. Tricentennial Committee.
Westchester Co. Emergency Work Bureau. *Historical Development of Westchester Co.: A Chronology ....* White Plains. 1939. 2 vols.

ARDSLEY, Westchester Co.

Quick ... (ed.) *Village of Ardsley,*

an *Historical Sketch.* Ardsley. 1903. illus. 66 pp.

BEDFORD, Westchester Co.
Barrett ... (town historian) *The Town of Bedford 1680-1955.* 1955. wrps. illus. maps. index. 116 pp.
Luquer, E. *Old Bedford Days ... Recollections.* 1953. pvtly. prntd. 39 pp.
--- *Bedford & Bedford Village.* 1928. wrps. 8 pp.
Wood, J. *History of Town of Bedford 1681-1917.* 48 pp. (Reprntd. from French's *Hist. of Westchester Co.* See French's entry under WESTCHESTER COUNTY.)

BRIARCLIFF MANOR, Westchester Co.
Anon. *A Village Between Two Rivers.* 1977. pub. by Briarcliff Manor-Scarborough Hist. Soc. illus. map. 100 pp.
Anon. *Our Village, Briarcliff Manor 1903-1952.* ca 1952. 95 pp.
Pattison ... *A History of Briarcliff Manor.* 1939. wrps. illus. 20 pp. (Reprntd. from the *Briarcliff Weekly* newspaper.)

BRONXVILLE, Westchester Co.
Ferris, L. *Tales of Other Days 1853-1879.* NY. 1939. 48 pp.
Mays, V. *Pathway to A Village. History of Bronxville.* Bronx. 1962. illus. 153 pp.

CHAPPAQUA, Westchester Co.
Nicolaysen, E. *Chappaqua. Past, Present, Future.* ca 1940. illus. 20 pp.

CORTLAND, Westchester Co.
Horton, S. *1609-1870. Early Hist. of Manor of Cortland & More, Especially of Town of Cortland & Village of Peekskill.* Peekskill. n.d. 205 pp.

CROTON-ON-HUDSON, Westchester Co.
Hogue & Agne. *Brief History of Croton-on-Hudson, Golden Jubilee 1898-1948.* illus. advts. unpaged.

DOBBS FERRY, Westchester Co.
Hist. class of St. Cristopher's School. *A Brief Historical Review of Dobbs Ferry.* April 29, 1943. 14 pp. typed mss. in WCHS.
Parrell, M. *Profiles of Dobbs Ferry.* 1977. illus. map. 118 pp.

FORDHAM, Westchester Co.
Melick, H. *The Manor Fordham & Its Founder.* 1950. 191 pp.

GREENBURG, Westchester Co.
League of Women Voters. *This is Unincorporated Greenburg.* 5th ed. 1965. maps. wrps. 80 pp.

GREENVILLE, Westchester Co.
Buff, B. *A History of Greenville-Edgemont.* 1977. illus. map. 112 pp.

HARTSDALE, Westchester Co.
LeViness, J. *History of Hartsdale.* Hartsdale. 1948. wrps. unpaged. (Orig. pub. in *Hartsdale Herald* 1932. under pen-name of Sherwood Underhill. Repub. in *Hartsdale Times* 1945-47.) Enlrgd. ed. 1962. illus. unpaged.

HASTINGS, Westchester Co.
Anon. *Hastings Centennial Chronicle.* 1979. illus. 20 pp. (Accounts from several Hastings newspapers of town activities 1879 to 1979.)

HASTINGS-ON-HUDSON, Westchester Co.
Harvey, H. (village historian) *Hist. Notes.* ca 1961. 9 pp.

IRVINGTON, Westchester Co.
Gilchrist, K. *History of Irvington.* ca 1960. 12 pp. typed mss. in WCHS.
Graff, S. (ed.) *Wolferts Roost: Portrait of a Village, Irvington-on-Hudson.* 1971. illus. 151 pp.

JEFFERSON VALLEY, Westchester Co.
5th Grade, Thomas Jefferson School. *The History of Jefferson Valley.* ca 1960. illus. map. mimeo. unpaged.

KATONAH, Westchester Co.
Avery, A. *Historical Sketch of Katonah.* Katonah. 1896. advts. 24 pp.
(Avery, A.) *Sketches & Views of Old & New Katonah.* 1900. illus. map. wrps. unpaged.
Duncombe, F. & C. *Katonah, the History of a New York Village & Its People.* Katonah. 1961. illus. maps. 515 pp. Reprntd. in 1978.

LARCHMONT MANOR PARK, Westchester Co.
Tatum. E. *The Story of Larchmont Manor Park.* 1946. illus. maps. 48 pp.

LEWISBORO, Westchester Co.
7th Grade. *Lewisboro Then & Now.* Lewisboro. 1945-1946. 34 pp. typed mss. in WCHS.

LYNCROFT, Westchester Co.
Parsons, C. *Lyncroft. A Historical Sketch of the Lyncroft Neighborhood.* New Rochelle. 1940. illus. maps. wrps. unpaged. (Lycroft is part of New Rochelle.)

MAMARONECK, Westchester Co.
Brown, H. (ed.) *300th Anniv. of Town of Mamaroneck 1661-1961.* illus. map. wrps. 44 pp.
Danforth, E. *Address Delivered 250th Celebration of Purchase of Mamaroneck from the Indians Sept. 21, 1891.* Mt. Vernon. 1891. 26 pp.
DeLancey, E. *History of Town of Mamaroneck.* NY. 1886. illus. map. 43 pp. (Reprntd. from Scharf's *History of Westchester Co.* See Scharf's entry under **WESTCHESTER COUNTY**.)
Fulcher, W. *Mamaroneck Through the Years 1661-1936.* Larchmont. 1936. illus. map. 64 pp.
--- *The Story of a Friendly Town 1896-1946.* Mamaroneck. 1946. illus. 143 pp.

MOUNT PLEASANT, Westchester Co.
Horne, P. *Mount Pleasant. History of a NY Suburb & Its People.* Hawthorne. 1971. wrps. 58 pp.

MT. KISCO, Westchester Co.
Hyatt, E. *History of Mt. Kisco.* 1893. illus. wrps. 32 pp.

MT. VERNON, Westchester Co.
Anon. *Historical Review of Mt. Vernon.* Mt. Vernon. 1927. 38 pp.
Beach & Wood, *Daily Eagle Illus. History of Mt. Vernon.* Mt. Vernon. 1903. 124 pp.
Gordon, D. *The Social & Cultural Development of Mt. Vernon.* 1951. 34 pp.
Hufeland, O. *Early Mt. Vernon.* Mt. Vernon. 1940. illus. Lmtd. 500 copies. 36 pp.
Wintjen, J. *The Village of Mt. Vernon 1851-1891.* Mt. Vernon. 1940. Lmtd. 500 copies. 37 pp. (Continues Hufeland's hist. See entry above.)
--- *Along the Road ... To Bedford & Vermont.* 1949. 26 pp. (The account of a colonial highway.)

NEW CASTLE, Westchester Co.
Busselle, A. *The Story of New Castle*. 1942. mimeo. 35 pp.

NEW ROCHELLE, Westchester Co.
Anon. *A Guide to New Rochelle and Its Vicinity*. 1842. 71 pp. (Some hist.)
Augur, C. *New Rochelle Through Seven Generations*. New Rochelle. (1908.) prntd. for pvt. distribution. 63 pp.
Coutant, L. *New Rochelle Press Almanac 1880*. New Rochelle. 1880. (Has a 15 pp. article on New Rochelle hist.) 1882 ed. Has a 10 pp. article on New Rochelle hist.
(Dillon & others) *Modern New Rochelle & the National City Bank. 1899-1909*. 1909. illus. 64 pp.
Forbes, R. (ed) *New Rochelle, 250 Years Official Historical Program*. NY. 1938. illus. map. advts. 64 pp.
Lindsley, C. *The Huguenot Settlement of New Rochelle*. Photostat copy, dated 1928, of article in *New Rochelle Pioneer* Sept. 5, 1885, in WCHS.
Nichols, H. *Historic New Rochelle*. New Rochelle. 1938. illus. maps. 212 pp.
Pettit, G. *Today & Yesterday in New Rochelle*. NY. 1913. illus. 106 pp.
Seacord & Hadaway. *Historical Landmarks of New Rochelle*. New Rochelle. 1938. illus. maps. 135 pp. Lmtd. to 1500 copies.

NORTH CASTLE, Westchester Co.
Gerhard, M. *History of Town of North Castle. Bicentennial Celebration 1736-1936*. advts. wrps. unpaged

NORTH SALEM, Westchester Co.
Eichner, F. (ed.) *When Our Town Was Young*. Garden City. 1945. 170 pp.
7th Grade, North Salem. *More Stories of North Salem Yesterday*. 1944. wrps. mimeo. illus. with orig. photos. unpaged.

OSSINING, Westchester Co.
Anon. *Golden Jubilee, Ossining 1901-1951*. Ossining. 1951. illus. wrps. 64 pp.
Cornell, G. *The Ossining Story 1813-1963*. ca 1963. illus. advts. wrps. 80 pp.
Horne, *A Land of Peace. Early History of Sparta, A Landing Town on the Hudson*. Ossining. 1976. maps. wrps. (Sparta is a tiny area of Ossining.) 47 pp.
Oechsner, C. *Ossining, NY: An Informal Bicentennial History*. 1975. 138 pp.
Reynolds, F. (comp.) *Reminiscences of Ossining*. Ossining. 1922. illus. wrps. 54 pp.

PEEKSKILL, Westchester Co.
Anon. *Peekskill, A Journey Into History 1839-1965*. Peekskill. 1965. brochure.
Anon. *Republican Illus. History of Peekskill*. Peekskill. 1902. 65 pp.
Acker, C. *Around Old Peekskill Since 1882*. Brooklyn. 1961. illus. 116 pp.
Acker, C. (ed.) *This & That About Here & There Around Old Peekskill, Memories & Recollections*. Peekskill. 1963. 124 pp.
Couch, F. *Leading Contributions to the History of Peekskill*. 1953. Collected & ed. by W. Horton. brochure.
Fox, J. *The Story of Peekskill 1609-1876*. Peekskill. 1947. illus. 180 pp.
Horton, W. (city historian)

Pioneers, Patriots, & People ... A History of Peekskill. 1953. 355 pp.

Naylor, C. Civil War Days in A Country Village. 1961. illus. maps. 122 pp.

Patterson, E. Peekskill in the American Revolution. Peekskill. 1944. 184 pp. Lmtd. to 500 copies.

Scofield, C. (city historian) Echoes From the Hills. 1961. illus. 128 pp.

Scofield, C. Old Village by the River. 1969. illus. (Bits of hist. about Peekskill taken from newly discovered documents located in 1952.) 73 pp.

--- Historic Tales of Yesteryear. 1959. illus. mimeo. 89 pp.

--- Stories of Peekskill & the Hudson River. 1957. mimeo. 92 pp.

Smith, C. Peekskill, A Friendly Town 1654-1952. Peekskill. 1952. illus. map. 446 pp.

PELHAM, Westchester Co.

Barr, L. (comp.) *A Brief But Most Complete & True Account of the Settlement of the Ancient Town of Pelham ... Also the Story of the Three Modern Villages Called the Pelhams.* Richmond. 1946. illus. 219 pp.

PLEASANTVILLE, Westchester Co.

Osterhoudt, R. (ed.) *Pleasantville. An Historical Sketch and a Survey of the Village Today.* 1937. wrps. 20 pp.

POCANTICO HILLS, Westchester Co.

Owens, W. *Pocantico Hills 1609-1959.* 1960. 53 pp.

POUND RIDGE, Westchester Co.

Harris, J. *God's Country. A History of Pound Ridge.* 1971. illus. 540 pp. (A Supplement dated 1973 is laid in some copies.)

RYE, Westchester Co.

Baird, C. *Chronicle of a Border Town, History of Rye 1660-1870. Including Harrison & White Plains till 1788.* NY 1871. illus. maps. 570 pp. Reprntd. in 1974.

Dalphin, M. *Fifty Years of Rye 1904-1954.* 1955. illus. 162 pp.

Lewin, L. & W. *History of Town of Rye Tercentenary 1660-1960.* ca 1960. illus. wrps. 50 pp.

Sherman, A. *Old & Ancient Rye.* Rye 1912. illus. 27 pp. (Reprntd. from Rye *Chronicle.*)

SCARSDALE, Westchester Co.

Hansen, H. *Scarsdale, Colonial Manor to Modern Community.* NY. 1954. illus. map. 340 pp.

Hoben, A. (Ed) *A History of Scarsdale.* 1935. wrps. illus. map. 34 pp.

Reische, D. *Of Colonists and Commuters. A History of Scarsdale.* 1977. illus. index. 156 pp.

SOUTH SALEM, Westchester Co.

Anon. *Old South Salem. Being an Account of the Village from Settlement to the Present Time.* South Salem. 1907. illus. 28 pp.

Van Norden, T. *South Salem Soldiers & Sailors.* 1927. 172 pp.

Webster, J. *Annals of South Salem.* ca 1952. wrps. 18 pp. (Reprntd. from the *Katonah Record*, May 1952.)

TARRYTOWN, Westchester Co.

--- *Pictures of Prominent Residences and Buildings and Objects of Interest in Tarrytown and Vicinity. With Some Portraits. Compliments of*

Tarrytown Press-Record. ca early 1900s. (This is a folder of 37 loose plates, each 6 x 9 inches.)

Anon. *Centennial Souvenir. A Brief History of Tarrytown 1680-1880.* Tarrytown. 1880. map. 24 pp.

Anon. *Tarrytown and the Tarrytown National Bank and Trust Co.* Tarrytown. Feb. 1932. illus. maps. wrps. 71 pp.

Bacon, E. *A Short History of the Tarrytowns.* 1922. illus. map. 12 numbered copies. (A large folded sheet, prntd. on both sides. A brief description of homes and sites.)

Bacon, E. *Chronicles of Tarrytown & Sleepy Hollow.* NY. 1897. illus. map. 163 pp.

Black, J. *I Remember (1870's-1880's).* 1938. pvtly. prntd. 112 pp.

Canning and Buxton. *History of the Tarrytowns.* 1975. maps. index. 348 pp.

Conklin, M. *History of Tarrytown & North Tarrytown.* 1939. illus. map. wrps. 58 pp.

Duboc. J. *In the Days of Ichabod.* Ann Arbor, MI. 1939. illus. 69 pp.

VALHALLA, Westchester Co.

Vetare, F. (Ed.) *Valhalla Heritage. A Bicentennial History.* 1977. illus. 48 pp. (Essays by high school students.)

VERPLANCK, Westchester Co.

Kelleher, W. *History of Verplanck 1609-1914.* Peekskill. Nov. 1948. Lmtd. ed. illus. (Reprntd. from *Highland Democrat,* Peekskill, July-Nov. 1914.) 2nd. ed. Jan. 1949. mimeo. 77 pp.

WESTCHESTER, Westchester Co.

(Morris, F.) *The Borough Town of Westchester Co.* White Plains. 1896. wrps. 22 pp.

WHITE PLAINS, Westchester Co.

(Mitchell, J.) *History & Directory of White Plains.* 1891. illus. wrps. maps. advts. 64 pp. (This hist. is reprntd. from Scharf's *History of Westchester Co.* See **WESTCHESTER COUNTY.**)

Rosch, J. *Historic White Plains.* (White Plains.) 1939. illus. 395 pp.

YONKERS, Westchester Co.

Allison, C. *History of Yonkers.* NY. (1896.) illus. 460 pp. folio. Reprntd. ca 1980 with added material & index.

Atkins, T. *Indian Wars & the Uprising of 1655. Yonkers Depopulated.* Yonkers. 1892. wrps. 14 pp.

Brown, H. *Old Yonkers 1646-1922.* NY. 1922 illus. map. 192 pp. (Very small book.)

Dawson, H. *The Gazette Series.* Yonkers 1866. Lmtd. 26 copies. pvt. circulation. 4 vols. (Reprntd. from the *Yonkers Gazette.* Data on: Andre, Yonkers, state boundary, Westchester Co.)

Walton, F. *Pillars of Yonkers.* 1951. 347 pp.

WESTERN NEW YORK

(Ernie Wessen of the Midland Rare Book Co. of Mansfield, OH, was closely connected with western NY State. He knew many of the dealers in that area, had customers there, and travelled through on buying trips. He once said that as far as he was concerned one of the three top buying areas in the U. S. was NY State west of Syracuse. The other two were northwestern PA and OH. The copies of his famous and collectible catalog "Midland Notes," which I have seen from the 1950s and 1960s, are full of rare and unusual books, pamphlets, and broadsides, many with Ernies's delightful and informative descriptions. Some of them are of western NY interes. Ernie's personal letters were full of rare book lore, anecdotes about many dealers in the eastern U. S., and his opinions on a wide variety of subjects. After he passed away his stock was acquired by another dealer and moved to western NY.)

--- *The American Kourier*. Vol. 1 No. 4. Dec. 1926. This is a 4 pp. paper issued by the K.K.K. and pub. by the Intl. Music Co. of Buffalo, NY. (The Ku Klux Klan appeals for funds. Among the items advertised in the paper are: a Bible; a pocket knife with an illus. of a sheeted Klansman on one side, and Washington and Lincoln on the other side; and KKK phonograph records: Why I am a Klansman, Keep the Cross Burning, Klansmen, and Daddy Swiped the Last Clean Sheet. During the late 1920s or early 1930s I remember the Klan meeting in a field near my home in Poughkeepsie, NY. It was rumored that one of the prominent doctors in town was a member.)

--- *Anti-Masonic Almanac ... for 1829*. by Edward Giddins. Rochester. Prntd. for the Author by E. Scrantom. 48 pp. (An important almanac as it gives considerable data on the infamous Morgan affair. The cover has an illus. of a blindfolded candidate for induction into the Masonic order receiving his Obligation. There are 12 illus. representing the abduction of Morgan.)

Armstrong, L. *William Morgan Abducted and Murdered by Masons, In Conformity With Masonic Obligations; and Masonic Measures to Conceal That Outrage Against the Laws ... Illustrated and proved in a Sermon by ... A Seceding Mason, and Late Pastor of the Presbyterian Church ... Delivered in Edinburgh*, Saratoga Co. Sept. 12, 1831. NY. 1831. wrps. 32 pp. (An anti-Masonic sermon on the alleged kidnapping and murder of William Morgan on the Niagara frontier. It has an interesting woodcut of Morgan and a group of Anti-Masons attacking a hydra-headed monster representing the institution of Freemasonry.)

Barton J. *Address on the Early Reminiscences of Wester New York, and the Lake Region ...* Buffalo, 1848. 69 pp. + errata slip. (Barton lived on the Niagara frontier for many years, and knew many of the very early settlers.)

Bigelow, T. *Journal of a Tour to Niagara Falls in ... 1805 ... With an Introduction by a Grandson*. Boston. 1876. 121 pp. (The first printing of this excellent description of a trip to the early western NY frontier via the Mohawk valley and return via the St. Lawrence River, Montreal, and VT.)

(Bourne, A.) *Wonderful Works of God. A Narrative of the Wonderful Facts in the Case of Ansel Bourne, of West Shelby, Orleans Co., NY. Written Under His Direction*. 1877. wrps. 40 pp. (Bourne, born in NYC in 1826, eventually moved to

Orleans Co., NY. In 1857 he was in Westerly, RI, and in the midst of rebelling against God he was stricken deaf, dumb, and blind. He became converted and 18 days later in the presence of hundreds of people he was completely healed.)

Clinton, DeWitt. *Remarks on the Fishes of the Western Waters of the State of New York, in a Letter to Samuel L. Mitchill.* 1815. 8 pp. (Mostly on the fish of the Niagara River.)

--- *Cornucopia. Batavia, (Genesee County, New York) ... June 28, 1811.* This is a 4-page newspaper, pub. by Peek and Blodgett. (This newspaper was pub. from March 1809 until October 1811; but Brigham's *History and Bibliography of American Newspapers 1690-1820* lists only 7 known issues of this paper and none from 1811.)

--- *Croquet. Terms, Suggestions, and Rules, Made Uniform and Condensed Under Direction of the American Croquet Co. of Geneseo, NY.* Geneseo. 1871. Has two diagrams of arch settings. 43 pp. (This is a very early U. S. pub. on the game of Croquet, as the first U. S. League was not formed until 1880.)

Follett, F. *History of the Press of Western New York, With the Proceedings of the Printers Festival, Held in ... Rochester ... Jan. 18, 1847.* Rochester. 1847. 76 pp. (Follett, 1804-1891, was a newspaper publisher and Post Master at Batavia, NY, and was a Canal Commissioner. An obituary of him appeared in the *NY Times.* This book was reprntd. for Charles F. Heartman, NY, 1920, in an ed. of 111 copies, leaving out the Proceedings of the Festival. Wilberforce Eames, the noted librarian and bib., wrote a preface for it. In 1973 Harbor Hill Press, Harrison, NY, reprntd. the Heartman ed. The original work has never come my way, but I have had the Heartman production.)

Ford, P. L. (ed.) *A Short History and Description of Fort Niagara, With An Account of Its Importance to Great Britain, Written by an English Prisoner, 1758. With a View of the Fort, 1758.* 1890. wrps. 18 pp. (Originally prntd. in the *Royal Magazine* in 1759, this is the 1890 printing, lmtd. to 250 copies.)

Hardy, James E. *"The High Wire King". Most Wonderful Mid-Air Performance in Existence. Hero of Niagara Falls, 1896. Marvel of Genesee Gorge, 1897* .... (Letter written by Hardy on his letterhead with the above prntd. heading, dated March 1908. He was the undisputed champion high wire artist of the world, but apparently was thinking about changing careers: he is writing for a catalog of White Wyandottes, intending to go into the business of raising chickens.)

(Henry, G. W.) *Trials and Triumps (For Half a Century) In the Life of G. W. Henry ... With the Religious Experience of His Wife ... Added One Hundred Spiritual Songs, With Music.* Oneida (NY). pub. by the author. 1856 ed. port. 349 and 160 pp. (Henry was an itinerant bookseller and preacher in western NY in the early 1800s who approved of the shouting done in camp meetings and churches. There is a small embossed likeness of him on the cover.)

Henry, G. W. *Shouting: Genuine and Spurious ... Outward Demonstrations of the Spirit ... Laughing, Screaming, Shouting, Leaping, Jerking, and Falling Under the Power.* Pub. and bound by the author. Oneida, NY. 1859. port. 432 pp. (This book was reprntd. in 1903, with port. and illus. 305 pp.)

Holbrook, T. W. *Proclamation. To the People of the United States.* Rochester (NY). Thursday, Aug. 11, 1864. Broadside, 4 1/2 x 10 inches. (In this handbill Holbrook announces his candidacy for office of President of the U. S. He seems to have gotten his inspiration while meditating in Mount Hope Cemetery, and in the Cemetery at Geneseo. Sabin, 32458, says that foreword looking chap "nominates himself for President of the US, and in so doing, proclaims himself a fool.")

Honeywell, E. *Young Men of America ....* Handbill, prntd. on both sides, ca 1880. (Honeywell warns young men against the evils of Free Masonry. It mentions William Morgan who allegedly was murdered by the Masons near Niagara in the 1820s, and an anti-Masonic convention at LeRoy, NY. It declares that punishment for erring Masons includes, "scalping, scorching brains, rotting on the dung hill, gibetting, and ... Even the vengeance of lightning is imprecated ... Young men are the nutriment on which Masonry feeds. Defend yourselves ....")

Lockie, L. *Pharmacy on the Niagara Frontier. The Past and Present.* 1968. Illus. Map. Index. 264 pp. (A detailed history of pharmacy in Erie and Niagara Cos., NY; pharmaceutical company hist.; and directory lists of pharmacies.)

Mathies, J. *Rochester, a Satire; and Other Miscellaneous Poems.* Rochester (NY). 1830. 130 pp. (Satirical poetry on Rochester and many of its residents. American Imprints locates only one other copy.)

Matteson, Mrs. A. *The Occult Family Physician, and Botanic Guide to Health ... Plants ... Medical Virtues ... Valuable Receipts ... by ... Trance and Healing Medium.* Pub. by the author. Buffalo, NY. 1894. port. index. 322 pp. (The author claims to have healed thousands of indisposed persons in western NY by the use of medicinal plants, and by her psychic and soul force.)

(Maude, J.) *Visit to the Falls of Niagara in 1800.* London. 1826. illus. 313 pp. + index, and an 8-page insert titled "Additional Notes." (Maude travelled to Niagara from NYC via the Hudson Valley, Oneida Castle, Owasco Lake, Bath, Canadarqua, Genesee Falls, Buffaloe Creek ... and returned via Queenstown, Thousand Islands, Montreal, Lake Champlain, and the Hudson River. Larned's *Literature of American History* says "This charmingly intimate record ... by an Englishman of quick sympathies, keen appreciation, and intelligent observation, is unfortunately rare ...." Sabin, 46913, says that only about 300 copies were prntd.; and both Sabin and Howes *USiana* call for a 16 pp. insert added later.)

--- Mr. Fillmore's Political History and Position. Speech of Hon. E. B. Morgan, of NY, in

U.S. House of Representatives. August 1856. 7 pp. pamphlet. (An anti-Fillmore speech at the time Fillmore, former U. S. President from Buffalo, NY, was running for the U. S. Presidency on the Know-Nothing Party ticket. "There is not in all the Northern States a man more completely and irretrievably wedded to the South, by his sympathies on the one hand and his hatreds on the other ...." After his defeat in this campaign, Fillmore never held another major public office.)

--- (Morgan Affair) *North Star Extra. 'Vengeance!' Furthermore do I Promise and Swear ... Masonic Oath ... July 19, 1828.*" St. Johnsbury, VT. July 19, 1828. By Ebenezer Eaton. Broadside, 6 x 12 inches. (Eaton was ed. of the North Star newspaper of Danville, VT, and after the disappearance of William Morgan the famous anti-Masonic author of western NY, he pub. a highly anti-Masonic editorial about the affair. A Deacon Dana, a Royal Arch Mason, owned the press and type of the newspaper and hastily got an attachment on the press and type effectively shutting it down. Eaton had this broadside prntd. in St. Johnsbury giving a detailed account of his fray with Dana.)

--- *New State Road.* 1825. Broadside, 10 x 12 inches. (Benedict Brooks, of Covington, who is running for the NY State Senate, gives his views on the building of a State Road from the Hudson River to Lake Erie, a question "which so much interests our friends in the counties of Steuben, Allegany, Cattaraugus, and Chautque." This is a very early reference to a State Road in western NY.)

--- (Niagara Falls) *Upfostrings-Salskapets Tidingar. No. 45, 46.* Stockholm, d 21 Mart. 1782. Geographie. Norra-America. Niagara Vattufall. 8 pp. (This appears to be a small monthly pub. from Sweden. It has 5 1/2 pages on Niagara Falls. Not in Dow's *Anthology and Bibliography of Niagara Falls*, or in Sabin.)

--- *Notes on a Tour Through the Western Part of the State of New York.* 1916. wrps. 55 pp. Limited to 200 copies. (This was originally prntd. in the *Ariel* magazine, Philadelphia, Pa. 1829-30. This traveller of keen observation travelled the "Clinton Canal" much of the way, visited Niagara, and returned to his PA home via Ithaca and Owego. According to an article in *York State Tradition* magazine, Fall 1968, the author of these notes was Michael H. Jenks. It tells of the hist. detective work that led to the discovery of the author's name.)

--- *Red Bird Line. 1850. Packet Baltic, Capt. John Tanner, Leaves ... Rochester ... Buffalo.* (This is a small timetable ticket giving the departure dates and hours for May and June, prntd. by the Daily American Press of Rochester. It is only a small item, 1 3/4 x 3 1/4 inches. No doubt only a very few of these have survived.)

Richmond, A. *What I Saw at Cassadaga Lake: A Review of the Seybert Commission's Report.* 1890 ed. 244 pp. Plus: *Addendum to a Review of the Seybert Commission's Reprt.* 1890. 163 pp. Both items bound into one vol. (The Seybert Commission, funded by the University of PA, investigated Modern Spiritualism as Practiced at Cassadaga Lake in Chautauqua Co., NY, and exposed many frauds. A major work on spiritualism in NY State.)

--- (Rochester) *Dan Rice's Rochester Song. Tune - Landlord's Pet. Composed and Sung by Dan Rice.* This is a broadside poem of 8 verses of 8 lines each. 7 x 10 inches. ca 1850s. (The song is about a canawler who was put in the Blue Eagle Jail for calling another man a thief. The copy I had had a note in pencil "Bought May 31st. 1856." Dan Rice was a famous showman whose career began when he bought a half interest in an educated pig named Lord Byron. The DAB says that in later life he became a temperance speaker but "the water pitcher before him on the lecturer's desk frequently held gin.")

--- (Rochester) *Illustrated Guide to Reynolds Arcade ... Plans of Each Floor, Number of Each Office, Names and Business of Each Occupant, History of the Arcade from 1828 ...* ca. 1880 wrps. 30 pp. (When built this was the largest and most expensive building the the U. S. west of Albany.)

--- *Roycroft Hand-Wrought Copper. 1917-1918.* Huge folio broadside with over 130 illus. of copper ware made by the Roycrofters, of East Aurora, NY. (Includes Roycroft Sheffield which was sterling silver on copper.)

--- *Roycroft Inn. East Aurora, Erie Co., NY.* ca 1920s. illus. wrps. 32 pp. (Interior and exterior views of this Mecca, with descriptions and lists of activites for guests. "Without the door let sorrow lie, and if perchance it happens to die, We'll bury it deep in a Roycroft pie.")

Schild, J. L. *Silversmiths of Rochester. Rochester Museum of Arts and Sciences.* 1944. illus. 32 pp. (Has brief biog. data on over 40 Rochester silversmiths.)

Schmidt, C. *Architectural Mouldings.* 1967. 75 folio plates, plus illus., and text. Lmtd. to 300 copies. (Most of the plates are of mouldings in homes in the Rochester area.)

Schmidt, C. *Cobblestone Masonry.* 1966. illus. diagrams. index. 326 pp. (There are many fine examples of homes, and other buildings, built of cobblestones in the western and central NY areas. Schmidt made a detailed study of them, and wrote several books on the subject. This work describes many NY State houses, plus a few from other states.)

Schmidt, C. *More Cobblestone House Entrances. Part VII.* pub. by the Cobblestone Soc., Childs, NY. ca 1960s. (Besides his notable books on cobblestone architecture, Schmidt issued a series of folders with loose plates. This one is Part VII, with 7 plates of entrances to cobblestone houses, and a sheet with a brief description of them.)

--- *Silver Lake Assembly.* 1901. wrps. illus. 16 pps. (Official Program of the Silver Lake Assembly in Wyoming Co. for 1901. Has an illus. of Carrie Nation, one of the featured speakers. "Carrie had a little axe, Its edge was bright as brass, And everywhere that Carrie went, The axe was smashing glass." Carrie Nation, 1846-1911, was a temperance advocate who wrecked many saloons with a hatchet.)

--- *Special Report of New York State Survey on the Preservation of the Scenery of Niagara Falls.* J. T. Gardiner, Director. Albany. 1880. maps. illus. 42 pp. (The area around the falls had deteriorated and the state wanted to restore it for public enjoyment. One of the men involved in this campaign to preserve Niagara was Frederick Law Olmsted the noted landscape architect. This major work is illus. with 11 mounted heliotype prints, 3 folding maps, and includes a description of the proposed State Reservation.)

Stanton, H. B. *Random Recollections.* 1886. 2nd ed. wrps. 134 pp. (Stanton, 1805-1887, lawyer and reformer, worked for Thurlow Weed the noted publisher in Rochester, and was deputy clerk of Monroe County. He was the husband of Elizabeth Cady the famous reformer and woman's rights leader. It is interesting to note that the DAB says the word "obey" was ommitted from her marriage ceremony at her insistence. The preface of the first edition of the work, 1885, states "a few numbers printed for private circulation, but there will be none for sale.")

--- *Stephen's Fenian Songster, Containing All the Heart-Stirring and Patriotic Ballads and Songs, As Sung at the Meetings of the Fenian Brotherhood.* NY. Pub. by Wm. H. Murphy. 1866. pictorial wrps. 72 pp. words only. (The Fenians were a group of Irishmen who wanted to establish a republic in Canada, and in the spring of 1866 they crossed the Niagara River from NY State and seized Fort Erie in Canada. In the aftermath some were arrested, tried, and condemned to death. This songster was probably named after James Stephens, a leader from Ireland who was visiting the U. S. in 1866.)

Thompson, J. (ed.) *The Real Diary of a Rochester Boy.* 1864. pub. 1917. 104 pp. Limited to 500 copies. (Daily diary entries for the year 1864. It provides an excellent picture of juvenile life in Rochester: the diarist smelled up the church by putting skunk cabbage leaves under the pew cushions, put an eel in a picnic basket to hear the women scream, and told his mother he did not need to wash as he had fallen into the bay. You will have to read the book to learn about all his other capers.)

--- *The the Settlers of the County of Wayne ... Fellow Settlers ... Sodus. Oct. 4, 1831.* Sgd. in type: *Many Settlers.* Broadside, 5 x 14 inches. (The unnamed settlers accuse Hugh Jameson, who had been nominated for Co. Clerk, of being an agent and an attorney for the Pultney Land Office which owned vast lands in that part of NY State for speculation. They warn their Fellow Settlers against voting for Jameson, "... reflect before you clothe such a man with additional power to oppress you ... he is the agent of the most offensive landed aristocracy that ever disgraced a free country ...." The Pulteney Associates were in business for many years, and it is said their last transaction was

made in 1926.)
--- *True and Wonderful Story of Paul Gasford, Who, When Only About Four Years Old, was Lost in the Woods ... After Four Days Travel, Got Safe to His Parents at Niagara, 40 Miles From the Place Where He was Lost.* NY. Mahlon Day. ca 1830's? yellow printed wrps. illus. with woodcuts. 15 pp. (A toy book pub. by a noted NY pub. of children's literature. Little Paul followed the lakeshore, ate grapes he found, hid when he saw some Indians, and finally arrived at Niagara. "Even the Governor himself was so astonished at the fact, that he sent for the little boy, and would have kept him, if his mother had been willing to give him up." Not in Weiss's bib. of Mahlon Day pub. in 1941.)

Tucker, P. *Origin, Rise, and Progress of Mormonism, Biography of Its Founders and History of Its Church. Personal Remembrances and Historical Collections Hitherto Unwritten.* 1867. illus. 302 pp. (The author was ed. of the *Wayne Sentinel* newspaper at Palmyra, NY, knew Joseph Smith, and aided in the printing of the Book of Mormon.)

Turner, C. *Dark Days on the Frontier of Western NY. Descriptive of the Sieges, Hardships, Endurance, Privations of the Early Pioneers ... Unpublished Reminiscences of the Surrender of Fort Niagara ....* Buffalo. 1879. wrps. 39 pp. (Turner was early resident of western NY.)

Willis, C. *Pulteney Land Title. Genesee Tract.* 3rd Edition. 1921. wrps. illus. map. 29 pp. (A concise hist. of this major western NY State land company, which controlled over one million acres.)

Winner, J. *Belva A. Lockwood.* 1969. wrps. Colored Port. illus. 139 pp. (A biog. of Belva, 1830-1917, of Niagara Co., NY, who was a lawyer, women's rights activist, and the first woman candidate for the office of President of the U. S.)

WYOMING COUNTY

WYOMING COUNTY
Beers, F. (ed.) *History of Wyoming Co.* NY. 1880. 310 pp. (Complete name index comp. by Conley & French. ca 1950. Batavia. 83 pp.) Reprntd. ca 1976 with index.

Douglass, H. (comp.) *Famous Sons & Daughters of Wyoming Co.* Warsaw. 1935. 79 pp.

Historical Wyoming. Mimeo. Issued 4 times a year. Later issues had illus. Last issue was Vol. 21, No. 4, dated July 1968. ("... contains more history of that county than can be found anywhere else.")

Tomlinson, G. *From Youth to Seventy & What I Saw By the Way.* LeRoy. 1894. wrps. 70 pp.

ARCADE, Wyoming Co.
Anon. *Arcade 1808-1912.* 1912. illus. advts. wrps. unpaged.
Douglass, H. *Progress With a Past, Arcade 1807-1957.* Arcade. 1957. illus. maps. advts. 200 pp.

ATTICA, Wyoming Co.
Anon. *Attica Centennial Book.* 1937. illus. map. advts. wrps. 24 pp.
Murphy, H. (comp.) *Development of Attica.* NY. 1978. illus. index. 120 page typescript.
Tolles, J. *Early Recollections of Attica.* 1937. wrps. 16 pp.

(First prntd. in *Attica News*, April 1874. Reprntd. in *Attica News* Aug. & Sept. 1902. Reprntd. as pamphlet 1937.)

BENNINGTON, Wyoming Co.
Ripstein, A. *A Town of Country Folk*. 1977. pub. by author. illus. bib. 200 pp.

CASTILE, Wyoming Co.
Anon. *Castile Sesquicentennial 1808-1958*. illus. wrps. 24 pp.

PERRY, Wyoming Co.
Crocker, F. *Perry in the Civil War*. 1940. typed. mss. in Perry Pub. Lib.
Roberts & Clarke (comps.) *History of Town of Perry*. Perry 1915. illus. map. 380 pp.
(Roberts, F.) *First National Bank. 100 Years in Perry 1855-1955*. ca 1955. illus. wrps. unpaged.

PIKE, Wyoming Co.
French. R. *The Formation of a Pioneer Village, Once Nunda Hollow, now Pike*. Pike Library. 1971. a mss.

ST. HELENA, Wyoming Co.
Anderson & Willey. *St. Helena. Ghost Town of Genesee 1797-1954*. 1954. illus. wrps. 42 pp.

STRYKERSVILLE, Wyoming Co.
Douglass, H. *Strykersville Sesquicentennial 1808-1958*. Arcade. 1958. illus. advts. wrps. unpaged.

WARSAW, Wyoming Co.
Bishop, L. *The First Century ... A Brief History of the Incorporated Village of Warsaw*. Warsaw. 1946. wrps. 31 pp.
Robinson, L. (ed.) *Historical Centennial Celebration of Warsaw 1803-1903*. Warsaw. 1903. illus. 247 pp.
Young, A. *History of Town of Warsaw*. Buffalo. 1869. illus. 400 pp.

YATES COUNTY

YATES COUNTY
Aldrich, L. *History of Yates Co*. Syracuse. 1892. illus. 671 pp.
Cleveland, S. *History & Directory of Yates Co*. Penn Yann. 1873. illus. map. Vol 1 (all pub.) (It is said that the unbound sheets of Vol. 2 were destroyed by fire, only 6 copies saved.)
Another ed. Penn Yann. Sept 1951. illus. maps. Lmtd. 250 sets. 2 vol. (This ed. contains Vol. 2, with this notation: "The concluding section of the mss. was lost, the printed version ending with page 1168 ... pp. 1168 ends in middle of sentence.") (Index comp. by F. Bootes, Middlesex, 1954, 25 pp.) Reprntd. ca 1976.
Stork, W. (ed.) *Students' Handbook of Yates Co*. Penn Yann. 1898. illus. 158 pp.
Wolcott, W. (comp.) *Early History of Yates Co. Selected & Copied*. Penn Yann. 1930. A 32 pp. mss. of articles orig. pub. in Penn Yann *Democrat* in 1855. in NYPL.
--- *The Military History of Yates Co*. Penn Yann. 1895. 158 pp.

JERUSALEM, Yates Co.
Davis, M. *History of Jerusalem*. Pnn. Yann. 1912. illus. 103 pp.

PENN YANN, Yates Co.
Anon. *Penn Yann*. Penn Yann. 1915. illus. 128 pp.

STARKEY, Yates Co.
Sunderlin, A. *Starkey Township of Bonnie Dundee*. 1960. illus. map. wrps. 48 pp. (Includes: Shannontown, Starkey Corners, Lakemont, Glenora, Rock Stream, Dundee.)

INDEX

This index lists localities, subjects, and authors.

Abbatt, Wm 54
Abbott & McCausland, 123
Abbott, E (Mrs) 146 Henry 146
Aber & King, 52
Aboriginal occupation of lower Genesee country, 117
Abt, H 241
Acker, C 253
Ackerman, E 52
Ackert, A 40
Actors, 74
Adam's Basin, 200
Adams & Breed, 169
Adams, 179 225 C 55 Charles Francis 113 E 28 F 169 I 15 Israel adventures of 15 J 105 215 234 238 J T 180 John 190 John Quincy 111 O 178 S 84 W 12
Adamsville, 62
Ade, George 130
Aderman, W 51
Adirondack, 245 High Peaks & the Forty-Sixers 152 Adirondack hiking 48 Iron Works 149 Mountain Club 79 voices 147
Adirondack Mountains 54 83 147 150 152 155 156 158-161 181 182 186 187 212 227 birds 157 158 fires 150 health resort 159 illustrated 160 lumbering 151 photographs 146 prints 147
Adkins, E 237
Adrosko, Rita J 17
Afton, 30
Agassiz, 18
Aigonquin Indians, 93
Aiken, J 145
Aikman, Water A 135

Akerly, S 55
Akers, D 170
Al-Khayat, H 38
Alabama, 51
Albany, 1 2 9 26 55-58 62-64 66 69-71 76 77 84 85 90 108-111 120 148 158 162 166 185 188 222 242 260 Co 1-3 89
Albertson, C 240
Albion, 173
Alcohol, 73 103 125 149
Alden, 44 T 84
Alder Lake, 242
Aldrich, L 168 263
Ale, 62
Alexander, 51 H 111 I 236
Alexandria Bay, 97 150
Aley, L 242
Alfred, 3 4
Algonquin Indians, 186
Allegany Co, 3-5 12 27 114 259
Allen, 4 A 212 C 215 Ethan 246 F L 124 H 14 H A 14 M 43 R 214
Allison, C 255
Alliteraricus, 242
Allyn, D A 5
Alma, 3
Almond, 3
Altamont, 2 49
Amagansett, 234
Amazing Madame Jumel 129
Amenia, 41
Ameri, N 241
American, Agricultural Association 230 artists 1564-1860 dictionary 183 biographical sketch book 10 biographies 180 181 185 189 Congress biographical directory 180 directories

American (continued)
  bibliography 188 189 game
  mammals & birds 22 Guide
  Series 1 history dictionary 180
  Indians 184 Legion Post 394
  249 literature 184 lithography
  186 maps 186 newspapers
  1821-1936 183 newspapers
  bibliography 181 woods ex-
  hibited 151 152
Amesm, C 234 Ezra 19 Mr 73
Amherset, Jeffrey 119
Amherst, 44
Amityville, 234
Ammi, Phillips 57
Amsterdam, 118
Ancram, 36 Iron Mine 57
Anderson & Willey, 263
Anderson, A 27 D 46 G 189 213 J
  210 S 55 W 165 William 35
  220 221
Andes, 10
Andover, 3 4
Andre, John 191 198 206 Maj 199
  200 202 203 205 207
Andre's Hill, 199
Andrew, B 218
Andrews, Samuel J 116 W L 191
Angelica, 3 4
Angell, P 172 Sarah Ann 138 139
Anguish, L 166
Annandale, 41
Anne, queen of England 33 85
Anon, 1 3-5 12-14 27-32 36-40
  42-55 96-103 105 106 115 116
  118 121-124 144-146 163-167
  170-175 177-179 190 210-214
  216-219 233 235 237 238 240
  242-255 262 263
Anti-Masonry, 229 256 258 259
  See also Free Masonry
Anti-Rent, 25 39 55 56 59 60 63
  68 74 75 79 80 82 217
Antwerp, 97
Apples, 222 223
Arcade, 262
Arcadia, 248
Archdeacon, T 124
Ardsley, 250 251
Argyle, 246
Aristocracy, 56

Arkwright, 14
Armbruster, E 99 100 179
Armstrong, J 192 John 192 L 146
  256
Arnold, 31 66 192 Benedict 196
  198 203 206 I 175
Arnold-Andre affair, 193 196 120
  202 207
Arthursburg, 41
Asharoken, 234
Asher, G M 32
Ashokan Reservoir, 8
Ashton, J 101
Ashville, 28
Astor, 173 John Jacob 155 W 172
Athens, 52
Atkins, T 255
Atlanta, 233
Attica, 262 263
Atwater, M 116 Moses 116
Atwell, C 105
Auburn, 14 15 22 88 145
Auburn State Prison, 23
Audubon, John J 128 John James
  87
Augur, C 253
Augusta, 163 Township 163
Augustus, Williams 57
Auriesville, 85 118
Aurora, 44 219
Austerlitz, 36 81
Austin & Huntington, 174
Averill & Hager, 31
Averill, H 31
Avery, A 252
Avon, 102
Ayres, J 236
Babylon, 234
Bacheller, I 147 Irving 151
Back Number Town (Lewiston)
  145
Bacon, E 175 255
Bacon R & C 247
Bacon Hill, 214
Bagg, M 165
Bailey, H 41 J 99 L 120 M 218 W
  177 W W 56
Bainbridge, 30
Baird, C 254
Baker, 173 A 167 D 45 N 210 211
  O 45

Balcoms Corners, 14
Baldwin, 121 Jeduthan 192 M 241
 S E 56 Simeon 56 T 192
Baldwinsville, 166
Ball, L 16 Peter 10 S 45
Ball's Cave, 10
Ballston, 158 215 Spa 214
Balmville, 170
Bancroft, F 16 G 111 George 202
Bangall, 63
Bangor, 49
Bangs, R 100
Banks, A 1
Bannan, T 165
Banner Man Island, 78
Bannerman, F 192
Bannerman's Island, 192
Bannister, C 169
Bar bills at Crown Point, 149 150
Barbe-Marbois, 192
Barck, O T 192
Barclay, D 170
Barker, E 48 J 125 Jacob 125 P 46
Barkley, W 118
Barnerville, 217
Barnes, D M 125 T 1 W 14
Barnett, 31
Barneveld, 163
Barney, D 4
Barnhart's Pool, 11
Barnum, H L 193
Barr, L 254
Barrett, 251 R 28 Walter 187
Barritt & Jernegan, 244
Barry, T 47
Bartlett, W H 83
Barton, J 256
Bascom, F 49 R 246
Bashant, N 162
Batavia, 51 257
Batchellerville, 214
Bates, Barnabas 220 C 172
Bath, 16 232 233 258
Bath-on-the-Hudson, 190
Battle fought on snow shoes, 157
Battle of, Plattsburgh 149 154 162
 Prescott 154
Bay, John 120
Bay Ridge, 99
Bayard, N 32 Nicholas 32 33
Bayba, A 190

Bayles, R 209 234 T 235 236
Bayshore, 234
Beach & Wood, 252
Beach, L 171 S A 222
Beacon, 41 63
Bean, W 2 249
Beardsley, L 175
Bearsville, 9
Beastall, W 125
Beauchamp, W 165 167
Beautiful Bronx 5
Beautiful Hudson by Searchlight 57
Beaver Falls, 101
Beaverkill, 9 11
Beck, Dr 127 Lewis C 228
Becker, Charles 135 H 3 50 53 214 Howard I 214 J 219 John P 193 S 45
Beckwith, Oscar F 81
Bedell, C 210
Bedford, 251 252 Village 251
Bednarz, Julius 46
Beecher, L 235 R 51
Beekman, Cornelia 175 Judge 218
Beekmantown, 31
Beers, 51 F 3 51 53 118 262
Belcoda, 118
Belden, E P 125
Belfast, 4
Bell, A G 24 B 218 240
Bellamy, B 123
Belle Harbor, 122
Bellot, A 122
Bellport, 234
Belmont, 4
Belvidere, 4
Benedict, G 165
Benjamin, A 249 Franklin Lewis 1842-1828 63
Bennett, 130 A P 1 C 216 E 193 R 189
Bennington, 263 Co 1
Bensel, A 243
Benson, Egbert 129 223
Benton, Charles 57 Myron 80 N 53 R 147
Benziger, G 145
Bergen, 51 T 99
Bergh, Henry 141
Berlin, 189
Berne, 2

Bessboro, 49
Best, H 57 T 163
Bethany, 51
Bethke, R 147
Bethpage, 121 122
Beulah, 118
Bevan & Iron, 106
Bevier, A 245 J H 85
Bieber, Jack 86
Bien, J R 107
Big Indian, 242
Big Moose Lake, 53 54
Bigelow, S 234 T 256
Billings Gap, 63
Bingham, R 45
Binghamton, 5 58 225
Biondi, M 212
Birch Bark Books, 146
Birch, Harvey 193 J 216 J J 85
Bird, 110
Birdsall, 4 R 175
Bishop, L 263
Bissell, E 47
Bixby, W 194
Black, H 36 J 255 Jacob 19 M 57
Black Lake, 212
Black River Valley, 97
Black Rock, 8
Blackmer, C 170
Blacks in Albany, 1 62
Blair, H W 126
Blaisdell, T H 3
Blake, W 178 194
Blakely, S 177
Blanckman, E 212
Blasdell, 44
Blatchford, S 85
Blauvelt, E 15
Bleecker, 77 226
Bleeker, Leonard 200
Blenheim, 217 Hill 217
Bliss, H 217 M 233
Block Island, 235
Blockville, 28
Blodgett, B 38
Bloodgood, S DeWitt 193
Bloomingburgh, 239
Blue Mountain Lake, 52 53
Blue Stores, 66
Board of Water Supply Songs 8
Boatner, M M III 180
Bogardus, 77

Bolivar, 4
Bolton, R 126 250
Bombay, 49
Bond, R P 85
Bonner, W T 126
Bonnie Dundee, 263
Bonsted, C 213
Boonville, 163
Booth, J 213 John Wilkes 143 M 126 M A 8
Border Town, 57
Boston, 44
Boughton, F 36
Boundaries of NY State, 229 230
Boundary dispute between, NY & Massachusetts 57 NY & Massachusetts Bay 32 NY & Vermont 147 150 155 158
Boundary of NY & NJ, 80
Bourglay, Jules 68
Bourne, A 256 Ansel 256 M (Miss) 98
Bouton, N 38
Bovina, 39
Bowen, G 101
Bowlby, 233
Boyd, J 57 J P 85 Julian P 85 W 102
Boynton, E 173
Boyton, P 103
Bradbury, 36
Bradford, 233 William 33
Bradish, Luther 230
Bradley, C 44 H 214 K 13
Bradstreet, Col 119
Bragdon, G 116
Brahler, V 116
Brainard, 189 D C 220
Branch's Anaconda 141 142
Brandow, J 214
Brant, 45 Capt 205 Joseph 89
Braynard, F 126
Brayton, I 247
Breed, H 106
Breen, W 101
Brentwood, 234 Park 103
Brewerton, 174
Brewster, 178 A 166
Brewster National Honor Society, 178
Briarcliff Manor, 251
Bridgehampton, 234 235

Bridgewater, 163
Briggs, 46 A Jr 147 E 46
Brigham, A 169 C S 181
Brighton, 50 114
Brinckerhoff, T 41
Brink, B 244 B M 242
Brinkman, W 2
Brislin, A 246
Britten, E 215
Broadalbin, 50
Brockport, 114
Brockville, 98
Bronson J & R, 17
Bronx 5 Co 5 66
Bronxville, 251
Brookfield, 21 105
Brookhaven, 12 234 235
Brooklyn, 81 99 104 Borough 64 99 100 Eastern District 99 Village 99
Brooks, Benedict 259 C 102 E 234 M 13
Broome, Co 5 6 29
Brophy, Joseph Francis 103
Broughton, J 51
Brown, A 147 247 D 162 E 249 G 48 Grace 20 H 252 255 H C 58 J 216 John 158 Mr 230 S 27 T 85 163 Thomas 22 85 86 220 222 W 245
Brown Tract, 155
Brownell, C 97
Browning, C 175
Brownsville, 100
Brownville, 97
Brownyard, M 116 Mary Jane 116
Bruce, D 166 167 H A 126
Bruijkleen Colonie, 99
Brumberg, G 169
Bruni, S 145
Bruns, John 23
Brunswick officers, letters during the American Revolution 207
Brush, E H 86
Brutcher, C 17
Brutus, 15
Bruyas, J 86
Bryant, William Cullen 103
Buck, C 44
Buckley, E 15
Buckman, David 82
Budge, Henry 18 Priscilla 18
Buel, D 190
Buell, 77
Buff, B 251
Buffalo, 8 45 56 95 107 109 146 166 230 259
Buffaloe Creek, 258
Bufford, J H 147
Bull, W 232
Bullard, E 215 Otis A 138
Bulson, D 217
Bunker Hill Club, 112
Bunnell, A 102
Bunyan, Paul 10
Burgess, A 174
Burgoyne, 154 192 199 204 209 215 Gen 91 John 120 199 207
Burhans, M 44
Burke, 49 C 86 M B 147
Burned Over District, 75
Burns, John 23 Robert 127
Burr, 227 Aaron 129 137 195 208 Capt 134 David H 107 G 5 Madame 129
Burroughs, John 68
Burrville, 97
Burt, C H 147 O 224
Bush, H 118
Bushnell, C I 194
Bushwhackers, 83
Bushwick, 99 100
Buskist, 13
Busselle, A 253
Bussy, E 39
Busti, 27 Paul 109
Butler, 249 B 245 W A 112 Walter 208
Butterbut Valley, 175
Butterfield, R 175
Byrnes Tract, 25
Byron, 51
CLyde, 248
Cadbury, Warder H 53
Cadwallader, M 169
Cady, Elizabeth 261
Calder, A 9
Caldwell, A 123
Caledonia, 102
Calhoun, John C 188
Callender, J 99
Callicoon, 239
Cambridge, 156 246
Camden, 163

Camillus, 21 166
Camp Silas, 80
Camp meeting manual, 225 226
Campbell & Seward, 175
Campbell, C 239 D 177 W 242 W
    W 6
Camroden, 163
Canaan, 36 78
Canada Creek, 109
Canadarqua, 258
Canadasaga, 89
Canadice, 168
Canajoharie, 9 118
Canajoharie & Catskill Rail Road
    Company, 9
Canajoharie & the Sullivan-
    Clinton Expedition, 118
Canals, 6-8 230
Canandaigua, 19 168 233
Canasatego (Indian), 85
Canastigione, 3
Canastota, 105
Canfield & Clark, 162
Canning & Buxton, 255
Cannonsville, 39
Canoe Place, 238
Cantin, E 41
Cantine & Rainer, 9
Canton, 148 212
Canuteson, R 173
Cap-Tree Island, 236
Cape Vincent, 97 98
Caplise, J 168
Card, H 148
Cardiff Giant Humbug 18
Carey, Mathew 6
Carleton, Guy 199 Maj 208
Carman, H J 126
Caroline, 241 Street 248
Carpenter, M 190
Carse, R 234
Carthage, 97 148
Case & Smith, 106
Case, A 238 Henry 158 J 13 W 15
Casler, N 97
Cassadaga, 27 Lake 259
Castile, 263
Castle Creek, 5
Castle Town 114
Castleton, 56 189
Castorland, 101
Catharine, 218

Catskill, 9 52 56 Aqueduct 9 10
    Mountains 8-12 20 23 40 55 70
    79 93 95 182 226 227 Rivers 9
    Water System News ... 9
Cattaragus Reservation, 90
Cattaraugus, 12 13 Co 3 12-14 27
    259 Reservation 86 87 90 92
Cave of the Winds, 230
Cavert, W 214
Cawley, Tom 5
Cayuga, 14 Bridge 241 Co 14 15
    19 88 162 Indians 85 88 Lake
    20
Cazenove, Theophilus 109
Cazenovia, 105
Cedar Neck, 104
Cedarhurst, 122
Census 1790, 224
Census 1845, 224
Centerville 4
Central Bridge, 217
Central Islip, 235
Central NY, 14-27 162
Centuries in Elma 46
Century History of the Genesee
    Co Fair 1839-1939 51
Ceres, 4
Chadwick, G 52
Chalker, C 248
Chambers, Wm 195
Champion, 97 Simon B 17
Champlain, 31 73 192 201 Canal
    153 Valley 73 74 92 157 161
Champlin, J W 139
Chang, Li Hung 141
Chapin, L 13
Chaplain, 123
Chaplin, J 127
Chapman, M 213
Chappaqua, 251
Chard, L 28
Charles, C 243
Charlotte, 14 27 River Tract 25
    Temple 140
Charlotteville, 217
Charlton, 214 J 13
Chase, E 52 F 167 L 213 Mary M
    62
Chatham, 62
Chaumont, family 148 V Leray de
    148
Chautauqua, 27 28 Co 3 27-29

270

Chautque Co, 27 259
Chazy, 31
Cheektowaga, 45
Cheese making, 53
Chemung Co, 3 29
Chemung Valley, 29
Chenango, 5 Canal 30 Co 29-31 162
Cheney, T 29 167
Cherry Creek, 14 28
Cherry Valley, 26 86 175
 Methodists 18
Cheshire, 205
Chester, 170 171
Chichester, D 102
Child, 27 91 H 239 Hamilton 225
Childs, R 170
Chili, 114 115
Christian (Indian), 85
Christie, J 211
Christman, 68 H 59
Churchill, J 173
Cicero, 166
Cinderella Island, 46
Civil War, 82 125 132 138 141 145 151 158 166 239 254
Clarence, 45
Clarendon, 173 200
Clark, D 195 G 174 George W 35 H 29 J 102 166 Joseph 86 L 165 247 L G 224 Willis Gaylord 224
Clarke, C 168 M 121 T 96 165 T W 86
Clarkson, 115
Clarkston, T 36
Clarksville, 15
Claudius, 201
Claus, Daniel 148
Claverack, 36
Clawson, C 3
Clayton, 97 150 W 166 232
Clearwater, A 242
Cleaver, M 218
Clermont, 36 70
Cleveland, S 263
Clifton, 115 209 210 Park 214 Springs 168
Clinton, 41 163 Canal 259 Co 31 32 48 73 Square 163 166
Clinton, DeWitt 6 18 75 111 224 229 231 257 G 181 George 90

Clinton (continued)
 181 193 194 Gov 113 137 Henry 192 202-204 James 200
Clintondale, 242 243
Cloutier, I 50
Clove Branch, 41
Clowes, E 234
Clute, J 209 210
Clymer, 28
Coates, L 211
Cober, R 114
Cobleskill, 21 217 218
Cochecton, 239
Cochrane, C 243 M 30
Cocks, G 122
Coeymans, 2
Coffin, Alexander Jr 194 family 44 N W 148 R 44
Coghlan, Margaret 195 Mrs 195
Cohan, George M 132
Cohen, D S 59
Cohocton, 128 233
Cohoes, 2
Cold Spring, 178 Harbor 235
Cold Spring-on-Hudson, 178
Colden, 45 C 87 Cadwallader D 6
Cole, D 210 G G 181 H 42
Coleman, R 171
Colesville, 5
Colles, C 108 Christopher 107
Collier, E 37 F 35
Collins, 45 46 G 50 167
Colonial, charters, patents, & grants to NY City 35 highways of greater NY 34 NY 32-35 75 77 95
Colportage Wagon Work, 162
Colton, J H 59
Columbia Co, 1 35-38 59 63 70 74 79-81 83 84 120 197
Columbia Springs, 60
Columbiaville, 37
Colvin, Verplanck 160
Colwell, E 6 30
Comstock Prison, 70
Con Edison Power Co, 79
Concord, 46
Conde, E 216
Conesus, 102
Conesville, 218
Coney Island, 100 103
Congdon, 27

271

Conklin, M 255 H 195
Conlon, J 242
Connewango, 14
Conojohary Patent, 90
Conover, A 210 G 169
Constitution Island, 78
Conway, M 101 148 Moncure 80
Cook & Kaplan 5
Cook, 41 A 50 D 46 F 48 87
   Flavius J 49 J 49 M 148 Mr 6 T 249
Cookingham, H 162
Coolidge, Calvin 104 G 148
Cooney & Powell, 115
Cooney, E 54
Cooper, Fenimore 131 J 175 176 234 James Fennimore 23 67 95 Joseph (Mrs) 122 M 60 W 175 William 176
Cooperstown, 18 20 23 175 176
Copake, 36
Copeland, D 173
Coram, 235 236
Corbett, J 218
Corbin, J 212
Cordonnier, V 167
Corey, A 245
Corfu, 51
Corinth, 83 214
Corland, 21
Corn Island, 98
Cornbury, Gov 33 Lord 32 33
Cornell, A 250 G 253
Corning, 233 A 172
Cornish, C 38
Cornplanter (Indian), 85 86
Cornplanter, Jesse 87
Cornwall, 171 222 Co 33 District Club 60
Cortland, 19 38 251 Co 14 16 19 38 162
Cortlandville, 41
Cossayuna, 246
Cossville, 21
Cottage, 13
Cotter, O 103
Couch, F 253
Coughlin, J 96 R 98
County of Dutchess 40
Court of General Sessions, 125
Coutant, L 253
Couzens, M 250

Coventry, 30
Cow Neck, 235
Cowles, Caroline 168 G 247
Cox, Abraham Beekman 175 Lyman A 159
Coxe, 196
Coxsachie, 52
Cozzens, I 127
Crait, 189
Cranberry Lake, 212
Crane, M 118
Crapsey, E 128
Craven, C 236
Crawlier, 64
Cresswell, D 196
Crime, 128 136 185 224
Crocker, E 28 F 263
Crockett's Corners, 102
Crofut, D 172
Croquet, 257
Crosby, Enoch 193
Crosfields Purchase map, 109
Cross, 75
Croton Aqueduct, 60
Croton-on-Hudson, 251
Crown Point, 48 109 119 149 150 228
Crozier, Hiram P 20
Crumb Elbow, 71
Crysdale & Wait, 15
Cuba, 4
Culnon, Cornelius 149
Cumpston, D 114
Curley, E 240
Currie-Bell, A 238
Curtin & Hewitt, 87
Curtin, J 87
Curtis, G 212
Curtiss, G H 24
Cushman & Nichols, 250
Cushman, E 250
Cusick, D 87
Custer, E 99
Cutchogue, 235
Cutten G & M, 19
Cypress Hills, 100
Cypress, J Jr 66
DAR, 248 Sew-kat-si Chapt 213
Daily, F 50
Dairy industry, 224 225
Dalphin, M 254
Dana, 130 Deacon 259

Danforth, E 252
Daniel Gray Fishing Club, 76
Daniels, H 43
Dannemora, 31 Prison 70
Dansville, 102
Darien, 51
Dark Island, 98
Darling, Johnny Caesar Cicero 10
Darlington, O 120
Darrow, F 28
Darrow School, 220 221
Davenport, C 37
David, M 263
Davidson, H 39
Davies, J 128 T 174
Davis, 1 E 116 G 103 P 28 S 87 W 210
Davison, E 44
Dawes, E 87
Dawson, H 250 255 H B 196
Day, C 240
Dayton, 13 14 Township 13
DeBehr, Charles 127
DeBevoise, Henry S 179
DeCosta, B 196
DeCrevecoeur, 75 76
DeForeest, 33
DeGekruicigde, Christus 33
DeKalb, 212
DeKay, James 228
DeLancey, E 252 Oliver 202
DeLanoy, 179
DeLavergne, C 44
DeLisio, D 248
DeLong, H 102
DePeyster, John Watts 207
DePuy, Col 123
DeRonde, Lambertus 33
DeSille, Nicasius 34
DeVine, J 39
DeWitt, W 243
Decker, M 196 Spiketooth 239
Deerfield, 163
Deerpark, 171 172 235
Delavan, Edward C 55
Delaware & Hudson Canal 8 9 81
Delaware Co, 23 25 38-40
Delaware Indians, 88 95 120
Delaware River, 10 139
Delaware Valley, 8-12 240
Delhi, 39

Democratic Republican General Committee, 112
Dempsey, 171
Dencke, C F 88
Dengler, D 118
Denley, 110
Denniston, G 170 232
Depauville, 97
Deruyter, 105 Township 106
Dever, M 163
Devereaux, L 165
Devoll, J 168
Devoy, J 45
Devyr, T A 60
Dewey, Almira Melpomena 162 Anna Diadema 162 Armenius Philadelphus 162 Encyclopedia Britannica 162 Franklin Jefferson 162 Marcus Bonaparte 162 Octavia Ammonia 162 Philander Seabury 162 Pleiades Arastarcus 162 Timothy 162 Victor Mellenus 162
Dewitt, 166
Dexter, 97
Dexter, O P 155
Diamant, L 197
Diarpino, C 44
Dibble, Ebenezer 152
Dilley, B 27
Dillon, 253 J J 224
Dimitroff & Janes, 233
Dirlam & Simmons, 46
Disbrow, L 128
Disturnell, J 128
Dobbs Ferry, 62 251
Dobie, R 237
Dobson, H 118
Dockstader, Jacob 68
Dodge, 166 R 235 Tristram 235
Doig, A 178
Dolge, Alfred 156
Dominy, family 104
Donaldson, A L 181 T 88 Thomas 88
Donlon, H 118
Donohoe, M 219
Donovan, H 49 M 12
Dora & Keough, 49
Dornburgh, H 149

Dorsey, B 13
Dosoris Island, 121
Doty, 27 L 3 L L 101 L R 101
Dougherty, E 171
Douglas, 240 E 225
Douglass, 44 H 262 263
Dover, 41 Furnace 84 Plains 84
Dow, M 31
Downing, R 121
Downs, 27
Draft riots in NY (City), 125
Draheim, H 53
Drew, H 101
Drumlin Square, 249
Dryden, 241
Duanesburg, 216
Duboc, J 255
Dubois & Smith, 209
DuBois, A 100 C 244 Frederick Nelson 56 Gualtherus 33
Duck Rock, 71
Duer, Wm A 129
Duffy, J 129
Dugdale, R 60
Dumans, E 212
DuMont, Rachel 208 209
Dunbar, Duncan 127
Duncan, J M 88 W 129
Duncombe, F & C 252
Dundee, 263
Dunham, M 106
Dunkirk, 28 226
Dunn, E 118 J 176 N 61 Nathaniel 61 W 44
Dunseith, F 178
DuPont, Rosalie 193
Durant & Pierce, 96 212
Durant, S 162
Durham, 11 52
Durkee, C 215
Durlach & Blumin, 218
Durland, F 170
Durston, H 167
Duryea, 61
Dutch, 35 90 91 172 242 books & pamphlets 32 dialect from old NY 80 houses 75 settlers in Kings Co 100 trouble with Indians 90 91
Dutchess Co, 40-44 57 58 61 69 75 78-80 87 95 197 204 205 226

Duvall, R 237 238
Dyson, V 234 235
Eager, S 170
Eagle & Brooklyn 99
Eames, Wilberforce 144
Eardeley, W 179
Earth-Closets ... 143 144
East, Aurora 46 260 Fishkill 41 Floyd 163 Hampton 104 235 Island 121 Meadow 121 New York 100 Norwich 121 Randolph 14 River 110 133 Rochester 115 Rockaway 121 Unadilla 176 Williston 121 235
East River Bridge 129
Easthampton, 105
Eastlake, A 164
Easton, 246 247
Easton, John 119
Eaton, 105 106
Eaton, Amos 7 Ebenezer 259 H 249 Rev Mr 249
Eaton's Neck, 235
Eatonbrook Valley, 106
Ebenezer, 46 47
Ebenezer Society, 47
Ecclesiastical records ... NY ... 1621-1810, 33
Ecob, H 176 K 175
Eddy, A 19
Edelstein, D 182
Eden, 46 William 202
Edinburgh, 200 256
Edison, 130 Machine Works 61
Edmeston, 176
Edmonds, W 164 W D 197
Edsall, T 123
Edson, O 27
Edwards & Rattray, 103
Edwards, 212 C 237 E 176 Jonathan 84
Efner, 197
Eichner, F 253
Eights, James 84
Einhorn, Arthur 149
Eisner, J 122
Elba, 51
Eldredge, M 248
Elgin Botanic Garden, 147
Elizabethtown, 48
Elko, 13
Ellenville, 243

Ellicott, 28 B 109 Joseph 109
Ellicottville, 13
Ellington, 14 Geo 129
Elliott, Charles L 142
Ellis, E R 129 F 12 35 W J 61
Ellis Hollow, 241
Ellsworth & Richmond, 106
Elma, 46 47
Elmira, 29
Elting, I 244
Elwood, G 116
Ely, Edwin L 143
Emens, H 115
Emerson, 80 E 96 L 53
English, Crown Grants 71 land grants & shore rights 71
Entwistle, O 30
Environmentalism, 79
Eppes, Lyman 158
Erie Canal, 7 226 building 6 building errors expose 8 letters by DeWitt Clinton 6 map 8 medal 7 sesquicentennial pictures 7 survey by Stephen Van Rensselaer 7 termination at Black Rock vs Buffalo 8 tolls 6
Erie Co, 3 19 44-47 258 260
Erie Railroad, 228 232
Erieville, 106
Ernenwein, R 164
Ernewein, R 165
Erwin, C 233
Esopus, 243
Esopus Indians, 12
Esperance, 218
Essex, 48 49 Co 47-49 150
Estabrook, A 61
Estelle, 240
Estlake, A 19
Euphemia, 70
Evans, 46 C 182 E 163 M 97 Wm 106
Everest, 32 A 31 149 A S 149
Everett, Edward 55
Everitt, C P 129
Evers, Alf 11 182
Ewell, E 44
Faigle, E 167
Fair Plain, 13
Fairfield, 53
Fairhaven, 15

Fairport, 115
Fake, K 217
Fala, 75
Fales, E Jr 197
Famines, fires & festivals, 5
Fanning, Capt 84
Far Rockaway, 121 High School students 123
Farley, J 210
Farmingdale, 121
Farmington, 169
Farnham, C W 149
Fast, Howard 61
Faulds, C 211
Faust, R 174
Fayel, J 98
Fayette, 219
Fayetteville, 166
Feldman, B 239
Fell, H 213
Fellows & Roseboom, 168
Fellows, Moses 198
Felter, W 100
Fenians, 261
Fennessy, L 48
Fenwick, 27
Ferguson, H 236
Fernow, B 1
Ferris, F 240 L 251
Fiction, 88 104 140 147 151 157 193 247
Fiegl, E 4
Field & Waugh, 233
Field, 130 B 97 234 F 103 L 234 M 123 150
Fifth Grade Thomas Jefferson School, 252
Figliomeni, M 197
Fillmore, 4 141 Millard 19 202 Mr 258
Finney, 74 75 C G 224 Charles G 22
Fire Island, 235
Fish, 130 of western NY 257 preserved 140
Fisher, C 101 E 100 198 Elijah 198 J 168
Fisher's Island, 236
Fishkill, 41 58 63 73 128 133 197 Hook 41 Landing 41 Plains 41
Fisk, James Jr 141
Fiske, S 130

Fitch, A 246 247 J 98 M 50
Fitzgerald, C 1
Fitzpatrick, S 32
Flagg, J 130
Flagg's Flats, 130
Flanagan, M 3
Flatbush, 99 100
Flatlands, 99 100 105
Fleishmanns, 39
Fleming, 15
Flexner, J T 88 198
Flick, A C 182
Flint, The 244
Flora of the Adirondacks 159
Floral Park, 121
Floyd, 163
Floyd-Jones, E 178
Flushing, 81 179
Fluvanna, 28
Fly, J C 62
Flying pioneers at Hammondsport NY, 24
Follett, F 257
Folsom, G 102 M 30
Folts, A 163 J 233
Fonda, 118
Foote, C 216 J 177
Forbes, R 253
Forbush, W 123
Ford, P L 104 198 257 W C 150
Fordham, 251
Foreman, E 116
Forest fires of 1903, 150
Forest Road, 171
Forester, Frank 62 66
Forestville, 28
Forkey, D 50
Forman, S 173
Forrestal, M 41
Forsyth, M 243
Forts, Ann 62 Covington 49 50 Edward 88 91 150 152 159 162 198 202 246 247 George 196 Johnson 89 Montgomery 151 202 Niagara 91 257 Oswego 188 Plain 118 Putnam 200 Schuyler 165 206 Stanwix 91 206 Ticonderoga 203 Washington 198
Fortress West Point, 204
Foster, J 198 Nathaniel 94
Fouquet, L 150

Four Track Series, 227
Fowler & Nagel, 28
Fowler, 212 A 212 E 243 Edward 220 H 62 Lorenzo 128 Orson 128 R 33
Fox, Charles James 195 J 253 W 150
France, king of 86 87
Francis, A M 9 J 130 John W 130 131
Francke, K 176
Frankel & Dublin, 131
Franklin, Benjamin 85
Franklin Co, 31 49 50 97 212
Franklinville, 13
Fraser, J 190
Fraud, politics & the dispossession of the Indians 90
Frederic Harold, 147
Fredericksburg, 205
Fredonia, 28
Fredriksen, B 41
Free Masonry, 23 224 See also Anti-Masonry
Free Will Baptist, 21
Freedom, 13
Freeland, D 172
Freeman, A 210 J 19 20
Freeport, 121
Freeville, 241
Fremont, 239
French & Indian Wars 77 87-90 92 152 153 159 201
French Creek, 28 Yorkers 29
French, 17 21 A 198 250 Edwin Davis 135 143 J H 183 R 263
French occupation of the Champlain Valley ..., 148
French-Onondaga dictionary 94
Frenchville, 163
Freneau, Philip 131
Friars Club ... NY City ..., 132
Fried, M 243
Friendship, 4
Frisbee, P 37
Frontenac expedition, 90
Frontier lands handled for military veterans, 25
Frontier to 1825, 28
Frontiersmen, 207
Frost, A B 11 G 249 genealogy 122

Frothingham, W 50 118
Fulcher, W 252
Fuller, E 30 J 163 P 51
Fullerton, E 104
Fulton, 22 171 174 Chain 54 Co 1 50 118 215
Fulton, E 98 Robert 64 137 184
Furman, G 99
Gabriels, 50
Gaine, Hugh 134 198
Gaines, 173
Galatian, A 29
Gallatin, 36
Galloway, H 40
Gallt, F 52
Galpin, H 30 W 162
Ganaoque, 150
Gansevoort, 214
Garabrands, Peter 76
Garand, P 97 213
Garbutt, 118 P 118
Garden City, 121
Gardiner, 243 D 235 E 170 J T 261
Gardiner's Island, 236
Gardner, E E 9 H 15
Garrison's Landing, 179
Gasford, Paul 262
Gass, M 236
Gates, 115
Gay Head, 41
Gaynor, William 130
Gebhard, E 36
Geddes, 166
Geiger, L 46
Genesee, 263 Co 44 50 51 114 257 Country 3 51 Falls 258 Gorge 257 River 86 117 Tract 262 Valley 102 228
Geneseo, 102
Geneva, 169 233
Genoa, 15
Genung, A 241
George Washington Bridge, 111 132
Gephart, R M 183
Gerhard, M 253
German theater 136
Germans, 216
Germantown, 36
Gerrow, J 242
Gerry, P & R 123

Gerwig, H 179
Getman, M 15
Ghent, 36
Gibbs, I & A 121 R 62 Theron Zadock 62
Giddings, E 2
Gifford, F 168
Gilbert, J 4
Gilbertsville, 176
Gilchrist, A 244 K 252
Gilder, R 132
Gill, I 246 247
Gillet, W 97
Gillette, Chester E 20 S 28
Gilliland, Wm 49
Gilman, W 62 211
Gimelli, L 174
Girl Scouts, 45
Gleason & Nulty, 212
Glen Cove, 121
Glen, G 99
Glen Haven, 115
Glenco Mills, 36
Glenn, M 49
Glenora, 263
Glens Falls, 62 111 245
Glenville, 216
Glovack, J 45
Glover, W 44
Gloversville, 50 157 158
Goat Island, 145
Goddard, A 190
Golden Anniv of Sherill 164
Golden Era of Trenton Falls 164
Gomph, J 30
Goodenoughs, Joshua 92
Goodrich, G 241
Goodwin, H 38 241
Gordon, D 252 W 214
Gore, Obadiah Jr 208
Gorham, B W 225 F W 68 L B 68
Goshen, 171
Gotham, 135
Gould & Klaber, 236
Gould, 130 E 96 Edwin 138 J 39 Jay 39 64 138 139
Goulds, 64
Gouveneur, 212
Governor's Island, 123
Gowanda, 13
Grady, J 54
Graff, S 252

Grafton, 189
Graham, 41 J 239
Grand Canal, 229
Grand Island, 46
Grand-View-On-Hudson, 210
Granger, 4
Granger, Erastus 94 95 J 168 M E 150
Grant, President 182
Granville, 62
Grass Island, 236
Gravesend, 99
Gray & Savage, 62
Gray, E 88 K 177
Gray Man, 83
Great Card Game 25
Great Neck, 121
Great Sodus Bay, 249
Greater Ridgewood, 100
Greece, 115
Green, F 210 Hetty 141 J 42 W 249
Green Island, 2
Green Mountain Club, 79
Green River, 84
Greenburg, 251
Greene, 30 Co 1 11 51 52
Greene, G W 198 N 118 215 Nathanael 198
Greenpoint, 100
Greenport, 36
Greensville, 172
Greenville, 52 171 251
Greenwich, 247
Greenwood Lake, 171
Gregg, A 2 3
Gregory, W 183
Grenell Island, 97
Greylock, Godfrey 222
Grider, R A 206
Gridley, A 163 L 88 Luke 88
Griffen, C & S 63
Griffin, A 237 E 250 William Joseph 213
Griffins Mills 44
Griffis, W E 88
Grills, R 105
Groce & Wallace, 183
Grose, E 214
Groton, 241
Grymes Hill, 209
Guilderland, 2 3

Guilford, 30
Gulder, A 219
Gumaer, P 171 Peter E 172
Hadden, James M 199
Haddock, J 96 150
Hakes, H 232
Halcott, 52 Valley 52
Half Moon, 202 214
Hall & Patterson, 166
Hall, 14 C R 133 E 166 Edward H 161 H 14 150 James 84 228 L 12 M 236 R 151
Hallock, B 117 L 237
Halsey, A 238 Francis Whiting 178 G 178 Gaines Leonard 178 R 226 W 234
Hamblin, J 39
Hamburg, 46
Hamilton, 106
Hamilton, A 199 Alexander 199 M 183 W 100
Hamilton Co 52 53 110 151
Hamlet, 14
Hammersley, S 215
Hammerstein, Oscar 130
Hammond, 212 Jabez 229 L 105
Hammondsport, 24 233
Hampton Port, 237
Hampton, V 209
Hancock, 39
Hand, H 103 M 168
Hand weaving & dyeing 17
Hanford, F 114
Hankin, Montague 12
Hanna, A 151
Hannibal, 174
Hanover, 28
Hansen, H 250 254
Hanson, W 216
Harbor News Association, 133
Hardenbrook, L 37
Hardie, J 133
Hardin, G 53
Harding, V 100
Hardy, James E 257
Harlem, 123
Harmony, 28
Harriman, 75 173 family 171
Harriman-Bear Mountain State Park, 75
Harrington, H 63
Harris, G 88 J 254

Harrison, 112 254 B (Mrs) 135 F 33 Gen 160 William Henry 111 112
Harry Hills Dance Hall on the Bowery, 133
Hart, I 116 John 5 L 50
Harte, C R 200
Hartford, 62 247
Hartsdale, 251
Hartwick, 176
Hartwood, 239
Harum, David 26
Harvey, Geo 66 H 251
Hasbrouck & Heidgerd, 244
Hasbrouck, F 40 K 171 243 244 M 166
Hasbrouk, K 171
Haskell, C K 10 D C 108
Hasselbarth, 210
Hassett, W 63
Hastings, 251
Hastings, H 33
Hastings-on-Hudson, 66 251
Hatch, J 31 V 28
Hathaway, B 88
Hauppauge, 236
Hausner, K 218
Haverstraw, 71 207 210 211
Hawes, H 145 L 45
Hawley, C 89 219 J 116
Haydenville, 15
Haydock, G 63 George 63
Hayes, A 48 C 30 M 24 Simeon (Mrs) 155
Hayner, M 190 R 190
Hazard, T R 20
Hazes, Col 198
Hazletine, G 28
Hazleton, 64 H 99
Head of the Harbor, 236
Headley, J 151 R 170
Health & recreation in the North Woods, 152
Heartman, C F 133 134 Charles F 133 134
Heath, H 98
Heaton, G 29
Hebron, 62
Hedges, H 234 235 237 P 238
Hedley, 27
Hedrick, U P 183
Heffernak, K 167

Heidt, W 239 W Jr 241
Heimer, M 215
Heinemann, E 11
Heiner, G 98
Heitman, F B 184
Hell's Acres, 74
Hellebergh, 3
Hemans, M 234
Hemlock Lake, 102
Hempstead, 105 121 122
Henderson, 97
Hendricks, H 243
Hendrie, C 237
Henrietta, 115
Henry, G W 257 258 J Raymond 137
Hensley, P 212
Herbert, Henry William 66 Victor 132
Herkimer, 53 54 Co 1 53 54 156 215 Flood 53
Herrick, J 4
Hessians, 207 208
Heusser, A H 89
Heuvelton, 212
Hewitt, G 97
Hewlett, 122
Hiawatha, 81
Hick's Neck the story of Baldwin LI 121
Hickey, A 243
Hicks, A 134 C 42 239
Hicksville, 122
High Bridge, 5
High Rock, 9
Highland, 63
Highmarket, 101 148
Highways, 20 34
Hildebrun, C R 33
Hildreth, E 235
Hill, D (Gov) 1 H 45 52 J W 228 L B 63 W 151 246
Hillard, E B 200
Hillburn, 59
Hillery, 44 H 178
Hillsdale, 36 J 36
Hillside Lake, 41
Hilton, 115
Hinckley, 163
Hine & Davis, 209
Hine, C 209 C G 64 104 Thomas Avery 64

279

Hinman, M 5
Hiram, P Crozier NY 20
Hislop, C 1
Hitchcock, E 52 S 102
Hoag, 44
Hoben, A 254
Hochschild, H 52 53
Hodge, F W 184
Hodges, A 121 Jacob 19
Hoecher, R 241
Hoffman, C F 226 J 99 L 122 R 250
Hogue & Agne, 251
Holbrook, T W 258
Holcomb, H 14
Holden, A 245 Eben 151 J 245 Joseph 35
Holland Patent, 163
Holland Purchase, 109
Holland, R 46
Hollcroft, T 219
Hollenbeck, 77
Holley, G 145 O L 226
Hollis, E 233
Homan, L 239
Homer, 16 26
Honeoye, 115 169 Falls 115
Honeywell, E 258 R 50
Honeywood, Saint John 220
Hoosick Falls, 152
Hopewell, 41 63 Jct 41
Hopkins, Frank E 104
Hopkinton, 212
Hops, 20 22
Horicon Lodge, 153
Hornby, E 173
Horne, 253 P 252
Hornell, 233
Hornor, J W Jr 200
Horse racing, 171
Horseheads, 29
Horsford, C 238
Horton, 44 S 251 W 96 253
Hortontown, 41
Hosmer & Bruce, 151
Hotchkin, A 176
Hotels, 231
Hough, F 96 98 101 212 F B 33 73 89 120 184 200 Franklin B 101 149 155 R B 151
Howard, 138 E & V 146 H 99
Howe, A 178 Elias 153 M 4

Howell & Tenney, 1
Howell, G 215 238 N 234
Howes, W 184
Howland, Darius 77 E 14
Howlett, 13
Hoyt, E 64
Hubbard, Elbert 46 152
Hubbell, R 218
Hudowalski, G 152
Hudson, 36 37 80 81
Hudson Falls, 247
Hudson, Henry 64 184
Hudson Highlands, 64 65 79 173 179 200 226
Hudson River 2 58 65 69 70 76 83 86 108 120 128 171 184 192 196 204 226 228 244 253 258 259 chains 197 200 map 8 106 109-111
Hudson River, Telephone Directory 65 66 Valley 160
Hudson Valley, 10 54-84 184 193 200 203 207 258
Hufeland, O 66 250 252
Hughes, G 177
Huguenots, 231 253
Hull, N 189 232 R 173
Hultz, H 250
Hume, 4
Hummel, C F 104
Hungerford, E 51
Hunt, A 178 L L 201 T 36 121 W 10 W S 66 Walter 153
Hunter, Dard 73
Huntington, 229 236 W 177
Huntting, I 42
Hurd, D 31 175
Hurley, 243
Huron, 249
Husted, S 115 116
Hutchins, J N 21 134 John Nathan 134
Hutchinson, S A 2
Hutton, T 10
Hyatt, E 252
Hyde, J 30 John 30 L 245
Hyde Park, 41
Hydesville, 169
Ice Island, 98
Ilion, 54
Independent Salt Co, 26
Indian Lake, 53

Indian Pass, 48
Indians, 15 75 84-96 245 affairs 95 120 bead identification 91 bread root of the Senecas 88 Five Nations 90 in North Hempstead Township 122 medals 89 narratives of massacres & depredations 85 Six Nations of NY 87-90 92 96 treaties printed by Benjamin Franklin 85 wars 119 See also individual tribes
Industrial Advertising Co of America, 36
Industrial directory, 231
Ingersoll, R 30 R C 30
Ingraham, J H 66 P 215
Interbrook Lodge, 152
Inventors & inventions of Cayuga Co, 14
Inwood, 122
Ireland, J N 134
Irish, 165
Iron mines, 75
Iron Mountain, 152
Iron ore, 152
Irondequoit, 115
Ironmaking industry, 84
Iroquois Indians, 84 86-88 90-92 186 Confederation 87 games & dances 87 languages 86 87 League 88
Irvin, F 122
Irving, 28 226 Washington 10 55 66 67 111 131 202
Irvington, 252
Isaac Carow, 134 135
Isbell, L 106
Island Park, 122
Isle of Long Ago 68 69
Islip, 236
Israel, N 32
Ithaca, 23 241 259
Ives, H 49
Jackel, A 1
Jackman, W 46
Jackson, 246
Jackson & Gibbs, 177
Jackson, Andrew 232 C 248 F 177 Gen 61 160
Jackson Whites 59
Jacob, R 5

Jacobs, S 248
Jacoby, J 164
Jagendorf, M 10
Jagger, W 104
Jamaica, 104 179
James, F 217 H 36
Jameson, Hugh 261
Jamestown, 27 28 Academy 27
Jay, John 201
Jaycox, 179
Jefferson, 218 227
Jefferson Co, 96-99 146 157
Jefferson Valley, 252
Jefferson, W 235 238
Jeffrey, R 227
Jemison, Mary 86 93
Jenkins, S 5
Jenkinson, I 227
Jerusalem, 123 263
Jervis, C 233
Jessup's Landing, 214
Jesuit Missions, 89
Jewell, 163 I 100
Jewett, 52
Jews, 66 117
Jogues, I 33 Isaac 85
Johnson, 102 A G 68 C 44 174 246 E 49 F M 68 G 54 H S 36 Hiram W 74 John 207 P 117 P D 201 R 145 Richard M 114 W 209 William 85 88-90 92 94 120 148 157 160 189
Johnston, G 236 H 98 J 209
Johnstown, 50 68
Jones, Ignatius 2 37 L 176 Martha 127 Mr 230 P 163 247
Jordan, Dr 127
Joshua, a man of the Finger Lakes Region 17
Jr Hist Soc, 44
Juckett, M 153
Judah, S B H 135
Judd, O 30 Samuel 140
Jukes, family 60 61
Jumel, Madame 129
Junius, 21 219
Kaatskill Mountains, 230 See also Catskill Mountains
Kaiser, C 145 L 227
Kallicicki, E 30
Kalsbeck, E 115
Kanadesaga, 169

Kane, J 153 M 144
Kanisteo Valley, 232
Karaghtadie (Indian), 85
Katkamier, A 169
Katonah, 252
Kauterskill Falls, 231
Kayaderosseras Grant, 90
Kayaderosseras Mountains, 154
Kayderosseras, 154
Keeler, Morris 20
Keeney, 38
Keeseville, 48
Kelby, W 202
Kelleher, W 255
Keller & Little, 213
Keller, E 115 W 3
Kellogg, D S 31 F 21 L 247 S 118 Spencer 118
Kelsey, 29 J 117 179
Kemp, O 11
Kendall, 173
Kenmore, 46
Kennedy, J 51
Kenney, J 1
Kensico Reservoir, 66
Kensler, G 241
Kent, C A 122 Chancellor 56 137 142 E 68 172
Kerns, E 15
Keskachauge, 99
Keskequa Trail, 103
Kesse, G 176
Ketchum, R J 6 W 45
Keyser, L 218
Kiefer, W 211
Kielty, B 135
Kim, S 69
Kimball, F 1 H 145
Kinchen, O 153
Kinderhook, 37 111-113
Kinderuntie (Indian), 85
King, C 245 Francis S 135 H 241
King's Bridge, 64 123 250
King's Landing, 115
Kingman, L 240
Kings Co, 99-101 204
Kings Daughters, 48
Kingsbury, 159
Kingston, 62 85 98 190 208 243
Kinns, H 213
Kipsbergen, 41
Kirchwey, G W 70

Kirkland, 163 S 89 Samuel 89
Klein, H 135 M M 184
Klingel, M 46
Klock, E 54 J N 21
Knapp, E 104 family 104 Frances J 239 H & C 98 J 227 Jacob 227 S L 69
Knight, R 211
Knoepfel, W H 10
Knoepfel's Cave, 10
Koke, R J 65
Kolff, C 209
Krieger, A 115
Kruger, H 97
Ku Klux Klan, 19 21 256
Kurtz, D 38 M 241
LaRue, J 98
Lackawanna, 46
Lacy, I & A 145
Ladies Soc of Universalist Ch, 177
Ladue, D 115
Lafayette, 166
Lafayette & Lisle, 6
Lagrange, 41
Lakes, Champlain 86 150 152 158 159 195 258 Erie 145 226 228 259 George 71 89 148 150 152 153 156 157 158 160-162 188 192 194 197 230 245 Luzerne 196 Mahopac 179 Memphremagog 150 Mohonk 81 Ontario 148 188 Placid 48 153 158 Ronkonkoma 236 Tear in the Clouds 69 Titus 50
Lake Champlain Valley, 89
Lakemont, 263
Lamb, M J 135
Lamont, T 217 Thomas William 217
Lancaster, 47 B 202
Landauer, B 135 Bella C 135
Landesman, A 100
Landon, H 96 97 J 98
Lankes, F 46 47
Lankevich & Furer, 135
Lansing, 77 241
Lansing, R 97
Lansing Township, 241 242
Lansingburgh, 85 190
Lape, J 49
Lapham, E 238

Larchmont Manor Park, 252
Larned, J 45 J N 184
Larremore, T & A 104
Larson, H 176
Latham, C 14
Lathrop, J 37
Lauber, Charles 11
Laurens, John 199
Lautenschlaeger, M 170
Law, George 141
Lawrence & Andrews, 135
Lawrence, 122 Polly 220
Lawson, H 179
Lawyer, W 5
LeGallienne, R 245
LeRoy, 51 258
LeViness, J 251
Lea, George 77
League of Women Voters, 251
Leather, glove industry in the U S 157 tanning & currying 16
Leathersich, D 102
Leavitt, P 49
Lebanon, 106 232 Springs 37 158 220 Valley Church 221
Lee, C 227 F 114 H 240
Leete, C 213
Leetown, 41
Lefevre, R 244
Legend of Sleepy Hollow 67
Legend of the Bushwhacker Basket 82 83
Lehman, K 105
Leng & Davis, 209
Lenni Lenape Indians, 95
Lennox, Charlotte Ramsay 70
Lenox, 106
Leon, 13 14
Leonard, I 13 J 136 Stephen Banks 21 W A 21
Leptondale, 171
Leslie, E 167
Leuchs, F 136
Levy, S 171
Lewin, L & W 254
Lewis Co, 97 101 148 155 160
Lewis, Benjamin Franlin 63 F 6 J 41 69 Sinclair 57
Lewis Patent, 152
Lewisboro, 252
Lewiston, 145
Liberty, 239

Lichtenthaeler, F 10
Lieber, F 69
Lienhard, F 43
Lilly, 95 J 5
Lima, 137
Lincoln, (Abraham) 16 18 54 150 155 Maj Gen 206
Lincoln, (town) 106
Lindsley, C 253
Link, L 37
Linn, Wm 136
Linton, E 234
Lisle, 6
Littell, W 176
Little, Abraham 85
Little Africa, 132
Little Britain, 171
Little Falls, 22 54
Little Hoosick River, 189
Little Neck, 179
Little Nine Partners 42
Livermore, S 176
Liverpool, 166
Livingston Co, 3 101-103 114
Livingston, 37 77 79 E B 70 Edward 111 family 57 70 75 83 legacy 83 Manor 36 R R 70 Robert 70 Robert R 70 192 201
Livingstone, family 2
Lloyd Harbor, 236
Lloyd, 243 J P 239
Lock Street, 248
Locke, 15 172
Lockie, L 258
Lockport, 145
Lockwood, Belva A 262
Locust Valley, 105 122
Lodi, 219
Loesch, F 176
Loescher, B G 153
Log Cabin & Hard Cider campaign, 112
Log of, *Spendthrift II* 71 *Totem* 104
Lomas & Peace, 99
Lonergan, C 48
Long, Eddy 240
Long Island, 71 95 99 103-105 120 154 179 194 201 203 231 234 235 238 City 179 Colonial Patents 105 Sound 104
Long Lake, 49 53

Long, Peter H 220
Longellow, 81
Longstretch, T M 153
Loomis Gang, 17
Loomis, K 52
Loon Lake, 233
Lord, J 190
Lorillard, 173
Lorraine, 97 98
Lossing, B 136 B J 202 227 Benson J 112
Lott, R 236
Lotterer, E 40
Lotteries, 227 228
Loudoun, Earl of 150
Lovell, Gen 141
Low, 77 Isaac 190
Lowder, Mr 24
Lowe, E B 117
Lowi, T J 136
Lowville, 101 151
Loyalists, 120 187 202 205 207 209
Lucanera, V M 202
Lucas, F W 153
Luce, G 13
Luck, M E 152
Ludington, Henry 205
Ludlowville, 242
Lum, D 170 David B 170
Lumber trade, 55
Luquer, E 251
Luther, L 15
Lutz, E 219
Luzerne, 245 Chevalier de la 195 196
Lyman, H 97 Phineas 150 S 136
Lyme, 98
Lynch, C 29
Lyncroft, 252
Lyndon, 13
Lyon, C 248 Caleb 153
Lyons, 248 249 Falls 17 101
Lysander, 166 167
M'Alpine, J 154
MacCracken, 80 H 40 H N 40
MacLaren, W 102
MacMorris, M 246
Macatamney, H 136
Macedon, 248
Macedonia, 15
Machias, 13

Mackenzie, W L 113
Macleod, R 46
Madison Co, 14 30 101 105 106 162
Madison, James 231
Maghaghkamik, 172
Maguire, Robert 200
Maher, R 41
Malden Bridge, 37
Maleska, 95
Mallman, J 238
Malone, 50
Maloney, D 115
Malt houses, 55
Malverne, 122
Mamakatting Park, 240
Mamaroneck, 252
Manchester, 169
Mandeville, Rev 179
Manhattan, 105 126 127 Beach 100 Island 128 129 132 137 141 198 maps 108
Manley, H 90 238
Manlius, 26 166 167
Manly, J 12
Mann & King, 4
Mann, H 122 203
Manning, D 213
Manor of, Cortlandt 69 Rensselaerwyck 74
Mante, T 154
Manville, P (Mrs) 154
Maps, 106-111
Mara & Sachse, 240
Marathon, 38
Marbletown, 81 243
Marcellus, 167
Marcosson, I 164
Marcy, 163 Gov 153
Marengo, 248
Margaretville, 39
Marilla, C 47
Marion Press, 104
Marion, V 248
Markham, 13
Marks, David 21 M 21 22
Marlboro, 243
Marsh Island, 98
Marsh, Richard 16
Marshall, 163 164 M H 154 O 145 146
Martha's Vineyard, 104

Martin, C 114 242 E W 136 J P 203
Martinsburg, 153
Mary Powell, steamer, 64
Maryland, 176
Mason, H 245
Massena, 160 212 213
Massey, F 97
Masten, A 2 245
Mather, F G 203 J 228 W W 228
Mathews, J 137
Mathews-Northrup, 109
Mathias, F 210
Mathiasen, M 154
Mathies, J 258
Matinecock, 122 Indians 105
Matteson, A (Mrs) 258
Mattice, B 218
Mattituck, 236
Maude, J 258
Maurice, James 140
Maverick, A 137 Peter 137
Maxwell, 249 M 166
Mayham, A 217
Maynadier, G 70
Mayo, A D 71
Mays, V 251
McCabe, A 210
McCartan, C 106
McCarthy, B 4
McCartney, W 50
McClellan, George 113
McCrea, Jane 209
McCullough, E 100
McDade, T 185
McDermott, C 234
McDowell, W 90
McGee, James 197
McGinnis, E 118
McGrane, 196
McGrath, E F 70
McIntosh, F 14 W 114 168 248
McKelvey, B 117
McKim, C 136
McKinstry, Justus 132
McLellan, Hugh 31
McMahon, H 27
McMartin, D 50
McMaster, G 232
McNamara, A 5 T 164
McNamee, D 35

McRorie, W 177
McWatters, G S 136
McWhorter, E 173 246
Mechanicville, 214
Medicinal plants, 227
Medina, 173
Meier, E 237 238
Meissner, 179
Mel & Gene, 71
Melick, H 251
Mendon, 115
Ment, D 99
Mentz, 15
Merchantile union business directory, 229
Merchants, 228
Merrick, 122
Merrill, A 27 29 51 117 Asa 51 F 99
Merriman, C 15 122 M 116 R 176
Merritt, J 121
Mershon, S L 71
Methodists in Cherry Valley, 18
Metz, C 46 H 34
Mexican War, 11
Mexico, 174
Meyer, N 121 235
Meyers, A 240
Michilimackinack, 89
Middle Island, 236
Middleburg, 218
Middlefield, 176 177
Middletown, 39 171
Mielatz, C F W 135
Mikula, E 47
Milbert, J G 71
Milet, Pierre 90
Milford, 177
Milfordville, 23
Millbrook, 42 63 226
Miller, B 165 G 237 G A 1 M 235 P 29 S 36 247 W 36
Miller Place, 236
Millers Place, 110
Millerton, 63
Milliken, C 168
Millionaires Hive, 133
Millis, W 203
Mills Hotels ..., 142
Milne, A 155
Minard, J 3 4

Minerva, 48
Minisink, 91 171 172 Battle Ground 10 Indians 85 Valley 171
Minnewaska, 81
Minot, H D 157
Miriam 9
Missionary work, 228
Mitchell, J 255 P 242
Mitchill, Dr 194 S L 137 Samuel L 257 Samuel Lathan 133
Mix, Jonathan 194
Modena, 244
Moffat, A 170
Moger, R 123
Mohaques country, 90
Mohawk Baronet, 88
Mohawk Flatts Grant, 90
Mohawk Indians, 86 88 90 91 120
Mohawk River, 9 85 86 162 189 197 (River?), 71
Mohawk Valley, 26 86 95 147 163 197 215 231 256
Moira, 50
Moncrieffe, Maj 195 Margaret 195
Monell, J 172
Monroe, 172
Monroe Co, 3 114-118 261
Monroe, J 14 39 98 105 216 J A 169 J D 39
Montauk, 236 237
Montayne, F 218
Montgomery, 172
Montgomery Co, 1 118 215
Montgomery, Gen 195 204 Richard 201
Monticello, 240
Montville, 15
Moody, J 203 James 203
Mooers, 31
Moore, C 114 121 E 177 H 190 Pliny 73
Moravia, 15
Moravian Mission, 87
Moravians, 87 95
More & Griffin, 39
Moreau, 146 214 215
Morgan, 173 E B 258 William 225 229 256 259
Morhouse, Abraham 68
Mormons, 21 249 262
Morris, 177 F 255 I 209 W 240

Morris Purchase map, 109
Morrisania, 250
Morrison, 28 248 A & W 248 W 27 219
Morrissey, John 57
Morristown, 98
Morrisville, 22
Morse, E 169 H 43 R 178
Morton, 130
Moscow, H 137
Moscrip, A 246
Mott, E 228
Mounts, Beacon 73 Hope 172 Mount Ida 83 Independence 119 Kisco 252 Lebanon 35 221 Mansfield 150 Marcy 69 Morris 102 103 Pleasant 252 Vernon 252
Mount Hope Cemetery 258
Mount, W E 241
Mount'marcy, 161
Mountain Tulip legend, 82
Mountains, gazetteer 225
Mulconery, B 3
Mulford, H 166 U 233
Muller Hill, 106
Mumford, 118
Munro, Robert 51
Munsee, 84 85 Indians 84 85
Munsell, J 1 2 185 Joel 57 73 182 185 W 39
Munsell's historical series, 119 120
Munson, G 31
Murphy, H 34 262 Timothy 206
Murray, D 39 155 Jo 17 Sam 17 T 54
Muster Rolls of the NY Provincial Troops 1755-1764 90
Myers, H 177 J 3 T B 207
N E Precinct, 42
Nammack, G 90
Napanoch, 243
Naples, 169
Narrows, 133
Narrowsburg, 240
Nassau Co, 64 99 120-123
Nation, Carrie 261
Natural history of NY, 228 229
Natures Serial Story 76
Naylor, C 254
Neal, J 175

Near, I 98 232 233
Negro, equality 113 history source materials 1
Neilson, C 204
Nellis, C 53
Nelliston, 118
Nelsonville, 178 179
Nesponsit, 122
Nestigauni, 162
New Albion, 13
New Amsterdam, 34 109
New Baltimore, 52
New Berlin, 23 30
New Bremen, 148
New Castle, 253
New City, 211
New Harlem, 123
New Hartford, 164
New Hurley, 244
New Jerusalem, 132 133
New Lebanon, 37 74 220 222
New Lots, 100
New Markhams, 14
New Netherlands, 32-35 91
New Paltz, 244
New Rochelle, 253
New Steam Boat Rip Van Winkle ... 74
New Utrecht, 99 100
New Windsor, 172
New Woodstock, 106
New York & Albany Post Road ..., 64
New York & Erie rail road guide, 226
New York Bay, 123
New York City 35 56 60-63 69 71 76 79 83 104 106-111 123-144 148 153 156 161 192 202 203 230 231 256 258 architecture 123 atlas 106 colonial commissions claendar 34 map 106 110 merchants 187 188 water supply 9 10
New York Co, 123-144
New York gazetteer, 205
New York Island, 127
New York Ladies Southern Association, 138
New York land patents 1688-1786, 155

New York Ontario & Western Railway timetable, 22
New York privateers 1756-1763, 130
New York State, agriculture history 183 atlas 107 boundaries 229 230 canal system 189 gazetteer 183 184 188 history 182 183 185 186 189 map 107 109 110 military & bounty lands 16 names 223 printer 1785-1830 183 Register 226 227
New York Supreme Court, 138
Newark, 248 Valley 240
Newburgh, 55 71 120 172 192 197
Newcomb, 48 49
Newell, R 145 237
Newfane, 145
Newhouse, S 155
Newman, J B 10 L 3 W 167
Newport, 54
Newstead, 47
Newtown, 179
Niagara, 69 71 88 120 145 208 259 Co 3 44 144-146 258 262 Falls 45 128 188 227 256-259 261 frontier 145 146 River 257 261
Nicholl, H 234
Nicholls, H 145
Nichols, C 106 H 253
Nicolaysen, 251
Nile, 4
Niles, 15
Nimmonsburg, 6
Nine Little Partners 42
Niobe, 28
Niskayuna, 3 214 220 222
Niven, A 171
Noble, H 48
Nonemacher, B 176
Nordstrom, C 211
North, A 40 family 35 221 S 51
North, Castle 253 Chatham 37 Cohocton 233 Collins 46 47 Guilford 30 Harmony 28 Hempstead 122 Quaker Hill 43 River 110 Salem 77 253 Tarrytown 255 Tonawanda 146 Western 163 Wolcott 249
North Hempstead Township 122

Northampton, 115 116
Northern NY, 146-162 181
Northfield, 210
Northport, 237
Northrup, A 166
Northumberland, 146 214
Northup, J 13
Northwest Passage, 157
Norway, 54
Norwich, 30
Norwood, 213
Novum Belgium ..., 33
Noyes, John H 22 John Humphrey 25 164 M 217
Nunda, 103 Hollow 263
Nundarama, 103
Nutt, J 172
Nutting, Judge 22
Nyack, 211
O'Callaghan, E 163 E B 34 35 90 185
O'Connor, J 10 James 10 R 138 R F 76
O'Neil, E 50
O'Neill, 171
O'Reilly, H 117
O'Rielly, H 117 204
Oak Island, 236
Oakes, R 97
Oakfield, 51
Oaks Corners, 169
Oaks, M 169
Oblenis, C 211
Odd Natt, 6
Odell, Jonathan 120
Odessa, 218
Oechsner, C 253
Oehser, E 13
Ogden, 115 116
Ogden, David 91 L 172
Ogdensburg, 154 213
Ohio River, 94
Old Bay Ridge, 99
Old Forge, 54
Old Hellebergh ..., 3
Old Keeseville, 48
Old Matinecock, 122
Old Mine Road, 64
Old Ninety-Nine (Indian), 88
Old Ninety-Nines Cave, 88
Old Northampton, 115 116

Old Onondaga Valley, 166
Old Plattsburgh, 32
Old Purchase South, 234
Old Quaker Meeting House, 44
Old Roslyn, 123
Old Syracuse, 167
Olean, 13
Olive, 244
Oliver, J 233
Oliverea, 242
Olmsted, Frederick Law 261
Onderdonck, H 122 179 H Jr 204
Oneida, 18 22 105 Castle 86 164 258 Co 14 22 24 26 162-165 215 Community 19 20 22 24-26 164 Indians 85 86 88-90 164 200 Iroquois Glass Trade 91 Lake 22 155 174 Movement 19 Reserve 22
Oneonta, 20 177
Onondaga Co, 14 21 162 165-168
Onondaga Indians, 85 88 94
Onondaga Valley, 25 166
Ontario, 248 Co 3 114 168-170
Orange Co, 10 19 69 75 76 79 81 82 170-173 197 207 210
Orangetown, 201 202
Orchard Park, 47
Orient, 237
Orleans Co, 3 44 114 173 256
Osborn, 105 C 36
Osborne, D 14 T M 22
Osgood, H 114 117
Osseruenon, 85
Ossining, 253
Osterhoudt, R 254
Ostrander, S 99
Oswegatchie, 213
Oswego, 22 91 174 Co 14 97 173 174 Harbor 188
Otego, 177
Otisco, 224
Otsego Basse, 18 19
Otsego Co, 1 23 25 174-178 227
Otsego Lake, 18 20
Otten, M 37
Ottman, W 29
Oulcout, 110
Outland, E 23
Overlook Mountain House, 10 11 182

Ovid, 219
Owasco, 15 Lake 258 River Valley facts & folklore 15
Owego, 21 240 259
Owens, W 254
Owl's Head, 50
Ox Bow, 213
Oxford, 30
Oyster Bay, 122
Pleasant Valley, 114
Packard, 214
Page, F 6
Paine, Thomas 204
Painted Post, 233
Painter, L 45
Palatines emigrating from Schoharie Co NY to PA 10
Palen, I 30
Palisades, 211
Palmer, D R 204 L 166 P 32 R 50
Palmyra, 248 249
Paltsits, V H 205
Pamelia, 98
Panama, 28
Paper & paper making, 73
Paris, 164
Parish, I 241
Park, R 173
Parker, A 1 Arthur C 86 C 212 J 117
Parkhurst, F 46 47
Parma, 115 116
Parrell, M 251
Parsons & Rockfellow, 103
Parsons, C 252 I 167
Partridge, B 74
Patchinville, 233
Patchogue, 237
Patrick, L S 205
Patriots War, 153 154
Patten, J 139
Patterson, E 254 M 172 M S 139
Pattison, 251
Pauguaconsk (River?), 238
Paul Smiths, 50 Adirondack Park 156
Paulding, 226
Pavilion, 51
Pawling, 42 205 G 232
Payne, F 212 John 51 R 236
Peake, L 27
Peal, B 165

Pearce, N 42
Pearl River, 211
Pearson, J 216
Pechuman, L 145
Peck, J 175 W 114 117
Pecksville, 41
Peconic, 237
Peekskill, 61 62 251 253 254
Peenpack, 172
Pelham, 254
Pell, F 229 family 74 Joshua III 74 Polly 78
Pelletreau, W 178 236 238 250 W S 139
Pembroke, 51
Penet, Peter 98 200
Penet Square, 98
Penfield, 116
Penfold, S 210 211
Penn Yann, 263
Pennell, Joseph 135
Pepper, C Jr 74
Percy, J 47
Perinton, 116
Perkins, G 156
Perkinsville, 233
Perry & Pell, 74
Perry & Wilcox, 118
Perry, 263 Clay 10 J 14
Perry, 44
Perrysburg, 13
Perth, 50
Peru, 31
Peterboro, 77 132 164
Peters, H T 186
Peterson, A 28
Pettit, G 253
Pharmacy in western NY, 258
Phelps & Gorham's Purchase, 114
Phelps, 169 H P 74 O S 156
Phelps Old Mountain, 147 156
Philadelphia, 98
Philalethes, 74
Philip (Indian), 119
Philipse Patent, 90
Phillips, 22 A 30 Ammi 57 P L 186 Wm 199
Phillipstown, 179
Phinney, E 176
Phoenix, 174
Phrenology, 128
Pierce & Hurd, 240

Pierce, J 12 13
Piercefield Paper Co, 156
Pierceville, 106
Piermont, 211 226
Pierre, R P 90
Pierson, E 211
Pike, 263 Col 160 E 163
Pilat & Ranson, 100
Pilling, 86 87 J C 186
Pinckney, J 52
Pindar, John S 21
Pine Hill, 244
Pine Lake, 39
Pine Plains, 41 42 63
Pine Tree Corner, 77
Pine Valley Community, 13 14
Pine Valley Yorkers, 13
Pinney, E 239
Pitcairn, 213
Pitcher, 30 C 164
Pitts, H 170
Pittsford, 116
Pittstown, 170
Placid, P 91 Paul 91
Plains Road, 244
Plainview, 122
Planemakers, 230
Plank, W 242 243
Platt, E 42 H 236 J 7 Jonas 24
Plattsburgh, 32 109 149 150 154 162
Pleasant Valley, 42 48
Pleasantville, 254
Plum, D A 186
Plum Point, 63
Plumb, A 13
Pocantico Hills, 254
Poetry, 226
Poland, 54
Polhemus, M 243
Politics, 136
Pollard, R 217
Pollopel, 78
Pomfret, 28
Pompey, 167
Pondshiners, 83
Pontiac (Indian), 119
Pool, W 145
Pope, F L 75
Port, Byron 15 Henry 48 Jefferson 237 Jervis 9 91 172 Leyden 101 Washington 122

Portbay, 220
Porter, A 145 168 E 36 163 M 32 P 145 146
Portland, 29
Portville, 14
Post, A 15 R 237
Post offices to 1850, 227
Potsdam, 213
Pottery, 26
Pottle, E 169
Poughkeepsie 40-43 55 58 61 63 69 82 193 201
Pound Ridge, 254
Powell, Duncan 66 E 168
Powers, M 91
Pratham Church, 174
Pratt & Mann, 97
Pratt, E 97 J 173 Peter P 91 Zadoc 11 Zadock 10
Prattsburg, 233
Prattsville, 10
Presbyterian Meeting House, 23
Prescott, 154 C 164
Press history in western NY, 257
Preston, 30
Preston, J 1 M 102
Price, J H 75
Priest, J 2 91
Prime, Samuel Irenaeus 156 W 156
Prince, L 213
Printing in Washington Co 151
Printy, J 47
Prison, 9 70 78 79 204 ship 194
Pritchard, Z 241
Privateers, 130
Proctor, L 2
Prospect, 163 164
Prout, H 52
Prouty, Fremont 150
Provol, W 23
Pryer, C 250
Public welfare history, 230
Pugsley, F 116
Pulaski, 174
Pultneyville, 249
Purcell, E 121
Purple & Gulian, 30
Purple, G 240
Putnam Co, 40 178 179
Putnam, Gen 195 Israel 196 Rufus 87

Quaker, 14 90 41 140 Basin 106
  Hill 43 106 Meeting House 44
Quarry Hill, 172
Queen Anne's American kings, 85
Queens Borough, 64 99
Queens Co, 179 204
Queensbury, 245
Queenstown, 258
Quick, 250 Dorothy 105 F 102
  Tom 91 172 239
Quinlan, J 239 J E 91
Quinte Bay, 89
Quogue, 237
Racquette River, 156
Radcliff, W 111
Ragged Lake, 50
Railroads, 231
Rainbow Lake, 50
Raitt, J 39
Ramapo, 210 Mountain People 59 Pass 211 Valley 201 Works 211
Ramapough Indians, 59
Randall, Nehemiah 6
Randolph, 14
Ranlet, P 205
Ransom, C 123 J M 75
Rathbone, 37 T 164
Ratner, L 229
Rattray, J 235-237
Ray, F M 156
Raymond, C 75 H 49 Henry J 137 M 31 205 W 35
Raynor & Color, 172
Raynor, 205 J 53
Rayville, 37
Rea, Caleb 156
Read, D B 205
Real, David Harum 26
Reaman, G 92
Rebellion of 1837, 153 159
Red Creek, 249
Red Hook, 192
Red Jacket (Indian), 86
Redfield, T 92
Redford Glass Co, 157
Redmond, D 157
Reed, Calvin 35 N 41 R 145 W 50
Reeve, B 237
Reference books, 179-189
Reid, 130 Whitelaw 130
Reinstein, J 45

Reische, D 254
Remsen, 164
Renesselaer Co, 1
Rennsselaer Co, 61
Rensselaer, 190 Co 1 75 189 190 Manor 189 Polytechnic Institute 56
Rensselaerville, 3
Rensslaerville, 3
Renz, L M 92
Reukauf, C 45
Reusswig, H 38
Revolutionary War, 16 21 55 57 60 73 76 77 85 89 91 110 119 120 165 180 181 183 184 187 190-209 242 250 254 maps 195
Reynolds, C 2 F 253 H 43 H W 43 75 J 3 S 101
Rezneck, S 190
Rhinebeck, 41 43 Flatts 77
Rial & Westervelt, 51
Rice, Dan 260 H C 75 N S 76
Rich, A 116 Floyd J 97 H 157 Henry 134
Rich Valley, 14
Richards, C 168 Caroline Cowles 168
Richfield, 177 Springs 177
Richmond, 170 210
Richmond Co, 209 210
Richmond, A 259 M L 187 R 27
Rickard, C 217
Ridgewood, 123
Ridley, H 169
Riedesel, Gen (Mrs) 205
Riker, J 123 179
Riley, L 179
Ringling, John 132
Ringwald, D C 76
Rio, 172
Rip Van Winkle, 10 67
Ripley, 29
Ripstein, A 263
Risch, J 76
Riverby, 68
Riverdale, 144
Riverhead, 104 234 237
Rivington, 205 James 160
Roberts & Clarke, 263
Roberts, F 164 263 G 216 J A 205 K 157 K & J 230 M 232 R B 187

Robertson, C 164
Robeson, Paul 62
Robinson House, 201
Robinson, E 219 L 263 Mr 230 T 97
Robson, M 145
Rochelle, Roux De 72
Rochester, 45 81 114 116 117 260 261 industry & trade unionism 117 in 1827 116 in 1835 117 its founders & its founding 117
Rock, E 175
Rock Stream, 263
Rockaway, 122 123 Beach 122 Peninsula 122 Point 122
Rockefeller, John D 83
Rockland Co, 62 75 76 197 202 210-212
Rockville Centre, 123
Rockwell, A D 140
Rodman, 98
Roe, A 249 E P 76
Roebling, 130
Roebling cables for the Hudson River Bridge, 132
Roeliff, Jansen 36
Rogan, R 206
Rogatie, B 38
Rogers, A 124 B 238 F 157 H 164 Horatio 199 M 157 Robert 89 119 157 S 233 Wm 93
Rogers Rangers, 86 92 in the French & Indian War 92
Rogers Rock, 157
Rohman, D 165
Rome, 22 148 164
Romulus, 219
Rondout, 243 Creek 76 Valley 85 88
Roosevelt & Brough, 76
Roosevelt, Eleanor 76 Elliott 76 F D 76 family 74 Franklin D 63 Mrs 75 President 75 Teddy 130 Theodore 74 157
Roosevelt-Strauss ratification 74
Root, E 146 M 103
Rosch, J 255
Roscoe, 9 11 W 217
Rose, 249 W 245
Roseberry, C 76
Rosenberg, S E 117

Rosendale, 244 Township Assn 244
Roslyn, 123
Ross & Kozacek, 52
Ross, J 32 O J 158
Rosseel, F 145
Rossie, 212 213
Rotary Club Wolcott, 249
Round Lake, 214
Rouses Point, 32
Rouses's Point, 151
Rowson, S H 140
Roxbury, 39
Roy, Frank Austin 140
Royalton, 146
Royce, C 49
Rubin & Brown, 140
Rudge, William Edwin 71
Rumsey, H 241
Rush, 117
Rushford, 4
Rushmore, G 172
Rusk, S 11
Russell, 213 G 106 I 248 M 176 Mr 13
Rutland Co, 1
Ruttenber & Clark, 170
Ruttenber E, 170 172
Ryder, E 217 R 163
Rye, 250 254
Sabbath Committee, 225
Sabbath Day Point, 245
Sabin, J 187
Sabine, W 206
Sackets Harbor, 98 160
Sacondaga, 50
Sag Harbor, 237
Sager, I 13
Saint Clair, Maj Gen 206
Saint Elmo, 244
Saint Helena, 263
Saint Johnsville, 118
Saint Lawrence Co, 97 147 162 212 213
Saint Lawrence River, 98 150 256
Saint Lawrence Valley, 147
Saint Regis Indians, 88
Saint Regis Lakes, 157
Saint Regis River, 162
Salem, 83 220 247
Saliba, G 146

Salisbury, S 174
Salles, family 136 Laurent 136
Salmo Otsego, 18
Salsig, D 206
Salt Point, 44
Saltaire, 237
Salzmann, Laurence 138
Sammis, R 236
Sampson, Davenport & Co, 77
Sampson, Deborah 203 Joseph A H 220 Proctor 220 W 140
Samuel, Irenaeus Prime 156
Sanborn, J W 93
Sand Lake, 190
Sanders, D C 93 J 216
Sanderson, D 243
Sandy Creek, 174
Sandy Hook, 55
Sanford, 6 C 212 W 39
Sanger, J 24
Sangerfield, 16
Sant, R 15
Santway, I A 158
Saquoit (River?), 164
Saranac Lake, 48 49 158
Saratoga, 120 164 198 214 215 230 Co 146 151 213-215 246 256 Springs 158
Sardinia, 46 47
Sargent, W 206
Sauers, E 174
Saugerties, 244
Saunders, J 179 L 115
Savannah, 249
Sawyer, J 175 W 247
Saxton, K 50
Sayville, 237
Scaroon, 49
Scarouady (Indian), 85
Scarsdale, 254
Schadlach, M J 69
Schaefer, J 166
Schaldach, W J 11
Scharf, J 250
Schenectady, 61 90 162 216
Schenectady & Catskill Railroad, 77
Schenectady Co, 1 215 216
Schermerhorn, Maria 80
Schild, J L 260
Schmidt, C 51 118 260
Schoharie Cave, 10

Schoharie Co, 1 9 23 25 63 215-218
Schoharie (River?), 217
Schoharie Valley, 217
Schoolcraft, Henry 128
Schoonmaker, A 243
Schrabisch, M 93
Schram, B 36
Schroon Lake, 49 150
Schubel, G 100
Schults, C 13 28
Schulz, W 54
Schurz, 130
Schuyler, 54 family 77 G W 77 Gen 194 Philip 77 199 S 74
Schuyler Co, 3 29 218 219
Schuylerville, 215
Schwart, Cornelia Beekman 175
Schwartz, 175
Scio, 4
Scipio, 15 142
Scisco, L 168
Scnneider, D 230
Scofield, C 254
Scotch settlement, 213
Scotia, 216
Scott, G 215 J 164 206 212 R 77 Robert 77
Scottsville, 117 118
Scoville, J A 187
Scudder, H 121
Scully, V 248
Sea Cliff, 123
Sea Gate, 100
Seabury, S 235
Seacord & Hadaway, 253
Searing, A E P 11
Sears, L 242 R 215
Seaver, F 49 J E 93 W 51
Sedgwick, H 102
Seely, L J 24
Seese, M 170
Selijns, Henricus 34
Selivanova, N 210
Selkreg, J 241
Seller, E 47
Selyns, Henricus 34
Sempronious, 15
Seneca, 47 84 85 Co 218 219 Falls 169 170 219 219 fiction legends & myths 87 Indian myths 87 Indian revolution 93

Seneca (continued)
   Indians 84 85 87-91 93 94 96
   120 Lake 169 Snipe clan 91
Sennett, 15
Setauket, 237
Settle, L 240
Settlers revolt, 44
Seume, J G 208
Seventh Grade, 252 New Paltz
   Central School 244 North
   Salem 253
Severance, F 45
Seward, 218
Seward, Miss 207 W 5 William H
   16 229
Sewer systems & sewage disposal
   works maps, 108
Sexton, J 29
Seymann, J 35
Seymour, G 6 J 164
Shakers, 35 66 187 220-222
Shandaken, 244
Shannontown, 263
Shaping a City ... Brooklyn 99
Sharon Springs, 218
Sharpe, L 247
Sharts, E 171
Shaw & Shoemaker, 188
Shaw, 105 E 235 G 49 S 176
Shawangunk, 244 Mountains 93
Shea, J G 94
Shear, H 3 4
Sheeban, H 214
Sheep, 70
Sheffield, 73
Shekomeko, 95
Sheldrake, 219
Sheller, A 166
Shelter Island, 237 238
Shennandoah, 41
Shepherd, C D 37
Sherburne, 30 31
Sherill, 105 164
Sherman, 29 A 250 254
Sherrill, H 40
Sherwin, H 28
Sherwood Corners, 244
Sherwood, W 243
Shields, 31
Shikellamy (Indian), 85
Shinners, L 30
Shoebridge, S 167

Sholes, 110
Shonnard & Spooner, 250
Shore front rights in the State of
   NY 71
Shorey, M 214
Shurtleff, Robert 203
Shushan, 140 247
Sias, S 217
Sickler, V 244
Sidewalks of NY (City) 135
Sidney, 39 Plains 39
Sight-Seeing Map of the Hudson
   River 111
Sigman, F 46
Signor, I 173
Sigsby, Wm 206
Silver, 76
Silver Bay, 245
Silver Creek, 28 29
Silver Lake, 260
Silversmiths, 260 of Utica 19
Simcoe, John Graves 205
Simeon DeWitt steamer, 20
Simmons, L 49
Simms, J 217 J R 94 207
Simpson, E 174
Sinclairville, 27
Sing Sing Prison, 70 78 79
Sinnett, C 239
Sipprell, M 46
Skaneatales Lake, 25
Skaneateles, 167
Skenesboro, 109
Skillman, F 123
Skinner, C 98 J 240 Nathan 239 W
   Fishkill 41
Slade, W 158
Slave trade under the Dutch, 35
Sleepy Hollow, 255
Sleight, H 237
Sloan, 47 Margaret 61 Samuel 61
   William 139
Slocum, G 117 118 H 115 R 166
Sloop Landing, 249
Slosek, A 174
Smart & Noble, 246
Smith & Cale, 102
Smith & Husted, 114
Smith, 40 123 A 245 C 166 168
   254 C A 77 E 15 41 43 235
   Garret 62 Gen 141 Gerit 132
   Gerrit 20 25 77 H 5 38 45 48

Smith (continued)
  245 H P 158 J 30 105 215 238
  J A 123 J E A 222 J H 207
  Joseph 152 262 Joshua Hett
  191 207 L 46 47 233 M 52 106
  121 N 244 Nathan 24 P 40 249
  R 49 234 S 25 Sidney L 135 T
  54 V 121 122 W 169
Smithers, C 212
Smithers, N 212
Smithfield, 25 106
Smithtown, 105 238
Smits, E 121
Smyrna, 31
Snedens Landing, 62
Snell, C 207
Snow, B 14 D 14 J 45
Snyder, C 174 C M 94 J 100
Snyder Hill, 14
Sobel, R 207
Sodus, 220 249 Point 249 Village 249
Soldiers & Sailors Home, 16
Solvay, 167
Sonnontouan, 219
Sonnontown, 89
Soper, E 215
South Bay, 236
South Butler, 249
South Dayton, 13 14
South Glens Falls, 215
South Kortright, 40
South Nyack, 211
South Onondaga, 167
South Salem, 254
South Side Sportsmen's Club of Long Island, 103
South Trenton, 163 164
South Wales, 47
Southampton, 238
Southern NY, 201
Southern Tier, 27 29
Southold, 105 237 238
Southwick, S 29
Spafford, 167 H 219 H G 188 230 Horatio Gates 57 58
Spaight, F 41
Sparks, Jared 202
Spaulding, S 48
Spear, D & G 121 D N 188
Spencer, 240 A 37 J 25 Judge 56 L 46

Spencertown, 36 37 84 Academy 59
Spicklefisherman, 11
Sprague, H 50
Spraker & Carpenter, 176
Spring Valley, 211
Springer, A 2
Springfield, 177 179
Springport, 15
Springville, 46 47
Springwater, 103
Spurr, Norman 78
Squire, A O 78
Staats, 77 E 176 R 41
Stafford, 51 M 141
Stage, canal, & steamboat register for 1831 8
Stage route from Owego to Bath 1816, 21
Staley, G 164
Stamford, 40
Stanley, E 163
Stansbury, Joseph 120
Stanton, Elizabeth 261 H B 261
Stanyon, M P 53
Stapleton, E 2
Star Lake, 213
Stark, Cordelia 230
Starkey, 263 Corners 263
Starks, 158
State Prison, 22
State Road, 259
State wide, 222-232
Staten Island, 64 71 73 104 110 209
Staton, F 159
Steamboats, 76 231 for Rondout 76 of Lake Champlain 158 of Lake George 158
Steamer, *Mary Powell* 64 *Simeon DeWitt* 20
Stearns, A 43
Stedman, 28
Steele, Z 141
Steendam, Jacob 34
Steinmeyer, H 209
Stephen, H 141
Stephens, A 95 James 261 W 101 W P 159
Stephentown, 190
Sterling Furnance, 196
Stern, M 25

Steuben, 163 164 Co 3 16 21 24 27 114 138 232 233 259
Stevens, E 177 G 159 H 142
Stevenson, G 11
Stewart, J 47 Mr 25
Stickler, J 159
Stickley, Gustav 19 20
Stickney, C 172
Stiles & Stearns, 100
Stiles, H 99
Still, B 137
Stillwell, L 4
Stirling, Peter 104
Stittville, 163
Stobo, R 159 Robert 159 160
Stockbridge Indians, 86
Stockport, 37 40 60
Stockton, 29
Stockton, E L Jr 95
Stockwell, O 50
Stoddard, S 49 S R 160
Stokes, I 137 I N Phelps 142 O 78
Stone, 226
Stone Ridge, 244
Stone, W 142 215 246 William L 205 207
Stoner, Nicholas 94
Stonnes, E 31
Stony Brook, 238
Stony Point, 196 211
Stoodley, R 98
Stork, W 263
Storke & Smith, 14
Storm King, 79 Mountain 192
Stormville, 41
Stottville, 37
Stow, 28
Strang, J 78 Jesse 78
Stratford, 50
Street, 226 A B 48
Streeter, H 175
Streetroad, 49
Strickland, E D 86
Strong, A 117 G 168 George W 142 J R 142 Nathaniel T 94 R 100 T 100
Stroup, I 248
Struggle for Monroe Co 114
Strykersville, 263
Stuart, Harriot 70 W 232
Sturcke, A 79
Sturge, G 174

Stuyvesant, 37
Suffern, 211 Jr High School 210
Suffolk Co, 64 99 204 233-239
Suffrage, 56
Sullivan, 91 106 198 204
Sullivan & Flick, 208
Sullivan Co, 10 81 239 240
Sullivan, E 207 F J 79 J 189 John 87 93 198 William 23 Yankee 57
Sullivan-Clinton campaign, 118 208
Sulphur Springs, 168
Summer Hill, 15
Summerville, 118
Sunderland, L 31
Sunderlin, A 263
Sutherland, J 79 Joshua 79
Swalm, L 79 Levi B 79
Swan, C 28
Swarthout, L 167 233
Sweden, 118
Sweetland, H 14
Swiggert, H 208
Swinnerton, H 175
Sylvester, N 189 213 215 242
Sylvia Lake, 213
Symbols of the Capitol or civilization in NY 71
Symes, Lancaster 71
Symonds, J 222
Syracuse, 22 23 26 166-168 200 225
Syrett, H C 105
Tagashata (Indian), 85
Taghconic, 222
Taghkanic Mountains, 57
Tahawus, 49
Tahawus Newcomb & Long Lake 49
Tait, J 213
Talbot, A 79
Tall Ships ... (19)76 portfolio, 126
Talman, W 210 W B 211
Tammany Society, 136 194
Tanner, John 259
Tanney, D 105
Tanning & currying in their various branches from actual experience 16
Tappan, 64 199 201 211
Tarrytown, 54 64 205 254 255

Tatnall, Paul 66
Tatum, E 252
Tawger, R N 96
Taylor, 214 D 31 E 29 217 F 169
  H 29 John 55 62
Teall, S 166
Tefft, G 247
Temperance, 126 146 147 Society 55
Temple, Charlotte 140
Ten Broeck, 77 Abraham 201
Ten Mile River, 57
Tenney, J 2
Tenny, Joseph 16
Terry, R 37
Terwilliger, 245
Theresa, 98
Thistlethwaite, W 54
Thomas, A 43 173 242 Abner H 242 E A 242 H 164 165 J 142 R 25
Thomas King (Indian), 85
Thompson & Husted, 114
Thompson, E 4 44 J 261 K 116 Sally 18
Thomson, F 189 M 35
Thoreau, Sophia 80
Thorne, family 226
Thornton, 27
Thorp, John 73
Thorpe, T B 142
Thousand Islands, 98 227 258
Thrall, W 232
Three Mile Point, 23
Throopsville, 15
Thurston, E 247
Ti Street, 49
Ticonderoga, 42 49 91 119 151 152 194 198 202 206 208
Tiemann, Ex-Mayor 141
Tilden, 130
Tioga Co, 21 29 240
Titus, S 234
Tivoli Falls, 77
Toby, 230
Todd, J 53
Tokaaio (Indian), 85
Toler & Nutting, 123
Toll, D 216
Tolles, J 262
Tolman, W 97
Tomlinson, G 262

Tompkins, A 210 Daniel D 224
Tompkins Co, 29 162 218 240-242
Ton, E 189
Tonawanda, 47
Tooker, W W 95
Torrance, M 3
Tory Rangers, 208
Totten & Crossfield Purchase, 151
Tottin Purchase, map 109
Towner A 29
Township 34, 53
Township 40, 151
Tracey, W 163
Trade & customs records, 32
Trapper's guide for capturing fur-bearing animals 155
Trappers of NY 94
Trebor, H 179
Trees, 231
Trelease, A W 95
Tremain, L 11
Trenton, 164 Falls 163-165
Tribunus Populi, 80
Trolley, 25
Troopers, 231
Trost & DeLong, 48
Troupsburg, 233
Troy, 73 80 83 151 190
Truesdall, J W 25
Truman, George T 90
Trumansburg, 242
Trumbull, J H 208 John 199
Truxton, 38
Tryon Co, 242
Tschoop (Indian), 95
Tuck, G 215
Tucker, P 262
Tuckerman, H T 130
Tug Hill, 101 148
Turner, 145 A A 80 C 262 O 114
Tuscarora Indians, 86-88
Tusten, 240
Tuttle, 73 E 234 G 161 R 115 Wm D 19
Tuxedo, 82 172 173 201 area 69 Park 82 172 196
Twain, Mark 173
Twichell, H 172
Tyler, A J 87 R 174
Tysen, R 209
Ulmann, A 142

Ulster Co, 55 77 81 88 197 242-245
Ultan, L 5
Ulysses, 242
Unadilla, 23 177 178 Village 178
Underground Empire 10
Underhill Burying Ground, 105
Underhill, D & F 105 Sherwood 251
Union Springs, 15
Union Village, 62 247
Unions, 76
Upper Nyack, 211 PTA 210
Upson, R 218
Upton Lake Grange members 41
Utica, 19 22 26 45 73 147 165
Vail, 86 R W G 208
Valatie, 37
Valentine & Newman, 235
Valentine, D 142 D T 142
Valhalla, 255
VanAllen, G 122
VanArnam, L 101
VanBergen, R 52
VanBuren, 168 A 242 Martin 8 104 111-114 153 160 192 232
Vance, A T 26
VanDenbergh, J 170
VanDer Zee, H & B 35
Vanderbilt, 130 G 100
Vandercook, 81
Vanderpoel, A 37 A E 143
Vanderwerker, J 213 214
VanDeusen, Delia 80
VanDeWater, F 231
VanDoren, Carl 85
VanDusen, R 245
VanDuyne, A 169
VanEpps, 214 P 216
VanHoesen, R 13
VanHousen, I 233
VanLiew, B 236
VanLoon, L 80
Vann, J 81
VanNorden, T 254
VanNorman, I 81
VanPatten, John F 80
VanPelt, D 143
VanRensselaer, 77 229 manor lands 68 Stephen 7 77
VanSchaack, H 167
VanSchaick, J 218

VanSiclen & Hurd, 243
VanStantvoord, C 215
Vanuxem, Lardner 84
VanValkenburgh, F 233
VanWyck, F 81 99 105
Varney, J M 81

Varney Mountain, 81
Vassar College, 40 69 75 82
Vassar, John 82 T E 82
Vedder, J 52
Veldran, B 216
Venice, 15
Vernon, 105 165
Verona, 165
Verplanck, 255
Versailles, 87
Vetare, F 255
Victor, 170
Victory Mountain Park, 161
Vigilant Association of NY City 132
Villenova, 14
Vinal, T 145
Vindex, 8
Virgil, 38
Vischer Ferry, 3
Voegelin, 95
Volkmar, Charles 11
Volusia, 110
von Rensselaer, family 2
Von Steuben, Baron 228
Voyse, M 235
Vrooman, E 217 J J 95
W, H 28
WPA Guide, 40 121 122 189 245
Waddell, W 161
Wading River, 238
Wadsworth, Clement H (Mrs) 250 J 249
Wager, D 163 164
Waid, R 29
Wait, W 37
Waite, B 168 D 102
Walbridge, 158
Wales, 47
Walker, O 6
Walkill, 244 Precinct 171
Wallace, A 171 E 161 Robert H 171
Wallbridge, O 103
Waller, G 215 H 179

Walrath, F 241
Walton, 40 158 F 255
Walton, Starks, & Co hardware dealers ... 158
Walworth, H 161 J 231
Wampsville, 106
Wanakena, 152
Wantagh, 123
Wappinger confederacy (Indians), 184
Wappingers Falls, 44
War of 1812, 77
Ward, F 102 117 H 177
Waring, G E 143
Warner & Hall, 48
Warner, Anna Bartlett 78 G 217 H 146 Susan 78
Warren Co, 1 151 245 246
Warren, A 46 E 27 Geo W 159 R 27 U 179
Warsaw, 263
Warwarsink, 172
Warwick, 62 66 173 Woodlands 62 66
Washbon, H 3
Washington, 44
Washington, George 120 132 172 194 205 Gen 192 204
Washington, (pseud) 231
Washington Co, 1 62 151 156 245-247
Washington Heights, 56 125 126
Washington, I & P 208
Washington Township, 44
Water Mill, 238
Waterford, 106 110 214 215 Study Club 215
Waterloo, 169 219
Watertown, 22 98 146 150
Waterville, 23 165
Watervliet, 3
Watrous, H 219
Watson, 101 S 13 W 48 49
Watts Flats, 28
Watts, G 211 H 116 L 236
Waverly, 240
Wawarsing, 245
Wawarsink, 91
Wawasink, 85
Wayland, 233
Wayne, Anthony 194 196
Wayne Co, 3 114 220 247-250 261

Wayside Telephone Service, 26
Waywayanda, 10 172
Webb, F 36
Webber, K 105
Webster, 118
Webster, C 212 J 254 O 38
Webutuck River, 57
Wedd, S 31
Weed, Thurlow 111 229 261
Weeds Basin, 15
Weedsport, L 15
Weekes, A 122
Weeks, G 236 P 176
Weigold, M 250
Weise, A 2 189 190 214
Welch, E 30 38 39 105 163 174 177 218 219 241 248 250 S 45
Weld, R 99
Weller, E 45-47
Welles & Proios, 237
Wells, Gabriel 125 J 241 L 167
Wellsville, 4
Welsh, W A 97
Welsh settlement, 164
Werner, C J 26 E A 189
Wesley, 13
West Almond, 4
West Bank of the Hudson River 64
West Eaton, 106
West Falls, 44
West Farms, 144 250
West Geneseo, map 109
West Island, 121
West Islip, 238
West Monroe, 22
West Nyack, 212
West Park-on-the-Hudson, 68
West Point, 56 59 60 71 77 78 173 192 200 201 203 204 230 mob 77
West Seneca, 47
West Shelby, 256
West Taghkanic, 83
West Winfield, 54
West, M 115
West of the Cayuga 12
Westbrook, 41 M 208
Westchester, 81 255 Co 62 66 74 77 205 250-255 Co Emergency Work Bureau 250
Westcott, E N 26

299

Westerlo, 3
Western NY, 117 204 255-262
  map 109
Westernville, 163
Westfield, 27
Westford, 178 Union School 178
Westhampton Beach, 238 239
Westminster Park, 150
Westmoreland, 165
Westover, F 14 M 216
Westport, 49
Westville, 50
Wetherbee & Taylor, 82
Whaley Lake, 44
Whaling, 103
Wharton House, 197
Wheatland, 118 Center 118
Wheeler, C 14 F 39 Thomas 26
Whipple City, 247
Whipple, G 161 231 John 78
Whitaker, E 238 E & C 234
White, 173
White City, 118
White Creek, 53 246 247
White, F 11 J 98 P 31 T 44 166
  Tryphena Ely 21 166
White Plains, 76 206 254 255
White's Utica Pottery, 26
Whited, K 53
Whitehall, 109 149 247
Whiteman, J 161
Whitesboro, 165
Whitford, N 189
Whiting, Dr 73 Nathan N 23
Whitman, Walt 140
Whitmarsh, M 38
Whitmore, F 38
Whitney Point, 6
Whitson, S 144
Whittemore, H 231
Wiccopee, 41
Wickham, R 215
Wicks, P 38
Wightman, 161
Wilber, David 20
Wilber, F 30
Wilcox, A 101 G & J 238
Wilde, E 231
Wiles, R 83
Wiley & Garner, 145
Wiley, S 97
Wilkenfeld, B 144

Wilkinson, J 5
Willard, F 53
Willers, D 219
Willett, 38
Willey, N 237
William, king of England 32 33
Williams & Cardamone, 26
Williams & Palermo, 216
Williams, 44 C 51 E 145 Eleazar
  86 F 171 H 83 114 J 100 231 J
  C 26 John 83 M 36 145 O 163
  W 8 William 25 26
Williamsburg, 99 100 101
Williamsburgh, 99 100
Williamson, 249 C 51 J 231
Williamsville, 47
Willing, 4
Willis, C 262 N P 83
Willsboro, 49
Wilna, 99
Wilner, M 146
Wilshin, F 209
Wilson, 146
Wilson, Commissary 119 D 209
  247 J 144 M 178 W 43
Winans, 31
Winch, D 214
Windham, 52
Windsor Beach, 118
Wingdale, 79
Winkler, J 83
Winne, E 177
Winner, J 146 262
Wintjen, J 252
Wirt, 4 5
Wittmeyer, A 231
Wolcott, 249 250 W 263
Wolferts Roost, 252
Women of NY (City) ... 129
Women's Soc Western Presby
  Ch, 249
Wood, G B 231 George B 231 J
  251 Jonathan 220 L 39 L C 12
  S 234 236 Silas 236 W 105
  Walter Abbott 152
Woodbridge, Timothy 59 84
Woodbury, 173 G 162
Woodhull, 233 Nathaniel 206
Woodmere, 122
Woodruff, R 232
Woodstock, 9 182 245

Woodward, Charles L 144 J 27
Woodworth, J 190 John 162
   Samuel 139
Woolsey, C 243 M 162
   Melancthon Taylor 162
Woolworth Building, 126
Worcester, 178
World War I, 10 161
World War II, 9 63
Worman, 245
Worth, G 2 37
Wortis, H 238
Wray, S 144
Wright, A 96 115 171 C C 7 J 15
   Stephen S 154
Wurtsboro, 240
Wyoming Co, 3 44 114 260 262 263
Xulver, F 123
Yaphank, 236 239
Yates, 24 A 216
Yates Co, 3 114 218 263
Yawger, R 15
Yellow fever epidemic in NY City, 133
Yonkers, 255 Military Academy 84
York, 103
Yorkshire, 14
Yoshpe, H 209
Young, 158 A 27 263 David 16 John 55 56 R 44 S 44
Youngs, Isaac N 222
Youngstown, 146
Zacarra & Edwards, 84
Zacenovia, 105
Zierak, S 50
Zim, 29
Zimm, L 242

www.ingramcontent.com/pod-product-compliance
Lightning Source LLC
Chambersburg PA
CBHW052053230426
43671CB00011B/1891